THE

NEW ENGLAND STATES

By Neal R. Peirce

THE MEGASTATES OF AMERICA

THE PACIFIC STATES OF AMERICA

THE MOUNTAIN STATES OF AMERICA

THE GREAT PLAINS STATES OF AMERICA

THE DEEP SOUTH STATES OF AMERICA

THE BORDER SOUTH STATES

THE NEW ENGLAND STATES

THE PEOPLE'S PRESIDENT

THE

NEW

ENGLAND

STATES

People, Politics, and Power

in the Six New England States

NEAL R. PEIRCE

W · W · NORTON & COMPANY · INC ·
NEW YORK

FIRST EDITION

Library of Congress Cataloging in Publication Data
Peirce, Neal R
   The New England States.
   Bibliography: p.
   Includes index.
   1. New England—Politics and government.
2. New England—Description and travel—1951–
I. Title.
F10.P44   974   75–45345

ISBN 0 393 05558 2

1 2 3 4 5 6 7 8 9 0

For my New England mother
Miriam deSteiger Peirce

AND

in memory of Russell L. Bradley
1904–1975
critic, proofreader, and friend extraordinaire

CONTENTS

FOREWORD

THIS BOOK IS ABOUT THE New England States, part of a series covering the story of each major geographic region and all of the 50 states of America in our time. The objective is simply to let Americans (and foreigners too) know something of the profound diversity of peoples and life styles and geographic habitat and political behavior that make this the most fascinating nation on earth.

Only one project like this has been attempted before, and it inspired these books: John Gunther's *Inside U.S.A.*, researched during World War II and published in 1947. Gunther was the first man in U.S. history to visit each of the states and then to give a good and true account of the American condition as he found it. But his book is a quarter of a century old; it was written before the profound economic and population growth and societal change of the post-war era. Before he died, I consulted John Gunther about a new book. He recognized the need for such a work, and he gave me, as he put it, his "good luck signal."

But what was to be a single book became several, simply because I found America today too vast, too complex to fit into a single volume. A first book, *The Megastates of America*, treated America's 10 most heavily populated states. The series of eight regional volumes, completing the exploration of all the states in our time, began with publication of *The Mountain States of America* and *The Pacific States of America*, followed by *The Great Plains States of America*, *The Deep South States of America*, and *The Border South States*. Separate volumes are to follow on the Mid-Atlantic and Great Lakes states.

A word about method. Like Gunther, I traveled to each state of the Union. I talked with about 1,500 men and women—governors, Senators, Representatives, mayors, state and local officials, editors and reporters, business and labor leaders, public opinion analysts, clergymen, university presidents and professors, representatives of the Indian, black, and Spanish-speaking communities—and just plain people. Some of the people I talked with were famous, others obscure, almost all helpful.

I went by plane, then rented cars, made a personal inspection of almost every great city and most of the important geographic areas, and must have walked several hundred miles in the process too, insanely lugging a briefcase full of notes and tape recorder into the unlikeliest places. Usually I got names of suggested interviewees from my newspaper friends and other contacts in new states and cities and then sent letters ahead saying I would like to see the people. From the initial interviews, reference to still more interesting people invariably ensued. Rare were the interviews that didn't turn out to be fascinating in their own way; the best ones were dinner appointments, when the good talk might stretch into the late evening hours.

My initial travel and interviewing in the 50 states took a year and a half; there were return visits to some states, and telephone follow-up calls to many sources. The writing was complicated by the need to review hundreds of books and thousands of articles and newspaper clippings I had assembled over time. And then each manuscript, after it had been read and commented upon by experts of the state (often senior political reporters), had to be revised to include last-minute developments, and still once more given a final polish and updating in the galley stage.

Amid the confusion I tried to keep my eye on the enduring, vital questions about each state and its great cities:

What sets it (the state or city) apart from the rest of America?
What is its essential character?
What kind of place is it to live in?
What does it look like, how clean or polluted is it, what are the interesting communities?
Who holds the power?
Which are the great corporations, unions, universities, and newspapers, and what role do they play in their state?
Which are the major ethnic groups, and what is their influence?
How did the politics evolve to where they are today, and what is the outlook for the coming years?
How creatively have the governments and power structures served the people?
Who are the great leaders of today—and perhaps tomorrow?

A word of caution: many books about the present-day American condition are preoccupied with illustrating fundamental sickness in our society, while others are paeans of praise. These books are neither. They state many of the deep-seated problems, from perils to the environment to the abuse of power by selfish groups. But the account of the state civilizations also includes hundreds of instances of greatness, of noble and disinterested public service. I have viewed my primary job as descriptive, to show the multitudinous strands of life in our times, admitting their frequently contradictory directions, and tying them together analytically only where the evidence is clear. The ultimate "verdict" on the states and cities must rest with the reader himself.

For whom, then, is this chronicle of our times written? I mean the individual chapters to be of interest to people who live in the various states, to help them see their home area in a national context. I write for businessmen, students, and tourists planning to visit or move into a state, and who are interested in what makes it tick—the kind of things no guidebook will tell them. I write for politicians planning national campaigns, for academicians, for all those curious about the American condition as we enter the last decades of the 20th century.

From the start, I knew it was presumptuous for any one person to try to encompass such a broad canvass. But a unity of view, to make true comparisons between states, is essential. And since no one else had tried the task for a quarter of a century, I decided to try—keeping in mind the same goal Gunther set for *Inside U.S.A.*—a book whose "central spine and substance is an effort—in all diffidence—to show this most fabulous and least known of countries, the United States of America, to itself."

———

These books had to be, by their very character, a personal odyssey and personal task. But I owe a special word of thanks to those who helped me. In this volume, I am indebted to James Dickenson, a correspondent for the Washington *Star*, for assistance in preparation of the Connecticut chapter. My warmest thanks also go to those who read the draft manuscript in its entirety: Evan W. Thomas, my editor at W. W. Norton & Company; Jerry Hagstrom; Frederick H. Sontag, public affairs and research consultant of South Orange, New Jersey; and copy editor Calvin Towle. Various friends and associates helped with many details of research and proofreading, and for that I am especially indebted to Oliver Cromwell, Jean Allaway, Geneva Torrey, Barbara Hurlbutt, and DeMar and Claudia Teuscher. Credit goes to Russell Lenz, former chief cartographer of the *Christian Science Monitor*, for what I feel is the superb job he did in preparing the state and city maps.

Finally, I would like to express my thanks to the several persons in each state who consented to read and comment on the draft manuscript about their state. The names of these persons appear in the interviewee list at the back of the book; I choose not to list them here lest someone hold them responsible for something said or unsaid in one of the chapters, and of course the full responsibility for that lies with me.

A fellowship at the Woodrow Wilson International Center for Scholars, located in the Smithsonian Institution in Washington, provided intellectual and physical sustenance while this and other volumes in this series were being written.

THE

NEW ENGLAND STATES

NEW ENGLAND

PERIL AND PROMISE IN THE OLDEST REGION

To RETURN TO NEW ENGLAND and her mist-shrouded coast, her forested mountains, her Plymouth and Boston and town meeting villages, is like undertaking a voyage backward through time and history to the American touchstone.

In many senses, New England is to America what Old England is to the English-speaking world: the womb and starting place; the fountainhead of a culture's language, law, and learning; the smaller geographic entity from which great spaces were colonized. In centuries past, both sent ships in trade to the farthest corners of the globe; both became bankers and insurers and financiers of broad influence; both were early centers of manufacturing and tasted some of the bitter human fruits of the industrial revolution. Both, by determination and spunk, retained their economic position long after the centers of fresh growth had shifted to other realms.

In time, the pressures of competition began to close off the options for the "mature" economies of Old and New England. They lacked space, lacked natural resources, and lacked the requisite weight of population. By the mid-1970s, economists were projecting bleak years for both.*

* The lack of indigenous sources of energy was a major factor in this, though there was a curious parallel in the hopes of both Great Britain and New England that oil would help to offset their energy deficits—Great Britain's North Sea oil finds, and the less certain projections of oil in the Georges Banks, off New England's shores.

In matters of the spirit, one need not be as pessimistic. Both Old and New England retain a refinement of civilization, a special place for higher education (and even for intellectuals in politics), and a reverence for history and the social amenities all too often lacking in their brash competitors. And in New England, the moral flame lit by the Puritans has yet to be extinguished. The persecuted and rejected zealots of Old England in the 17th century, the Puritans came to the New World objecting to the formalism of the Church of England and intent on building a more pure Christian commonwealth on these uncharted shores. In time, the town meeting evolved out of the congregational setting, and so the idea of local, participatory democracy was born in America. As Henry Steele Commager once wrote:

What have Puritanism and democracy in common? Both respect the individual. . . . Both recognize the ultimate authority of reason. . . . Both respect the dignity of man. Both are equalitarian and leveling, for to the Puritan salvation was dependent on merit or grace, not on wealth or class or talents, and to the democrat equality was part of common humanity. . . . Both, finally, gave their allegiance to ideas or principles rather than to men or institutions.

Out of the Puritan culture and the harsh physical environment grew the legendary New England traits of character. Here, historian James Truslow Adams observed, "the gristle of conscience, work, thrift, shrewdness, duty, became bone." The Yankees became known as a people proud, willful, tenacious, stubborn, often taciturn, always self-reliant, men and women who demanded terribly much of themselves. They believed, with Henry David Thoreau, that the individual's first duty was "to live his life as his principles demand." The tradition of nonconformity that had given the culture its birth lived on, too—a perverse independence of mind that would cultivate the flames of the American Revolution (starting with Massachusetts' famed "Committee of Correspondence") and lead the Abolitionist cause in the years preceding the Civil War. The same spirit has evidenced itself in myriad forms straight down to the firm rejection of McCarthyism by Senators like Margaret Chase Smith and Ralph Flanders, New England's status as a center of the most vocal opposition to the Vietnam war, and Massachusetts' refusal, among all the American states, to vote for the ticket of Richard Nixon and Spiro Agnew in 1972. All this has been a kind of fulfillment of Ralph Waldo Emerson's counsel that there should always be "a minority unconvinced."

Historians like to point to the towering group of thinkers and writers born in New England in the first two decades of the 19th century, and who made their careers there: Emerson and Thoreau, Nathaniel Hawthorne and John Greenleaf Whittier, Harriet Beecher Stowe, James Russell Lowell, William Lloyd Garrison, John Bartlett, and others. A high proportion of these were rebels and reformers, fathers and mothers of the Transcendentalist and Abolitionist movements. Others in their ranks were Theodore Parker, Wendell Phillips, Massachusetts Senator Charles Sumner, and Margaret Fuller, one of America's earliest and most effective feminists. Later, in a somewhat less rebellious age, New England spawned or harbored such literary figures as William and Henry James, Henry Adams, Emily Dickinson, Edna St. Vincent Millay, Amy Lowell, Robert Lowell, and yes, Horatio Alger. Then there were such diverse figures as Mary Baker Eddy, Robert Frost, John P. Marquand, the elder and younger Oliver Wendell Holmes, and John Dewey.

There have been low points in the intellectual history of New England, especially the 1920s and '30s, the times of the Sacco-Vanzetti trial and book burning in Boston. But from Franklin Roosevelt's presidency onwards, large numbers of New England intellectuals, starting with Justice Felix Frankfurter, were drawn into the national government. More came under Massachusetts' President John F. Kennedy. A very condensed list from recent years must include Henry A. Kissinger, Daniel Patrick Moynihan, James Killian, Edwin O. Reischauer, Elliot L. Richardson, and Jerome B. Weisner. Some of the world's leading scientists are based in the region's universities; especially in Boston, the literary and artistic scene is a thriving one, often represented to the country through the *Atlantic Monthly* and Boston's public television station, WGBH, and the *Christian Science Monitor*. In 1974 *Time* magazine assembled a list of 200 outstanding young American leaders (aged 45 or younger) who were making a strong civic or social impact on the nation. An astounding 34 percent of them were either New England-educated and/or professionally active in the region.

For 200 years, New England's Puritan-Yankee stock remained virtually undiluted, permitting the development of a remarkably homogeneous culture. Then, starting in the first half of the 19th century, the repercussions of the Irish potato famine and the search of Yankee managers for a source of cheap labor resulted in a vast migration of people from the Catholic nations of Europe and French Canada. In 1850 one out of every ten New Englanders was foreign born. In the decades which followed hundreds of thousands of additional Irish arrived; the manufacturing boom in New Hampshire, Maine, and Rhode Island in particular fostered a steady growth of the French-Canadian population; and over the Atlantic came great quantities of Italians, Poles, Germans, Lithuanians, Portuguese, and Russian Jews. By 1920, almost a quarter of New England's people were foreign born, while another 36 percent had one or more foreign-born parents. No other region of the United States began to approach these percentages.

Later in this book, and especially in the Massachusetts chapter, we will review the fierce antagonisms that arose between the Yankee and Irish— a conflict only approaching solution in our own time. Also worth noting, as writer Joe McCarthy has pointed out, is that "the newcoming Italians, Slavs, Russian Jews, and French Canadians found that the long-established Irish in New England were almost as aloof and as difficult to deal with as the chilly Yankees."

The interethnic rivalries are still acute in present-day New England, as the Italians and others seek to topple the Irish from the bastions of political power. Historically, however, the more essential conflict was between the Protestantism of the Yankees and the Catholic faith claimed by most of the immigrants. The newcomers, George Wilson Pierson wrote, "knew not the Puritan code." Eventually the mass of the population worshipped "in that church the old Puritans most abominated and feared." The immigrants and their descendants were to enrich New England's culture in countless ways. Yet, as Pierson observed, the residue of Puritanism proved remarkably hardy:

> The New England independence of mind is not dead. Nor is the New England conscience. . . . Just as with the philosophy of the Greeks, or the laws laid down by the Romans, the moral attitudes of the New England culture persist, though the people who gave them birth have long since passed away. . . .
> Everyone knows that the center of the population has moved inexorably west: New Haven's carriage industry to Detroit, Amoskeag's textiles to the South, the millionaires to Texas, and the lunatic fringe to Southern California. But the moral basing point of the nation is still in the Puritan tradition.

Pierson made those observations two decades ago, but I heard a direct echo of the same one day in the spring of 1974 talking with a sprightly non-agenarian, Wilbert Snow, the Pulitzer Prize-winning poet and former governor of Connecticut. The country was in the midst of the Watergate turmoil, and Snow remarked: "New England has to set the ethical standards for the United States today, in clean politics. We bank on our Puritan heritage and the Ten Commandments." That same year the whole nation had seen an example of New England rectitude in the decision of Massachusetts' Elliot Richardson, then the Attorney General, to resign his office rather than break his word and discharge Special Watergate Prosecutor Archibald Cox (another Massachusetts man). Finally, in the dénouement of the disgraced Nixon presidency, old New England virtues seemed to be precisely the prescription the nation wanted: honesty, conscience, candor, and simplicity. It was not the first time the Puritan spirit had been re-evoked in the American experience, and surely not the last.

About the Land

Just as New England bespeaks the old and established in the terms of America's short human history, so it constitutes one of the oldest continuously existing regions in the geologic history of the world. The Green Mountains of Vermont were created some 425 million years ago, in the mists of Cambrian times; some 75 million years later the ancestors of New Hampshire's White Mountains were born as a great mass of molten granite was thrust up from the innards of the globe. Far beyond our scope here is the story, pieced together by the geologists, of the tiltings, depressions, and risings of the earth's crust, of the repeated intrusions and retreats of the sea over the hundreds of millions of years, and finally of the age of the glaciers, which began their recurrent movements across the whole face of

New England from one million until only 12,000 years ago, scraping, grinding, carving the essential face of the region as we know it.*

What the early white explorers and settlers found as they opened New England to European settlement three to four centuries ago was a land more exciting to the eye than susceptible to the plow. Most of the soil of pre-glacial times had been scraped away, buried under rocks or deposited in the ocean, leaving much rocky and barren territory and vast deposits of moraine —the rubble of clay, sand, gravel, and boulders deposited by the melting or "rotting" glaciers. Scattered among the hills, however, were pockets of rather flat, rock-free soil. These marked the spots where great blocks of ice or ice-gathered debris had dammed up the valleys, forming lakes and allowing the incoming streams to lay down a mantle of silt and sand. When these lakes finally drained a few thousand years ago, patches of land friendly to the settlers' plows were formed. The greatest of these was in the valley of the Connecticut River, where the glacier formed a dam near the present site of Middletown, Connecticut, creating a broad lake between the mountains, running 157 miles to a point about halfway up the modern-day New Hampshire-Vermont border. The lake existed some 4,000 years until the water, in a single great spring break-up at Middletown, burst its prison and rushed to the sea. As the water level dropped 90 feet, the rich, sediment-laden valley of the Connecticut, today New England's best farming area, was left exposed.

Many of the lakes never drained, of course, thus creating a prime attraction for the visitors who have found New England a cool and beckoning oasis for well over a century now. Nor did the glaciers eradicate the mountains, though they are geologically old and worn; the highest point in the Green Mountains, for instance, is Mount Mansfield, only 4,393 feet above sea level, compared to a height of some 12,000 feet at the time of its birth. The glaciers also carved an exceptionally ragged and irregular seacoast, running no less than 6,000 miles if one counts the total shoreline from Stamford, Connecticut, to Passamaquoddy Bay, Maine. That long sand spit called Cape Cod, together with the nearby islands of Nantucket and Martha's Vineyard, owe their existence to the workings of the last glacier, 12,000 years ago.

Contrary to popular impression, the face of New England as the 17th-century settlers found it was not one great impenetrable forest. There were substantial tracts of open land, some of which the Indians, all of whom were part of the great Algonkian relationship, had cleared for their crops of corn and beans. As the immigrants arrived, they snapped up the most accessible and fertile lands, along the coast and in the Connecticut River Valley. Thomas Pownall, writing in 1796, observed that the land between New Haven and Hartford was "a rich, well cultivated vale thickly settled and swarming with people. . . . It is as though you were still traveling along one continued town for 70 or 80 miles on end." As later waves of immi-

* For a particularly exciting geologic history, the reader is referred to Betty Flanders Thomson's *The Changing Face of New England* (New York: Macmillan, 1958).

grants arrived, the thrust of farming went farther and farther north and higher and higher into the region's stony hills. The years between 1830 and 1880, Betty F. Thomson noted in her history of New England land and folkways, were the heyday of the region's self-sufficient farms and little villages.

This happy state was not to last long. The hillside farms, which seemed to grow rocks better than any crop, taxed men's energies and patience; the hard winters began to take their toll; and when crops failed, the livestock suffered. Farmers began to desert their old homesteads, looking for broader lands. The Connecticut hill town of Hartland, for instance, had progressively fewer people in every Census from 1790 to the mid-20th century. At first the farmers pushed on to the less settled parts of northern New England, where they could obtain more acreage. But soon the tide turned to the broad, fertile fields of the Midwest, which received mass settlement after the opening of the Erie Canal in 1825. Then came the railroads, which could bring Midwestern crops back to the East at low freight rates, and the economic underpinnings of New England agriculture came unglued. By the thousands, New England farmers set off for the West; as Henry Ward Beecher once put it, the New Englanders came across the continent driving their lowing herds and schools and churches, their courts and lyceums before them. In the Western Reserve, in Michigan, Wisconsin, Kansas, Oregon, and many other regions, New England accents and customs cropped up.

Back home, there were the abandoned farm houses. For a season or two or three they would stand, but then the process of decay would start, to be finished off by fire or violent windstorm. Robert Frost, the great American poet who had been born in California but lived most of his life in New Hampshire and Vermont and came to symbolize New England for millions, caught the familiar scene in his poem, *The Need of Being Versed in Country Things*:

> The house had gone to bring again
> To the midnight sky a sunset glow.
> Now the chimney was all of the house that stood,
> Like a pistil after the petals go.
>
> The barn opposed across the way,
> That would have joined the house in flame
> Had it been the will of the wind, was left
> To bear forsaken the place's name. . .
>
> The birds that came to it through the air
> At broken windows flew out and in,
> Their murmur more like the sigh we sigh
> From too much dwelling on what has been. . .
>
> For them there was really nothing sad.
> But though they rejoiced in the nest they kept,
> One had to be versed in country things
> Not to believe the phoebes wept.

The verses have a special poignancy for anyone who has ever walked through the woods in New England, coming not only on mile upon mile of stone walls that once bordered fields, but also the old cellar holes. I remember them, as a child, a first startling lesson in social history, wondering whatever, whatever became of the people who once lived there. Then, in later years, in an old mountain graveyard near our New Hampshire summer home, I discovered a set of headstones that told something more of the story. Lined up neatly, the stones revealed the lifespans of Charles Adams, his wife Melinda, and their family: Charles had died in 1885 at the age of 73, and Melinda 13 years later at 82. But their son Eben had died in 1848 at the age of 7 years, Ocenia in 1850 at 11 months, Eben George in 1856 at 1 year and 5 months, Ocenia Melinda and Mary Ann, both in September 1863 at 5 and 11 years respectively, and Charles in 1864 at 20 years. In 16 years, Charles and Melinda Adams had buried *six* children. Early death from childhood diseases and epidemics was not peculiar to New England in the "good old times," but against the backdrop of New England's cruel winters, and the odds against a farmer's succeeding on those rocky hillsides, the human tragedy seems to take on epic proportions.

Whatever viability there may once have been in hillside farming in New England has long since disappeared. In the earlier days, former Congressman Richard W. Mallery of Vermont pointed out in an interview, the natural fertility of the soil in hardwood areas was not great, but enough humus had been laid down over the years so that a farmer could get several good crops once he had cleared off the trees. "If you were using a scythe and oxen, it didn't make much difference if the land was sloped or level, or whether you had one acre in a field or 20," Mallery observed. If there was a great boulder in a field, the farmer using a walking plow behind horses could easily go around it. But in the age of tractors and other large farming equipment, few suitable areas are left.

To this, one must add the fact that most New England soils, according to state and federal soil surveys, are of poor quality. The only significant exceptions are the Connecticut River Valley and large acreages of potato-producing land classified as "Caribou loam" in Maine's Aroostock County. Only 9 percent of the region's land surface is in crop or pastureland, compared to 56 percent in the U.S. as a whole. New England farming tends to be highly specialized and localized—tobacco in Connecticut, apples in Massachusetts and New Hampshire, cranberries near and on Cape Cod, potatoes in Maine, maple sugar in Vermont and New Hampshire, and milk in Vermont. In terms of volume, dairy and poultry products account for the lion's share of farm sales—62 percent of the six-state total of $670 million in the last Census of Agriculture. (Vermont, predictably, leads the pack in dairy products, while Maine is the leader in eggs and poultry.) A number of new specialty crops have been tried in recent years. Sugar beets, attempted in Maine, turned out to be a colossal failure, but there have been good results with nurseries in Massachusetts, bedding plants in Connecticut, sod in Rhode Island, vineyards in New Hampshire, and a unique newcomer—resort farms.

New England agriculture has suffered in recent years. Total acreage has dropped sharply; there are less than a quarter as many farms as there were at the end of World War II; with 5.8 percent of the national population, New England produces (in terms of dollar value) only 1.5 percent of the nation's farm products. Nor are the future prospects thought to be bright. Because of increasing pressure on agricultural land to accommodate housing, new shopping centers, factories, and the like, government economists predict additional declines in farm acreage. This will be offset in part by increased productivity, but still the total food output in the year 2000 will be the same as in the 1970s—while the region's population increases by as much as 50 percent. At a 1974 region-wide meeting called by the New England River Basins Commission, Hugh Tuttle, whose family has farmed in Dover, New Hampshire, for almost 350 years, argued that despite the likelihood of a continued decrease in farmland, production could be increased through high-intensity specialized cultivation. Even such previously untapped resources as hot water discharges from power plants, he said, could be used to let New England agriculture prosper into the next century.

There are those who worry about New England's extreme dependence on other regions for foodstuffs; at any given time, for instance, the region has only a few days' supply of agricultural goods. With a renewal of interest in backyard gardens and the exurbanites who have taken up farming in states like Vermont and Maine, some agrricultural resurgence in the region may be taking place. But in relation to New England's overall food needs, such countertrends to the long-term agricultural decline are frail indeed.

The face of New England has been radically altered by the long-term downturn in farming. In 1830, about 60 percent of New England's land was cleared for agriculture. As the farms were abandoned, or farmers let their pasturelands return to forest, the trees began to return to their primeval dominance. First came the pine forests, only to be decimated by the rapacious splurge of logging around the turn of this century; now the pine and hardwood forests are in good balance in the region. According to the U. S. Forest Service, 83 percent of the surface of New England was in forest by the early 1970s. The figures ranged from 65 percent in Rhode Island to 90 percent in Maine and New Hampshire. The forests should be a prime economic asset for the region, but the fact is that they are very poorly managed. A principal reason is that 62 percent of the forest acreage is held by private citizens in small lots averaging 75 acres. Endemically, these small landowners—ranging from clubs and housewives to business and professional people—lack the knowledge for professional classification and selective harvesting of their woodlands; often they hold the land simply as a retreat, and are offended by the idea of cutting. So New England grows more lumber than it harvests, and most of the wood used in the region has to be imported from elsewhere. Badly needed are government-fostered forest management programs, which can actually increase the aesthetic appeal and long-term recreational use of woodlands. It is hard to underestimate the importance of woodlands as a natural resource. I especially like the definition of the New England Natural Resources Center: "Forests are renewable solar energy converters."

In the chapters which follow we will take a closer look at the immensely variegated face of New England's six states. Their total land area of 66,608 square miles is less than half the size of Montana, a fourth of Texas, and a scant 11 percent of Alaska. Yet in that space one can move from the comparatively placid waters of Long Island Sound to the high cliffs and turbulent sea of the Maine coast, from the fertile Connecticut Valley to the granite top of storm-thrashed Mt. Washington, from close-packed suburbia to the vast, unpeopled stretches of northern Maine. I have met hundreds of Americans who have never seen New England, and who wonder what those of us with roots there see in it. One can do no better than quote the words of Henry Cabot Lodge, Sr., the Massachusetts Senator of the early part of this century. "New England," he said, "has a harsh climate, a barren soil, a rough and stormy coast, and yet we love it, even with a love passing those of dwellers in more favored regions."

Parsing New England

That New England is a distinct region of America, long recognized as having a unity and individuality of character granted few, if any, others, there should be little argument. As early as 1789, in his seminal work on the sections of the United States, Jedidiah Morse noted the states east of New York had "the general name of New England" with "several things" in common including "their religion, manners, customs, and character; their climate, soil, productions, natural history, &c . . ." The other states of the fledgling country, by contrast, Morse described and discussed separately without any sectional groupings.* In a later edition, he did separate the United States into three "grand divisions"—Eastern, Middle, and Southern States, the first of which was "that part of America, which, since the year 1614, has been known by the name of New England."

Common grievances, as the American South was soon to prove, help to forge regional identity, and in the early 19th century New England certainly felt it had much to complain of in the dominance of the Virginian dynasty, Jacksonian democracy, and the fall from power of the Federalist party. Indeed, when the British extended their blockade to the New England states during the War of 1812 and brought shipping to a standstill, the Federalist-controlled legislature of Massachusetts called a convention of all the New England states at Hartford. There was even talk of secession—the same sin for which New England would later castigate the South so soundly. The Hartford convention finally settled for a severe scolding of the Madison administration, but the point of a special New England identity in the Union had been underscored.

* Jedidiah Morse, *The American Geography; or, A View of the Present State of the United States of America* (Elizabethtown, New Jersey, 1789).

"Every school child," John Gunther commented in *Inside U.S.A.* three decades ago, "knows what the six New England states are, and what is the knifelike boundary of the region as a whole." In contrast to the loose and conglomerate geographical expression "the Middle West," Gunther suggested, New England was the epitome of clear-cut regional identity. A Yale University study of New England regionalism, published in 1947 under the leadership of Professor Maurice E. H. Rotival, suggested that "in tradition no area of the United States, other than perhaps the Old South, has been better known for uniqueness and self-consciousness. . . . New England is a region, in a most fundamental sense, because its people think it is. For three centuries, there has been a self-consciousness in the area that many peoples fight wars to obtain."

Heretics do, from time to time, dare to challenge the idea of New England, the single entity. Pointing to the topographic differences (from oyster beds and salt meadows to mountains) and other centrifugal forces in the area, George Wilson Pierson suggested only half in jest: "On the map it looks as if New England *ought* to be a region. Whereas, in sober truth, geographically New England is not so much a region as an optical illusion." Elliot Richardson counseled me to take notice of the sharp subdivisions of New England. Most of Connecticut, he said, was in the New York orbit, with very little communication with Boston, and virtually none with Providence. Vermont, in its day-to-day dealings, he said, related primarily to New York State. That leaves only four states that do have relatively close economic ties and other needs for communication—New Hampshire, Maine, Massachusetts, and Rhode Island. "And in them," Richardson said, "you're only talking about a relatively small area embracing Providence around through eastern Massachusetts, southern New Hampshire, southern Maine, and maybe as far north as Portland." A lot of Maine and New Hampshire, he suggested, remains "real hinterland."

Withal, Richardson and others point out, New England does have certain common cores of interest, among which are its fuel and railroad problems (to which we shall return later). Unless it be Atlanta for the new South, no other section of America has a single "capital" of such generally acknowledged stature as Boston, long the spiritual and economic leader of New England. For the first time in decades, Boston now has a quality newspaper with aspirations to be the voice of an entire region—the Boston *Globe.*

A theme which does appear and reappear in writing about these six states is that there are really two New Englands—the rural, lightly populated and heavily forested northern tier of Maine, New Hampshire, and Vermont, contrasted to the heavily industrialized group of Massachusetts, Rhode Island, and Connecticut. The "northern" New England image is one of quaint village greens, clean, white church spires, and miles of stone walls attesting to the struggle of farmers of yore to carve out fields for their crops. That of "southern" New England is more of heavily industrialized cities, peopled in the great majority by foreign ethnic groups, and of New York-oriented suburbs.

In a sense the north-south dichotomy is correct. Rhode Island, Massachusetts, and Connecticut, for instance, rank from second to fourth among all 50 states in density of population, with 923, 739, and 634 persons per square mile, respectively. In New Hampshire, by contrast, there are only 85 persons a square mile, in Vermont 50, and Maine 33. In percent of the population living in urban areas by the Census definition, Rhode Island ranks third, Massachusetts fifth, and Connecticut 14th among all the states; the comparable rankings for New Hampshire, Maine, and Vermont, are 37th, 41st, and 50th respectively. Likewise, the percentage of ethnic minorities in southern New England is significantly higher than in the region's northern tier.

Nevertheless, some caveats must be entered to a north-south division. Over great stretches of Massachusetts and Connecticut, and even sections of little Rhode Island, one can find large tracts of forest, farmlands, and little villages that look like a chapter out of yesteryear. Perhaps the most exquisite, perfectly preserved town green of all is in Litchfield, Connecticut, and there are many like it in the southern tier. By contrast, the percentage of the working force that spends its days in factories is not much lower in northern New England than in the southern three states. (In New Hampshire the factory employment percentage is even higher than in Massachusetts.) And for gloomy mill town scenes, one need look no farther than Manchester, New Hampshire, or Lewiston, Maine.

One should also take note of the portion of New England that can be considered part of the United States' east coast megalopolis. There is no commonly accepted definition of megalopolis, but the fact is that 88 percent of New England's people already live within a metropolitan area, or within a 20-mile drive of the borders of one. All of Rhode Island and almost all of Connecticut and Massachusetts are now "megalopolitan," and the northern borders of this remarkable agglomeration of population now appear to have extended into southeastern New Hampshire and Maine's Portland area. Some also see its influence in Vermont's ski and second-home boom, and project its eventual growth as far north as Montreal. In terms of the most dense type of population concentration, government economist Jim Wallace has predicted that by the year 2000 there will be a tightly knit, interdependent urban area from New York through Hartford to Springfield. Another will run from Providence, through New Bedford, Boston, and Worcester, to the Manchester and Concord areas of New Hampshire. The rural stretches between cities, which even megalopolis enjoys, will have disappeared unless stringent land use regulations are imposed in the next few years.

Thus, whatever the indigenous economic problems of New England may be, the northward thrust of the eastern megalopolis is expected to keep the population increasing from now to the end of the century. One government projection is for the addition of four million people by the year 2000—about 3.5 million of that total in the three southern states, where the population pressures from the eastern megalopolis are by far the greatest. That means from a population total of about 12 million in 1970, New England would rise to roughly 16 million by the start of the next century.

The chart below shows the growth of New England's population in the 30-year period from 1940 to 1970, and the rough projections to 2000:

	1940	*1970*	*Projection for 2000*
All of New England	8,437,290	11,841,663 (+ 40%)	16,000,000 (+ 35%)
Southern tier	6,739,399	9,667,604 (+ 43%)	13,100,000 (+ 36%)
Massachusetts	4,316,721	5,689,170 (+ 32%)	
Connecticut	1,709,242	3,031,709 (+ 77%)	
Rhode Island	713,346	946,725 (+ 33%)	
Northern tier	1,697,981	2,174,059 (+ 28%)	2,900,000 (+ 34%)
New Hampshire	491,524	737,681 (+ 50%)	
Maine	847,226	992,048 (+ 17%)	
Vermont	359,231	444,330 (+ 24%)	

The figures make it clear that the great weight of population growth since 1940 has occurred in the southern parts of the region, especially heavily suburbanized Connecticut, which lies close to New York, the heart of megalopolis. The projections to 2000 indicate more of the same, even if the rate of growth, in percentage terms, will be more nearly equal than in the recent past.

There was a time, of course, when New England had numbers of people, and resultant political power, of immense proportions. Close to one out of every four Americans lived in the region in the year 1800. By 1900, the figure had dropped to only 7 percent. It then declined gradually to 5.8 percent in 1970. The region's population growth rate was about 70 percent of the national average in the 1940s and 1950s, and 95 percent in the 1960s. It then dropped to 63 percent of the national average between 1970 and 1975, contemporaneously with a sharp decline in the region's economy. The demographers' projections for the last decades of this century could prove to be much too high if that trend were to continue, and so it is to the economic problems of the region that we turn next.

Life in a "Mature" Economy

In the nineteenth century, saws and axes made in New England cleared the forests of Ohio; New England ploughs broke the prairie sod; New England scales weighed wheat and meat in Texas; New England serge clothed businessmen in San Francisco; New England cutlery skinned hides to be tanned in Milwaukee and sliced apples to be dried in Missouri; New England whale oil lit lamps across the continent; New England blankets warmed children by night and New England textbooks preached at them by day; New

England guns armed the troops; and New England dies, lathes, looms, forges, presses and screwdrivers outfitted factories far and wide. But by the twentieth century, New England plants were closing up and laying off workers. To most New Englanders the cause of the region's economic decline seemed obvious—loss of industry. They brooded upon reasons for this loss: cheaper labor in the South, obsolescence of the old brick factories along the rivers and beside the waterfalls, the decay of Boston's docks, imports from Switzerland and Japan.

—Jane Jacobs, in The Economy of Cities

New England is the American prototype of a "mature" economy, in vivid contrast to the nation's South and West. As the economists tell it, a mature economy is one in which the transition from agriculture to industry is long since accomplished, a major manufacturing base is in place, and wages have worked themselves up to a high level, at least in comparision to other regions. The capital stock tends to be aged, costs of operations high, and new job opportunities scarce. Such an economy is likely to be an exporter of capital, dependent on the interest and dividends it receives from it; this leads in turn to a more cautious approach to investment, aversion to risk-taking, and a drying up of the entrepreneurial juices.* The region with a mature economy is seriously disadvantaged in competing with areas that are still moving to an industrial base, where plants are newer, wages lower, the average age of the population lower, and there is less of a public burden to be carried in terms of retirees, the unemployed, and the welfare population.

The once mighty New England textile industry, a bulwark of the region's industrial prosperity in the 19th century, is Exhibit No. 1 of the problems of the mature economy. The industry had its genesis in 1790 in a daring act of industrial espionage by a young British immigrant, Samuel Slater, who brought to America, in his head, the secret design of the first power looms ever made. It was capitalized by shrewd Yankee businessmen, largely out of capital generated by New England's seafaring successes. Power came from the region's abundant, fast-flowing rivers. And low-cost manpower was available—from Yankee yeomen who could no longer make a living on the region's rocky soil, and later from hundreds of thousands of immigrants from Canada and Europe.

By the early 1900s, at its peak, the New England textile industry employed more than 400,000 men and women, located in mill towns large and small including the massive operations at cities like Massachusetts' Lowell, Lawrence, and Fall River, New Hampshire's Manchester, and Rhode Island's Woonsocket. Trouble began to brew, however, when New England's southern competitors perceived that synthetics were about to cut into cotton textiles and began to branch into the new products. In typically

---

* There are many business start-ups in modern New England, but many of them die on the vine from the harshness of the economic climate. The region's greater problem, economists say, lies in the lethargic attitude toward growth of its established firms.

stubborn style, the Yankees refused to move to new lines. Even more serious, the Southern textile magnates could hire mill hands at much lower wages than those in New England. Textiles began to move southward in such proportions that between 1929 and 1950, no less than 149,000 textile jobs were lost in New England. That still left 264,000 in the region but the decline was just gaining steam. By 1954 only 179,000 textile jobs would be left, by the early 1970s not much more than 75,000.

In 1953, serving his first year in the U. S. Senate, John F. Kennedy produced some solid evidence of the type of inducements the Southland was using in the pirating of New England textiles. He cited a letter from a Southern community leader to a leading Massachusetts textile manufacturer, promising a tax-free modern factory financed by tax-exempt municipal bonds, inexpensive TVA power, and cheap nonunion labor. The Southern firm, Kennedy said, "could utilize a federal tax amortization certificate for its machinery and subminimum learner rates for its initial work crew, while taking advantage of lower unemployment compensation taxes and cheaper transportation rates."

The Southern tactic worked so well that in 1949 the unemployment rate had soared to 26 percent in Lawrence, 18 percent in New Bedford, 12 percent in Fall River and Lowell, and 13 percent in the Providence-Pawtucket area. A quarter century later, the unemployment rate in these areas —defined as "chronically depressed" by government economists—would still be well above regional and national levels.

By the early 1970s the New England textile industry was still a factor to be reckoned with, each year producing some $2 billion worth of shipments. The long decline in employment had finally leveled off. It seemed that the plants that had survived the siren song of the South, survived the waves of Japanese and other foreign imports in recent years, survived antipollution regulations, and still could find enough labor at the industry's rather low wage levels, would find a way to persevere in the future. New England textiledom is split into 800 separate firms, but as inefficient as that may seem, and often is, the cloud has a silver lining. A goodly number of the smaller firms have carved out a niche for themselves in very specialized kinds of textile products that no competitor—Southern or foreign—can make quite as well or economically.

Leather and shoemaking is an even more venerable New England industry than textiles; in fact, the first shoemaking shop in the country was opened in Lynn, Massachusetts, in 1635. For close to three centuries New England shoes dominated the national market; at the start of this century, for instance, Massachusetts alone made 47 percent of the nation's footwear.

The first significant reversal came in the 1920s, when most of the mass-produced, cheap shoes produced in cities like Lynn, Haverhill, and Brockton were lost to plants in the Mid-Atlantic and Midwest regions. A steady erosion in the New England shoe industry reduced employment from 145,-000 in 1929 to just under 110,000 in the first years after World War II. Still, shoes were an underpinning of the economy in scores of Massachusetts, Maine, and New Hampshire communities.

Then came a sudden flood of foreign imports which knocked the bottom out from under this rather staid, steady industry in the 1960s and early '70s. In 15 years foreign imports, including finely crafted Italian and Spanish shoes, jumped from less than 5 percent to 40 percent of American production. The competition from lower-paying European and Southern plants, rapid fashion changes, the lack of process and production technology in New England's undercapitalized shoe factories, and the stiff pollution controls imposed on tanneries all fell like a storm on the region's footwear industry. Major producers like Bates, French, Shriner, and Stetson all abandoned New England. Thirty-five percent of the region's shoe jobs disappeared between 1958 and 1971. The remaining New England firms scrambled to modernize and automate their plants, but the future remained uncertain for the remaining firms and their 60,000-odd workers.

All of this was a grim portent for New England because even after the massive loss of shoe jobs, the footwear industry remained the biggest single employer in Maine, number two in New Hampshire, and a subsidiary but still important factor of the manufacturing mix in Massachusetts.

There are, of course, other major industrial segments to the New England economy. Electrical machinery, including communications equipment and electronic components, accounts for 12 percent of the region's factory jobs. Almost as much employment is provided by the traditional sector of nonelectrical machinery—metal-cutting tools, machine tool accessories, engines, and turbines, an area in which the region got an invaluable headstart in the 19th century. Other important elements are transportation equipment (aircraft and the remnants of the shipbuilding industry), fabricated metals, rubber and plastics, paper, printing, and publishing. Space precludes reviewing all these industries here, but it is worth noting that their 1974 "pre-recession" employment—1,427,000—was 135,000 less than seven years before, and not much different from the total a generation ago.

"Structural" Unemployment and the Energy Deficit

Over the span of the region's history, New Englanders have been able to overcome the adverse odds posed by their location and sparse resources through a remarkable mix of pluck, luck, the China trade and clipper ships, technological innovation, cheap immigrant labor, tariffs, smart financing, wartime stimuli, and the momentum built by the region's headstart in the industrial revolution.

For most of the 1960s it appeared that New England would be able to luck it out again—to make a relatively painless and rapid transition from outmoded styles of low-wage factory employment to better-paid production jobs and a high-technology, export-oriented type of economy.

As it turned out, however, the New Englanders were too optimistic, too soon. They failed to take account of the degree to which the soaring job levels of the early 1960s in electronics, machinery, and university-research related employment were linked to the Vietnam war and the space race. Starting in the last years of the decade, the federal government began to cut back in defense and aerospace orders. Then came the national recession of 1970–71, accelerating the trend. To their horror, regional economists noted that the New England unemployment rate, which for two decades had scarcely varied from the national level, suddenly began to diverge up and away from the country as a whole. The region failed to register any significant recovery from the 1970–71 recession. By 1973 there were 65,000 more people unemployed in New England than had been projected just three years before. The regional unemployment rate from 1971 to 1974 was 25 percent higher than the rate in the rest of the nation. And to top it all off, major defense base cutbacks occurred in 1974, especially in Massachusetts and Rhode Island. The immediate and direct impact was the loss of more than 30,000 civilian jobs and a loss to the regional economy of half a billion dollars in personal income.

Then came the national recession of the mid-1970s, which affected New England more seriously than any other region of the nation. By May 1975, for instance, the regional unemployment rate was 11.6 percent, compared to 9.2 percent in the country as a whole. The most serious jobless rates of all were in Massachusetts, at 12.6 percent, and poor little Rhode Island with an astronomical 16.2 percent rate. Most alarmingly, economists doubted whether the region could recover as quickly or easily as the nation at large. The suggestion was that New England had entered an era of structural—that is, basic, long-term—high unemployment, which would keep the region behind the nation for a period of years. The reasons lay in a list of interrelated economic disabilities that would be enough to make a less resourceful people throw up their hands in despair. Foremost among these were those relating to raw materials and energy:

■   Scarce natural resources. New England has virtually no indigenous mineral resources outside of garden variety products like granite, sand, gravel, limestone, and marble. The value of minerals mined is scarcely one half of one percent of the national total. Missing are such resources as iron, copper, gold, or silver, which have permitted other areas to prosper. The region does have abundant wood resources, but, as I noted earlier, they are so poorly managed that New England is a net importer of timber.

■   Dearth of fuels. This, of course, is the region's gravest resource problem. The general assumption is that the six states have no mineable coal.* Even more serious, no oil or gas reserves have ever been discovered under New England's soil. The bitter irony is that this region, at the very end of the fuel distribution lines, uses more oil, and pays more for it, than any other part of the nation. The region is 70 to 75 percent dependent on petroleum to power its utilities and heat its homes, factories, and public buildings. For the same uses, no other region of the country has a petroleum de-

---

* Anthracite was dug in Massachusetts in early times, but it is not known whether the deposits there are close enough to the surface to be commercially feasible.

pendency of more than 25 percent; the other regions, of course, are closer to coal and natural gas reserves. And in addition to lacking local sources of oil, New England has no refineries and no deepwater ports. In the words of Charles Burkhardt, a New England oil expert, "the only other part of the world more dependent upon petroleum than New England [is] Japan. . . . If someone had sat up nights for a generation trying to find ways to confound New England's petroleum economy by design, he couldn't have done better than we have done by accident!"

High prices of industrial fuel have long been a deterrent to the growth in New England of such high-energy users as glass, aluminum, and steel. For a number of years, the region did benefit from low-cost home heating oil because it could import that fuel, technically defined as "middle distillate," from Mideast and South American countries that sold it for substantially lower prices than U. S. oil producers. In 1959, however, the federal government imposed a mandatory oil import quota program, purportedly for reasons of national security. New Englanders, however, thought it was a sop to Texas and Louisiana oil interests, so powerful in Washington under Republican and Democratic administrations alike.* Not long after President Nixon took office in 1969, he created a high-level Cabinet committee to study the problem. The committee recommended discontinuing the oil import quotas, but Nixon refused, a move that had every appearance of a paying off of some of the big oil contributors to his campaign. The quotas were not lifted until 1973—and even then a high tariff was imposed. In the words of New Hampshire's Senator Thomas J. McIntyre, "even in those years when there was not a threat of shortage, prices [of heating and heavy industrial oil] were held artificially high and we [in New England] were denied any substantial competition which would have resulted if lower-priced foreign oil had been permitted."

New England's vulnerability in petroleum use, however, was thrown into bold relief, as never before, when the world price of crude oil started to rise rapidly at the start of the 1970s, capped off by the Arab oil embargo and enormous price increases of 1973–74. The chairman of Northeast Utilities, for instance, said that the cost of 24 million barrels of oil in 1969 had been about $50 million, but in 1974 had risen to $325 million! Between 1973 and 1974 alone, New England's total energy bill rose by 139 percent, or roughly $1.2 *billion*. On a per capita basis, the increase in New England was close to three times the national average. According to studies by the First National Bank of Boston, total manufacturing costs in the region began to

---

* The ostensible reason for the oil import quota program was to stimulate domestic oil exploration and production, but all it really did was to increase costs to New England and the Midwest and bolster profits for some segments of the oil industry. Some members of the New England congressional delegation complained lustily, but lacked the political clout to do much about it. On the other hand, the New England Congressmen may have outsmarted themselves in fighting to keep the price of natural gas regulated. Paul London, director of the New England Research Office, argues that "we sealed most of the natural gas in other regions by making it unprofitable to put the gas into interstate pipelines." There were enough pipelines constructed to reach throughout the Southwest and South and many other parts of the country. But they never quite made it to New England, with the result that the other regions had the advantage of a particularly inexpensive fuel, putting New England at a severe competitive disadvantage.

rise at an annual rate of 2.2 percent because of higher energy costs alone. In some manufacturing areas, the bank warned, higher energy costs could drive firms "close to a financial crisis stage."

And all of that was before President Ford in early 1975 announced his plan to place a $3-a-barrel tax on oil imports to reduce domestic consumption. To New Englanders, the move looked like the most callous step imaginable, one that would darken for years the chances of a real economic recovery in the region.

In the face of the oil shortages and blackmail prices, New England began to scramble for alternative energy sources—and found obstacles at every turn. Some utilities sought to convert to coal, but any broad expansion of coal burning threatened to violate ambient air standards. The region was already more advanced than any other part of the country in nuclear power generation, but serious environmental problems with the nuclear plants already on line hampered any rapid advancement. There was talk of the possibilities of solar and wind power, but both were relatively untried. (Solar energy, in particular, could be beneficial for New England, but it will take time to perfect the technology.)

"So we end up with oil for our current use and foreseeable future," John Buckley, vice chairman of Northeast Petroleum, commented. "Without oil," he said, "we can have no growth, no upward social mobility; the inevitable result will be severe social tensions." Buckley pointed to paper and pulp, an energy-intensive industry, as an example of potential problems. Typically, the ownership of paper companies in New England is outside the region, with headquarters in places like Philadelphia, New York, and Chicago. With their power costs in New England practically quadrupled, and without the alternative of natural gas or coal open to them in other regions, the paper companies would certainly not be likely to expand their New England facilities. And when the paper industry encounters a future downturn, the corporate managers would be likely to close down New England operations first. (Despite the energy shortage, however, the paper scarcity and high prices of the mid-1970s were stimulating hundreds of millions of dollars of investment in pulp and paper mills by big corporations in states like Maine.)

The region's sky-high fuel costs also threaten the future of other high-energy users, such as brickmakers or florists (the largest rose-growing company in the U.S. is located in Massachusetts). And while energy represents a smaller share of the costs of blue-ribbon firms like General Electric, Raytheon, Polaroid, and Monsanto, some of their New England operations could be jeopardized as well. As an example, the turbine division of GE at Lynn, Massachusetts, employing roughly 10,000 workers, uses a million barrels of oil a year, generating its own power. That oil bill rose from $3.5 million to $12 million a year in late 1973—a not insignificant factor in the profit and loss sheet for that plant.

The energy crisis served to heat up the already spirited debate about the need, envisioned by the oilmen and others, for New England refineries, deepwater ports, and possible drilling for oil offshore on the Georges Bank. Potential supplies of oil and gas from its own continental shelf, the oilmen argued, would guarantee New England a secure fuel source and avoid the high tariffs on refined foreign petroleum. With or without its own offshore oil, they said, New England ought to construct refineries for purposes of self-sufficiency in processing, and as a way to escape the high fees on oil product imports from abroad. Modern refineries, they argued, can be built with safeguards to stop odors and other unpleasant side-effects. Opponents replied that benefits from offshore development would be canceled out by damages to biological life on the Georges Bank, the lifeblood of New England's $100 million fishing industry.* The environmentalists foresaw, according to one summary, "coastlines daubed with oil and spreading industrial blight, which would deface scenic coastal areas and threaten the region's valuable tourist industry."

The "yea" or "nay" on Georges Bank oil development was effectively removed from New England control, however, when the Supreme Court in 1975 ruled that the federal government had exclusive right to control oil development on the outer-continental shelf. The Interior Department quickly set in motion the machinery to lease tracts to the oil companies for exploration and later development. If oil in sufficient quantities were found, coastal regions of New England would be obliged to accommodate the whole infrastructure necessary to oil extraction, including warehouses, rigs, platform construction, inland shipment of oil, and possibly refineries. Richard Dowd of Connecticut's department of environmental protection said that "a juggernaut is coming our way, piloted by the oil companies and fueled by the federal government"—for which the region was ill-prepared. Dowd suggested a New England interstate authority to compete on leases with the oil firms, build refineries, provide housing for oil workers, and the like. The region needed that kind of innovative action, he said, "to grasp the off-shore oil issue and turn it to our economic advantage and environmental protection."

Many New Englanders would like to avoid oil development altogether. They argue that in 20 or 30 years new sources would be depleted, or irrelevant because of new energy sources, and that in any event there would be no real savings to New England consumers. At the first meeting of the New England Energy Council in 1974, the group's vice chairman, K. Dun Gifford, said the stated world price of oil would control the price of oil from the Georges Bank, and that even at full production, Georges Bank could produce only one-thirtieth of New England's oil demand. Gifford, who is also chairman of Massachusetts Common Cause and vice president of Boston's Cabot, Cabot & Forbes, said conservation was the key to a sensi-

---

* The oilmen can argue, with good evidence, that the huge growth of offshore drilling in the Gulf of Mexico has done nothing to harm that region's thriving fishing industry. New England fisheries are already in dire straits, for quite different reasons—the region's antiquated fishing fleets, and the aggressive competition of the foreign trawlers and huge "factory ships" for fish processing that have invaded New England coastal waters in massive numbers in recent years. That story is treated in more detail in the Massachusetts chapter of this book.

ble regional energy policy. Even in the absence of a needed federal policy, he said,

The New England states could prohibit the sale of automobiles of certain sizes [high gasoline consumption models] in the region. The states could establish their own gasoline tax and, with the proceeds, build solar energy collectors for heating and cooling. . . . They could require a reduction in energy consumption by residential, commercial, and industrial users. . . . They could jointly decide the location of a refinery or nuclear generating stations. But none of this is happening. . . .

■ High electric power costs. Even before the phrase "energy crisis" entered the vernacular, New England homeowners and factories had learned to pay far above the national average for their electricity. The differential was variously reported as high as 50 percent in the 1940s, 15 percent around 1960, and 33 percent in 1968. The high cost of power, according to a 1970 study of the New England Regional Commission, had been due to the large number of individual utilities and the small size of their service areas and loads. The commission recommended a single agency with authority to locate and construct new generating and transmitting facilities in the region —thus reviving the public power controversy that erupted a half century ago over the suggested Passamaquoddy tidal-power project in Maine and has continued in various forms since. As recently as 1973 the voters of Maine overwhelmingly rejected a proposed state public power authority. But in the same year a Massachusetts Congressman, Michael J. Harrington, followed up on the Regional Commission's report with a bill to set up a New England regional power and environmental protection agency, modeled after the Tennessee Valley Authority. The idea was to create a "quasi-public" agency with directors appointed by the President, "to compete with private utilities and thereby bring down the price of power." The economies would allegedly be achieved by taking advantage of mass purchasing, avoiding large profit dividends and corporate salaries, and soliciting federal subsidies for power plant construction.

That approach has worked magnificently in the Tennessee Valley—a story reviewed in a prior volume of this series, *The Border South States.* But it has never been given a chance in New England.* Public power advocates claim the obstacle is the influence of New England's private utilities, whose massive propaganda campaigns, financed indirectly through customer electric charges, have defeated them repeatedly in the legislatures and at the polls.

Problems of Cost, Location, and Apathy

Fuels and electric power are not the only unusually expensive commodities in New England. The overall cost of living is higher than in any other

---

* Public power, in fact, accounted for only 2.7 percent of New England's installed electric generating capacity in the early 1970s. Vermont is the only state with a significant share of public power (21.4 percent), a cause championed over the years by former Governor and Senator George D. Aiken and others.

part of the coterminous U.S.A. According to the U. S. Labor Department's Bureau of Labor Statistics, Boston is *the* most expensive city; an average family of four there must have an income of $14,893 a year (in 1973 dollars) to maintain an "intermediate" standard of living. The figures are not much lower in Hartford or Portland, and even small cities and rural areas of New England have higher living costs than the rest of the country.

The high cost of doing business in the region is underscored by high construction costs, high land prices, and environmental controls stricter than the U. S. average in most New England states. Taxes also top the national rankings. In Massachusetts and Connecticut, with the bulk of the regional population, per capita state and local taxes rank third and fifth highest, respectively, among all 50 states. Vermont comes in first, and Maine seventh, in the ranking of taxes as a percentage of personal income. The principal reason for New England's high tax rates is the advanced level of government-financed social services, including welfare, unemployment compensation, health, and education. Even before the 1973-74 energy crisis, it was estimated that it would cost a company 63 percent more to do business in Massachusetts than Texas, based on cost of unemployment and workmen's compensation, state taxes, and power costs.

A few New Englanders see a silver lining in the high social service and tax picture. President William Brown of the First National Bank of Boston, for instance, has been quoted as saying that Massachusetts' social costs have already been factored into the economy. "We've had our problems, and California and the South will get them later," he said. In the interim, however, it is hard to see how New England will not suffer in the stiff interstate and interregional competition to hold or attract new job-producing plants and capital investment.

Finally, two other regional disabilities must be noted: New England's location, and the apparently heavy odds against coordinated economic problem solving.

▪   Locational disadvantages. "Located here in the northeastern corner of the country," Robert Eisenmenger of the Federal Reserve Bank of Boston has noted, New England plants find themselves "distant from national markets." There are many cases, he points out, in which competing manufacturers are located between the New England producer and both his suppliers and potential customers. The point is easily overdrawn, because the markets of the eastern megalopolis *are* close to New England. Probably the greater problems relate to the region's problems in transportation, both within New England and in its contact with the outside world.

In contrast to the 19th century, when the great fleet of New England sailing ships were among the fastest in the world, New England shipbuilding has stagnated and New England ports have fallen into disrepair. Almost all water transportation in the region is coastal—in an era when other regions, tapping federal funds, have made spectacular advances in river- and canal-borne shipping. Most of the coastal shipping is involved with fuel transportation, and the region exports few of its own manufactures by water. The only notable exception to deterioration of the ports has been a new container port in Boston (though in view of the region's compactness, a modern port facility at Boston should be sufficient except for oil).

Highway building in the region has proceeded well. Among other things, new superhighways have made it easier for people from the rest of megalopolis to reach northern New England for skiing and summer vacations. But in competing with other regions, the new highways have not been much of a plus, since the rest of the nation has received the same infusion of federally financed interstate roads. In fact, New England probably "exported" a lot of interstate mileage to other regions because its residents, with comparatively high incomes, pay more than an equal per capita share of federal taxes, and New England itself had much shorter distances to be connected by the interstates. In any event, large-scale highway building would be a bad prescription for New England in the next decades. There are air pollution problems in the congested areas, and already there are enough roads in New England to pave over the entire state of Rhode Island.

Railroad service is a disaster in the region. The system is working at only one-third capacity; stations are decaying; only the most minimal passenger service remains;* hundreds of miles of track lie abandoned; and the two major railroads of the region—the Penn Central and Boston and Maine —are bankrupt, along with five other Class I railroads and numerous small carriers. Something may be salvaged as a result of the Northeast Regional Rail Service Act, passed by Congress in 1973, but any solution is likely to involve the abandonment of more uneconomical runs. The consequences of a final demise of the railroads can scarcely be exaggerated. Factories would be closed, thousands would be put out of work, and many busy communities would become ghost towns. According to a study of the bankrupt Boston and Maine, for instance, the loss of its rail service would cost 51,250 jobs in the five states it serves. In addition, the shutdown would trigger a 1–5 percent increase in the price New Englanders pay for basic commodities. The economies of rail service, particularly in a fuel-scarce era, are impressive. According to Frank Geremia, Rhode Island's supervisor of transportation planning, the rails can carry, for each gallon of fuel expended, three to five times as much freight as trucks, or 125 times as much as air cargo. In addition, a single rail track can carry 40,000 people an hour, 20 times the capacity of a highway lane.

Passenger air service, vital to any region's economic well-being, presents a mixed picture. Boston's Logan Airport is one of the country's most heavily used, with frequent connections to other parts of the nation and Europe. There is a good level of passenger service to Hartford-Springfield and mediocre service to cities like Portland, Bangor, Burlington, and Providence. After that, the picture is depressing in the extreme. Northeast and

---

* Over 54 million passengers passed through Boston's North and South Stations in 1945, but by 1970 the figure had sunk to 9 million. Maine and New Hampshire have no passenger service whatever, and Vermont is serviced by only two passenger trains a day.

Mohawk, two principal regional trunklines, were merged into Delta and Allegheny, which in turn have viewed service to smaller New England cities as an unnecessary encumbrance and received permission from the Civil Aeronautics Board to discontinue numerous lines. Vast areas of New England must now depend on commuter airlines, which at least have the advantage of being locally owned. But the commuter lines are not certified by the CAB, lack copilots, do not have to fly fixed schedules, and are not given the route subsidy and protection afforded major carriers. Again, one sees an area in which the combination of intraregional lethargy and federal indifference imperils New England's present and future.

▪ Apathy, fragmentation. "I used to tell New Englanders the one thing you could touch, feel, and smell when you got off the plane at Logan was apathy." Dr. James M. Howell, who made that remark, is a Texas-born dynamo who took over the "proper Bostonian" research department of the First National Bank of Boston in 1970 and started a one-man crusade to convince New England business and political circles of the dire prospects for the region's economy and the need for coordinated region-wide planning.

The obstacles are formidable. New England has a surfeit of old, capital-deficient, and rather inefficient manufacturers,* many of them family-owned, known for their lethargic attitude toward growth possibilities. Many of the region's banks fit into the same category. There are notable exceptions to the rule, but not enough to give New England a progressive business climate. During the 1960s the national conglomerates had a field day snapping up the family-owned businesses, especially in northern New England. By the early 1970s, 19 of the 22 Vermont plants with more than 500 workers were owned by out-of-state corporations. In Maine, all of the six firms with 2,000 or more workers were absentee-owned. The same applied to 16 of New Hampshire's largest firms. Some executives, like G. William Miller, president of the Providence-based Textron Corporation (itself a conglomerate), believe that the influx of competent, professional managers from the outside has sharpened the region's competitiveness.† If Miller is right, however, New England would be an exception to the general rule I have observed across the country in which the sale of factories to outside interests dampens the possibilities for progressive economic or civic planning within states or communities. Geoffrey Faux, co-director of the Cambridge-based Center for Community Economic Development, put the case especially well:

There are rarely any employment benefits from absentee ownership in a small community. Some studies show that the immediate direct effect of a merger on jobs is negative, and there's evidence that outside ownership has a deadening effect upon

* According to figures assembled by Howell's research department, the average age of capital equipment in New England is 11-plus years, compared to eight years for plants of the same companies outside the region. In the Massachusetts textile industry, the average age of machinery is over 17 years.
† Quoted in *Business Week*, August 4, 1973.

growth. For example, between 1958 and 1969, firms headquartered in Maine with over 500 employees expanded employment by over 82 percent while firms owned outside the state grew only eight percent. Absentee corporations tend to bank and purchase accounting, engineering and other professional services in the corporate headquarters, rather than in the vicinity of their plants. They also encourage purchasing of supplies and materials from national firms. Absentee corporate personnel have little interest in the community from which they derive their profits, and an absentee firm is quicker to lay off workers at the slightest sign of a downturn than is a local firm whose management feels some responsibility for the community.

Regardless of the character of business ownership in New England, forceful leadership to deal with region-wide economic problems has been lacking. The small, locally owned firms have evidenced a parochial point of view, while the conglomerates have other problems to attend to. Except for the 15-odd big corporations that have moved into Connecticut's Fairfield County from New York (and thus have no special orientation to New England), the entire six-state region has headquarters of only 14 of the 500 largest industrial corporations on the *Fortune* list. The dearth of regional leadership potential is also reflected by the small number of the country's large banks, retailers, utilities, or transportation firms which consider New England "home." (The major exception, of course, is life insurance; New England is headquarters for a fifth of the largest national firms.)

James Howell complained that New England's public policy makers were infected by "a wide belief that there's little we can do to help the local economy—that we in New England are the tail of the [national] dog." "They can't come off the idea," he added, "that politics is first and economics second, third, or fifth." The region's governors, Howell argued, should be able to influence 25 to 30 percent of the economic activity in their states. His bank, he said, had done a substantial amount of forecasting to show which industries, if encouraged, could be expected to expand significantly in the near future, making up for the region's glaring job deficit. But he despaired that the six governors, acting singly or in unison, would utilize that information to create actual new jobs. Traditionally, the New England state governments have invested very little, compared to national averages, in industrial development.

That old-style lethargy, however, may be breaking down. In the final section of this chapter, I will review the impressive array of governmental and private organizations now examining, and trying to develop solutions for common New England problems. Howell himself has advanced by several notches the quality and extent of research into the region's economy. Like a missionary, he has criss-crossed New England spreading the message that the region desperately needs new jobs, fewer people on unemployment and welfare, and reduced state spending (particularly in Massachusetts). He views his role as helping to fill a void left by the death of two famed Harvard economists, Sumner H. Slichter and Seymour E. Harris. These two economists "and all the great men who write about the New England economy," Howell said, "lamented the fact that there was no cohesive and coordinated business relationship here." Howell thinks the region needs intensive economic planning involving both private and public sectors. He believes the planning process must break down the traditional adversary roles of business and organized labor. He has done some of that himself at the First National Bank, bringing in labor leaders, for example, for lunch and talk with bank executives about the region's economy. This must have come as a special shock to some of the staid and proper Yankee aristocrats of the First National. On the initial occasion Howell invited the union men, a first vice president of the bank objected: "Jim, you better not do that, because they're going to steal all the silver."

Points of Growth and Strength

So far I have accentuated the negative about New England's economy. Now it is time to turn to the region's very real assets. Briefly stated, they are these: a tradition in making precision products; long experience in accumulating capital and putting it to work; a base in higher education unequaled in the United States (except, perhaps, in California); a proven capacity to pioneer in the 20th century's most advanced types of services (ranging from research and development to management consulting); and finally, a superb, still largely inviolate natural setting, with immense possibilities for recreational development in an affluent national economy.

- Precision products. From the days of the Puritans onward, New Englanders had been producing such goods as clocks, rifles, and jewelry on a handicraft basis. Starting in the late 18th century, these activities became formalized in larger shops capable of high levels of production. The typical mix, in classic economic terms, was a large number of man-hours employed on a small volume of raw materials to create a low-bulk, high-value product. The key words were quality, precision, craftsmanship, and durability. New England machine and hand tools, firearms, and clocks won renown. Some of the most ancient plants are still in operation—for example, the Springfield (Massachusetts) Armory, which has been producing rifles for the U.S. Army since 1795. Connecticut's concentration of specialized metal-working plants is another example.

New England thus had the industrial leadership and pool of skilled manpower to branch out into some of the most important new products of the 20th century—specialized papers and plastics, photographic instruments, biomedical instruments, electronic components, mainframe computers and computer peripheral equipment,* missile and space systems, jet aircraft engines, and sophisticated instruments for pollution monitoring and control. The heart of these new-wave industries has been the Route 128 area around Boston, with major spillover into the Hartford area, southern New

---

* Some examples of biomedical equipment are artificial organs, implantable devices, and nuclear medical instruments. Computer peripheral equipment involves graphics and plotters, visual display systems, and the like.

Hampshire, Rhode Island, and even Vermont's Burlington area. The companies most dependent on defense and space contract work encountered severe reversals in the late '60s and early '70s, though a number—like United Aircraft and Raytheon—were quite successful in readapting their product mix and marketing strategies for the civilian market.

■ Finance. Out of its historic role in maritime trade, New England developed into a major banking and insurance center. The banking evolved to handle the region's trade accounts; the pool of capital acquired from trade in turn was used to finance textiles and other factories. Insurance had its genesis in the sharing of risks in sea voyages, and before long the insurance houses branched out into life, accident, and liability policies. "Thanks to Yankee shrewdness and conservatism," writer Joe McCarthy has noted, "stability and growth went hand in hand" in the region's banks and insurance companies. (My own maternal grandfather, Everett S. Litchfield, was a Boston insurance man in the early part of this century. He had the conservatism McCarthy alluded to, and sufficient shrewdness to build a solid practice for himself. But he had another, less celebrated Yankee quality— a streak of warmhearted generosity under the stolid veneer. Thus he helped many promising young people make their way through college and passed a much smaller inheritance on to my mother than a harder-headed man might have done.)

Today Massachusetts and Connecticut hold one of the nation's greatest pools of capital. The money management firms of the region are estimated to have $85 billion in assets. The First National Boston Corporation, for instance, has assets of more than $6 billion. Boston is considered the mutual fund capital of the nation. Ten large New England life insurance companies, led by John Hancock Mutual of Boston and Aetna Life of Hartford, have combined assets of $46 billion. "Such large financial institutions," according to one economic analysis, "not only give the region a rich lode of venture capital but they also generate considerable employment both directly and indirectly." Insurance company payrolls have increased dramatically in the past several years; if these gigantic firms were suddenly to disappear from the scene, the New England economy would be the poorer by literally hundreds of thousands of jobs.

■ Education and "export" services. The universities of New England, incubators and protectors of the region's distinguished intellectual history, are also an economic asset of no mean proportion. Here is the heart of the Ivy League and the home, in fact, of some 10 percent of the total number of colleges and universities in the country. These institutions have countless graduate departments of high repute, including many of the nation's leading schools of law, medicine, and business. Harvard, MIT, and Yale may lead in stellar faculty and extensive research operations, but the fact is that tens of thousands of students, many from outside New England, also attend the high-quality smaller colleges like Brandeis, Dartmouth, Williams, Smith, Mt. Holyoke, Bowdoin, Colby, and Amherst, as well as the vastly expanded campuses of institutions like the Universities of Massachusetts and Connecticut, and Boston University. In terms of student enrollment, Boston's Northeastern University has ranked in several recent years as *the* largest private university in the world. In the words of Frederic Glantz of the Federal Reserve Bank of Boston, "Eastern Massachusetts is just one big college town." His studies indicate that private higher education is the "industry" which draws the most dollars into Massachusetts, outranking all manufactures.

The other important "export" services—almost all of which draw off the region's lead in scientific research—include hospitals, health and allied services, finance and insurance, business consultation, architectural and engineering services, "think tanks," research and development work, and headquarters of national-level corporations. Tourism, likewise, draws immense amounts of outside dollars into the region, though it is not a "spin-off" of the university-scientific complex like so many of the others.

A sign of the times is that between the early '60s and early '70s the number of jobs in Massachusetts' specialized export service industries grew by 69 percent, at the same time that manufacturing employment declined by 11 percent. Somewhat less spectacularly, the same trend was apparent in the regions other five states.* Like high-technology and low-bulk manufactures, export services are not retarded significantly by the area's tough winters, energy costs, and long distances-to-market. Understandably, New Englanders look to them as the keystone of their economic future.

• Natural setting. However much New Englanders over the years may have talked of the harshness of their climate and the barrenness of the soil, the fact is that this region, in its own quiet and often understated way, is one of the most beautiful on the North American continent. No one who has ever spent time amidst the lakes and mountains of New Hampshire and Vermont, watching their changing mood as the seasons and weather cycles roll by, or walked through New England's forests and pristine villages in the dazzling clarity of the autumn foliage season, or felt the pulse of the ocean against Cape Cod's beaches and Maine's craggy coast, can doubt the conclusion.

The economists are not so caught up in their statistics that they fail to recognize the value of all this. They point out that the eagerness of so many highly skilled and professional workers to locate in New England, often at lower wages than they might demand in other regions, is directly tied to the region's amenities—physical and cultural. According to Martin Katzman of Harvard's School of Urban Design, the economic health of New England depends in great measure on attracting creative people who can produce innovative and specialized products and services. With a despoiled natural environment, such people would be repelled rather than attracted, and New England would lose its best hope to make the delicate transition from quantity to quality growth—i.e., its only chance to survive as a viable

* The region-wide figures for the 20-year period ending in 1970 show that while New England was suffering a net loss of 234,000 jobs in its traditional exporting industries, like textiles and leather, it was adding 191,000 jobs in durable goods and new-style exporting industries, and 78,000 jobs in export services.

place to live and work. Economist Robert Eisenmenger has suggested, in fact, that maintenance of the natural landscape may be *the* most important base for the long-term development of the region.

Environmentalists take the same view, of course, and I heard similar sentiments expressed in several talks I had with New England businessmen. This remarkable commonality of view, provided it can go beyond lip service to actual accommodation in nitty-gritty decisions, could be the most exciting development of all in modern New England.

The areas of actual and potential conflict are formidable. They involve complex costs and trade-offs in (1) developing adequate environmental controls, and particularly in formulating an intelligent land use policy in a region with little excess acreage in which to make mistakes; (2) deciding how much growth is necessary, desirable, or achievable, and finally (3) the question of which levels of government, or mix between them, will be the most appropriate forum in which to thrash out the region's problems and apply solutions.

The Environment and Land Use Issues

Putting the "environmental" issue in perspective in present-day America is a perplexing task, because the definition of the problem and the scope of proposed solutions are constantly changing.

Less than a decade ago, for instance, one could have surveyed New England's performance in cleaning up its polluted waters, discussed some localized air pollution problems, added a few fillips about flood plains and coastal wetlands, and left the analysis at that.

Those traditional issues, however, are already becoming a trifle passé. As John A. S. McGlennon, the regional administrator for the U.S. Environmental Protection Agency, pointed out, New England "already has the mechanisms in place to protect the coastal wetlands and to clean up the rivers." All major discharges were under permit by the end of 1974, and many municipal sewage plants were under construction.

By the 1970s, however, it was clear to New England planners that they faced an infinitely more complex set of problems. Some related to the splurge of second-home development in northern New England. Some had to do with urban sprawl in the southern tier. Others related to the demands conjured up by the energy shortage—refineries and deepwater ports, nuclear plants and their omnivorous use of water, power plant discharges into the air with conversion to coal. Finally, they all resolved themselves to the use of land. For each man, woman, and child in New England, there are only 3.6 acres of land and fresh water; with population growth there will be only 2.6 acres per person by the year 2000. Each citizen, McGlennon said, needed to ask whether those few acres "can provide the support I need—provide my food and water, dispose of my waste, accommodate my house and my share of school and office and shopping and highway space, process the fuel and power I use, and provide for my recreation?" In those terms, he suggested, "our land is a very finite, limited resource."

Forward-looking New Englanders have shown that they are well aware of the kinds of land and resource conservation efforts that ought to be undertaken in the immediate future to assure a humanly decent environment into the next century. A Boston-based environmental group, "Massachusetts Tomorrow," in 1973–74 assembled a group of task forces on land use, energy, transportation, and housing. Each task force presented two alternatives for the state. One was a continuation of trends as they have emerged from the past, and would continue to the year 2000 without major alteration. This scenario was called "Massachusetts One." The second, "Massachusetts Two," spelled out the kind of new policies needed to give the state a more promising future. One can argue with several details of the study, but the essential choice is hard to argue with:

Massachusetts One: The current land use pattern of the state, and its densely populated eastern third in particular, consists of intensive development in the renewed Boston city core, profligate use of land in the new suburbs, and a gray area of decay between. The reasons for this lie in an interlocking pattern of wasteful use of energy, overreliance on the automobile, inadequate mass transit, exclusionary zoning, scarcely existent planning above the town or city level, and the baleful consequences of overreliance on the property tax. These patterns and trends, if unmodified, will leave the commonwealth in a sorry state in the future.

One may expect that a scattering of local master plans, together with zoning, will save some towns from utterly jumbled development. But high property taxes (in lieu of a state income tax) will continue to force farmers to sell their land for house lots, and will induce many towns to oppose low income housing because the taxes from poor people do not pay for their school costs and other municipal services they require.

As in recent years, the dynamic that initiates and primarily determines land use will continue to be developers in pursuit of profit. Random local moratoriums on growth will have no broad-range effect on the region. The prospect is for more of the seemingly endless succession of shopping malls, parking lots, and commercial establishments that distinguish modern-day suburban development. In the close-in suburbs, the proliferation of dumps and junkyards, rundown industrial sites, billboards, litter, and abandoned neighborhoods will continue. Downtown Boston will have 17 more high-rise office buildings, which will add more vitality to the inner core. But 174,000 additional commuters, mostly white collar workers coming from the ever-more-distant suburbs, will attempt to drive 100,000 cars into the already clogged city streets each day. Expanded mass transit might be an answer, but suburbs resist new lines for fear they will change the nature of their communities (i.e., bring in center-city blacks). The heritage of poor management could well lead to the complete elimination of commuter rail service (presently carrying more than 600,000 passengers per day) by the year 2000.

Moreover, continued profligacy in the use of energy, together with the anticipated population rise, will increase the total energy demand of Massachusetts two and a half times by 2000. Prices will be much higher, there will be more frequent shortages, and six or seven huge 3,000–3,500 megawatt electric generating plants will be necessary. At least half of these will be nuclear. The strain of this rapid increase of electric generation will produce an erosion of environmental quality and increased vulnerability to disruptions and disasters.

Present trends also point to a seriously deteriorated housing situation. With government aid continuing at past levels, or declining, the supply of low-income housing will continue to diminish. Many old residential areas of the state will be forced into rapid deterioration and turned into slums. The result will be increased suburban sprawl and spreading urban blight. Industry will eventually heed the westward pull, establishing jobs beyond reach of many poor urban families. The cost of privately built housing will rise to such a high level that only a small portion of the state's people will be able to afford new unsubsidized housing.

Massachusetts Two: With a fundamental shift in public commitment and social policy, keyed to careful management of resources, greater economic equality, and environmental improvement rather than deterioration, the alarming trends of Massachusetts One could be brought under control.

Land would be recognized as a finite resource to be developed according to its nature for social good. A Massachusetts land use commission would inventory the state's natural assets—forest, agricultural land, watersheds and water bodies, and man-made features that ought to be preserved (historical buildings and humanly significant urban neighborhoods, for example). The eventual goal would be a land use plan indicating how all land in the commonwealth would be utilized at various levels of population growth. The plan should present alternatives for public discussion and political decision on major policy questions. Municipal governments would be required to implement at the local level the requirements of the state-wide land use policy.

Tax reform would be necessary—a graduated state income tax, with revenues redistributed to reduce municipalities' dependence on the property tax, and a policy of tax assessment on land to reflect its designated use in the state and local land use plans, rather than the most profitable potential use.

The normal mode of suburban development could be shifted from single-family houses to low-rise, high-density settlements in which at least 20 percent of the units would be for low-income families. These settlements would be clustered around public transportation (bus or mass transit lines) and contain within themselves schools, shops, and recreational facilities for a variety of income groups. Surrounding land, which might have gone into grid development, would be saved as open space. Residents should be able to get along without a car for commuting. Mass transit would be upgraded and extended to supply downtown Boston and its surrounding high-density communities with fast, clean, and reliable service. Lines could be built to more distant suburbs, and a circumferential mass transit line might be constructed.

Given time, variants of the cluster form of development could be applied to old suburban communities and urban neighborhoods. Zoning and other incentives, for instance, could reverse the trend toward supermarkets, encouraging a proliferation of smaller shops in each neighborhood. A general objective of the state land use plan could be rehabilitation of old buildings and neighborhoods, in place of leaving them to decay while development leapfrogs to new fresh green acres. To keep Boston livable, policies could be developed to put an eventual limit on high-rise development and ban autos from many of its streets.

Energy demand might be held in check through thoroughgoing conservation measures, intensive research into better and less environmentally hazardous ways of producing power,* mass transit, and the land use policies increasing the proximity of people's homes, jobs, and shopping places.

To anyone familiar with the political, social, and funding obstacles to any change faintly resembling the Massachusetts Tomorrow plan, the whole scheme on first blush seems wildly utopian and impractical. But unless such a plan, or equally satisfactory variants, are applied in the next years, Massachusetts will be a far less desirable place to live in 2000 and beyond than it is as these pages are written. It is also clear that Connecticut and Rhode Island face problems of equal gravity, as will southern New Hampshire and Maine within the foreseeable future.

Moreover, the more one looks at the environmental and land use problems New England faces, the clearer is the essential interdependence of the whole region—densely populated southern New England and the northern vacationlands alike. If the north is to be preserved as an adequate recreational ground for southern New Englanders, for instance, strict controls will have to be placed on big-scale land and second home developments. The danger is that helter-skelter vacation area development can destroy the natural environment that draws visitors from the urban areas in the first instance. Just as with suburban development to the south, the northern mountain areas need regulations against dividing large parcels of woodland into individual lots, a practice that often has disastrous effects on watersheds and natural vistas. The more intelligent vacation area developers already realize that cluster-style development, leaving large areas of land untouched, is aesthetically more pleasing and also more economical than running roads, water, and sewer lines to dispersed home lots.

There is also a common interest, both north and south, in preserving New England's dwindling stock of farmland. Poet and literary historian Malcolm Cowley, who owns a farm in Sherman, Connecticut, argues that one need not justify retaining open farmlands by the ecological argument

---

* The Massachusetts Tomorrow group estimated, for instance, that with an intensive research and development effort to reduce capital costs of solar heating and cooling, solar energy could heat and cool over 10 percent of the state's homes by 1985. The Cambridge-based consulting firm, Arthur D. Little, in 1973 inaugurated a long-range program, financed by 28 major firms, to develop a billion-dollar solar house-heating and cooling industry within a decade and a half.

—that one needs meadows and streams, woods and wetlands to depollute the air and maintain drinkable water. Open farmland, he points out, is like a breath of fresh air after forest or town, and also a tourist inducement. And "every good field is a loss to the community," whether it reverts to scrub and maybe a meager future firewood or pulpwood crop, or whether it becomes part of a residential development, in which case it "produces nothing" except new residents who seldom pay enough taxes to pay for what they receive in services, and whose arrival forces up property values so that the taxes of farmers and other old-time property owners triple or quadruple. (Cowley recommends the creation of "agricultural preserves," the purchase by the state of "development rights" to open lands, and other economic steps to keep producing, well-kept farms in business.) Forests are another case in point. They are so important to the whole region, as watersheds and recreation areas and sources of timber and income, that there should be stiff controls to prevent large parcels of woodland from being broken into residential or commercial grids.

Water supply problems underscore the theme of regional interdependence. With prospective population growth in the southern states, formidable amounts of additional water will be needed from the important drainage and reservoir sites in the northern tier. Unless early steps are taken to preserve broad areas of the Connecticut and Merrimack River basins for watershed drainage and reservoir sites, the water will simply not be available. It is not difficult to envision struggles over water allocation in New England reminiscent of those that have sparked the fiercest debates in the politics of the American West.

Similar issues are posed by the siting of power plants, which frequently ship their product across state lines. The private utilities have formed a New England Power Pool which decides where new plants will be located, where the power will flow, and which companies will get it. The public regulatory function occurs only at the state level or, in the case of nuclear plants, in part through the federal government. By 1983, 12 new fossil fuel and eight additional nuclear units will come "on line" in New England, occupying thousands of acres of land and using 20 million gallons of water a minute for cooling. But there will be no public regional overview or control of the siting decisions, which are clearly interstate in their implications for the environment and quality of life of all of New England's people.

This section is perhaps best concluded by the understated but highly relevant comment of the New England River Basins Commission, based on its 1974 conference, "New England in the Year 2000":

It is unfortunate that the natural or physical world was not organized in the form of New England townships. If rivers, mineral deposits, groundwater supplies, wetlands and so forth conformed to town boundaries, management would be considerably simplified. But of course they do not. . . . If we are to deal with the movements of masses of people and the conflicts they cause as the megalopolis moves northward; if we are to understand the implications of trends toward greater leisure time and stricter conservation of energy resources and how these trends will affect patterns of development at the local level, a much greater level of inter-town as well as interstate and regional cooperation and analysis will be necessary.

Growth vs. No Growth: Economics and Life Styles

When the question of growth vs. no growth was posed at a conference on "Prospects for New England" which this writer chaired in autumn 1974,* one of the participants rose to say that the real problem for the region, in view of the gloomy economic turn of events in the early 1970s, was merely "maintenance"—to keep the economic base it had.

Still, there is (and was at that conference) a clear dichotomy on the essential issue of whether the region can best survive by continuing to stress conventional economic development, or whether it should opt for quite a different life style based on the expectation of a "low-energy" economy in future years.

The assertion of a business economist like James Howell is that in a stagnant economy, the "growth dividend" that has made American society viable is removed. It means that the pie isn't getting any bigger, and that "the slice I got last year may have to be given up this year." With a growing pie, the wealthy can stay wealthy while a large part of the lower income group can be (and has been) sucked up into the middle class through rises in productivity. "Once an economy stagnates," according to Howell, "economic redistribution is not social progress, it is flat out revolutionary." His conclusion is that New England (and the U.S. in general) have no choice other than to find ways to continue economic growth, both in manufacturing and other sectors.

New England, in particular, the growth advocates warn, has a "bimodal" income distribution pattern in which a substantial group of very wealthy families, who have built their fortunes over a century or more, coexist with a substantial group of the working poor who still await their first entry into middle income ranks. Almost 6 percent of New England's families, for instance, earned more than $25,000 a year in the late 1960s, a figure 20 percent above the national average. The group of New Englanders earning $10,000 to $25,000 a year was 15 percent above the national figure. But at the same time, about 25 percent of the families of the region were earning less than $7,000 a year. Examples of dire poverty can be found in Maine's distant Washington County, in Vermont's hardscrabble "Northeast Kingdom," and in communities like the Portuguese at New Bedford, a people with a great deal of pride who nevertheless are obliged to work at an almost biologic subsistence level. In a study of 31 major U.S. cities in the early '70s, Boston was found to rank second (and Hartford 13th) in terms of the intensity of income *in*equality between poor and wealthy families.

According to the growth advocates, New England may well have a rosy "post-industrial" future and should actively promote the glamorous knowledge-based industries that give it a competitive edge compared to other regions. But New England in 1974 still had some 256,000 people in labor-intensive (i.e., rather low-skilled) industries. Most were older workers, likely

* At the Woodrow Wilson International Center for Scholars in Washington.

to spend the rest of their days on welfare if not in a factory. "I think we have almost a moral obligation to nurture manufacturing" of the traditional type to accommodate these workers for another generation, according to Howell. "If we couldn't dynamite the people out of Appalachia 20 years ago, we sure as hell aren't going to get the New Englanders to leave New England today."

The reply of the "no growth" or "slow growth" camp is that New England, along with the rest of the United States, must adapt itself to a future in which there will be severe energy shortages and astronomically rising costs for energy, in which the population will stop growing and may even decline, and in which the appearance of new manufacturing enterprises with large payrolls will be reduced to a mere trickle. In that less affluent, low-energy future, they suggest, the big second-home recreational developments so recently envisaged for northern New England will never be expanded beyond their mid-1970s level, and the rapidly escalating land prices of recent years will actually decline. This view was taken at the 1974 conference, to which I have referred, by such persons as Dennis Meadows of Dartmouth College, a co-author of the 1972 book *Limits to Growth*, and by John Cole, editor of the *Maine Times*. Both suggested that the region forsake the industrial and recreational development rat race in favor of greater emphasis on community and environment and, in Cole's formulation, on small, locally based manufacturing and service industries which require little energy.

Neither man, however, could suggest more than a bleak future for the thousands now laboring in New England's low-skill, low-wage factories. Perhaps it is significant that both are non-natives drawn to northern New England for its unique social and physical setting.

The resolution of the argument about growth, its desirability and/or feasibility, is beyond our scope here because it depends, first, on totally uncertain future turns in the national and international economic scene, and, second, on one's perception of what the future of the New England and national society *ought* to be.

What can be said with certainty is that class attitudes underlie a great deal of the debate going on in New England in the 1970s. It is not too gross an exaggeration to say that on the side favoring rapid economic development is the bulk of New England's huge Catholic-ethnic population, together with some lower-income Yankees. On the anti-growth side are the affluent Yankees, some medium- and low-income natives opposed to almost *any* kind of development and megalopolitan refugees who are either independently wealthy or prepared to get along with comparatively little. This latter group, in Elliot Richardson's words, "reflects the middle class set of values and the whole ecological point of view." It is, he suggests, "the cultural gap between the cross-country skier and the snowmobiler."

State senator C. Robertson Trowbridge of New Hampshire, the publisher of *Yankee Magazine*, whose district is on the rubbing edge between southern and northern New England, observed a typical confrontation of the two New England types:

The second-home folks—many of them are here now—are environmentally concerned because they want to be the last persons to get in and then close the door. When they arrive here, they land on top of a stratum of workers and loggers and the lower-paid group whose concern about the environment is nowhere near the same. They are resented when they try to tell the locals not to let in any more people, and to stop highways and bypasses the locals want. The new people coming in here are the ones saying "Stop." And the old ones are saying "To hell with you, we're just beginning to sell."

Six States' Cultures: Studies in Contrast

The division of social classes in the arguments about growth and environmental preservation in New England stem from, and help to throw light on, the profoundly different political cultures of the six New England states.

I doubt if it is an accident, for instance, that Vermont, the most old-style Yankee and rural-small town state of the region, has—at least in northern New England—been the most advanced and daring in environmental measures like the banning of billboards and non-returnable bottles and creation of commissions to control future vacation home and recreation developments. Until 1974, when local-control advocates and real estate dealers mounted a successful countereffort in the legislature, it appeared that Vermont was on the road to early adoption of a comprehensive statewide land use plan. Land use appears stalled at this writing, but it is hard to imagine that the pressures for it will subside. Vermont's most influential leaders, including most top elected officials of both political parties, share the idea that Vermont has something unique and precious in its quiet, nature-oriented, tolerant life style. New immigrants to the state take precisely the same view, whether they be wealthy retirees, counterculturites, or former Wall Street bankers who have opted for subsistence farming in place of the urban rush. Among the vast majority of Vermont people, there seems to be a common determination that the thundering herds of skiers and second-home owners from New York will not trample the precious land to death.

Next-door New Hampshire is a study in contrast. Big mill towns, heavily populated with cautious and conservative French-Canadian workers, sprang up here in the 19th century. The state's Yankee aristocracy, which helped found some of the earliest conservation organizations in America, has found itself increasingly outgunned. The dominant newspaper, the Manchester *Union Leader*, is screamingly prodevelopment, anti-planning, and antitax in a state with low social services and the unique status in present-day America of having not a single broad-based tax. The state has tried, instead, to subsist off "sin" taxes (liquor, tobacco, racing, sweepstakes, and the like), all designed to draw in out-of-state money to pay New Hampshire's bills. Environmental legislation has lagged seriously. Land use controls, if they come in the near future, will only be possible because the developers have become alarmed by the complete shut-out they are experiencing in some towns with choice property. A measure of state character is that the most revered New Hampshire Senator of recent decades was Styles Bridges, an archconservative, friend of the China lobby, and vindictive man. In Vermont, the style was set instead by George D. Aiken, a liberal Republican, convinced conservationist, and, most important, a person of immense personal integrity and respect for the views of others.

Maine falls between these two extremes, but much closer to Vermont than New Hampshire. The state's intrepidity, honesty, humor, and Down East matter-of-factness are all legendary, but for close to a century after the Civil War, when Maine lost the flower of its youth, there was a tendency, even on the part of its own citizens, to downgrade the state as a rural backwater. The manipulation of government by the timber interests and utilities contributed to a low assessment of self. This began to change after World War II when the Democrats, under Edmund Muskie, sprang out of their narrow Irish-French Canadian ethnic base, bringing bright young people to positions of leadership. Artists, writers, and intellectuals moved into the state as they decided the urban civilization of states to the south left much to be desired. A consciousness of Maine's coast and villages as a treasure to be preserved began to thrive, leading—as in Vermont—to a strong bipartisan environmental movement. Great battles have been fought in recent years over oil refineries, water pollution, wetlands preservation, and billboards, with the conservationists usually victorious. But the timber interests remain exceedingly strong, resisting state control of their vast lands, and public power is still more a hope than a reality. Land use planning has advanced significantly, but not to the level of sophistication of Vermont's.

Massachusetts has a very mixed record on environmental protection, for reasons that hark back to the old Yankee-ethnic rivalry that burned so intensely and so long. The ethnics, mostly Democrats with the Irish in the first rank, finally upset the old Yankee-Republican political machine in the 1920s and '30s. But they had difficulties with political corruption in their own ranks, symbolized by the likes of James Michael Curley. This permitted the Yankees—men like Leverett Saltonstall, Henry Cabot Lodge Jr., Christian Herter, Francis Sargent, and the black who thinks Yankee, Edward Brooke—to win many elections for governor and U.S. Senator. These Yankee leaders, from a background of fiscal conservatism, were also civil libertarians because of their abolitionist ancestry, and in recent years they have turned out to be strong environmentalists. On many policy issues they are close to the wave of more highly educated, less patronage-oriented "new Irish"—of which Senator and then President John F. Kennedy was the great exemplar. The political mix has been further influenced by a remarkable generation of professionals, the leaders of Massachusetts' universities and high-technology service areas, an articulate group with unusual political influence.

As a result of all these political shifts, Massachusetts has become, to my mind, the most "liberal" state of the Union. Its heavily Democratic legislature and Republican governors have been responsible for an impressive list of socially advanced laws, ranging from "no fault" insurance to "anti-snob" zoning legislation. The state also enacted an environmental policy act, modeled after the federal Environmental Protection Agency. It passed the first wetlands act in the country and has especially strong state-wide air pollution control. But for reasons in large part political, the ethnic-based Democrats controlling the legislature were leery about giving Francis Sargent, the Yankee Republican governor of the 1969–74 period, the authority he wanted to put the broad range of environmental programs under the control of his newly created cabinet department of environmental affairs. The logjam was apparently broken in summer 1974, when Sargent's impending electoral defeat loomed on the horizon. But the question of environmental coordination had so preoccupied the legislature that in this sophisticated state, where some of the country's most advanced discussions about environmental and land use planning go on, laws and plans to protect the future of the land were still in the study stage.

Connecticut politics have long been marked by political boss control, colorful ethnic rivalries (in which the old WASPs have constantly lost influence), and a strong home rule tradition. The per capita income is the nation's highest, due principally to wealthy Fairfield County in New York's posh northern suburban belt. But there are hundreds of thousands of blue collar working folk of Irish, Italian, and Polish background, who are not normally attuned to forward-looking social programs. The state has a poor budget system and no income tax. Intellectuals have occupied high positions in government, but in much lesser degree in recent years. The setting is not one in which one would expect heady breakthroughs in environmental and resource planning.

In fact, Connecticut's environmental laws, up to 1971, were a case study in fragmented authority. The various functions were split into multitudinous boards and commissions, none of which was functioning well. Air and solid waste control were under the particularly pusillanimous direction of the state health department. Citizen environmental pressure was limited to a few rather traditional conservation groups, pursuing their special interests in a low-keyed way.

Then came the rapid rise of national concern about the environment in 1970, "Earth Day" and similar events, pressure from college students and other activists, and the formation of a group known as "Connecticut Action Now," headed by Fairfield County's Dan W. Lufkin. At 40, Lufkin had already amassed a fortune of some $35 million as the founder and prime mover of a very unconventional Wall Street investment house. Lufkin, a Republican, gave dash and élan to the environmental movement, and Connecticut Action Now gave it a single, strong voice. But in the 1971 legislative session, the key leadership came from Democrat Stanley Pac, chairman of the joint environmental committee, who was a Polish Catholic liquor salesman from New Britain—scarcely the picture of the elitist environmentalist.

The net result was that the legislature, with strong bipartisan support, created a comprehensive state department of environmental protection with impressive powers over virtually every aspect of pollution control, forest and park lands, fish and game, flood plain encroachment, and coastal wetlands. Lufkin became the first commissioner of the new department. The environmental push continued in 1973 with Connecticut's first-in-the-nation approval of a plan to recycle, statewide, all solid waste into electricity, fuel, and reusable metal and glass. Through its broad powers, the environmental protection agency was creating a *de facto* land use plan for all of Connecticut, though the planning was primarily negative—in stopping ecologically hazardous development—rather than positive in terms of prescribing the most desirable forms and location of new communities and commercial enterprises.

Finally, we come to Rhode Island, America's smallest, most Catholic, and most heavily ethnic state. From the Civil War until 40 years ago, the state was in the iron grip of an unscrupulous Republican machine which represented an alliance of the Yankee aristocracy and textile magnates. For decades, the ethnic groups—the Irish, French-Canadians, Italians, and others—were neutralized politically by shocking limitations on the right to vote, and the divide-and-conquer tactics of the ruling clique. This ended abruptly in the 1930s when the old order was overthrown in a "bloodless revolution," led by Governor Theodore Francis Green, a Yankee who threw his lot in with the working man. The Democrats and their close union allies proceeded to tax business at high rates and to favor organized labor through high workmen's and unemployment compensation laws.

Rhode Island is a picture of arrested political development, the election of men like former Governor John Chafee or U.S. Senator Claiborne Pell notwithstanding. Here the antagonisms of the 1930s linger on—a Democratic-Catholic-ethnic party, now an overwhelming majority, versus a tiny Republican-Protestant-capitalist party. The ruling Democrats are bread-and-butter liberals but social conservatives, and they have not had much interest in environmental laws. There is a powerful coastal resources management board. But police powers over air and water pollution are submerged within the department of health, and statewide planning within the department of administration. Rhode Island has its environmental groups but lacks a large, affluent intelligentsia to give them power. In 1975 the state finally seemed on the verge of enacting a statewide land use plan, but as Governor Philip Noel acknowledged, that plan was coming *after* the development of his tightly packed little state.

New England's New Regionalism

No American region is comparable to New England in the number and scope of organizations, governmental and private, concerned with a clearly defined group of states in the federal system.

Only the most confirmed no-sayer could argue against the desirability of some form of coordination in a region so compact and beset by common problems. In the words of Vermont's former Governor Philip H. Hoff, "New Englanders are traditionally an independent and self-sufficient lot, traits to be nurtured and encouraged. But it is clear that in an era of increasing interdependence, independence can creep into a form of provincialism which works to the disadvantage of everyone."

If New England were a single state, it would rank third in population in the country (behind only California and New York) and presumably exercise the power of one of the mightiest megastates. Wilbur Cross, Connecticut's great governor of the 1930s, in fact once suggested quite seriously that the six states should combine into one—at that time, for reasons of economy and efficiency of administration. As John Gunther noted in *Inside U.S.A.*, Cross "was violently shouted down." The spirit of state independence is deep-rooted; on the walls of the Vermont State House, for instance, are inscribed the words of Ethan Allen: "I am as determined to preserve the Independence of Vermont as Congress is that of the Union and rather than fail I will retire with my hardy green mountain boys into the caverns of the mountains and make war on all mankind."

Presumably, any suggestion of merging the New England states would be as fiercely opposed by state leaders now as in the past (though one wonders if the people themselves would find the idea so appalling). Some lonely voices in the region have called for union; economist Rudolph W. Hardy, a veteran of work in the regional planning, states the case quite directly: "We must arrive at a point perhaps within the next 20 to 30 years when we have an effective general purpose government at the New England level with all three branches represented and including regional elections." As an interim step, Hardy has urged creation of a comprehensive New England-wide planning authority based on state-federal participation; its final decisions, he suggests, should be enforceable in both state and federal courts.

Almost three decades ago the Yale University Committee on Regional Planning was thinking along the same lines, urging creation of a New England Regional Development Administration as a public corporation with powers similar to that of the Tennessee Valley Authority to achieve coordinated planning and action on problems of truly regional implications, including land use regulation, the management of population centers across state lines, forestry and recreation improvement, and the rationalization of transport and communication.

In 1975 a single, powerful New England Commission was suggested by Charles H. W. Foster, professor of environmental policy at the University of Massachusetts and the Bay State's former cabinet secretary for environmental affairs. Such a new England Commission, Foster said, would incorporate into its structure the multiplicity of existing state- and federal-sponsored New England-wide agencies into a single organization consisting of the governors and regional administrators of the principal federal cabinet agencies. It would be the equivalent of a cabinet agency for the whole region, he said, assuring that every major new program and policy was sub-jected to regional scrutiny. Foster was not proposing a common govern-ment for the region, however; the New England Commission he recom-mended would serve as a program and review, but not an operating agency, even though it would be heavily involved in overseeing planning efforts carried out by functional agencies at state, interstate, and federal levels.

To others, the question of state merger or common planning misses the point. As banker James Howell lamented: "New England is really run by 1,600 cities and towns and, except for Connecticut and Massachusetts, has weak governors—a system spawned by the original political framework, which was the town. I cannot foresee our ability to make the leap to co-ordinated planning with those 1,600 towns and cities retaining the power they do." Howell was not original in noting the incredible political frag-mentation of New England, of course. The Yale committee of the '40s called for "enactment of state statutes providing for the automatic exten-sion of municipal boundaries upon the occurrence of stated conditions (density of contiguous population, intensity of use of common urban cen-ters, utilities, etc.), or . . . providing for the creation of new planning and development districts." Ingrained and stubborn "home rule" sentiment has thwarted all such efforts. New England in the most extreme form, but all the older sections of the nation in the East and Midwest have refused to permit annexation by established cities with growing suburbs. The result has been inequalities of tax base, not to mention a thwarting of the common planning essential to any successful society in the complex and interdepen-dent world of the latter 20th century.

There are also those, even beyond political leaders whose existing power bases and offices could be threatened by a unified New England, who question the practicability or the desirability of expending immense amounts of political energy and scarce planning energies on multistate gov-erning mechanisms. New Englanders, they suggest, can get together to de-fend their common interests in the national arena through conventional, pragmatic, interest politics. But the state and local governments, they point out, are in place, each with its own history, traditions, basic charter, and accepted democratic processes. Governmental scholar Richard Darman has suggested that "to attempt to undo or redo this pattern would be—if it were possible—inefficient at best." In answer to the assertion that common regional planning is a highly desirable goal, Darman replies that (1) plan-ning is difficult; (2) qualified planners are a scarce resource (and a bad economist, for example, may be considerably worse than no economist); and (3) "that it is not at all clear that *regional* planning should have a high priority claim upon limited planning resources."

However one would resolve those arguments, the fact is that the formalized regional structures of New England have advanced by leaps and bounds in recent years. A review of them is in order: *

* This review will omit the plethora of regional organizations in functional areas—some 70 by recent count—whose interests and activities are fairly narrow in scope. These range from

- New England Council for Economic Development. This entirely private businessmen's organization, founded in the 1920s to counter the exodus of textile mills to the South, did much of the pioneer work in forming a common regional consciousness on economic problems. In the past it has advertised itself as "the recognized spokesman for New England," but its more important role has been as the catalyst for the launching of other regional efforts, ranging from the New England Governors' Conference in the 1930s to the New England Congressional Caucus and Research Office in the early 1970s.

The industries making up the latter-day Council, then-Governor Kenneth Curtis of Maine noted, are less tied to narrow family dynasties and more responsive to broad community needs than their predecessors. The Council is divided into numerous subcommittees, working in every field from marine resources to government affairs. It took early, courageous stands in New England oil and transportation problems, and has been especially active in promoting the region's tourist industry. Yet with the increasing complexity of regional problems, a common pattern has been to spin off special organizations to deal with such problem areas as higher education and a regional criminal intelligence system. The Council itself, some feel, is moving (or returning) to a more standard chamber-of-commerce approach.

- New England Governors' Conference. Since its formation in 1937, this group has been the leading forum for governmental coordination among the six New England states, and the common political voice of the region. Its programs have ranged from cooperative agreements on controlling forest fires and adult education programs to shared facilities for female prisoners. The governors led in developing a unified New England position on the oil import quota problem, leading to a change in national policy.

The Governors' Conference is a strong examplar of the importance of regional cooperation, but it also illustrates the weakness of any group that must operate on consensus alone. Its executive director, Chapman (Chip) Stockford, has pointed out that its successes have come primarily on "issues that are very small," including transfer of prisoners, in-state tuition rates for all New England students, and the like—but that the governors have not, because of the problems of achieving unanimity, addressed more serious problems like long-range regional planning. Governors speak only for themselves, not their state legislatures, and only for administrations elected for two or four years. Some resist anything but the blandest common positions. Two governors of the early 1970s were cool if not hostile to the idea of regionalism itself—Connecticut's Thomas Meskill and, even more notably, the stormy reactionary from New Hampshire, Meldrim Thomson, Jr. After

the New England Aviation Commissioners Conference and New England Technical Services Board to such groups as the New England Board of Higher Education, the New England Heritage Trail Foundation (a key tourist promotion organization), and the Northeast Drug Abuse Conference. Several of the New England interstate compacts, through which the six states enter legal relationships among themselves with the concurrence of the federal government, have served as models for other regions of the nation.

Meskill's retirement, Maine's independent governor, James B. Longley, joined with Thomson on some issues. The disruptive tactics of these governors were highly disturbing to their fellow chief executives.

Until the mid-1960s the Governors' Conference depended on the New England Council for a part-time secretariat. But in the 1960s, as its meetings expanded from a couple of times a year to five or six, the organization broke away from the Council and formed its own small staff. By 1974, the Conference's budget was still below $50,000 a year and the governors were working in large measure through the:

■   New England Regional Commission (NERC). This is one of the so-called "Title V" commissions, designed to promote regional economic development, created in 1965 as a result of Senate logrolling at the time the Appalachian Regional Development Act was passed. As Martha Derthick of the Brookings Institution has written, "Whereas in Appalachia's case the regional organization resulted from a major spending program, in the Title V case the organizations came first—and then the spending programs failed to follow." The NERC and its counterparts for the Ozarks, Coastal Plains, Four Corners region and others have never received more than a fraction of the massive funds pumped into the Appalachian Regional Commission. Lacking either the big dollar or the big stick (which could only come if the White House ordered the federal funding agencies to follow their prescriptions), the Title V commissions are political eunuchs. They are also neither fish nor fowl in terms of the federal system. The six New England governors, for instance, direct the NERC, governed by majority vote and trying to operate by consensus. There is also a federal co-chairman who has a veto power yet is exceedingly nervous about mentioning the fact that he does.

Politicians do like cash to underwrite their public works programs, of course, and several of the regional commissions avoided political flak by putting whatever appropriations they received into sewage treatment plants, industrial parks, and the like. The NERC, however, put practically all its money into research and planning and demonstration grants—as one critic put it to me, "into a lot of way-out infrastructure stuff in education and the environment, the wrong kind of priorities." A lot of money also went into a master plan for New England's future. All of this went relatively unnoticed until the Boston *Globe* in 1972 kicked off a muckracking exposé with the headline: " 'Do-Nothing Bureaucracy' Squanders Millions of Tax Dollars." The article depicted the NERC as a "high-level pork barrel operation" funding bloated salaries, "stacks of reports that collect dust," and "studies that usually recommend more study." Over the commission's five-year history, the paper said, it had spent less than 1 percent of its $23 million appropriations on industrial development—at the same time that regional unemployment had doubled and 2,800 businesses had failed in New England.

The governors responded by firing NERC's executive director, shaking up and slimming down the rest of the staff, and creating the position of state co-chairman's special representative—a governors' man on the scene to rescue the commission from its morass. Grandiose master plans were scuttled in favor of concentration on a number of critical and immediate problems—fisheries, railroad transportation, energy, and steps required to fill New England's growing job deficit.

In August 1974, the NERC announced a $448,000 international trade program including a reverse investment mission to pinpoint and then call on likely European investors, assistance in export promotion for the many small New England firms which cannot afford an in-house foreign marketing capacity, and NERC trade offices in Europe and New York. Another noteworthy NERC spin-off was the New England Municipal Center, the only regional municipal center in the country, which has a staff of 12 professionals concentrating on community development and human resources problems.

By 1975, as the six governors made increasing policy pronouncements and ordered increasing numbers of studies and projects in their capacity as members of the NERC, it was clear that the commission was on much sounder footing politically. Still, however, its inherent structural difficulties remained.

■ Congressional Caucus and Research Office. Late in 1972 the New England delegation in Congress became the first regional congressional group in the nation's history to open a professional staff office in Washington. The innovation was made all the more unique by the addition of an associated New England economic research office, headed by a professional economist, to draw on and coordinate relevant research done by the region's major universities and financial institutions.

Prior to 1972, members of the New England delegation—25 Representatives and 12 Senators—had cooperated, informally, on a crisis basis as issues of compelling importance to the region reached a head. But there were no regular meetings of the kind held by delegations like those from California, Texas, New York, and Pennsylvania. In staff work and voting, the New Englanders, in typical Yankee individualistic style, went their own ways. As Republican Representative Silvio Conte of Massachusetts, who had carried on the often lonely battle against mandatory oil import quotas for several years, commented: "The Southerners always hang together. Why can't we?" Another leading figure in launching the joint caucus-research office on Capitol Hill put the issue in a wider context:

It was really Northern savings through a graduated federal income tax that financed Southern industrial development in the massive economic redistribution from wealthy states to the poorer ones that began with FDR. Now we in New England have a mature economy, and we have to ask the question: "Is the evolution of national economic policy leaving us behind?

We think it's being aimed at growing parts of the country. In other words, that's leaving large chunks of New England out of it. It's not leaving much of Boston out of it. But it sure as hell is leaving these mill towns out of it. It's leaving out a big chunk of Providence, Brockton, Fall River, Lowell, Gardner, and Lawrence.

The question is: How can we get a good national economic policy that doesn't discriminate against Lawrence? Massachusetts pays $1.12 in federal taxes for every dollar it gets back, while Alabama pays only 57 cents. The problem isn't too serious for affluent New England cities. But it's another matter when Lawrence and other towns that have had 20 years of chronic unemployment are shipping their money to Alabama.

A prime mover in organizing the New Englanders was a freshman Democratic Congressman from Massachusetts, Michael Harrington, along with the delegation's co-chairmen, Conte and House Majority Leader Thomas P. O'Neill, also from Massachusetts.* The operation had a very youthful tone: Harrington was only 35 at the time, and the person selected to be executive director of the New England caucus, Jill Schuker, was only 27. Paul London, the research office director, was 36. The delegation began to meet regularly and coordinate its efforts on issues like oil policy, passage of the Regional Rail Reorganization Act, and the proposed 200-mile economic zone to protect the region's fishing industry.

The "lobbying" effort, if one wanted to call it that, was especially effective because of the sophisticated research built into the effort. In the words of New Hampshire's Congressman James Cleveland, commenting on the new caucus-research operation, "The real currency in Washington . . . is information. . . . The most effective lobbyist in Washington is the one with a head full of facts, not a fat expense account." Cleveland was certainly right about the New England office lacking big dollars to pass around—the annual budget for the caucus was only $30,000, for the research office $60,000 (the latter sum raised by the New England Council). The region would ultimately have to put up much more money than if it wanted an ongoing, highly professional Washington office; in the meantime, it was benefiting from its lucky draw of first personnel. As George Brown, Massachusetts Governor Francis Sargent's aide for regional matters put it, "It's amazing how much difference good people can make. Schuker and London have really made it go."

■   New England River Basins Commission (NERBC). This is one of the so-called "Title II" commissions for coordinated river basin planning set up under the federal Water Resources Planning Act of 1965. Several independent studies have identified the NERBC as the most successful of the lot; unlike its counterparts in other regions, it has displaced the Corps of Engineers as the coordinator of multipurpose river basin development in New England. Its other asset is an activist, highly professional chairman with a conservationist background, R. Frank Gregg.

Gregg jokingly refers to the various studies which give the NERBC high marks because the authors consider him a pleasant and effective man —but invariably add that Title II commissions are just information and coordination forums, without real power, so that the case is essentially

* From the private sector, chief assistance in setting up the New England office came from James Howell; James G. Hostetler, Washington counsel for the New England Council; and John G. Buckley, an economist and vice president of Boston's Northeast Petroleum Corporation, the largest independent petroleum marketer in New England.

hopeless. "The hypothesis of political scientists, that an institution is most effective if it has authority, is perhaps false," he told me. One first has to define the elements of regionalism, Gregg suggested, naming information, planning, technical assistance, federal-state liaison functions, conflict resolution, coordination, and management. "You may need different institutions for different functions," he said. "Clout in regional authorities may not be the measure of their effectiveness. My thought is that if you can provide sound information, you're a long ways down the pike. The information function in New England is not adequately performed yet. If it were, existing decision-making mechanisms might be far more adequate."

The long and short of it is that some of the most advanced thinking and planning about New England's overall natural resource base, including the most compelling case I have ever seen for comprehensive land use planning, has taken place under the aegis of the NERBC. Much of this chapter is based on that splendid resource, as is a great deal of other analysis of the region.

It has been suggested that the NERBC, working closely with the Governors' Conference, be given the responsibility for central planning within New England on natural resource and land use problems. Clearly the NERBC has the expertise and leadership potential to do the job. It might be strengthened by having more elected officials, including not just state officers but also state legislators, officially represented on its board. The state land use planning departments could be closely associated with the commission in its region-wide planning work. Federal legislation could expand the title and function of the river basin commissions across the country to include all natural resources. And finally, the federal government could help if the Office of Management and Budget were to refuse to budget projects of federal agencies unless they were planned and coordinated through the regional planning institution.

All that, however, would still spell just more coordination and fall far short of the concept of a New England-wide land use commission with power to enforce its decisions, even against the will of a recalcitrant state government.

▪ Federal Regional Council of New England. Like its counnterparts in other regions of the country, this federally sponsored group seeks to coordinate the grant flow of the major federal departments active in the region. It works with state and local governments, but is hampered by the fact they they have no official role within it.

▪ New England Natural Resources Center (NENRC). If one were constructing a list of the kinds of organizations needed to provide the dynamic and catalyst for change in a modern region, a totally independent group, unencumbered in its scope by private charter or governmental mandate, would surely be included. The young New England Natural Resources Center may fill that role in this region. Led by men like former Vermont Governor Hoff and Charles H. W. Foster, it is a nonmembership organization free to take an independent view. Its board consists of two trustees from each New England state, including conservationists, businessmen, academicians, and professional people.

"Our concern," director Perry Hagenstein said, "is with environmental and land use problems across state lines." The word "bridge" seems to be a key to NENRC; as one of its trustees, Hartford attorney Russell L. Brenneman, described it, the organization "is a bridge between the environmental and the government and business communities over which the environmentalists have traveled to gain greater awareness of economic and political interests and over which businessmen and bureaucrats have traveled to gain sensitivity to environmental issues."

The NENRC has undertaken some impressive studies, including a careful listing of close to 5,000 New England "natural areas"—sections of land or water unaltered by man and harboring native plant or animal life or important natural features that ought to be saved for future generations. The information was all stored in a computer bank and has been made available to conservationist groups and to state governments in making inventories of areas to be protected under land use regulations. The organization is also the only New England group which seriously advocates that land use planning must extend to the regional level, both in protecting the natural landscape and in the siting of power plants. A skeptic might say the Resources Center is ahead of its time, but that may be precisely its value.

New England: America's Tomorrow?

Surveying New England's important regional organizations, one is impressed with how very young most of them are. The New England Council and Governors' Conference antedate World War II, but the Regional Commission did not come into being until 1965, the River Basins Commission until 1967, the Natural Resources Center until 1970, and the formalized Congressional Caucus and Research Office until 1972. Thus the oldest region, in a time of economic crisis and environmental hazard, has taken unto itself a fascinating new set of mechanisms for coping.

The nagging question remains, however: are they adequate? Must a unified regional planning or governing mechanism be established in the years ahead? I believe that the economic problems facing New England are so grave that the answer must be "yes." The time may not be far distant when a dramatic further advance in regionalism may be vital, if for no other reason than to convince New England's own people that there *is* hope for this region with its proud traditions of excellence harking back to the time when it had "books on the slope of Beacon Hill" while "the wolves still howled on its summit."

New England may be unique among American regions in its common history, its close interrelationships, and physical compactness. But the phenomena it is experiencing today—the "mature" economy, the groping for a "post-industrial" alternative, the worry about accommodating so many millions of people in a fragile life space—may be, if they are not already, the problems of the rest of the United States tomorrow. If New England "fails," its failure might presage a failure of the whole nation. Thus New England presents a fascinating laboratory and test case in the United States of the metes and bounds of what can be accomplished on a regional basis.

Some 40 years ago, Bernard DeVoto wrote that "New England is a finished place . . . the first American section to achieve stability in the conditions of its life." If nothing else, I hope this chapter, and those to follow, will show that DeVoto was wrong for two reasons: first because New England's wellsprings of creativity still run fresh and new, at least in so many sectors of life; and second because if New England does not adapt and adjust to its new realities in the next decades, it could fail as a viable region, to the profound loss of us all.

MASSACHUSETTS

DISTINCTION IN ADVERSITY

As AMERICA EMERGED from World War II, Massachusetts seemed headed into a long decline. Its cities and its industries were obsolescent, its politics ethnic-oriented and patronage-ridden, its leadership tired and unimaginative. Only its universities continued to show some of the vitality that had made Boston the Athens of America in the 18th and 19th centuries, and now they seemed oddly cut off from the political and governmental life of the state. A patina of historic preciousness, of proper Bostonianism contraposed to Irish sentimentality, lay over Massachusetts. The state would have been anyone's last candidate for a center of American growth and thought in the post-war period.

But while the nation was looking westward and away, some remarkable things occurred in the old Commonwealth:

▪ Its people began to discard the ancient enmities between Protestant and Catholic, Yankee, and Irish, that had corroded public life for a century.

▪ Old Boston began to rebuild itself, becoming one of America's most handsome and livable cities.

▪ The universities in Cambridge became vital and advanced intellectual centers, not only on the national scene but in the political life of the state.

▪ The economy emerged from the trough of despair created by the flight of textiles to the South. Massachusetts evolved into a preeminent state in electronics and industry based on imaginative scientific research.

■   A new class of highly educated and progressive-minded people was drawn by the science-based industries, and Massachusetts became perhaps the most liberal state, politically, in the Union.

■   The tradition-encrusted Massachusetts legislature began to pioneer in field after field of social legislation—albeit at such a heavy cost that in the recession of 1975, the state was plunged into one of the severest financial crises ever to face an American state.

■   Great strides were made in purging corruption from government.

■   And Massachusetts furnished a President who could fire the ideals of a nation.

Now it must be acknowledged that not every progressive change took place rapidly or was totally effected in the Massachusetts of the mid-1970s. There remain several grave drawbacks to life in the state. Its center cities have been deserted by their natural elite and by their middle class. Many old mill towns have yet to recover from the loss of their great factories, and the slowdown of the space race and research in new weaponry has raised serious questions about the future of Massachusetts' scientifically based industries. Since 1969, unemployment has been a grim specter, for both mill hands and scientists. Indeed, as these lines were written, the state was suffering under an unemployment rate of close to 13 percent, one of the worst in the entire United States. Though the 1970 Census found that of the Bay State's 5,689,170 people,* only 3.1 percent (175,817) were Negroes, and despite remarkably progressive state legislation written to enhance the opportunities of minorities in schooling and busing, racial discord has grown and reached a crescendo with the ugly disturbances in South Boston that attended orders for full school desegregation in 1974–75.

But with time, it seemed likely that the basic enlightenment of public life in the state would ameliorate, if not solve, the racial problems. Unemployment and fiscal problems seemed likely to remain severe for some time, but Massachusetts still had the scientific and intellectual reserves to make it a prosperous entity in the "post-industrial" world of the future. Those same reserves gave it the basic capacity (if it demonstrated the will) to contain the suburban sprawl of the post-World War II era and to create an energy-conserving, physically attractive urban environment. The Bay State was thus facing new and difficult challenges in the 1970s, but it still had the capacity to build on its remarkable advances of the years since World War II to create a Golden Age of the Commonwealth.

Overcoming Ethnicity

"The modern history of politics in Massachusetts," political scientist Murray B. Levin wrote a few years ago, "begins with the great Irish potato

---

* The population grew by 1.4 million, or 32 percent, between 1940 and 1970, but by only 139,000, or 2.4 percent between 1970 and 1975.

famine of 1845." In five years, an estimated million Irish died of starvation and another 1.6 million left their native land, a high percentage of them to settle in New England and especially the state of Massachusetts. By 1860, 61 percent of the population of Boston was foreign born, and the percentage was not far different in cities like Lowell, Lawrence, and Fall River. Starting in the 1880s, large numbers of Italians, Poles, Lithuanians, Portuguese, Scandinavians, and Germans began to follow the Irish. By 1920, more than two-thirds of the people of Massachusetts were either foreign born or of foreign parents. Boston elected its first Irish-born mayor in 1885, Massachusetts its first Irish Catholic governor in 1918.

The Irish and their fellow immigrants did not enter a political vacuum. For more than 200 years, a homogeneous Yankee Protestant population had held sway on the shores of Massachusetts Bay. The story of that civilization, begun on the November day of 1620 when the hardy Pilgrims first touched the bleak shore at Provincetown and "fell upon their knees & blessed ye God of heaven, who had brought them over ye vast & furious ocean," is so classically American as to barely require retelling here. In those two centuries Massachusetts had grown from one of the strictest theocracies the world has ever known to a seedbed of sedition in the days of John Adams, John Hancock, and Paul Revere. It had been the site of the Boston Tea Party, the Boston Massacre, and the shots from Lexington and Concord "heard 'round the world." From a colony of hardscrabble farming and modest cottage industries, it had grown in eminence as an Atlantic fishing center, as the home port of prosperous seaborne commerce in the West Indian trade (including rum and slaves), then even greater profits in the China and East India trade and the brief, colorful era of the Yankee clippers racing at full sail across the world's oceans. The great New England insurance industry had arisen from a pooling of maritime shipping risks in the late 18th century, and the textile industry from a pirating of secret English mill techniques around 1800. Transcendentalism, America's first major intellectual movement, had begun to flower in Massachusetts, expounded by writers like Bronson Alcott, Ralph Waldo Emerson, and Henry David Thoreau. And this was the leading American state in the move to abolish slavery under the American flag. In every part of life, Massachusetts deserved the region's title of "New England"; as Yale President Timothy Dwight wrote of the Bostonians in 1796: "They are all descendants of Englishmen and, of course, are united by all the great bonds of society—language, religion, government, manners and interest."

The clash between old Yankee and Catholic immigrant was predictable, bitter, and lasting. Both sides abhorred the other's religion. The Puritan settlers of early New England had gained their name because their sect wanted to "purify" the Anglican Church of all vestiges of popery, and they had persecuted and driven from Massachusetts nonconformers to their narrow way, including Baptists and Quakers. The Roman Catholic Irish viewed all Protestantism as apostasy; writer Joe McCarthy quotes one of their spokesmen as saying that "a *Christian* Protestant . . . is a contradiction in terms." The Yankees were proud of their British ancestry; the Irish, remembering cen-

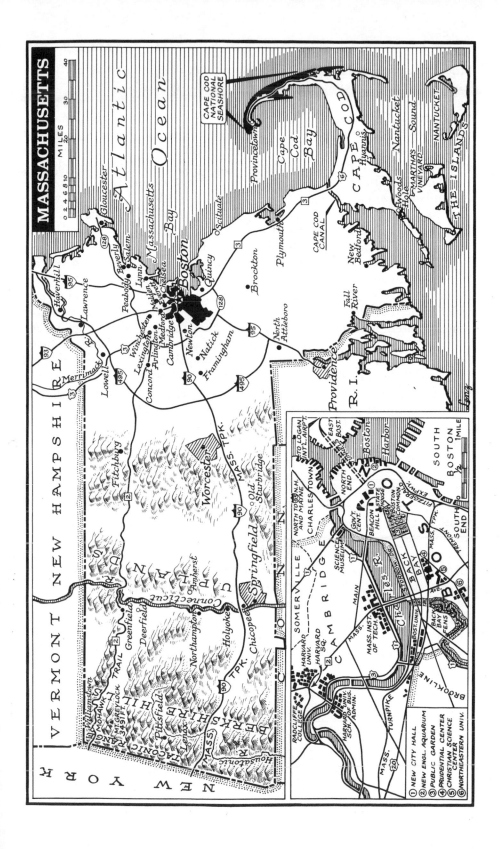

turies of English exploitation of their homeland, despised everything British. The Yankees were reform-minded, fond of causes like abolition, women's rights, and improving conditions in the prisons; their philosophy was one of the perfectability of man. The Irish Catholics viewed true salvation as an occurrence of life after death; they feared job competition from Negroes and were proslavery; they believed in hierarchy and authority and rigid class lines and a politics based on personal loyalties rather than abstract philosophies.

The old Yankees stopped at nothing to subjugate the Irish immigrants. An unskilled workman would earn a mere $4.50 to $5.50 a week, a woman working as a domestic as little as $1.75 a week, of which 75 cents was taken for board. The Irish were crowded into the mudflats of the cities and waterfront slums. Five to 15 might live in a single basement; as James MacGregor Burns writes of the time that John Kennedy's grandfather came to Boston, "One sink might serve a house, one privy a neighborhood. Filth spread through courts and alleys, and with it tuberculosis, cholera, and smallpox, which thrived in the poorest sections, where the Irish lived." Election laws were purposely rewritten to delay the day that the immigrants might vote.

But with the professions and economic advancement closed to them, the Irish turned to their favorite avocation—politics—and made a grand success of it. Because the Yankees were Republicans after the Civil War, the Irish were automatically Democrats. As the Irish and their fellow immigrants began to outnumber the Yankees, they gained offices. The ward political organizations provided loyal voters with jobs, licenses, street lights, emergency welfare aid. The system flourished right up through two World Wars and into the 1950s. James Michael Curley was a symbol of it all, a kind of Robin Hood whose stealing from the rich was tolerated because he "took care" of his own. Robert C. Wood (now president of the University of Massachusetts) said in 1961 of the Democratic party in Boston: "The 'in' group in politics here is still playing 19th-century politics. They see the problem as dividing the spoils, not how to manage society."

The cleavage between Irish and Yankees plagued Massachusetts life for more than a century. Up to World War I, the Boston newspapers segregated social items about Yankees and Irish Catholics in different pages. Yankees looked down on Irish as a kind of social scum. Irish detested Harvard because, as John Gunther observed, "Harvard is the great rival of the archbishopric for intellectual control of the community." It was at a Holy Cross alumni dinner in 1910 that Irishman John Collins Bossidy first recited the satiric jingle:

> And this is good old Boston
> The home of the bean and the cod
> Where the Lowells talk to the Cabots
> And the Cabots talk only to God.

A few years later Boston experienced its famous police strike, pitting the two groups against each other. (My own Boston grandfather was one of the citizen strikebreakers, and proud of it to his life's end. But my friend Robert

Healy of the Boston *Globe* reminds me *his* grandfather was one of the leaders of the strike.)

Between the world wars, the Irish became so strong that they controlled both Boston politics and much of the state's politics. After voting Republican in every Presidential election from the Civil War (except the three-way race of 1912), Massachusetts cast a final sentimental vote for its own Calvin Coolidge in 1924 and then switched to Al Smith and the Democrats in 1928, to remain in the Democratic column (except for the Eisenhower elections) ever since. Curley served not only four terms as mayor of Boston, but one as governor of the state of Massachusetts (1935–37). Yet the success of the Irish, outside of politics, was limited. After visiting Boston in 1944, John Gunther reported:

> Only one small Boston bank is Irish owned, and only four out of 30 directors of the chamber of commerce are of Irish descent. There are few dominating Irish figures in law, medicine, or finance, and none of the big department stores is Irish controlled; not a single Irishman is an officer, a committee chairman, or a member of the executive committee of the New England Council.

The first Irishman to make a strong breakthrough into the Yankee-held State Street banking and financing community was Joseph P. Kennedy, father of President John F. Kennedy, son of Patrick J. Kennedy (an East Boston Democratic leader, owner of three saloons and a wholesale liquor business), and grandson of Patrick Kennedy (native of County Wexford, Ireland, who had arrived penniless in Boston in 1848). Joseph Kennedy was the first of his clan to attend once-hated Harvard, graduating in 1912. Two years later, he was a bank president; five years later he penetrated the Yankee stronghold of the board of trustees of the Massachusetts Electric Company; in the 1920s, he became phenomenally successful in the stock market and moving pictures and acquired the famous Kennedy fortune; in the 1930s President Roosevelt made him first chairman of the Securities and Exchange Commission, and later Ambassador to Great Britain.

The rise of the Kennedy family as Green Brahmins and the climactic election in 1960 of John Kennedy to the Presidency, the first Roman Catholic ever to hold that post, were grand symbols of what was happening more quietly and more importantly for the civilization of Massachusetts. Thousands of young Irishmen took advantage of the GI Bill after World War II; they emerged as talented professionals, pragmatists, able to communicate and work with the Yankee aristocracy as equals. Their interest in petty political patronage was minimal. The "new" Irish, one might say, won out by co-opting the Yankees' value system. "The old Yankee," Robert Wood told me, "won out in terms of attitudes. The desires for probity, for effective government won out in the mind of most of the voting population. . . . With Kennedy and other Massachusetts figures of national stature, you see the rational, problem-solving, consensual politician."

The vital turn from old ethnic to new pragmatic politics seems to have occurred in Boston city government with the election of John Collins as mayor in 1959 (a story we will return to later). On the state level it emerged through a series of political scraps, Irish versus Yankee, Yankee versus Italian, and Irish versus Italian, in the late 1950s and early 1960s. It should be remembered that when the Irish became dominant in the 19th century, they turned as cold a shoulder on the Italians and Poles and other ethnic groups as the chilly Yankees had turned on them. The fierce inter-ethnic rivalries have remained strong, especially in Democratic party conventions and primaries. In 1960, the Democrats nominated an "All-Green" statewide ticket that offended Italian, Jewish, Polish, and other voters and opened the way for the election that year of a Republican governor, John A. Volpe, the first Italian and Catholic ever to be nominated for that office by his party. In 1962, the Kennedys intervened indirectly to secure the Democratic gubernatorial nomination for a Yankee Democrat, Endicott Peabody, just so there would be no "All-Green" ticket in the election when Edward M. Kennedy was first running for the U. S. Senate. Peabody, Wood points out, was a symbol of "the nonethnic probity." But Peabody failed to perform effectively as governor and was upset two years later for renomination by his own party in a primary charged with ethnic animosity. The man who beat Peabody, Lt. Gov. Francis X. Bellotti, seemed to have no discernible qualifications save his desire for higher office—and being Italian. That was enough to beat Peabody in the primary. But Volpe (just as Italian and ambitious as Bellotti, but a lot more capable) recaptured the governorship in that year's general election. Massachusetts was not to elect another Democratic governor until 1974, and when it did, the winner was a liberal Greek-American who defeated a standard-type Irish politician to win his party's nomination. By the 1970s, everyone seemed to agree that a lot of the juice had been drained out of the old ethnic issue.

But not all. As Robert Wood points out:

> The successful practitioner of politics, operating on old ethnic/personal principles he knew, continues to play an outmoded game. Publicly, there is much talk of ethnic tickets—while the public has gone on beyond them. The result is a gap, much greater than in most states, between voter expectations and actual performance. It increases the disillusionment, cynicism, and skepticism with politics. . . .
>
> The guys who want to do the right thing will get more support than they expect to get. But they are always trapping themselves by falling back into ethnic politics more than they really have to. It is still a factor in primaries, but not so much in general elections.

An overnight transformation from ethnic to issue-based politics is more than one could reasonably expect in a state with 52 percent Roman Catholic population (highest of any state except Rhode Island), a 5 percent Jewish population (third highest in the country), and a 1970 "foreign stock" population figure of 24.6 percent (second highest of all the states). Of the 1.4 million Massachusetts citizens in 1970 who were immigrants or children of immigrants, the largest single group was Canadian (largely French-Canadian), numbering 357,288. The French-Canadians lack the political effectiveness of other ethnic groups, however. Unpublished Census surveys have shown that 13 percent of the state's people name their own background as Irish, and another 10 percent as Italian. These, and to some extent the Poles (3 percent), are the groups politicians mean when they talk of "ethnic" Massachusetts.

The days when rivalries between these ethnic groups could be exploited for political purpose are beginning to wane. A key factor was the high amount of intermarriage, following World War II, between Irish and Italians. Congressman Silvio O. Conte, himself a son of Italian immigrants and a war veteran who broke the old ethnic lines by marrying a girl named Corinne Duval, recalls: "The guys came back from the war with a completely different attitude. Irish parents could no longer tell Irish boys and girls just to marry Irish. Hell, the guys had been all over the world and seen every kind. They weren't about to let their parents tell them whom they could marry. This had a great effect in breaking down the barriers among the nationalities."

As the intermarrying got underway, so did the postwar suburban housing boom. Today, the settled, generations-old ethnic communities still exist in Boston and other cities, but more and more of the descendents of immigrants live in a homogenized suburbia where ethnic loyalties, like straight ticket voting, are out of style. Yet on occasion, old-style ethnic politics bubble up in an ugly way. In 1971, house speaker David Michael Bartley was willing to tell a Boston *Globe* reporter, for attribution, how he had "learned to dislike Yankees" as a golf course caddy in his youth (they didn't tip well) and accuse the Holyoke *Transcript-Telegram* of being "viciously anti-Irish Catholic" (an exaggerated if not utterly false charge). One close observer of the Boston political scene told me that on election day, "an Italian can't do well in an Irish district, but an Irishman can do well in an Italian district." But the Boston city council, once an Irish stronghold, was neatly split up in the early 1970s: four Irish, three Italians, one black, one Wasp.

The overall Protestant-Catholic animosities of Massachusetts were tremendously lightened by the changes within the Roman Catholic Church in Massachusetts, especially the Archdiocese of Boston. William Cardinal O'-Connell, leader of the Boston flock until his death in 1944, has been described by John H. Fenton as a "haughty, aloof figure . . . who could freeze a dissenter at 50 paces with a baleful glare. . . . One of his primary aims was strengthening the Catholic parochial school system. His acknowledged intent was to protect the children of the archdiocese from the heretical influence of Protestantism." Richard Cushing, O'Connell's successor, was an open, warmhearted man of quite another temperament. Born in 1895 in a third-floor flat of a cold-water South Boston tenement, he had made his mark in church work as an indefatigable and amazingly successful fund raiser, an activity he continued as Archbishop and later as Cardinal (raising, by some estimates, $300 million over his lifetime). But what Cushing will longest be remembered for is his tireless work to build bridges of understanding between Catholics, Protestants, and Jews. "We are told there is no salvation outside the church—nonsense!" he once said. "Nobody can tell me Christ died on Calvary for any select group." Cushing candidly admitted he was "no scholar," but at the Second Vatican Council his impassioned plea for religious liberty and condemnation of the doctrine that the Jews, as a people, are responsible for the crucifixion of Christ, led the assembled bishops to break the rules of silence and applaud the crusty, warmhearted man from Boston.

The potential power in heavily Catholic Massachusetts of the leader of the Boston See is immense, though it is easy to exaggerate the extent to which church influence is actually exerted. Cardinal O'Connell had a registered lobbyist and other emissaries to the legislature who carried his messages concerning birth control bills, a proposed state lottery, and child labor. Under Cushing, the influence was much less direct, perhaps because he had much less interest in pushing traditional church doctrines in politics. Cushing did, however, once pronounce in a pastoral letter that "When a Catholic fails to take a stand against race intolerance or prejudice he is a slacker in the army of the church militant." He was a lifetime member of the NAACP but by the same token endorsed the John Birch Society for its outspoken anticommunism. The Catholic hierarchy was a major defender of the 1879 law forbidding dissemination of birth control information in the Commonwealth, and helped defeat proposed abolition in two referenda (1942 and 1948).* Despite his ecumenicism, Cushing opposed the rise in the late 1960s of the "underground church" in which Catholics and Protestants join together for holy communion in their homes.

Through the Kennedys, with whom he had a close association over many decades, Cushing became something of a national figure. Few will forget his raspy voice (which was likened to the sound of "coal rattling down a chute in a South Boston basement") delivering a seemingly interminable invocation at President Kennedy's inauguration in 1961 (while white smoke poured from the lectern from a small fire). But then there was the private Cushing, weeping alone in his private chapel the day he received word of John Kennedy's assassination, and his prayer cracking with grief at the funeral, as he called on the angels to carry his "dear Jack" to Paradise.

Cushing's 26-year leadership of the 1.9 million Roman Catholics of the Boston area came to an end with his resignation, at age 75, in 1970. Two months later, he was dead. Rome's choice for a new archbishop was a surprise—Humberto Sousa Medeiros, a 55-year-old native of the Portuguese Azores who had for five years been bishop of Brownsville, Texas. For the first time in 124 years, Boston had a non-Irish archbishop. But Medeiros was no stranger to Massachusetts; he had grown up in Fall River, where he once swept floors at 62 cents a day and gave up a promising career as an artist to become a priest. In Texas, he had become a sturdy friend of the impoverished Mexican-Americans, and was a close friend of César Chávez. His selection was a sign of the changing times, since Boston has experienced in recent

* The law was finally declared unconstitutional by a federal court in 1970. The court found that the statute "conflicts with fundamental human rights." A similar Connecticut statute had been nullified earlier, leaving no state with anti-birth control legislation.

years a heavy influx of Spanish-speaking Puerto Ricans and Cubans.

While a friend of the poor, Medeiros is no flaming liberal on other church issues. Soon after assuming his new job, he attacked efforts to liberalize abortion laws as "a step backward" and "a new barbarism." Massachusetts' old anti-abortion law became a dead letter when the U.S. Supreme Court in 1973 ruled that early abortions were part of the mother's constitutional liberty and privacy right. Medeiros gave active encouragement to "right-to-life" groups which successfully pressed the Massachusetts legislature, with its two-thirds Roman Catholic membership, to enact a bill—of questionable constitutionality under the Supreme Court's guidelines—prohibiting all abortions after the sixth month of pregnancy, except to protect the life and health of the mother. The opposition in the legislature came almost entirely from Protestant and Jewish members, and the bill passed over Gov. Francis Sargent's veto.

The abortion issue was exacerbated again in 1975 when Boston city prosecutors, all Roman Catholics of Irish ancestry, prosecuted and convicted Dr. Kenneth C. Edelin on manslaughter charges in connection with an abortion he had performed in October 1973 when he was chief resident obstetrician at Boston City Hospital. The prosecutors alleged that the fetus, 24 weeks of age at the time of the operation, could have survived if Edelin had taken appropriate steps; Edelin said that it could not have. After his conviction, Edelin charged that racial and religious prejudice in Boston had made a fair trial impossible; "it was a witch-hunt," the black physician commented.

While the Roman Catholics get the most public attention, other religious groups continue to prosper in Massachusetts. The Mother Church of the Christian Scientists is there, and that group's newspaper, the *Christian Science Monitor*, is one of the finest in America and distributed nationally (201,000 copies daily)—an organ with more influence outside of Boston than within it. Fresh vigor was brought to the *Monitor* in the early '70s when its Pulitizer Prize-winning overseas correspondent, Welsh-born John Hughes, became editor and undertook a reconstruction of the news staff to correct what he perceived as a "hardening of the arteries" in staff and approach. In the prestigious 125,000-member Episcopal Diocese of Massachusetts, a change as momentous as the Catholics' shift to a non-Irish bishop took place in 1970. To succeed retiring Bishop Anson Phelps Stokes, Jr., the Episcopalians chose the Rt. Rev. John M. Burgess, son of a dining-car porter and the first black man to head an Episcopal diocese in the United States.

The Political Cultures

The confusing cross-currents of modern Massachusetts politics are easier to fathom if one keeps in mind the four principal political strata of the state, defined by Edgar Litt in his valuable book, *The Political Cultures of Massachusetts:*

THE PATRICIAN ELITE. These are the Lodges, Herters, Saltonstalls, Websters, and Elliotts of Massachusetts, born to wealth and high social status, members of the elite religious groups (often Episcopal or Congregational), educated at the best private schools and usually Harvard University, residents of high-grade Boston suburbs like Lincoln, Bedford, or Weston. In fiscal matters, they have traditionally been conservatives who, "like their Puritan forefathers, strive to carry out the handiwork of God with a modest profit [and] a balanced budget." They are also conservatives on many educational issues. Their political interests rarely conflict with those of State Street and the First National Bank, but first and foremost, they are interested in honest, decent government. On questions of civil liberties, they have been liberals since the days of the abolitionist movement. This Yankee community, Robert Healy of the *Globe* told me, is "the main force of the liberal stream" in the state today. "The kids of Yankees are furthest to the left," he said. "The highly politicized campuses are products of New England prep schools." Their parents, of course, are more cautious. Litt describes them as "brokers of a changing economic society [who] mediate between the larger world of Washington and the confines of the town and the ward. Their links with the past and their confidence in mastering the future provide experience with which to meet the impact of international cartels, common markets, and automation on the home, the family, and the job."

THE YEOMEN. Once the numerical majority in Massachusetts and now a fast-declining minority, these are the rural and small-town businessmen and workers of old Protestant stock. They are to be found in the small towns and villages of nonmetropolitan Massachusetts, which contain only 15 percent of the population. Litt describes their prevailing ethos as that of 19th-century America "with its emphasis on individual initiative, its distrust of bigness in government, corporations, labor unions, . . . and a personalized, informal attitude toward friends and neighbors." Here we catch a glimpse of old town meeting New England, even, as Litt suggests, *Saturday Evening Post* New England. It is staunchly Republican and conservative on social welfare, civil liberties, and governmental reform; its representatives have frequently held leadership positions in the legislature, reflecting those attitudes. Litt observes: "Replaced by a young managerial stratum, bypassed by the industries, turnpikes and shopping developments of a consumption-oriented society, the yeomen have lost their sense of usefulness, their participation in the mainstream of American society." Yet, he might have added, they feel they preserve some quintessence of Old America in their little towns and villages, quiet and pastoral, which have a peace and dignity no suburb or city has ever approached.

THE WORKERS. This is Ethnic Massachusetts, the urban-based Irish Catholic and their sometime friends, the Italians, Poles, and assorted other European arrivals of the past century and a quarter, as they are still embodied in ethnic neighborhoods. "They are localists," Litt observes, "with a deep resistance to governmental, social, and economic change because they perceive, often correctly, that the strategies of constitutional reform and urban renewal threaten their entrenched positions in the neighborhood [and] the legislature." The story is told of the city of Boston's proposal a few years ago to put an urban renewal project into Charlestown. At a public meeting to discuss the idea, a man stood up and told the Boston Redevelopment Authority: "I have an unalienable right to be a slob." What he was saying, in effect, was that he was part of an Irish or Italian immigration movement, that by the sweat of his brow he'd acquired his place in the sun, and that whether some elitists thought his community an eyesore or not, he liked it and wanted to keep it as it was. The resistance to black encroachment in Massachusetts is strongest in such neighborhoods, of which the most famous example of all is South Boston. Such places are parochial, resistant to all change, and liberal only in regard to social welfare issues (as long as their communities are not disturbed). Unions are their champions, and their party (especially among the Irish) has been, is, and most probably will remain the Democratic.

THE MANAGERS. Here is the new postwar society: highly educated and professional—the administrators, teachers, lawyers, clergymen, scientists, technicians, advertising and communications specialists. Here the lines of ethnicity disappear: they may be Yankee, Irish, Italian, Jewish, or whatever. They earn well but they have yet to acquire the social status, reserves of wealth, or corporate power of the patricians. While their heritage, Litt observes, is "Democratic, urban, immigrant, blue collar," they are highly independent in politics, the proverbial ticket splitters. They were attracted to John Kennedy, but often vote Republican in contests for statewide office in Massachusetts. Many were attracted to the peace movement, a small minority to political conservatism in the model of Orange County, California. But they see themselves as rational men, and believe in social and economic welfare measures to improve society.

The long hegemony of the Massachusetts Republicans—from the Civil War to the late 1920s—was attributable to the power and prestige of the patricians and the then-still-strong numbers of the yeomen. The Democratic era that began with Al Smith's victory in Massachusetts and continues to this day has been due (1) to the emergence of the Democratic workers as Massachusetts' majority group, and (2) to the general inclination of the new managerial class, all other things being equal, to vote Democratic. Beguiled by the presence in the high Massachusetts offices of Republicans like Leverett Saltonstall, Christian Herter, Edward Brooke, John Volpe, Elliot Richardson, and Francis Sargent (governor 1969–1975), outsiders have been prone to think of the Bay State as a two-party state. In some ways, the thesis is correct. While the Democrats have a 2–1 registration lead, the number of independents, when added to the Republicans, forms a majority:

Registration (1974)		
Democratic	1,226,824	43.4%
Republican	476,491	16.8%
Independent	1,124,994	39.7%

But the Republican registration has declined precipitously in recent years (down 13 percent just between 1970 and 1974), and most of the party's enrollees are over 40 years of age.

Without the independent vote, Republicans would long since have been closed out entirely from effective participation in Massachusetts political life. It gives them the potentiality of winning, but only with candidates who represent the liberal wing of the party and have strong personal appeal, or when the Democratic opponents are exceptionally weak. When one looks behind the façade of the GOP glamor candidates, one finds a dry rot has infected every part of the GOP organization. The grass roots party, still strongly yeoman-oriented, is old and tired. The Republican state committee has begun only in the last few years to add ethnics to its heavily Yankee Protestant ranks. The party's yeoman-oriented legislative leaders were as likely to oppose as to support the progressive programs of Republican governors, fearing more taxes. And the patricians, as Litt notes, are caught up in the changing economy as establishment forces like the John Hancock Insurance Company and the First National Bank of Boston cooperate with Harvard and MIT. The party's successful statewide candidates are obliged to create their own highly personal organizations. But the loyalty—as with the many Italians whom Volpe brought into the Republican activity—is to the man, not the party, and the result is highly divisive. The Democrats' factionalism, dividing into camps of rival warlords, is similar, but the Democrats have the vote cushion and think they can afford the luxury (though they sometimes end up losing elections for statewide office as a result).

The Republicans' anemia is so dire that it has been almost 20 years since they had a plurality in the legislature and among statewide elective offices. In the space of one decade, 1954 to 1964, the Republican strength in the legislature declined from 53 percent to a mere 29 percent of the seats. The Republicans were even worse off after the 1974 election, with only seven of 40 seats in the state senate and 46 of 240 seats in the house. In the same election, the Democrats won all eight seats on the governor's council. The outcome was largely foreordained by the Republicans' appalling failure to recruit candidates.* Only two of the eight Democratic candidates for the governor's council were opposed, and there were Republican candidates for only 108 of the 240 house seats and 13 of the 40 senate seats. The Boston *Globe* in 1971 quoted an anonymous but loyal State House Democrat as hoping the Republicans would show more spunk. "It would be better, not only for the two-party system but for Democratic party discipline, if the Democrats got cut back to say, 150 [house] seats," he said. "You can't appeal for a party-line vote now; they say, 'Hell, there are 169 others. You don't need me.'"

Even the occasional statewide victories for the Republicans might not be possible if it were not for the "Massachusetts Ballot," adopted years ago and now a model for several other states. Under it, there is no single party column or voting machine lever, and the voter is obliged to make an

* Another factor was the past action of the Democrats in the legislature to redistrict many Republican seats out of existence. In the Boston area, for instance, there are wedge-shaped senate districts with a safe minority of suburban voters, deliberately designed to keep Democrats in office.

individual choice for each office. In the top two or three offices, where the candidates are familiar as individuals to the voters, Republicans occasionally have a chance of winning; in voting for most other posts, however, many have a tendency just to seek out the candidate with the word "Democratic" written beside his name and vote for him.

Things have been steadily getting worse for the Massachusetts GOP in the last several years, not only because the party's base is so small, but because it is split into bitterly quarreling liberal and conservative wings. Governors Volpe and Sargent generally kept the conservatives in check, but Sargent deeply offended the conservatives by his scarcely disguised disdain for figures like Spiro Agnew, his support of a graduated income tax, and his cavalier attitude toward Republicans in the appointments he made to state offices. All of this boiled to a head at the 1974 Republican state convention, just two months before President Nixon's eventual resignation, when the delegates repudiated Sargent and Brooke by thunderously approving a resolution supporting the imperiled President after rejecting a Sargent-Brooke draft that would merely have declared Nixon "like any other American, subject to the law of the land."

But when a Massachusetts Conservative party was formed in March 1971, to fight the "rush to liberalism" of the regular Republican leadership, it proved to be very short-lived—quite simply, one would have to say, because its constituency was so thin. A Conservative party might be viable in New York State, but Massachusetts simply lacks large number of conservative voters comparable to upstate New York, some of the New York boroughs, or parts of Long Island. Nor is it an easy matter to lure working-class Massachusetts Democrats into a conservative movement, because of the strong emotional ties which the Irish and other ethnic groups have to the Democratic party.

The Presidential elections of 1968 and 1972 provided compelling evidence of that loyalty. In 1968, Hubert Humphrey swamped Richard Nixon by a margin of 702,373 votes (63 percent) in Massachusetts. It was Humphrey's biggest numerical majority in any state of the Union. Then, in 1972, while 49 other states were voting for Nixon's reelection, Massachusetts went for George McGovern by a solid plurality of 220,462 votes (54 percent). (Interestingly, Brooke was reelected to the Senate the same day by a margin of 682, 654 votes—63.5 percent of the total cast.)

Humphrey's victory could be explained in terms of the ethnics' unflagging Democratic loyalty, plus the remarkable shift of Massachusetts' affluent and intelligentsia to the Democratic column over the years. Almost 60 percent of Humphrey's plurality came from Boston and its suburbs, many of which are very urban in character. But once-Republican suburbs had also turned Democratic. Wellesley, which went 79 percent for Dewey in 1948, was only 57 percent for Nixon in 1968. Between the same two elections, Concord dropped from 71 to 48 percent Republican, Brookline from 56 to 26 percent Republican. The Democratic switch was almost as dramatic in western Massachusetts cities like Springfield and Pittsfield.

In 1972, McGovern failed to do quite as well as Humphrey had in ethnic and suburban communities. But there were other factors that kept the Bay State in the Democratic column: a heavy pro-McGovern student vote, strong support for McGovern by organized labor in the state, Boston *Globe* endorsement, and the deep support of the anti-Vietnam war movement in the state. Asked about the Democratic victory, the 24-year-old McGovern campaign head in the state, John McKane, said: "I think it has something to do with the atmosphere [Senator Edward M.] Kennedy has made possible. He has made liberalism respectable. A lot of people who would be Archie Bunkers are more progressive here than elsewhere."

Writing in 1975, after Senator Kennedy had been subjected to constant heckling on his trips back home because the South Boston Irish associated him with the pro-busing cause, one had to wonder if the Kennedy magic would hold forever among the Archie Bunkers of Massachusetts.

Even if it didn't, however, the Republicans seemed spiritually and numerically incapable of filling the gap, and there was the continued vitality of Massachusetts Democratic party to consider. This was illustrated in the 1974 gubernatorial contest. The favorite of the Democratic leaders in the legislature was the state's attorney general, Robert H. Quinn, the burly son of an Irish immigrant who had battled his way up in the Democratic hierarchy to become house speaker before his election as attorney general. But in the primary, Quinn was decisively defeated by Michael S. Dukakis, a cool-headed, tenacious former state legislator whose parents had also been immigrants (in his case, Greek).

In the legislature, Dukakis had scarcely been one of the "club," but his performance had been impressive, including his successful effort to pass Massachusetts' pioneering no-fault auto insurance law over the strong opposition of the insurance and trial-lawyers lobby. Defeated for lieutenant governor in 1970, he had remained in the public eye as moderator of the public education television program "The Advocates." Dukakis started full-time campaigning a year before the primary, built up a coterie of dedicated followers, and successfully sold the voters on his reform program in the areas of fiscal management of state affairs, criminal justice, mental health, and a promise to eliminate the patronage system in Massachusetts, "lock, stock and barrel." His strong primary victory over Quinn gave him the momentum he needed to defeat Sargent, one of the Republicans' most effective campaigners of recent years, by a margin of 207,931 votes (52 percent). Taking office in January 1975, at the age of 41, Dukakis enjoyed the sterling liberal credentials and popular mandate a Massachusetts governor needed to impose the kind of austerity program the state would need for fiscal survival in the late 1970s.

Before the 1974 elections, the Democrats did themselves a large favor by passing (over Governor Sargent's opposition) a bill abolishing Massachusetts' mandatory pre-primary endorsing conventions. The conventions had had the effect of dramatizing and exaggerating the splits within the party; in fact they were raucous, emotion-packed affairs whose handiwork

—especially in nominations for governor and U.S. Senators—had frequently been reversed by the party rank-and-file on primary day. In 1970, for instance, then-Democratic party chairman David Harrison scheduled the convention in the sylvan setting of the University of Massachusetts campus at Amherst. His intent was to avoid the stigma of "booze, broads, and boodle" that had surrounded earlier conventions, but he might as well have put the meeting in South Boston. A single ballot for governor took more than six hours, at least two major fistfights broke out on the convention floor, and there were scuffles, dead microphones, and a woman who fainted as her delegation was called to vote.

"The delegates," R. W. Apple, Jr., reported in the New York *Times,* "were overwhelmingly Irish-American, overwhelmingly insiders, overwhelmingly middle-aged." He spotted one of them, an oldtimer in a black suit with a two-day growth of beard, who shrugged his shoulders during a shouting match and said of the candidates for the nomination: "Kevin's my cousin, I play handball with Frank Bellotti, and I went to school with Maurice Donahue. I gotta make a connection with Kenny O'Donnell." The candidates referred to were Mayor Kevin White of Boston (who was short on delegates but longest on popular support), state senate president Maurice Donahue (favored with the delegates but disadvantaged with the voters because of his boss role in the widely scorned legislature), former Lt. Gov. Francis X. Bellotti (who ran in the vain hope that a split in the Irish vote would permit him to slip through to a minority vote victory in the primary), and former White House aide Kenneth P. O'Donnell (still trying to cash in on his association with the Kennedy family). Donahue turned out to be the convention winner, but one of his backers predicted: "We know Mossie will lose in September and Kevin will lose in November. That's the way it always is." He was right.

The only real winners in the convention charade were the Republicans, who benefited immensely from the publicizing of their opponents' feuds, and a well-known Democratic politician by the name of Edward M. Kennedy. Up for reelection in 1970, Kennedy did appear at Amherst, but only long enough to deliver a brief speech of high moral tone accepting renomination. Then he got out of town. Kennedy, and his brother John before him, have never sought to bring order out of the chaotic tribal warfare of the Massachusetts Democrats. When party chairman Harrison asked him to take a strong stand in 1970, Ted Kennedy replied: "How can I? Maurice Donahue is a friend of mine, Kenny O'Donnell was a friend of my brother, and Kevin White's a good Democrat."

Dukakis told me after his election that he thought he could have won even if the convention system had remained intact. Whether true or not, the fact is that the passing of the conventions and the nomination and election of a remarkably independent Democratic governor coincided quite neatly. Another sign of the times was that a strong reformist state legislator from Newton, Paul H. Guzzi, defeated the old-line secretary of state, John F. X. Davoren, by a margin of almost 100,000 votes in the Democratic primary, and then went on to win the general election with more than half a million votes to spare. It was the first time that an incumbent of that office had been defeated for renomination. (Davoren richly deserved the defeat. A one-time car salesman who rose to be speaker of the state house before achieving statewide office, he had a record of egregious absenteeism as secretary of state. The Boston *Globe* revealed in 1973 that he spent most of his time in his home town of Milford, where he controlled local politics for years "through a political machine fueled by his powerful positions in [state] government.")

Massachusetts voters continue, however, to love a familiar Irish name. Elected lieutenant governor on the ticket with Dukakis was a freshman state legislator named Thomas P. O'Neill III, whose father was well known as a veteran Congressman and Majority Leader of the U.S. House of Representatives. The younger O'Neill was put to work by Dukakis as his chief liaison officer with the state legislature *and* the federal government.

Some miscellanea on Massachusetts politics:

- The state has a Presidential primary that used to be a fairly meaningless nonbinding write-in preference poll but in recent years has been strengthened to require that names of leading candidates be placed on the ballot. In 1972, Maine's Edmund Muskie was strongly favored by the state's Democratic hierarchy and had a four-to-one lead over George McGovern in a Boston *Globe* poll taken in January. But it was McGovern, buoyed by antiwar sentiment and a strong grass-roots organization, who emerged the victor in April with 51 percent of the Democratic vote, compared to only 21 percent for Muskie. In the 1976 primary, Massachusetts Democrats turned around and gave conservative to moderate candidates 54 percent of the vote. Washington Sen. Henry Jackson won with 23 percent, forcing the party to take him seriously as a candidate. Alabama Gov. George Wallace got 17 percent, Georgia's Jimmy Carter 14 percent. Arizona's Morris Udall, with 18 percent, came in second and led a string of liberal candidates.

Prior to the 1976 Presidential primary season, Massachusetts was the center of an effort to establish a common New England regional primary date in early March. The effort, pushed by liberal Democrats including Lt. Gov. O'Neill and state representative Barney Frank of Boston, had three goals: to put some sense into the primary process by letting national candidates concentrate their efforts in the region at the same time; to magnify the effect of Massachusetts' liberal constituency, which selects nearly half the region's national convention delegates; and to sap some of the attention from the bizarre New Hampshire primary setting. Predictably, however, New Hampshire refused to go along, setting its primary for the last Tuesday in February, a week before Massachusetts' new date.

- The Ripon Society of independent and progressive-minded younger Republicans was founded in Cambridge early in the 1960s and has continued to exercise an influence substantially beyond its numbers—a thorn in the side of the conservative, contented national Republican establishment and the nemesis, of course, of groups like Young Americans for Freedom, which are also strong in Massachusetts.

▪   The peace movement blossomed in the Bay State, starting on a quite modest scale in 1962 when independent candidate H. Stuart Hughes polled 2.4 percent of the vote for the U. S. Senate against Ted Kennedy and George Cabot Lodge. A few years later Massachusetts began to send to Congress two men who personified a freewheeling, antimilitary liberalism—Michael Harrington, from 1969 onwards, and a Jesuit priest, the Rev. Robert F. Drinan, first elected in 1970. Both these Democrats owed their elections to the small armies of students from eastern Massachusetts' activist universities who poured in to help, plus the support of the new managerial class in sophisticated, liberally oriented suburban towns. Vietnam was the issue Drinan used to win initially; the issue that almost defeated him, despite a distinguished record as an educator and lawyer (including several years as dean of Boston College Law School), was the fact that he was also a priest. Roman Catholics especially appeared to resent his entry into the active political arena. By 1974 he appeared to have solidified his hold on his district, winning a majority of the vote against two opponents (one Republican, one independent). Drinan is the first Catholic priest to serve in Congress since the Rev. Gabriel Richard served as a territorial delegate from Michigan in 1882; in his first election he was also the second person in a whole century to defeat an incumbent Massachusetts Congressman in a primary.* Since the Harrington and Drinan elections, the ranks of very liberal Bay State Congressmen of their stripe have been augmented by the election of two others: Garry E. Studds from the Cape Cod-New Bedford district, and Paul E. Tsongas from the Lawrence-Lowell area.

Does all the evidence point to Massachusetts being the most liberal state, politically, in the U.S.A.? The answer, based on all the evidence we have reviewed, may well be "yes," and the most important reasons may be the strong intellectual influence of Massachusetts' many universities, whose faculties are often direct participants in public life, the liberality of the Yankee elite, and the progressive attitudes of several leading Democratic state legislators.

But there is another side, symbolized in recent years by a woman named Louise Day Hicks. A dowdy attorney in her fifties, Mrs. Hicks rose to power in Boston on a single issue: ethnic white Bostonians' concern about the incursion into their neighborhoods of Negroes, whose numbers increased from 9.8 to 18.2 percent of the city population in the decade of the 1960s alone. Mrs. Hicks's first and most loyal supporters were the blue-collar Irish of South Boston—"my people," as she calls them. But she gained national prominence by her fight against school busing to achieve racial balance while she served on the Boston school committee. "You know where I stand," was her rallying cry. In 1967, she lost a bitter mayoralty campaign to Kevin White

---

* The only other Bay State primary upset was in 1966 when Mrs. Margaret Heckler upset an aging Joseph W. Martin, Jr., in the Republican primary in Martin's southeastern Massachusetts district.

by a vote of 102,706 to 90,154; two years later she led the pack to win election to the Boston city council; in 1970 she was elected to Congress from the Boston congressional district that John W. McCormack had represented for 40 years. In 1971, she ran for mayor as the candidate of those who want to preserve white neighborhoods and stop crime on the streets—"the fact that people don't dare walk out of their own doorway." But Mrs. Hicks's performance in Congress had been lackluster, and Mayor White defeated her the second time around by a resounding 112,875–70,214 vote. She was defeated for reelection to Congress in 1972 but remained a potent political force in the Boston area—particularly as the school busing issued crested in 1974–75.

State Government: Glory and Travail

Being the old and tradition-bound state it is, Massachusetts has had to struggle through most of the 20th century to bring its archaic structures of state government into line with the needs of the times. Finally, substantial success is in sight.

As a legacy from colonial times, Massachusetts entered the century with a form of government deliberately designed to restrict the governor's authority. The system had originally been intended to prevent executive abuse, a remembrance of the conflicts with the Crown before the Revolution. The 20th-century results were less desirable. The governor had to work with an independently elected governor's council that could reject any appointment he made and pass on *every* state contract—an invitation to partisan maneuver or graft, with no commensurate policy responsibility to the public. Secondly, there was a large, domineering legislature that controlled the executive departments by overlapping appointments to commissions, which in turn had to return to the legislature for their money and could easily bypass the governor.

The system was palatable enough to the Republicans who dominated state government up to the late 1920s, since divided authority mitigated against any strong governmental programs that might mean more taxes or an impingement on private capital. Then, when the Democrats took control of the governorship and the governor's council in the 1930s, they used those offices to circumvent the rural-dominated legislature, increase the power of labor, and enhance the interests of a patronage-oriented, ethnic coalition at the expense of the Republican patricians. During World War II, there was something of a hiatus in politics and state government, and that truest of bluebloods, Leverett Saltonstall, was governor. As the postwar era opened, the patricians of the business and financial community became preoccupied with national and even international economic issues and felt some despair in controlling state government because of the preponderant numbers of the Democratic-ethnic coalition. They did, however, furnish one distinguished governor—Christian A. Herter (who was later U. S. Secretary of State). And in time, the patrician-managerial strata discovered they needed, in Edgar Litt's words, "integrated centers of political power within the state to which they [could] relate national policies and economic developments. . . . They [found] that the governorship and the party systems are vital instruments for bringing about rational, managerial changes." As it turned out, their principal opponents were the very groups most entrenched in the legislature—the yeomen and core-city politicians, both intent on protecting their particularistic economic and social interests. And the managers and patricians faced another problem: the harm to Massachusetts' national image that stemmed from corruption in government. There was a distinct danger that without corrective action, Massachusetts' prospects for business deals, new industries, and government contracts might be seriously impaired.

Official skulduggery had been a problem in Massachusetts since the 1920s, occasionally among Republicans but mostly among Democrats. By the end of World War II, political corruption—payroll padding, kickbacks on contracts, payments for jobs—was taken for granted. In 1945, Curley was elected mayor of Boston even while under federal indictment for mail fraud (a charge on which he was later convicted and sent to prison). In 1956, Congressman Thomas J. Lane, a Democrat from Lawrence, was convicted of income tax evasion, served four months in federal prison, and then returned home to be reelected by his understanding constituents. In 1960, Democratic state representative Charles Iannello's Boston South End district reelected him by a 2–1 margin after he had been tried, convicted, and sentenced for a year to the house of correction on charges of larceny from the state by his family-owned firm.

The revelations of widespread public malfeasance began in 1958 when the Boston *Herald* uncovered a broad pattern of corruption in the rental of equipment by the state department of public works from private contractors. William F. Callahan, then chairman of the Massachusetts Turnpike Authority and a man who exercised vast power in the legislature and through job patronage, became a leading target of investigators and newspaper writers. Democrat Foster Furcolo, governor from 1957 to 1960, was eventually indicted on charges of conspiracy to arrange a bribe. The case was thrown out of court for lack of evidence, but several persons who had served in Furcolo's administration were convicted and went to jail. In 1960, following the income tax evasion conviction of a consulting engineer named Thomas Worcester, who agreed to tell what he knew in exchange for a lighter sentence, federal Judge Charles E. Wyzansky issued a report scoring what he called a "sordid racket of extortion, bribery, and corruption." He suggested that the same unsavory practices might have affected broad areas of the Massachusetts body politic.* The corruption issue was a key factor in the election of John A. Volpe as governor. Once elected, he proceeded to establish a state crime

* An apparent end to the whole bizarre era was reached in 1969 when FBI agents in Atlantic City arrested a six-year fugitive from justice, George L. Brady, ex-head of the Massachusetts Parking Authority and a man under indictment on charges of larceny in the disappearance of $784,480 in construction of an underground garage beneath Boston Common. According to an account by John Fenton in the New York *Times*, Brady had been trudging forlornly back to a dreary rooming house with a bundle of groceries when his captors accosted him. *Sic transit gloria.*

commission that eventually reported: "Corruption permeates the state, from town governments to the State House and involves politicians, businessmen, lawyers and ordinary citizens."

Today official corruption is less of a problem than it was in Massachusetts, but by no means expunged. Some people in Massachusetts claim that the corruption issue was blown up far beyond its true proportions; as state legislator William Bulger of South Boston told me in reference to the crime commission and its $589,000 budget, "When you have a Manhattan Project, you have to explode the bomb." Some decent men found their public lives ruined just by being mentioned in the reports of the time, he says, and Callahan was even named in one indictment after he was dead. Nevertheless, public morals had declined so far in the late 1950s that ordinary citizens had to make political payoffs to get such minimal services from government as licenses to be hairdressers, electricians, or plumbers. I worked myself as a salesman for political printing in 1958, visiting many politicians in the state house in Boston, and the place reeked of corruption. Members of the governor's council sat at their desks between sessions bargaining over the telephone for jobs for favored constituents and mentioning suspicious cash sums. (Four former councilors were among those later indicted and convicted on charges of bribery, based on evidence the crime commission gathered.) This was the same era during which a bookie operation was found to be flourishing within the very corridors of the State House.

The crime commission findings have borne important fruit. While Republicans benefited most from them politically, it was Democratic Governor Endicott Peabody who capitalized on them to have the governor's council stripped of all its powers except approval of pardons and ratifying judicial appointments. At the same time, state officers were switched from the archaic two-year terms to four-year terms, starting in 1966. These proposals were approved by a referendum vote of the people in 1964 by a vote of 1,-133,624 "yes" to 589,219 "no" votes. Peabody later told ex-Governor Terry Sanford of North Carolina (as quoted in Sanford's *Storm Over the States*):

These amendments to the constitution have considerably overhauled the executive in Massachusetts and given him real authority to match his responsibility. I think that the outlook for the long run—in giving Massachusetts effective government, in restoring the confidence of the alienated voter, in eliminating corruption—is tremendous.

The next logical step would be the total abolition of the governor's council. But, like that other dangerous anachronism, the electoral college feature of the federal Constitution, it seems to hang on, and on, and on. (In 1975 Governor Dukakis began a new push for a constitutional amendment to abolish the council once and for all, but was rebuffed by the legislature).

Massachusetts has, however, recently completed the first major overhaul of its executive branch in half a century. Ten cabinet-level departments have been created, each with its own secretary appointed by the governor and serving at his pleasure. They have absorbed 300 previously independent agencies of state government, 170 of which reported directly to the governor. The new structure has eliminated numerous examples of duplication and fragmentation. For instance, there were 21 separate agencies handling youth services, 30 dealing with environmental problems and 17 responsible for aid to needy families. The reorganizational proposal was first put forward by Governor Volpe and brought to fruition under Governor Sargent. "We surprised even ourselves by being able to get it through the legislature," Sargent said. (Later, the legislators renewed their image of obstinacy by slowing down the required legislation to complete reorganization under the cabinet system—partly, it appeared, because of their political differences with Sargent. By the start of the Dukakis administration in 1975, however, it appeared that the drawn-out process of implementing the reorganization might soon be completed.) Both Sargent and Dukakis appointed outstanding cabinet secretaries of both sexes. Dukakis filled a campaign promise by appointing four women to his cabinet. He claimed that his cabinet was made up of "first-rate generalists," and most observers seemed to agree he had succeeded. In 1975, as the state's budget grew tighter, there was some sentiment in the legislature to abolish some of the cabinet positions. Critics of the cabinet system argued that it was simply another bureaucratic layer which may actually slow the delivery of services to the public.

Change has come a lot slower to the legislature, familiarly known by the bombastic name of the Great and General Court of Massachusetts. Big city ethnics and Yankee yeomen sometimes combine to defeat the will of reform-minded governors who reflect a broader and more modern constituency. The house membership, 240 since 1857, has made it second only to New Hampshire in size among all state legislative bodies. For years the house fought obdurately against any reduction in its unwieldy ranks, resisting the efforts of the strong, reform-minded Massachusetts League of Women Voters to cut its size to 160. In 1970, for instance, the legislature refused to permit a referendum of the people on the proposed cut, even after the League had gathered 150,000 signatures on an initiative proposal. In the following election, however, a substantial number of house members who had voted against the cut were unseated. The legislature then voted the proposed amendment (as required by the Massachusetts constitution) in two successive sessions, and in 1974 the people voted the reduction by a thundering margin of 1,128,315 to 302,008. The change was to go into effect in 1977.

The legislative membership says a lot about Massachusetts life and politics. The Democratic leadership is all Irish-American; the Republican, Wasp. With its size, the membership reflects every age, color, profession, ethnic, and professional group imaginable, though there are some imbalances: only 15 women out of 280 house and senate members, but heavy numbers of lawyers and, oddly enough, funeral directors. When I looked around the house floor one day in 1970, I saw five gaunt snowy-haired Irishmen who were spitting images of the then aged and ready-to-retire House Speaker, John W. McCormack. But the legislature is moving fast to incorporate youth, with many members in their twenties and early thirties. The state constitution sets no minimum age for officeholders, and perhaps the hoary old Commonwealth will be first with teenage legislators.

The General Court is characterized by an unusual constitutional right of free petition by all citizens, together with the custom of giving all the petitions a hearing before a legislative committee.* But the "democracy" in the system tends to end there. Party discipline is strong, the speaker and senate president often exert heavy-handed leadership. Until a 1973 reform, it was standing practice for committee meetings, including the crucial executive sessions of joint legislative committees where many of the gut decisions are made, to be closed to the public and the press. Even the 1973 rules change left an escape hatch by which a committee could go into executive session by a majority vote of its members. There are so many bills (close to 10,000 each session) that most legislators rubber-stamp committee recommendations. The legislature has some modern features, like annual unlimited sessions (which now tend to run most of the year until they are "prorogued"), and a legislative reference bureau of exceptional quality. But the Council on State Legislatures in 1971 gave it a rather mediocre rating of 29th in the U.S.A. in terms of its overall effectiveness. One drawback is terribly limited office space. As then-Representative Martin F. Linsky of Brookline wrote in 1969:

> Being a Republican, I have no legislative office. I am privileged to share a five-girl secretarial pool with my 239 colleagues, I answer my phone calls in one of a row of telephone booths lining one side of the House Lobby and discuss personal matters with constituents in a large waiting room which doubles as a corridor between the phones and the chamber. And so in an atmosphere of privacy comparable to Boston Common during the lunch hour, I discuss welfare checks, jobs, getting speakers recruited, retrieving suspended driving licenses [a favor much demanded of legislators], and conduct a bit of informal psychiatry. Such are the perquisites of power.

Now each legislator is guaranteed at least a desk and a place to park his briefcase, an achievement for which the youthful house speaker of the late '60s and early '70s, David M. Bartley of Holyoke, could take substantial credit. Sometimes Bartley knocked heads in a manner that could be likened to that of the late speaker John Thompson of Ludlow. But any resemblance between the two men stopped there. Thompson was a big, burly personification of the Irish boss, a tough, partisan figure who never forgot to collect a political debt. He called himself a "delightful rogue," an apparent excuse for his heavy-drinking ways and wicked temper. (In 1963, Governor Peabody tried to purge Thompson—and failed.) But Bartley, by contrast, was extremely concerned about his own image and that of the entire General Court. He traveled about the state giving speeches on how the legislature was being

---

* The bills filed by common citizens have often, in the words of one legislative leader, been "pretty flaky." Examples: proposals to heat the sidewalks or to impeach every judge on the Massachusetts bench. But a handful of excellent bills got their start by this unconventional method. House clerk Wallace Mills was quoted as saying in 1972: "You know, it's funny. I look back at the 25 years of bills I've seen and recall how many laws today were once thought just the harebrained scheme of some idiot."

modernized—in rules, staff help, computerization, and office space—so that it could be one of the advanced ones of America. Under his tutelage, the house changed its rules to give rank-and-file members more time to study appropriations bills, and thus have a real say in state budget priorities.* In addition, Bartley and his counterpart, senate president Kevin B. Harrington, secured passage of a much tougher lobby control law.

There is little question that the General Court has passed some remarkably progressive legislation in recent years. Some examples:

■ America's first "no-fault" insurance law, authored by Dukakis, which was passed in 1970 in an attempt to cut down on Massachusetts' auto insurance rates, then the highest in the nation. The law has been a stupendous success; in its first year of operation, insurers paid out 43 percent less to accident victims than they had under the old system. The law has undergone steady revisions, including the addition of property damage in 1971. Premiums have been sharply reduced, and payments are quicker. Attempts by the Massachusetts Trial Lawyers Association to revoke the law have been hooted down.

■ A 1970 "bill of rights" for the protection of consumers, a consumer protection unit-pricing law, and a generic drug law. Earlier, Massachusetts passed a truth-in-lending act that served as a basis for subsequent congressional legislation.

■ An "environmental bill of rights," numerous antipollution laws, and huge bond issues for environmental protection.

■ Even before Watergate, what was then the toughest campaign spending law in the country, except for Florida and Kentucky. This was followed in 1973 by a so-called "omnibus" campaign reform bill requiring very full spending reports by candidates and political committees. But reform forces in the state thought even that law too weak, and in a 1974 statutory initiative approved by the people mandated even stricter reporting requirements and a bipartisan corrupt practices commission to enforce compliance.

■ The 1970 Vietnam bill, which said Massachusetts inhabitants need not fight abroad unless Congress declared war, and instructed the state attorney general to file a complaint in the Supreme Court. (The court, by a 6–3 vote, refused to hear the case, but Massachusetts had made its symbolic point.)

■ A pioneering public-school racial imbalance law, passed in 1965, which gives communities a 15 percent bonus in state school-construction aid if they place new schools in locations that will relieve or eliminate imbalanced classroom enrollments. (The law remains a major point of contention in the state, and if it were not for gubernatorial vetoes, it would have been repealed altogether. In 1974 the statute was modified to encourage voluntary, rather than forced, busing. The most vocal opponents of the measure are blue-collar ethnics whose leaders claim it was imposed on their inner-city communities by suburban and rural legislators. Nor is it especially popular with some

* The legislature in 1974 approved an open budget act, requiring both department heads and legislative committees to hold public hearings and furnish more supporting data aimed toward a program budget. The stated goals of the act were more complete public scrutiny and less clandestine decision making. Bartley relinquished the house speakership in 1975 to accept an academic post.

blacks, who are more interested in having more black teachers and principals and additional "black studies.")

■   A Massachusetts housing finance agency, established in 1968, which subsidizes low-income housing by granting low-cost loans to developers and has a unique rule that developments include both full-rate renters *and* at least 25 percent low-income tenants. The result has been a real mix of income groups and a program that ought to be a model housing program for the nation. The housing finance agency, however, ran into trouble in 1975 when it could not sell bonds for new construction due to Massachusetts' suspect financial condition.

■   An "anti-snob" zoning law, passed in 1969, designed to break down suburban resistance to low-income housing, and hundreds of millions of dollars in bond issues to encourage construction of housing units for the less affluent. The "anti-snob" law gave the state's housing appeals committee power to override local zoning boards' rejection of housing projects for the poor. By the mid-1970s, however, it had failed to have measurable results and the vast majority of Massachusetts' 111,842 blacks continued to live in Boston, four of its close-in suburbs, and New Bedford, Springfield, and Worcester. A 1975 joint federal-state report, entitled "Route 128: Boston's Road to Segregation," charged that housing, employment, and transportation development within the suburbs had formed a pattern leading to Boston's school busing crisis.

■   Gun control laws, passed in 1968 and 1974, which were hailed as the toughest in the nation. Massachusetts citizens must register all firearms and anyone convicted of carrying an unregistered gun receives a minimum of one year in jail, with no hope of probation, suspension of sentence, or parole. Proposals were still active in 1975 to ban "Saturday night special" handguns, or the possession of any kind of handgun except by police and military personnel.

■   A number of rather advanced laws in the civil liberties area. In 1974, for instance, the legislature adopted a local option "bill of rights" for public high school students. The measure permitted them to express their views through speech and symbols, to publish and disseminate their views, to assemble peaceably on school grounds to express their opinions, and to enjoy a wide latitude in personal dress. Another 1974 act banned discrimination in providing credit because of sex or marital status. And in 1973, then-Governor Sargent icily refused to let Massachusetts participate in the compilation of the FBI's national-level computerized criminal history file on persons with any "significant" contact with law enforcement agencies. The system, Sargent said, posed "one of the biggest threats to our democratic system—the invasion of one's privacy."

■   A 1970 mental health treatment and commitment reform act—an attempt to build on Massachusetts' reputation of having one of the best mental health treatment systems in the U. S.

■   An omnibus 1972 prison reform measure establishing community corrections centers and authorizing work-release programs. The intent was to provide inmates with education, training, and employment outside prison walls. Implementation proved very slow, however, in the wake of prison riots, strikes, and a mass outbreak that forced Governor Sargent to dismiss his reform-minded corrections commissioner, John O. Boone. Nevertheless, the state pushed ahead in the early '70s with furloughs and other reforms, even in the face of opposition from some conservative legislators. In a landmark move, Massachusetts in 1971 began to abolish its institutions for youthful offenders and place them in community-based work and educational programs instead.

Massachusetts also began to clear away its huge backlog of court cases with establishment of an appeals court under the supreme judicial court. Sargent was able to name an almost entirely new set of judges to the supreme judicial court, which claims to be the nation's oldest, predating even the U.S. Supreme Court. The appointees proved to be outstanding jurists who moved into social fields under the new chief justice, G. Joseph Tauro. "Tauro's court," the Boston *Globe* reported, swept away many archaic legal rules and found "for tenants over landlords, consumers over businesses, citizens over government agencies, homeowners over banks and employees over employers."

▪ 1975 legislation, advocated by Dukakis, replacing the old department of public utilities, which was often charged with toadying to the utilities on rate increase demands, with a new commission which Dukakis promised would be "aggressive, consumer-oriented," and willing to grant rate increases "only when they are clearly merited." In 1975 pressure was also building for a state-run public power authority that would be responsible for the construction of all new power plants and transmission lines in the state and would sell wholesale power to private utilities—the intent being to lower Massachusetts sky-high electricity rates.

All of this is not to suggest that Massachusetts has become a Utopia of progressive legislation. Many of the bills cited have serious defects. And the lobbies have not lost their teeth. Some of the big, powerful statewide lobbies like the Associated Industries of Massachusetts have succeeded—even in a heavily Democratic legislature—in bending tax legislation to the benefit of business. Organized labor is also a factor to be reckoned with, though its power is considered less now than in the early 1950s, when it was a potent force in elections and got a substantial amount of pro-labor legislation passed. The state's union heritage is more one of conservative craft unionism of the AFL variety than militant industrial unionism of the CIO type; in fact, Massachusetts lacks any mass union like the UAW or ILGWU. The leadership is heavily "ethnic," involving many of the same factions as the Democratic party.

A formidable new element was added to the labor picture in the early 1970s, however, with the rise of potent government employee unions which were authorized to bargain collectively with the state in 1974. A new public union coalition called "Alliance," consisting of the state chapter of the American Federation of State, County and Municipal Employees and the Service

Employees International Union, seemed on the verge of winning elections to represent a substantial majority of the some 70,000 state workers. With state workers facing the very real prospect of massive layoffs because of the commonwealth's fiscal crisis, there was a prospect of serious strikes by the once-quiescent public work force. All of this seemed likely to spark major political battles as well. State representative Barney Frank, in an interview with the Washington *Post*, said he thought there was "no bigger issue" than that of the public workers. "The balance has tipped much too far in the direction of the public employee," he asserted. "The mistake we made was to give them collective bargaining on top of civil service. Now they are triply protected. I'm not so worried about the money they earn, but productivity —you just can't get any. And the most progressive programs get hurt the most." (Ironically, Frank's brother David was one of the leaders of the Alliance.)

For all its liberality, Massachusetts has a tax structure in distinct need of reform. About half of all governmental revenue, counting state and local government together, comes from the local property tax, which is at the highest per capita level in the United States. Yields are vastly disparate, depending on the wealth of individual communities, and the rates are close to confiscatory in Boston and some other cities.* Not until 1971 did Massachusetts move toward some type of direct state subsidy for cities—based on a so-called "equalized municipal grants" system, designed by the ever active League of Women Voters. Massachusetts' per capita tax collections of state and local governments, as a share of personal income, reached 14.2 percent in 1973—the fourth highest level in the nation. (The only states exacting a greater toll were New York, Vermont, and Wisconsin.)

Massachusetts' per capita income, relative to the other states, has slipped a bit in recent years, but in 1974 still ranked a respectable 12th. The problem is that the heavily relied upon property tax fails to tap that income growth adequately. The state government does impose an income tax, but Massachusetts voters have three times refused in public referenda to make it a progressive income tax. There are exemptions which allow low-income voters to avoid most of the income tax, but the wealthy escape fairly lightly. Thus the heaviest burden falls on middle-income taxpayers, the same group which is hit most heavily by the property tax and quite heavily by the sales tax. The middle-income, ethnic Democrats so thoroughly in control of the legislature should be ashamed not to have done better for their own people.

The Massachusetts state budget has literally sextupled since 1960, to $3.2 billion for fiscal 1975. The increase reflects higher costs for all phases of government, but especially education and welfare. The education increases were long overdue, but even with major advances during the 1960s, Massachusetts still ranked only 44th among the 50 states in per capita state gov-

---

* The typical tax on a house with a sale value of $25,000 in America's 30 largest cities in 1973 was $547; in Boston the rate was $2,220, the highest of any of the 30. A Boston family earning $10,000 a year paid $1,721 a year for real estate, sales and income taxes, and auto registration—17.2 percent of its income—again the highest of any of the 30 cities. Rates in the suburban Boston communities are also among the highest in the nation.

ernment expenditures for all education in 1972. The Massachusetts state government in 1969 became the first in the Union to assume the full burden of welfare costs in the state, a vital point of relief for the sorely pressed municipalities which had borne much of the burden before then. But the lawmakers did not anticipate the fantastic increase in welfare benefits which would follow as more eligible people applied and recession-time unemployment hit the state. By early 1971, one out of every five persons in Boston (21.2 percent) was receiving some type of welfare, compared to 9.6 percent in 1966. In the 1974–75 recession, the welfare budget began to soar out of control. "This welfare thing is drowning us," Dukakis told me shortly after he took office. He said Massachusetts' welfare spending per capita had risen above the other industrialized Northeastern states, and that while he was willing to see Massachusetts among the four or six leading states in welfare aid, he saw no reason it should be far above them. "There's a lot in that department [human services] that has nothing to do with real need," Dukakis said.

The problem of slashing hundreds of millions of dollars from the human services—which made up 60 percent of the state budget—fell to Secretary of Human Services Lucy Benson and particularly the bright young management specialist she recruited to head the welfare department, Jerald Stevens. Some welfare services were sharply restructured, others eliminated altogether. Employable persons were cut from relief rolls, several medical services jettisoned, and the central welfare office cut by 10 percent. Stevens also said he was trying to establish "some coherence" in a small army of welfare social workers who were often ill-trained and unresponsive to management directives. Finally, in late 1975, Mrs. Benson resigned, feeling that she was not receiving proper backing from the governor. Welfare Commissioner Jerald Stevens was named by Dukakis to succeed her.

All those steps reduced the welfare budget from $1.8 billion to $1.4 billion, but the legislature then proceeded to lop off another $400 million, including a sharp cut in welfare for AFDC families and total elimination of the program which gives medical care to the working poor not actually on welfare. Even before that, because of severe staff cutbacks, there were a few instances of mental health patients rioting and terrorizing other patients in the state's mental hospitals. All the hospitals were in danger of losing their accreditation. Mrs. Benson said that the massive cuts in human services made "a mockery of the commonwealth's commitment to help persons in need."

Indeed, the fiscal gloom of the Bay State as it struggled through the 1975 recession was almost overwhelming. "Massachusetts today," Dukakis told the legislature, "faces the most serious budgetary crisis in memory—the largest current fiscal deficit of any state in the nation and an economic base that is stagnant and eroding." First he made what seemed a Herculean effort to reduce expenditures, eliminate waste, and reexamine old programs and priorities. But even then, the budget for the 1975 fiscal year could only be balanced through a $450 million bond issue, a $350 million tax increase (the largest in the state's history) and deep cuts in human services which the state legislature insisted on.* The budget, according to the Boston *Globe*, was thus balanced—"on the backs of the poor and needy. . . . Massachusetts is not exactly broke, but its progressive drive and spirit have been broken."

In the face of that dire situation, and the real hardships the poor and ill were being made to suffer, it was hard to see a silver lining. But the process was forcing Massachusetts to effect some long-overdue savings—"an opportunity to do some cutting and leaning," as Dukakis told me. Ironically, that was precisely the very policy that many of the state's business leaders, fearful of the commonwealth's growing competitive disadvantage among the states because of ballooning budgets, had been advocating for some time.

For fiscal 1977 Dukakis proposed a balanced budget, no new taxes, and the restoration of a few of the human service programs.

While the tax and welfare issues in Massachusetts have been getting the headlines, some believe that another issue—reform of the civil service system—ought to be next on the Commonwealth agenda. The problem is that so many state and local jobs are frozen into protected civil service status that governors and mayors and their department heads lack flexibility to bring in their own people at the top, especially at the appropriate level for "bright young men." A self-perpetuating bureaucracy, Robert Wood told me, captures effective control of government. "It doesn't protect you from patronage abuses and at the same time it doesn't allow you the techniques of modern management."

Many national experts consider Massachusetts civil service the most ossified, rigid, and unresponsive system in the entire United States. Placement in jobs, for instance, is uniformly preceded by civil service tests that have no discernible relation to an applicant's real skills or aptitude for a position. According to state representative Frank, the system makes for inefficient, uncivil servants. "The system is full of excuses for everybody not to do anything," he said. "The manager can say, 'Why should I try to manage? I have civil service—if I tried to disappoint them, I couldn't.' And the employee says, 'How the hell can I function when this guy isn't even trying to manage?' And they're right. There are so many points where the system can bog down that it's impossible to fix responsibility."

Howard Smith, secretary of economic affairs in the Dukakis cabinet, told me it was so excruciatingly difficult to fire a tenured civil service employee that he didn't consider it a productive use of his time to make the effort. Dr. William Goldman, the former commissioner of mental health, said shortly after leaving office in 1975 that the state personnel office, which administers civil service in the state, "implements the biases of its very parochial and reactionary leadership, and has clearly overstepped itself so that it has become one of the most secret, powerful, hidden agencies of government."

* Part of the problem was fiscal, but the other part was human and political. Instead of fuzzing over massive budget gaps and then coming in for supplemental appropriations, Dukakis insisted on portraying the fiscal crisis in its starkest light. The legislators, many fearful of losing their seats in the impending reduction of size of the house, found him unwilling to make the most innocent concessions to their political needs. A well-placed source said: "The legislators think the governor is hard-nosed, arrogant, insensitive and unfeeling—and he does act that way."

To those adjectives one may be able to add "corrupt"; in September 1975 Governor Dukakis said an investigation of the civil service system had turned up evidence of payoffs and other criminal activities in the fixing of examinations.

The Massachusetts government is rife with excess jobs and incompetent people at the lower rungs. There is a kind of hangover of the ethnic era, in which government service is doled out to cronies or acquaintances on a preferential basis. Just a single example: by 1973, 22 of the state legislators elected in 1970 had deserted the Great and General Court for better-paying and generally more comfortable positions on the public payroll. Thus it was almost incredible to hear Dukakis announce in winter 1975 that "the old patronage system has been destroyed." He claimed that an absolute end had been made to the system by which vast numbers of state government jobs were dispensed through a gubernatorial patronage office. Under that system, Dukakis said, there was "no way a citizen could walk in the door and compete on equal terms with anybody else for a job. Political sponsorship was the order of the day." By contrast, he claimed that his administration was in the process of developing the first modern personnel system in the history of Massachusetts state government, including a new judicial nominating commission to remove judgeships from politics and an end to summer jobs dispensed to the relatives and friends of legislators. "These are really revolutionary changes," Dukakis asserted. One could only conclude that if he were really serious, and did end the patronage system in state government, the change in the old commonwealth's ways would indeed be revolutionary.

A Leadership Roundup

The names of some Massachusetts politicians, especially those named Kennedy, have been household words in America for more than a decade now. The name of Edward Brooke strikes a bell with Americans because he is the first black Senator of this century—though there is a lot more to Ed Brooke than that. Elliot L. Richardson, a former state lieutenant governor and attorney general, was well enough known nationally before his celebrated departure from the Nixon Justice Department in the "Saturday night massacre" of 1973 (referred to in the introduction to this book). He had already served as Deputy Secretary of State, as Secretary of Health, Education, and Welfare, as Secretary of Defense, and Attorney General, gaining a reputation as one of the most competently cool and farsighted administrators any state has offered the nation in modern times. After his break with Nixon, Richardson was frequently mentioned as a possible future Republican Presidential candidate—a possibility he did not reject but admitted was unlikely. In 1974–75, he was a fellow of the Woodrow Wilson International Center for Scholars in Washington, specializing in state and local government; then he went to London, appointed Ambassador to the Court of St. James by President Ford only to return a few months later as Secretary of Commerce. No one expected the Richardson career to end there; among the future possibilities was the position of Secretary of State, a seat on the Supreme Court—or the Vice Presidency.

Mention should also be made of John A. Volpe, who left the governorship to serve creditably as Secretary of Transportation in the first Nixon administration. After the 1972 election, Volpe was sent off to be Ambassador to Italy so that the White House could install a more pliable conservative in the Cabinet post. An ex-contractor and onetime Federal Highway Administrator, Volpe had surprised everyone by moving to curb indiscriminate freeway construction and foster mass transportation.

Massachusetts in recent decades has contributed three prominent leaders to the U.S. House of Representatives—John W. McCormack, who was Speaker from 1962 through 1970; Joseph W. Martin, Jr., Speaker during the Republican 80th Congress (1947–48) and his party's spokesman as Minority Leader for many years; and Thomas P. O'Neill, Jr., who became Majority Leader in 1973.

Both McCormack and Martin were able, honorable men, and in their prime skillful negotiators in the personalized world of the U. S. House. But neither will long be remembered for any substantive contribution to American government. Both lingered too long in public life—McCormack as Speaker into his 79th year of life, when the intellectual tides of national life had long since passed him by, Martin as a House member until he was 82, though he had been deposed as minority leader eight years previously.

O'Neill is a big (six-foot-two, 260-pound), bluff Irishman, gregarious and knowledgeable, at once a page out of *The Last Hurrah* and an issue-oriented Congressman who surprised everyone by breaking with the Johnson Vietnam policies in 1967 to become an avowed, persistent dove. His district, in somewhat different configuration, was represented in earlier times by such legendary characters as John F. ("Honey Fitz") Fitzgerald, James Michael Curley, and John F. Kennedy. On his legendary Saturday walks, O'Neill mixes with an ethnic-social polyglot with few if any competitors among the nation's congressional districts—Irish and Italian working folk by the thousands, Portuguese in Somerville and East Cambridge, blacks in East Boston housing projects, Armenians in Watertown, the remnants of Back Bay and Beacon Hill Protestant elite, the cerebral Democrats of the Harvard and M.I.T. communities. In the House, O'Neill is known for his parliamentary finesse and a pragmatism and genial sense of humor which earn him many friends and few enemies.* Having ridden with (and occasionally led) the House reform movement of recent years, he was in a strong position to win

---

* O'Neill was primed for a key role if the Nixon impeachment had reached the House floor in 1974. Writer Jimmy Breslin relayed this delightful O'Neill story about the night that Gerald Ford was sworn in as Vice President, following the Agnew resignation. At the White House, Secretary of Housing and Urban Development James Lynn said to O'Neill: " 'Tip, did you ever think we'd be standing here in the White House with history being made, the Twenty-Fifth Amendment working for the first time? There's probably never going to be another like it in the country's history.' 'Not for about eight months,' Tip O'Neill said. Lynn's mouth opened. Tip O'Neill gave this great street laugh of his and jammed a Daniel Webster cigar in his mouth. James Lynn went away from the night with cement in his stomach."

the Speakership whenever Carl Albert of Oklahoma relinquished that post.

There is little one can add now to the familiar record of John F. Kennedy, the President who enunciated so many goals but had a chance to implement so few. As a Senator for Massachusetts, his record was passing but not brilliant; before he had had a chance to build seniority, in fact, his sights were set on the Presidency. Kennedy's initial election to the Senate, in 1952, had the byproduct of retiring from elective office the Republicans' great white hope of the first postwar years and the Eisenhower preconvention campaign manager of that year, Henry Cabot Lodge, Jr., grandson and namesake of the famous Massachusetts Senator who had led the successful fight to prevent U. S. entrance into the League of Nations. The defeat did not end Lodge's career; he went on to be U. S. Ambassador to the United Nations, Richard Nixon's Vice Presidential running mate in 1960, Ambassador to Vietnam and Germany and U. S. negotiator at the Vietnam peace talks in Paris. Finally (in one of those superb ironies of history), President Nixon made Lodge his personal envoy to—the Vatican. The present-day vogue is to see Lodge as an outmoded Cold Warrior, and politicians belittle his 1960 campaign on the Nixon ticket. Lodge was an early and strong advocate of the liberal brand of Republicanism which later triumphed in Massachusetts, however, and certainly an unselfish public servant.*

Senator Edward M. Kennedy, youngest of the three famous Kennedy brothers, is by most standards a conscientious and able Senator, a stalwart liberal who has grown immensely in his grasp of national issues. It is easy to forget now that in 1962, when he first ran for the Senate at 30 years of age, his candidacy was seen by many as crude capitalizing on the family name by a very inexperienced young man. But he easily defeated his Democratic opponent of that year, Edward J. McCormack, nephew of the Speaker, and won the general election with a smashing 71.8 percent of the vote. Then came the years of tragedy: his brother John's assassination in 1963, his brother Robert's assassination in 1968, and the death of his auto companion and pretty secretary, Mary Jo Kopechne, at the bridge at Chappaquiddick Island in 1969. Before the latter incident, Kennedy had been the all-but-certain next Presidential candidate of his party; after it, he won a second Senate term in 1970 by 58.8 percent—13 percent less than six years before. The following January, Kennedy was deposed from the position of Senate Whip he had won just two years before. His decisions not to seek the Democratic Presidential nominations in 1972 or 1976 appeared based in part on concern for his family in view of the assassinations of his two brothers, in part on the political fallout of Chappaquiddick, which in the public mind seemed revived as an issue following the Watergate scandals. By the mid-1970s, Kennedy had taken a new grip on his Senate duties, leading a fight for nationalized health insurance and fighting effectively for the liberal cause among Senate Democrats (helping secure an enlargement of the Senate Democratic Steering

---

* Twenty years after Kennedy took his Senate seat away from him, Lodge told me the defeat was "a blessing in disguise" because the United Nations job proved to be far more challenging "than just being one of 96 in the Senate."

Committee in 1973 and persuading that body two years later to provide choice assignments for liberal and freshman Senators).

The Kennedy saga often recalls the extraordinary statement of John Kennedy when he was a Senator in the 1950s—words that once sounded so arrogant, and now so strangely prophetic: "Just as I went into politics because Joe [the oldest brother] died, if anything happened to me tomorrow Bobby would run for my seat in the Senate. And if Bobby died our younger brother Ted would take over from him."

An interesting comment about Edward Kennedy's peculiar political position in the nation was made by author Richard J. Whalen in 1974. "He is the candidate," Whalen wrote, "of a waning national nostalgia, rooted in the legend of his martyred eldest brother. . . . [But] beneath the evocative name, face, voice and style stands a politician whose views on public policy clash . . . with the only Kennedy presidency we are ever likely to have. If the Senator were not a Kennedy, he would be ranked among the leaders of the left-liberal assault on JFK's world view, foreign policy, and defense program."

Presidential speculation about Kennedy may go on for years to come. As a Washington *Post* headline proclaimed in September 1974: "With '76 Ruled Out, Kennedy Could Run in '80, '84, '88 or '92." The article pointed out he would not reach the age of 60 until the 1992 campaign year.

Edward Brooke is a calm, articulate legislator, carrying on in the liberal Republican tradition of Massachusetts, a clear reflector of thought in his state. The son of a bourgeois Negro family and a successful lawyer, he built his home-state reputation fighting corruption, first as chairman of the Boston Finance Commission (1961–63) and then as attorney general of the state (1963–66). President Nixon twice offered him a Cabinet position, which he declined; while his stands on the Vietnam war and social issues were well to the left of the President's, Brooke took care to keep the lines of communication open to the President and his party. "I do not intend to be a national leader of the Negro people. I intend to do my job as a Senator from Massachusetts," Brooke said in 1966, the year he ran for the Senate. He has kept that promise, but national black leaders nonetheless consider him an effective agent for their cause. A leader of the Black Caucus of Negroes in the House told me that "too many blacks stay hung up on the race issue, which is one reason we don't win more elections in districts without black majorities. This is the reason we don't put pressure on Brooke. He needs a Black Caucus like a hole in the head."

The man Brooke succeeded, veteran Senator Leverett Saltonstall, was a perfect model of Yankee probity and moderation. Saltonstall had been an able wartime governor of his state but never made a strong mark on the Washington scene. He did do a superb job of representing special Massachusetts interests, like fishing, electronics, and the military. Brooke's effort is not comparable on that score, nor does Ted Kennedy's staff—despite the campaign slogan of doing "more for Massachusetts"—take the initiative on state issues. That role has now switched to the House side, particularly through Michael Harrington and one of the two remaining Republicans, Silvio O. Conte, a member of the Appropriations Committee. Conte, a liberal who attracts broad Democratic support in his western Massachusetts district, is a scrappy fighter for New England interests on energy matters and has fought over the years against big farm subsidies.

Among the more influential members of the delegation is Edward Boland of the Springfield area, who shares a Washington apartment with O'Neill. He is on the Appropriations Committee and was formerly a House spokesman for the Kennedys. Representatives James A. Burke and Torbert Macdonald have advanced to second-ranking positions on the Ways and Means and Interstate Commerce committees respectively, and have bright prospects for becoming chairmen in a few years. Macdonald, whose first claim to fame was that he roomed with Jack Kennedy at college, compiled one of the worst attendance records in the House but has recently made a more substantive mark chairing a subcommittee on communications and energy resources.

Economy: From Mill Town to Route 128

As these pages were written at the height of the 1974–76 national recession, unemployment in Massachusetts had soared to 14.4 percent, more than a third higher than the national rate. With a touch of real despair, Bay State economic analysts suggested that the state's recovery from the recession would lag well behind the nation as a whole, principally because of Massachusetts' large reservoir of poorly trained blue-collar workers and the continuing decline of traditional industries such as textiles and shoes.

The economic history, problems, and future prospects (or non-prospects) of the Bay State are essentially those of the New England region of which it is the keystone—the story told in detail in the introductory chapter of this book.

The economic woes of the mid-1970s, of a severity unknown since the Great Depression, were familiar to Massachusetts to the extent that they were rooted in the half-century decline of nondurable goods manufacturing. They differed markedly in the extent they were based on growing, huge energy price differentials between New England and other parts of the country, as well as higher tax rates than in other regions. But in a way the future seemed brighter because one could no longer say—as one could in the 1940s —that the great preponderance of Massachusetts wealth, built up in the days of the China trade and textile-mill ventures along the rivers, was tied up in restrictive "Boston trusts" that limited heirs' ability to do much constructive with their fortunes. The postwar economic renaissance in Massachusetts had built up new, viable pools of capital and a willingness to take risks.* The Boston banks, for instance, had become aggressive in lending to

* Just between 1972 and 1974, according to the First National Bank of Boston, 115 manufacturing firms began operations in the state, while 18 closed down.

research-based companies, which all perceived as the state's and region's hope for the future. The new problem was that high-technology enterprises required fairly modest numbers of workers—particularly of the low-skill type who were fast losing their jobs as the old-style factories folded, or retrenched.

At the end of World War II, the first serious efforts were made to utilize Massachusetts' remarkable university-based scientific brain power for promising, innovative economic enterprises. In 1946, Ralph Flanders (later U.S. Senator from Vermont) persuaded a few Boston capitalists to launch a new firm called American Research and Development, which was founded to invest in (but not control) promising new enterprises. The initial customer was Tracerlab, the first of Boston's postwar science-based industries. Tracerlab was the creation of three young Harvard scientists, working out of a decrepit old building in downtown Boston. They bought radioactive isotopes from Oak Ridge, Tennessee, and packaged them for the numerous hospitals and medical centers of Boston for use in diagnostic and treatment work. Boston banks turned down Tracerlab's request for capital to grow to meet its market, but American R & D quickly moved in with a $150,000 expansion loan that put Tracerlab on the road to prosperity.

In the years that followed, hundreds of electronics and highly technical research and development companies sprang up in Cambridge, drawing on the scientific talents at Cambridge and MIT. In the early 1950s, a new circumferential expressway—Route 128—was built to divert through traffic from Boston's streets. Critics said the road was an unnecessary extravagance and criticized the governor of the time, Paul Dever, for building it. They could not have been more wrong. Route 128 in a few years had become a foremost world center of space-missiles-electronics technology. It grew to have 30 industrial parks and over 700 firms.* The Air Force, which is the nation's largest purchaser of electronic equipment, placed its Electronics Systems Division at Hanscom Field in Bedford, near 128, and the Air Force's Cambridge Research Lab, Lincoln Lab, and MITRE Corporation, plus the Draper Lab at MIT, were all within easy reach. NASA's Electronic Research Center also went to Cambridge—some said as an act of political favoritism by President Kennedy to his brother, Senator Edward M. Kennedy, who had promised in his 1962 campaign to do "more for Massachusetts." By the late 1960s, nearly 50,000 professional engineers and scientists worked in the Cambridge–128 area. Fed by military contracts (in which Massachusetts ranked seventh in the country) and the outpouring of funds for research in connection with the moon-landing program, eastern Massachusetts was enjoying the greatest economic boom of its history.

Then, in 1969, recession struck. The reasons were the same as for the great letdown that began at the same moment in California: NASA cutbacks with completion of research and equipment manufacture for the Apollo

---

* Some of the principal electronics and related scientific firms of the 128–Cambridge complex are RCA, Avco, Minneapolis-Honeywell, Raytheon, Polaroid, General Electric, Geodyne, Textronic, Thermo Electron, Actronics, Litton, Adcole, General Radio, Xerox, Sylvania, Hewlett-Packard, and the two fiercely competitive leaders of the mini-computer industry—Digital Equipment and Data General.

missions, and a rapid reduction in Defense Department orders. In Massachusetts, there was not the accompanying blow from cutbacks in air frame construction, but the state may have been harmed by what some saw as a deliberate Nixon administration policy of punishing Massachusetts Senators Kennedy and Edward M. Brooke for their lack of support on the ABM, Supreme Court nominations, and other key issues in Congress. Just before Christmas 1969, NASA announced closing of the Electronic Research Center at Cambridge that had been the political *cause célèbre* of the early 1960s.* In a year and a half, no less than 10,000 of the scientists and engineers in the Cambridge–128 area lost their jobs. By spring 1971, total Massachusetts employment in electrical equipment and supplies manufacture, which had peaked at 103,000 in 1967, was down to 80,800. Virtually every company in the electronics field laid off workers; some closed down entire branches; several firms went bankrupt.

By the eve of the later and more serious 1974–75 recession, however, the Bay State's R & D-electronics industry had effected a significant comeback. The painful shake-out had eliminated weaker firms unable to make the transition from primary reliance on military-aerospace business to commercial accounts. This required development of such free-market skills as market research and sales promotion, and an end to the salad days of overloaded payrolls based on cost plus-fixed fee government contracts.

An example of the new flexibility was provided by the giant of New England electronics, the Raytheon Company. Founded in 1922 as a radio tube manufacturer in Newton, Raytheon began its great era of prosperity in World War II when it cooperated with MIT to develop microwave tubes to be used to power radar systems. For 16 years, up to 1964, Raytheon was headed by Charles Adams, a great-great-great grandson of John Quincy Adams. He steered the firm ever deeper into defense work and toward its contracts of recent years to develop the Hawk and Sparrow missiles, the sonar system for Navy submarines, the SAM-D and Sidewinder missiles, and a subcontract for ground-based radar for the Safeguard system. But then Thomas S. Phillips, a Boston-born design engineer who joined Raytheon in 1958, became its president and proceeded to turn the company toward acquisition of marketing-oriented commercial firms like Amana Refrigeration, the textbook publishing firm of D. C. Heath, and Caloric Corporation, which makes dishwashers and kitchen equipment.

Across the high-technology spectrum, the firms enjoying the most significant Massachusetts growth in the early 1970s were those engaged in the manufacture of computer peripheral equipment, minicomputers, and medical instrumentation. By mid-1974 all but a few thousand of the jobs lost in the electrical and electronics manufacturing industry had been regained, and a high proportion of the laid-off scientists and engineers had been rehired. The new recession which followed bit heavily into the improved employment figures, but with national recovery there was every expectation that

---

* ERC subsequently got a second life as Transportation Systems Center for the Department of Transportation.

Massachusetts would resume its growth as a national leader in electronics. The continuing input from the universities seemed likely to offset competition from the nation's newer high-technology areas—primarily the San Francisco Bay area, as well as Houston, Dallas, Los Angeles, and North Carolina's Research Triangle. For instance, the MIT Development Foundation, established in 1972, was busily at work translating unexploited ideas coming out of that university's research activities into viable new enterprises. Among the newer firms is Cambridge Survey Research, the innovative attitudinal research company founded by Patrick Cadell, a young Harvard graduate who became famous as Sen. George McGovern's pollster in his presidential race in 1972.

And to its scientific skills, Massachusetts in modern times has added amazing entrepreneurial talents. A $400 million empire in food, liquor and wine, shipping, oil, and real estate, for instance, has grown out of a one-room grocery store opened in Boston's North End in 1910 by two young Greek immigrants, John and Thomas Pappas. This vast enterprise is now run by James Pappas, John's son, who took over in 1972 at the tender age of 26. It is really still a family affair, though, because James's two brothers and cousin share in the management. They have eschewed the heavy political involvement of their fathers (Thomas a big Eisenhower and Nixon supporter, John active on the Democratic side).

An even more dazzling Bay State entrepreneurial story is that of Dr. Edwin Land, inventor of the Polaroid camera. As founder, chief executive officer, and director of research of the Polaroid Corporation, Land saw its total assets rise past the half-billion dollar mark with annual sales of $750 million. The secret has not just been the ever improving technology of his cameras that develop their own pictures, but brilliant merchandising—like the $19.95 black and white "Swinger" camera, of which more than five million were sold within two years of their introduction on the market in 1965, and equally successful subsequent low-priced color models. The firm seemed to have stubbed its toe in the mid-1970s, however, when its SX-70 camera, on which it spent a staggering $600 million (or possibly more) in perfecting as a breakthrough to a "clean" development process, sold poorly and caused profits and stock value to decline precipitously.

Edwin Land's achievements should not be discounted by one possible market failure (however grandiose). An ever-creative man, he has more than 100 inventions in the field of optics to his name, and developed cameras (like those used in the U-2 espionage plane) that can capture ground detail from 70,000 feet altitude. He lives in a modest Cambridge home. As Frederick Lundberg noted in *The Rich And The Super-Rich*, "Like Pasteur, Edison and other creators, he lives mainly in order to work." That work will doubtless continue, despite his 1975 decision to turn over the presidency of the firm to a long-term associate, William J. McCune, Jr.

Through his long career at Polaroid, Land emerged as an advanced social thinker, anxious to find ways of humanizing machine society and solving the "problem of mass boredom and mental stagnation" in American life. In the field of social action, Polaroid has few peers among major American corporations. It is deeply involved in the politically dangerous area of prison reform through Robert Palmer, the firm's director of community relations, who was president of a Massachusetts movement that wrote and helped win legislative approval of the state's landmark correctional reform act. The firm has hired more than 150 ex-convicts over the past several years and worked hard to persuade other Massachusetts firms to do the same. About 12 percent of the company's work force are blacks, with a sizable number in salaried jobs. Another 3 percent are physically or mentally handicapped, or have a poor grasp of English. The firm has a subsidiary in Boston's black neighborhood of Roxbury, staffed largely by "unemployable" workers. And Polaroid is involved with dozens of community projects in the Greater Boston area and New Bedford.

The most pervasive human tragedy of modern Massachusetts is the fate of its thousands of no-longer-young blue-collar workers who grew up with the textile and shoe industries or other now-declining industries. James Howell of Boston's First National Bank cites the case of the stitchers and cutters in that city's apparel industry, who are stuck at wage rates just above the minimum wage for their entire working lives. "Yet these people—perhaps because they're Europeans—still have a high sense of personal integrity and pride in their work. But we're failing to provide them with meaningful jobs," he said. Others point out that there is a narrow margin between wages in the older industries and welfare or unemployment benefits, with grave consequences both for the affected industries and the numbers of citizens for whose sustenance the state must pay. (Despite the growth of its universities and junior colleges, the state has paid insufficient attention to developing good trade-vocational schools that could turn out workers with a prospect for higher wages merited by higher productivity.)

When factories close down, textile and shoe workers most often have no realistic career alternatives. The Boston *Globe* reported the story of Mrs. Mary Scott, one of 300 workers to lose a job when the Bori Shoe Co. folded in Lynn in 1969. A 64-year-old widow, she had spent 12 years doing fancy stitching on women's shoes and was earning $77 a week when the plant closed. Running to the end of her period of unemployment compensation, Mrs. Scott despaired of finding work anywhere. She lived frugally, rarely venturing from her $18.50-a-week apartment. Some Social Security and old age as a ward of the state were all that seemed to await her.

Governor Dukakis said that the major focus of his economic recovery plan for the state would be on "the older communities" like Lowell, New Bedford, and Lynn, "who really want and need" expanded job opportunities. It did appear that state economic development activity—a long-neglected area—would receive professional, high-level attention under Dukakis's secretary of economic affairs, businessman trouble-shooter Howard N. Smith.

The opportunities for improvement in economic promotion are rife. Albert J. Kelley, dean of Boston College's school of management and chairman of the state's board of economic advisers, had observed in 1974 that Massachusetts "strangely" lacked a master economic plan worked out cooperatively by state government, citizens, and business. Job-producing businesses, he said, needed to feel that they were wanted in Massachusetts and would be treated well and fairly. One major failure, he said, was the lack of coordination between state and local tax systems, which he likened to "wild horses competing for the individual and business tax dollar." A master tax plan, he suggested, could coordinate property taxes levied locally with state income and sales taxes and give businesses a definitive basis on which to make their future plans in the commonwealth.

Howard Smith seemed to be picking up on Kelley's advice in 1975 when he announced a "back to basics" economic recovery program that realistically discounted the possibility of attracting many new plants to the state and concentrated instead on intensive field work to make it clear to existing Massachusetts industries that their presence in the state was valued, and that his department would work to clear away frustrations they encountered in dealing with the state or local governments. The objective was to close the 3 percent gap between unemployment in Massachusetts and that in the rest of the nation within five years by trying to encourage each of the state's 10,000 firms of significant size to add an average of just one employee a year—an objective which, if reached, would add 50,000 jobs by 1980, with an additional 25,000 through the "multiplier" effect.

Other notes on the Massachusetts economy:

▪ Important income is earned from out-of-state visitors—businessmen and tourists—who number about 8.5 million (one and a half times the resident population) and bring $1.25 billion into the state each year.

▪ Value added by manufacturing is close to $10 billion, putting Massachusetts 10th among the states, precisely where it stands on the population scale too. Some major industries, in addition to those already mentioned, are machinery, apparel, printing, publishing, and rubber and plastics. The Massachusetts economy, Albert Kelley observed, is heavily dependent on the skilled engineers and craftsmen who man the manufacturing industries. "While engineers get much of the credit," he said, "one of the more important, in fact maybe the most important factor has been the skilled blue-collar craftsman. While the engineer tends to be migratory, the skilled technician and craftsman has been a more stable factor and one of the strongest attributes of the labor force in Massachusetts. These skills have ranged all the way from electronic technicians to ship builders, from shoe machinery operators to machine tool operators."

▪ Agricultural produce brings in a rather insignificant $170 million a year, 42nd in rank among the states. But Massachusetts does grow about half the cranberry crop of the entire world, and has small but thriving dairy, tobacco, fruit, and maple syrup industries.

▪ Boston remains one of the great medical centers of the Western world, with institutions like the Harvard Medical School, Peter Bent Brigham Hospital, Boston City Hospital, the Children's Hospital Medical Center, and the Lahey Clinic. The struggle to modernize and meet rising budgets is a whole story in itself, especially acute in a municipal hospital that has become a famous national institution, like Boston City Hospital.

■ The port of Boston, its illustrious history notwithstanding, has limped from crisis to crisis in recent times and many of its dock facilities are in disrepair or disuse. Logan International Airport, by contrast, is the eighth busiest in the world and has rapidly increased its position as an embarkation point for transatlantic passengers from the northeastern U. S. and the Midwest. The airport's physical expansion and noise pollution have blighted life in the heavily Italian North End of Boston; on the other hand, it is the transportation nexus that has helped to make Boston–Cambridge–128 an intellectual and economic national and world force. From Logan's easily reached runways, the area's academicians, scientists, businessmen, and government experts commute easily to Washington, New York, other U. S. cities, and abroad.

■ "The Massachusetts fishing industry," according to Frank Donovan of the Boston *Globe,* "is like a ship without a rudder, bobbing aimlessly on a stormy sea and in danger of sinking." In fact, the New England fishing fleet is in such poor condition that 119 vessels have been lost at sea in the past decade. Problems include foreign competition, especially in frozen fish; incursion of Russian and Canadian ships on the Georges Bank, which has contributed to overfishing that has dangerously depleted the stocks of haddock; trawling by Russian ships that cuts the lines laid by New England lobstermen; and the fragmented condition of the industry, which leaves each fisherman in competition with his neighbors and foreign fleets. The big ports are New Bedford, Gloucester, and Boston, with New Bedford the clear leader. But despite recent addition of some modern trawlers with huge nets, the total catch is valued at only $40 million a year. In an ironic twist, many jobs and substantial income for an historic old fishing town like Gloucester are provided by reprocessing of ground fish shipped to the city in 50-pound frozen blocks—from the very foreign fishing fleets that have put so many Gloucester fishermen out of work.

Collegia Massachusettensis

Massachusetts has education resources rivaled only by California's. It has 117 institutions of higher learning, including 15 which grant Ph.D. or equivalent degrees. Massachusetts attracts more students from out of state —80,000 at last count—than any other state.

Harvard and MIT stand at the apex of the pyramid. As Ford Foundation president McGeorge Bundy told me: "You can't get away from the Cambridge complex. There's no doubt that just for sheer first-class intellectual manpower, it's the most powerful single nexus in the country." Bundy's remarks have a lot more behind them than the sentimentality of an Ivy Leaguer. A survey appearing in *Science* magazine indicated that of the 41 major advances in the social sciences made in America between 1930 and 1965, nine occurred in Cambridge, compared to only five each in New York and Washington, the two runner-up cities. The electronics-technology boom of Route 128–Cambridge industries would have been inconceivable without the concentration of scientific talent at MIT and Harvard.

Concomitant with this has been the shift in the role of the intellectual in Massachusetts politics. The traditional town-gown antagonisms, part of an anti-intellectualism that was next to anti-British sentiment, were overcome by John F. Kennedy. His brain trust of 50 to 60 Cambridge academicians working on national problems has been copied within Massachusetts, with each major politician of subsequent years gathering his own brain trust of bright men and women. Massachusetts intellectuals have been active both in campaigns and in program policy development, a fruitful new relationship in the state's development that has been only partially disturbed by new tensions arising from the era of campus revolts.

First, a view of the major Boston area universities:

■   Harvard (15,602 students in 1974). Many people view this oldest of all American universities as also the greatest, even if early 1970s studies of the American Council on Education gave it slightly lower marks in its graduate department quality than its only serious competitor, the University of California at Berkeley. Harvard faculties were rated ahead of all others in the U. S. in classics, music, sociology, biochemistry, zoology, geology, and mathematics, and scored in the top rankings in almost every other discipline (engineering excepted). The university's law, medical, and business schools continue foremost in their fields, and now turn out a high complement of very socially conscious graduates. Listing the Harvard faculty who have achieved international reputations or contributed importantly to American government would take pages.

The postwar era has been one of rapid change for Harvard. Its student body has shifted from a preponderance of private prep school graduates to a broad cross-section of the U.S.A. Through association with Radcliffe College, the university has become fundamentally coeducational. While campuses of other prestige universities like Berkeley and Columbia exploded in the mid-1960s, Harvard remained calm; then came 1969, the occupation by radicals of University Hall, the early morning raid by 400 policemen, the subsequent shocked reaction by faculty and students, and a student strike. The following years featured a number of protests, particularly on Nixon administration Far East policy in 1972. But after that the quiet "normalcy" typical of most U.S. universities in the mid-1970s set in; a high proportion of students spent their time working long hours to achieve grades that would get them into good medical or law schools. Under the calm exterior, however, there was strong and continuing student resentment against the faculty's concentration on advanced scholarship and publication at the price of time for teaching or spending informal time talking with students. Social scientist Seymour Martin Lipset, coauthor (with David Riesman) of a 1975 book, *Education and Politics at Harvard*, told an interviewer that "colleagues who think calm means the return of the good old days are kidding themselves." The absence of war, he said, had defused visible protest, but surveys showed student attitudes on armed conflict, civil rights, and the economy were almost identical to those recorded in the 1960s. Harvard, he suggested, creates an "intelligentsia" opposed to prevailing powers and authorities because of the interaction of a nonconformist faculty with students whose well-educated and liberal parents have encouraged them to be critical of established institutions.

Harvard has had three postwar presidents, each in a way symbolic of his times. James B. Conant has been described by Harold Taylor, a reviewer of Conant's memoirs, *My Several Lives,* as "the first of the new breed of scientist-administrators produced by the Second World War, . . . a liberal-minded conservative, . . . a supporter, in some ways a leader, in cold-war doctrine" but also "one of the first to urge a liberal and long range policy for the control of atomic energy." His view of education was conservative, rooted in the European ideal of the university as "a collection of eminent scholars." Conant was succeeded in 1953 by Nathan M. Pusey, a former president of Lawrence College, who increased student enrollment by a third and doubled the faculty to 6,000, vigorously defended Harvard against the attacks of Senator Joseph McCarthy of Wisconsin, proved a phenomenally successful fund raiser, and succeeded in keeping Harvard from becoming too financially dependent on the federal government. But he proved aloof and ineffective in dealing with the student uprising of 1969 and took early retirement in 1971. Derek Bok, who succeeded Pusey, is a Stanford graduate who joined the Harvard faculty in 1958, built an innovative record as dean of its law school, but was only 40 years old when he became president—an outgoing, approachable man popular with both students and faculty, perhaps the right man to heal Harvard's internal divisions and confirm its historic position as the moral leader of higher education in America.

Despite its $1 billion endowment, unequaled in any other university, Harvard has had to deal with severe fund shortages in the 1970s with warnings of "operating deficits," "austerity," and "record shortfalls" in the face of inflation.

The accent on youth symbolized by Harvard's Bok is also strong at Radcliffe, which chose Matina Souretis Horner, then only 32 years of age, as its sixth president in 1972. Dr. Horner, ironically, had made her academic mark as a psychologist studying reasons why women fear success. The Cambridge community has observed the interesting phenomenon of this daughter of Greek immigrants, raised in the Roxbury community, presiding over the trial integration of Radcliffe with Harvard under one university umbrella.

■   Massachusetts Institute of Technology (7,888 students). In engineering, MIT remains preeminent in America. Its physical sciences departments are also outstanding; its economics department is rated best in the nation by the American Council on Education and is headed by Paul A. Samuelson, recipient of the 1970 Nobel Prize for his efforts to "raise the level of scientific analysis in economic theory." James R. Killian, who became the first White House science advisor, under President Eisenhower, was the primary figure in building MIT to its position of excellence in the postwar years, although the widening of its role from the physical sciences to humanities, creating a true university, had begun under his predecessor, Karl T. Compton. MIT has made distinct national contributions in a multitude of fields, including time-shared computers, automated libraries, and an imaginative program in secondary school physics instruction. In 1974 the university, with a $1.2 million National Science Foundation grant, opened an "innovation center" to encourage participants—ranging from freshmen through doctoral candidates—to learn and apply basic skills needed for developing new products and getting them into production. Royalty income is shared by the inventor and MIT.

Institute scientists have been at the forefront of science political activism in recent years, including the fight against the antiballistic missile system in the late '60s and early '70s. Student and faculty criticism of the university's deep involvement in war-related research (it remains the largest defense contractor among U.S. universities) reached a crescendo in the same years. Under Jerome B. Wiesner, the former science adviser to President Kennedy who became MIT's president in 1971, the effort to supplement the university's basic science and engineering pursuits with a major effort in the arts has expanded. "A person is much less of a human being if he thinks of himself only as a technocrat," according to Wiesner. "Society needs the cognitive reaction of a poet as well as a technologist."

▪ Boston University (18,958 students). BU is the nation's fourth largest private university but has one of the smallest endowments ($14 million compared to Harvard's $1 billion-plus).* It has a dynamic and controversial president who seems likely either to make it into a distinguished university or lead it to disaster—John R. Silber, former dean of the college of arts and sciences at the University of Texas. Silber took the job on the condition he would have a free hand to go out and hire dozens of outstanding teaching professors and actually speculate with BU's unrestricted $12 million endowment in the hope it might generate at least $5 million a year.

▪ Boston College (13,000 students). This Jesuit institution, situated in Chestnut Hill to the west of Boston proper, is remarkable for its diverse and intensive efforts to improve the Boston community. Its citizen seminar program, begun in 1954 by the Rev. W. Seavy Joyce, S.J., then dean of business administration and now president of BC, was perhaps *the* most crucial single element in bringing together the differing religious, ethnic, political, and racial groups of Boston who simply were not talking with each other at that time. Joyce used the issue of economic revival to get the Yankee businessmen and Irish businessmen communicating, and the citizen seminars have continued ever since, covering a myriad of problems that face the Boston area.

An example of BC's continuing deep involvement in state issues is the leadership role which the director of its bureau of public affairs, Robert J. N. O'Hare, has taken in investigation of possible routes to regional or metropolitan-wide government in Massachusetts. In 1971, he suggested

---

* Boston is also home of *the* largest private university in the world, Northeastern, with 33,557 students in 1974.

abolishing the existing counties of the state, which tend to be perpetually short of funds and lacking in effective powers, and replacing them with seven new regions, each with its own popularly elected government having broad powers in areas such as water supply, sewage, and solid waste disposal, law enforcement, conservation and open space, mass transit, health services and public education.

■   Brandeis University (3,030 students). This Jewish-sponsored but officially nonsectarian institution has been characterized by *Newsweek* as "a veritable *wunderkind*" among American colleges. Founded in 1948 on a tree-shaded campus in suburban Waltham, it received a Phi Beta Kappa chapter more rapidly than any other university in the past century and is widely respected for its academic excellence. But in the late '60s it became one of the most radical and agitated colleges in America. It was early in accepting substantial numbers of deprived black and white students, many of whom were party to a series of sometimes violent demonstrations. The scene was marked by seizure of buildings, vandalism, disruption of classes, and intimidation of students and professors.

The Boston area picture is rounded out by Tufts University (6,000 students), known chiefly for its Fletcher School of Law and Diplomacy. Tufts also takes pride these days in an improved engineering school, headed by Dean Ernest Klema of atomic bomb discovery fame. Wellesley College (1,963 students) is a good quality women's residential college but is outshone by Radcliffe.

■   Western Massachusetts has a set of distinguished small colleges where the emphasis is strictly on good teaching—Williams (1,850 students), Mount Holyoke (1,962), Amherst (1,252), and Smith (2,564). The ideal was summed up by President James Garfield, talking about Williams: "The ideal college is Mark Hopkins on one end of a log and a student on the other." All attract exceptionally well qualified students and have in small, unpublicized ways been drawing abreast of or even moving ahead of the times. Williams, for instance, was once a strong fraternity college, but the students lost interest in them and in effect disestablished the fraternities in the early 1960s. (And now Williams, like many others, has gone coed.) Williams also instituted the first college-level environmental studies program in the mid-1960s. Mount Holyoke developed a strong women's rights orientation decades before the term "women's liberation" was invented, and has long had strong woman presidents. One of its political science faculty members, Victoria Schuck, exemplifies the combination of exceptional teaching skills, sound scholarship, and political activism. Williams' James MacGregor Burns, author of distinguished historical and political science works, is perhaps the best known academician of the western colleges.

A "four-college" plan, allowing students to interchange institutions in the courses they take, was begun a few years ago by the four colleges in close proximity in the rolling Connecticut River Valley—Amherst, Smith, Mount Holyoke, and the main campus of the University of Massachusetts at Amherst. In 1958 these four also conceived the idea of a completely unstructured college for gifted and highly motivated students. Called Hampshire College, it opened its doors in 1970 with 268 charter students. At Hampshire, faculty and students are intended to shape the curriculum together.

The University of Massachusetts was long the proverbial stepchild of higher education in Massachusetts, dedicated mainly to agriculture and completely overshadowed by the great private institutions. But in 1960, Dr. John W. Lederle was brought in from Michigan and began the difficult process of transforming UM into a university in the tradition of the great public institutions of the Midwest and West. The main campus at Amherst was expanded to an enrollment of 22,500 by 1974, and projected for an eventual 25,000 figure. It is intended to be detached, residential, academic, and excellent. A medical school was opened at Worcester, to evolve around the idea of providing instruction in total health service delivery. And in 1971, construction was begun on a $355 million Boston campus of UM, to be located at Columbia Point, the site of a former city dump and a big public housing project in Dorchester, 2.5 miles from center city. (It was the largest construction program ever undertaken in Massachusetts.) UM Boston, which had 6,100 students when it moved from temporary downtown quarters to Columbia Point in January 1974, was planned to be a thoroughly urban-oriented institution, primarily serving students from the low-income neighborhoods of the Boston area. But according to chancellor Carlo Luigi Golino, an Italian immigrant who graduated from New York City College: "Just because this is an institution for poor kids does not mean that it should not be as good as those places across the [Charles] River."

Lederle resigned in 1970, to be succeeded as UM president by Robert C. Wood, a man we have quoted earlier in this chapter. Wood was director of the Joint Center for Urban Studies of MIT-Harvard, former board chairman of the Massachusetts Bay Transportation Authority, and had been undersecretary of the federal Department of Housing and Urban Development in its development years—one of Massachusetts' outstanding scholar-administrators. By the mid-1970s, annual expenditures for the state's institutions of public higher education had topped $200 million a year, five times the level of a decade before. With several of the private universities suffering declines in enrollment and financial crises, Wood and his colleagues faced arguments that the time had come to stop the fast growth in public universities—together with the prospect of severe financial cutbacks because of the state government's fiscal woes.

Massachusetts has 11 state colleges and an expanded network of community colleges, some of which are of exceptional quality. The state is considered a national leader in the field of vocational education. It was a pioneer in the development of public schools in America and recently has ranked fourth among the 50 states in its annual per capita expenditures for elementary and secondary school students. Appropriately with its high Catholic population, the state has been strong in parochial schools. The fame, however, has gone to the select college preparatory schools like Phillips Andover,

Groton, Deerfield Academy, Milton Academy, and the Boston Latin School. Some of the less richly endowed private boarding schools are in serious financial straits these days, and one, the Northampton School for Girls, was simply closed and its campus put up for sale in 1971.

The New Boston

Boston, the tired old city where cowpaths became streets, "Last Hurrah" politics reigned, and municipal tax rates first turned astronomical, has suddenly become one of the two or three most livable and exciting cities of America. For one who once lived in the closed old Boston, and now returns to the new Boston, the experience is a continual wonder. With its neighbor Cambridge across the Charles River, Boston has opened up—physically, spiritually, ethnically, economically. It is no longer an historic relic, but a vital center of the U.S.A. in our times.

Yet the old charm lingers on. You will find it in the lovely old red brick homes of Beacon Hill, with cobblestoned Acorn Street and Louisburg Square, where a little green park is ringed by stately 19th-century houses and gas lampposts. Historic Boston can be seen in an hour or two along the mile-and-a-half Freedom Trail in this most walkable of all American cities: the State House with its 23-carat gold dome, begun from designs by Charles Bulfinch in 1795; the pleasant expanse of the Boston Common, which the town bought as a "trayning field" for the militia and for the "feeding of Cattell" back in the 17th century, and where pirates, witches, and Quakers were hanged from an elm near the Frog Pond; Park Street Church, where William Lloyd Garrison delivered his first antislavery speech in 1829; the Old Granary Burying Ground with the graves of John Hancock, Samuel Adams, and Paul Revere; the Boston Athenaeum, the literary *sanctum sanctorum* of old Boston; King's Chapel, which was the Episcopal place of worship of early British governors and later the first Unitarian church in America; the Old State House and scene of the Boston Massacre; the Old South Meeting House where Bostonians met to protest the British tea tax before staging their famous Tea Party; Faneuil Hall, where Sam Adams and James Otis delivered the fiery speeches that led to Revolution; the Paul Revere House, Boston's oldest wooden frame building (1677); and the Old North Church, immortalized by Longfellow's poem about Revere's midnight ride ("One if by land and two if by sea"). Add to all this Bunker Hill, the Charlestown Navy Yard where the old frigate *Constitution* rests, Back Bay, the Public Garden, and Lexington and Concord not far distant—well, there can only be one Boston, and America needs one.

Writing in the Boston *Globe* in 1970, Ian Menzies suggested that Boston and San Francisco—especially among young Americans today—are "the two most exciting cities in the nation." There are certainly strong similarities. Both have water on three sides, strikingly similar skylines, almost equal land areas (Boston's 45 square miles, San Francisco's 47), and similar populations (Boston's 641,071—16th largest in the U.S.A.—and San Francisco's 715,674—13th largest). And both, Menzies observes, "have that mix of academe, of history and of the arts. While one has a Puritan heritage, the other Spanish, both today are managed by a rambunctious Irish-Italian political culture sitting uneasily over new militant minorities while a Waspish establishment watches on the sidelines with the ultimate weapon of money." Neither city, he points out, overawes one as a New York, Chicago, or Los Angeles may. "People know each other in San Francisco and Boston. They talk to each other, eat with each other, banker and cultural entrepreneur, student and newspaper editor, professor and legislator, architect and community leader. They are walkable cities, centralized, physically compact, friendly." Both have a big academic suburb—Boston's Cambridge, San Francisco's Berkeley.

Of the two cities, of course, San Francisco is more raucous, given to the new no-matter-what, while Boston reveres tradition. Topless and bottomless could not have happened in Boston; they did in San Francisco. In Boston, even the Old Howard Burlesque has fallen before the renewers' iron ball; but gone too, happily, are the days of book burning, the Sacco-Vanzetti trial, and "banned in Boston." And there is a final difference: San Francisco is not a capital, Boston is. Boston is ultimately more important to its state than San Francisco is to California. "We are virtually alone among the states" Massachusetts' Martin Linsky notes, "in that our capital city is also our most significant city in terms of culture, sports, population, sin, food, and fun."

There is always danger in attributing too much of the change in a city or state to one man, but by almost universal consensus, the vital turnaround from the "old" to the "new" Boston occurred during the reign of John F. Collins, mayor of Boston from 1960 to 1967. I have heard more than one person refer to Collins as "the best mayor Boston ever had."

When Collins became mayor, Boston was in near-desperate straits. As long as James Michael Curley and his type had been mayor, there was no chance that the Brahmin-dominated business community would invest in downtown Boston. Curley left City Hall for the last time in 1950, but John Hynes, the mayor of the next decade, while a pleasant and well intentioned man, lacked the skill to bring even his good ideas to fruition. In Collins' own words, these were the conditions in 1960:

In the prior 25 years, Boston had lost $500 million worth of assessed property. In terms of Manhattan, that may not be a staggering figure, but it was in fact 25 percent of the potentially accessible tax base. In the 10 years between 1950 and 1960, Boston had lost 100,000 people, so its population had dropped to less than 650,000. And they were the people whom we could least afford to lose—the better educated and more affluent. Beyond that, blight and decay had been given such a headstart that the place was simply dilapidated. The citizens of Boston had essentially lost faith in the government of their city—they simply felt hopeless about the whole thing. The postwar building boom had bypassed Boston entirely, and there had been only one major building built in 25 years —the John Hancock Life Insurance Company building. The tax rate had been going up at an average annual rate of $8 a year. Boston was heading for insolvency.

Collins' own election was a major upset in which he defeated John Powers, an influential, classic type of politician who had support from prominent clergymen in the Boston Archdiocese and was considered the all-but-sure winner in the contest. Collins, however, brought fresh approaches and thought to his campaign. Five years before, Boston was struck by a polio epidemic, and he and three of his children contracted the disease. "I was to have died, and didn't, and then I was not to have been able to get out of bed into a wheelchair, and never be able to walk, but thanks be to God, all of those things didn't happen," Collins told me. "I mention that only because during the period of enforced convalescence, I had an opportunity to read just about everything that had ever been written about Boston, urban problems, and Boston's history and contemporary situation. I was determined in 1959—though I was still confined to a wheelchair—that Boston was entitled to one last clear chance to see whether or not it could commence to modernize its structure, physically, sociologically, and fundamentally."

As soon as he took office, Collins instituted a number of new policies which helped to bridge the traditional walls of distrust between City Hall, State Street, and the Cambridge academia. To avert fiscal insolvency, he ordered a belt-tightening in city government, beginning with a no-fire, no-hire policy that made it possible to eliminate 1,250 permanent city jobs. This enabled him to win the support of Brahmin business leaders like Charles A. Coolidge, president of the Boston Chamber of Commerce and a former member of the Harvard Corporation. Unlike his predecessors, Collins had a crisp, businesslike way of doing things; at a crucial set of meetings with the business leaders, held "at the vault" (one of the Boston banks), he lined up their support for numerous reforms. Both business and academic talent were obtained to help reorganize several departments of city government. Boston's perennial shortchanging by the state legislature was righted to a degree, after some very acrimonious sessions, by enactment of a limited sales tax to be used for aid to education on a formula favoring the poorer, older cities. And an income tax was passed, which in turn permitted the state to take over the responsibility for the municipal share of welfare.

The most visible monuments to the Collins regime emerged in the area of physical reconstruction of the city. "The blight and decay had received such a headstart," he explains, "that we could not afford the traditional and comfortable manner of almost finishing one job before undertaking another in urban renewal. I determined we should commence eight to 10 projects simultaneously. So I needed the best man in the country to run the program, and I finally settled on Ed Logue." At the time, Edward Logue was urban renewal director for the nationally acclaimed effort in New Haven. (At the end of the Collins administration, Logue ran unsuccessfully for mayor of Boston and was then selected to head the New York State Urban Development Corporation.)

Logue's presence in Boston helped to stir up investors' interest and draw federal dollars. As a first step, he and Collins resolved the tax problems that had stalled, for five years, the plans of Prudential Insurance Company to erect a huge office building complex in the Back Bay area with plazas and arcades on the scale of New York's Rockefeller Plaza. The problem was that under Boston's existing tax rate, Prudential would have been obliged to pay an annual tax bill of $15 million or more—even after spending $150 to $175 million to build the center. Yet it was obvious that if national corporations of the dimension of Prudential could be induced to spend hundreds of millions of dollars in Boston, the economic multiplier effect in terms of jobs and other construction would accrue to the city's benefit. Under Mayor Hynes, the idea had already been developed of a "capitalization of income method" to tax the new Prudential Center. But the proposal was bogged down in economic infighting and legislative bickering. Collins and Logue helped persuade the legislature to enact it in the so-called "Prudential law," permitting a payment of 20 percent of gross rental income in lieu of taxes, with a guaranteed $3 million annual fee. The Prudential project then rose rapidly. Its 52-story tower, completed in 1965, became the highest building in New England or, in fact, in the entire U. S. outside of Chicago and New York. A "skywalk" on the 50th floor became an important tourist attraction in itself. The complex included a new Sheraton hotel, Boston's first big new hotel since 1927.

The new tax formula used for the Prudential Center was subsequently copied for numerous new buildings in Boston. As a result, Boston has suddenly become a highly attractive center for insurance companies, banks, professional services, and corporate headquarters. Some major new buildings have included the 34-story State Street Bank Building, the 40-story New England Merchants National Bank Building, Center Plaza (eight stories tall and 900 feet long), the 41-story Boston Company Building, and several other smaller office buildings. The momentum carried forward in the early 1970s with construction of a $50 million First National Bank Building, the $105 million new home office of the John Hancock Life Insurance Company, the $20 million new Keystone building, and a $35 million Christian Science Center adjacent to the Prudential Center. (The Christian Science Church, to its credit, has also leased land to private developers to build $70 million worth of middle- and low-income apartments near its Back Bay headquarters.)

More than the Prudential Center, perhaps, Collins and Logue will be remembered for the massive and dramatic Government Center built on 60 acres of land in the heart of the city, where scabrous old Scollay Square once stood. Again, Hynes had had the idea of a government center, but Collins had the skill to implement it. The victory was won and I. M. Pei was commissioned to draw up the overall area plan, replacing 22 old streets with six new ones, two of them broad thoroughfares leading to a vast central plaza before the new City Hall.

The City Hall design was chosen by open architectural competition, thought to be the first such contest for a public building in America in this century. "This was the only area really of disagreement that Ed Logue and I ever had," Collins told me. "He didn't believe in architectural competitions.

For one thing, they take too long, and they result in delays and acrimony and controversy. I thought, however, that we only build a city hall once in a hundred years, and that it was appropriate we build something of a monumental nature." The challenge stimulated an outpouring of preliminary designs from 256 architects. Of the 10 finalists, none was a major, established firm—and thus it can be assumed that none would have had a chance under normal selection procedures. The final award went to Architects Kallmann, McKinnell & Knowles, two of whose members were then professors of architecture at Columbia University and had never designed a major building.

The resulting structure, completed in 1969, is architecturally the most exciting city hall in America and certainly one of the most successful public buildings of our times—on a plateau, perhaps, with a few other modern achievements like the St. Louis Archway and the new Hawaii Capitol. The designers eschewed any kind of boxy, office-building-like creation that could be torn down without qualm in 30 or 40 years. Nine stories high, the structure has a free-form exterior and many interior elements of simple rough concrete, supplemented within by red New England brick. It is most reminiscent of the style of the French architect Le Corbusier, with asymmetrical façades and deep recesses. It is a hollow rectangle built around a court with a lobby which rises on two sides to skylights nine stories above. At a distance, the building seems terribly solid, but in fact the red brick of the great courtyard before it follows through the lobby, and city pedestrians are constantly running in and out of the building. At ground level, half buried in City Hall Plaza, is the "mound" part of the structure, with city offices most used by the public. Suspended at a second level, and defined by massive frames on the exterior, are the city council chambers and mayor's office. The third and highest portion, identified by a frieze around the perimeter of the building, contains floors of departmental offices. Amazingly, despite the mass of the structure, it does not seem to overwhelm nearby Faneuil Hall and in fact enhances the much less exceptional architecture of the many other buildings in the Government Center. The New York *Times*'s Ada Louise Huxtable has written of this city hall: "Virtually no changes have been made in the prize-winning design. The result is a tough and complex building for a tough and complex age, a structure of dignity, humanism and power. It mixes strengths with subtleties. It will outlast the last hurrah."

Interestingly, many Bostonians were highly skeptical of the building when it was completed, but seem to be liking it more and more as time wears on. Given a chance, it seems, people's taste may indeed rise to a higher common denominator. One thing is sure: the City Hall Plaza in front, while it may be windy and deserted on an icy winter day, turns into a mass of relaxed people, lolling in front of the large fountain and sunken pool, on a spring or summer day. It has quickly become a favorite place for demonstrations and big public gatherings. A truly civic place, one might say.

The full Government Center complex consists of some 30 buildings, worth $260 million (including $21.6 million for City Hall itself). The location is crucial, bordering the State Street financial center, Beacon Hill, and Faneuil Hall and the waterfront. When the entire area's development is complete around 1980, Bostonians will have a "walkway to the sea" from Government Center Plaza through the restored Faneuil Hall Market district, scheduled to have outdoor cafes, restaurants, and shops, to the new Boston waterfront with parks, marinas, three 40-story towers by I. M. Pei, hotels, a nautical museum, and a new aquarium.* In extending the pedestrian link to the waterfront, however, Boston must cope with the massive barrier of the elevated Fitzgerald Expressway, which separates both the waterfront and the North End from downtown, an ugly reminder of the 1950s when the highway planners were rampant.

Many people looking at Boston, Collins claims, "see the Prudential, the new dramatic city hall and Government Center. But they fail to realize that we built more low-income, moderate-income housing in the 1960s than any city in America. . . . Take a ride through Roxbury, and through Washington Park, and you will discover nonprofit, neighborhood-oriented housing. Now Charlestown is underway, and the South End and a number of other neighborhoods." That account, however, fails to take account of the high rates of vandalism, drugs, narcotics, and crime which afflict some of the housing projects that have gone up. The city, moreover, continues to face a grim shortage of decent housing at reasonable rates for poor and lower-middle income people—a result, at least in part, of relocation forced by urban renewal.

Boston's problem, John Warner, then director of the city's redevelopment authority told me in 1970, is that "the work-save-reward ethic for low and middle income people isn't working any more. You simply can't buy a house on that kind of income." Between 1960 and 1970, the number of owner-occupied units in Boston valued at less than $20,000 dropped by almost 50 percent and the number of units available for rental at less than $100 a month by 46 percent. Yet a third of the families in Boston earned less than $7,000 a year in 1970. By 1975, some 6,000 housing units in Boston were under foreclosure as landlords complained that city rent control prevented them from getting enough revenue. Over 200,000 middle-class people have left Boston in the past two decades, leaving behind two groups—those people who had enough money to enable them to ignore the unpleasantries of city living, and those with so little money that they just couldn't get out.

The only bright spot is the return to the city of middle-upper and upper income people, noted in apartments on Tremont Street, along the Charles River, and in the Back Bay. The idea of attracting tenants for some 1,500 new luxury apartments was one of the key selling points for Park Plaza, the $266 million high-rise project on the south side of the Boston Commons and Gardens which was being pushed hard in the early- and mid-1970s as the biggest single urban renewal project in the city's history.

* The same general area has some of America's most colorful restaurants, including Durgin Park, the Union Oyster House, and Locke-Ober Restaurant.

Problems in City Government

The Collins era, focused on physical renewal and economic city admin-istration, came to an end in 1967. (Collins moved over to MIT to become a professor of urban studies.) The new mayor was Kevin H. White, then 38 years of age, Ivy League graduate, Irish Catholic and the son of a veteran city councilman. He had been Massachusetts secretary of state for six years when he entered the race for mayor, narrowly defeating Louise Day Hicks.

Once installed, White tried to turn the focus of the city toward the neighborhoods, establishing a series of little city halls throughout the city,* and undertaking a tremendous amount of new school, fire and police con-struction. The real estate tax almost doubled in four years, to the highest rate for any large city in the United States. In 1971 White switched to an "austerity" budget, forbidding new hirings and attempting to institute some economies and productivity measures in one of the nation's more inefficient municipal bureaucracies. A U.S. Census survey in 1972 showed that the average number of municipal government employees per 10,000 inhabitants in Boston was 213, 76 percent above the national average of 121. The city spent about four times as much per capita for public safety as cities of com-parable size, and even twice as much as New York City. Through use of computers, the White administration was able to deploy personnel and re-sources more efficiently in several areas of city government. The size of the Boston City Hospital was cut back severely, with major economies resulting. Still, if it had not been for federal revenue sharing, the tax rate per $1,000 of assessed valuation would probably have risen well above $200 by 1973 or 1974. As it was, the rate was held at $196.†

Boston's government problems hark back to the first part of this cen-tury, when the Yankees, "retreating to Beacon Hill" in the face of the Irish onslaught, tried to limit the city government by setting up a Boston finance commission, appointed by the governor, to watchdog city expenditures, as well as a state-controlled Boston liquor-licensing agency and a state civil service commission with power over the qualifications for city employees. A Boston home rule commission, appointed by White shortly after he took office in 1967, said that such bodies, plus separate boards for housing and

---

* The neighborhood city halls provide a good way for citizens to get their requests and complaints heard, but they do not represent a true decentralization and coordination of city service delivery. Departments are administered from "the top down," with insufficient co-ordination between the departments. Officials of the neighborhood city halls program in the mayor's office refer to this, according to a report by government scholar John Mudd, as "the rat problem." If a rat is found in an apartment, it is a housing inspection responsibility; if it runs into a restaurant, the health department has jurisdiction; if it goes outside and dies in an alley, public works takes over.

† These Boston tax rates, as fearsome as they are, should be taken with a slight grain of salt because of habitual underassessment of real value. Older industrial and commercial property has been assessed at 80 percent of full market value, and residential properties at only 20 to 30 percent. In 1975 the state supreme court ordered a statewide reassessment of property at 100 percent of real value, possibly presaging a full reconsideration of the whole topsy-turvy system.

urban renewal set up in later years, tended to dilute the authority of the mayor and the city council. The commission recommended a number of steps to streamline city functions, making departments more accountable to the mayor and the mayor more accountable to the city council and the people. The commission also envisioned "a long process of developing community self-government in Boston" by giving elected district councils considerable input in determining local emphasis of various municipal services. Mayor White backed some of the proposals, including abolition of the independently elected school board—a step he proved unable to effect. But the council resisted some of the suggested changes, and White himself, while backing "input" from individual communities of the city, remained dead-set against community control.

In 1971 White was able to win reelection with an impressive 62 percent of the vote, again against Mrs. Hicks. A major part of his victory stemmed from his success in making common cause with hard-pressed ethnic communities, building a unique alliance of blacks, Wasps, Italians, and even some South Boston Irish. Facing reelection in 1975, he had to deal with the violent political emotions generated by actual implementation of city-wide school busing. But White's opponent, Joseph Timilty—a former city councilman of limited education—declined to make school busing a central part of his campaign, and White slipped through to a narrow victory. White's victory apparently lay in his success in stabilizing the Boston tax rate, together with his opposition to a court ruling that all municipalities must bring property assessments up to full value. Following the election, White announced that the goals of his third administration would be "civic harmony" and financial self-reliance.

White has envisioned himself as a politician of national stature. In 1972 he came close to being selected as the Vice Presidential nominee on George McGovern's ticket. In 1974 he seemed to be launching a low-key Presidential bid as he invited leading national figures in Democratic politics, the media, and academia to discussions about the national future in cozy sessions at the city-owned George Francis Parkman House, overlooking Boston Common on the crown of Beacon Hill. The sessions were financed by the "Faneuil Fund," his private political checking account that some critics said was regularly replenished by direct and indirect gifts from the large patronage army (22 Democratic ward committeemen and 4,000 non-civil service City Hall employees) at his command.

Some of Boston's problems are unique, at least in degree, to the city. Between universities, churches, libraries, hospitals, museums, and the like, 60 percent of the property in Boston is not on the tax rolls at all. The area universities have been expanding by leaps and bounds in the postwar era, appropriating huge chunks of commercial real estate for tax-exempt academic institutions. Bills proposing taxation of dormitories and faculty housing have been introduced regularly in the legislature, but have yet to pass. The Boston housing shortage is aggravated by the rapidly rising number—now

20,000—of area students who live off campus, driving up rents.

The problem is compounded, Thomas Moccia of the Boston Chamber of Commerce noted, because "we spend a lot of money policing this town for a population that doubles during the day. A helluva lot of our uncontrollable costs—police and fire protection, museums and libraries, for instance—are metropolitan or regional in nature." Boston is the classic case of 100 suburbs around a small center city. The city's population, in fact, is only 23.3 percent of the Boston metropolitan area count (2,753,700 in 1970), a smaller percentage than any other major U. S. cities except San Francisco and Newark. What keeps the parts from cooperating are traditional hostilities—between city and suburb, Catholics and Yankees, and now blacks and whites.

Yet oddly enough, in a rudimentary way, Boston began metropolitan planning before any other region of America. The start was 1889, when the Metropolitan Sewerage Commission was created as an independent state agency to serve Boston and nearby towns. Later, two more autonomous state agencies were set up, to handle water supplies and the preservation of publicly owned parklands. In 1919, all three services were then consolidated under the Metropolitan District Commission. MDC has survived for a half century, perennially the whipping boy of municipal officials who criticize its independence (commissioners appointed by the governor) and lack of initiative in improving its facilities. Other regional bodies of the Boston area include the Metropolitan Air Pollution Control District (another pioneer effort, dating from 1910), the Massachusetts Port Authority (familiarly known as Massport, which runs both the port and Logan International Airport), the Metropolitan Area Planning Council (1963 vintage), and the Massachusetts Bay Transportation Authority.

What one discovers in urban politics today, Robert Wood says, is a similar demand in both suburban and ghetto neighborhoods. In one, the call is for governmental autonomy; in the other, for neighborhood participation and control. But the essential goal is identical.

The real issue in regional development these days, [Wood says], is not what we talked of in the 1950s—a single, consolidated government for a region—but the problem of how you decentralize some functions like police and welfare that touch people's lives so intimately and terrifyingly, and at the same time centralize and regionalize developmental programs like those in air, water, transportation, and pollution. What you really want is a simultaneous diffusion of power to the people—we'll never put the cork back in the bottle of citizen participation that was taken off in the mid-1960s—while at the same time we have some consolidated developmental programs.

An area of particularly perplexing problems, despite effective regionalization, is Boston's mass transit system. The city had the first subway in the U. S. (1897) and with its narrow streets and confined land area proved to be an ideal city for rapid transit. Between commuter rail lines, subways, and buses, the Boston region had an annual passenger load of 456 million passengers in 1942. But then, in the postwar period, new patterns of sub-urban settlement and work locale, plus more universal car ownership, made mass transit less and less desirable. Commuter rail lines began to go out of business and Boston's subway-bus system was in financial trouble. In 1964, the legislature created the Massachusetts Bay Transportation Authority to own and run all public transportation in a 78-town area that embraces the entire Boston metropolitan area. On the map, the MBTA seems to have lines going everywhere one might want to go; moreover, from a planning point of view, it looks like the perfect model of a single authority, transcending all jurisdictional lines, with power to tax the people of the serviced communities.

Some farsighted planning has gone into MBTA, including work on lines extending its rapid rail connections to the north and south. The system's boosters say that with that improvement, MBTA will have more miles than San Francisco's BART and will be the country's most effective system in terms of service and cars and combinations of rail and bus. With the help of federal mass transit funds, the MBTA in 1974 was planning $1.3 billion in capital improvements within a decade.

Nevertheless, there are chronic problems. Much of MBTA's equipment is old—trolleys over 25 years old, for instance, and three major repair facilities over 40 years of age, some dating from the 1800s. MBTA chairman Henry S. Lodge (son of Ambassador Henry Cabot Lodge) said in 1971 that the situation "requires an enormous amount of ingenuity, dedication, and just plain hard work from our workers to keep the system together and running." The labor situation is incredibly complicated with 6,500 employees in 27 unions. The system has long been a dumping ground for political patronage, with the Irish heavily favored. It has the highest paid bus drivers in the world. When Robert Wood, Lodge's predecessor, took over as chairman in the 1960s, he asked where the equal opportunity office was. The reply: "Equal opportunity office? We don't even let the Italians in." (Wood then instituted a lottery system to pick new bus drivers.) A spokesman for the authority told a New York *Times* reporter of unusual work rules which often result in four or five men doing the same job:

To simply replace a broken windshield on a bus, and make a slight adjust-ment on an engine [the spokesman explained], this is what has to happen:
The bus is driven to a repair shop by an operator of the carmen's union. At the apron of the garage, a member of the machinists' union has to take over and drive it inside. A member of the pipefitters' union then removes the wind-shield wiper. The windshield is then removed and replaced by a member of the sheetmetal workers' union. Then a diesel mechanic would work on the engine after its doors have been opened by a sheetmetal worker.

The region's people, frustrated by irregular MBTA service and preferring their own autos, particularly after a fare rise in the late '60s, were taking only 146 million rides a year on the system in 1973—only 32 percent of the 1942 figure. The MBTA deficit shot up from an annual figure of some $20 million in the mid-1960s to about $140 million in 1975, necessitating massive state subsidies. In fact, a subsidization of almost 40 cents was required for every quarter paid at subway turnstiles.* A large part of the problem lies in huge salary increases won by the unions; from $9,973 in 1970, for instance, the pay for an "operator" went up to $14,575 in 1975. There were some signs in 1975, though, that the MBTA had begun to turn the corner on its huge deficit increases, partly through economies, partly through the more direct control which the state government, through the secretary of transportation, had secured over its operations.

Support for mass transit was also growing steadily at the highest levels of state government. Governor Dukakis—who continued to ride the MBTA line to downtown Boston from his Brookline home, even after taking office —had made a great point of the need for a statewide transportation system in his campaign. He looked forward to a network of regional transit systems all over the state, together with an increasingly heavy state involvement in the rail system, including state ownership of some freight lines.

Highway building is another area in which Boston is moving to regional cooperation, though this is a case of city and suburbs unifying to *stop* the growth of new facilities, not to foster them. Boston highway planning used to be controlled in the typical American pattern of single-purpose technicians with a powerful construction industry lobby behind them, well insulated from public pressures. There were plans for a superhighway cutting the city from north to south, a loop encircling the city and another in its heart. The only protest came from small and uncoordinated community groups, without technical expertise. Then, in 1963, Frederick Salvucci, a planner for the Boston Redevelopment Authority, began to question the engineering analysis that led to the plan for an inner belt that would dump thousands of autos into the crowded, narrow streets of Boston. Help was enlisted from architects, sociologists, and graduate students and faculty at the local universities.

When the Department of Public Works began to move ahead with plans to build a highway through part of a wildlife sanctuary in the suburbs, the conservationists and environmentalists were drawn into the battle. This meant cooperation from middle- and upper-class suburbanites who had a powerful lobby in the State House. Thus a unique coalition emerged of inner-city blacks, ethnics, academics, suburban businessmen, housewives, and professionals. It could not be ignored by the politicians. In 1969 Governor Sargent, onetime hearty supporter of the inner-belt concept, privately told his highway administrator: "The old highway building game is over." The next year, he went on television to announce: "I have decided to reverse the transportation policy of the Commonwealth. . . . [Our] plan will be based on an answer to the question, . . . not where an expressway should be built, but whether an expressway should be built." The net result was

* This treadmill of fiscal frustration brings to mind the Kingston Trio's record of a few years back about the unlucky Charlie who lacked the nickel for a transfer when the old MTA (Massachusetts Transportation Authority) raised the fare on the subway. So Charlie was stuck on the train forever, "and his fate is still unknown. He may ride forever 'neath the streets of Boston, he's the man who never returned."

to halt work on a major segment of the inner belt (I-95), on expressway construction through Cambridge, on a new two-mile-long runway at Logan International Airport, and half a dozen other major highway projects in the Boston area. Public anti-highway, pro-mass transit sentiment was so strong by 1974 that a proposal to divert money from the highway fund for mass transit, submitted for a vote of the people, won by a landslide margin. Fittingly, Dukakis appointed Frederick Salvucci as his secretary of transportation.

Bostonian Culture and Communications

The arts organizations of Boston, Bernard Taper has written, "live a life of exquisite misery"—superb in quality and variety but limping along with chronic deficits, low support from the city's people, and an almost invisible level of government support. In the late 1960s, when the San Francisco city government was expending $3.6 million to subsidize the arts, the figure in Boston was less than a tenth as much. In fact, even such cities as Buffalo, Rochester, Fort Worth, and Seattle do much better by way of supporting the arts than does Boston.

The city's two preeminent cultural institutions are the Boston Symphony Orchestra and the Boston Museum of Fine Arts. The orchestra was begun in 1881 by Henry Lee Higginson and personally supported by him for three decades thereafter, at a cost of some $1 million. Still regarded as one of the world's best orchestras, the symphony plays a long Boston season (33 weeks) and then eight weeks in the summer at Tanglewood in the Berkshires. Its celebrated pops concerts and free outdoor performances on the Esplanade beside the Charles River Basin make it an integral part of Boston's life. Between them, the symphony and the justly renowned Fine Arts Museum (a treasure trove of the great Impressionists and the country's leading museum of Oriental art) have in recent years accounted for some 70 percent of the entire expenses for the fine arts in Boston. In 1970 the legislature was arguing over whether to give the Massachusetts Arts Council $160,000 or $100,000 in what the Boston *Globe* described as "a tawdry display of philistinism and ignorance as, even from the point of commercialism, surveys have shown that history and culture draw more tourist dollars than any other attraction, including sports."

In the performing field, major contributions are made by the Opera Company of Boston, the Boston Ballet, and the Theater Company of Boston, which has given actors like Dustin Hoffman and playwrights like Sam Shepard their start in the years since it started in the early 1960s. And for those with less sophisticated tastes, there are two magnificent scientific-type museums—the Museum of Science, with its Charles Hayden Planetarium at Science Park, and the New England Aquarium, since 1970 in a splendid $6.5 million concrete-and-glass home on an abandoned Boston wharf, the blue-green lit interior evocative of undersea life.

Boston does have a lot of private art galleries (Back Bay, Cambridge), some of America's most delightful bookstores, shops to please the most discriminating and off-beat purchasers, and establishments like "The Restaurant at the Orson Welles" Theater in Cambridge with hippie waiters and waitresses and slide light shows; in all, one of America's most sophisticated urban mélanges. There is a thriving "alternative" press (*The Real Paper, The Phoenix*) and even a station (WBCN-FM) that broadcasts very sophisticated rock for the younger generation. WGBH-TV, the public television station, has had the guts to broadcast some imaginative programming, including shows oriented to black life and women's liberation; in fact, it is regarded as one of the country's outstanding public television stations. In sports, the city no longer has a National League team but it can boast the Red Sox (1967 and 1975 American League pennant winners), the Bruins of the National Hockey League (1969–70 Stanley Cup winners), the Celtics (frequent world champions in basketball) and the Patriots in football. And what other city has anything like the annual Boston Marathon foot race? As many as 1,000 people enter, from some of the world's greatest long distance runners to pure amateurs from all over the United States. The 26-mile race is run every April 19, Patriot's Day, and attracts some quarter million people, one of the largest crowds to watch any athletic event anywhere.

For years, the quality of Boston's newspapers (the *Christian Science Monitor* excepted) was dismal indeed; by commonly accepted practice, a good third of every front page was covered with advertisements, and news coverage was rarely distinguished. The old Boston *Post* was perhaps the worst of the lot. Catering, apparently, to the market of people who could not afford eyeglasses, it ran most of each story in big heads and subheads, with a runty little story in small type beneath. What happened first to change all this was that Boston papers began to die off—the *Transcript* in 1941, after 111 years of publication, the *Post* in 1956 after 125 years. The *Daily Record* and *Evening American* merged in 1961, the *Herald* and *Traveler* in 1967, and the *Record-American* and *Herald Traveler* (into a single Hearst-owned paper eventually called the *Herald American*) in 1972. The latter merger was the result of a distress sale of the *Herald Traveler*, which had been losing money for years but was sustained by profits from a Boston television channel which the FCC had awarded to the Herald Traveler Corporation in 1957. What the FCC bestows by way of a television license it rarely takes away, but in this case it did, ostensibly not because of alleged "ex parte" contacts between Herald Traveler executives and the FCC when the license was originally given, but because "it is important in a free society to prevent a concentration of control of the sources of news and opinion." As soon as the Herald Traveler formally relinquished its television license (WHDH-TV), it sold its newspaper plant and title to Hearst. The result for Bostonians: a new television station (WCVB-TV), not much better or worse than the old WHDH-TV, and the loss of the *Herald Traveler*, once New England's leading newspaper, the voice of Brahmin Boston, after 126 years of publication.

The new *Herald American* is a thoroughly unspectacular paper—a mish-mash of the heavy use of New York *Times* News Service stories which dominated the *Herald Traveler* in its emaciated final years and the sensationalized local crime and race-related stories that were the staple of the old *Record-American*. The paper, dwindling in circulation, managed to make it onto journalism magazine [MORE]'s list of the 10 worst papers in the country in 1974.

The good news in Boston journalism lies in the spurt toward excellence of the *Globe* since the mid-1960s. The paper has hired aggressive reporters willing to dig up scandals in government, write frank coverage about city problems, and even move into the national bigtime (through publication in 1971, for instance, of some of the disputed Pentagon Papers stories). Chief credit for the bright new era apparently goes in the first instance to editor Thomas Winship, who has put a heavy emphasis on youth in his hiring policies and then permitted the talent he hired to bloom. Robert Healy, who acts both as executive editor and political editor, shows amazing skill at remaining conversant with Massachusetts and national political developments despite his administrative duties. On public issues like the Vietnam war, race and community relations, the *Globe* has become as "sensitive" or "to the left" (the reader may choose his own word) as any major city daily in the U. S. today. Editor Winship believes the paper can exert strong weight for reform, its power second only to the Archbishop or Cardinal. The policy upsets some conservatives, who argue that the paper writes more for dilettantish suburban liberals than the hard-pressed low-income whites left in the center city, where the gut problems really are. And it may be that a young, highly educated writing staff and heavily suburban circulation influence the *Globe* in that direction. But it has tried hard to give fair coverage to the city's ethnic neighborhoods and to respond to criticism from antibusing forces and others who have challenged its coverage of their concerns. The *Globe* endorsed Humphrey for President in 1968 and McGovern in 1972, but provided fair news column coverage of Nixon in both years. The paper has a strong Washington bureau and aspirations to one day be a regional paper for all of New England. The *Globe* is written with integrity and enthusiasm, and may in itself have something to do with Massachusetts' complexion as the country's most liberal state today.

Outside of Boston, mediocrity often reigns in Massachusetts papers, but there are some bright exceptions, particularly the *Berkshire Eagle* (Pittsfield) and the Quincy *Patriot-Ledger*.

Geoethnic Boston

Old Boston, as every schoolchild is supposed to know, was built on a diminutive 783-acre peninsula, connected to the mainland by a narrow neck of land. This is where one finds the historic buildings of the Freedom Trail,

State Street, and the Government Center we have touched on.

Big chunks of present-day Boston, however, are built on land created by landfill operations which occupied the city during the latter half of the 19th century. The greatest of these was the reclaiming of the dark and evil-smelling tidal reaches of some 450 acres to the west of Beacon Hill, creating the area known as Back Bay. "The draining and filling and building up of the Back Bay," Lewis Mumford wrote in an essay for the centennial year of the Boston Museum of Fine Arts, "marked a turning point in Boston's existence. Here the self-contained provincial town, with its mainly English ancestry and background, turned into a multinational metropolis reaching out far beyond New England for cultural sustenance." The physical process of landfill alone, he notes, must be considered a "triumph of geotechnics" made possible only by invention of the steam engine and railroad, a feat unmatched before the 20th century. A special railway was built from the gravel pits of Needham, nine miles away, and for almost 40 years gangs of men worked 24 hours a day to fill the whole area to a depth of 20 feet.

What arose in the Back Bay was a landmark in American city planning. Frederick Law Olmsted, the designer of New York's Central Park, articulated the idea of a green belt stretching from the Public Garden, up wide and tree-lined Commonwealth Avenue, westward through the Fenway and Jamaicaway to Franklin Park, a distance of eight miles. Commonwealth Avenue, with its central pedestrian mall, was the first American boulevard actually to be built. Around Copley Square, the center of Back Bay, some of the architectural gems of the past century, including the classic revival Public Library and Romanesque Trinity Church, were built. Here too, the Conservatory of Music, the Boston Symphony Hall, the Mother Church of the Christian Scientists, sought a home. There were famous residents like Oliver Wendell Holmes, who moved to 296 Beacon in a fit of what he called justifiable domicide, the great philanthropist Henry Lee Higginson, Augustus Lowell, who was president or treasurer of 10 cotton companies, and his son Abott, who later became president of Harvard.

Yet from the start, parts of Back Bay have been blighted or imperiled. The very railway line that brought the landfill created a corridor of run-down buildings and pollution. One of the most creative aspects of Back Bay was the Charles River Embankment, a river park that turned the edge of the one-time mudflat, as Mumford puts it, "into a great public pleasance." But in the 1930s most of that parkland was destroyed to build Storrow Drive along the river. (Still, some of the views along the Charles, which separates Boston from Cambridge, must be considered among the most exhilarating cityscapes of our land.) In our time, the Massachusetts Turnpike has come plowing through Back Bay—within two blocks of Copley Square, right over Fenway Park, and actually tunneling beneath the massive Prudential Center, built in the 1960s.

As for the Prudential Center itself, there is some truth to Mumford's criticism of it as "an architectural nonentity, more worthy of Detroit or Los Angeles than either Boston or the Back Bay." Others said that its 52-

story scale dwarfed the nearby buildings of Copley Square and the Christian Science Mother Church, and that it was a fatal mistake to build it on an elevation that isolates it from its neighborhood. Similar criticism greeted the 60-story John Hancock Tower, completed in the early 1970s directly on Copley Square beside Trinity Church. But the architects, by sheathing the Hancock's rhomboid tower in mirror-glass, were able to reflect the church and other surroundings. This writer finds the new Hancock tower so tall, thin, and graceful that it seems to occupy a very different environment than that of surrounding Copley Square—a situation in which both the older buildings and their lofty new neighbor have satisfactory, separate presences. The Hancock edifice was delayed two years in opening by one of the most celebrated snafus in the history of skyscraper construction—the mysterious shattering of the expensive mirror-glass panes after they had been put in place. After suffering the ignominy of installing temporary plywood windows to replace the 3,500 which broke, the company and its architects finally solved the problem by installing 13 acres of new, stronger glass at a cost of $6 million. This was followed by a monumental law suit by Hancock against the architect (I. M. Pei), the glass company, and the general contractor. Countersuits and cross-claims were anticipated in a case likely to line lawyers' pockets for years and years.

The Back Bay is also packed with social contrasts and contradictions. There is the magnificent old Ritz-Carlton Hotel, where the Kennedys and other celebrities always stay when they visit Boston, where every suite has a wood-burning fireplace stocked with birch logs, and the management supplies on stiff folded paper an information sheet showing the driving time to posh private educational institutions like Milton Academy, Phillips Andover or Exeter Academies, and Miss Hall's School. The ballroom of the Copley Plaza is the scene of periodic Waltz Evenings, a first-family tradition in Boston. But even along Newbury Street, with its art galleries and patina of "class," there are surprising numbers of vacancies. The Back Bay, *Boston* magazine reports, is plagued with a surfeit of "tax exempt properties, gouging landlords who pile the students into decaying buildings, fast-food joints and garish boutiques where the kids hang around nickel-and-diming themselves to death." Boylston street is filled with "panhandlers, gypsy children, hawkers, freaks, students and the displaced [who] roam the streets discouraging and even frightening shoppers." On Hemenway Street, filled with walk-up apartments heavily frequented by students and other young people, a May 1970 block party of about 300 persons stopped traffic in the area and was broken up by angry local gendarmes who surged through the area clubbing young people in their apartments in a gruesome display of police brutality.

But a purge of the young from Back Bay would be a fatal error, and one that Boston is not about to embark upon. As Lewis Mumford writes:

It is not by accident that Harvard's rejuvenation in science and scholarship under Charles Eliot coincided with the constructive enterprises of the Back Bay, in the generation between 1870 and 1900. With the waning of those energies, metropolitan Boston for a time began to fall apart, riddled with traffic but empty of life.

In a word, it was in the Back Bay that Boston first established itself as one of the centers of world culture in the arts and sciences that it has again, in the present generation, so preeminently become. To forget the part played by those cultural advances is to overlook the most essential functions provided for in any future scheme of urban renewal for the Back Bay: that of higher education and popular culture.

Boston remains one of the great medical centers of the Western world. Several of the important institutions (including Harvard Medical School, Peter Bent Brigham Hospital, Boston City Hospital, and Children's Hospital Medical Center) are located in the Back Bay and others (including Massachusetts General Hospital) downtown. The saga of attempts to modernize and meet rising budgets in the area's hospitals is a whole story in itself, a problem especially acute in a municipal hospital which has become a famous national institution, like Boston City Hospital. Actual delivery of health services leaves much to be desired. For all of Boston's magnificent facilities, for example, writer Selig Greenberg discovered a slum neighborhood with an infant mortality rate of 111.1 per 1,000 live births—exceeding the level of the Biblical plague inflicted on ancient Egypt, when every tenth newborn child died.

Ethnically speaking, Boston divides into a series of communities with quite clear identities. Most people think of the city as being heavily Irish, but a 1970 study by the Harvard–M.I.T. Joint Center for Urban Studies found that the Irish represent only 22 percent of the city's population. There are Irish pockets in many areas of Boston, but the greatest single concentration is in South Boston. Before World War I, "Southie" had a population of more than 70,000, which dipped by the early 1970s to 38,500. Those who remained constituted perhaps the most isolated ethnic community in any American city. The isolation is physical: the area is surrounded by the bay on three sides and cut off from downtown by railroad tracks and a six-lane expressway on the other. But South Boston's "separateness" is primarily psychological. When someone is sick, or his house burns, or there is a death in the family, the outpouring of neighborly help is astounding. Many residents of "Southie" who deserted its drab frame row houses for the suburbs have returned, complaining that people are "cold" out there.

The other side of the close-community coin is the parochialism, the narrow-mindedness, the fierce suspicion of outsiders one finds in "Southie." And if one leaves color aside, the community's income, occupation, education, and other statistics are closer to black Roxbury than any other Boston neighborhood. Alcoholism, mental illness, early pregnancies, venereal disease, and school drop-out figures are all high. And while South Boston's St. Patrick's Day parade, *de rigueur* for any Boston politician, has long been famed,* there are large contingents of Lithuanians, Poles, and Italians in the

* According to oldtimer Clem Norton, who was the Charlie Hennessey in Edwin O'Connor's *The Last Hurrah,* the St. Patrick's Day parade has "lost its gimp" since the days of James Michael Curley. Norton reminisced with a reporter in 1971: "He'd ride in the back seat of an open car in a big fur coat with a big silk top hat and the nuns and priests would rush out to his car and stop the parade to shake his hand."

community, each with its own churches. What is common to all the ethnic groups (now intermarrying in increasing numbers) is the blue-collar employment of their breadwinners.

The first great threat to South Boston was the state's public school racial imbalance law, passed in 1965. One of its goals was to prevent any school from having more than 50 percent black students. For years the law went unenforced, but in the meantime elections to the Boston School Committee were decided almost entirely by candidates' willingness to denounce it. Repeatedly the school committee refused to take steps to desegregate the city's schools. (South Boston High, for instance, was 99 percent white, while schools in some nearby areas were 100 percent black.) In 1972 the NAACP filed a school desegregation suit, leading to a 1974 decision by Federal Judge W. Arthur Garrity (who had been sponsored for appointment to the bench by Senator Edward Kennedy) finding that the school committee had "intentionally" segregated its schools and "knowingly carried out a systematic program of segregation." The first-phase desegregation, which Garrity ordered for autumn 1974, concentrated on South Boston and Roxbury. In retrospect, it seems small wonder that South Boston erupted in ugly racial violence. Vile epithets were hurled at black students bused into the area; a black man from Haiti was assaulted by a white crowd and would probably have been killed if police had not intervened; Senator Kennedy was spat on at an antibusing rally and heckled in other appearances. Above the door of South Boston High a white student tacked a sign: "Little Belfast."

In one respect, one could say that South Boston's people had been betrayed by the politicians who had told them it would "never happen." But psychiatrist-writer Robert Coles had a sound point when he said that the busing in Boston was "a scandal" because it was imposed "on working class people exclusively. . . . These people sense that they have no control over the destiny of their lives." Suburban Bostonians, Cole said, should have been forced to share in the change. William Bulger had made the same point a couple of years earlier when he commented to me that South Bostonians "feel they're being put on to bear the whole brunt of social change."

In autumn 1975, desegregation, under orders issued by Judge Garrity, took on a citywide coloration (although the suburbs remained inviolate). The all-white Boston School Committee maintained a policy of not cooperating with Garrity except when specifically ordered. In December 1975, Garrity placed South Boston High School under federal court receivership and stripped the school committee of jurisdiction over security in all the schools and of implementation of the citywide desegregation plan. But the violence continued, and 18 months after busing began, the public schools had lost nearly a third of the white enrollment. Most of these students went to private anti-desegregation academies, parochial schools or dropped out.

The most promising element of the desegregation plan was a system of 22 magnet schools that students could choose voluntarily. Roxbury's William Monroe Trotter School, established in 1970 to draw white students on the basis of educational excellence, is recognized as the best elementary school in Boston and has a waiting list.

With 18 percent of Boston's population, blacks are now second to the Irish in numbers, concentrated in center-city areas—principally Roxbury and the South End. Much younger in average age than most other ethnic groups in the city, the blacks are primary (but by no means exclusive) beneficiaries of the various programs of the city's strong community-based antipoverty agency, Action for Boston Community Development (ABCD). Such crumbs, however, are scant substitute for political power, which the city's blacks have never achieved. By 1975, only one black had ever served on the Boston city council; significantly, no black had ever been elected to the school committee. Conditions for blacks in poor city neighborhoods are not much better than in most big city ghettos. There have been incidents of savage attacks on whites by black gangs. Theoretically, Boston, with its historic record of tolerance and a white population still four-fifths of the whole, should be able to accommodate its black and Puerto Rican populations better than any other major East Coast or Midwestern City. But its record to date gives grounds for deep discouragement.

Some 11 percent of Boston's people are Italian in ancestry. One major concentration is downtown Boston's North End, a congested and deteriorated neighborhood that nonetheless has life and vitality that has been likened to Mulberry Street on Manhattan's Lower East Side. Another is East Boston, a neck of land jutting into Boston Harbor and connected to downtown by the Sumner and Callahan Tunnels. The 39,000 Italians in East Boston have fought a desperate battle against being engulfed by Logan International Airport, their unwelcome neighbor. In all America, it is difficult to find a more poignant story of the conflict between a city neighborhood, the economic exigencies of the jet age, and the heavy-handedness of a public authority. Forty-five years ago, just as the great Italian immigration wave into America was subsiding, East Boston had some 60,000 people and Logan was a 1,200-foot cinder runway. Today busy Logan's runways extend over 10,000 feet in length and its area has been expanded by landfill to reach three miles into Boston Harbor.

East Bostonians profit in one way from the airport, since they have almost 1,000 jobs there. But their community has paid a gruesome price. Airport expansion and highway connections have taken the homes of more than 1,000 people. Now East Boston's population is less than 40,000. The Massachusetts Port Authority (Massport), the quasi-public body which runs Logan, for years used its contract-letting and patronage powers to keep a friendly legislature and quash proposals to curb its powers, limit its runways, or include citizens in planning and development. In the mid-1960s, the authority swallowed up Wood Island Park, a large wooded area that was East Boston's most popular recreation site, and for a while it appeared that nothing would stem its appetite for new land, at East Boston's expense The infuriated East Bostonians, however, fought back through lawsuits, petitions to the state and city governments, and even sporadic demonstrations delaying airport traffic. Gradually they won high-ranking officials over to their side, and in late 1974 the freewheeling executive director of Massport, Edward J. King, was forced out of office. A new era of citizen- and environment-conscious leadership seemed in the offing, and if Governor Dukakis had his way, a conversion of Massport and other independent authorities into agencies directly responsible to the governor.

East Boston has also won a new lease on life with new housing projects, a new school, two new parks, and the like—mostly through its own community development corporation, with help from the Boston Redevelopment Authority. And for most citizens, life goes on as it has for generations in this little transplant of old Italy, the people rubbing elbows in the gay hubbub of the fruit-and-vegetable market on Maverick Square and living on in decaying old "triple-decker" houses with laundry fluttering from the back porches. (Inside, one finds rooms as spotless as a Back Bay doctor's waiting room.)

Yet another ethnic Boston stronghold, traditionally Irish but with significant Italian and French-Canadian minorities, is decaying old Charlestown, the site of Bunker Hill, just north of downtown Boston across the Charles River. Charlestown benefited tremendously from the Boston Naval Shipyard, oldest in the nation, but the yard was finally closed down in the early 1970s, depriving Charlestown of 6,000 jobs. There has been some debate about moving the U.S.S. *Constitution* from Charlestown to a site on the downtown Boston waterfront, but Charlestownians responded with the idea of a national historic park to incorporate Old Ironsides with a marine museum of shipping and structures of Revolutionary-era history and architectural merit at the Navy Yard.

Our ethnic review of Boston is rounded out by two other elements— white Protestants (13 percent of the total population) and Jews (6 percent).* The Wasps are scattered generally around the city, with special pockets in the Back Bay and Beacon Hill areas (though most wealthier old Bostonians have long since fled to the suburbs). Jews, who include a quite high percentage of young unmarried adults, are found in Back Bay, Brighton, and Dorchester-Mattapan (the latter an area of vivid conflict with the blacks).

The proud, liberal old town of Brookline, which is geographically but not politically part of the city, has shifted to about 50 percent Jewish in recent years (Irish and Wasps splitting the other 50 percent). Brookline is located just west of Back Bay and has many lovely residential streets—including Beals Street, where the birthplace of John F. Kennedy stands. My own maternal grandparents moved to Brookline to raise their family and live the rest of their lives; the memories remain vivid of holiday seasons with a magically lit Christmas tree towering to the high ceilings. Brookline in recent years has been proving that it cares about its many old people

---

* The growing Puerto Rican community, Greeks, Chinese (Boston has the country's fourth largest Chinatown) and others represent an aggregate of 30 percent of the city population, but no single group is as high as 5 percent.

living in rooming houses on and near Beacon Street in the Coolidge Corner area. At the Devotion School, they can get a good, hot lunch for just 50 cents, the program financed through a federal subsidy. Brookline also has Sussman House, a government-subsidized apartment-hotel for senior citizens, beautifully furnished with a warm atmosphere. Here the old people can exchange lifetime experiences in a genuinely human setting denied so many today. To get in, one must have lived in Brookline for 10 years, and even at that, there is a waiting list of 500.

A postscript might be added on Cambridge. Aside from the vital role it plays in the worlds of letters, science, and government, it is also a geographic place of 100,361 permanent residents, according to the 1970 Census. A rapid MBTA subway line and numerous bridges tie it closely to Boston, across the Charles River. Physically, Cambridge's two great universities are as different as they could be. Harvard evokes images of the Yard with its blending of Georgian stateliness and mellowed red brick, the incomparable Widener Memorial Library, America's preeminent Law School, and architectural gems like Walter Gropius' Harkness Commons and Graduate Center (1950), Le Corbusier's sole design on the North American continent in the Carpenter Center for the Visual Arts (1963), and Minoru Yamasaki's William James Hall (1964).

M.I.T., which moved to Cambridge from Back Bay in 1916, is housed in rather forbidding, huge buildings of Greco-Roman theme, though it has an attractive great dome and many handsome modern buildings have been added in the post-war era. Among them are Eero's Saarinen's striking Kresge Auditorium and the impressive cylindrical brick chapel he designed. Even private Cambridge contributes notably to American architecture with a prize-winning building like the glass-vista Design Research building on Brattle Street.

Industrial Cambridge, characterized by old ethnic politics, busy factories, and crowds at Central Square, is not unlike the type of urban community that one might expect to find anywhere in Massachusetts. It has traditionally abhorred university Cambridge, an antipathy strengthened by the deviant campus ways of the last several years. Cambridge city councilman Albert Vellucci has demanded more than once that the Yard be turned into a giant parking lot. But while Harvard and M.I.T pay no taxes (except voluntarily, for 20 years on new properties), they do provide thousands of jobs for the local economy.

Sociologically, the most phenomenal place in Cambridge (and perhaps all of New England) is Harvard Square. Once a bustling but low-keyed place of choice shops and carefree students, the square in the late '60s and early '70s seemed more like a kind of Haight-Ashbury or Telegraph Avenue reincarnate, a powerful magnet for the dissentious young street people of America. The pot-smokers, hairy wonders, *Hare Krishna* chanters, and other crazies have subsided some since, but no one can envision the square returning to its staid self of old.

What will *not* happen to the Harvard area will be the monumental

John F.Kennedy memorial, including a museum, park, library, and archives, that had been planned for a site beside the Charles River. Local residents had complained that hordes of tourists would inundate the area, and eventually forced the JFK Library Corporation to abandon the plans so grandiosely announced a few years before.

Boston Suburbia

Boston's multitudinous suburbs vary from industrial towns that are virtually undistinguishable from parts of the city proper to privileged sanctuaries of big-lot zoning to which the elite and semi-elite have migrated to guarantee themselves some greenery and keep the city at a safe, long distance. In the latter category there are even some towns that paid moving expenses of poor people into Boston and outlawed kindergartens because they didn't want large families coming. In more recent years, the familiar weapon of zoning has been used to exclude low-income residents.

Immediately north and northwest of Boston is a belt of industrial-residential cities which have functioned primarily as support cities for Boston for two centuries—places like Chelsea (30,625), Revere (43,159), Somerville (88,779), Everett (42,485), Medford (64,397), Malden (56,127), Watertown (38,531), and Arlington (51,319). Like Boston, virtually all have heavy ethnic populations and most have been losing population in recent years. They are crowded and generally (though not altogether) unattractive physically. Driving through, one has to check maps and city-limit signs, since the places all run into each other. The people either work in local factories or commute to jobs in Boston or on route 128. Usually they vote Democratic, but they may best be viewed as Massachusetts' real "silent majority"—people engrossed in typical small-city problems, reading their small daily newspapers, seldom gaining prominence in the metropolitan press like the more vocal communities where there are strong liberals. Somerville proved an exception in 1969 when it surprised the state (and perhaps itself) by electing an Episcopal priest as mayor. Malden is an example of a city that has pulled itself up by its bootstraps. Until a decade ago it was deteriorating badly, in both its residential and industrial sections. But Mayor Walter Kelliher then brought it back through urban renewal, housing improvement, and New England's most outstanding program of code enforcement.

Further north, on an arc running from the North Shore of Massachusetts Bay to the Merrimack River Valley northwest of Boston, lie many old cities that are within the Boston orbit geographically but enjoy very independent existences on their own. In between are a number of smaller residential towns, all of which have been growing rapidly since 1950. The North Shore cities—Salem (40,556) and Beverly (38,348), with their rich lore of witchcraft and the merchant princes and shipmasters in the West Indies and China trade, and Gloucester (27,941), still an important fishing port, and surrounded now by choice summer resorts—still have a special kind of magic about them. Beverly is surrounded by towns like Wenham, Topsfield, Hamilton, and Manchester, with large estates and the homes of some of Massachusetts' richest families—the "martini and manure crowd," some say. Even within Beverly itself there is wealth enough: production workers averaged $178 a week in 1970. The city is the home of statesmen like Henry Cabot Lodge. The reader is referred to the excellent modern updating of the American Guide Series book, *Massachusetts: A Guide to the Pilgrim State*, edited by Ray Bearse and published by Houghton Mifflin Company of Boston in 1971, for colorful detail on these places.

Lowell (94,239), Lawrence (66,915) and Haverhill (46,120), all sooty children of the industrial revolution, have had a hard time of it since World War I. Lowell and Lawrence were two of the greatest textile cities of the 19th century but saw that industry move south decades ago; Haverhill, a self-proclaimed "shoetown," is just now entering its worst depression as foreign competition decimates the market for domestically manufactured shoes. To a degree, the electronics and computer industries have helped the economy of these areas, which are close to the new outer belt (Route 495). Still, their unemployment is far ahead of the national average, and even concerted city renewal and industrial recruitment programs have not returned solid economic health. The physical plant of these cities is corroded and outmoded, they suffer from sagging tax bases and have an unusually high percentage of women in the labor force (four out of 10 in Lawrence, for example).

Lowell, which had the reputation of being a model industrial community between 1825 and 1860, is hoping for a new lease on life by a transformation into an "industrialized Williamsburg." Having escaped the federal bulldozer to date, there is hope that a substantial portion of the old city can be turned into a National Urban Park, which would feature restored textile mills, indoor and outdoor museums with artifacts from the Industrial Revolution, and recreational walkways along the 5.6 miles of canals originally built in the early 19th century to harness the power of the Merrimack River for the textile mills. Several tens of millions of dollars of local, state, and federal money would go into the project, a major part of the money for restoring the now-decaying canals. Congress in 1974 passed legislation to create a Lowell Historic Canal Commission to investigate the possibilities, including placing the area in the national park system.

The city of Lynn (85,018), much closer to Boston, is a shoe and leather town like Haverhill but has also benefited from the big payroll of General Electric, which has manufactured jet engines at its huge River Works plant there. But now troubles are closing in. The city has found itself almost bankrupt with soaring tax rates, inadequate housing, and even a general move-out by General Electric (which once employed 30,000 workers in the city).

Peabody (48,080), close to Lynn, has long billed itself as the "largest leather-processing city in the world." Until recent years, seven out of every 10 workers were employed in the leather trade. If that were still true,

Peabody might profitably be closed down and abandoned. But Peabody has been able to get some new industries going, and it was selected for the site of the North Shore Shopping Center. Its population has almost doubled since World War II and the town has not been able to keep up with demands for schools and expanded public facilities and public services.

Although Route 128 makes a complete loop around Boston, from Gloucester on the north to the Quincy area in the south, the concentration of research, electronics, and weaponry plants is in the area northwest and west of the city. Route 128 has been a phenomenal economic success, but it ought not to be regarded as the perfect model for good industrial-residential planning. "It's essentially strip development," John Collins said. "Doggone successful strip development, but nevertheless strip development." The traffic is incredibly heavy, even though the road is eight lanes wide on many stretches. The stories are that many politicians made a lot of money on zoning shenanigans and that much of the housing thrown up rapidly near the corridor was really substandard. The planners hope that development along Route 495, the new outer ring, will be better executed, and that corridors of green space will be created to avert thoughtless sprawl obliterating the natural landscape.

Several towns along 128 have benefited immensely in (a) new tax-producing industry and (b) an influx of a highly skilled, well educated population element. Waltham (61,582), an old industrial town with a heavy ethnic population where the illustrious Waltham Watch Company folded due to foreign competition after World War II, got a new lease on life through electronics manufacturing, including a big Raytheon facility. Historic Lexington (31,886), with its lovely Green, where the Minutemen statue still stands guard, and Concord (16,148), town of the "shot heard 'round the world," of Emerson Thoreau and Walden Pond, have doubled to tripled in population in recent decades without losing their essential flavor (provided one is willing to overlook some not-very-Colonial shopping center developments). Smaller old Massachusetts towns like Lincoln and Bedford, in the same area, have grown at like pace, filling up both with Route 128ers and many of the people who play prominent roles in the destiny of Boston, commuting from their handsome homes to the city each day. Burlington is a pivotal town in this stretch of Route 128, where the highways coming down from New Hampshire tie in. The town had barely more than 2,100 people in the 1930s, but 21,980 by the latest Census count. Industrial centers and the big Burlington Mall shopping center have gone up there. Many long-time residents naturally oppose proposed changes in the town, and thus town meetings may run for 12 to 15 sessions instead of only one or two nights.

(A brief diversion on the town meeting is in order. John Burke, the Boston *Globe's* suburban editor, points out that most of the 317 towns in Massachusetts still have the classic town meeting where each voter can attend and voice his opinion. This remains the purest form of direct democracy in the land, facilitating extremely personal, close control of government by the people. Some of the larger towns, however, have gone to representative town meetings. One man represents 50 or 60 voters. These meetings are more representative, to be sure, but may turn into debating contests as members looking toward a run for town-wide office use them to gain public exposure. Long sessions, in which issues are frequently blown out of proper proportion, often result.)

Towns of affluence and high social consciousness lie immediately west of Boston. The two which stir up the most controversy are Brookline (52,882), to which we alluded previously, and Newton (88,556), noted for its splendid public school system, the Boston College campus, posh estates and tree-lined streets, and the New England Industrial Park, a forerunner of Route 128 development. Both Brookline and Newton have many Jewish families and they have very definite ideas about current social problems and they bring them right to the voters through referendum and debates. Newton gave Father Drinan his winning edge in his first race for Congress.

Framingham (60,623) and Natick (31,057), about 20 miles west of Boston, are bedroom towns, small manufacturing centers, and retail centers in their region. Framingham has Shoppers' World, one of New England's first shopping centers. Both towns have doubled in population since 1930. The western suburbs have been avid participants in programs to bus Negro children to the suburbs for school, and their residents generally have more sensitivity to city needs than many other suburbanites. But Newton (and Lexington, too) have proven as obdurate about actually setting land aside for low-income housing, especially when faced with concrete proposals, as the most conservative suburban strongholds.

The South Shore, stretching from Boston to Plymouth, has never had the social distinction of the North Shore, even though the seashore is just as attractive and the visitor will find choice little bayside communities like Cohasset, Scituate, and Duxbury. But instead of receiving the Boston elite, they were traditionally the goals of one-day excursions by Dorchesterites and other less pretentious Bostonians.

Yet if one treasures history and tradition, it is hard to outpoint the town of Plymouth, "America's home town," where a visitor seeking directions may be told to "go down past the Mayflower until you come to Plymouth Rock, then take a right." The town, which not long ago celebrated the 350th anniversary of the time when the hardy Pilgrims landed and made their first settlement, offers some fascinating contrasts. Just south of town, Plymouth Plantation, a full-scale recreation of the Pilgrim's Village, was completed in 1958, with a modern replica, *Mayflower II,* anchored offshore. Yet quite close to it one can also find a huge new nuclear plant, with a 300-ton reactor core, built by Boston Edison Company. The nuclear plant, a possible precursor of two more to come, tripled the town's tax base in five years—but also triggered a wave of rapid, unplanned, and in some cases slipshod development, along with pressures for new schools and other facilities. Some townspeople were left wondering if the advantages of the big atom would be so wonderful in the long run as they had appeared on first blush.

If any place in America might be expected to be a Yankee Protestant stronghold, it is Plymouth, but in fact the town is now heavily populated by Portuguese, Italians, Germans, and Irish, descendants of another century of immigration. Like other New England towns, Plymouth has suffered from death of the old mill-city economy, especially the recent closing down of one of the world's largest rope manufacturers there. But urban renewal has taken hold, and just to the west, a new industrial park has opened up. And with the fast auto connection by the Southeast Expressway (Route 3), there are some people who make their home in Plymouth but work in Boston.* The town's population actually grew by 4,161 in the single decade of the 1960s—almost as much as its total population after its first two centuries of settlement. The 1970 total was 18,606.

The biggest city directly on the South Shore is Quincy (87,966), one of New England's most progressive medium-sized settlements. Quincy is heavily Irish but also has ample complements of Italians, Jews, Finns, Scots, Greeks, and Syrians, attracted over the past century and a half to work its quarries and shipyards. In recent years, Quincy has been attracting commercial business to balance the gigantic Fore River Shipyard of General Dynamics. Interestingly, this old ethnic community is considered by educators to have one of the most innovative school systems in the nation.

Sometimes considered part of the South Shore area, though it is several miles inland, is Brockton (89,040), an old shoe city that was said to have shod half the Union Army in the Civil War. With the present-day depression in the shore industry, Brockton is suffering, but early enough it saw the trouble ahead for leather and managed, with moderate success, to diversify its economy into electronics and other industries.

The Other Worlds of Massachusetts

Now the time has come to review the geological variety of Massachusetts, a small state by national standards (it ranks only 45th) but pleasing to the eye of man for all its recorded history. The eastern third of the state, including all of the Boston orbit, the North Shore, South Shore, New Bedford area and Cape Cod, is part of a coastal lowland that was once submerged beneath the sea. Bedrock pokes up through the land surface in the northeast, giving the North Shore a rugged, picturesque character. To the south, the shores are sandy and more level. The unique hook-shape of Cape Cod was created by glaciers which swept down from the north 10,000 to 30,000 years ago, halting at the line of what is now the Cape and depositing

---

* Suburban housing and light industry are springing up all along the Expressway, with rather tasteless large-scale development of small houses in some burgeoning little towns like Norwell and Hanover. In a few more decades, the South Shore might begin to rival the North Shore in overall population.

a load as "terminal moraines" to create land which the wind and waves would reshape.

Starting around Worcester, the land becomes hillier—an upland region which is actually a southerly extension of the White Mountains of New Hampshire. Further west, the Connecticut River flows from north to south across Massachusetts. It has created a broad plain with deep, alluvial soil, interspersed with traprock ridges that have resisted erosion and form sharp hills of more then 1,000 feet on the valley floor. The Connecticut Valley offers a rich harvest of tobacco, onions, and potatoes and is heavily settled in places like Springfield, Holyoke, and Greenfield.

West of the valley rise the Berkshire Hills, a continuation of Vermont's Green Mountains. These rugged hills were long a barrier to easy commerce; today they are favorite summer vacation places, interspersed with small upland farms. Still further west, the land dips again into the pleasant Housatonic River Valley, rather broad in the south but only six miles wide in the stretch from Pittsfield north to the Vermont line. Finally, Massachusetts ends with the Taconic Range along the New York border, reaching a high point of 3,491 feet in the northwest (the highest elevation of the state).

More must be said of Cape Cod, that low-slung spit of sand and scrub pine that ranks high among the vacation meccas of modern America. The Cape has almost 300 miles of coastline, 121,000 permanent residents and some 450,000 on a typical July day. The Kennedys, repairing in times of triumph and tragedy to their compound of houses at Hyannis Port, helped draw national attention to the Cape. But the place needed little advertisement. For years, the people have been pouring in, and still are. The Cape has been subjected to incredible growth pressures in recent years: the headiest building boom in Northeast America (and not just for summer vacationers, but for Boston suburbanites as well), an alarming strain on the Cape's fresh water supply, and real estate prices so high that the native Cap Codders (a mixture of English stock, Portuguese, and Cape Verdean stock whose ancestors came to man the fishing fleets or work in the cranberry bogs) can't afford to buy homes for themselves. The per capita income of the natives is a scant $4,049 a year. In the summer, many are thrown out of their rented quarters to make way for well-heeled tourists; in the winter, many end up on the unemployment rolls or welfare.

The visitor to the Cape, as he drives along the stretch of Route 28 between Hyannis and Harwich Port, is greeted by a tawdry jumble of motels (with which the Cape is now saturated) and neon lights in a show of commercialism as unnecessary as it is tasteless. Yet, writes Edward Garside:

> Beneath the recent overlay of vulgarity the Cape's ancient nature lives on. . . . The land is small, subdued; its colors are low in key. The salt marshes, the low houses at their margins, the woods beyond, the hidden ponds, the suddenly revealed harbors have a comforting dimension. But look outward and there is always the sea, a great presence fraught with sublimity.*

* In a review of Walter Teller's *Cape Cod and the Offshore Islands* (Prentice-Hall, 1970), in New York *Times Book Review,* (June 14, 1970).

And this generation has done a magnificent thing in the creation of the Cape Cod National Seashore, covering all of the Great Beach that runs without interruption for 30 miles from Nauset Harbor to Provincetown on the ocean side of the Cape. Too much of the rest of the Cape is tightly held, a province of the wealthy (and increasingly, outside investors); this great seashore is preserved for the people.

There is so much else to the Cape—its quaint towns like Falmouth and Yarmouth, Chatham and Orleans, its *nine* summer theaters (a concentration of summer stock unique in America), its hoarse Portuguese fishermen on the wharfs at Provincetown, its painters, writers, steeples, oysters, and saltbox houses—that we can only hint at the story here. Among the embellishments is the famous Woods Hole Oceanographic Institution, key to Massachusetts' prominent position in the world of ocean research. And the Cape has a sense of place: as Thoreau wrote of a Cape height he had stood on: "A man may stand there and put all America behind him."

We dare not overlook the picturesque islands south of the Cape—Nantucket and Martha's Vineyard. Their days of isolation are gone, with regular air connections to New York and Boston, together with onslaughts of autos (arriving by ferry), hippies, hikers, and gawking tourists.* The islands are no place for poor people: at Edgartown on Martha's Vineyard, for instance, summer homes cost from $50,000 to $200,000. Private landowners have preempted so much beachfront that only 9 percent of Martha's Vineyard is open to the public—a sample of the alarming trend all along the eastern seaboard.

Another threat lies in the land rush which hit the islands in the early 1970s, as real estate values soared and many islanders began to fear the onslaught of huge subdivisions and condominiums sponsored by off-island developers. This prompted Senator Kennedy to introduce legislation "to establish the Nantucket Sound Islands Trust to preserve and conserve the Islands." Four categories of land development ranging from town-controlled development to no development at all would be established; the whole would be administered by a commission under the Secretary of the Interior. Federal intervention, proponents suggested, was necessary because of obdurate Yankee attitudes that had blocked adequate local zoning and subdivision controls. But many islanders (and not just developer interests) objected to such a strong federal incursion into local affairs. A sensible compromise for Martha's Vineyard was found when the Massachusetts state government in 1974 set up a regional planning authority with the majority of members elected from that island's six towns. Unlike most regional planning commissions, it was vested with full regulatory and zoning powers and control over individual town zoning decisions. Early indications were that the state-created commission would reject unfettered development in favor of preserving the unique "island culture"—that special am-

---

* The gawkers have b_en especially offensive at Martha's Vineyard, where they have descended on nearby Chappaquiddick Island to see the crude little bridge from which Senator Edward Kennedy's auto fell on a summer night of 1969.

bience of open seashore, of placid ponds and green forests and little white houses that has made these islands so alluring to off-islanders for generations.

Southeastern Massachusetts is home of two desperately depressed and troubled communities—New Bedford (100,221) and Fall River (97,882). Both cities date from the mid-1600s and New Bedford especially has a colorful history as a great whaling port (an industry in which it seized leadership from Nantucket after the War of 1812),* a station on the Underground Railway smuggling slaves north to Canada, a big textile city, and still an important harbor for deep-sea fishing vessels and coastwise freighters. Fall River remembers days of glory, too, including the time when the Fall River Line provided direct passenger boat transportation to New York. Starting around 1870, textiles became the vital industries of both cities; then came a flight to the South and the Great Depression, almost obliterating New England textiles and throwing Fall River and New Bedford into a slump from which they may never recover. In recent decades, the "needle trades" have provided more jobs than any other industry in each city, but the employment is highly seasonal and oriented to jobs for women, not men. Congresswoman Margaret Heckler, who represents Fall River in Congress, points out that in that city "women comprise 40 percent of the manufacturing labor force; 38 percent of the mothers with children over six years old are working and, incredibly, 37 percent of mothers with children under six years are also part of the work force." The median education level in the city is eighth grade.

Despite their historic harbors, both New Bedford and Fall River are physically depressing, chock full of abandoned warehouses and mills, old and often dilapidated wooden frame houses. Poverty and unemployment are rampant in the large Portuguese communities of both cities. (I have heard one estimate that there are as many as 10,000 illegal immigrants in New Bedford, principally Portuguese.)

New Bedford's problems have been exacerbated by its 12 percent population of nonwhites—Afro-Americans, Cape Verdeans (Portuguese-black Creoles), and Puerto Ricans. The city sprang into the national news in 1970 when riots, burnings, and shootings occurred in the tragically overcrowded West End, where 1,200 housing units formerly occupied by poor blacks were torn down in highway and urban renewal programs. High unemployment (almost 30 percent in the ghetto), almost nonexistent recreation facilities, summer heat, and seriously deteriorated police—minority relations were blamed for the violence.† "New Bedford is, for a very large

* New England's whaling industry was doomed by the discovery of oil in Pennsylvania in 1857, which resulted in a quick national shift from whale oil to kerosene for lamp fuel. There is still a small business in blackfish oil, derived from a series of small whale. The oil is refined as a lubricant for clocks and watches.

† Massachusetts Attorney General Robert Quinn, in a report on the New Bedford disturbances, said there was "a distinct pattern of excessive force and abusive treatment being directed upon the citizens of the black and Spanish communities," and that police guilty of misconduct were being protected by their superiors from accountability.

part of our population, an absolutely miserable city," the local Urban Coalition said in a 1970 report—"a city where many can't make a decent living, can't get a decent house to live in, can't get a good education for their kids, can't find a decent place for their kids to play."

No one has yet figured out a way to improve New Bedford's economy substantially, but there is some hope on the physical renewal front. Under the direction of the city's urban renewal director, Howard Baptista, himself a black reared in the West End, construction finally began in 1974 on an extremely ambitious program to rebuild the downtown, waterfront and West End areas. The plans included new docks, high-rise apartments, a shopping mall, a hotel and pedestrian mall, and more than a thousand new low- and middle-income housing units.

The first thing to know about Massachusetts' third largest city, Worcester (1971 population, 167,462), located in the east central part of the state, is that the name is pronounced WOO-ster. The second is that its design and tone have led many people to liken it more to a Midwestern town than an Eastern city. The overwhelming impression is industrial, and in fact the city has some 500 factories producing a myriad of products. Some of America's most unique inventions, from the steam calliope to the first successful liquid-fueled rocket, have emerged from Worcester. Hills rescue the city from physical monotony, and important strides have been made in downtown renewal. (Worcester Center includes a two-story shopping arcade à la 19th century, the inevitable high-rise, and a reflecting pool and park incorporating the old city hall with the new structures. The whole is a tasteful blend of eras that has, in effect, made downtown Worcester a new town.) There are a number of institutions of higher learning, including Clark University, the Worcester Polytechnic Institute, and Jesuit-run Holy Cross College, and the new University of Massachusetts Medical School.

From an unsavory governmental history, Worcester has risen to the ranks of well-administered municipalities in the past 20 years under an exceedingly able city manager, Francis J. McGrath. The city has, for instance, used its federal revenue sharing funds to preserve social programs, rather than following the lead of most New England communities, which opted for building sewers and new town halls with the windfall money from Washington.

The driver traveling west from Worcester toward Springfield will pass close to Old Sturbridge, one of Massachusetts' prime tourist attractions. Old Sturbridge is New England's answer to Williamsburg, a recreation of an old Colonial-era town. The difference is that Williamsburg is a reconstruction of an actual town, Old Sturbridge pure invention. But the attention to olden days detail is meticulous, a tourist trap but a good one. If one yearns after something legitimate, one answer is Hancock Shaker Village, a few miles west of Pittsfield, where the structures of the Shaker community that prospered in the early 19th century have been preserved and restored—in the words of one critic—to provide "a very clear impression of the ways in which a given community joined a scrupulous esthetic sensibility to the arduous, workday tasks of social and religious salvation."

Far better known, and also entirely authentic, is Deerfield in the Connecticut River Valley. Deerfield really suffered through the French and Indian Wars, became an agricultural center in the 18th century, was a favorite spot of literati in the 19th century and still has Old Deerfield Street, set under an arch of 200-year-old elms, where preservation of Colonial homes has been underway for a century. Past the houses, one has glimpses of open country and far hills. The visitor feels transported back over time, into the milieu that makes New England such a precious part of America.

Springfield is the center of the generally prosperous Connecticut Valley metropolitan area, the home of more than half a million people. The city's population decline turned around in the early 1970s, reaching 169,027 and surpassing Worcester, previously the Bay State's second largest city. But over most of the postwar era, the principal Connecticut Valley area growth has come in the suburbs and academic communities centered around Northampton.

Since George Washington decided in 1794 to put an armory in Springfield to provide small-arms manufacturing for his army, it has been primarily an industrial city. By latest count, there are 236 manufacturing plants, turning out firearms, plastics, chemicals, paper, and electronic equipment. Former Defense Secretary Robert McNamara ordered the closing down of the Springfield Armory, a step completed in 1968 with a symbolic burst of fire from four M-14 rifles, the last of an illustrious line of weapons (if one may say that of instruments of death) produced there for the U.S. military. By normal standards, the loss of 2,400 jobs and a $27 million payroll would have been a crippling blow, but the armory was no sooner given up by the government than it became a technical school campus and industrial park (including a General Electric machine-gun plant), helping to sustain the local economy.

Springfield also subsists as the principal trading center of the Connecticut Valley and has the Eastfield Mall, the largest enclosed shopping center of western Massachusetts. Its downtown business center has been redeveloped quite successfully, and the industrial centers are set off by parks and boulevards and tree-shaded streets that convey an aura of substance and dignity that is lacking in many of the older industrial cities. Its government was encumbered until a few years ago with a weak mayor and bicameral city council, but then it shifted to a strong mayor form and elected an outstanding reform mayor, Frank Freedman. (Freedman was a bit of an oddity—a Republican, Jewish mayor in a Democratic, Catholic city.)

Ethnically, the Springfield area has many more Polish and French-Canadians than most of Massachusetts, though the strength here of Irish and Italians (especially in local politics) is not to be discounted. The city also has a significant black community and a growing number of Puerto Rican immigrants—a racial mix that has led to some clashes. School integration, however, has been accomplished quite peacefully in recent years. Part of the reason, according to School Superintendent John Deady, is that "we don't have the same history of bitterness and hostility in this city that has occurred in Boston."

Chicopee (66,676), just north of Springfield, has a much more diversified economy than many Bay State cities, ranging from sporting goods and surgical dressings to electronic components and a plant that prints the *Wall Street Journal*. The big Westover Air Force Base, largest SAC base in the eastern U.S., helps to sustain the local economy.

Neighboring Holyoke (50,112) is a prototype of the deteriorating Massachusetts mill town—old textile and paper mills lining the banks of the Connecticut; red brick tenements nearby (called "The Flats"), where the Irish, Polish, French-Canadian, and German immigrants were concentrated in the 19th and early 20th centuries; gracious homes of the successful old Yankee mill owners, built high above the city and overlooking the valley with its river, mills, and tenements; and middle-class housing of more recent decades. The lack of physical renewal in Holyoke stands in stark contrast to the success of Springfield and other western Massachusetts cities. Now many of the Puerto Ricans who came up the valley to pick tobacco, and moved into Holyoke, are combining with local blacks to pose a serious social problem for the old ethnic communities. Most of the once-booming pulp and paper industry has been lost, and the future looks grim. The insularity of Holyoke is hard to believe; a Boston *Globe* writer discovered that before House Speaker David Michael Bartley of Holyoke first took his seat in the legislature in 1962, he had never seen the State House in Boston.

Up north in the Connecticut River Valley is the small city of Greenfield (8,116), a place of wide, elm-shaded trees justly called one of the most beautiful of all Massachusetts towns. Greenfield is the eastern terminus of the Mohawk Trail, a picturesque mountain road extending over the Berkshire Hills to Williamstown in the state's northwestern corner. On an early October day, the trees vibrant in their red and orange autumn tones, the drive can be an unforgettable experience. (The main east-west connecting road, however, is the more southerly 131-mile-long Massachusetts Turnpike, which was completed in the 1950s and opened up the western part of the state as never before.)

The placid life of an earlier time goes on in the Berkshires, including little "hill towns" like Florida and Peru, known for their beauty and cool year-round weather. The small towns remain heavily Yankee, but the cities, especially Pittsfield and North Adams, have the same strongly ethnic complexion of the rest of urban Massachusetts. Pittsfield (57,020), set between the upper branches of the Housatonic, has a big industry in General Electric (manufacturing heavy transformers) plus a variety of light industries. But this is no typical factory town. Elms shade the streets, there are many beautiful homes, and almost everywhere a glimpse to the Berkshire hills. Downtown, a successful urban renewal program has been carried out, and there is even a Hilton Hotel.

North Adams (19,195) enjoys a lovely hill setting like Pittsfield's, but for years was the prototype of a withered, listless community. By the early '70s, its mills long since fled to the South, North Adams had an unemployment rate of 13 percent, one third of the housing was dilapidated or deteriorating, and the high school (built in 1867) was literally crumbling. After years of squabbling about proposed solutions, the town finally seemed to be taking hold of itself. Hundreds of units of low- and moderate-income housing, some of it sponsored by a nonprofit group, were constructed. A bond issue was passed to build the new high school that had been talked of for 20 years. And a community resources corporation took over the 19th-century Windsor Mill complex and began to lease space for artisans (potters, glass blowers, weavers, and the like), integrating the project with courses offered at North Adams State College. This wave of activity was a small beginning at solving the community's economic ills, but the new spirit—including reports that one out of seven adults in North Adams were doing some type of community volunteer work—did win the city an All-America Cities award and some hope for the future.

The Housatonic River has the bright distinction of being Massachusetts' cleanest waterway. General Electric at Pittsfield and several paper mills have installed sophisticated anti-pollutant equipment, and towns like Dalton, Hinsdale, Great Barrington, Lee, and Pittsfield are advanced in their sewage treatment facilities. But all seem to agree that top honors should go to Crane & Co. of Dalton, a 175-year-old family firm that makes high-grade writing papers and the parchment-like paper on which U.S. currency is printed. Crane & Co. began its clean-up of objectionable discharges even before World War II and has since invested well over $1 million to eliminate pollution. Company president Bruce Crane, an aristocratic gentleman of the first order and for years Republican National Committeeman for Massachusetts, is able to boast that "we probably have the cleanest paper mill in the country."

A few miles down the valley from Pittsfield one comes on Lenox, one of the most charming old Berkshire summer resorts, a place rich with memories of the days when writers like Nathaniel Hawthorne, Catharine Sedgwick, and Henry Ward Beecher lived or visted there. Thirty-six years ago, the 210-acre private estate named Tanglewood (after Hawthorne's Tanglewood Tales) was given to the Boston Symphony Orchestra. That same year, the Berkshire Festival was born, and each summertime the Boston Symphony presents 24 weekend performances. The rich cultural diet is supplemented with concerts by the orchestra's chamber players and guest concerts. From 15,000 persons the first season, attendance has risen to more than 200,000. Even in the face of some competition from the Philadelphia Orchestra playing at Saratoga, Tanglewood is likely to retain its informal title of "pastoral music capital of the United States."

Like other resort areas, the Berkshires have a share of summer stock theatres specializing in syrupy Broadway revivals. Something different is going on at the Berkshire Theatre Festival in Stockbridge, close to Lenox. Under the leadership of William Gibson, an outstanding modern playwright himself, the Berkshire Playhouse there has adopted the unique policy of doing new plays by serious playwrights. Several Berkshire Theatre plays have gone on to Broadway. But, Gibson told a visiting reporter, "our object is not to try things that will be successes in New York. It's helping people of talent open up and develop. So much of theater life is just the opposite of that. God, people are machine-gunned to death on Broadway. Here, we don't have to worry about what Clive Barnes will say."

And on that cultural upbeat, our story of Massachusetts, a remarkable civilization at once dying and being born anew, is finished.

RHODE ISLAND

"CITY STATE" AND ETHNIC LABORATORY

"LITTLE RHODY" is a unique world. Physically, it ranks as America's smallest state. Until New Jersey surpassed it recently, it was the most densely populated of all the states. It has by far and away the highest proportion of Roman Catholics of any state and can safely be called the "most ethnic." Finally, it is the most consistently Democratic state in its voting habits.

The compactness is illustrated by Rhode Island's measurements: only 48 miles from north to south, and an even more modest 37 miles from east to west. These 1,214 square miles could be contained in New York State 41 times, in Texas 227 times, in Alaska almost 500 times over.

James Bryce once suggested that Rhode Island might become the first American "city state." Socially the description fits. Many of the Rhode Islanders with whom I spoke described their home as a communal, tight-knit little state where everyone seems to know everyone. One young professional lamented that Rhode Island was so much like a small town that there was no real privacy, no matter where one went, and thus no opportunity for riskless peccadillos.

Geographically, the city-state theme is borne out by the fact that except for the residents of Block Island, no Rhode Islander is more than 45 minutes by automobile from Providence. Yet, to the eye, Rhode Island does not strike one as a densely packed city stretching from border to border. Its industrialized and urbanized image notwithstanding, the state actually seems fairly spacious. Lovely Narragansett Bay, intruding 28 miles from the sea and cutting the state into two quite uneven parts, contributes to the open feeling. There is also the fact that 64 percent of the state's land surface is in woodland, and another 5 percent in crop and pasture land.

Tolerance and Prickly Independence

Founder Roger Williams, fleeing the oppressive Puritanism of the Massachusetts Bay Colony, planted a tradition of religious toleration, along with prickly resistance to all forms of tyranny, in his new colony on the shores of Narragansett Bay. Before many years the "democraticall" government which Williams founded was undermined by aristocratic elements. But his spirit of religious toleration flourished and endured.

Only Maryland, among the colonies in the 17th century, would rival Rhode Island as a society open to freethinkers, nonconformists, and religions of every sort. In 1638 the first Baptist Church in America was established in Providence by dissenters from the Puritan Church in Massachusetts. Soon came the Congregationalists—though in Rhode Island they would never, because of the strict separation of church and state, achieve the dominance they had in Massachusetts and Connecticut. Quakers and Methodists arrived in the early years, too, as did the Jews, who a century later would build the second synagogue in America at Newport. (The old synagogue still stands—ironically, in a setting of Egyptian obelisks, reflecting the influence of Newport Jews who had formed the first Masonic Lodge in America.) Only later, around the time of the American Revolution, did the first significant numbers of Roman Catholics, who were destined to become the dominant sect of modern Rhode Island, arrive in the state. They were welcomed, in the manner of the many sects before them, as Rhode Island sought to honor the inspiration of Roger Williams, spelled out in the Royal Charter of 1663—"to hold forth a lively experiment that a most flourishing civil state may stand and best be maintained with full liberty in religious concernments."

Williams' spirit of revolt against oppression has also reappeared, time and again, through Rhode Island's 340-year history. Rhode Islanders like to remember that they were never subjected to the authority of royal governors, and that they declared their independence from Great Britain two months before the assembled colonies took that momentous step at Philadelphia in July of 1776. Chafing at the idea of a strong central government, Rhode Island refused to send delegates to the Constitutional Convention 11 years later; it joined the Union only belatedly, in 1790, and then only by two votes.

Despite an oppressive political order, the independent tradition survived into the 19th and 20th centuries. Rhode Island's common people found themselves under the control of a narrow elite and powerful mercantile interests, groups which used all means, fair and foul, to thwart the development of full-fledged democracy. The ruling circles, for instance, sought to remain in power by denying the right to vote to persons without property, and later to the foreign-born. The Colonial Charter of 1664, which restricted

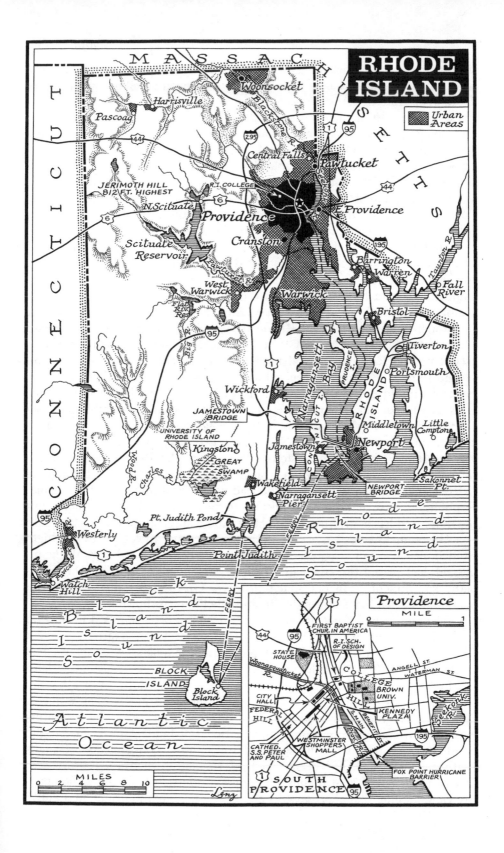

RHODE ISLAND

Urban Areas

MASSACHUSETTS

CONNECTICUT

Woonsocket
Harrisville
Pascoag
Central Falls
Pawtucket
JERIMOTH HILL
812 FT. HIGHEST
R.I. COLLEGE
N. Scituate
Providence
E. Providence
Scituate
Reservoir
Cranston
West
Warwick
Warwick
Barrington
Warren
Fall
River
Flat
Riv.
Res.
Bristol
Tiverton
Portsmouth
Wickford
Narragansett Bay
RHODE ISLAND
Prudence I.
Middletown
Little
Compton
JAMESTOWN
BRIDGE
UNIVERSITY OF
RHODE ISLAND
Jamestown
Newport
Kingston
GREAT
SWAMP
NEWPORT
BRIDGE
Sakonnet
Pt.
Wakefield
Narragansett
Pier
Pt. Judith Pond
Rhode
Island
Sound
Westerly
Watch
Hill
Point Judith
Block Island Sound
BLOCK
ISLAND
Block
Island
FERRY
Atlantic
Ocean

Blackstone R.
Pawtuxet R.
Big R.
R.I.
Charles R.
Wood R.
Pawcatuck R.
Sakonnet R.
Taunton R.

MILES
0 2 4 6 8 10

Lyng

Providence

MILE
0   1

FIRST BAPTIST
CHUR. IN AMERICA
R.I. SCH.
OF DESIGN
STATE
HOUSE
Woonasquatucket R.
ANGELL ST.
WATERMAN ST.
COLLEGE
HILL
BROWN
UNIV.
CITY
HALL
FEDERAL
HILL
KENNEDY
PLAZA
Seekonk R.
CATHED.
S.S. PETER
AND PAUL
WESTMINSTER
SHOPPERS
MALL
FOX POINT HURRICANE
BARRIER
SOUTH
PROVIDENCE

access to the ballot box to a privileged few, was kept in effect for years after Rhode Island became a state. Only a threatened rebellion—the so-called Dorr War—forced the writing of a new constitution, broadening the franchise, in 1842. Even then, immigrants were not allowed to vote until 1888, and non-property holders could not vote for the Providence city council until 1928. A boss-ridden and often corrupt Republican party, fronting for the mill owners and representing what John Gunther called Rhode Island's "glacially aristocratic families," controlled the state from the Civil War down to the 1930s, buying and stealing elections and rigging state law to ensure its own dominance. Perhaps the only true parallel in American history was the powerful and heartless oligarchy that controlled Louisiana for so many decades.

In Louisiana the downtrodden were of native stock—poor white and black, Roman Catholic and Protestant alike. In Rhode Island they were the foreign-born—Irish, French-Canadian, Italian, and others—who had been imported to man the sweatshops of the textile mill owners. Louisiana's liberator was the volcanic Huey Pierce Long, a man soon perceived to have dictatorial tendencies himself; Rhode Island's was a mild-mannered Yankee Democrat, Theodore Francis Green. The change Green brought to Rhode Island was no less fundamental than Long's in Louisiana, however. In his second term as governor, Green led a "bloodless revolution" that broke the back of the old order. Election returns were tampered with to give Democrats control of the eternally Republican state senate; the all-Republican supreme court, on which no Democrat had sat for 63 years, was purged; in a 15-minute flurry of action on New Year's Day, 1935, the state government was reorganized from stem to stern, cleaning out the Republicans who had held it in an iron vise for so long. Since then, a heavily ethnic, labor-dominated Democratic party has been the leading political force of Rhode Island. Republicans have returned periodically to power in state government, but the new breed has borne little resemblance to the autocrats of old.

Governor Green, it is worth noting, offered no apologies for his high-handed maneuvers of 1935, which bordered on a *coup d'état*. Roger Williams, he said, had placed the "right of rebellion" among the "principles of democratic government." "In our state's history," Green said, "there have been many times when that spirit of dissent and rebellion has shown forth."

The dominant Democrats of recent times have been standard liberals on issues like workers' benefits, but they are ideological conservatives. Though Rhode Island has a fairly small black population, it took seven years of effort in the 1960s before a fair-housing bill could win approval. Rhode Island fought tooth and nail against relaxing its ban on abortions, even after the U.S. Supreme Court had seemed to resolve the issue in favor of women's right to make their own determination on that issue. And the legislators most fervently against abortion, claiming that full human life begins at the point of conception, were the strongest for a restoration of Rhode Island's death penalty, which had been wiped off the statute books a century ago. One of my Rhode Island friends who opposes abortion takes quite the opposite view, arguing that abortion kills an innocent, capital punishment a guilty person. Whatever one's point of view, it seems certain that Roger Williams, suddenly returning to the Rhode Island of the 1970s, would find the issues of tolerance, human dignity, and separation of church and state as vital in our time as they were three centuries ago.

Special Assets: The Bay, Brown, et al

Over a memorable Italian dinner in Providence one evening, my friend John Hackett, veteran political writer for the Providence *Journal-Bulletin*, ventured the view that Rhode Island has four principal assets: the Bay, Brown, the State House, and his own newspaper. And he was probably right. Flying into Providence on a clear spring morning, I was immediately impressed with the loveliness of Narragansett Bay, the most striking feature of the little state's geography. Its sparkling blue waters are dotted with pleasing islands, coves, and beaches. This is one of the best sheltered harbors on the Atlantic Ocean, with a long-exploited but still real potential for industry, recreation, and tourism. Newport is only one of several meccas for gracious living along its shores.

Brown University, housed in mellowed brick buildings that look down on working-class Providence from College Hill, is a venerable member of the Ivy League and the alma mater of many of Rhode Island's most famous sons and daughters. Founded in 1764, it is the nation's seventh oldest university and was known for years as one of the more conservative of the Eastern colleges. In 1969, however, Brown had the courage to undertake a radical reform, called the New Curriculum. The program jettisoned many traditional academic approaches in favor of allowing students to design their own programs of study and enjoy close contact with faculty in small, informal classes from their freshmen year onwards. Because of the financial crunch encountered by all universities, plus faculty traditionalism and normal academic lethargy, the program was not fully implemented. But enough of it remained to allow students a free environment for learning, rather than mere preparation for graduate school.

Few would dispute Hackett's categorizing of the State House as one of Rhode Island's greatest assets. Its radiant white marble outshines every other building in the capital city of Providence; in some atmospheric conditions it seems almost to float over the city. Its style is of the Early Republican period, of architectural power and simplicity. The unsupported marble dome was the first in America (later Minnesota followed suit); the interior has the opulence of an ancient European court, perhaps more than a modest little state needs, but still a delightful extravagance. (It was not until 1900, incidentally, that Rhode Island decided on a permanent capital; from 1740 until the construction of the State House, the legislature alternated between the Old Colony House in Newport and the old Capitol at Providence.)

The Providence *Journal* and *Evening Bulletin*, according to the foundation-supported 1974 *New England Daily Newspaper Survey*, "are very good newspapers. They are head and shoulders above almost all in New England in the depth and breadth of their total coverage, their standards, and their professionalism." Remarkably for papers of their total circulation (219,000), the Providence papers not only do a good job in covering all areas of the state—which they long ago decided to cover as a single city, with bureaus in all the major towns—but provide highly creditable national and international coverage.

The papers bear, of course, a special responsibility because they so dominate the public discourse in this little state. A. J. Liebling once characterized them as "a benevolent despot." (There are dailies in five other smaller Rhode Island cities, but their combined circulation is only a third as large.) The history of the Providence papers is a Republican and conservative one, reflecting their ownership by a few of the older Yankee and Republican families. But the papers have moderated their politics and philosophy over the years, and exhibit an exemplary division between news and editorial columns. Balance in campaign coverage, editor Charles Spilman told me, was attempted "even to the extent of putting a ruler on coverage." * Though the *Journal* and *Bulletin* endorsed Richard Nixon for the presidency, they won a Pulitzer Prize for breaking the story of his scandalously low income tax payments. They called for Nixon's resignation several months before he finally left office in 1974.

Lawrence P. McGarry, the personification of old-line Democratic politics in the state, said the *Journal* and *Bulletin* were "Republican-oriented papers with a lot of Democrats working for them as reporters. The staff are a good bunch. If they have something on you, they'll belt you. If you do something half decent, they'll give you a fair shake. I've got to be honest —they do a good job. I say that even though over the years they've been more against me than for me."

McGarry's words suggest that a spirit of civility and fair play, more in accord with Roger Williams' tolerant philosophy than the bitterness and discord which plagued Rhode Island public life over such long stretches of its history, may have emerged in our time.

Yankees, Ethnics, and the Political Wars

For at least a century, religion and ethnicity have been the vital factors of Rhode Island politics. Once a stronghold of Yankee Protestant stock, the

* Spilman's point has been borne out by independent studies. In 1972, for instance, the papers gave almost equal column inches of coverage to U.S. Senator Claiborne Pell, a Democrat running against former Republican Governor John Chafee, whose family is one of the owners of the papers. Nor was there any discernible distortion of news coverage to favor Chafee. The *Journal-Bulletin* endorsed Chafee but then gave prominent coverage to the Democratic outcry over the endorsement. All this is in strong contrast to the days when Republican Senator Jesse Metcalf (1924–37) and his brother were substantial stockholders, and his brother president of the papers. The doctrine was uncompromisingly Republican—in both news and editorial departments—in those days. As late as the 1940s, there was the celebrated case of an editorial board meeting in which eight of the nine men present voted to support the Democratic candidate. Managing editor David Patten, a shrewd operator closely tied to the ownership, cast the single vote for the Republican. The meeting broke up as he announced, "OK, the one vote wins."

state began to draw strong numbers of foreign immigrants from the 1810s onwards. First came the Irish, servants and workers initially, destined to be the masters of Rhode Island politics for so many decades. Then came the French-Canadians, imported to man the textile mills in heavy numbers from 1860 to 1895. Next were the Italians, largely of that country's peasant class, who flooded into Rhode Island in a gigantic population wave between 1900 and 1915. Significant numbers of Poles and Portuguese, together with a scattering of Swedes, Germans, Armenians, Greeks, Lithuanians, Finns, and Syrians, added to the foreign influx. By 1920 the Census showed that a phenomenal 71 percent of the state's people were either foreign-born or the sons and daughters of one or two foreign-born parents. In the third and successive generations, the foreign groups are no longer counted separately by the Census Bureau, so that the foreign stock figure dropped to 41 percent in 1950 and 33 percent in 1970. Appropriate statistics are not available, but I imagine that if a careful survey were made, Rhode Island would still be far ahead of all other states in the proportion of its population from the identifiable European ethnic groups. The state's exceedingly high Roman Catholic population share—64 percent at latest count—is illustrative of the point.* Not even in Massachusetts or Connecticut are the old WASPS (white Anglo-Saxon Protestants) in such a hopeless minority.

The Yankees did not acquiesce lightly to a transfer of political power to the immigrants; in fact they fought a spectacularly successful rearguard action, over the better part of 100 years, to retain their hegemony. An overwhelmingly Protestant group, the Yankees relied on the most restrictive voting system outside the old South, a rotten borough system that kept them in control of the legislature, and corrupt political bossism. We have already touched on the limited franchise; one of its features was to bar foreign-born persons from voting in city elections until the late 1920s, thus retaining Republican control of the cities even when the city populations were overwhelmingly immigrant and Democratic.

The rotten borough system was so egregious that in 1900, 28 of the smallest towns and cities, representing a scant 18 percent of the state population, elected 28 state senators, a majority of nine. The state house of representatives was also malapportioned, though not quite as heavily, to favor the Republican small towns, and the Democrats were unable to take control of it until 1930. There was always the possibility that the Democrats might elect a governor, but even when they did (and they controlled that office for only eight years between 1856 and 1932) it did them little good. Under the state constitution, Lincoln Steffens wrote in 1905, the governors were "administrative mummies." They had no veto and practically no control of administration. After 1901 the state had a remarkable law providing that if the senate chose not to confirm the governor's appointments within a period of three days of submission, it could select its own men for the jobs. "Thus the

* The regular Protestant denominations account, by contrast, for only 11.7 percent of the population, and Jews for 2.5 percent. The remaining 22 percent of the people have no religious affiliation.

important factor of patronage," political scientist Erwin L. Levine has noted, "rested in the senate's collective hands, in reality the Republican party bosses', and not in the governor's."

The prototype Republican boss was Charles R. Brayton, a corpulent, affable, almost blind man of blueblood Rhode Island stock who had been a general in the Civil War. When Americans think of political bosses, they normally think of big-city types like the Curleys, Hagues, and Pendergasts. Brayton proved that an equally ruthless, efficient regime could be built on a rural base. He had an alliance with one of the most powerful Republican Senators of the late 19th and early 20th centuries, Nelson Aldrich. But in matters internal to Rhode Island, Brayton's rule was supreme. With impunity, he bought the voters in the small towns, who sent Brayton men to the legislature. Lincoln Steffens wrote that Brayton controlled legislators by advancing them "to judgeships and other political jobs, threw them law business and, if they were not lawyers, contracts and other business. He had pull enough to get men jobs with his client corporations." Brayton was a lobbyist for the multimillion-dollar corporation which ran street railways in Providence, for the New Haven Railroad, the Providence Telephone Company, and other firms doing business with the state. His base of operations was the State House office of one of his satraps, the High Sheriff of Providence. From there he controlled the state legislators like marionettes.

Brayton's corporate clients provided him with all the cash he needed to control elections. "That bribery exists to a great extent in the elections in the state," Democratic Governor Lucius Garvin told the General Assembly in 1903, "is a matter of common knowledge. No general election passes without the purchase of votes. . . . Many assemblymen occupy their seats by means of purchased votes." Even in Providence, where the Democrats had substantial strength, many of the elected officials were "yellowdog" Democrats, paid by the Republican machine and obedient to its commands. As the immigrant groups began to rise in numbers, Brayton and the other Republican bosses cleverly played one group off against another. There was considerable resentment among the French-Canadians, for instance, at the Irish dominance of the Democratic party, so that Brayton engineered the nomination of Aram J. Pothier, a prominent Franco-American, as the Republican gubernatorial nominee in 1908. Pothier and another Republican French-Canadian, Emery San Souci, ended up serving for 11 years as governor. Similar stratagems were used to peel off some Italian support for the Republican party.

In the long run, however, the Republican strategy of divide and conquer was to prove untenable. Few are the states in which there was such rancor between a capitalist class centered in one religion and a working class based in another. The mill owners paid their employees substandard wages and were part of the cabal denying the foreign-born the right to vote for so many years—thus inspiring, in Duane Lockard's words, "a deep and rankling hatred for the upper classes, the monied interests, and the Republican party." As late as the 1950s, Lockard reported, the very mention of "mill owner" in the poorer Italian wards of Providence was enough to bring a stream of invective.

Teaching political science at Rhode Island College in the 1970s, Professor Victor Profughi told me his students—largely from Rhode Island ethnic backgrounds—still saw the "East Side crowd" and the mill owners as the enemy. "They may have no clear image of the Democrats," Profughi commented, "but they certainly do of the Republicans."

Though the Democrats of Rhode Island had long offered a haven for the underprivileged immigrants, it took the presidential election of 1928 and the candidacy of Alfred Smith, the Catholic candidate from the streets of New York, to tie the state's Catholic ethnic groups into a cohesive voting bloc. Smith became the first Democrat—except for Woodrow Wilson, when the Bull Moose movement divided the Republicans—to carry Rhode Island since the birth of the Republican party. Then came the Great Depression, and the rise of a powerful labor movement of heavily Catholic-ethnic composition, to cement the relationship. Only Eisenhower, in 1952 and 1956, and Nixon, in 1972, have since carried Rhode Island for the Republican presidential ticket. In 1960, when Catholic John F. Kennedy was running for President, Rhode Island gave him 63.6 percent of its vote—Kennedy's highest percentage in any state. Democrats Lyndon Johnson in 1964 and Hubert Humphrey in 1968 also received their highest percentages among all states in Rhode Island—80.9 and 64.0 percent respectively. Even George McGovern, who was anathema to some of the state's old-line Democratic politicians, received 46.8 percent of the vote in Rhode Island, his best showing in any state except Massachusetts. Well over half the present-day inhabitants of Rhode Island were not even born when the state last elected a Republican to Congress (in 1938). The last time Rhode Island chose a Republican U.S. Senator was 1930. At least on the national level, no other state offers a comparable record of blind one-party loyalty.

In state voting, however, the picture has been more mixed. After Boss Brayton died in 1909, a group of lesser Republican bosses maintained general control until the 1930s, and even after that a coterie of small-town Republican legislators sustained a major voice for their party in state affairs through their rarely broken control of the malapportioned state senate, clear down to the advent of court-mandated "one man, one vote" in the 1960s. Three times since the dawn of the Democratic era Republicans have been able to take control of the governorship—though as John Chafee, one of those Republican governors, told me, "for a Republican to win, you have to have a tarnished Democrat." The first Republican breakthrough was William H. Vanderbilt of the famous Vanderbilt clan, who won in 1938 after a run-in between the Democratic governor and a racetrack operator in which charges of bribery flew left and right and martial law was employed to close down the operator's track. Vanderbilt, however, pushed through a civil service system for state employees, a step which offended the rural-based conservatives of his own party and helped bring about his defeat in 1940. The second Republican governor was Christopher Del Sesto, elected in a wave of sympathy in 1958 after he had been counted out of an apparent victory in 1956 by Democratic legal stratagems that invalidated hundreds of absentee ballots. Del Sesto's candidacy was also significant because he was the first Italian-American nominated for a high Rhode Island office on the Republican ticket. But, like Vanderbilt, he lasted only one term in office.

Then, in 1962, John Chafee inaugurated an unusual GOP winning streak. Three factors played a part in that win, by the slimmest margin of just 398 votes out of 325,000 cast. First, Chafee was one of the most personable Yankee bluebloods to seek office in a long time—as one Democrat described it to me, "he had that country-boy, apple-eatin' charm." Second, the incumbent Democratic governor, John Notte, was a lackluster figure who critics said had spent more time getting measured for clothes than in running the state. Third, organized labor, a mainstay of Democratic victories since the '30s, felt Notte was a lightweight incapable of doing anything to relieve the high unemployment rates the state was then suffering. So labor, to the Democrats' consternation, sat on its hands, and Chafee won.

(The relationship between organized labor and the Democrats, as close as it may seem to an outsider, has had its rough spots. As Edwin Brown, secretary treasurer of the state AFL-CIO, explained: "There's been a closeness, but it hasn't been a true association. The Democrats have passed liberal laws and handed out some patronage to the labor guys. But the labor movement hasn't had the input it should in developing overall policy and in the selection of candidates. I've always felt as if we've been used." One has to be reminded of the feeling of many partners in marriages.)

Once in office, Chafee proved unusually skillful in maneuvering issues so that the solidly Democratic legislature would pass his programs. He prided himself in bringing in new industry and some 50,000 jobs. In 1964 he was reelected with 61 percent of the vote, in 1966 with 63 percent. In both those elections, at least a third of the voters split their tickets to vote for Chafee while supporting Democratic presidential or Senate candidates. But Chafee proved that his pulling power was more than a personal affair by helping two Republican candidates, both of whom were Roman Catholics, win election as lieutenant governor and attorney general in 1966. Two years later, the bubble burst when Chafee was unwise enough politically to say that the state would need an income tax to meet its financial needs. Democrat Frank Licht campaigned against the income tax and defeated Chafee.

As it turned out, Licht was either uninformed or a deceiver, because two years later, shortly after being reelected for a second term, he backed and put through the legislature the income tax he had denounced so roundly. Licht's apologists claim he was misinformed by subordinates concerning the state's finances when he campaigned against Chafee and the tax. Rhode Islanders thought they had been double-crossed, however. As it was, the Democratic state chairman, Lawrence P. McGarry of Providence, told Licht he would be "committing political suicide" if he ran again, in 1972, so Licht chose to retire gracefully.

John Chafee, in the meantime, had gone off to Washington to serve for three years as Secretary of the Navy under President Nixon. In 1972 he returned to run against Democratic Senator Claiborne Pell, hoping to benefit from the "guilt factor" voters might feel for turning him out of office on the tax issue. The Chafee campaign made every effort to tie Pell to a so-called "McGovern-Pell" plan to cut the defense budget, which Chafee said would cost Rhode Island 7,000 Navy jobs. Chafee's uncharacteristically strident attacks on Pell boomeranged, and he lost by a substantial margin. But the Nixon reelection campaign, with which Chafee was so closely associated, succeeded in putting Rhode Island, for the first time since General Dwight Eisenhower's campaigns, into the Republican column. McGovern's liberalism on social issues was clearly to the left of the Rhode Island Democratic mainstream,* but the defense issue doubtless played a role in the Nixon victory. During the campaign, for instance, the Committee to Reelect the President ran scare ads in Rhode Island papers saying that McGovern-backed defense cuts would cost Rhode Island thousands of Navy jobs, both military and civilian, resulting in a "staggering" blow to the state's economy. "Fortunately," the ads said, "none of this will come to be if the man who's President right now remains President."

Five months later, it became obvious that Rhode Island voters had been the victims of yet another great double-cross. The Nixon administration announced a large group of military base closings, including its intention virtually to sweep the Navy out of Rhode Island—a body blow to the little state's economy. Chafee later told me that if he had been elected, "the President wouldn't have closed all those bases to welcome me to Washington." Perhaps so, but Rhode Islanders had swallowed the strong-defense argument and given Nixon their votes, only to be hoodwinked again, as they had been on the income tax issue.

In the mid-1970s, there seemed little reason to expect Rhode Island politics to change from the mode prevalent since the 1930s: a dominant Democratic party, tied closely to organized labor, heavily ethnic in leadership and composition, winning the vast majority of elections over the minority Republicans. The Republicans have accepted an increasing number of Catholics and ethnics as their candidates, but barring some massive split or snafu on the Democratic side, that is generally not enough.

As an example, in 1972 practically every pre-election poll showed that Herbert DeSimone, a Republican who had served four years as attorney general of the state in the late '60s and barely missed election as governor in 1970, would win the governorship. DeSimone emphasized the need to get new industry and jobs for the state and had what in other states were good issues for the times—a promise to make all government meetings open to the public and the press, and to push conflict-of-interest legislation. DeSimone also made much of his Italian background, thus appealing to a huge ethnic bloc in the state. His Democratic opponent, Mayor Philip Noel of Warwick,

* It is true that McGovern won Rhode Island's first-ever presidential primary in May 1972. This was because the student-liberal activists backing him put on a blitz campaign in the three weeks immediately preceding the primary, while the regular Democratic-labor forces were lethargic and uncertain about their preference. The McGovern victory should not be taken too seriously. He won 41 percent of the Democratic vote, but the cumulative vote for Edmund Muskie, Hubert Humphrey, and George Wallace was 56 percent. Interest in the primary was so low that fewer than one in ten voters bothered to go to the polls at all.

at the time was little known outside his own city. Noel also refused to disassociate himself from the McGovern candidacy. But Noel was ethnically safe: his father was French-Canadian, his mother of Italian background. And on election day, despite the Republican win at the presidential level, Rhode Island's normal Democratic habits carried Noel to victory with 53 percent of the vote. In the next election year, 1974, the Democratic tide was running so strongly that Noel won reelection with an astounding 78 percent of the vote.

When I asked John Chafee about the long-term Republican outlook in the state, he acknowledged: "We're in a lot of trouble. We don't have that much basic strength. We do have the small towns—but so what, especially after reapportionment of the legislature?" Chafee pointed out that the Republicans did win some elections, including the attorney general's post in every election from 1966 through 1972. There was a special reason for that, however: each of the losing Democrats was an Italian-American, apparently suspected by many voters of having Mafia connections. No ethnic group has been willing, in recent decades, to transfer its loyalties to Republicans. Chafee, for instance, made a big play for the Portuguese, who had long enjoyed small bastions in the Fox Point area of Providence and the town of Bristol (a phenomenon going back to the state's seafaring days). After a great earthquake in the Azores in the early '60s and an opening of the federal immigration laws, the Portuguese began to expand in numbers and potential political influence. But by the early '70s it was apparent that the Democrats were once again monopolizing the support of a vital ethnic element, though the Portuguese had yet to be paid off with a significant number of public offices.

The Democrats' secret of success has been a careful ethnic balancing of their statewide tickets. This was particularly easy as long as Rhode Island law called for nominations by party conventions, rather than in open primaries. Even after the institution of primaries in 1948, however, ticket balancing remained an easy enough matter because the law allowed party conventions to endorse candidates who in turn received preferential placement on the ballot.

The Democratic tickets, from the early 1930s onward, were well balanced among four groups—the Irish, Italian, French-Canadian, and Yankees.* (The first exception came in 1972 with the nomination of Frank Licht, who was Jewish.) Among these "equals," there has consistently been one group more preferred than the others: the Irish. The proclivity of this group for political success—even if the Italians have now outstripped them numerically—is one of the wonders of American politics. John Gunther, passing through the state at the end of World War II, noted how so many positions of political power were in Irish hands. In 1974, I was reminded of his observation when I noted that the majority leaders in both houses of the legislature, as well as the Democratic state chairmen, were Irish.

* The four-man congressional delegation, for instance, has for years had one representative of each of those groups.

That same year, an enterprising university student, Laraine L. Laudati, interviewed 47 of the 50 Rhode Island state senators about their ethnic background and that of their districts. She was told that in terms of ethnic dominance, nine districts were Irish, nine Italian, nine French, nine Yankee, seven Portuguese, two Jewish, and one Swedish. But there were 19 senators of Irish background, 10 Italian-American, six French, six Yankee, three Portuguese, two Jewish, and one German. Ms. Laudati reported that eight of the nine predominantly Irish districts had Irish-American senators, the highest correlation of district and senator. She also reported that "the Irish represent more Portuguese districts than do the Portuguese, as many Yankee districts as do the Yankees, and nearly as many French districts as do the French." The study bore out not only the Irish genius in politics but also the importance of Roman Catholicism. In several cases where a Catholic ethnic district did not elect "its own kind" to the senate, in almost all cases it elected a Catholic from one of the other major ethnic groups.*

The reasons for the "underrepresentation" of several of the ethnic groups bear examination. The Portuguese, as we noted previously, are just now starting to make themselves felt politically. Many Yankees who might succeed in politics apparently never make the try, feeling they have little chance in such an overwhelmingly Catholic state. And of course the Yankees, through their wealth and educational advantages, have ways to make their influence felt in Rhode Island affairs. Democratic politician Lawrence McGarry gave me a view from Irish eyes: "There's an old Wasp power structure—the Metcalfs, the Sharps, the Browns, the Chafees. It's the Rhode Island Hospital Trust Bank, the Providence *Journal*, the Rhode Island Hospital board of directors. The patriarch of the whole outfit is John Nicholas Brown—he's allegedly a Democrat, but you couldn't prove it by me. Remember they had a governor—Chafee—and have a Senator—Pell. They're both bluebloods."

The Italian-Americans, while proportionately represented in the senate, are often bought off and co-opted for lower elective and appointive positions by the Irish. This is not to say that the Italians are not a potent force. One of their number, John O. Pastore, was the nation's first elected Italo-American governor in the 1940s and went to the Senate, to win by consistently overwhelming margins into the 1970s. Numerous other Italians have won top positions. In the 1950s, when Republican Christopher Del Sesto won office by splitting off a big segment of the normally Democratic Italian vote against an Irish opponent, a correspondent for *The Economist* of London provided this explanation:

[The Italians] did not shift blindly, as a block, simply because Mr. Del Sesto is an Italian, but for deeper-reaching, in some respects almost subtle, reasons. The passage of the years has created a new kind of Italian-American society in Rhode Island, sophisticated, economically and culturally advanced, mixed with other blood, spread more widely through the state, but always remaining in some degree Italianised in its politics. The Irishmen running the Democratic party failed to recognise the change in this "Italian vote." They did not see, or would not admit, that in

* Not only shared Catholicism, but also intermarriage may account for this. The Italians and Irish in particular have intermarried heavily—unions which produce quite beautiful children.

important matters like money to spend on politics, and the influence provided by group leadership, there are as a practical matter more millionaires among the Italians today than there are ditchdiggers, more doctors and lawyers and artists than costermongers, more successful businessmen than factory hands.

In the 1970s, I heard, the Italians had become the wealthiest ethnic group in the state (excepting, perhaps, the Jews in professions). Among their principal sources of prosperity were the law, jewelry, real estate, construction, and, for a certain minority, the rackets.

The French-Canadians present a prime case of retarded social and political development. Large numbers of them have stayed on in the mills; others have gone into construction work. To other Rhode Islanders, they seem to be a provincial, ingrown group. But they have remained very loyal Democrats. When Governor Chafee wanted to appoint a qualified Franco-American Republican to a judgeship, he could not find one.

All this leaves unanswered, still, the reason for the phenomenal long-term success of the Irish in politics. One explanation, of course, is that they got into politics before any of the other ethnic groups and, having mastered the art, were happy to stay with it. But the luck of the Irish would have dimmed without exceptional political talent. A clue to what that is came to me in an interview with 75-year-old Harry F. Curvin, who "retired" to the chairmanship of the state board of elections in 1964 after a quarter century as the speaker of the Rhode Island house. I asked this patriarch to explain the secret of his success in remaining the presiding officer of a state legislative body longer than any other person in American history. Curvin replied with generalities on approach and specifics on tactics:

I was always an uncompromising Democrat. That was my politics, all the way. I played fair and honest with the Republicans, my opponents, but never gave them any of the best of it—couldn't, wouldn't, and didn't think they were entitled to it.
I made a practice of trying to study human nature, especially in my own party. I observed the new members, and I could distinguish the wheat from the chaff. I was a bit selfish, and when I became speaker I amended the rules so that the speaker, rather than the membership of each committee, would appoint the chairman and vice chairman. We were in session 30 days before I appointed committees. I didn't want any clinkers on important committees.

Curvin went on to explain how he withheld any worthwhile committee assignments from new members who associated with his opponents—"a half dozen disgruntled guys, all cliqued together, who sat down in the rear of the chamber" and tried to convince new legislators not to be "rubber stamps." Starved for important committee work or patronage, the smarter fellows, Curvin said, would eventually come to him on bended knee. After appropriate apprenticeship, they would be admitted to his team and receive their rewards.

The heart of Curvin's explanation of success came, however, in a story he told of how he became speaker by outfoxing, outpoliticking, and physically threatening James H. Kiernan, a nimble-witted operator and master of political invective who had been a state legislator since 1915 and majority leader with brief interruptions since 1935. Kiernan would later serve as majority leader again for practically the whole 25 years Curvin was speaker. Curvin's words:

No one ever had a more loyal friend, no people were ever more closely knitted together than the majority leader (Kiernan) and myself—after we both aspired for the office of speaker in 1940.

The background was that in 1936, Kiernan had engineered the defeat of the then-speaker, Edward Flynn. He did it by secretly sewing up the support of the 11 Italo-Americans in the house, by promising them choice committee assignments and other patronage.

(Kiernan, Curvin explained, became speaker in 1937–38, but lost the post when the Republicans took control of the house in 1939–40. Curvin himself was Democratic leader of the house during those four years, so that after the Democrats regained control in the 1940 elections, the question was who would then become speaker.)

Right after the 1940 election, Jim Kiernan and I met at a funeral. Kiernan said to me—he always referred to me as a kid, an upstart—"Kid, I understand you're going to run against me for speaker."

I said—friendly as the flowers in May—"That's a funny thing, Jim, fellows are telling me you're running against me for speaker. Who's running against you?"

He said: "Why don't you remain as [Democratic] leader?"

My reply was: "I don't want to be leader if you're speaker. And don't you try to do with me, Jim, what you did with Ed Flynn. If I catch you making one commitment . . . I don't intend to make any commitments. If I can win it clean, I'm going to make it. If I catch you making any commitments for a choice committee appointment, a major piece of patronage, or anything, Jim, it will be a real dogfight. Flynn, he took it like a gentleman. Me, I was born and brought up in an area where you had to fight your way up all the time. And Jim, when I talk this way, I mean it. One of us will wind up in a morgue or a hospital. Don't pull it on me."

Kiernan then made a canvass, and found out he'd lose. So he called me the next week and said: "How would you like me to nominate you for speaker?" I replied: "I would like that very much."

Then Kiernan asked: "If I support you for speaker, can I be [majority] leader?"

I replied: "Positively." I didn't care. I was conceited enough to think I'd be the speaker, the leader, and the whole ballgame.

But, I asked Curvin, hadn't he been obliged himself to make commitments to get the support he needed from the Democratic members? This question triggered an emotional response as the old man, now white haired but still powerful of voice, threw his arms up into the air and exclaimed: "No, not a commitment, as God is my judge. It's over now, and I swear I made no commitments. I'd been Democratic leader for four years. I had good people working for me. I never broke my word to any of them."

And how did he and Kiernan get along together for the next 25 years? "He was a good guy, and we got along beautifully."

One didn't need to read *The Last Hurrah*, I concluded, to understand the genius of the Irish politician.

Rhode Islanders in Washington

Rhode Island's political and social development since the late 19th century is nicely capsulated in the careers of four men it has sent to the United States Senate—Nelson W. Aldrich, Theodore Francis Green, John Pastore, and Claiborne Pell.*

Aldrich was the personification of the old Republican machine, a master operator in the use of political power for private gain. The influence over the entire nation which he exercised from a Senate seat is scarcely imaginable in our day, when the executive has so overshadowed the legislative branch. (A member of that executive at this writing, of course, is Vice President Nelson Aldrich Rockefeller, the old Senator's grandson, no mean purveyor of power himself. The line of descent was through, Aldrich's daughter, Abby, who married John D. Rockefeller, Jr., in 1901.)

Nelson Aldrich sat in the United States Senate for 30 years, beginning in 1881. A quarter century into that long career, when Aldrich's power was at its zenith, the great muckraker Lincoln Steffens described his role for *McClure's Magazine* (issue of February 1905):

> The United States Senate is coming more and more to be the actual head of the United States government. In the Senate there is a small ring (called the Steering Committee) which is coming more and more to be the head of the United States Senate. The head of this committee is Senator Nelson W. Aldrich, who has been described as "the boss of the United States," "the power behind the power behind the throne," "the general manager of the United States." . . .
>
> Everybody knows that Senator Aldrich, a very rich man and father-in-law of young Mr. Rockefeller, is supposed to represent "Sugar," "Standard Oil," "New York," and, more broadly, "Wall Street." [He is] our leading legislative authority on protective tariff, he speaks for privileged business; the chairman of the Senate Finance Committee, he speaks for high finance. . . .
>
> We have in Senator Aldrich the commercial ideal of political character and— if not the head—at least the political representative of the head of that System which is coming more and more to take the place of the passing paper government of the United States.

Steffens went on to document Aldrich's close political and business ties to General Charles R. Brayton and the other corrupt figures of Rhode Island Republicanism in those years. It was in this era of such gross misuse of the public trust that the necessity of some kind of "revolution" in Rhode Island became apparent. And it came, as we have previously noted, with the near *coup d'état* engineered by Theodore Francis Green and his ethnic-labor allies in the early 1930s.

The parallel development on the national scene, of course, was the advent of the New Deal, the beginning of the end of "congressional govern-

---

* Fewer of the House members have made much of an imprint on the national scene, though mention should be made of two who contributed significantly in the health field—John E. Fogarty as the Appropriations subcommittee chairman who was instrumental (along with Alabama's Senator Lister Hill) in the fantastic growth of the National Institutes of Health, and Aime J. Forand, the man who first introduced Medicare legislation in Congress.

ment." It was a greatly subdued U.S. Senate which Green entered in 1937; in any event he was already 69 years of age and past his rebelling prime. He would remain in the Senate until 1961, becoming, at 93, the oldest man ever to serve in Congress.* Green did, in fact, overstay his time in the Senate. Rhode Island respected him as a "grand old man" of its politics, but he was already losing his grip on affairs by the time he ran for his last term in 1954. His Senate staff fronted for him so well that it was said that if Green died, they could have put his body in a closet and everything would have gone on normally. The workings of the seniority system elevated Green to chairman-ship of the Foreign Relations Committee in those years, but Majority Leader Lyndon Johnson eventually persuaded him to become "chairman emeritus" so that a younger and more alert William Fulbright could take over in his stead.

John O. Pastore and Claiborne Pell, Rhode Island's two Senators of recent years, are alike in being "liberal" Democrats. Aside from that, they have been studies in contrast.

Pastore grew up in a $20-a-month tenement in Providence; his father, an immigrant Italian tailor, died when Pastore was eight, and his mother went to work as a seamstress to support him and his three brothers and two sisters. Though Brown University was convenient, regular college was out of the question for a son of this poor family. So Pastore clerked days for an electric power company and attended night classes in the local branch of Northeastern University. He received his law degree in 1931.

Pell, by contrast, was born into an elite family. His father was elected to Congress the year young Claiborne was born, and later held high political posts in New York before becoming U.S. Minister to Portugal and then Hungary. Pell's wife, from the city of Newport, is the niece of A & P heir Huntington Hartford. As he told an interviewer in 1972, he felt himself "fortunate in being able to pursue a public service career" without the necessity of worrying about making a living. His secondary education was at St. George's, a Rhode Island school for the socially prominent, followed by Princeton (cum laude 1940) and a master's degree in international administration at Columbia (1946). For seven years he was in the U.S. Foreign Service, and he participated in the 1945 conference in San Francisco at which the United Nations was founded.

Pastore found it tough to make a living as a lawyer in Providence of the early 1930s, so he turned to politics. A local ward politician, Tommy Testa, helped him win election to the legislature; after three years there, he became a fifth and then third assistant to the state attorney general, making a name for himself by prosecuting a big murder case. By a stroke of good luck, he decided to run for the lieutenant governorship in 1944 (when the post, re-served in those days for Italian-Americans, was only part-time, with a $2,500-a-year salary). Soon after Pastore won the office, Governor J. Howard

* Green died five years after his retirement, at age 98. His friends recall affectionately how he played tennis and wrestled until his eighties, and walked two miles to his Senate office up to the day he left Washington. To his credit, the old man had the foresight to advocate U.S. recognition of Communist China 20 years before it became a reality.

McGrath left to become U.S. Solicitor General, and a still little-known John Pastore was suddenly chief executive of the state. In 1946 and again in 1948 he was overwhelmingly reelected. As Sam Lubell wrote in those years, "Pastore hit the 20-to-1 jackpot in time to synchronize with the arrival at voting age of the heavy Italian-American economic power as a result of the wartime boom." In 1946, the story is told, Dennis Roberts, then mayor of Providence, sent a delegation to Pastore telling him he should not think of running for a full term on his own, since it wasn't yet time for an Italian-American governor. According to a reporter who listened through a keyhole, Pastore replied: "This is one Wop who's going to run!" He took care, however, not to show favoritism to Italian-Americans when he was in the State House, and in 1950 he won election to the U.S. Senate.

Pell dabbled in Rhode Island politics, without any elective offices, until 1960, serving simultaneously as a limited partner in the banking firm of Auchincloss, Parker, and Redpath. His 1960 nomination for the Senate in the Democratic party was a stunning surprise, because he carried 61 percent of the vote against two seasoned Irish politicians who had served as governor—Dennis Roberts and J. Howard McGrath. Roberts, however, had been discredited politically by the controversial disenfranchisement of absentee ballots that permitted his reelection over Christopher Del Sesto four years previously. And McGrath, serving as U.S. Attorney General, had been fired by President Truman following a series of tax scandals involving one of his subordinates, T. Lamar Caudle.* Pell came on as a fresh face; personal wealth permitted him to run a lavish campaign; moreover, he proved no slouch at ethnic politics, since he had learned fluent Portuguese while his father was in the diplomatic service there, and could also converse easily with Italian-American and French-Canadian voters in their own language.

By character, Pastore is cocky and incredibly energetic, a man of slight stature (five feet, four inches) and fearsome oratorical skills, called by some "The Mouse that Roars." Though a master of parliamentary tactics and a party regular who has been the floor manager for many pieces of major legislation, he was defeated when he ran for Democratic Whip in 1965. E. W. Kenworthy of the New York *Times* observed that Pastore's "caustic tongue" may have operated against him: "When his exasperation reaches flash point, he will leave his [Senate] seat, stride aggressively up to the offender, thrust his beak under his chin and wither his opponent with shouted scorn. As the opponent tries to stammer a reply, Mr. Pastore whirls on his feet, throws his arms up in despair of such folly and stalks back to his seat."

Pell, on the other hand, is courtly, soft-spoken, an almost invisible member of the Senate who eschews publicity. "I was a diplomat for seven years," he explained to the Ralph Nader Congress Project interviewers in 1972. "I remember the old rule of diplomacy which is 'always let the other person have your way.' You can't approach an idea frontally. I go up and down the

* In fairness to McGrath it should be pointed out that he had taken over the Justice Department from Tom Clark, inheriting the problems which Clark left behind and which led to McGrath's downfall. In 1948 he had served as Democratic National Chairman and was one of the few party higher-ups who believed Truman could defeat Thomas E. Dewey.

halls trying to explain my ideas to others. I've done most of my work quietly."

Both Senators have been sometimes effective legislators, but again in quite different ways. Through his long seniority, Pastore gained positions of major influence: chairman of the Communications Subcommittee of the Commerce Committee (and thus the key man to see or influence on matters regarding the Federal Communications Commission, which regulates television and radio licenses); chairman, in alternating years, of the Joint Committee on Atomic Energy; and chairman of the Appropriations subcommittees dealing with Housing and Urban Development and Space and Science. Despite his many liberal votes, critics sometimes said he was too close to the interests of private businesses. In 1969, he stirred up a hornet's nest of protest when he sponsored a bill that would have made it virtually impossible to take broadcasting licenses away from television station owners, no matter how miserable their programming, and thus their use of the public's airwaves, may be. He has been, however, a friend of public television and was the chief sponsor of the legislation to limit campaign media spending which went into effect in 1972.

Pell's most important committee post is Foreign Relations, in which he quietly but firmly opposed the Vietnam war from 1966 onwards. Typically, Pell takes on an issue long before it has risen to much public notice, and then works on it, year after year, until he succeeds. He was the person really responsible for a treaty among 85 nations to ban placing "nuclear and other weapons of mass destruction" on the ocean floor. He sponsored the bill to set up the National Foundation on the Arts and Humanities, which provides millions of dollars of grants to artists and writers—a first in American history. He was the first Senator to take a deep interest in rapid rail transportation in the Northeast corridor, introducing an eight-state authority to operate rail service there as early as 1962, and later the successful bill to fund the New York-Washington metroliner and New York-Boston turbotrain projects. He introduced successful legislation to encourage research and training in the marine sciences, with important facilities in Rhode Island. And several major college aid measures, including a landmark 1972 bill to enable young people to obtain aid to go to college, with the money funneled directly to them rather than through the universities, originated with Pell.

John Pastore emerged as the prototype of the reactive politician, the liberal-labor Democrat who made his peace with big business, a man who always saw his opportunities and moved with vigor to seize them. One could fault him for blind spots about his role, or that of Congress as a whole; for instance, he opposed a proposal to give Congress the right to reply to presidential telecasts by noting: "If you give Congress the right to reply to the President, you may have to give everybody else the right to reply to the President—and to Congress, too." (This, Pastore evidently thought, was too great a disturbance of the system of presidential superiority so widely accepted before the ultimate excesses under the Nixon regime came to light.) No faults of vision, however, can detract from the fact that Pastore was one of the most successful Italian-Americans ever to emerge on the American political stage. Had he not chosen to retire voluntarily with the close of the 94th Congress (in January 1977), it seems inconceivable that Rhode Island voters would not have returned him to Washington as long as he wished.*

Claiborne Pell, by contrast, is living proof that the federal system remains flexible enough to permit important and innovative reforms, in both domestic and foreign policy, to originate in Congress rather than the executive branch alone. A few Senators and Representatives of his farsightedness are the leavening that prevents the worst ossification in official Washington. It remains a wonder that the voters of Rhode Island's ethnic-cultural mix permit Pell to remain in the Senate. Political circumstance has a lot to do with this, of course; after his first win, Pell tended his home state political garden with an active Providence office and spread money around to local party committees in years he wasn't running himself. Then he could benefit from the Democratic custom of almost always endorsing incumbents for reelection.

Nevertheless, if ethnic politics in Rhode Island were as brutal as an outsider might assume, some Irishman or Italian might have risen up to upset Pell in his own party. Pell's continued political success does suggest that in Rhode Island, as in so many states, the American voters are not predictable automatons based on their social and economic backgrounds. They do *think* —not always, but often enough, to make both Rhode Island's "lively experiment," and that of the United States as a whole, a viable one.

State Government: Missed Opportunities

The State of Rhode Island and Providence Plantations provides a quite average government, reflecting the nature of a heavily Democratic-ethnic-labor-dominated state of narrow geographic confines. Overall taxes are almost precisely at the national average, but somewhat heavier on businesses than on individuals; the amount spent on schools and universities is just below the rest of the nation, on a per capita basis; welfare expenditures are quite high; outlays for highways are understandably the lowest in the nation.

In the early 1970s the Midwest Research Institute undertook a complex rating of state and local governments on such measures as the professionalism and overall performance of administration. Rhode Island came out slightly behind the national average with a grade of "B," somewhat inferior to neighboring Connecticut and much worse than Massachusetts (a finding to

* Pastore's 1970 Republican opponent, whom he trounced with 68 percent of the vote, was the Rev. John McLaughlin, a Jesuit priest who had been raised in a traditional Democratic Providence household. Pastore was enraged by being challenged by a priest in full clerical regalia; as he said in declining face-to-face encounters with McLaughlin, "How can I debate with a man my religion teaches me to call father?"

After his defeat, McLaughlin was hired as a speechwriter in the Nixon White House, where he eventually went to absurd lengths in defending Nixon's role in the Watergate cover-up. (Justifying the presidential profanity revealed by the Nixon tapes, for instance, McLaughlin said it was a justifiable "form of release, almost therapy.") The Very Rev. Richard T. Cleary, New England provincial of the Jesuits and McLaughlin, publicly disassociated the order from McLaughlin's defense of Nixon. McLaughlin's interesting rejoinder was to tell a reporter: Father Cleary "is at the geopolitical center of liberal thinking, isn't he? That's Massachusetts, the only state out of step with the rest of the country."

which Rhode Islanders take violent exception because of their low view of government in Massachusetts).

The historical record shows that Governor Green, taking over a badly outmoded state government in the early 1930s, was able to make the governor the real chief executive of the state by solidifying the various state agencies into 11 broadly defined departments directly responsible to him— rather than to the legislature, which had run the state before through more than four-score boards and commissions. Green was limited by the highly political environment of Depression times, however. Vast numbers of people depended for their livelihood on some type of political job and department heads were chosen because they were "damned good Democrats." This began to change some when civil service was instituted by Republican Governor William Vanderbilt on the eve of World War II. By the 1950s, with the Depression past and people earning good incomes, the climate was ripe for even more reorganization, including consolidation of financial controls, tighter overall administrative supervision from the governor's office, and the institution of home rule.

With fits and starts, the process of professionalizing Rhode Island government had continued down to the 1970s. After Roberts, the best governor was probably John Chafee in the 1960s; his appointments were of especially high quality. Governor Noel, first elected in 1972, brought (as we will discuss later) the first professionalism to the economic development area. But still, the problem of obtaining the very best people to head a broad range of state agencies and departments remains. As Roberts told me, "You can't hire enough good professionals. Who the hell wants to come to Rhode Island?"

Rhode Island has failed to capitalize on its unique compactness by becoming a city state in fact. Though its total population (927,000) is only that of a good-sized urban center, it insists on maintaining 39 cities and towns with complete governments.* There are no county governments to serve as hindrances to efficient administration, but still there is the confusion —and cost—of so many governments in a geographically limited space. Only in very limited areas has consolidation even been attempted, the most notable of which may be the statewide solid waste management corporation, similar to Connecticut's, approved by the legislature in 1974. That is just one example, of course, of how a state-municipality consolidation could improve the quality of services, save Rhode Islanders many tax dollars, and provide a valuable experiment in the American federal system. The best-run metropolitan area governments in the U.S. (such as Nashville and Jacksonville) could be looked to for models of simplified governmental structure. And then, to assure efficiency and citizen voice at the local level, administrative districts could be drawn up with local coordinating committees of major government departments and citizen advisory groups.

Nothing like this has ever been seriously proposed for Rhode Island, however, and the state has had the most serious problems in even changing

---

* The population of Rhode Island actually dropped by 2.4 percent from 950,000 to 927,000 between 1970 and 1975.

its state constitution to conform to the realities of modern times. During the 1960s, for instance, a constitutional convention droned on for almost five years—an all-time endurance record in U.S. history. Its final document was resoundingly defeated by the voters. In 1973, by a razor-thin margin, the voters approved calling another convention; its only really important recommendations were to require campaign finance disclosures of candidates, permit state lotteries, extend the terms of major state officials from two to four years, and increase the pay of state legislators from an incredibly low $300 a year (in effect since 1900) to $2,000. The voters approved the lottery provision (which the legislature rushed to implement). And they voted for the campaign finance article (which the legislature, after prolonged in-fighting, watered down so much that most candidates for lower offices would not have to report at all).* But the voters refused to increase statewide officials' terms to four years, remaining in a lonely minority among the states on that score; moreover, for the seventh time in 13 years, they refused the legislative pay hike, leaving the salary at the lowest amount of any state except for New Hampshire (where it is $200).

For years organized labor † has had more power in the legislature than practically anywhere else in the country, even Michigan. The AFL-CIO's historic close ties to the Democrats, and to Democratic governors, are the principal reasons for this. Moreover, labor has been able to put many of its leaders into key positions. Back in the 1950s the president of the state AFL (prior to merger with the CIO) was director of the state labor department, while Frank Sgambato, a textile workers' vice president, was chairman of the state senate labor committee. Sgambato subsequently became senate majority leader from the mid-1960s to 1973, while the Rubber Workers' John J. Skiffington became house majority leader in 1969, a position he still held in the mid-1970s. Bill Castro, a member of the bus drivers' union, was chairman of the senate labor committee and J. Howard Duffy, a field representative for the State, County, and Municipal Workers, was chairman of the house labor committee. The net result of all this is that Rhode Island laws are more friendly to labor than those of almost any state; alone with New

---

* Rhode Island had previously had no corrupt practices or campaign spending law. The legislation finally written in 1974 exempted from reporting all candidates spending less than $5,000. Thus statewide and major city mayoralty candidates were the only ones seriously affected.

† The biggest unions in the mid-1970s: Steelworkers (about 7,000 members in the state); Machinists (4,500); State, County, and Municipal Workers (6,000); Electrical Workers (6,000); Rubber Workers (2,500); building trades (7,500, split into several unions); schoolteachers (5,000); and Meat Cutters (2,100). There are only 4,000 members of the Textile Workers left—down from a peak of 20,000 in the 1930s and early '40s. The state AFL and CIO were merged in 1958, three years after the national bodies; "once merged," according to secretary-treasurer Edwin Brown, "we achieved the best amalgamation of any of the states."

At Brown's instigation, the Rhode Island AFL-CIO in 1971 launched a Health Maintenance Organization providing comprehensive medical care for $50 per family per month. Prudential Insurance eventually stepped in with major funding and management skill, but the HMO—the first and only one in the state—was able to grow only slowly (to 14,000 members in 1974) in view of the active opposition of the Medical Society, most of the hospitals, and Blue Cross-Blue Shield. "It's a helluva formidable opposition," Brown said, "but in my judgment the HMO is the greatest way of delivering health care and it's the next step to prevent a socialized medical program." The HMO is proof that the Rhode Island AFL-CIO, despite its reputation as a bread-and-butter labor movement, has the capacity to raise its sights to broader social objectives.

York, for instance, Rhode Island has a law permitting workers out on strike to draw unemployment compensation benefits—from a fund set up by taxes on their employers in the first instance! Another Rhode Island law permits retirees, simply by announcing they are seeking work and can't get it, to draw on the unemployment compensation fund.

Some of the more thoughtful labor leaders, in fact, believe that the union movement may use the legislature too heavily—trying to get by legislation what they should be bargaining for. Using as an example 1973 legislation stipulating that no worker could be required, even on overtime, to work more than 54 hours a week, AFL-CIO secretary-treasurer Edwin Brown said he didn't "care to have the legislature accomplish for the unorganized workers what the unions are accomplishing for the organized workers." The legislature, he said, should set some minimum standards for working conditions but stop there. "We bargain enough for the unorganized workers as it is, on unemployment and workmen's compensation, wage collections, and the like," Brown said. For all of organized labor's success in the legislative halls, the fact is that only 27 percent of the Rhode Island work force is unionized— no more than the national average.

Seeking to counteract labor's influence in the legislature are the normal array of business lobbies—chambers of commerce, the utilities, banks, and insurance interests. Rarely can they defeat labor in a head-on clash, but as in all states there are broad areas of wheeling and dealing and special arrangements. Traditionally, the most venal lobby was that of the racetracks. In his 1959 book on New England politics, Duane Lockard observed that many legislators—including the veteran house majority leader, James Kiernan— were on the payroll of the racetracks as attorneys or clerks at betting windows. Legislators and paid legislative staff were often observed working at the tracks, even when officially recorded as "present" at the State House. With the decline of citizen interest in horse racing in recent years, the racetracks have become less influential. But the state lottery, enacted in 1974, opened up the prospect for a new era of official hanky-panky.

The overall level of malfeasance in Rhode Island government does appear to have abated since the 1950s, when Lockard observed widespread frauds in elections and "a sordid picture" of bribery and corruption in regular state business. Rising levels of education and voter sophistication are probably the chief reason for the improvement. Later generations of immigrant families are not as desperate for patronage crumbs as their fathers, and are thus not as tolerant of corruption. The Yankees, deprived of effective political power, no longer look to state government as an object of manipulation for personal gain. (The last bastion of Yankee power evaporated when the state senate was reapportioned along straight population lines in the 1960s.)

Some observers complain that gross corruption is still present but hidden from public view because of the lethargy of the press (although the Providence *Journal* and *Bulletin* occasionally set up teams of investigative reporters). The smallness of Rhode Island is often named as a reason for little corruption in recent years; I heard such comments as "everyone is looking through the other fellow's window," and "outright graft here is like stealing from your neighbors." Former Governor Roberts pointed to the tight fiscal controls on state and local government enacted under his administration and still on the books. Correspondent John Hackett observed that "the pickings are so thin—the penalties are the same as for stealing millions in New York, so that the potential offenders feel the stakes are too high for any possible gain."

The apparent waning of outright corruption does not mean that the old political patronage system is dead in Rhode Island. Civil service notwithstanding, connections and favoritism play a big role in hiring for state government. And the city of Providence is an exquisite museum piece of the patronage system as it functioned in an earlier day across this country.

A final word needs to be said about the sad state of representative government in Rhode Island. The bright spot is that the days are now gone when the governor was virtually powerless at the hands of a totally dominant legislature. Governor Green's "bloodless revolution" put much more power in the hands of the executive, as did Roberts' administrative reforms and the fall of small-town, Republican control in the senate. John Chafee said that as governor he felt he had all the power he really needed, with no boards or commissions or governor's council (on the model of several other New England states) to limit his authority.

One legacy of the past remains, however: individual legislators' subservience to their leadership. "The legislative leaders in both houses," Duane Lockard noted in the 1950s, "are respected, feared, and followed by the membership." (Former Speaker Harry Curvin told me that was a very apt description.) To this day, it is said that "whatever the speaker wants, the speaker gets." The senate has generally not been as disciplined, but the man who became majority leader in 1973, former Providence fireman John Hawkins, began to exercise authority like the house speakers. All of this makes for perhaps the most undemocratic legislature in the country.

Rhode Island, until 1975, was the only state in which both houses' committee hearings could be and frequently were closed to everyone except the witness presenting testimony. (The Virginia senate has a similar provision; otherwise all hearings in all states are customarily open.) Moreover, Rhode Island shared the distinction with Mississippi of keeping *all* committee deliberations and all final votes secret from the public. Until 1974, party caucuses were also closed, and especially in the house there were few recorded votes—"no Democrat wants to argue with the speaker," one heard. In 1974 Governor Noel ventured into this quagmire by suggesting that a "new openness" in the legislature would help to dispel widespread cynicism resulting from national scandals. The legislative leaders responded initially by saying that open meetings might impede progress; they would, the house majority leader alleged, attract "cranks" who would interfere with committee business.

Apparently some of the public displeasure about all the secrecy was getting to the controlling Democrats in the legislature, however, because in 1975 the Democrats in both chambers followed their leaders' suggestions to open their committee sessions to public attendance and scrutiny. A new electronic voting system in the house also resulted in many more publicly recorded votes.

I asked Victor Profughi to assess the legislature. "The quality of legislative output is very good—much better than we have a right to expect given the lack of staff, low pay, and poor facilities," he said. Is the legislature effective? I asked. "Sure, it's effective in passing what the leadership wants."

A Problematic Economy

Rhode Island has a colorful economic history, reaching back to the first two centuries in which she was a great seafaring and shipbuilding state, deeply involved in the slave and molasses and China trade and the legendary time of the great whale catches. Sailing ship wealth helped to capitalize early factories, however, and Rhode Island was to become and remain the most heavily industrialized state of the Union. (One reason for this, of course, was that there was so little space for agriculture. There has been farming since the colony's start, and the history books tell of great estates owned by a landed aristocracy, using slave labor, in pre-Revolutionary times. But agriculture has been a subsidiary factor for two centuries now, yielding, at latest report, a negligible $20 million a year—less than any state except Alaska. The catch of Rhode Island fisheries, chiefly in lobster, clams, and flounder, is only $15 million a year.)

With some justification, Rhode Island claims to be the birthplace of the American factory system. And it was at Pawtucket in 1790 that Samuel Slater —financed by Moses Brown of the famous Rhode Island merchant family —reproduced the Arkwright machines of England, starting the young country's first mechanized cotton mill. Within 25 years of Slater's coming, according to one account, Rhode Island mills were turning out more than 27 million yards of cloth a year and providing jobs for 26,000 operatives (including many child laborers). Together with cotton milling, the woolen and worsted industry flourished in 19th- and early 20th-century Rhode Island. Until the 1940s, when the exodus of mills to the South hit its peak, spinning and weaving was the dominant industry of Rhode Island. It was also the state's Achilles heel, because the ethnic stock workers were paid appallingly low wages; the image of the old textile industry, as one labor leader described it to me, was of dim 25-watt lighting and creaking old elevators in rambling, often decrepit mill buildings. In the 1920s, 90,000 men and women—three-fifths of the Rhode Island factory employment—were in textiles; in the last few years, the total has been scarcely 18,000. This remnant work in small, specialized plants and turn out synthetics and over half the United States' production of lace.

A century before textiles, Rhode Island made a start with the casting and fashioning of metals; from a first forge near the Pawtucket Falls in 1671, the industry grew so successfully that at the start of the Revolution,

Rhode Island led all other colonies in iron and steel production. Growing in part by virtue of textile plant instruments, the iron foundries and metal-working shops grew through the 19th century. One of the most famous of these, Brown and Sharpe Manufacturing Company, was founded in 1833 and today has a 16-acre machine-tool factory in North Kingston which it calls "Precision Park." The firm's product line ranges from metal tools to delicate micrometers. Altogether, some third of the state's factory workers are employed in metals, machinery, and electrical equipment manufacture.

A close cousin is the jewelry and silverware making business, which dates back to 1794. Rhode Island calls itself "the costume jewelry center of the world," and since 1880 no state has had as many jewelry workers (some 20,000 by latest count). The great bulk of these are in the Providence area, where one out of three workers is said to be directly or indirectly involved. There are some large firms, including Gorham (the world's largest producer of sterling silver products), Speidel, Coro, and Trifari. But mostly the field is atomized into small plants; there are 795 in the state, in fact.

Rhode Island has a smattering of powerful national corporations and aggressive financial institutions operating within its borders. Raytheon, for instance, manufactures oceanographic hardware there, North American Philips turns out electro-optical devices, and the state hopes to capitalize on its "Ocean State" history and potential through an oceanographic research industrial park adjacent to the University of Rhode Island's Graduate School of Oceanography on the Bay. The Industrial National Bank of Providence, which holds about 55 percent of the state's banking assets, began in the late 1960s through its holding company to acquire major consumer loan and mortgage banking operations across the U.S. Providence is also the headquarters of a major U.S. conglomerate, Textron, Inc., which through careful acquisitions of thirty-plus relatively small but successful firms in their own fields,* had by the early '70s reached $1.7 billion in total annual sales. This success was due largely to the managerial skill of G. William Miller, who took over Textron at age 35 in 1960.

The high finance schemes of Industrial National or Textron may not be of much importance to the average Rhode Islander—though the state would dearly love some more headquarters of major firms because of the high-income employment those central offices furnish. What *is* of pressing concern to the state's citizens is what can be done to modernize and improve the industrial mix and to diversify the economy in general. During the late 1960s, when factory jobs in the state hit an all-time high of 127,000 and unemployment, for the first time since the postwar textile exodus, dipped below 4 percent, Rhode Island economic leaders were boasting that the state had licked its essential economic problems. A serious decline began in 1970, however, with unemployment back to more than 6 percent and factory jobs off by several thousand (especially in defense-related industries).

This situation prompted some soul-searching, starting with a Providence

* Examples: Bostitch in stapling devices, Homelite in chain saws, Speidel in watchbands, Talon in zippers.

Journal-Bulletin article headlined: "What's Wrong with Rhode Island Today
—An Economy Misdirected and Lacking Leadership." Business groups, with
some labor participation, then formed a "Project Rhode Island" to identify
the problems and suggest solutions. A study commissioned by this group,
written by Harvard economics professor Robert A. Howell, destroyed any
remaining complacency. Howell noted that the average grade completion for
Rhode Islanders was 11th from the bottom in the country (leading only
the Southern agricultural states). His report said Rhode Island exhibited
many of the characteristics of a "secondary labor market" in which "workers
tend to display a high degree of casualness toward full-time, long-term employment," where "marginal" firms pay low wages in inefficient facilities, and
in which "unemployment compensation, public assistance, and other forms
of supplemental income substitute for regular employment."

The Howell report also noted that the average factory wage in Rhode
Island was 20 percent below the national average, and had been declining
steadily, in relation to the rest of the country, since 1947. (Not since the
1870s, in fact, have average manufacturing wages in Rhode Island matched
the national average.) The average manufacturing firm, it was noted, had
only 40 employees, and many of these were privately held companies with
unambitious management. As opposed to the official 6.7 percent unemployment rate of 1972, the report said, a realistic level of unemployment plus
underemployment would be 12.5 percent to 15 percent of the work force.
Several reasons for the state's "weak economy" were listed: low-skilled labor
force, shortage of industrial sites, lack of tax and financial incentives, ineffective development efforts, and poor image and attitudes.

Predictably, "Project Rhode Island" listed "upgrading the labor force,"
including ongoing vocational training programs and special programs aimed
at the needs of individual companies. "Land use planning," with special attention to the fishing and recreational resources of Narragansett Bay, was
listed. A long list of tax reforms to encourage business, including elimination
of the sales tax on machinery and electrical equipment and abolition of the
corporate excess tax, were proposed. (Rhode Island's corporate income tax
of 8 percent does place it two to three percentage points above most other
states.) The group also recommended that Rhode Island repeal its laws allowing payment of unemployment compensation to strikers and retirees.

In fact, labor-related legislation is probably the strongest point of real
disagreement between Rhode Island Democrats and their labor friends on
one side, and the state's Republicans on the other. Former Governor Chafee
went to some length in an interview to blame Rhode Island's poor economic
performance on features in state law that discourage businesses, especially
ultraliberal unemployment compensation benefits. "The Democratic governors and legislature and their labor allies have reduced the state to a weekly
wage that's far below the U.S. average," he said. He also cited figures showing
Rhode Island's per capita income, in relation to both the rest of the United
and New England, had slipped rather seriously over the past generation. Referring to Tony Policastro, president of the Rhode Island AFL-CIO, Chafee

said: "Look at that guy Policastro riding high—I'd say he's the strongest nonelected official next to the [Roman Catholic] bishop in this state. And this is what his policies have done."

The Democrats take quite an opposite view, of course, claiming the state's labor laws have little to do with its economic problems. They also tend to be fiercely defensive of their ties to labor. Former Democratic Governor Dennis Roberts said he had used labor support to get job-producing legislation and "not to remove a tax from a banking institution that did a thousand stockholders some good." Warming up to the issue, Roberts went on to say: "Some people think labor has a horn on its head. Who the hell is labor? The poor guy who's got a family, who's contributing to the productivity of the economy, and is perhaps the most intelligent, skilled, moral citizen in the world. Why shouldn't he participate in government?"

(After such exchanges, the visitor to Rhode Island comes away feeling he is rehearing the battles of the '30s—from both sides.)

The "Project Rhode Island" report did make observations about the role of the governor in economic development that I have never heard quite so strongly stated: "The most important individual for a strong economy in Rhode Island is the governor. If he makes economic development the central thrust of his administration, works hard to make Rhode Island attractive to industry by both proposing legislation and utilizing key business executives to help him attract industry, and holds his department heads responsible for high performance, then Rhode Island stands a good chance of moving toward a strong economy."

This message apparently struck home with Philip W. Noel, the governor elected in 1972, who made economic development the central thrust of his administration. Noel did not buy the proposed law changes on unemployment compensation—that could have amounted to political suicide in his own Democratic party, of course. But he did take the unusual step for a labor-backed Democrat of supporting the tax breaks for industry, approved by the legislature in 1974.

(Noel, a powerfully-built, outspoken political figure with a keen sense of national as well as state issues, rose rapidly in national Democratic circles, winning selection as chairman of the Democratic Governors' Association for 1975–76 and chairman of the platform committee for the 1976 Democratic National Convention. His backers entertained hope he might one day end up on a national ticket. During the 1975 recession, however, Noel's own Democratic-controlled legislature rebuffed him on an austerity program, which included a 5 percent reduction in the work week and compensation of state employees. Instead, the legislators raised income, gas, and cigarette taxes.)

By the mid-1970s, in fact, it was clear that there was an entirely new attitude about business development in the state. What made this possible was an event that at first seemed to spell economic doom for Rhode Island— the great Naval pullout announced by the Defense Department in April 1973. Rhode Islanders had anticipated some cutback in Naval installations but were totally unprepared for the sweeping nature of the cut, to be accomplished within a single year. "State's Economy Sails Off with Navy," one newspaper headline read. At Quonset Point, the Naval Air Station and the Naval Air Rework Facility—the state's largest employer, with 3,600 workers—were closed down. The adjacent Davisville Seabee base, with about 600 civilian workers, was also phased down to a warehousing operation, with Seabee activities transferred to Gulfport, Mississippi (shades of Senator John Stennis) and Port Hueneme, California. On the other side of Narragansett Bay, the Atlantic Fleet Cruiser-Destroyer Force was moved out of Newport, causing that city and neighboring Middletown and Portsmouth to lose 40 percent of their jobs, 50 percent of their payrolls, and close to a third of their total population. Altogether the state lost 18,000 military personnel, who had had an annual payroll of $200 million, and 5,000 civilian jobs for the Navy, plus another 6,000 to 7,000 in secondary unemployment.* The effect could scarcely be underestimated on a state with a total payroll of less than $4 billion and only one metropolitan area and labor force to absorb the blow. Some observers likened the disaster to the now legendary hurricane of September 1938, which swept into the Bay with 135-mile-an-hour winds and two 30-foot tidal waves, taking 260 lives and causing $100 million in damages, in 1938 dollars. Others compared it to the great textile exodus of the 1940s. There was fear that the state unemployment rate of 6 percent could double—which indeed was a low guess, since it almost *trebled* in the 1975 recession.

Protest marches on Washington and bitter complaints by the congressional delegation failed to deter the Defense Department in making the announced cuts. But there were some in Rhode Island who saw a silver lining. Governor Noel said "it was unwise for the state to have been so heavily dependent on the military." Dennis Roberts, who had been governor at the height of the textile pullout, was even more direct: "Back then, the South was taking all our textiles, and silently we were happy they were doing it. The Navy moving out of here is the same—a bitter pill to swallow, but eventually a good thing. With the Navy, we were too dependent on the federal budget and a defensive war machine not really contributing to the economy of Rhode Island."

As it turned out, the Navy pullout was softened by rapid action, starting with the governor. Taking office only four months before the Naval move was announced, Noel had set up in his office a small "policy and program review team" of highly trained professionals. One of these was Glenn Kumekawa, a former University of Rhode Island academician in urban planning, who was made team leader of the recovery effort. Within two weeks a broad task force of government and private sector leaders had been assembled to

---

* All that was left was the Naval War College, the Officer Candidate School, and the Underwater Systems Center at Newport. (The Naval Academy Preparatory School was returned to Newport in 1974.) Some Rhode Islanders read dark political significance into the fact that the Newport fleet was transferred to bases in the South, including Newport, Virginia, and Mayport, Florida. They felt this reflected the Nixon administration's "Southern strategy" and antipathy for New England.

assess the impact and offer policy advice. An immediate priority was to short-circuit the usually laborious and drawn-out process of transfer of abandoned military facilities, so that they could be used for civilian employment. Noel and his recovery team then began a round-the-clock search for a single big employer that could take up a big part of the employment slack with well-paying, labor-intensive jobs. This effort met with success when the Electric Boat Division of General Dynamics Corporation, holder of the contract for the Trident submarine, agreed to transfer part of its submarine facilities from Groton, Connecticut, where it was cramped for space, to Quonset Point. The governor of Connecticut objected heatedly about this "hijacking of a major Connecticut employer," but by mid-1974 the deed was done and 2,000 Rhode Islanders had new jobs with Electric Boat.* This was made possible in part by a major state training program for welders, in which every trainee could be assured a job.

The recovery effort did not stop there, however. Noel and his staff were well aware that Rhode Island had a bad name in business circles as a labor-dominated state where political decisions harmed the industrial climate. So Noel, in Kumekawa's words, "moved to coalesce business and labor for the first time to hammer out an economic program to make Rhode Island as competitive as any eastern state in business taxes and the conditions of work." The new tax breaks for industry were one part of this effort; another was to upgrade the state's development effort from a branch of the governor's office to major status as a new department of economic development with a "strongman" director. Instead of filling that post with a standard Rhode Island politician, a national search was conducted to find a topnotch man; the person eventually selected was James O. Roberson, who was becoming bored with his job of recruiting new industries for the Denver Chamber of Commerce, and welcomed the challenge of revitalizing a mature economy "without the wild entrepreneurship you find in the West." The new department was put through the legislature with labor and management unified in support. The absence of a really strong environmental movement made this relatively easy; as Roberson told me, "in the Mountain or Western states, the environmentalists would have raised a great hue and cry."

Roberson's office won *de facto* control of a new Port Authority and Economic Development Corporation, which he said would exploit a great deal of the abandoned Naval facilities in a "Southern New England Technological Center." High-paying industries, including multinationals with European headquarters, would be solicited to set up new plants, Roberson said. The goal would be technologically oriented growth industries in such areas as ocean products, health products, electronics, and chemicals. Even steel mills could be constructed without harm to the Bay, he said, if they used electric furnaces. (There was also talk of an oil refinery; while it could also be constructed in an environmentally "clean" fashion, the state seemed less interested because not many jobs would be involved.)

---

* Already, some 3,000 Rhode Islanders crossed the Connecticut border daily for jobs at Electric Boat's Groton plant.

The economic development department also planned a major push to expand tourism. Rhode Island lacks sufficient "terminal" vacation complexes to draw large conventions and the like, but new money was pumped into a recreational building authority to make this possible. (Leonard J. Panaggio, chief of the tourist promotion division, said the state had never had a professional survey of its tourist business, variously estimated at between $18 million in 1950 and $100 million in 1973 from the many cottage colonies, marinas, camping grounds, and historic sites.)

Finally, Roberson said there was no reason that Rhode Island, with its location along the main stretch of the "Boswash" megalopolis, its supply of open fields and countryside, and its easy air access to Manhattan, could not in time become a corporate headquarters area to rival western Connecticut.

Many of these plans might well come to something. But Rhode Island's economic bootstrap operation could not stop the unemployment rate, by spring 1975, from rising to an alarming 16.2 percent. Nevertheless, it did seem certain that the Navy pullout had prompted Rhode Island to more serious thought and planning about its economic future than the formerly complacent state government and feuding camps of business and labor had ever contemplated before.

The City: Providence

The city of Providence, where Rhode Island began and the nexus of the state's successive stages as an agricultural, shipping, and industrial civilization, is New England's second largest urban center. But the city's 1970 population count, 179,213, was a long ways down from the peak of 253,504 recorded just before World War II. Seventeen percent of the city's people departed in the 1950s, another 14 percent in the '60s, populating sprawling suburbs which at latest count had 76 highway-oriented shopping centers.

The city today remains, the population drain notwithstanding, what the writers of the WPA Writers' Project described in the 1930s—"an agglomeration of contrasting and often antagonistic regions and influences."

There remains College Hill, where the four famous Brown brothers (John, Joseph, Nicholas, and Moses), along with other leading merchants made rich on the rum-slave-molasses trade, built their magnificent mansions, filled with art treasures from the far-flung world ports to which they dispatched their vessels. Much of College Hill was badly run down by the 1920s; then, however, came a renaissance sparked by the Providence Preservation Society, so that today on old Benefit Street and nearby streets more than 200 houses have been privately restored—a veritable outdoor museum of the American architectural heritage. Here one finds the John Brown House, which John Quincy Adams called "the most magnificent and elegant mansion I have seen on this continent." Here is the old State House (dating from 1792); the First Baptist Meetinghouse, near the spot where Roger Williams founded his church in 1638; the charming but more recent Fleurs de Lys studio (1886); Brown University's buildings; the Rhode Island School of Design—the list goes on and on.

Across an ugly slash of railroad tracks from College Hill is the glistening white State Capitol of 1900, mentioned previously in this chapter. Governor Chafee wanted to make an acropolis of the Capitol area and got Edward Durrell Stone to make a plan for it; a handsome building for the Rhode Island Health Department, in Stone's typical style, had been built there when Chafee showed me around it in 1974, but a lot of cheapish construction in the area remained to be cleared. Cheek-by-jowl with the Capitol is one of the great white elephants of American architecture—a fortress-like building put up by the Masons in the 1920s. The crash came before the interior could be finished, and it remains unfinished. There are sloping floors and other strange features, designed for Masonic services, and no one can figure how to convert the structure (which Governor McGrath bought for the state, thus capturing the Masonic vote) for office use. It would cost a prohibitive $500,000 just to tear the building down, so solidly is it built.

Providence's traditional "downtown" lies across the Providence River from College Hill and is separated by both the river and railroad tracks from the Capitol area. The city leaders have been sorely perplexed about the vitality of downtown, which lost two of its major department stores in 1973 alone. Westminster Street, the major shopping artery, was transformed from a traffic-filled street to a pleasing pedestrian mall in the 1960s in a partly vain effort to stop shoppers from driving out to the shiny new shopping centers. Two great new high-rise office buildings now dominate the skyline—the Rhode Island Hospital Trust Tower and Old Stone Bank, both constructed since 1970. A large luxury apartment complex, the Regency, has brought a lot of people back into downtown. A big new Civic Center was constructed for ice shows, basketball, and the like; it has been accounted a real success, except for the fact that $40,000 in ticket sales mysteriously disappeared during its first year of operation and the conviction of the center's executive director on charges of having solicited a $1,000 bribe from a rock show promoter. On the high culture circuit, the Rhode Island Philharmonic and the State Ballet of Rhode Island were joined in the mid-1960s by the excellent Trinity Square Repertory Company, one of the best of its kind in the U.S. The interior of the old Majestic Movie House was gutted for the repertory company, making two theaters out of the structure, one in the round. All of this activity has brought some life into the town at night, symbolized by a rash of new restaurants.

Downtown also has Kennedy Plaza (formerly Exchange Place), a central city square of quality abutting a handsome City Hall Park. Through urban renewal the litter of old flophouses and rundown movie theaters was cleared away in front of the Cathederal of St. Peter and St. Paul (the site of the first Roman Catholic church of Rhode Island, in 1838); the result is a beautiful plaza with European flavor.

Some of the best improvements, however, have been on the periphery of the old downtown (including the only new hotel of any size*); in between are bleak urban spaces. It may be that Providence simply lacks the "critical mass" of population, business, and cultural activity to make it a strong center city in the peculiar economic conditions of our time. Strong exception to that view, however, was taken by the Providence Foundation, an affiliate of the Greater Providence Chamber of Commerce, in an extensive market analysis of downtown Providence accompanied by a lengthy report on various options for the city's physical face by the year 1995. The report said center Providence was unlikely to regain the retail sales lost to suburban malls. But there was a real potential (and unmet need in existing facilities), the report said, in making downtown a vital convention, specialty-shop, and entertainment center.

To be sure, Providence has in the last 25 years cleared a great deal of land for urban renewal and added some impressive industrial parks. But the effort has been too weak, on the whole, and at the same time the city administration has let Providence's real strength—its ethnic neighborhoods —run downhill.

The worst eyesore of the city by the 1970s was the South Providence neighborhood, which until the 1940s had been the mainstay of the Irish and Jewish middle class. Then came urban renewal; a substantial number of blacks moved in, and City Hall stopped caring for the area.

"The creeping blight," Democratic city chairman Lawrence McGarry said, "is now into West Elmwood, East Elmwood, Smith Hill, Providence Park, and South Providence. The blight is spreading like any germ or disease. Not enough is done for the people, their homes and neighborhoods. There's a lack of playgrounds, or equipment for the playgrounds we have. We're not spending the kind of money we should to make this a city you'd be proud to live in. Because the truth is, if you went around Providence and looked, you wouldn't want to live here."

McGarry's words might be discounted in part, because he was backing a candidate against the incumbent mayor in a tight primary, and because he was frankly upset about the transformation he saw from "a predominantly Irish and Catholic city" to one with many blacks and Puerto Ricans. But the physical deterioration in the neighborhoods was clear to me as I drove about Providence.

Sad to say, much of the distinctive old flavor is going in the process. The Federal Hill area is an example. Heavily Italian in composition, it was described in the WPA Guide as offering

an Old World atmosphere, especially at night. Along the streets are carts piled high with fruits and vegetables. Indoors are displays of cheeses, meat and fish cured in the Italian manner, olive oil, a wide variety of typical farinaceous [starchy] products, and all manner of other foodstuffs pleasing to the Italian palate. Shrill cries, excited

---

* That hotel is—ugh—a Holiday Inn. But a new, large Marriott Hotel was also scheduled to open in 1975 in a new development area, Randall Square.

crowds, mingled odors and colors, to which occasionally arises the whine of a grind organ, render this gustatory paradise an exciting experience for those who enjoy the more vivid aspects of human activity.

Now, 40 years later, one drives through Federal Hill in the evening, and the streets are largely deserted. Remnants of the culture are still there, in excellent Italian restaurants, but countless sons and daughters of the Italian heritage have moved to the suburbs, or buy their food now in supermarkets like everyone else.

(Federal Hill, it should be added, has been considered by many the center of Mafia activity in New England, complete with a share of hoodlum executions. At this writing, however, the alleged Mafia leader, Raymond L. S. Patriarca, was in prison, and many of his cohorts were out of circulation.)

A word should be said about Providence's watery site and its port. The city is located on the Providence and Seekonk Rivers, which flow into and form the head of Narragansett Bay. This was traditionally Providence's "window to the world," and the history books are replete with romantic references to the era when tall-masted Indiamen and other ships crowded the harbor. The port remains one of fair importance, especially for oil tankers, but in recent years little has been done to refurbish the port or exploit its income potential. (This might change with the new state-run Port Authority and Economic Development Corporation.) One important improvement of recent years was the construction of a hurricane barrier across the Providence River, a sensible insurance against the disasters which befell the city in the Great Gale of 1815, which swept sailing ships on a great tide into the center of the old central city, and the hurricanes of 1938 and 1954, when Providence again wallowed in sea water.

Providence politics long resisted the change apparent in other phases of Providence life. Except for one two-year hiatus, the old Irish Democratic machine controlled the mayoralty continuously from 1912 to 1974. In all those years, there was never an Italian mayor, a fact which rankled not a little. Old-fashioned patronage was the bulwark of the Democrats' power. The city had no civil service system; in 1964 Joseph A. Doorley, Jr., running for his first term as mayor, promised to institute one, but in 10 years in office he never made good on his pledge. All this was buttressed, up to 1974, by the fact that Rhode Island law permitted officeholders to hit up their city and state workers for campaign contributions, allowed government employees to campaign for their bosses, and required no campaign spending or contribution reports from candidates.

The 1974 elections proved a watershed of sorts. The Democrats engaged in a bitter primary fight which opened the way for election of a Republican Italian-American, Vincent A. Cianci, Jr., as mayor. And there were signs that a civil service system for the city was finally about to become reality.

Until they split in the primary fight that led to his eventual defeat, Doorley shared his patronage powers with Lawrence McGarry, the long-time director of public works for Providence and city Democratic chairman. McGarry could offer 500 to 600 jobs in the public works department to the party faithful. At any given time, up to a third of the Democratic city committeemen were found to hold city jobs on the side.

When I talked to McGarry, he was in the twilight of his career, confined to a wheelchair with multiple sclerosis. But the Irish charm was undiminished, and so was his fervent belief in political patronage and opposition to civil service in any or all forms. "If any man is interested in taking a part in politics," McGarry said, "should he be barred from state or municipal government?" Patronage, he suggested, was the rule of the day in national government, under administrations of either party. "It's been going on since the beginning of politics, and not only in politics *per se* but in business and in the church. There's politics in everything. It's a fact of life." He said he had watched civil service at the state level and believed it merely encouraged each party to freeze in its followers, thus ballooning the payrolls. "But with patronage," he said, "you can always eliminate jobs." He said he had done that in Providence—an assertion others told me was true. "Why," McGarry asked, "should someone who works for state or local government be guaranteed a lifetime job when a man in private enterprise is not? I don't see the reason for it."

McGarry did say that the patronage system was not as helpful to the party in power as outsiders believed—that except for some 50 or 75 top-level positions in a city like Providence, all the rest were lowly positions like garbage collector or street sweeper, paying up to $3.40 an hour, and that he had often been obliged to hire noncitizens "because the average person doesn't want a job in the incinerator or sewer disposal plant." Often when he put a man to work as a laborer for a councilman, McGarry said, he made an enemy rather than a friend, because the employee would eventually "be dissatisfied and want a better job I didn't have for him."

(When I asked former Governor Roberts, a firm backer of civil service, for a reaction to McGarry's argument, he said that civil service that locks people into jobs without incentives for improvement is wrong, but that there can and should be opportunities for in-house training and constant upgrading of civil servants' performance. He dismissed McGarry as "a purely political figure with political concepts.")

McGarry celebrated his "Last Hurrah" in 1974 in a vain attempt to overthrow Mayor Doorley, who he thought had become stale at the job, in the primary. Doorley responded quickly by transferring all patronage powers to his own office and firing most of McGarry's supporters, turning the old man's weapon against him. As I talked with McGarry during that campaign (while his political lieutenants passed through to meet in a proverbial smoke-filled room in the rear), he indicated he would have few regrets, even if his candidate turned out to be the loser. (As it turned out, Doorley did beat McGarry's man in the primary; then in the general election McGarry sat on his hands, many of his cohorts backed Cianci, and the stage was set for the Republican upset.)

I've lived politics [McGarry said]. I started out as a kid going out to houses to get signatures, and driving voters back and forth to the polls. At 23 I was put on the ward committee in South Providence, where I then lived. Years later I became vice chairman, then chairman of the party in the city, and then state chairman. I've truthfully lived the whole thing from the lowest to the chairmanship. I've been through more battles than you could shake a stick at, from the ward up to presidential campaigns.

McGarry then recalled the incident of the 1972 Democratic campaign, when he tangled with George McGovern over a disputed convention delegate deal, causing McGovern, after a showdown in the governor's office, to apologize to McGarry for denying a commitment. "It didn't make McGovern a great man to me because he finally told the truth" about their deal, McGarry said. "And when they asked me after the convention and the Eagleton affair if I'd back McGovern, I said, 'Yes, 1,000 percent.'" The remark made the national news and certainly did McGovern no good in an already hopeless presidential campaign.

Politics [McGarry continued] is a great life if you can take it. You have to develop a tough exterior and interior, and be able to laugh it off.
In politics, I say, the cardinal rule is "Only give your word when you have to, and when you give it, keep it." If you do that, you'll always come out with the respect of the people you deal with.

Even Presidents of the United States, I reflected, might do better if they kept that wisdom from the Providence wards in mind.

The Newport Scene

Historic old Newport, when I visited in 1974, was a town in heavy trouble because of the Navy's pullout. Some 14,000 Naval personnel had left; more than a thousand civilian jobs had vanished; the real estate market was glutted with hundreds of vacant apartments and homes; the unemployment rate was climbing toward 10 percent; and the business that had been most dependent on the paychecks of Navy personnel—restaurants, bars, new and used car dealers, laundromats, and the like—were tightening their belts or closing their doors permanently.
Newport, however, will survive very nicely in the long run. Since its founding in 1639, spectacular ups and downs have characterized the town's history, and always the natural assets—especially the magnificent seascape, the mild climate and deep water harbor—have, in time, rejuvenated this jewel of the New England coast.
By the mid-18th century, shipping and commerce had made Newport one of the three largest cities on America's Atlantic flank. Newport skippers pioneered the famous and infamous triangular trade route—to Africa for humans, then to the Caribbean for sugar, and then to the rum distillers at home. Fishing was important, too, and the making of sperm oil and sperma-

ceti candles added to the city's prosperity. The resulting wealth made New-
port into a showplace of New England. Choice shops, theaters and teas, and
a thriving literary society were all part of the scene. And Newport became
America's first summer resort as wealthy planters and merchants from the
Southern states and the Caribbean went there to escape the heat and fevers.
Even in Europe the town was noted for the elegance of its society.

Then came the Revolution and three bleak years of British occupation,
from 1776 to 1779. The seaborne commerce collapsed and the British, when
they departed, left the town in ruins. More than half the population was
gone; according to one history, many families "had emigrated to Providence, retired with the British army, or remained broken in fortune and
spirit." Until the Civil War, the social life would remain restrained; little
building was seen; and the focus of shipping on the North Atlantic coast
turned decisively and permanently to New York.

It was in the 1830s, however, that some farsighted men began to realize
that the pasture and meadow lands sloping to the sea south of Newport's
old town center could be used for elegant summer cottages. Oddly enough,
the first "cottages" were cheap structures designed to last only for a season. But in 1839 the Jones family of Savannah, which had been summering
in Newport for 120 years, commissioned the building of "Kingscote"—a
"rustick Gothick" mansion that is said to be the oldest summer-resort cottage in the nation. A great rash of "cottage" building ensued in the following years, to hit its zenith in the "Gilded Age" following the Civil War.
Now the Southerners, subdued and impoverished by the Recent Unpleas-
antness, were supplanted by the Northern "royalty" of America's era of unfettered capitalism and conspicuous consumption—the Vanderbilts, Astors,
Belmonts, Wideners, Burdens, Dukes, Goelets, and many others. Along
Bellevue Avenue they put up their summer cottages with an extravagance
rarely dreamed of by the European nobility. According to the *American
Guide Series*,

> Probably America will never again see such lavish entertaining as took place
> at Newport during the summer seasons of the "gilded years," 1890–1914. Into six
> or seven weeks of each season were crowded balls, dinners, parties of every descrip-
> tion, each host or hostess striving to eclipse the others in magnificence. Huge sums
> were spent in the prevailing spirit of rivalry. Mrs. Pembroke Jones set aside $300,000
> at the beginning of every Newport season for entertaining, and some hostesses spent
> even more. . . . So much prestige was attached to spending July and August at
> this exclusive resort of the period that to have neglected to do so would have
> exposed a definite gap in one's social armor.

The greatest social event each summer was at Mrs. William Astor's
"cottage"; she was the social arbiter of the period, and since her ballroom
held only 400, the legend of the Four Hundred at the very peak of the social pyramid was born. Jokes and decadency played a part in all this, however, including one ball given for "Prince del Drago from Corsica," who
turned out to be a small monkey in full evening dress, and the great "Dogs'
Dinner" at which 100 canines of the elite gorged themselves on stewed

liver and rice and other delicacies—while, as critics pointed out, thousands were starving elsewhere. The ostentation of the Newport scene, in fact, was offensive to many of the elite themselves. As Stephen Birmingham wrote in *The Right People*, "Older people of 'refinement, wealth, and fashion' took a horrified look at what was happening, and began moving quietly away." Some retreated to Saunderstown, across the bay from the glitter of Newport; others headed to Bar Harbor on Mount Desert Island in Maine.

By the 1920s the society leaders of the Gilded Age had dispersed or died; with them disappeared the dinner parties for 80 or 90 guests, the most elaborate cotillions and fashion parades. A new kind of money came to Newport—people who made their money on Wall Street. They were a less stable group, since their fortunes were tied to the ups and downs of the ticker tape, and after the crash of 1929 most of them disappeared. The resort to this day has a goodly number of wealthy summer visitors, but they represent a much more discreet kind of wealth.

The economic slack caused by the end of the select and gaudy summer trade was taken up by the U.S. Navy, which expanded its base in Newport following 1918 and by the mid-1930s employed 3,500 civilians in Newport, many of them natives who had previously worked on the grand estates in the summers but faced unemployment during the winter months.

The preoccupation of modern Newport buffs has been the preservation and restoration of Newport's historic buildings, both the palatial cottages and colonial-era structures in the old town center. The 30-year-old Preservation Society of Newport County, for instance, owns and opens to the public such great old mansions as The Breakers (Newport's most stunning summer residence, built for Cornelius Vanderbilt), The Elms, Chateau-sur-Mer, Kingscote, and Rosecliff (where the 1973 film *The Great Gatsby* was filmed). The Newport Restoration Foundation, founded in 1968 by tobacco heiress Doris Duke, has bought and restored some 75 historic dilapidated houses and put them in prime condition, renting them out at nominal fees to Newport tenants.* Miss Duke has reportedly spent many millions on the venture. Another 50 old houses have been bought since 1963 by "Operation Clapboard," which sells them to buyers who will promise to rehabilitate them.

Thus Newport's architectural heritage is being tended and preserved, and opened to all who will come to see, in a manner far more appealing than the haughty and exclusive way the grand summer cottages were developed up to World War I. And the architectural treasure trove forms only one part of a multifaceted development of Newport as a fun place for broad masses of people. The range of things to do seems endless—viewing

---

* So three cheers for Doris Duke. She does, however, appear to be a recluse and authoritarian in her own way. According to press reports, she spends her Newport weekends in an estate surrounded by 10-foot-high barbed wire and guarded by a dozen German shepherds. She refuses all interview requests; when an enterprising Providence *Journal-Bulletin* reporter snapped her picture on a street in 1975, she demanded the film back and relayed a threat to suspend all restoration projects, thus throwing 81 carpenters out of work, if she was defied. The newspaper never ran the picture, one editor commenting: "We don't like to yield to blackmail, but we don't want to be known as the outfit that spoiled it for Newport."

historic sites, enjoying "all-around-town" sculpture exhibits, watching the grand and colorful America's Cup races and the annual sailboat show at Fort Adams, bicycling along Ocean Drive, eating lobster, shopping along the wharf, swimming on the splendid beaches, or walking along the spectacular Cliff Walk that skirts the old summer cottages on one side and the foaming green-blue sea on the other. The Newport Jazz Festival was lost to New York, but the weatherbeaten Newport Casino, built in 1880 by New York *Herald* editor James Gordon Bennett, Jr.,* is home of the National Lawn Tennis Hall of Fame and host to important sports events like the Women's Professional Grass Courts Championships.

For all its glamor, Newport has long been and remains a predominantly blue-collar town where 80 percent of the churchgoers are Roman Catholics. Not everyone is affluent; in fact there were some 1,000 people on welfare even before the Navy sailed away. In the early 1970s the town chose as its mayor Humphrey J. Donnelly 3rd, a father of six who earns his living cutting grass and trimming hedges for the Newport Electric Corporation. Donnelly does not actually run the city; there is a city manager for that. But he is a good vote getter and proud of being Newport's first blue-collar mayor. "I guess it all started," he told a reporter in 1974, "when I finally realized that the world is just as much mine as anyone's."

Rhode Island's Other Worlds

For most Americans, Providence and Newport (not necessarily in that order) are all there is to Rhode Island. The image is false, for several other worlds are tucked into corners of this Lilliputian state:

▪ The Blackstone Valley. This is a heavily industrialized and suburban corridor which stretches between two declining textile cities, Pawtucket (on Providence's north side) and Woonsocket (on the Massachusetts border). Pawtucket, where Slater built his famous cotton mill, is a working-class town, heavily French-Canadian and Irish. The population, 76,984 in 1970, has declined in three of the four past decades. Recently an urban renewal project, with the restored Slater Mill as its centerpiece, has made Pawtucket's congested downtown quite attractive.

Woonsocket is reputed to have more French-Canadians than any other city south of Montreal. French is the prevailing tongue in the streets, shops, and mills, and only a foolhardy soul would try to run for office in Woonsocket if he did not know the language. With the flight of the textile mills —this used to be one of the country's leading woolen manufacturing centers —Woonsocket found a high proportion of its workers unemployed. But an industrial development foundation has bought up old factories, started an industrial park, and alleviated most of the unemployment. The 1970 population was 46,820, down from 50,211 in 1950.

* Bennett is said to have built the Casino out of pique because a staid old Newport club, the Reading Room, expelled him after a guest of his rode a horse into the club.

■ Northwestern Rhode Island is lightly populated and attractive to the eye, with many lakes, streams, forests, parks, and farmlands. This is where Thomas Dorr made his last stand in the famed rebellion of the 1840s.

■ Southern suburbs. Cranston (73,037), an older, still expanding suburb, and Warwick (83,694), which has tripled its population since 1940, are the heart of Providence's postwar suburban growth, now with many large shopping malls and industrial parks.

■ East Providence (48,151) is a growing industrial suburb where tasteful little parks and tree rows hide oil tanks facing onto Narragansett Bay. One of the secrets of the state's livability, in fact, is the chain of small parks constructed around Providence earlier in this century; they relieve the industrial monotony and provide sorely needed breathing space. At East Providence, too, a knowing guide can lead one to Squantum, an exquisite dark-paneled Victorian clubhouse built in the 1870s to be—as it has remained—one of Rhode Island's most desirable clubs. (Others are the Hope, Turks Head, and University Clubs, all in Providence.) Squantum perches on a rocky abutment, overlooking the bay; on the land side one discovers a railroad spur which used to bring American Presidents and other dignitaries for visits. (Another bit of lore about Presidents is that Rutherford B. Hayes made the first telephone call by an American President, from Rocky Point to Providence.)

■ Eastern bayshore. An attractive chain of small cities, together with white houses looking down on the Sakonnet River and a sprinkling of quiet farmlands, characterize this part of the state hard up against the Massachusetts border. (Indeed, a goodly portion of it was once part of the Bay State). At Barrington there are miles and miles of lovely estates and *the* Rhode Island Country Club. Warren's history includes visits by Washington and Lafayette during the Revolution. Several of Rhode Island's famous whaleships were made in Warren and sailed from there in search of whale bone and oil. Textiles and a heavy ethnic population came later; in a later generation, one now sees a great textile mill converted to the manufacture of American Tourister luggage.

Bristol, where legend says the Vikings visited as early as the year 1000, is a quiet, tree-lined old town of much grace, filled with many lovingly preserved examples of colonial and early 19th-century architecture. The location is directly on the Bay, and Bristol in fact was once the fourth busiest seaport in the country. There the shipyard of Herreschoff Manufacturing Company built the fastest steam and sail yachts in world history, and developed the first torpedo boats. More recent industries include Kaiser Aluminum. The people are a mixture of Yankee, Italian, and Portuguese stock, with some Irish and French-Canadians; no matter what their heritage, they all join in what must be the grandest Fourth of July celebration anywhere in America. There are block parties, dances, carnivals, visits by naval ships, and, on the Fourth itself, speeches and bell ringing and a mammoth parade. (One wishes more Americans could still enjoy such uncomplicated, old-fashioned patriotism. It would do our jaded souls good.)

■ The Islands: Rhode Island, Jamestown. I include these here to clarify
a confusing terminology. "Rhode Island" is the official name of Aquidneck
Island, the site of Newport, Middletown, and Portsmouth; ergo the state
name "Rhode Island and Providence Plantations," referring first to the island, then to all the rest of the state. Jamestown is the other major island
in Narragansett Bay, with the town of the same name, connected to Newport
since 1969 by a new bridge that rises 215 feet above the water.

■ South County. Running westerly from Narragansett Bay to the Connecticut border on the west, and covering the southwesterly third of the
state, is Washington County, affectionately known as Rhode Island's "South
County." The eastern anchor is Quonset Point and the historic town of
Wickford; the western extremity the little city of Westerly; the area's total
southern flank is onto the Atlantic, with Block Island, the state's ocean island
resort, lying several miles offshore. Fortunately not too many people live
in the South County (only 84,000, or an eleventh of the state total), so
that the rolling hills, the "salt ponds" and swamps and woodlands and bird
sancturaries remain relatively unscathed by human development. This was
Rhode Island's "plantation country" in earlier times, and something of that
relaxed tempo remains.

The South County includes the Great Swamp, a 2,600-acre morass
where flora and fauna are protected against man-made encroachment. The
swamp witnessed a bloody battle of King Philip's War in 1675, when Rhode
Island's early settlers attacked the Narrangansett Indians and their allies,
killing some 600 and virtually annihilating the once-powerful Narragansetts.
Not far from the swamp is the thriving town of Kingston, home of the
University of Rhode Island, and the Gilbert Stuart birthplace at Saunderstown. Surprisingly, Rhode Island has four ski areas, and two of them are in
this region.

All along the South Country's seaward flank, thin long arms of white
sand, among them some of the best beaches of the country, embrace salt-
water lagoons and marshes. By ferry from Point Judith or Newport, one
can reach Block Island, a pear-shaped piece of rolling land, moorlike in
character with seemingly countless salt-water and fresh-water ponds. The
island, which has fewer than 500 permanent residents—many of them descendants of the first settlers from Massachusetts in the 17th century—is
named for Adrian Block, the Dutch navigator who went ashore there in
1614. The *National Geographic* tells us that Block Island "once reared huge
oaks, glowed with fields of wheat and corn, and harbored sheep and cattle
on its softly folded hills." Most of that is gone now; the visitor will find
shingled old hotels of Victorian vintage, but the moors are closer to their
primeval state than they have been for centuries. Together with the white
beaches and towering bluffs they bespeak a refreshing timelessness and solitude that densely packed little Rhode Island would do well to preserve for
all time to come.

CONNECTICUT

STATE OF STEADY HABITS

JOHN GUNTHER, IN *Inside U.S.A.*, described Connecticut as a "worthy little state." There is ample reason to think the residents of "The Nutmeg State" heartily agree. To some outsiders, Connecticuters' pride in their state is matched only by that of Virginians. This is as true of the Southern and Eastern European immigrants who now make up a majority of the population as it is of the old Yankees.

Indeed, Ella T. Grasso, a two-term Congresswoman who made political history by becoming the first woman ever elected governor of a state on her own as well as becoming the first Italian-American to be governor of Connecticut, indicated shortly after her inauguration that her preference for her home state over Washington, D.C., was more a factor in her candidacy than the ambition to run for higher office.

Connecticut is also described as a "land of steady habits," and this is demonstrated in many ways. One is that the state, third smallest and fourth most densely populated in the nation with an area of 4,956 square miles, is fighting a constant—although not always successful—battle to retain as much of its small-town New England charm as possible against the encroachments of New York City from the south, Boston from the northeast, and its own industrialization and urbanization. Between 1940 and 1970, the population rose 77 percent—from 1.7 million to 3.0 million—while that of New England as a whole increased only 40 percent. The population surge leveled off after 1970, however; in 1975 the Census Bureau estimated that the rise in five years had been only 2.1 percent (to 3,095,000). (This compared to an increase of 3.0 percent in all of New England in the same four years, and 4.8 percent in the country as a whole.)

Particularly in the sparsely populated eastern counties and the spectacularly beautiful western hills, the people of Connecticut have succeeded to a remarkable degree in maintaining the beautiful old Revolutionary homes and towns. The poet Wilbert Snow, a former governor, spoke for many in his poem, *Connecticut Tercentenary Ode:*

> These homes our fathers cherished like their laws,
> Reveal the steady minds of men who caught
> Life's dignity and beauty: freezing, thaws,
> Time's negligence and scars blind worms have wrought
> Have sagged their oak foundations, yet they stand
> The architectural glory of the land.

Connecticut is also a state of contradictions. Except for Alaska, it has the highest per capita income in the country but no state income tax and one of America's lowest levels of state aid to the public schools despite some recent reforms. It has been a leader in urban renewal and environmental protection but is quite conservative in many ways because of the paradoxically parallel influence of the Roman Catholic Church, the Congregationalists, and the banking and insurance industries.

Connecticut prides itself on its clean politics and government—"we are surrounded by evil on every side except the water," says one of Connecticut's top political reporters—but it has produced little sharp political debate on the issues and few distinguished political leaders. Its only presidential candidate was Sen. Brien McMahon, who was a favorite son in 1952, and Theodore H. White once described it as a state that exports political "power brokers."

These characteristics are due partly to the state's history and partly to its diversity. In the course of driving across Connecticut—a little more than an hour north and south, two and a half hours east and west on its turnpikes and Interstate highways—the traveler will encounter the urban industrial belt running north to south from Hartford down the center of the state through New Haven, then curving west to Bridgeport; wealthy suburbs such as Fairfield County, which has closer emotional and political ties with New York City than with Connecticut; old seafaring towns such as Mystic; and the beautiful colonial small towns of the eastern and western sections of the state, reminders of that cherished past of which Snow wrote.

In addition to such colorful names as Cow Shandy, Jangling Plains, and Dark Entry, there are English place names—Greenwich, Cornwall, Avon; Biblical—Canaan and Goshen; and Indian—Yantic, Cos Cob, reflecting the state's history. The state's name derives from the Indian word "quinatucquet," meaning "upon the long tidal river," referring to the Connecticut River, which flows to the Atlantic Ocean.

The statisticians tell us that in addition to its high per capita income, Connecticut has the lowest percentage of poor people among the 50 states, the highest average federal income tax payment, the highest percentage of households with telephones, the second highest assessed value of property per capita, and the third highest average of life insurance value per family. Teacher salaries, library books per capita, median school years completed, and if one considers the measure important, news magazine readership rank near the top of the list of states. Only two other states have more of their college graduates in *Who's Who* (thanks almost exclusively to Yale, one would guess). Per capita, the state is fourth in physicians, first in nurses. The highway death rate is the country's lowest.

So Connecticut has a lot of things going for it. The question is: does this proud and historic little state really measure up to its potential? Is the pride justified? There the answer is not so sure.

Historical Notes

Connecticut's tradition as a "state of steady habits" is rooted in the strong-willed men, such as the Reverend Thomas Hooker, who settled this territory in the 1630s, mostly because of land hunger but also to escape the autocratic and theocratic government of Massachusetts. Connecticut is also known as "The Constitution state" because the Fundamental Orders, drafted in 1638 from a Hooker sermon as a governmental framework for three Hartford Colony towns, represented the first constitution drafted in the New World.

In 1662 Gov. John Winthrop Jr., son of the governor of Massachusetts, obtained a charter ratifying the Orders from King Charles II. In 1687, when Sir Edmund Andros, the Crown-appointed governor, demanded the return of the charter at a meeting in a Hartford tavern, the lights, according to legend, were blown out, and the charter was hidden in the trunk of a great oak tree nearby. The colony remained under the Fundamental Orders until a new constitution was adopted in 1818, and this early act of resistance is celebrated by gavels, chairs, and other objects formed from the tree. Mark Twain noted that he had seen a "walking-stick, dog collar, needle-case, three-legged stool, bootjack, dinner table, tenpin alley, toothpick, and enough Charter Oak to build a plank road from Hartford to Salt Lake City." Whatever the validity of Gunther's judgment that Connecticut is a "worthy (i.e., virtuous) little state," Twain knew it had had its share of sharp-eyed Yankee peddlers and traders. The nickname "Nutmeg State" came from their practice of selling wooden nutmegs to the unwary, but Connecticut's overseas trade started because it was the port for trading Connecticut onions for Indian spices.

The Fundamental Orders established a government with close ties to the Congregationalist church. During its early history, Connecticut was almost as theocratic as Massachusetts. In 1708 Congregationalists and the more moderate Presbyterians worked out the "Saybrook Platform," which provided for biennial meetings of the ministers in each county and began

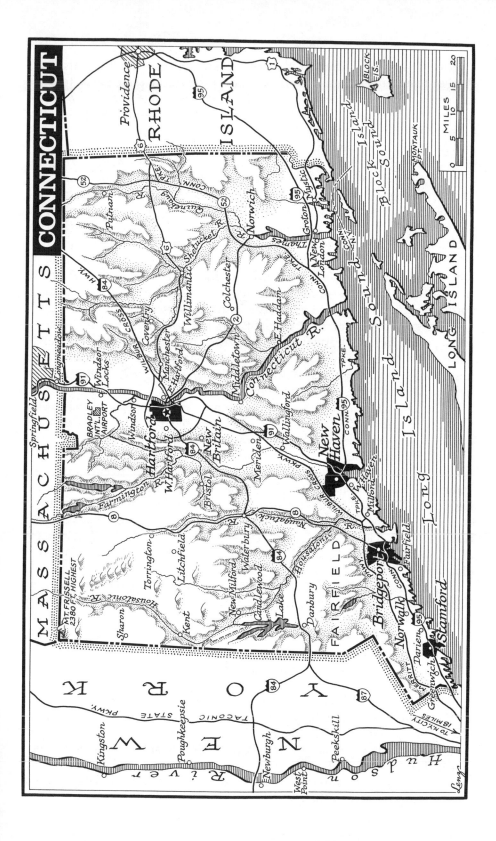

a state religious establishment that contributed, along with the harsh soil, Puritan temperament, and traditional independence of each town, to Connecticut's stability and conservatism. Property ownership was a prerequisite for the franchise; early Connecticut was well able to control its enthusiasm for pure, unsullied democracy.

A political "revolution," which was rooted in a religious "revolution" of members of the Anglican Church, in 1818 disestablished the Congregationalist Church, whose expenses had been paid out of state funds. For years it was against the law to belong to any other church, and there were no colleges except the Congregationalists'. Drafted by a combination of Jeffersonian Republicans (and later Democrats) and Episcopalians, the constitution of 1818 was partly the result of changes due to the Napoleonic war—Jefferson's embargoes cut off the sea trade and forced the state to turn to manufacturing—and it remained in effect until 1965, when the U.S. Supreme Court "one man, one vote" ruling forced the state to reapportion the state legislature and rewrite its basic charter.

The constitution of 1818 strengthened the governor, separated the executive, judicial, and legislative departments, and gave all religious groups status. The lower house representation remained the same, however, because each town, regardless of size, had either one or two representatives each, which they were allowed to keep.

The present constitution puts representation in conformity with population, requires redistricting and reapportionment every 10 years, and further strengthens the governor by requiring a two-thirds rather than simple majority for the legislature to override a veto.

In the Revolutionary War, as in every one since, Connecticut was known as "The Nation's Arsenal" because it was an early arms manufacturing center. Col. Samuel Colt started out in Hartford and the Winchester company in New Haven. Along with other early Connecticut manufacturers of guns, clocks, and other products, he pioneered the development of interchangeable parts, which was a major element of the industrial revolution.

Jonathan Trumbull, who was colonial governor when the Revolution began and became the first governor of the new state, was a towering figure during the war, marshaling men, supplies, and matériel for George Washington's army. In the Silas Deane house in Wethersfield, a favorite of Washington's, Washington and the Count de Rochambeau, commander of the French forces in America, made a decision in 1781 to combine their armies. The result was the defeat of the British at Yorktown.

Nathan Hale, the schoolteacher who was hanged as a spy by the British in the Revolution, was from Connecticut, as was Silas Deane, the first envoy of the Continental Congress to France. Benedict Arnold's roots were in the same Nutmeg State. Harriet Beecher Stowe, author of *Uncle Tom's Cabin*, her father, the theologican Lyman Beecher, and her brother, Henry Ward Beecher, came from Hartford. Mark Twain settled in Hartford and wrote *Huckleberry Finn* there.

Other famous sons of Connecticut were John Brown, the abolitionist, J. P. Morgan, the great financier, and P. T. Barnum, the circus impresario. Three other famous sons had more long-lasting impact on Connecticut, however. They were Eli Whitney, Seth Thomas, and Eli Terry. Whitney invented the cotton gin, but more importantly, with Colt, he developed the techniques of mass production and interchangeable parts. Thomas and Terry, the clock men, put these techniques to use. Henry Barnard was the first U.S. Commissioner of Education.

Cursed with unproductive farmland that increasingly was unable to raise grains competitively with western lands, whose crops were available to Eastern seaboard markets with the opening of canals, Connecticut became—and is—one of the first centers of mass production in the New World and one of the most highly industrialized states in the nation. About three-fourths of its union membership is involved in metal working, which is a high precision industry, and Connecticut is one of the nation's leading producers of aircraft components, electronics, and other sophisticated products.

Hartford is known as America's "Insurance Capitol." Its first insurance company was incorporated in 1795, and its best known, the Hartford Fire Insurance Co., was organized in 1810. Much of the early insurance business developed from Connecticut's seafaring and shipping history. Connecticut lays claim to many firsts—the first American public election (1640), the first turnpike, the first warship (the 16-gun *Oliver Cromwell*), the first use of anesthetic, the first American Ph.D. degree (at Yale), the first telephone switchboard, the first football tackling dummy (invented by Amos Alonzo Stagg at Yale), the first fish hook, meat grinder, steamboat, and lollipop. Inventive Connecticut always was, but a national leader in politics—almost never.

Ethnicities and the Bosses

Connecticut was the product of the first New England emigration, from Massachusetts, and it seems historically appropriate that in later times it was to receive, in relation to its land area and population, a particularly high concentration of the great wave of European immigration that began to reach these shores in the mid-19th century. These were the "ethnics," filling the gaps created by the old Yankees who had left depopulated towns and farms as they departed the flinty soil of their birth to seek their fortunes westward.

First were the Irish, fleeing the potato famine of 1846–47. Soon they were building roads, canals, railroads and dams—and working, as would the other immigrant groups, in the factories that would make Connecticut an industrial state of note. Germans came about the same time as the Irish, the Scandinavians after 1870, then the Italians between 1900 and 1915. The Poles became one of Connecticut's most important ethnic groups, along with their East European cousins, the Lithuanians and Czechoslovakians.

By 1920 Connecticut had the third largest proportion of first- and second-generation immigrants of any state in the nation. Almost 70 percent of the population was either foreign-born or born of foreign or mixed parentage. (Only Rhode Island and Massachusetts were higher.) By 1950 the figure was 48.1 percent, and the 1970 Census showed that 32 percent of the population, fifth highest in the nation, were first- or second-generation immigrants. Because this does not include their forebears, the fourth- and fifth-generations, the proportion of ethnics actually is considerably higher.

The first wave of black migration reached Connecticut from the South beginning around 1870, attracted by work in the tobacco farms of the Connecticut Valley. This population surge was to end shortly after World War I, followed after World War II by an even greater tide of Southern-born black folk. Between 1960 and 1970 Connecticut's black population increased from 111,000 to 196,000, reaching 6 percent of the population. Jews have been present in the state since the Revolutionary War and early replaced the Yankee peddler as purveyors of goods and worthy competitors in commerce. Today they are 3.4 percent of the population. During World War II thousands of French-Canadians moved to Connecticut and there are more than 100,000 Puerto Ricans, most of whom arrived after 1960.

It took nearly a century for the ethnic groups, primarily from Catholic nations, to wrest control from the old Yankees. In the 72 years between 1858 and 1930 the Republican party dominated Connecticut politics. This was due partly to the state's ingrained conservatism, which was bolstered by a distrust of the Democrats inherited from the Civil War. It was reinforced by fears generated by William Jennings Bryan's Populist—some called it "radical"—Presidential campaign of 1896, which shook many small towns loose from their pre-Civil War Jacksonian Democracy. It was also due in part to the drastic malapportionment of the state legislature in favor of the small towns, which, in contrast to the increasingly immigrant and Democratic cities, were Yankee Republican.

Connecticut's conservatism, stemming from the Establishmentarian Congregational Church and the propertied quasi-aristocracy, was reinforced by the rising manufacturing interests who preferred the Republican party because of its protectionist stance (a position shared by the workers almost as much as the owners). Industry dominated as agriculture declined steadily on the state's inhospitable rock-strewn soil, with the exception of the chicken farmers, many of whom were Jewish immigrants, and the tobacco farming in the rich Connecticut River valley.

The political upheaval caused by the Great Depression was to have as marked an effect on Connecticut as on any state. Following the election of Democrat Wilbur Cross in 1930, state-wide elections became close and the two parties, tightly organized and led, were strong and in balance. The governorship shifted from the near-Republican monopoly of earlier years to an almost even division for a quarter century, during which elections were rarely won by a vote of more than 51 percent. Following the 1954 election of Abraham Ribicoff, however, the Democrats began to build a registration advantage that was more than 150,000 by the time Mrs. Grasso was elected in 1974. They actually controlled the statehouse for all but the four years, 1971 to 1975, when Thomas Meskill was governor.

The Republicans lost an enormous political advantage in 1965 when the U.S. Supreme Court's "one man, one vote" decision forced a reapportionment of the state legislature. Prior to that the one-tenth of the people living in the smallest towns had half the representation in the house of representatives, because each town was allowed at least one representative and none, however large, had more than two. This system was a vestige of the New England tradition of fiercely independent towns and town meeting democracy, and it gave the Republicans, who were politically dominant in about 90 percent of the towns, control over the house and the power to neutralize Democratic victories in the state senate and constitutional offices. Thus, the little town of Union (population 261) had the same representation as Hartford (population about 180,000), a ratio of about 682 to 1. This made the Connecticut legislature the least representative—and the least democratic—in the country. In 1936, for example, the Democrats got a total of 1,238,072 popular votes to 368,816 for the Republicans, but the Republicans elected 167 representatives to the Democrats' 100. The cities were overrepresented in the senate, and the suburbs got the short end all around.

When this apportionment was made in 1818, it was not so unreasonable; at that time, for instance, Hartford had less than 9,000 population. Even as the cities grew, Republicans for years far outnumbered Democrats, although their margin steadily decreased because of immigration. From 1912 until his suicide in 1937 Connecticut Republicans were led—"bossed" is a better term—by J. Henry Roraback, one of the great political bosses of this century whose benevolent dictatorship has been likened to that of the Byrds in Virginia—"efficient, conservative, and in absolute control," in the words of one writer.

Roraback was a lawyer and former railroad lobbyist who became chairman of the Republican State Central Committee in 1912. A big, forceful, mustached man, he looked the part, as one observer noted, of a "ruler of corporate empires." He ran the Republican party with absolute power, partly because of his personal force, but partly because Connecticut's decentralized, local nature meant there were no power bases strong enough to challenge a strong leader. One reason for the discipline that held in both parties was the practice of running senatorial and gubernatorial campaigns out of the state party headquarters. Another was the absence of any state primary whatever until a post-convention challenge primary was enacted in 1955.

In this tradition Roraback exerted iron control over nominations, legislation, and almost everything else. A staunch conservative, he was generally able to keep his lieutenants from directly stealing public money, although one was sent to prison in the infamous Waterbury scandal of 1938. The city was looted of about $3 million by some of its officials—the last major scandal in the state.

Roraback's scruples did not extend to conflict of interest, however. He was president of the state's leading utility and with his control over legislation was able to greatly help the interests he represented. This included giving the utilities controlling membership of the public utilities commission and the "oversight" legislative committees. His power to discipline subordinates was awesome, even by the standards of the time. He denied renomination to two Republican governors who disagreed with him. In 1922 when Vice President Calvin Coolidge was the featured speaker at a party gala in Hartford, Roraback further humiliated one of these governors, Everett J. Lake, by not allowing him to sit at the head table.

Roraback committed suicide in 1937, after showing signs of emotional stress. In 1936, although still GOP state chairman and national committeeman, he shocked the Democratic state convention in Groton by appearing and attempting to endorse the Democratic candidate for governor, Wilbur Cross. After his death GOP leadership shifted from faction to faction, primarily between the towns and the growing suburbs. "Roraback was a great oak and nothing grew under him except little fledgling bushes," remarked John Alsop, Republican National Committeeman, brother of the newspaper columnists, and a member of an old-line Yankee Republican family. "When the oak came crashing down it was in a colorful way."

Cross's election in 1930 marked the emergence of the Democratic party as a competitive force in Connecticut politics. Until that year they had not had a U.S. Senator since 1876 and only two governors since 1900. Cross was the retired dean of the graduate school at Yale, a gray-haired twinkly-eyed man known affectionately throughout the state as "Uncle Toby." Nominated as a sacrificial lamb, Cross was elected partly because of the Depression, partly because he campaigned as an "unbossed" candidate.

A great raconteur and connoisseur of good food and cigars, Uncle Toby faced a Republican-controlled legislature but turned out to be a savvy politician with a Yankee horsetrader's sense, able to work out compromises with Roraback on legislation. Until his tenure the governorship had been treated as a ceremonial office. (The governor's office was just a room in the prestigious Yankee Hartford Club, where the inaugural parades used to start, until the election of Abraham Ribicoff, a Jew, necessitated "other arrangements.") Cross's predecessors would show up on Thursdays, meet with party and legislative leaders, hear what they had planned, and then disappear until the next Thursday. Cross broke precedent by working at the job full time.

He was defeated by a Republican in 1938. Coincidentally, that was the year a couple of upcoming young Democrats, John Moran Bailey, the future national chairman and backer of President John F. Kennedy, and Abraham Ribicoff, the future governor and U.S. Senator, began making their presence felt in party affairs. Contributing to Cross's defeat was the 28 percent of the gubernatorial vote received by Jasper McLevy, the Socialist mayor of Bridgeport from 1933 to 1957. McLevy, a fiscal conservative and a socialist in name only, had been elected mayor as a protest against the local scandals of the major parties.

There were other political changes besides the New Deal at this time. One was the growth of the labor union movement, which since then has almost always supported the Democratic party in Connecticut. Although there is no evidence that labor leaders can deliver their members' votes, labor provides money, campaign workers, and Democratic propaganda at union meetings and in labor newspapers. The unions' 290,000 members (1972 figures) make up nearly one-tenth of the state's population and about one-sixth of the eligible voters.

The emerging dominance of the Democratic party was the result of another factor: the assimilation of the ethnics and their participation in politics. The Democrats gained control of the cities where the ethnic groups settled while the Republicans' strength was in the small towns and suburbs, particularly Fairfield County, the wealthy bedroom county of New York City commuters. The harbinger of the Democratic rise was actually the defeat of Al Smith in 1928. The election was not a happy occasion for the Democrats, but behind the returns there was good news for these perennial Connecticut losers. Smith ran strongly in the cities of the Catholic immigrants, breaking the old Republican hold. It soon became clear how strongly Democratic power was centered in the larger cities of Hartford, New Haven, Bridgeport, and Waterbury. By the 1970s, Hartford, New Haven, and Fairfield County each had about one-fourth of the Connecticut voters. Not surprisingly, the big city bosses tended to overlook the needs of the smallest towns, just as before, the town-dominated GOP had neglected urban problems.

Bailey became chairman of the state Democratic party in 1946 and served until he died in 1975, the longest tenure of any state chairman of either party in Connecticut's history. He was in the tradition of Irish control of the party as the immigrants settled into the New Country. But Bailey not only participated in the election of the first Irish (or Catholic) President; he was also the prime mover in the election of a Jewish Senator and presided over the election of a woman governor of Italian ancestry and the first blacks to Connecticut statewide office. Under his leadership the Democrats completed their long climb from a distant second to the dominant political party of Connecticut.

Bailey was from a fourth-generation Irish family. He was a Harvard graduate who acted as though he wanted to hide the fact and look like the stereotyped Irish political boss. His classmates at Harvard Law School included John Davis Lodge, later Republican governor of Connecticut, and Alger Hiss. Bailey was seldom seen without his cigar (which he only chewed at Lent) and generally had his spectacles pushed up on his forehead. In the words of his biographer, Joseph Lieberman, a state senator in the mid-

1960's: "Bailey was tall, bald, and beefy and walked in a heavy, flat-footed way with his shoulders slightly slouched and his black pants up and over what Chicago politicos call 'the alderman.' "

This remarkable mid-20th-century political leader started out as a precinct worker in Hartford, was elected precinct chairman, and became the protegé of the city's political boss, T. J. Spellacy, who arranged for Bailey's election to the state central committee. In 1938, however, Bailey helped defeat Spellacy's candidate slate; one of Bailey's candidates for the state house of representatives was the 28-year-old Ribicoff. In 1940 Bailey was defeated in his race for probate court judge, his only attempt at elective office, partly because $1,000 in court funds during his tour as court clerk were unaccounted for. After the election he was absolved of any guilt and by 1946 he was the man to see for any Democrat who wanted a state-wide office nomination. Twenty years later Bailey was accused by opponents of conflict of interest in awarding state insurance business to members of his family and for the method of purchase of land for a state medical school site. Like the earlier charges, they were embarrassing for the boss but not lethal. Indeed, the level of corruption in Connecticut during the Bailey years was amazingly low. "By restraining his own hunger for glory and gain," political columnist David Broder wrote after Bailey's death "he avoided for 30 years the stain of scandal that has destroyed so many other dominant party organizations." The hunger for office never subsided, however. Bailey wanted to be Senator when Raymond Baldwin resigned in 1949, but Chester Bowles, then governor, refused. Bailey held it against Bowles for a long time.

As a statute revision commissioner, Baley got to know the state legislators well, and in 1946 he demonstrated the political power that resulted in his being elected state chairman. With the help of political allies, including Katherine Quinn, a former colleague in the Young Democrats and a future Democratic National Committeewoman, he succeeded in neutralizing Sen. Brien McMahon (whom he helped get elected) and won the gubernatorial nomination for Lt. Gov. Wilbert Snow over Chester Bowles. Snow, a tall, white-haired poet and scholar, lost the general election but helped Bailey win the state chairmanship. "Bailey loved politics more than anyone I ever knew," Snow said later. "I started him on his career."

As state chairman, Bailey effected a rapprochement with Bowles by helping him become governor in 1948. Later he persuaded Ribicoff, then governor, to join him in supporting John Kennedy. In 1956 Bailey circulated the famous "Bailey Memorandum," which was written by Kennedy's aide, Ted Sorensen. The memorandum, an entirely pragmatic document, flew in the face of then conventional political wisdom by arguing that a Catholic would be more of an asset than a liability on the national ticket. It analyzed recent elections and 14 important states in terms of their percentages of Catholic votes. In his book on Kennedy, Sorensen conceded that the memorandum probably claimed more than its evidence would bear, but he insisted that it was more valid than critics such as Hubert Humphrey contended. Since politicians are more concerned with probabilities than certainties, he concluded, it had the value of opening up the previously closed assumptions about a Catholic on the national ticket. "I was the responsible person to give it out," Bailey told me years later. "I was on safe ground. The organization wanted it."

Bailey was the first state chairman outside Massachusetts to come out for Kennedy, and he was rewarded by being included in the original inner circle that began planning Kennedy's successful presidential drive. In January 1961, the day after his inauguration, Kennedy appeared at the Democratic National Committee to nominate Bailey as national chairman. Bailey was a cautious politician, and John Kennedy was the only man to whom he ever surrendered his political heart. (Bailey kept the only promise he made to Kennedy when JFK made him national chairman: "I won't get you into trouble." Later Presidents were not to be so fortunate in the behavior of their political aides.)

The years between 1958, when the Democrats first won control of the Connecticut state legislature, and 1972, when they lost control of the state senate, were the peak years of Bailey's career. The 1962 off-year elections, in which a small town mayor, car salesman, and party workhorse named John Dempsey was elected governor, Ribicoff was elected U.S. Senator, and the Democrats finally outnumbered the Republicans by 396,000 to 382,000 (more than 500,000 were registered as independents).

At the height of his control, nothing was done in Connecticut politics and state government without Bailey. As national chairman he spent a good deal of time in Washington but was always available to fly home and rescue his floundering colleagues from the stalemates of their own creation. John Alsop remembers going to one of the traditional parties celebrating the end of a legislative session and finding Bailey sitting and smiling. "I came back and straightened everything out," Bailey said.

Bailey's success was due, in addition to his talents, to his 24-hour-a-day industry and attention to detail. "A good political manager never sleeps," one of his Republican opponents noted. He was always available and put great store in that quality all politicians value over any other: loyalty. In 1948, for instance, the postmaster's job in Hartford became vacant. A worker in the city street department, who was also a precinct captain, asked for the post. His support had helped Bailey get control of the city organization and then to nominate Snow. Bailey, who never forgot a political debt, mustered overwhelming support for his old ally before anyone else could develop support for the position.

Bailey understood as well as anyone that patronage is the glue of politics, and for the most part it served him well. "Ribicoff wasn't too interested in patronage, though he recognized it was necessary," he said. "So we built the organization and came up with good people." Constant care of detail, he continued, included "making sure everybody felt they were a part of it, no matter how little they might be." It meant being constantly on the telephone and available for people to see him at the Capitol, probably at his "office"—leaning against a pillar in his favorite spot in the building, or at

Parma's, a legendary Hartford restaurant specializing in Italian food and Connecticut politics.

Unlike Roraback, Bailey ruled by consensus. In the opinion of Homer Babbidge, former president of the University of Connecticut, Bailey had to have a governor or a legislative body to work through. Otherwise, Babbidge said, there really wasn't a tangible party organization. "I've tried to touch it, smell it, feel it, call it on the telephone, write to it—it just doesn't exist."

Above all Bailey was a political pragmatist. "Bailey's system was to try and stay off all horses until he was reasonably sure which the party wanted —and then throw all his weight behind him," John Alsop said. "And then it really got rough. It was a good system." Bailey was also master of the old tactic, observers noted, of "kill off your enemy and then resurrect him— bring them into camp."

Bice Clemow, editor of the West Hartford *News*, expressed a more jaundiced view. "We've never had a candidate for President. Connecticut exports power brokers. When you're a power broker you can't get trapped with ideologies. You have to go with the guy you can move with. The reason John Bailey made John Kennedy had nothing to do with how he felt about Jack's 'liberalism.' It had to do with his salability." Another way of expressing this is Ribicoff's statement concerning Chester Bowles, one of the most liberal men of 20th-century politics: "Chet believes too hard." Clemow concluded: "That's the trick in Connecticut. Don't believe too hard. . . . This never was a state of passionate beliefs except those rooted in the Catholic hierarchical domination."

With a few exceptions, however, Bailey's candidates can be said to compare favorably enough with the average public servant of the times in America: Senators Brien McMahon, William Benton, Thomas Dodd, and Abraham Ribicoff; Governors Chester Bowles, Ribicoff, John Dempsey, and Ella Grasso.

McMahon, who died in 1952, managed to become well-to-do while in office, however, and Dodd seemed to take a cue from him. A liberal on domestic issues, a militant anti-Communist (he was also an ex-FBI agent), Dodd took the lead in pushing for controls on handguns despite Connecticut's large arms industry. He was censured in 1967 by the Senate when a former aide, James Boyd, accused him of using campaign funds for his own personal use, and the charges proved irrefutable.

Another duty of a political leader is to judge and choose among the demands of various factions. In Connecticut, as in most other Eastern states, this had much to do with ethnic groups. No one was more sensitive to ethnic considerations than Bailey. From 1932 to 1962 Connecticut had an at-large congressional seat that was traditionally held by a Polish-American. In 1958 Bailey forced the nomination of Frank Kowalski, an Army officer unknown to Connecticut Democrats. In 1962 Kowalski turned on Bailey by challenging Ribicoff for the senatorial nomination. Despite Kowalski's insurgency, there was no stopping Ribicoff, because he had Bailey's powerful support. One measure of Bailey power and control over the party was his choosing another Polish-American, Bernard Grabowski, for the at-large seat. Grabowski was a totally obscure young lawer of whom the convention delegates had never heard—he was "grabbed from a bag" in the words of one observer—until Bailey foisted him on them. Ribicoff and Grabowski won handily.

(Lieberman provides a colorful vignette of Bailey at work in the convention setting. Shuttling in and out of the back rooms at Hartford's Bushnell Auditorium, the ever-present cigar lit, "he would grab an arm, look straight into the eye of its owner, and regardless of how far he was standing from the other, manage to sound as if he was whispering a very important and confidential piece of political information into his ear. His voice had a rusty quality which has been described as 'whiskey tenor'"—though Bailey, according to his biography, limited his drinking "to an occasional brandy and soda.")

Abraham Ribicoff, the figure who will be remembered as Bailey's most enduring contribution to the Connecticut political scene, is a liberal—and usually a very cautious man. A native of New Britain, he made a fortune in real estate and business investments in his early adulthood. In politics, he showed splendid instincts for survival by anticipating issues, from safety to consumer protection. "When Ribicoff moves, people don't say here is a guy who is far out," Ralph Nader, the consumer advocate, once said. "They say if Ribicoff is moving, the tide can't be far behind." Perhaps the only moment of high passion in Ribicoff's career—and it was a memorable one—came during the 1968 Democratic National Convention in Chicago, when he accused Mayor Richard Daley's police of "Gestapo tactics."

Elected to the state legislature in 1938 at the age of 28, Ribicoff established an early alliance with Bailey and later with the Kennedys. As governor he was a moderate, refusing like all the others to back a state income tax. As Secretary of HEW he was more a lobbyist than a missionary, reassuring Southerners about not withholding federal funds in segregated school districts and making a reputation of being cautious on civil rights generally.

As U.S. Senator, Ribicoff has never authored a major piece of successful legislation. He did back a form of the Family Assistance Plan the Nixon Administration pushed for a while, but finally gave up in disgust as the administration's interest steadily waned. He also proposed a 12-year, $20 billion program to integrate suburban and center city schools in all metropolitan areas, North and South. A year before, in 1970, he had supported a similar proposal by Mississippi Senator John Stennis, and during a debate with New York's Jacob Javits, also a Jew, Ribicoff accused Javits of "hypocrisy" concerning desegregation in the North.

When running for governor in 1954, Ribicoff countered an anti-Semitic whispering campaign with a well-timed election-eve telecast on which he said: "Any boy, regardless of race, creed, or color, has the right to aspire to public office. . . . The important thing is . . . that Abe Ribicoff is not here to repudiate the American dream, and I know that the American dream can come true."

By 1968, Bailey had begun losing control in Connecticut. One reason was that he had spent so much time in Washington as Democratic National Chairman. Another was that 1968 was a year of Democratic insurgents, particularly the supporters of Sen. Eugene McCarthy, in revolt against the old regulars on the issue of the Vietnam war. In addition, there were two reforms that weakened regular party control and made challenges to the regulars much easier than in earlier years. One was the challenge primary which permitted any candidate who received the vote of 20 percent of the delegates at the nominating convention to take the issue to all of a party's voters.* The other, enacted in 1966, was elimination of the peculiarly stringent straight-ticket voting method in which the voter had to pull the straight party lever and then, if he wanted to vote for any candidate of the other party, go back and change each individual vote on the voting machine. Connecticut now has an optional party lever.

In 1970 the Rev. Joseph D. Duffey, an antiwar Congregationalist minister, beat Bailey's candidate for the Democratic senatorial nomination in Connecticut's first state-wide primary and then lost to Republican Lowell Weicker in a three-way general election. The third candidate, running as an independent, was the incumbent, Sen. Thomas Dodd. Weicker won with 455,000 votes to 368,000 for Duffey and 266,000 for Dodd.

The 1970 election was a bad one for Bailey and the Democrats in general. Republican Congressman Thomas J. Meskill, an Irishman, beat Emilio Q. Daddario for governor, the first time the Democrats had lost the Statehouse since Ribicoff won it in 1954. The Democrats had been stunned by the surprise decision of Ribicoff's successor, John N. Dempsey, a gregarious and soft-hearted man who was born in Ireland, not to seek reelection. After the election they indulged themselves in a great deal of breast-beating about whether the party could survive.

Survive it did. In 1974, thanks partly to the Nixon Administration scandal, the Democrats won back the governorship and won overwhelming control of both houses of the legislature. Ribicoff was reelected with 61 percent of the vote over a black airline pilot, and the Democrats picked up the House of Representatives seat that had been held by Robert Steele, the losing Republican gubernatorial candidate. It was captured by Christopher Dodd, son of the late Senator.

The Democrats also made political history when Mrs. Ella T. Grasso, a two-term Congresswoman and long-time party regular, became the first woman and first Italian ever elected governor of the state. She was, in fact, the first woman ever to be elected governor of any state completely on her

* The challenge primary had actually gone on the statute books 13 years earlier, one of the rare victories of reformers in those times. It succeeded partly because one faction of the Republican party wanted to prevent opponents from seizing party control at the next state convention, but more importantly because the attempts of leaders of both parties to "amend it to death," the time-honored legislative tactic, became so flagrantly embarrassing that Bailey changed his mind and swung the Democrats in the legislature behind it.

own without inheriting the office one way or another from her husband. And she was elected by the second highest margin in a state history—by 200,000 votes, receiving about 60 percent of the 1,060,000 cast.

This provided an ironic last hurrah to Bailey's career as the ultimate ethnic politician. The contest for the nomination had been between Mrs. Grasso and Attorney General Robert K. Killian, both of whom Bailey considered members of his political family. "I brought Ella into the picture 20 years ago," he recalled in a conversation during the preconvention maneuverings. "I brought Killian back and made him town chairman in Hartford. I sold Dempsey on the idea of appointing him attorney general." One of his children, he noted, was for Grasso, while another was for Killian.

The 1974 Irish-Italian fight over the gubernatorial nomination was particularly vivid. Jack Zaiman, veteran political editor of the Hartford *Courant*, told me that ethnic bitterness "was at an all-time high." Killian, described as "a professional Irishman," went on television to denounce the "power brokers"—Arthur T. Barbieri, Democratic chairman of New Haven, Nicholas R. Carbone, the party chief in Hartford, and Frank A. Santaguida, the party leader in Waterbury. All hoped to replace Bailey as state chairman, but part of Killian's bitterness could have been because Mrs. Grasso beat him in his home town of Hartford.

In the past, Bailey and other party leaders had defused the issue by putting a Wasp or Jew on the ticket. After 1974 party members could only hope that, as one put it, "the one-time election of an Italian as governor could draw the boil." One of Bailey's last services to his party, a role he had played long and well, was to patch up, temporarily at least, the rift in his "family." He negotiated a compromise whereby Killian agreed to drop his challenge to Mrs. Grasso and run for lieutenant governor on the ticket with her. In April 1975, three months after Mrs. Grasso and Killian were sworn in, Bailey died of cancer.

The election of Mrs. Grasso was the climax of the Italians' steady climb to party dominance—an inevitable victory, it would seem, because they are the largest ethnic group in Connecticut. According to the 1960 Census there were 237,000 first- or second-generation Italian-Americans, about one-fourth of the foreign stock in Connecticut. By 1974 the Democratic house and senate leaders were Italian and the party leaders in Hartford, New Haven, Waterbury, Stamford, and Meriden were Italian. Italians ran the Republican party in Hartford, New Haven, and Bridgeport.

Until 1970, however, no Italian had ever run for governor. Mrs. Grasso's victory, to Zaiman, was "the last Hurrah for the Irish domination of the Democratic party," although others thought the Irish would prove more durable politically. Fewer in number than the Italians, Poles and other Eastern European groups, the Irish had dominated because they got there first. By the 1970s, however, they were no longer hungry, and in Connecticut many were moving over to the GOP.

Mrs. Grasso, who was 55 when elected, was a veteran of 22 years in active politics, as a state legislator, a popular and well known secretary of state, and two-term Congresswoman. Except for her Washington service she lived all her life in Windsor Locks, a mill town she loved and for which Washington was no proper substitute. "I hate not sleeping in my own bed," she once said. There were other drawbacks to Washington, however. The crucial factor was her frustration as a junior Congresswoman and the difficulty of getting a handle on a good issue.

Ella Rosa Giovanna Oliva Tambussi Grasso was the only child of a baker who migrated from the Piedmont area of Italy. He worked 14-hour shifts in the bakery to send her to a private girls' school, Chaffee, and then to Mt. Holyoke, where she made Phi Beta Kappa, graduated magna cum laude in 1940, and got a Master's degree in economics in 1942.

Like many other Connecticut natives she loved the state and described her childhood in her parents' white house with green shutters as an "idyllic existence." One thing she learned in college, according to her roommate, was that education carried with it a social responsibility. In the early 1950's she ran for the General Assembly.

During her gubernatorial campaign her critics contended that Ella Grasso was as ambitious, temperamental, egotistical, and short-tempered as any male politician, but the image she projected was of a no-nonsense, rather conservative woman of deep beliefs who said of her *Newsweek* magazine cover story: "Oh, it's very nice but I'm still just a girl from Windsor Locks." She campaigned generally in pants suits and crepe soled lace-up oxfords with her glasses (like Bailey's) pushed up on top of her head. She made her acceptance speech wearing what some observers thought bore a suspicious resemblance to sneakers and delivered her inaugural speech carrying a single long-stemmed red rose that had been given to her at mass that morning in Windsor Locks.

As a staunch opponent of abortion, she disappointed feminists and as a U.S. Representative was ranked among the lower third of women in Congress by the Women's Lobby, a full-time lobbying organization. She was by no means a women's libber. She referred to her husband, Thomas Grasso, a retired school principal and constant campaign companion, as "my best friend." Once elected, she appointed relatively few women to major state jobs. Asked what she called her mother, her daughter (she also has a son) joked: "Usually I call her 'Sir.'"

Mrs. Grasso was publicly opposed to any kind of state income tax, which is an emotional question in Connecticut, and campaigned on a promise to "finance Connecticut's budget within the existing tax structure," despite inheriting a $180 million budget deficit. Many critics believed that an income tax was the only way to finance the social services the state demanded, but Mrs. Grasso serenely shrugged off challenges that her programs were impossible without it. (There were reports that she privately conceded the need for such a tax.) Her strongest campaign issue was a charge that three major public utilities had cheated consumers out of $11 million by not passing on the savings from more efficient operations. She proposed abolition of the public utilities commission and its replacement with a new regulatory authority, stronger consumer and environmental protection, mass transit, and a program of assistance to failing industries and tax incentives to strengthen the state's economy.

In her political career Mrs. Grasso learned well the art of balance. She was able to work with Bailey and the party regulars and with party liberals as well. In 1968 she endeared herself to the late Robert Kennedy's supporters by sponsoring a minority platform at the national convention opposing Lyndon Johnson's Vietnam policies. She also initiated, as secretary of state, campaign contribution disclosure reforms. "She's a political artist in a sense that she has been able to maintain credibility with the full range of the Democratic party," according to Lieberman. "As a result there are few people who agree with her 100 percent, but most Democrats in Connecticut agree with her enough so they can support her. . . ." The Connecticut Women's Political Caucus finally endorsed her gubernatorial candidacy after a long, stormy debate during which Bella Abzug, the strong-minded New York Congresswoman, urged them to forgive Ella Grasso her "one mistake" on abortion. The Permanent Commission on the Status of Women called her refusal to allow Medicaid funds to be used for abortions "discriminatory, inhumane, and unjust to poor women."

All this annoys her political foes. "Ella is a standard machine-type politician, but she gets away with it because she maintains that image of Mt. Holyoke serenity," an aide to Killian complained. During her first year in office, Mrs. Grasso battled frequently with the overwhelmingly Democratic legislature. Late in 1975, the Assembly refused to cooperate with Mrs. Grasso's proposal which would have lengthened the work week for Connecticut's 40,000 state employees from 35 hours to 40, saving $8 million or more in overtime and encouraging early retirement by employees who did not want to work a longer work week. But earlier in the year, Mrs. Grasso forced down the throats of reluctant state legislators a bill granting state employees promotion and cost of living increases in violation of her own austerity budget.

When the Assembly failed to lengthen the work week, Mrs. Grasso dismissed 500 state employees and threatened to lay off as many as 5,000 eventually. As these pages were written in early 1976, Mrs. Grasso planned to continue her campaign for a longer work week.

Mrs. Grasso also backed a bill forcing city and town officials to submit their disagreements with government employee unions to binding arbitration (a procedure which robs local officials, as representatives of the public, of their right to have a final say over public expenditure).*

Mrs. Grasso did fulfill her campaign promise to replace the old public utilities commission with a new public utilities control authority instructed to hold monthly public hearings for complaints, with a consumer council. But due to budgetary pressures, she has had to move slowly in assigning en-

---

* The broad concessions to the public employees were the result of heavy union pressure which neither Mrs. Grasso nor the legislature seemed to know how to resist. In discussing the binding arbitration bill with legislative leaders, for instance, the mayors asked if the state government would impose the same system on itself. Greeted by an incredulous response, Mayor Donald J. Irwin of Norwalk commented: "That's just saying, 'If you want to cut my throat, why don't you try cutting your own?'"

gineers and other experts to the control authority to give it a chance to hold its own in technical arguments with the utilities when they ask for rate increases.

She allowed the state sales tax to rise to 7 percent, but did promise the business community she will seek a repeal of the tax and will ask the Assembly to raise the state tax on gasoline another two cents to 12 cents a gallon.

She effectively gutted the department of environmental protection through appointment of a weak-kneed commissioner, but did nominate an advocate of mass transit to head the department of transportation, normally a haven for highway zealots, and she named a political liberal rather than a contractor as director of public works.

Weicker, the Republicans, and Political Miscellanea

U.S. Senator Lowell Weicker, a Yankee accustomed to drawing hard, sharp moral judgments, is an appropriate inheritor of the old independent Yankee political tradition. By the mid-1970s he had become the best known figure in his state's Republican party, which was deeply divided over him. He was also a commanding figure in Connecticut politics generally, partly because of his service on the Senate Watergate Committee and his early denunciation of President Richard Nixon. This made him unpopular with many Republicans but won support from independents and Democrats.

In many ways the Connecticut Republican party is as liberal as the Democrats, if not more so. John Alsop, whose forefather helped draft the 1818 constitution, ascribes this to the tradition of direct, participatory, small-town democracy, which the Republicans have always controlled. There were paradoxes in addition to the gross malapportionment that was only ended with the 1965 reapportionment. One was that the GOP was more centralized statewide than the Democrats, whose city bosses each had enough strength to force a sharing. Thus, Bailey was never able to rule with such authoritarianism as Roraback.

"The country Republicans tended to be fairly liberal, and this in turn transmitted a fairly liberal cast to the Connecticut GOP," Alsop told me. "This translated itself to heavy Willkie support in 1940, 1952 leaders in the fight for Ike, in '64 for Scranton, and in '68 for Rockefeller."

After Roraback, the party was led by, among others, Clarence "Cappy" Baldwin, a liberal Republican, and then John Davis Lodge, the brother of Henry Cabot Lodge, the 1960 GOP vice presidential candidate and later ambassador to South Vietnam. John Lodge was the last Republican governor before Meskill; his political career ended when Ribicoff defeated him in 1954. "A sillier man we've never had," a highly respected Republican leader recalled. "He got in and behaved roughly like an emperor." (Remembered far more fondly among former Republican officeholders is Raymond E. Baldwin—no relation to the onetime Republican state chairman —who served with distinction as governor in the early 1940s and later as

U.S. Senator, the state's chief justice, and as chairman of the 1965 constitutional convention.)

The Republican Old Guard and liberals fought all during the 1950s, and the 1962 state convention was torn by personal rivalries that Alsop says contributed to his own defeat for governor. The Connecticut GOP has also been torn between the "Hartford Establishment" (led by Roraback and then Lodge and Alsop) and the "Fairfield County Establishment." Fairfield County Republicans, many of whom supported Barry Goldwater in 1964, traditionally complain that while they raise the money the Hartford leaders wield political power and make the tickets. But Frederick K. Biebel, who was elected party chairman in 1975, was from Stratford in Fairfield County.

Alsop believed that while the malapportionment looked bad on paper it contributed to good state government. "I always predicted reapportionment would be very bad for the state of Connecticut and very good for the Republican party," he said. "The leaders from small towns had been broad in their view, sound and moderate men." Reapportionment meant that the Republicans had to broaden the base of the party, however. Many opposed reapportionment on the grounds that the old system allowed them to keep control of the house of representatives.

Starting in the 1920s, the GOP always had some ethnics on the ticket. An Italian traditionally ran for state treasurer, for instance, and like the Democrats, the party's nomination for the at-large Congressional seat was a Polish-American preserve. Italians eventually worked into control of some of the city organizations. Right after World War II William Celentano was mayor of New Haven, and in the late 1960s Ann Uccello was a courageous reform mayor of Hartford. There were others, such as Nicholas Panuzio, the first Republican to be mayor of Bridgeport in nearly 50 years, whom President Ford in 1975 appointed to head the federal General Services Administration.

Until 1970, however, the Republicans nominated only two non-Yankees —Lieutenant Governor James C. Shannon in 1948 and E. Clayton Gengras in 1966—for governor. In 1970 an Irishman, Republican Thomas J. Meskill, was elected at the head of a ticket that had only one Yankee on it. Loss of the Statehouse threw the Democrats into deep confusion. To Alsop, the ultimate Yankee himself ("perfect Yankee cold roast beef," Zaiman described him), it meant the GOP was coming of age. "Until Watergate and Meskill's decision not to run again in 1974 we were really moving to a realignment of forces in the state," Alsop said. "Then we were really knocked in the jaw."

Meskill defeated Daddario by about 80,000 votes and inherited a Democratic-controlled legislature and a budget deficit of more than $200 million from his predecessor, John Dempsey. He set out to balance the budget with an enthusiasm that led some to call him "The Reagan of the East." His first year was marked, however, by a prolonged and bitter fight over a tax package that resulted in Connecticut's sales, cigarette, and gasoline taxes being among the highest in the nation. This was necessary because the state has no income tax.

Meskill subsequently did cut the sales tax back—from 7 percent to 6 percent—partly by paring social services and community development programs. Still, for all his budget balancing efforts, he passed on a $180 million deficit, which he had inherited, to Mrs. Grasso. His decision not to run for reelection contributed indirectly to Mrs. Grasso's election.

With Meskill's departure, Weicker, an heir to the Squibb drug fortune, became the dominant figure in the GOP. And the most controversial, because of his vehement criticism of the Nixon Administration and its Watergate scandals. After the 1974 elections he debated becoming an independent. Weicker already had something of a reputation as a maverick. A one-term member of the House of Representatives before being elected to the Senate in 1970, he opposed the Nixon Administration on the ABM system, the supersonic transport, and the Lockheed loan, and criticized the Administration for not backing mass transit.

"Weicker is full of missionary zeal," said Alsop. "He really believes what he says. He said the Nixon crew was wicked, and he turned out to be right." Bice Clemow described him as a reasonable man but with a lot of fury underneath. Weicker's fury, when aroused, knows few bounds. He assailed the Nixon Administration for "garbage politics and gutter goals" and told Charles Colson, a Nixon aide who went to prison because of the Watergate scandals, to leave his office during the Senate Watergate Committee hearings with the words: "You can just get your ass out of my office because you make me sick."

In interviews and on the live telecasts of the committee hearings during the summer of 1973, Weicker rejected the argument that dirty politics, wiretapping, big campaign contributions, and other corruptions were justifiable because everyone else, including Democrats, had done the same in the past. A big man, six feet, six inches tall, Weicker bellowed his dismay and disgust. "I don't want to hear that everybody does it. Believe me, everybody does not do it. This country is a decent place, peopled by honest, decent men, and that includes politicians." What particularly infuriated Weicker was "the incredible abuses committed by our law enforcement and intelligence community—the FBI, the Justice Department, the Internal Revenue Service, the CIA, the Secret Service, the military." Angry as some Republicans got at this, Weicker got standing ovations on his trips home after the committee's hearings.

It made no difference to Weicker that Nixon had campaigned for him and Meskill in 1970. He was also personally indignant with Thomas Dodd in that campaign because he felt Dodd had misused the political system. He would challenge Dodd personally in debate, jabbing at Dodd with his finger for emphasis. Ironically, Connecticut politicians believe that more than half of Dodd's votes would have gone to Weicker if Dodd hadn't made the race.

The voters in Connecticut have consistently maintained a comparatively high degree of participation. In the 1960, 1964, and 1968 presidential elections they ranked 10th, 11th, and 10th again among all states in voter participation (76 percent, 71 percent, and 68 percent of those eligible). In 1972 they ranked fifth with 65.7 percent participation.

In 1964 these voters went overwhelmingly for Lyndon Johnson over Barry Goldwater, giving him 68 percent of the 1,217,690 votes cast; in 1968 they gave Hubert Humphrey 50 percent to 44 percent for Richard Nixon and 6 percent for George Wallace; in 1972 they went for Nixon over George McGovern by 59 percent to 41 percent.

In 1974 Connecticut enacted a strict campaign contribution and expenditure law, despite strong opposition by labor and its Democratic supporters, who called it a "Republican ripoff" and an attempt to "emasculate organized labor." Individual contributions to either party central committee, candidates, or other organizations could not exceed $5,000; spending for a gubernatorial campaign was limited to 15 cents for each resident of the state, which according to the 1970 census would limit spending for a gubernatorial candidate to about $450,000. By comparison, Meskill spent $600,000 in 1970, and his opponent, Daddario, spent about $775,000.

State Government: A Fiscal Cripple

Connecticut has generally enjoyed relatively clean politics and a reputation for responsive state government. It has turned itself inside out to avoid a state income tax, however, and the result has been a distortion in the state's tax structure and public policies.

Rich and poor alike have opposed the income tax, the rich for obvious reasons of self-interest, the poor because they have been convinced that the tax would be an open-ended, insatiable monster. The Democratic party has defaulted in educating its lower- and middle-income constituency to the fact that an income tax would be much less regressive—and adverse to their own interests—than the sales tax, which is consistently the highest in the country. No governor has had the political courage to back the income tax—Ribicoff forcefully opposed it for fear of offending Fairfield County, and Mrs. Grasso campaigned on a promise to veto any attempt to enact it, thus tying her hands just before Connecticut headed into one of the most severe financial crises of its history. When I pressed Governor Grasso on the point shortly after she took office, she finally replied tartly: "Well, I guess the people of Connecticut had just decided they want a woman governor and no income tax." Most income tax opponents justify their position on the grounds that its absence has helped Connecticut attract new industry; proponents scoff and counter with the argument that resulting high property taxes discourage industry.

Bice Clemow put it most bluntly: "We were hoodwinked into thinking there was some magic in not having an income tax, that it would bring us a lot of wealth. It brought us a lot of chintzy New Yorkers who wanted to escape the tax. No industry came to Connecticut because it didn't have an income tax." Wilbert Snow, still keen and alert in his 91st year and three decades after his brief fling at statewide office (he was lieutenant governor for a term and governor for 13 days), told me in an interview one day in 1974 at his Middletown home: "Not having the income tax is a sop to Fairfield County. It's our Alsace-Lorraine."*

Connecticut had an income tax for about a month in 1971 but never collected a cent from it. Acting on the recommendation of a bipartisan tax study group, the legislature reluctantly enacted a graduated tax of 1 to 6 percent that was expected to fill the $260 million budget deficit the state faced. The reaction was explosive. The legislators' offices were deluged with angry letters and obscene telephone calls, and those with the temerity to make public appearances in behalf of the tax were booed and jeered, a response historically appropriate for a state that had refused to ratify the Constitutional Amendment establishing the federal income tax.

After protest petitions were circulated throughout the state, the legislature repealed the tax and raised the sales and excise taxes to generate the income—sales tax to 6.5 percent, the gasoline tax from 8 cents to 10 cents per gallon, the cigarette tax from 16 cents to 21 cents a pack.

Despite the polls that showed the citizens of Connecticut opposed to the income tax by 3 to 1, the violence of the reaction shocked the legislators. It didn't matter that economists argued that a graduated income tax was the most equitable. As one legislator put it: "You don't really see the sales tax or the tax on cigarettes and gasoline the way you do an income tax."

Despite the lack of an income tax, Connecticut's tax burden in the mid-1970s—taxes as a percentage of personal income—was the fifth highest in the nation, after Maine, Massachusetts, Vermont, New York, and Wisconsin. In the previous 20 years the tax burden had risen 111 percent, faster than in any other state except one (Delaware), from 6 to almost 13 percent of personal income. The chief reason was that property taxes per capita ($273 in 1971) were the third highest in the nation (after Massachusetts and California and tied with New Jersey). The property tax was 51.2 percent of all state and local taxes, compared to 40 percent in the country as a whole. Only three states had taxes less responsive to a rise in personal income. Per capita state aid to local governments in Connecticut was 29 percent less than the national average.

One result was increasing disparities in the money available for schools between the rich and poor communities. When Mrs. Grasso took office she was forced to ask that the sales tax be raised back to 7 percent and that it be applied to personal services, that the cigarette and corporate income taxes be raised (to 25 cents per pack and from 8 to 9 percent).

In the early 1970s Connecticut ranked 25th in per capita expendi-

* The life story of this thoroughly delightful poet-professor-politician, who still recalls with gusto the radicalism of youth and was a close friend of Rubert Frost, is told in his autobiography, *Codline's Child* (Middletown: Wesleyan University Press, 1974). "There have been three things in my life," according to Snow: "poetry, education, and politics—in that order."

tures for all state functions at $505.92 per person. In per capital expenditures for highways it was 32nd at $88.89, for public welfare it ranked 17th with $89.90, and for health and hospitals it was 23rd at $51.86. In per capita expenditures by both state and local governments it was 15th with $826.20. These figures can sometimes be misleading. Connecticut highways are generally good because the state is small, and there is no necessary correlation between expenditures and the quality of individual performance in a field like education. Robert Franklin, executive director of the Connecticut Public Expenditure Council, a group of businessmen organized in 1941 to monitor and study the state government, argued that performance in school has more to do with family income and attitudes.

Because of the large disparities between the wealth of cities—in Canton, for example, there is $38,000 worth of taxable property for each student but in Greenwich there is more than $170,000—citizens of Canton sued to get more state aid to the poorer cities. State aid was distributed primarily as a flat grant of $250 per pupil and the complainants wanted this weighted in favor of the poorer communities. A superior court judge in Hartford agreed and ruled the old system unconstitutional.

Connecticut's financial problems of the 1970s were the result of the low revenue elasticity of its property taxes, which produced about three times the revenue of the state sales tax, and of course the continued absence of an income tax in the face of ever-escalating demands for public services. Many citizens were duped into thinking that a state lottery, approved in 1971, would rescue Connecticut government from its fiscal morass. But by 1974, despite a $29.4 million gross, the lottery was still providing a profit equal to only four-tenths of one percent of total state and local government revenues in the state. Incredibly, when the legislature in 1975 finally decided to start a school equalization fund to aid poorer districts, it relied on a *second* state lottery for the financing.

After the Fundamental Orders of 1638–39, the Charter of 1662, and the constitution of 1818, Connecticut's fourth great political document was the constitution of 1965, which was precipitated by the U.S. Supreme Court's one-man, one-vote rule. It corrected the gross malapportionment of the state legislature, required redistricting and reapportionment every 10 years, guaranteed home rule to the municipalities, and strengthened the powers of the governor by requiring a two-thirds majority rather than a simple majority to override a veto. Wilbert Snow described the passage of the one-man, one-vote formula in Connecticut as "a day of rejoicing."

That ruling didn't guarantee strong, effective governors, however. The governor's office originally was primarily ceremonial, with the governor meeting once a week to get his orders from the party bosses. It was strengthened by the sheer force of will of Cross in the 1930s and later by Bowles, who fought for progressive programs, including low-cost housing, labor laws, improved mental health facilities, and governmental reorganization.

Their successors, according to Babbidge (who made an unsuccessful and badly under-financed bid for the Democratic gubernatorial nomination in 1974), did not provide very impressive leadership. Lodge, Ribicoff, Dempsey, and Meskill, he argued, "rather than educating the people to the archaic tax structure we have in Connecticut, have played to public weakness and exploited public ignorance of the effect of an income tax and have poisoned the public mind against any significant tax reform. We could correct a lot of inequities in the tax structure and could enjoy a more stable and predictable pattern of state services with it."

Reapportionment changed the attitudes of the state legislature as well as its geographical distribution. "With the single town representatives there was knowledge on the part of many that they had no political future," according to Babbidge. "Many dedicated their lives to the General Assembly, some for 30 years, and fairly conservative, stable government was the result. After one-man, one-vote, there were much younger legislators, a greater level of turnover, and a much higher ambition level. They all seem to be scrambling for some higher office. Service in the General Assembly is seen as the first rung on the political ladder." According to Franklin: "After reapportionment, the legislature began to feel its oats."

Before reapportionment, the party bosses, such as Bailey and his Republican counterpart, Searle Pinney, conferred and worked out legislation. After 1965, however, they couldn't get warring factions together for compromises and increasingly were not invited to the legislative leadership meetings to decide things. There often was less need, however, as one party often controlled both houses, depending generally on which was strongest at the top of the state and national tickets.

Before, the Republicans generally controlled the house, the Democrats the senate, and the party chairman acted as their spokesmen and negotiators. "Out of the bargaining and haggling that result from this divided control come some of the more disgraceful scenes of Connecticut politics," Duane Lockard, a political scientist, wrote. "Confusion reigns supreme as the atmosphere begins to resemble an oriental bazaar." Under the old system, party leadership was strong and cohesive, and Lockard's examination of roll call votes indicated consistent party regularity in the voting and powerful, decisive party caucuses.

Although there were and are powerful lobbies in the state—the Connecticut Business and Industry Association, the banking, insurance, trucking, utility, and liquor interests, the educators and then AFL-CIO—bribery was rare. And the parties occasionally disciplined irresponsible pressure groups, a unique occurrence in American politics. Since reapportionment, however, Democratic leadership of the house has tended to be weak and divided.

Party control figures indicate the sensitivity of the one-man, one-vote legislature to national trends. After the 1970 elections the Democrats controlled both houses, the senate by 19 to 17, the house by 99 to 78. After the 1972 Nixon landslide, the Republicans controlled both houses, the senate by 23 to 13, the house by 93 to 58. The Democrats won the post-Watergate off-year election of 1974, however, with a landslide of their own, winning the senate by 29 to 7, the house 118 to 33.

In 1973 the U.S. Supreme Court accepted a reapportionment of the house that reduced the number of districts from 177 to 151, with each representative representing about 20,000 people and each senator about 84,000, based on the 1970 census. The larger General Assembly was considered unwieldly, but the smaller number of representatives was not easily reconciled with the tradition of one representative for each of the 169 towns. (Reapportionment, it should be noted, has been no great boon for the cities in the competition for state favors vis-a-vis the smaller municipalities. The newly-dominant suburbs, indeed, sometimes appear paranoid about the cities.)

The state government in the mid-1970s still had a hard-to-manage total of 180 executive agencies, loosely grouped under 22 major executive departments. It is worth recalling that in 1943 Connecticut became the first state to create an official civil rights agency.

The tradition of town governments remains strong, as elsewhere in New England. It is Home Rule in its simplest form: "This is our town, we know how to run it. Don't tell us how." In 1975 the cities and towns were given broad new powers to borrow money and give tax breaks to attract industry to decaying areas if approved by the voters. But the problems of local government have outgrown the old town government structure in many areas, including education, water supply, sewage and refuse disposal, environmental protection, and the jurisdictional problems created when people live in one community and commute to work in another. The resulting problems of coordination are only partly met by a number of regional planning agencies, mostly centered around an urban core. The county governments were eliminated in 1960.

The state's justice system needs reorganizing, with the supreme court as its weakest link. The corrections system gets high marks, partly because of the elimination of the county governments and their jails. Now prisoners are under one state agency that operates maximum and minimum security prisons and regional correction centers and is able to recruit good professionals. The ultimate answers to the crime problem, according to Robert Franklin, whose organization pushed for a unified prison system, are sociological and concerned with racial and economic matters.

Consistent with its problems of raising funds because of the lack of an income tax, Connecticut also has a poor state government budget system. The financial reporting and personnel systems have remained unchanged since the early 1950s, and the budgeting system tells little of what the state governmental agencies do, quantitatively or qualitatively.

The state welfare system also gets failing grades because the bureaucracy often is ineffective, clients don't get the personal contact they should, and as a result there is an unsatisfactory rate of getting people off welfare and training them for jobs. "Many agencies are working uncoordinated with others, and there is lack of follow-up in placing people in jobs," Franklin noted. "The shortage of trained people for the jobs available is a Connecticut tragedy."

One area of government in which Connecticut seemed out in front of most others—at least until 1975—was reorganization to protect the natural environment. According to one ranking, Connecticut is 10th among the states in environmental quality, but this does the state something of an injustice. Connecticut is first among the states in tax incentives for pollution control equipment, fourth in number of water quality control programs, and ninth in percentage of population served by municipal water treatment plants.

The state passed a tough water pollution act in 1967 and followed with a strong air quality control act in 1970 and a solid waste management law in 1972. In 1971, with widespread support by many environmental and conservation-minded citizens and organizations, it reorganized its environmental programs under about 25 separate state departments into one state department of environmental protection. Its second commissioner, Douglas Costle, described it as "one of the most comprehensive reorganizations of environmental programs of any state" and in a sense as a "mirror image" of the federal Environmental Protection Agency.

The first commissioner was Dan Lufkin, a young Yale graduate who had amassed a fortune of more than $35 million on Wall Street at the age of 40. Lufkin, who had moved to Connecticut and bought a 480-acre dairy farm while commuting to New York City, formed an urban and environmental group called Connecticut Action Now and put up $250,000 to finance it. A member of the steering committee for Earth Day, he had also raised money for Republican politicians such as Richard Nixon and former Mayor John Lindsay of New York City. In 1970 he worked for Meskill, who made environmental protection a campaign issue and rewarded Lufkin by appointing him the first environmental protection commissioner.

Connecticut Action Now had united all the disparate conservationist elements into one strong voice and under this pressure the legislature passed a comprehensive bill. "It was a real motherhood issue," said Rita Bowlby, a close associate of Lufkin who later became director of government relations for the Connecticut Resources Recovery Authority. "The legislators on the committee got a lot of good publicity. Business saw the handwriting on the wall and cooperated." Lufkin and the legislative leaders had to make a few compromises, but the bill carried tough enforcement and penalty powers.

The problem wasn't hard to detect. When Lufkin took office Connecticut was creating seven billion pounds of solid waste annually, pouring 461 million gallons of partly treated sewage and 13 million gallons of raw sewage into Long Island Sound alone every day, and had one million tons of carbon monoxide, 324,000 tons of sulphur dioxide, and 52,000 tons of sooty particles in its air.

The new department of environmental protection took control over all pollution control programs—air, water, solid waste, radiation, thermal, and pesticides. It was entrusted with administration of all state forest lands, park systems, hunting and fishing laws, fish and game propagation, dredging and structures in navigable waters, flood plan encroachments, coastal wetlands, Indian affairs, commercial fishing, boating safety laws, and sports licenses. This has been done with a staff of 750, 175 paid by the federal government.

Much of the commission's problem lay in the fact that 30 percent of the industrial plant facilities in Connecticut were more than 50 years old, and a lot were small metal-finishing facilities. Yet in the first four years of the commission, more than 600 Connecticut firms had completed expensive abatement facilities, and the rest were expected to be in compliance within less than two years later. Although there was some resistance to the reforms by business, the utilities, entrenched bureaucrats, and some state legislators, it was not serious, according to Costle, even after the energy crisis of 1974. There was a greater problem with municipal officials because they had to go out and raise money for the programs through extended and complicated processes. By 1975 more than half a billion dollars worth of waste water treatment plants were under construction, some in anticipation of federal grants; as in many states, the slowing flow of funds from Washington was a delaying factor.

Because the environment is an interconnected element, the various towns had to cooperate on a regional basis; rivers and watershed areas, for instance, are regional. "The home rule tradition is very strong but the commission forced towns to cooperate in regional systems," Costle said in 1974. "We're beginning to intrude on local development decision-making on the basis of an overriding state interest. So, the tradition is still alive, but there have been steady erosions of that as a result of both state and federal law."

The reward is cleaner air and water. The Connecticut River is now swimmable, except after heavy rains, and when upstream plants in Massachusetts are completed it will be even cleaner. By the mid-1970s the state was also stocking fish, including trout and Atlantic salmon, in rivers for the first time in more than 20 years. As one old man pointed out to Lufkin: "The grass has come back on the [Naugatuck] river bank for the first time in years." The state was also beginning to meet federal air pollution standards and was beginning to consider a mass transit plan. It also had drafted a first effort to define a state-wide land use plan to control the nature and location of development, which is the major factor in controlling the environment.

"There's a lot of room for development, but if it's in the wrong place we wind up with environmental damage and damage to the taxpayers' pocketbooks in cleaning it up," Costle said. "Coastal and inland wetlands have a function as a flood control system for underground water or simply because of its unique wildlife habitat characteristic. The laws treat the environment like a sponge. It has a lot of assimilative capacity but if you overtax it you saturate it, and it turns those poisons around back at you. The law says, squeeze that sponge—restore some assimilative capacity."

It is impossible to prevent all pollution or development, of course. For example, environmentalists, who had managed to kill a circumferential highway around Hartford, lost a battle to prevent a highway from being built through the Still River flood plain between Danbury and New Milford, and tankers still occasionally spill oil into Long Island Sound. Moreover, the strong leadership of the department of environmental protection exercised by Lufkin and Costle was noticeably lacking under the commissioner appointed by Governor Grasso (Joseph Gill, a former agriculture secretary in the Dempsey administration). At one point in spring 1975 Gill even fired all the lawyers working for the department, suggesting that conciliation and voluntary compliance would be all-sufficient.

In 1974 the state began building a $295 million state-wide recycling system of 10 "resource recovery" plants to recycle the 10,000 tons of solid wastes produced daily by the 169 towns and cities. The plants were to separate metals and glass and convert trash and garbage into enough fuel to supply 10 percent of the electricity needed in their regions. Annual operating costs were originally estimated at $50 million with the system becoming self-supporting through the sale of recycled materials and user fees.

The waste recovery and energy generation plan was the first statewide plan of its kind in the United States—the type of imaginative planning and action which Connecticut, with its high levels of income and compact geography, could undertake in many fields such as mass transit and comprehensive land use planning. Indeed, compared to its potential, Connecticut's performance in government and planning is a distinct disappointment. Governor Grasso even believes that in this highly interdependent state, with its tightly packed metropolitan corridors, land use planning can be left to the almost total discretion of localities. In the words of Bice Clemow: "We had a fantastic opportunity to be the first effective city-state. The scale is right, the place is right, the contiguity to markets is right. If we'd adopted an effective tax structure we might have made it."

City and Town: Geographic Connecticut in Our Time

Geographic Connecticut is a study in contrasts. One of the most densely urbanized and industrialized states, it has ranked fourth in population density since 1880. Yet 70 percent of the land surface is in woodland, more than there was 100 years ago. The state is a combination of industrial cities, postwar suburbs (by 1970, 57.4 percent of the population was suburban, 16 percentage points more than just a decade previous), historical small towns, and farms. Despite its high population density, three-quarters of Connecticut is sparsely populated. More than 1,000 lakes dot the landscape.

The coastline is typically New England, rock-bound and rugged with sandy beaches and salt meadows backed by a mildly rolling upland. In the western highlands of the Berkshire Hills, one finds some of the wildest and most spectacular scenery in eastern America. The point of highest altitude is Bear Mountain, elevation 2,355 feet, in the northwest corner of the state. The gorge of the Mianus River near the New York state line is one of the most primitive areas near New York City. The state also contains such beautifully preserved towns as Litchfield, Stonington, Lyme, and Roxbury. The farms have corn, tobacco, orchards, and dairy pastures, although more and more farmland is being swallowed up for residential and commercial development.

The country east of the Connecticut River Valley is less rugged than in the west, but it is sparsely populated and airline pilots note it as one of the few dark spots at night on the urbanized Eastern seaboard corridor from Washington, D.C. to Boston. This is the area of the textile mills that went South in search of cheap labor in the late 19th and early 20th centuries. With the exception of areas such as New London, with its Navy installations, it is much less prosperous than the rest of Connecticut. For instance, the median income of Plainfield in 1969 was $8,954 compared to $19,956 in Greenwich. This eastern section has also suffered in recent decades because of migration to areas of greater opportunity.

Many of the small towns of old Yankee stock in central and western Connecticut have experienced declining population as well, primarily because of the decline of agriculture. The populations of 10 of the 22 towns in Litchfield County are smaller than in 1900, a fact that distresses traditionalists because Litchfield, the birthplace of Harriet Beecher Stowe, is regarded by many Northern New Englanders as the last Yankee bastion in a state they see becoming a New York City suburb. Anyone who has lived in Connecticut a day longer than his neighbor looks down on him as an interloper. The residents of Fairfield County are not regarded as Connecticut Yankees at all by those in the rest of the state. The people of Litchfield, with their gracious old Colonial homes and beautiful streets, consider themselves the *crème de la crème*. The center of the town, in fact, has been declared an "historical district."

Near Hartford, Windsor, and Wetherfield probably have as many well-preserved pre-Revolutionary houses as any town in Connecticut. In the southern part of the state are the port cities of New London (population 31,630) and Groton (38,523), and Mystic, an old whaling port and site of one of the nation's leading maritime museums. Highlights are the *Charles W. Morgan*, the last of the great wooden whaling ships, which sailed for 80 years and earned $2 million, and the *Joseph Conrad*, one of the last of the square riggers and now used as a training ship.

The southern half of the state also features summer resorts as well as factory towns and the exurbia of Fairfield County. One tourist attraction is the P. T. Barnum mansion and Seaside Park museum in Barnum's home town of Bridgeport. One of the state's leading attractions is the American Shakespeare Festival Theater in Stratford, which is modeled after the famous Globe Theatre in London. Always in the spring there is a riot of laurel, rhododendron, and dogwood, although the fall display of maples, oaks, and other hardwood trees, blazing in scarlet, russet, yellow, and orange is even more spectacular. Skiing, of course, is a major winter tourist industry in western Connecticut.

The geographic and economic spine of Connecticut is the urban corridor that runs from north to south down the center of the state, roughly along the Connecticut River valley, from Windsor Locks and Hartford through New Britain, Bristol, Waterbury, Middletown, and Meriden to New Haven. The corridor then extends from New Haven along the Long Island Sound through Bridgeport, Fairfield, Norwalk, and Darien to Stamford and Greenwich. It contains most of the state's population and an estimated 90 percent of its resources.

By 1972, Hartford County, Fairfield County, and New Haven County combined had almost 78 percent of Connecticut's population; Hartford County had about 817,000, or 26.9 percent; Fairfield County had about 793,000, 26.2 percent; and New Haven County had about 745,000, 24.6 percent. Hartford, the capital and the state's largest city, had a population of about 160,000 (6.4 percent of the state); Bridgeport, the second (after Hartford) most industrialized city, showed a population of about 156,000; New Haven had about 138,000; Stamford and Waterbury had about 100,000 each, and New Britain 83,441.

Many of the corridor cities are old milling and manufacturing towns. Waterbury is known as the "brass capital" of the nation, and some of the companies that made brass buttons for Revolutionary war soldiers' uniforms are still there. New Britain is renowned as the "hardware city," Hartford is the insurance capital, and Danbury (50,781) is a smaller city that was once the hat center of the country. Darien (20,311), Fairfield (56,-487), and Greenwich (59,755) are expensive suburban residential areas for many people who work in New York. In recent years these towns have attracted many large corporations which have moved their headquarters out of New York City. Almost all the towns in the urban corridor have a population density of 500 per square mile or more; in most the figure is actually 1,000 or more.

With suburbanization has come difficulties for the central cities, primarily because of the flight of the white middle class and the influx of blacks and other generally poor and uneducated minorities. Urban Connecticut, however, has not experienced the degree of urban core rot that has afflicted many East Coast Revolutionary-era cities (particularly in New Jersey). By the 1960s the six largest cities, plus Norwalk, Bristol, and New London, had embarked on urban renewal projects. The leader, not only of Connecticut but of most of the nation, was New Haven under its dynamic and persistent mayor, Richard Charles Lee, who was elected in 1953 and served for 16 years.

When Lee was elected, no new private office or hotel buildings or any public buildings, except two schools, had been built in New Haven for 30 years. The downtown, particularly in a three-block radius from the ancient

City Hall, was decayed and increasingly deserted as factories moved to open areas and more and more downtown shops became vacant. Lee had run unsuccessfully twice before on traditional themes of paving, playgrounds, honesty, and efficiency. Compaigning on a promise of urban renewal and with the support of Yale faculty members and Democratic party leaders such as Arthur T Barbieri and John Golden, Lee finally won at the age of 37.

Rebuilding New Haven immediately became the center of Lee's existence. He worked from a master plan drawn up by a French urban planner, Maurice Rotival, who was on the Yale University faculty during the 1940s. It envisioned New Haven as a traffic center with the renewal planned around the Connecticut Turnpike (Interstate 95) and other new highways. Lee hired as his renewal chief a like-minded young lawyer named Edward Logue. The two were equally dedicated and enjoyed a stormy but brotherly relationship before Logue went on to mastermind Boston's urban renewal (and later the New York State Urban Development Corporation). They clashed constantly over money—Lee controlling the purse—and Lee had to strive mightily to keep the aggressive and often abrasive Logue under control.

Together the two men achieved a great deal, although their quarrels frequently ended with Logue either quitting or being fired, minicrises which often required several days of mediation. Lee managed to whip the city bureaucracy into line, and he and Logue assembled an aggressive young staff which they encouraged to compete among themselves, somewhat in the way Franklin D. Roosevelt did with his dedicated but often perplexed New Dealers. They would throw a problem at several aides and the one who came up with the best solution got to solve it, with the full backing of the boss. As Lee's chronicler, Allan Talbott, noted: "Problems were not merely solved; they were crushed to death." Lee and Logue publicly encouraged each other's successes and taunted failures. The result was an atmosphere of competitiveness and high pressure; the problem was not to arouse enthusiasm but to control it.

Lee mustered the support of the Yale University Law, Political Science, Architecture, and Planning Departments (Nicholas Katzenbach, the future U.S. Attorney General, was on Rotival's staff) and got his people appointed to key positions in the New Haven city government. He also cut Golden and Barbieri in on decisions about patronage and contracts and managed to keep these powerful men—whose political power had been built partly on their reputation for keeping their word—from overwhelming him. This was done by playing off the two politically jealous figures against each other and often against Logue. To help sell urban renewal to the city, particularly the difficult problem of moving businessmen and residents to make room for new building projects, Lee formed the Citizens Action Commission, a group of civic and business leaders.

One vice president of the group was Alfred Whitney Griswold, the president of Yale from 1950 until his death in 1963. Lee had been director of the university news bureau before his election, and a warm friendship developed between the ebullient Irish Catholic mayor and the seemingly more restrained but equally mercurial Yankee. Both were maverick reformers, each with a rich, full-blown sense of humor. Griswold hated the grime and decay of downtown New Haven, and their friendship resulted in Yale's helping Lee on several occasions, including a role in bailing Lee out of a financing crisis in the building of the new Malley department store. Lee in turn helped Griswold when the new Yale hockey and skating rink was threatened by a conscientious bureaucrat's close interpretation of the fire code.

Under Lee's driving leadership the state was persuaded to build the Oak Street Connector, a six-lane link between downtown New Haven and the Connecticut Turnpike. The Oak Street project was the first. About 900 families were moved into new low-cost housing, and the slum was rebuilt with office buildings, a retail shopping plaza, high-rise apartments, and an industrial park. The Church Street project is a 96-acre area with a new hotel, department store, and apartment and office buildings. Lee persuaded Macy's to locate in the building of an old department store in the Church Street center after he learned that J. Richardson Dillworth, a friend and nephew of the former mayor of Philadelphia, was on the board of Macy's.

Neighborhood renewals followed. Wooster Square, one of the nation's first, is probably the most successful. In a sense, the Wooster Square project spilled over into nearby towns because Interstate 91 after it passed Wooster Square ran through a park and game preserve that aroused residents of suburban towns. Afraid that it might delay his projects, Lee proposed a regional corporation, which eventually became the Quinnipiac Valley Development Corporation, named after the river that flowed through the towns. Although it never became the full-fledged regional development corporation its proponents hoped for, signs of the development it proposed are evident along I-91.

Such initiative and flexibility were part of the reason for Lee's success, but another was his ability to inspire popular support. He was one of the first politicians to employ public opinion polling techniques and was the person responsible for introducing John F. Kennedy to pollster Louis Harris. Lee had an extraordinarily sensitive political antenna and a finely tuned sense of timing. His polls showed that more New Haven schoolchildren knew who he was than could identify the President and that 50 percent not only liked him but considered him a close friend of the family.

At home, Lee had a knack for personally involving many voters. "Under his administration urban renewal became as comforting as a new home, as useful as a handsome new school, as liberal as an antipoverty program, as commercial as a department store . . . as convenient as a new expressway, and as understandable as a neighborhood playground," Talbott writes. In Washington, Lee was extraordinarily aggressive in seeking out the new federal urban renewal funds and by 1965 had got more than $110 million, sixth in total amount in the nation after New York, Philadelphia, Chicago, Boston, and Detroit. Per capita, New Haven was first with $745; the second in per capita grants—Newark, N.J., with $277—wasn't even close. By 1970 the city received $180 million in public funds and another $250 million in private investment. Lee became known as the "beggar with a bushel basket." Before getting government funding, however, urban renewal got started with $2 million Mitchell Svirdoff, another key man, got from the Ford Foundation.

New Haven's renewal was an impressive pioneering effort that was well ahead of the rest of the nation, but Lee retired in 1970 a bitter man, according to Homer Babbidge. Part of the reason is that the reform impetus of the 1950s and 1960s had waned by then. "The 1950s and 1960s were dynamic years, exciting and full of change and controversy," Lee told me in a 1974 interview. "It was a glorious period and whatever we needed in the way of instruments and appropriations, we just had to sing our song and people listened." John Kennedy was in the White House and "with people like me barking at their heels . . . we were given special attention. You just had to spell it out for Bobby [Kennedy] and he understood it—and he would go all out for an idea." In 1968, however, Lee recognized that Richard Nixon would be elected. "All the bad things I feared came true. The 1970s is an era of caution. Apathy has settled in."

Another problem of the New Haven effort was that physical renewal at first took precedence over human renewal, a criticism leveled by increasingly militant blacks and conceded in more recent years by Lee himself. "The human renewal programs didn't come until we began to find these families who were tucked away where they had been lost for 20 or 30 years," he said. "We discovered that we had a lot more poor than we realized and a lot more problems than we realized. . . . So we were really moving the slums from one neighborhood to another."

New Haven's black population increased from 9,500 at the end of World War II to about 40,000, plus about 5,000 Puerto Ricans, in the early 1970s. To deal with these problems, Lee formed Community Progress, Inc., a private antipoverty organization. The city inaugurated preschool programs and then found that parents who had been charity wards for two or three generations had to be taught how to raise their children and what their responsibilities as parents were. A corps of homemakers was established to teach the residents of the new housing how to take care of it. "When people moved they took their slum habits with them," Lee recalled. "Our workers would go into the gin mills and pool parlors and confectionary stores and bookie joints and roust these people out to our van to register. We persuaded as many of them as possible to enter our work training center."

One big criticism common to all urban renewal is that appropriate housing is never found for all who are displaced. Despite the construction of 7,314 new units during Lee's tenure, the city ended up with an estimated 1,350 fewer than when the renewal began. Road and business construction, the key to the renewal, took a tremendous toll of housing, but many small businessmen were also driven out because they were unable to rebuild their clientele in new locations

The housing burden fell disproportionately on the minorities, but another complaint was that the urban managers had too much faith in technology and not enough in democracy. A major complaint of blacks was that they had had too little say in the decisions affecting them. The city was shaken by the black riots in the summer of 1967, the same time as the great disturbances in Detroit and Newark. By comparison, these disturbances didn't amount to much. There were no fatalities or extensive property damage. But they disrupted New Haven's self-image as a model city. They also, as elsewhere, hastened the flight of whites to the suburbs, weakening the prosperous middle class base that is the key to any city's survival and prosperity. There are now more blacks than whites in the city school system. New Haven's overall population dropped by some 20,000 between 1950 and 1970.

During the 1970s CPI came under increased challenge from the eight neighborhood "corporations" it had spawned in an attempt to get more local participation in decision-making. The protests were particularly vocal from such areas as the Hill, which had become something of a dumping ground for people who had been displaced, sometimes more than once, by the renewal.

For all its problems, however, New Haven has demonstrated considerable social stability. The potentially explosive Black Panther murder trial in 1970 was defused by the acquittal of one of the defendants by a calm, judicious, predominantly white jury—even after Kingman Brewster, the president of Yale, expressed his doubts about the possibility of a black man getting a fair trial in New Haven. Brewster's attitude, plus the students' maturity and the wisdom of Police Chief Jim Ahern, kept a May Day 1970, pro-Panther rally at Yale from exploding, a considerable feat because demonstrations against the Cambodia invasion were sweeping many of the nation's campuses at the time.

As in all university towns, there is town-gown conflict. New Haven's is not as bad as many say, although Yale's constant need to expand and the consequent pressure on nearby real estate creates a problem. About 60 percent of the city's population is of Italian descent, and many have class resentments of the Yalies. But as one member of the city government, which by the 1970s was dominated by Italian-Americans, put it during Lee's tenure: "Without Yale, New Haven would be just another Bridgeport and none of us wants that." In September 1975 the city's regular Democratic organization, long headed by a flamboyant Italian politician named Arthur T. Barbieri, received a stunning upset when the incumbent mayor, Bartholomew F. Guida, was upset in the Democratic primary by Frank F. Logue, the younger brother of Edward J. Logue. The result was a victory for the Irish over the Italians, but perhaps more significantly, for Yale students, blacks, and residents of the politically independent middle-class neighborhoods, who apparently agreed with Frank Logue that the Barbieri-Guida regime had been marked by secrecy, machine politics, and cronyism.

For all the retrospective criticism of his administration, Lee was still able to note when I spoke with him in 1974:

"A lot of the things that were problems 20 years ago are not problems today. In Connecticut we were at the bottom in central cities. We used to be third or fourth in retail shopping. Now we're first in Connecticut in retail shopping." So there seems to be some vitality still in this old city that likes to boast of its historical "firsts"—the first meat grinder, the first steamboat, and, of all things, the first lollipop. Now one must add, if not the very first, at least the nation's most ambitious effort to apply every conceivable resource to save a proud old city that could easily have become another Newark of our times.

Hartford was about 10 years behind New Haven in renewal but it landed running, and its projects are if anything more ambitious than New Haven's. Like nearly every city, Hartford has suffered the post-World War II syndrome of drugs, crimes, rising taxes, a steadily deteriorating old center city, white flights to suburbs and an influx of Southern blacks and Puerto Ricans seeking jobs in the city's industries. By the mid-1970s, the 45,000 blacks, mostly concentrated in the North End, the slum area north of the old State House, and more than 20,000 Puerto Ricans made up more than one-half of Hartford's population. Nearly three-fourths of the pupils in the public schools were black or Puerto Rican. In 1969 and 1970 widespread rioting and looting erupted as a result of grievances ranging from high prices charged by merchants in the tightly impacted slum to police treatment. As in so many cities, thousands of blacks had been uprooted by the renewal projects.

In the mid-1960s the city's decaying downtown section of tenements, small businesses, and pawnshops was rejuvenated by the construction of Constitution Plaza, at the cost of $40 million, mostly in private funds backed by the Travelers Insurance Co. The Plaza is dominated by a hotel, a television broadcasting center, and four high-rise office buildings. The most distinctive is the Phoenix Mutual Life Insurance Building, an oval-shaped glass skyscraper known as "The Boat" because its oval shape resembles a ship's hull.

Hartford built Constitutional Plaza with remarkable speed. One reason for the pace and scope of the plans was the involvement of the top executives of the city's insurance companies and banks who can commit their corporations' resources and cash. The city followed Constitution Plaza with a downtown civic center that includes a sports arena for the New England Whalers of the World Hockey Association, a convention center, an exhibition hall, and a new hotel. The Financial Center, a 26-story office tower, is near Constitution Plaza. Despite all this building, retail business in the Plaza has been, in the words of one observer, "a continuing disaster."

Next was the Windsor Street project, which now contains the Hartford branch of Rensselaer Polytechnic Institute and several office buildings. These two projects forced the relocation of blacks and Italian-Americans, however, and in early 1969 civic-minded business leaders organized the Greater Hartford Corporation to deal with urban blight and suburban sprawl. They included William P. Gwinn of United Aircraft, which is located in East Hartford; Henry R. Roberts of Connecticut General Life Insurance, who was one of the prime movers; Olcott D. Smith of Aetna Life and Casualty; and Roger C. Wilkins of Travelers.

This in turn led to creation of the Greater Hartford Process, Inc., 1970, an organization that two years later presented an $800 million, 15-year plan to renovate the city area. GHP's ultimate goal was an integrated plan for growth in the 29 towns in the north-central area around Hartford, an area that at the time had a population of about 670,000 and was expected to be more than 800,000 by the 1980s. Another nonprofit organization, the Greater Hartford Community Development Corporation, or "Devco," was established at the GHP's operational organization.

The first phase of Hartford's future rejuvenation, contemplated for completion by the mid-1980s, calls for construction of 6,500 new housing units and 10,000 rehabilitated units, new elementary schools, parks, recreational areas, and more hotel, retail, and restaurant facilities.

In the north end there are a number of GHP neighborhood projects aimed at integrating the crucial elements—housing, with low and moderate income housing evenly dispersed to break down economic segregation; land use planning for open spaces and to eliminate wasteful suburban sprawl; schools that also serve as community, health, and recreational centers (an idea borrowed from New Haven); and transportation, employment, and social service programs. All these efforts are aimed at breaking down residential and economic segregation.

The leader was the South Arsenal area, which was the first to get new housing—274 units of low- and moderate-income housing—schools, and a community center. One of the schools was the Everywhere School, an experimental institution serving the entire city. Facilitating this development was the formation of the South Arsenal Neighborhood Development Corporation (SAND). It was formed prior to the Hartford Process as a medium for legal action for neighborhood residents, mostly blacks, who viewed urban renewal with some justification as primarily a process of moving the ghetto from one area to another.

The Hartford Process also extended technical assistance in land use planning to the nearby town of Farmington, at that town's request. But its most ambitious idea was the proposed new town in Coventry, about 20 minutes northeast of Hartford. The corporation purchased more than 1,000 acres there to create a business, industrial, and residential community of about 20,000 residents and had business leaders such as Olcott Smith and Roger Wilkins meet with the local people to try to sell them on the idea. The idea was quite appropriate because James Rouse, the Hartford Process's godfather, was one of the creators of Columbia, Md., a new town created outside Washington, D.C. in the 1960s.

Hartford Process officials also argued that the plan would help Coventry's tax rate, employment, recreation, health facilities, zoning and land use planning, and housing. A lot of people worried that the new town, with its provisions for low- and moderate-income housing, might become a dumping ground for low-income residents. The project finally fell victim to the economic recession of the mid-1970s and the withdrawal of support by the business community when it became apparent that the project would involve major financial losses.

Peter Libassi, president of the Greater Hartford Process, predicted beforehand that "we're going to have very little success if the national government doesn't offer us some help. It's very hard to bring about the economic integration of suburban communities without major public support." The Process also received a serious setback in 1975 when a staff memorandum suggesting consideration of reducing Puerto Rican migration into the city was made public.

Despite the inability or unwillingness of the Hartford business community to finance a development as massive as the Coventry project from its own resources, the fact is that the presence of that huge pool of capital, with so many leaders dedicated to a better future for the Hartford area, has made many projects possible in Hartford that would never move forward in the typical "branch town." This, in turn, has often meant Hartford did not need to wait for slow-moving federal aid and its attendant red tape, detailed regulations, and guidelines. "We're a very unusual city," Libassi said. "We can raise . . . capital for long-term development activities from the private sector. The business community has remained extremely supportive." (That support, one should note, might not have been as constant without the charismatic leadership and proven business acumen of James Rouse, who came to Hartford every two months or so to give heart to the business leaders, telling them, in effect. "Yes, you can do it.")

The recession and inflation of the mid-1970s eventually forced an 180-degree turn from GHP's initial approach—from a suburban-city cooperative mold to assisting the city in its financial struggles with the suburbs, and from large-scale real estate development to an emphasis on inner-city neighborhood revitalization, assistance for local government, and attracting private developers to undertake modest-scale inner-city developments. GHP's budget, indeed, dropped from $800,000 in 1975 to $450,000 in 1976—though Libassi claimed the organization was becoming "more influential" through its shift from real estate development to a "more supportive, catalytic and causative role."

The growing alienation between Hartford and its wealthy suburbs was symbolized by the legal action taken by the city in 1975 to block $4.4 million in federal community development funds scheduled to go to seven suburbs which the city claimed had failed to offer plans to build low-cost housing. In essence, the city's lawsuit claimed that the suburbs were using community development money to enhance their job-producing potential—while leaving it to the city of Hartford to house the region's low-income families.

One of the major problems of the Hartford area, Libassi said, was that "the essential structural change" to make Hartford a viable city had not taken place "at the local, city, state or federal level." A specific weakness—in addition to those of all center cities—is that Hartford has a modified council-manager form of government. Because the mayor is not the city's chief executive officer, he is not eligible to serve on the regional council of elected officials. Nor does he or the city manager appoint any of Hartford's five representatives on the Capital Regional Planning Agency to act as their spokesmen for long-range planning. Although there are 36,000 Democrats to about 8,000 Republicans, Hartford had a Republican mayor, Ann Uccello, in the late 1960s.

Hartford does have a rich tradition to build on. Mark Twain built his delightfully inventive home in the city (because his publisher was there) and the Harriet Beecher Stowe House is next door. In West Hartford, one of the most beautiful residential communities in the country, is the modest saltbox house where Noah Webster, compiler of the first American dictionary, was born.

For years the Hartford skyline was dominated by the Travelers Insurance Company's skyscraper, the tallest building in New England until the erection of the Prudential Tower in Boston in 1965. Hartford residents approaching the city at night knew they were getting close when they saw the green glow of the Travelers Tower light.

Past Constitution Plaza is the Old State House, a lovely colonial masterpiece designed by Charles Bulfinch in 1796, and now a museum featuring the beautiful Council Chamber and a graceful unsupported spiral staircase. The seat of State government was transferred in 1879 to the present State Capitol, a domed Victorian structure sometimes described as a "Gothic Taj Mahal." On Main Street is the Wadsworth Atheneum, America's oldest public art museum, which recently was renovated and got a new wing for $4.7 million, the Avery Art Memorial, and the Morgan Memorial, which was a gift of the famous financier, J. P. Morgan, a Hartford boy. The Morgan Memorial has a gun collection that includes the wooden model of the original Colt revolver, invented in Hartford by Samuel Colt. There are three museums that feature Colt's works. The others are in the Colt building south of town with its onion-shaped dome and in the imposing State Library, whose collection includes the six-shooters of Wild Bill Hickok and Bat Masterson. Another memorable building is the Bushnell Memorial, on the Capitol's east flank, where symphonies, operas, and ballet play, and the State Armory. Trinity College, with a tree-shaded neogothic campus, is in the southern part of the city.

The experiences of Hartford and New Haven have been shared by some of Connecticut's other cities. Middletown (population 36,924), the home of Wesleyan University, suffered racial tensions in the late 1960s. The same happened in Waterbury, where the older Irish and Italian ethnic groups who long have run the city and the Democratic party found themselves under more and more pressure from increasingly militant blacks.

Bridgeport, a factory town that has been the butt of jokes since Mark Twain poked fun at it in *A Connecticut Yankee in King Arthur's Court*, has also been struggling desperately with its problems. It has knocked down thousands of decaying tenements and small stores and put up housing projects, shopping plazas, and office high-rise buildings. But it sometimes seems that little has gone right. Many of the housing projects soon become barely habitable, the Lafayette Plaza shopping center did poorly when it first opened, and discount stores have replaced stylish shops on Main Street. The city's pride, its parks, have had swaths bulldozed through them for new streets to funnel business into the downtown area. Lafayette Plaza, in addition to being a business disappointment, is the target of criticism by blacks and Puerto Ricans who were displaced by its construction. The 1970 Census showed about 25,000 blacks and 14,000 Spanish-Americans in the city's population, but racial tensions have generally been contained.

Bridgeport was the home of P. T. Barnum, who donated a museum and the Seaside Park recreation center. The city was insulted by former New York Mayor John Lindsay, who called it "dirty," a bad rap because it is as clean and litter-free as any in the country and certainly more so than New York City. Bridgeport was also described as "terribly depressing" by actor Paul Newman, who later apologized.

In a happy tradition of cultural trivia, the Barnum Institute of Science and History features mementos of Jenny Lind, the Swedish Nightingale, and Tom Thumb, the circus midget. Tom Thumb's house is in Bridgeport. The Beardsley Park Zoo, appropriately, contained the only pair of dwarf mongoose on the East Coast and two spotted palm civets, an animal that's part cat, part dog. Industrially, Bridgeport is the home of Remington Arms, the Singer sewing machine, General Electric, and Dictaphone.

In the Torrington Valley, west of Hartford, is the industrial town of Torrington, home of abolitionist John Brown. Climbing into the Litchfield hills is the altogether pleasing town of Litchfield, to which I referred earlier. Litchfield's Green is dominated by the white-steepled Congregational Church and the elm-lined streets have some of the most magnificent white clapboarded colonial homes in America. The birthplaces of Harriet Beecher Stowe and Henry Ward Beecher are in Litchfield, as is the Tapping Reeve House. On its grounds is a small white building that was the first law school in the country, where men like Aaron Burr (Tapping Reeve's brother-in-law) and John C. Calhoun studied.

In Fairfield County, Connecticut's "Gold Coast"—its "Alsace-Lorraine," in Wilbert Snow's memorable phrase—one finds that Stamford, once a sleepy, decaying little city that had a large proportion of factory workers, is undergoing renewal largely because many big corporations are moving their headquarters to the area from New York City. They include Xerox, Pitney Bowes, American Cyanamid, Barnes Engineering, Olin Mathieson, Schweppes, Continental Oil, Marx Toys, Litton Industries, and many others. They provided impetus for the $200 million 130-acre downtown renewal project that was begun in 1965. By 1974 Stamford could boast a business community with assets of $26 billion, a white-collar payroll of 14,000 people, and a median annual income of $16,000. High mark of the renewal area is a 21-story obelisk on Landmark Square that has offices, a sunken skating rink, and a rooftop restaurant with a view of Long Island Sound. It is the tallest building between New York and New Haven.

The desire of business to move to the environs of Stamford helped get the renewal plan underway and once started the plan attracted more. They have been an immediate as well as long-term help. When the city's New Home Towers housing project for moderate-income families was about to go bankrupt, several of the companies provided financing that enabled the project to avoid defaulting on its $850,000 debt, which would have adversely affected the entire urban renewal project.

Stamford is just one goal of New York corporations that look for headquarters outside the city. More than 100 moved to Greenwich alone in 1970 and 1971, and while they contributed more than $2 million a year in taxes and made little additional demand on city services, the residents of Greenwich were not enthusiastic. They had moved there to avoid the city and didn't want the city to follow them. They successfully resisted efforts of Xerox to settle in the town, even though the company spent $4.5 million for a 104-acre piece of land and mounted a public relations campaign that included a $250,000 planning study. One developer, trying to build an office complex in the center of downtown Greenwich, sued members of the city legislature for opposing the project. A $10 million office and store complex towering over the railroad station prompted some to complain that it looked as though it was transplanted from "Park Avenue."

A proposed move by RCA to New Canaan stirred a similar zoning controversy and eventual defeat. New Canaan in 1970 was the wealthiest town in Connecticut, with an average annual household income of $24,073, but many residents didn't relish the prospect of a couple of thousand new residents and the added strain on town services.

Some critics contend that Connecticut's lack of a state personal income tax appeals to well-paid executives, but this is a questionable motivation for corporate moves. More important is space to expand office and manufacturing activities and less traffic, noise, pollution, congestion, and other urban aggravations. Unfortunately, most of the fugitive corporations from New York have opted for parklike suburban settings rather than moving into the city centers, where their presence would add vitality and where their workers could more easily reach their places of work by mass transit rather than energy-consumptive private automobile travel. The move, of course, meant that many had to buy automobiles.

Fairfield County is not just a prestige address. Traditionally, it has been one of the Eastern Seaboard's most attractive and desirable residential locations. Whether this will always be true is another question. By the 1970s, as the pressures of commercialism increased, so did pollution. Traffic congestion was causing smog, and the osyters and clams from Long Island Sound were no longer edible. These and other urban problems made the residents of the county increasingly defensive.

Fairfield County is not the richest county in America (in fact, it ranks only 9th), but it has within its borders the two richest metropolitan areas in the nation—Stamford, where five-bedroom homes sold for $125,000 and had a vacancy rate of only 0.2 percent in the mid-1970s, and Norwalk. Among its towns are such luxurious enclaves as Greenwich, Darien, Westport, and Fairfield, which have been the homes of such people as composer Richard Rodgers, industrialist and art collector Joseph Hirshorn, actresses Bette Davis and June Havoc, and writers Peter DeVries and Hamilton Basso. The county contains industrial cities such as Bridgeport, Stamford, Danbury, and Norwalk, but it also has a landscape of rocky coastlines, beaches and harbors, sailboats, and wooded hunt country. It is an area of New York executives in Brooks Brothers suits commuting to their jobs, and much of it has remained very Wasp in character. There is a story that one resident of Greenwich, a writer, was asked by visitors in an automobile if she could tell them where the Rich family lived. Her puzzled response was: "Well, I think that adjective would really apply to every family here."

Jews have not always been made welcome or allowed in the county and beach clubs or allowed to buy homes wherever they wished. Mrs. Richard Rodgers once told how she and Mr. Rodgers were kept from joining a beach club because they were Jews and good-naturedly speculated on how many Christians would have entertained them if her husband had not been who he was.

Fairfield County also suffered the problems of drugs and youthful alienation that afflicted much of affluent America in the late 1960s and early 1970s. The pressures to break up the multi-acreage exclusionary zoning may have caused the residents the most grief, however. The campaign against Fairfield's existing zoning policies was led by civil rights groups and advocate planners who protested that the county allowed only wealthy whites to live there and that pressure for housing and dwindling land made it imperative to open the area to low- and moderate income housing. Needless to say, the established residents resisted opening up their towns to the problems of race and poverty. Some, such as literary critic and historian Malcolm Cowley, denounced proposed moderate- or low-income housing as "the worst threat to the environment next to strip mining (or) opening up the open farmland to the bulldozer."

Many communities faced the problem. In New Fairfield there was a proposal for a 253-acre new city of 8,000 on Candlewood Lake which its proponents said would open up the suburban American dream to a variety of races and backgrounds. Established residents countered that it would be a land speculators' dream and a pollution nightmare, and most signed a petition against it.

The zoning requirements for large lots, mostly written in the early 1930s, were originally intended to maintain the New England character of the towns. Under the pressures of urbanization and desegregation, however, this idea has come under increasing assault. New Canaan was the target of the most serious test case, which ironically was led by a former New Canaan town planner named Paul Davidoff, who became director of the Suburban Action Institute. The suit charged that the town's land-use regulations were discriminatory; the residents countered that anyone who could afford to live there was welcome. Davidoff argued that many zoning laws in the nation were illegal: "The suburbs are where we are building America, an America we can be proud of, rather than the segregated America we have been putting up."

Economics of the Nutmeg State

Although the manufacturing sector is decreasing, Connecticut is one of the most heavily industrialized states of America; indeed there are only seven other states (including, interestingly, its New England neighbors of Rhode Island and New Hampshire) in which a larger proportion of the work force is employed in factories. The "workshop"—and productive—complexion of Connecticut is underscored by the fact that there is not a single other state of the Union where a lesser percentage of the work force is employed by local, state, or federal government. The list of products in which the state has long played a leading or major role in the nation includes brass, firearms, machinery and machine tools, silverware, hats, clocks, and, in times past, textiles. Here one finds one of America's leading centers of the production of airplane engines and helicopters, electronic equipment, and nuclear submarines. Though New York City in fact outshines it in total value of outstanding policies and assets, Hartford has long been considered the insurance capital of the United States.

All of this stems naturally from Connecticut's history. The first ship built in the state was "Tryall" in Wethersfield in 1649, and shipbuilding began in New London in 1664. New Haven became an early port for the West Indies and the China trade, and the insurance industry grew out of agreements between groups of merchants in Boston and New Haven to share the financial losses when their ships were lost to storms or pirates. In time these underwriting partnerships evolved into insurance companies and their business expanded into fire, casualty, and life insurance. The earliest known policy issued in America was written on February 8, 1794, by the Hartford firm of Sanford and Wadsworth giving a local homeowner £800 of fire insurance for a year at .5 percent.

Connecticut has no mineral resources except for lime and silica used in making low-grade glass, although in the 18th century there was low-grade iron and copper ore. Its manufacturing industry is the result of the ingenuity of men such as Eli Whitney and Samuel Colt who pioneered mass production techniques. A not inconsiderable factor in Connecticut's manufacturing is the state's location in relation to the nation's major market centers such as New York and Boston. One-third of the country's population lies within 500 miles of Connecticut.

Almost every important Connecticut industry got its impetus from the salesmanship of the Yankee peddler who steadily pushed the markets west. The state leads the nation in numbers of patents granted in relation to population and has been called "The Gadget State." In addition to Whitney's invention, Connecticut's Charles Goodyear developed the vulcanizing process for rubber with its implications for the automobile, industry, and electricity. The stone crusher by Whitney's nephew, Eli Whitney Blake, revolutionized road building. The precision measuring instrument invented by Francis Pratt and Amos Whitney was accurate to 1/100,000 of an inch.

The latter-day fruits of all this were apparent in the early 1970s when Connecticut ranked first in the nation in number of people employed in manufacturing aircraft engines and parts (about 41,000, 35.8 percent of the U.S. total), submarines (16,000 or 100 percent of the national total), bearings (15,000 or 28.8 percent), and helicopters (12,100 or 46.5 percent). It was second in numbers engaged in manufacturing typewriters and office machines, electrical equipment such as switches and conductors, and appliances. It was third in hardware, guns and ammunition, watches and clocks, and optical instruments. United Aircraft with its Pratt Whitney (jet engines) and Sikorsky (helicopters) divisions is one of the state's leading employers.

Of the state's 60,000 manufacturing firms, an astoundingly high total of 2,400 are engaged in work with metal—bending, polishing, drilling, cutting, or fabricating it into something. Of the 433,000 Connecticut workers in manufacturing in the mid-1970s, 308,000 were in metals and metal products. Connecticut ranked first in the ratio of skilled workers in the total labor force, first in per capita value added in manufacturing (to a great extent because of the number of nuclear submarines, jet engines, machine tools, and firearms manufactured in the state) and first in per capita value of defense contracts. It was second to California in total dollar value of defense contracts.

By the mid-1970s Connecticut's gross state product was close to $21 billion. According to Mark Feinberg, director of development for the state's department of commerce, some 90 percent of the goods the state produces—including such services as insurance and research and development—is exported to out-of-state purchasers. Of this some $750 million in goods and services goes to foreign nations, with Pratt Whitney's jet engines accounting for about half the amount.

Connecticut is not a state of cheap labor—there are only 12 states, in fact, where factory workers earn more on the average. Yet, paradoxically, there is often (in nonrecession years) a shortage of skilled labor. A major reason is the unwillingness of today's young people to undergo apprentice training. "Younger people are not going to spend the time apprenticing, learning tool and die making as their fathers did," Feinberg said. "They don't want any part of working in oil up to their elbows. Also with the military cycle people work five or six years—then the contract ends. So they look for something more stable."

Total union membership in the early 1970s was about 290,000, approximately one-fourth of the nonfarm work force, putting Connecticut 17th among the states in the extent of unionization. The first industrial union in this country, the New England Association of Farmers, Mechanics and Other Workingmen, was organized in Lyme in 1830, and the first strike in the state was by weavers against the Thompsonville Carpet Manufacturing Co. in 1833. Labor organization declined in the state during the early 1870s, primarily because of the depression, but was rejuvenated when the first local assembly of the Knights of Labor was organized in New Britain in 1878. It was given another boost with the formation of the Connecticut Federation of Labor in 1887, the same year the state established the 10-hour day and 60-hour week.

Labor began to flourish under the New Deal legislation of the 1930s, and in 1945 Wilbert Snow, as lieutenant governor, helped push through a "Little Wagner" Act. "In 1921 it was an antilabor state," Snow told me. "I saw sweatshops from New York coming up to New England and giving these women 20 cents an hour—making slaves of them. I got pro-union."

The contrast to more recent years, when organized labor has been able to get almost anything it wants out of Connecticut and its Democratic administrations, could hardly be more striking. In the 1975 legislative debate about state employee pay raises that exceeded Governor Grasso's budget, union leaders sat in the galleries and shouted at Democrats who dared to argue against the increases. One of the few state senators who refused to go along, J. Martin Hennessey of Wethersfield, said afterwards: "Politically, I cut my throat."

Because of the large defense and aerospace contracts, Connecticut's unemployment rate is subject to wide swings. In the late 1960s the unemployment rate was a low 3 to 4 percent because of Vietnam war contracts. As the war wound down in the early 1970s, joblessness rose to a level between 8 and 9 percent, then it sank to about 6 percent as industry adjusted to the peacetime situation, only to soar upward again in the 1974–75 recession (to 9.8 percent in May 1975).

In addition to its skilled work force and strategic location in relation to markets, Connecticut attracts industry through the quality of life it can offer new residents. "They want to know how far they have to commute, how happy their wives will be with the area, and what the recruiting potential of an area will be," Feinberg said. "Management and workers can be 10 or 15 minutes away from whatever life style they want—high-rise apartments, garden apartments, or single homes with swimming pools."

Executives considering new plant locations want to see where their people will live, the quality of the schools and roads and retail shops, Feinberg added. "This is probably the biggest sales appeal we have in dealing with business. We got spoiled in the corporate office competition because we were winning about 85 percent of those deciding to leave New York City. Generally it was a question of New Jersey, Long Island, Westchester County, or Connecticut, and I don't think we lost more than four or five we were working on." Because of this Connecticut is increasingly attracting corporate headquarters and service industries.

Connecticut has also attracted a great deal of foreign investment, ranking fourth among the states after California, South Carolina, and New York. Foreign executives are as concerned as their American counterparts over the quality of life, and often they are more insistent on specific figures about labor productivity than American executives. This is particularly true of the major German firms, including Telefunken, that have moved to Connecticut.

Most of the corporate moves are from New York, however, partly because, as Feinberg says, "many companies have had problems in New York City, handling new and middle management people who don't want to go to New York which is a primary reason many have come here." Of the 58 major corporations that moved to Connecticut between 1969 and 1973, 46 were from New York and 20 were in *Fortune* magazine's top 500.

With the downturn in the economy in the early 1970s, these New York City moves slowed down but Connecticut still had much to offer over New York, according to Feinberg—higher quality high school graduates and a stronger work ethic, less corruption with public officials, less complexity in doing business, no state and local income taxes. No company by the mid-1970s had moved back to New York, and there was a likelihood of a new spurt of corporate moves in view of New York's fiscal crises.

The urban renewal programs, such as Stamford's, have attracted business as industries have expanded into the older towns. Many of the cities are also land poor, so the state in some cases has made land available—as in New Britain—for industrial parks and shared the cost of their development.

Out-state immigration accounts for only 30 percent of Connecticut's annual economic growth, however; the rest is internal. The state department of commerce is one of the oldest in the country and has a "battle plan" not only to encourage out-of-state business but to enhance opportunities for those already in Connecticut. This is not to say that praise for the state's economic development policies is universal. Pointing to an overall loss of manufacturing jobs—from 482,940 in 1968 to 394,700 in 1972—editor Bice Clemow blamed "a quarter century of lousy political leadership in terms of economic development." One result was that many companies, particularly in machinery, machine tools and textiles, found themselves noncompetitive because their plants had become obsolete.

The exporting of insurance returns an enormous amount of capital, however. Insurance employment rose about 50 percent between 1963 and 1973 and accounted for more than 47,000 employees by the latter date. According to University of Hartford economists, that means an additional 100,000 jobs were generated indirectly by the insurance industry for the Connecticut economy.

Thirty-five insurance companies have their headquarters in Connecticut, with more than 50 million policies in force and annually paying out more than $5.5 billion in benefits. Hartford became the insurance center it is today partly as a result of its response to the disastrous fires in New York

City in 1835 and in Chicago in 1871. Eliphalot Terry, president of the Hartford Fire Insurance Co., got the promise of unlimited backing from the Hartford Bank, then sledded to New York in below-zero weather to promise that he would pay in full every claim made on one of its policies as a result of the 700-building blaze. After the Chicago fire Marshall Jewell stood on a packing box to make the dramatic announcement that Hartford's Phoenix Insurance Co. would pay off immediately.

In the 1960s the insurance companies were tempted to diversify by the booming economy and the reluctance of people to tie their money up in long-term, low-interest policies. Many firms went into computers, housing development, mutual funds, and others. Connecticut General Life loaned the $23.5 million which the Rouse Co. used to purchase the 15,000-acre site of the new town of Columbia, Md. Rouse, of course, subsequently participated in the Greater Hartford Process. Cutthroat price competition and inflation in the 1970s hurt the insurance industry, however, as many of those alluring investments turned sluggish and sour. After-tax underwriting profits plunged from about $500 million in 1972 to an annual loss of about $500 million in 1974 because of the price competition and rising claims costs.

Connecticut farmland is some of the most pleasing in America to behold. One thinks of the rich bottomlands of the Connecticut River Valley and, in the hillier sections, farms with their stone walls and barns that provide such a pleasing backdrop to the wooded areas and bring natural old New England charm to the center of the East Coast megalopolis. Thus it is sad to report that the number of Connecticut farms has been dropping rapidly—from 22,241 in 1945, for instance, to only 4,490 in 1969. In a single five-year period in the 1960s, the total acreage on the state's farms dropped from 721,315 to 541,372. At the same time the value per acre climbed from $560 to $921—the highest per-acre value for farmland in the country. In large part, of course, this reflected the pressures on farmland from commercial and industrial developers. Partly because of the decline in farming Connecticut has twice as much wooded area as in the late 19th century.

In the overall economic picture, Connecticut agriculture, with annual sales around $165 million in recent years, is not very important. Most of the income comes from poultry and dairy products, but the interesting product is tobacco. Because the climate and soil of the Connecticut River Valley near Hartford are congenial, tobacco used as the wrappers for cigars is shade-grown under wide white and yellow cheesecloth tents. Southern blacks, West Indians, and Puerto Ricans moved to Connecticut to work as field hands. Right after World War II there were about 300 tobacco farmers on more than 15,000 acres, but by the early 1970s this number had dwindled to about 50 farming 4,700 acres. They employ about 7,000 workers seasonally at $2.28 an hour, which with the unemployment levels of the mid-1970's attracted 2,200 more applicants than there were jobs. Their tobacco was used in about 90 percent of the eight billion cigars smoked in the U.S.

Schools and Colleges

Connecticut was a seedbed of free public education in America. A public school system was established in New Haven in 1642 and in Hartford a year later. Henry Barnard, the state's first school superintendent, became the first U.S. Commissioner of Education in the mid-19th century. Across America, in the great westward trek of the 1800s, went Connecticut teachers and ways of learning.

Today the picture is more mixed. The interstate rankings show on the one hand that the state is sixth among the 50 in the teacher/pupil ratio in public schools, fourth in the percentage of high school graduates going on to college, and seventh in expenditures per public school student. But if one takes the percentage of all personal income invested in education at all levels, the Connecticut figure of 5.9 percent in 1972 was 48th in the entire nation. "It's our values," one critic told me. "Look at our per capita consumption of booze—closest to the most in the United States."

Part of the problem may be the preference that the state's heavy Roman Catholic population has shown for parochial schools. In the early 1970s the state attempted two plans to channel tax dollars to the church-run schools. The first provided direct state aid to nonpublic schools and was struck down in the courts as unconstitutional. The second provided for reimbursing parents for expenses in sending children to nonpublic schools up to $75 annually for each child through grade eight and up to $150 a year for each student in high school. This second plan was successfully challenged by the Connecticut Civil Liberties Union on constitutional grounds and also with the argument that it would ultimately lead to a dual school system, one public, black, poor, and inadequate, the other white, affluent, and superior.

There also was generally a city-suburb schism. In 1972 Hartford sued the state to break down the boundaries between inner city and suburban school districts on the grounds that the city schools were economically and racially segregated because of faulty school districting and the exodus of white, self-sustaining families and businesses to the suburbs. The Hartford schools were almost 70 percent black and Puerto Rican and about 40 percent were families on welfare. In the eight contiguous suburban towns, however, the minority populations were 5 percent or less. At the end of 1975 this suit was still awaiting trial, however.

Connecticut, like most of the other New England states, does boast excellent preparatory schools. Among the most famous are Choate, among whose alumni were John F. Kennedy and Adlai Stevenson, and Miss Porter's in Farmington, of which Jacqueline Kennedy was an alumna. Others include Hotchkiss in Lakeville, Kent at Kent, the Taft School in Watertown, and Pomfret at Pomfret. This writer would be an ingrate if he failed to mention South Kent School, an institution with no endowment but much spirit located close to Kent in the Berkshire hills, where a wonderfully dedicated group of "masters" helped him learn most of the English (and many of the values) reflected in the pages of these books.

If Connecticut had the earliest public school system, it was late coming to the idea of state-supported universities and to the idea of very many universities at all, for that matter. Until 1818 the only non-Congregationalist university was Yale, the second-oldest college in the nation (after Harvard) and of course a national university that has had a marked impact on Connecticut—through its alumni, research resources, and faculty—over the years. Locally, however, Yale has not been as closely interlocked with New Haven as Harvard with Boston.

Yale, of course, is one of the best and most famous of the nation's universities. Its law school may be second only to Harvard's and its other professional and graduate schools are among the nation's finest. Yale's undergraduate school traditionally has been somewhat more conservative and social than some of the other Ivy League universities, but students can get a superior education with Yale's high standards, superior faculty, excellent research and physical facilities, and a favorable teacher-student ratio. Its endowment of $500 million (second only to Harvard's, which is more than $1 billion) generated an annual income of $25 million in the mid-1970s. In the late 1960s, however, Yale began to be caught in the squeeze that afflicted many private colleges and universities, and before long its annual deficits were approaching $2.5 million. One problem is that unhappy alumni began cutting Yale out, in the late 1960s because of student demonstrations, in the 1970s because athletes and alumni offspring were not being admitted in the numbers they wanted.

Although many of Yale's wealthy and conservative alumni, upon whom it depends for endowments, were outraged by the student activism of the late 1960s and early 1970s and by Brewster, its personable president, Yale and the other Connecticut campuses remained relatively quiet during that turbulent time. In the case of Yale, this was partly because Brewster was generally popular and managed to defuse a lot of the emotion by not fighting everything to the last ditch. Brewster's controversial remarks that he was skeptical about Black Panther Bobby Seale's ability to get a fair trial on the murder charges against him united the student body behind him. So did Vice President Spiro Agnew's rather intemperate attacks on him. Brewster was able to anticipate most student demands and kept the university abreast of the times without lowering its high standards or alienating the faculty.

After the constitution of 1818 which granted a measure of religious freedom, Yale was followed onto the stage of higher education by fine colleges such as Trinity (Episcopalian) in Hartford and Wesleyan (Methodist). This is not to say that everyone in Connecticut greeted this expansion of colleges; when Trinity was formed, one public leader said a second college was superfluous, that the craze to build colleges was like the turnpike craze—just a passing fad.

Eventually, though, the time came for *public* higher education. The state established a normal school in New Britain in 1849 and what is now the University of Connecticut in 1881, as a result of a gift from Charles and Augustus Storrs. But Connecticut's public higher education, as in the rest of New England, lagged badly over the years—and still has a lot of catching up to do. It took years, for instance, to tear the University of Connecticut away from its original status as an agricultural school—or to get the state legislature to view it as an institution of any substance or importance. In 1925, for instance, the legislature passed a resolution (sponsored by a Yale man) decreeing that there should never be more than 500 students at the Storrs campus. A major impetus for change, of course, was the precipitous climb in enrollment that followed World War II as a result of the G.I. Bill of Rights. Then, in the 1960s, Connecticut seemed to take its higher education responsibilities really seriously for the first time in the state's history. From $13.8 million in 1960, state appropriations for higher education increased to $87.8 million in 1970. (Much of the credit for persuading the legislature to loosen their pursestrings for the University of Connecticut apparently went to former Governor Raymond Baldwin, who sold his plan for university expansion to legislators at sessions well lubricated with whiskey.) Enrollment rose rapidly in the '60s and was 24,000 by 1974. "When I left the presidency of the University of Connecticut in 1972 after 10 years," Homer Babbidge noted, "my name was on the diplomas of more than half the graduates in the history of the institution. The exponential growth was that great."

By the early 1970s, however, Connecticut still remained 47th among the states in per capita expenditures for higher education and in the amount spent per college-age resident. From an exceedingly low level of 5.6 percent of state revenues, expenditures for higher education rose to 12 percent in 1968—only to drop back to 9.7 percent in 1973, largely because of belt-tightening by the Meskill administration. Yet in 1973 the average American state expended 18.1 percent of general revenues for higher education.

"All Northeastern states are playing catch-up ball in terms of higher education," Babbidge said. "The University of Connecticut has an uneven profile. Its greatest arguable strength is that though a university and devoting an increasing fraction of its time to graduate and professional studies, it had not fallen victim to neglecting undergraduate education."

The enrollment figures showed more than 20,000 students enrolled in Connecticut's four state colleges in the early '70s, of whom 94 percent were natives of the state. (One could wish there were more out-of-staters, to broaden the vision and contact of Connecticut youth a bit.) In addition, the state could boast 13 two-year community colleges and its bevy of private colleges and universities, now numbering 25.

A Postscript on the Press—and Connecticut Awareness

Among the 28 daily newspapers in Connecticut, the historic and present leader is the venerable Hartford *Courant,* the oldest continuous daily in the

U.S., dating back to 1764. It is practically an institution. The *Courant* also prides itself on being the newspaper of record. It is not an easy paper to read, being stuffed with information. Its bland editorials often ignore the hot issues. But the *Courant* has a large and aggressive news staff that often probes below the surface of official statements.

Few Connecticut papers have head-to-head competition. Most are either the only newspaper in town or are morning and afternoon combinations under the same ownership—as in Bridgeport, Meriden, New Haven, and Waterbury. Some are mediocre, others excellent. The Waterbury papers have a reputation for good local government reporting, the Danbury *News-Times* for good suburban news, the *Day* of New London for good writing, the Vernon-Rockville *Journal Inquirer*, a newcomer formed in 1968, for its feisty local coverage.

Nevertheless, Connecticut suffers to a degree from the same problem New Jersey faces in the communications field—dominance of outside newspapers and television stations. Except for the Hartford area, opinion leaders are likely to rely as heavily on New York or Massachusetts papers as any printed locally. Only Hartford and New Haven have VHF television stations; all others are UHF—again resulting in heavy viewing of stations with only the most casual interest in Connecticut affairs. Nor have the state's own two VHF stations been particularly aggressive in state and local reporting. This is changing, at least in Hartford, where the Washington Post Company in 1974 bought WSFB-TV. The possibility of a strong, liberal-oriented station in the capital city, its signal reaching most of the population-heavy urban corridor, is of potentially great import in this state of steady habits. For when all is said and done, Connecticut remains a civilization which has yet to learn enough of itself, and the shortcomings in its own public life, to reach the distinction among American states that could be its.

VERMONT

THE BELOVED STATE

VERMONTERS LOVE Vermont, and with good reason.

The state's physical charm is beyond dispute. Vermont is a pastoral place, with a marvelous juxtaposition of meadow and forest land. The mountains are rounded, friendly, and quiet; as a former governor told me, "man is welcome on our mountainsides." And there are the village greens, with their white-spired churches and sturdy little meetinghouses and an architecture as graceful as this nation has ever produced; the barns in red or white; the maples, ready for their yield of sap in spring and flaming red in autumn; stands of white birches and forests of evergreen; dazzling arrays of wildflowers; and beckoning lakes, large and small. Vermont is perhaps the only place in America a stranger can feel homesick for—before he has even left it.

Then there is the image—some say the myth—of the Vermont Yankee: hardy, spare, independent, factual, thrifty, shrewd, self-reliant. That character did not come about by accident; as Bernard DeVoto noted back in the 1930s, it developed from Vermont's ancestral religion of Calvinism. "Its philosophy, that life is an endless struggle against evil and necessarily a losing one, exactly agrees with the experience of a people who settled on a thin, boulder-sown soil in a ferocious climate, where mere survival was success,"

DeVoto commented. And then he related a story, passed on through Robert Frost:

You are to picture the usual group at evening on the porch of the general store, and talk has grown nostalgic about the old-time education, when you studied under the invitation of the whip and book-learning was larruped into you to stay. It is agreed that that was the soundest technique of instruction and that in those days what a man learned counted for something.

But there is one protestant. His dissent is packed with a feeling of the irremediable injustice of this world, the evil and frustration that are integral in human life. With the hopelessness of mortality to avert the injuries inflicted on its innocence, he says, "The only time I was ever licked, 'twas for telling the truth." Silence while his neighbors receive this fact, examine it, and check it against the teachings of experience. Then, quietly, judicially, with an air of rendering exact justice in the light of eternal truths, one says, "Well, Sam, it cured ye."

There are those who say, and have been saying for years, that those noble Vermonters are a virtually extinct species, and that all the talk about them, together with the promotion of dubious antiques, maple syrup, Calvin Coolidge, covered bridges, and patchwork quilts, is one great tourist trap. Perhaps so, but the melody of the real Vermont, like the melody of Puritanism in America at large, lingers on. One can still say, with conviction, that there are values that set Vermont apart in America: pride and independence, stemming from the pioneer heritage; tolerance, which grew out of respect for others' privacy; conservatism, usually in the best sense—to conserve a way of life that let the individual be what he would, for good or ill, since, as Dorothy Canfield Fisher once wrote, "nobody can help him do his breathing; it is an intrusion to try"; a preference for gradualism over hectic or drastic change; and a deep love and respect for the precious land. The latter, as we shall see, has been translated into the most dramatic political controversy of Vermont in our times.

Vermonters, of course, are only human, and they have their prejudices. Those feelings welled up in the past century as the dilution of the native stock set in. First were the Irish, who came in the wake of the horrifying potato famine in their native land, first to build the railroads, then to settle. Later there arrived several thousands each of Italians, Poles, Finns, and Slavs, and, in the greatest numbers of all, the French-speaking from neighboring Quebec. But never were more than 15 percent of Vermont's people foreign-born, and if the newcomers were at first viewed with leery eye (especially for their Roman Catholicism in this very Congregationalist state), the fact is that it was not long before those who wanted to be were accepted as true Vermonters. The assimilative process has worked more smoothly in Vermont than in any other state, even though there are clear-cut geographic divisions—the countryside remaining primarily Yankee, the cities with their markedly Catholic-ethnic concentrations.

In recent years there have been isolated instances of ugly prejudice against blacks, though with a near-invisible four-tenths of one percent of the state population, they are scarcely the central social issue. (In 1968, George Wallace's racist appeal won him only 3.2 percent of Vermont's vote, his lowest showing in any state save Maine.) The more important Vermont

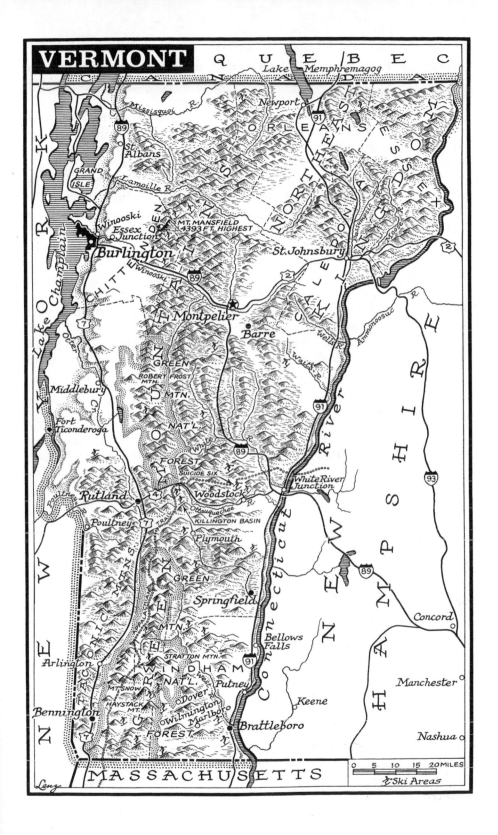

VERMONT

QUEBEC

Lake Memphremagog

CANADA

Missisquoi R.

Newport

St. Albans

GRAND ISLE

Lamoille R.

Winooski

Essex Junction

MT. MANSFIELD 4393 FT. HIGHEST

Burlington

St. Johnsbury

Winooski

Montpelier

Barre

Wells R.

Ammonoosuc R.

GREEN

ROBERT FROST MTN.

Middlebury

MTN

Fort Ticonderoga

NAT'L.

White R.

FOREST

SUICIDE SIX

White River Junction

Rutland

Woodstock

Poultney

Ottauquechee R.

KILLINGTON BASIN

Poultney

Plymouth

GREEN

Springfield

Concord

MTN.

Bellows Falls

Arlington

STRATTON MTN.

MT. SNOW

NAT'L.

West

Putney

Manchester

HAYSTACK MTN.

Dover

Keene

Bennington

Wilmington

Marlboro

Brattleboro

FOREST

Nashua

Lenz

MASSACHUSETTS

0 5 10 15 20 MILES

Ski Areas

Lake Champlain

Otter Cr.

CHITTENDEN

Wells R.

Waits R.

CALEDONIA

NORTHEAST

ORLEANS

KINGDOM

Moose R.

Passumpsic R.

NEW YORK

NEW

TACONIC MTNS.

GREEN MTNS.

WINDHAM

NAT'L. FOREST

Connecticut River

HAMPSHIRE

prejudice, if there is one today, is against the affluent out-of-staters who have moved in to buy up (and outrageously drive up the price of) Vermonters' own land. The state has had to pay a price for being, as writer Robert Taylor described it not long ago, "a soft green oasis amidst a metropolitan Sahara." Woodstock ecologist Richard Brett contends that Vermont's overcrowded megalopolitan neighbors ought to compensate the state for *not* developing—in effect, a survival easement.

Vermonters count themselves lucky in having a civilization where the person still matters, where there are no lonely masses yearning for identification. Their resistance to the incursions of megalopolis is based primarily on their desire to preserve that civilization and the hitherto-placid natural environment in which it has flourished. In a professional survey taken in 1971, a representative cross-section of Vermonters was asked what kind of a place they found their state to live in. A remarkable 81 percent found Vermont "one of the best" states, or clearly above the average. In an era of national disillusionment, I would be surprised if similar polls in other American states would show such positive feelings.

And, as corny as they may seem to some, there is still validity to the oft-quoted words of Coolidge in a speech he made at Bennington in his later years:

I love Vermont because of her hills and valleys, her scenery and invigorating climate, but most of all, because of her indomitable people. They are a race of pioneers who have almost beggared themselves to serve others. If the spirit of liberty should vanish in other parts of the Union and support of our institutions should languish, it could all be replenished from the generous store held by the people of this brave little state of Vermont.

Geography, Places, and Some Customs

Vermont is rather neatly delineated by the Connecticut River, which flows along its entire eastern border, and lovely Lake Champlain, which serves as its western border for 112 miles. But it is the ancient Green Mountains that are Vermont's salient physical feature; they stretch from south to north, from the Massachusetts border to Quebec, thus dividing Vermont into eastern and western portions with a high mountain mass between. For generations there was an unwritten "mountain rule" in politics, which decreed that governors must come alternately from the eastern and western sides. This practice has subsided now, and despite their differing historic patterns of settlement, eastern and western Vermont are much alike.

A more important modern-day distinction, writer William Moran has suggested, is between southern and northern Vermont. Southern Vermont is booming because of its thriving ski areas and easy access to megalopolis; northern Vermont, except for the Burlington and Barre Montpelier areas, is poor and remote. Politically, progressive political candidates fare better in southern than in northern Vermont.

The exception for Burlington, in particular, is a vital one, however. In a three-county area there one finds 155,000 people, 35 percent of the state total, with the major retail center of the state, its greatest concentrations of wealth, higher education, hospitals, and new-generation industries like IBM and General Electric. Burlington proper had 38,633 people in the 1970 Census, the only Vermont city with more than 20,000 people. The city is located directly on Lake Champlain, with a spirit-lifting view of the lake, its islands and mountains. The city was an old lumbering and port community, and then a working town; some of the old-style brick factories are still in evidence, but there has been a strong spurt of urban renewal and fresh downtown building to rival the suburbs. Burlington is the most mobile, transient city in the state, and many non-Vermonters, French-Canadians and Americans alike, are in evidence. They come to the University of Vermont (8,000-odd students) and four other colleges, for the facilities of New England's third largest medical center, to bank, for shopping (close to $400 million in annual retail sales), to visit government offices (the city is a kind of capital away from Montpelier), and to work in the new plants and industrial parks. So by Vermont standards, this is a very cosmopolitan place, although local politics generally boils down to the Irish and French fighting it out for dominance within the Democratic party, with the Republicans capitalizing on the splits for occasional breakthroughs.

One day when George Aiken was governor, back in the 1930s, he remarked he thought he would go up to the "Northeast Kingdom." So the three-county area along the Canadian and New Hampshire borders, the most deeply rural part of a rural state (there are only two towns of any size at all, St. Johnsbury and Newport), received its enduring nickname. The Kingdom is heavily populated with people of Vermont pioneer stock, some of whom can trace their ancestry in the region back five or six generations; mixed in with them are a goodly number of French-Canadians.* The people are lumbermen and farmers, and they live in an area of many charms—Lake Memphremagog, the covered bridges of Lyndonville, lovely Craftsbury Common, Peacham with red barns in eye-catching round and octagonal forms. But they are Vermont's poorest people—as recently as 1970, a fifth of them lived below or close to the poverty line, and social welfare agencies have to cope with problems of malnutrition and hunger. "We used to say," Aiken commented, "that everyone in the Northeast Kingdom was born with a fishpole in his hands." The problem has been that fishing is not enough to hold a region's young people. There are some 49,000 people left in the Kingdom today, but Orleans County has 15 percent fewer people than it did in 1920, Caledonia 13 percent fewer than it did in 1910, and Essex 36 percent fewer than in 1890.

---

* The Kingdom's ties to French-speaking Canada are very close. Aiken recalled that when a school burned down on the Vermont side, the kids promptly went over the line and went to school in Canada until a new school could be built for them. In the town of Norton, he said, the international boundary went right between the two counters in Ed Nelson's store. The American side had oranges and cotton goods, cheaper in the United States; the other side had woolen goods and meats, which at the time were much less expensive in Canada.

Remembering all the while that most Vermonters live in small villages, some cities and towns outside the Burlington area, running from north to south in the state, may be mentioned.

Montpelier, despite the state capital and the offices of the National Life Insurance Company—its two important enterprises—has only 8,600 inhabitants. One apt description I heard was that Montpelier is a place "where everyone wears a necktie and gets paid little"; or one may refer to the description of a generation ago, in the WPA Vermont *Guide:* "Montpelier, serenely indifferent, is a true Vermont town, sleeping in the shadow of the hills." Nearby is Barre (1970 Census count 10,209); "the granite center of the world" with a strong spirit but slightly grubby appearance. Barre has many Italian-Americans, and once elected Vermont's only Socialist mayor; these days it is routinely Republican in local elections.

Rutland, in center state, had 19,293 people in 1970, second only to Burlington. It was a railroad town with a lot of esprit de corps in the old days; now it is principally a regional shopping center (drawing even from New York State), but the population has not grown appreciably in recent years. The Rutland *Herald* is a lively, well-edited paper, with a young staff sometimes given to advocacy reporting; its liberalism on issues like public power and ecology are the bane of the state's conservative politicians. The *Herald* has a circulation second only to the Burlington *Free Press*, the only other morning paper in the state. The *Free Press*, now owned by the Gannett chain, covers Vermont news thoroughly and dispassionately and has been mellowing its traditional conservatism. (Until 1975, when both expanded their operations, neither the *Herald* nor *Free Press* had a Sunday edition; that was left exclusively to the paper in St. Albans, which is owned by William Loeb of Manchester *Union Leader* fame. "It's a blessing that Loeb pays less attention to Vermont than New Hampshire," a moderately conservative state politician told me. Hate journalism is clearly out of step with the Vermont ethos.)*

Among Vermont towns, none is more justly famous than Woodstock, between Rutland to the west and White River Junction on the Connecticut River. The heart of Woodstock, pristine and graceful, is its Green, bordered by lovingly preserved homes of brick and white clapboard, some dating back as far as the late 1700s. That placid scene, however, belies the fundamental change that has come over Woodstock as it changes from a trading center for local farmers and home for quiet retirees into what the Vermont *Times* calls "a suburban town for the tourist and the very wealthy." The ski culture (of which more anon) is one reason for that; an even more important catalyst has been Laurence Rockefeller, one of the famous Brothers, who is (through various corporate fronts) the town's largest employer, has 20 times the capital investment of anyone else in town, and is the community's largest benefactor. Rockefeller's intent seems to be to make (or preserve) Woodstock as a New England Williamsburg; unfortunately, Woodstock, with a popula-

---

* Vermont also has a number of quite adequate papers in cities like Barre-Montpelier (The *Times-Argus*, now owned by the Rutland *Herald*, with which it publishes a joint Sunday edition), Bennington (the *Banner*), and Brattleboro (the *Reformer*).

tion of 2,600, is now so "desirable" (with a covey of millionaires and a number of people who commute weekly to New York by air) that zooming land values and property taxes are squeezing out the less affluent indigenous Yankees.

South of Woodstock lies Springfield (population 10,063), a machine tool city with a lively intellectual history. An example of Vermont's far-reaching contacts in the modern world is that the firm of Jones and Lamson has been producing computer-controlled tool-making machines for sale to the Soviet Union under a multimillion-dollar contract.

Down to the south lie Brattleboro (9,050), historic for Vermont as the site of its first white settlement but today quite oriented to nearby Massachusetts, and Bennington (14,586), which looks to nearby New York State. Bennington College, founded in 1932 to stress independent study—a pioneering institution in that respect—now has some male students as well as women, and is considered one of Vermont's two most prestigious schools of higher learning.

The other is Middlebury, in west-central Vermont, which boasts a world-famous summer language school. Middlebury also sponsors the illustrious Breadloaf Writers' Conference, which over the years has attracted such luminaries as Sinclair Lewis, W. H. Auden, Wallace Stegner, Eudora Welty, Catherine Drinker Bowen, and Bernard DeVoto. Until his death in 1963, Robert Frost had a summer cabin nearby and took an active part in the Breadloaf sessions each August.

"Vermont has never given a first-rate artist to the nation," Moran wrote, "but the charm of life in these green hills and valleys has lured many of them here." Robert Frost was drawn to Ripton, Pearl Buck to Winhall, John Gunther and Greta Garbo to Greensboro, and Sinclair Lewis and his wife Dorothy Thompson to Barnard. Pianist Rudolph Serkin chose Marlboro College as the place to found the Marlboro Music Festival, which used to draw Pablo Casals each summer. Three famed American economists spend their summers in Vermont—Arthur Burns, Milton Friedman, and John Kenneth Galbraith. The townspeople of the little town of Arlington often showed up on *Saturday Evening Post* covers by that town's famous resident, Norman Rockwell. Also from Arlington was Dorothy Canfield Fisher, one of the most sensitive writers from and about Vermont.

Two quotes suggest the reason for Vermont's closeness to the arts. In the words of realist painter Luigi Lucioni: "Vermont is beautiful but not romantic. You have to go to it, it won't come to you." Or Sinclair Lewis: "I have never spent more than eight months in any one place, have traveled through 36 states and lived in eight or ten in addition to visiting 18 foreign countries, but Vermont is the first place I have seen where I really wanted to have my home—a place to spend the rest of my life."

A very native Vermonter, George Aiken, had this to say about his home town of Putney: "I call it the intellectual center of the world. It's where people from Harvard come to get the rust rubbed off. We have a small college, two private elementary schools, and a preparatory school (Putney

School) where distinguished people from Washington send their kids. And we have the Experiment for International Living." Aiken said all that as he prepared for his retirement; it was clear he feared no intellectual isolation in the distant Vermont hills.

History and Tradition

In 1609, 11 years before the Mayflower arrived at Plymouth, the French explorer Samuel de Champlain became the first white man to see Vermont. Sailing down the lake which now bears his name, he was captivated by the sight of Mount Mansfield and Camel's Hump towering over the Green Mountain range. But his interest was fleeting and for another 60 years the white man left Vermont, inaccessible by sea and so far from the promising shores of Massachusetts and Virginia and New York, to the Algonquin Indians.

To the traditional historians we must leave the details of the first permanent settlements, the French and Indian Wars, the contrary royal charters which caused New Hampshire and New York to feud so violently over the territory, and the Revolutionary War battles fought there. The early settlement of the state proceeded slowly because most of the early Vermonters were trappers, not farmers; this began to change in the mid-18th century, however, as a craftsman-agrarian society took hold. A large portion of the early citizens of this New England frontier were from Connecticut; as historian Earle Newton has written of them: "They were a restless, independent folk, a strange and contradictory combination of visionary and realist. They were adventuresome, dreaming ever new dreams of rich lands and great wealth just over the horizon. Yet they knew how to buckle down to the dirty, laborious job of drawing a living from the soil. Few of weak will or tender fiber survived; the frontier acted in some respects as a sorting process."

As the dispute over New Hampshire's and New York's competing claims to the lands between the Connecticut River and Lake Champlain reached its zenith in the years before the American Revolution, a number of settlers in the disputed area decided that they alone had the rightful claim. They hired a colorful, brash 27-year-old native of Connecticut, Ethan Allen, to be the colonel-commandant of a military company to defend their interests. Allen, his brother Ira, Remember Baker, and Seth Warner became the leaders of the Green Mountain Boys or, as the New Yorkers called them, "the Bennington mob." They did well in skirmishes with New York, which posted a bounty for Ethan and some of his followers. The Green Mountain Boys later scored a stunning success in the Revolutionary War by defeating General Burgoyne's troops at the Battle of Bennington. Burgoyne reported in a letter to England that this territory, "a country unpeopled and almost unknown in the last war, now abounds with the most active and rebellious race on the continent, and hangs, like a gathering storm, on my left." (Indeed, deprived of his supplies and his morale shattered after the Battle of Bennington, Burgoyne was soon to lose the battle of Saratoga, a turning point in the war for independence.)

New Hampshire dropped its claim on Vermont during the war, but New York refused to follow the example and blocked Vermont's admission to the Continental Congress. The indignant Vermonters proceeded to proclaim their independence from New York in 1777 and to declare themselves a sovereign republic. For the next 14 years, they issued their own currency, ran their own postal service, and carried on diplomatic relations. In typically Vermont fashion, the legislature of this independent state decided as its first official act "to adopt the laws of God until there is time to frame better."

The constitution of the Republic of Vermont, adopted in 1777, was heavily influenced by the liberal views of William Penn and included two provisions then unique in America—a complete prohibition of slavery, and universal manhood suffrage without property or taxpaying requirements. But, as writer William Moran has noted, while Vermont's constitution was modeled on and went further than the democratic Pennsylvania document, "the legislature drew heavily on Connecticut law that was conservative, and Vermont's legal history became one long struggle to reconcile a liberal constitution and a conservative body of laws."

Ethan Allen, a freethinker and opponent of organized religion, never sought office under the republic because he objected to the religious qualification it contained. He died in 1789, at the age of 52, apparently after an all-night drinking party. Only the most naive could regard Allen as an unblemished figure. A notorious braggadocio, he was even willing during the Revolution to carry on secret negotiations with the British Crown with an eye to rich trade agreements if the American cause failed. But if it had not been for Allen's fierce pride and determination, Vermont might never have shaken New York's claim on its territory and emerged as an independent state. Moreover, Allen and his followers wrote a constitution, grounded in the ideals of free and untrammeled personal liberties, which has formed the bedrock of the Vermont tradition ever since. He is as legitimate a folk hero as any American state has ever had.

In 1790 Vermont was finally able to settle its land claim with New York for an indemnity of $30,000 to New Yorkers who had lost property there. The next year the spunky little republic decided to ratify the newly written Constitution of the United States and petition Congress for admission as the 14th state. The record shows that the state's population was 85,539 that year, scattered through 185 towns—contrasted to only 300 people 30 years before.

The population almost doubled in Vermont's first decade of statehood, but a century would pass before it doubled again. In some decades the number of Vermonters in Vermont even slipped backward, as thousands deserted their homeland for more promising opportunities far afield. The list of famous Vermont emigrants is almost endless. The great Mormon prophets, Joseph Smith and Brigham Young, were from Sharon and Whittingham, respectively. Stephen Douglas, who would later contest Abraham Lincoln for the presidency, was born in Danby. Chester Arthur, later to be President, was born in a Fairfield cabin. Henry Wells, founder of the Wells-Fargo Express, the great newspaperman Horace Greeley, the famed Reconstruction politician Thaddeus Stevens, founder Franklin Olin of the Olin Mathieson chemical empire, educator John Dewey, Admiral John Dewey, President Calvin Coolidge—were all born Vermonters. John Gunther discovered a tally showing that this tiny enclave had produced, by the 1940s, two American Presidents, 80 college presidents, 31 chief justices, 33 United States Senators, 144 congressmen, and 60 governors of *other* states.

A heavy strain of radicalism runs through Vermont's early history. This state, for instance, opposed the ruling Federalist party in Washington because it believed the Federalists were primarily interested in serving the well-born and the rich. A fellow conspirator of Ethan Allen, for instance, was the Irishman Matthew Lyon, publisher of a "rabidly republican sheet" called the *Scourge of Aristocracy*. Elected to Congress in 1796, Lyon attacked President Adams and the other Federalists with such fervor that he was convicted and jailed under the Alien and Sedition Acts. Vermonters approved of him so thoroughly, however, that they reelected him over four opponents while he was in jail and raised enough money through a state lottery to secure his release from jail. Sitting again in Congress in 1801, Lyon cast the deciding vote to make Thomas Jefferson President. Vermont's radicalism was strongly agrarian, and thus linked to Jefferson's philosophy. In the first half of the 19th century, Workingmen's Societies were formed in Vermont to fight licensed monopolies and press for land reform to protect the poor; when the reformers were frustrated in the legislature, they formed farm cooperatives to sell their produce—a forerunner of the co-op movement so important in 20th-century Vermont agriculture.

Vermonters differed from Jefferson, of course, in that they were unencumbered by dependence on slaves. As hill people they had no need for chattels, and they had no seaports to provide profits through the slave trade. In 1803 a judge of the state supreme court refused to return a fugitive slave unless the owners could produce as proof of ownership a "bill of sale from Almighty God." By the 1820s emancipation sentiment was rampant in the state, fired by petitions from the churches and editorials which William Lloyd Garrison wrote for the Bennington newspaper. Each year, the legislature passed resolutions protesting slavery and dispatched them to the other states, prompting explosive replies from the South.* As Duane Lockard has written:

By 1856 the antislavery feeling was so deep in Vermont that John C. Frémont, candidate of the newly born Republican party, won the state by a margin of nearly four to one. At this point in time a man named Abraham Lincoln joined the party with some hesitancy, which presumably proves beyond all doubt the legitimacy of

---

* The Georgia legislature voted to return a copy of one Vermont resolution "to the deep, dank and fetid sink of social and political iniquity from which it came." Another Georgia resolution proposed to President Franklin Pierce that "able-bodied Irishmen be hired to dig a ditch all around Vermont, till the thing could be detached from the rest of the Union and towed out into the middle of the Atlantic Ocean." (This proves, of course, how old the "Southern strategy" in American politics is. A century later Barry Goldwater would propose sawing off the entire Northeastern seaboard and letting it float off to sea.)

Vermont's Republicanism—to be "more Republican" than Abraham Lincoln ought to be evidence enough. And as the twig was bent, the tree has been inclined.

In the Civil War Vermonters were to prove that their dedication to the antislavery cause was more than talk. Half of the men of military age—a total of some 35,000—joined the Union Army; of these, one out of every seven was to lose his life. In relation to its population, Vermont lost more of its youth in the Union cause than any other state. The dreadful toll is reflected in these Civil War statistics from two communities:

Plainfield	Stowe
68 enlisted	208 men served
5 deserted	40 died, 12 in battle
1 killed in action	4 wounds
2 died of wounds	1 suicide
11 died of disease	22 died of disease
12 discharged	1 died in prison
37 served their term	

The Civil War also cost Vermont dearly in economic terms. At the start of the war, responding to President Lincoln's appeal, the legislature appropriated $1 million for the Union war effort. This was 110 percent of the state's tax-raising capacity; in Pennsylvania the comparable figure was only 34 percent, in New York 20 percent, in Ohio 31 percent. In the four years that followed, the state appropriated $8 million for the war effort, a huge proportion of its native wealth.

In the midst of that painful conflict, a Vermonter in the U.S. House was making a contribution to higher education that has led to the creation of 70 colleges, among them some of the most important institutions of higher learning in the United States. His name was Justin S. Morrill, and the legislation, the Land-Grant College Act—familiarly known as the Morrill Act—was his personal conception, and one he fought through to passage himself. President Lincoln signed the bill in 1862. In 1867 Vermont advanced Morrill to the U.S. Senate, where he served for 31 years, a towering figure in his time styled by his contemporaries "The Father of the Senate."

Economy and Farming: Civil War Aftermath, and Later

The effects of the Civil War were to be felt for years and years in Vermont. As William Moran has written:

The effort in men and money made Vermont's people tired. The tide of people leaving for the West cut down the percentage of improved land in the state from 63 percent to 45 percent as brush and forest covered the pastures of abandoned farms; land values soared in other parts of the country but tumbled in Vermont, where farmland was sold for as little as $3 an acre, buildings included. Less than two-thirds of the natives stayed in Vermont and in each decade during the second half of the 19th century, two out of five natives left the state. The number of

Vermonters over 50 years increased from 14 to 21 percent; the people who stayed behind were unwilling to make innovative economic adjustments. The buoyancy of the young was gone and with it went a crucial ingredient of growth. Despondency replaced the spirit of radicalism and willingness to experiment so typical of Vermonters in their early history. Schools and roads and land fell into neglect, life in the "back beyond" or rural country deteriorated, there was inbreeding and illegitimacy and the start of serious welfare problems.

There was, of course, a kind of self-sufficiency in the simpler Vermont life style that enabled the state's people to ride out national depressions and recessions with relative equanimity. As Dorothy Canfield Fisher wrote in a 1922 book, *Our Rich Little Poor State:*

Now, when times are hard and manufacturers are flat and the mills in the industrial states about us are shut down, and newspapers are talking about bankruptcies and bread-lines, the Vermont family, exactly as rich and exactly as poor as it ever was, remarks with a kindliness tinged with pride, "Well, we'd better ask Lem's folks up to stay for a spell, till times get better. I guess it's pretty hard sledding for them."

A certain amount of industry did come to Vermont. Lumber, which had been Vermont's earliest export, grew so much in importance that by the 1880s only two cities in the country worked and sold more lumber than Bennington. There were many paper mills in the state. Vermont marble became nationally famous; available in about a hundred varieties, from white to jet black, it was chosen for more than 70 percent of the country's monuments and statuary. Vermont granite and slates, also of an exceptionally fine quality, were discovered and exported in large quantities. Asbestos and talc mines were opened in northern Vermont. Woolen mills sold millions of dollars worth of goods to outside markets. The machine-tool industry grew in Springfield and Windsor; scales were manufactured at Rutland and St. Johnsbury; and in Montpelier Dr. Julius Y. Dewey, Admiral Dewey's father, helped to found the National Life Insurance Company.

But Vermont was and remained distant from the main railroad lines and the country's centers of commerce and industry. The state remained an overwhelmingly rural society, tied to the land. In 1900, when only 31 percent of the people in New England as a whole lived on farms or in villages of less than 2,500 people, the comparable percentage in Vermont was 78 percent; in 1960, when the New England-wide rural population figure had dropped to 24 percent, 63 percent of Vermonters were still living on the land or in tiny towns. To this day, there is not a single other American state as "rural" in complexion.

Thus, for their livelihood, Vermonters continued to depend on agriculture during the century when the United States as a whole was rushing headlong into industrialization. Given the rocky nature of the soil, Vermont farming was never an easy affair; the state arrived at its present status as a milkshed for Boston and New York only after more than a century of trial and error with any crop or animal that could be raised in the hills. Potash, a by-product of land-clearing operations, was exported in the early years. Beef raising was important in the early 19th century, when large numbers of cattle were driven overland to market in Boston and New York. Then, in 1810, a diplomat who had served in Portugal introduced the famous Merino sheep of Spain to the state. Sheep raising reached its peak before the Civil War, when there were six sheep to every Vermonter. In the decades after the war, however, railroad lines to the West brought vast areas of free grazing land in states like Montana and Wyoming within reach of eastern markets, and western wool largely displaced that from Vermont and Ohio.* This caused a deep depression in Vermont agriculture, to be relieved only as the sturdy farmers changed again, this time to dairy cattle. Until World War I, most of the dairy produce was in the form of butter or cheese processed in the state; then came liquid milk shipping to the Boston and New York markets, still a mainstay of the state's agriculture. Much backwardness, including deep poverty in the hill farms, characterized Vermont agriculture through the years. Even in the late 19th century, according to one account, "Some Vermont farmers were still using oxen for work in the fields, growing flax for bed linen, carding wool from their sheep for homespun clothing, and making their own wooden maple-sap and milk buckets and farming tools."

To this day, Vermont remains the country's most intensive dairy state. In 1963 the number of people in the state finally exceeded the number of cows, but the obedient bovine still has her place of honor on the state seal. One still sees those placid scenes of herds of cows grazing on rich green pastures, and milk and butter still account for the lion's share of the state's annual farm sales of more than $200 million a year. Distant competitors to dairy produce are eggs, apples, vegetables, and the famous Vermont maple syrup. Since the 1930s, maple syrup production has dwindled from more than one million gallons a year to 300,000 gallons annually, though there has been a recent upturn through better marketing and technological breakthroughs like plastic tubing and vacuum pumps that permit sugar farmers to feed their sugar houses intravenously from the maple forests. (Maple sugaring is, of course, a quintessential cottage industry, consisting of some 900 dairy farmers and assorted entrepreneurs who venture out with their pails and spouts on snowy March and April days and return to rustic sugarhouses to become cooks and chemists. A measure of the obstacles to making much money in this trade is that it takes 40 gallons of sap to make a gallon of syrup, and the average yield from a single maple is only 12 gallons of sap in a season.)

Formal Vermont farming is now largely restricted to the long thin strip of land in the Connecticut River Valley, to substantial lands in the Champlain Valley, and some areas along the Canadian border. The hillsides

* The sheep, however, left a kind of calling card in Vermont: high pasture land, still occasionally visible, on which they grazed and prospered. Robert Babcock of South Burlington reminds me that sheep raising, even in the last half of the 19th century, produced the wealth for the mansions that still exist in the southwestern part of the state. In addition to western competition, sheep raising is thought to have died off because of the gradual decline of trace elements, like boron, in the soil through overgrazing.

of the Vermont interior, once intensely farmed, are returning to woods or, more likely, brush fields. In 1850, 75 percent of the land face of Vermont was cleared land, being farmed; by 1970, the figure had dropped to 25 percent, with half of the state gone back to trees. Vermonters lament the change, as the rolling farmed hills that once made the state so distinctive return to woodland.* But as a practical matter, Congressman Richard Mallary said, "If you try to preserve some of those farms, what you're doing is condemning someone to a lifetime of hard labor at submarginal pay." He suggested that the state might have to create agricultural parks, "maintaining a few hundred or thousand acres in farmland, so that people can see what Vermont was like in the middle 1800s."

An astounding number of Vermont's smaller farmers have sold out to their bigger competitors, abandoned their land, or sold it to housing developers and summer residents since World War II. In 1945, there were still some 26,000 farms in the state, down from 31,000 in the 1870s. But by 1964 the number of farms had dropped to 10,000 and, by 1973, to some 4,000, and there were fears of still more foreclosures and farm sales to come. This does not mean that overall milk production, for instance, is falling. But where Vermonters used to produce from herds of from five to 40 head, any viable operation now needs 100 head or more. "It used to be possible," Senator George Aiken noted, "to go into dairying for a few thousand dollars. Now it would cost you $250,000." One reason is the way the second-home industry has driven up land values.

Some people believe that truck farming for nearby New England markets may hold a bright future in Vermont, though that day has hardly dawned. What is certain is that a lot of informal, "marginal" farming is going on, not only among Vermont natives with factory jobs in nearby towns, but with the newcomers. "They try to subsist on the land as much as they can," Aiken said. "I've got four young neighbors in Putney. Two of 'em have hives of bees and raise their own honey and they have their gardens and raise all they need and a little more—and work maybe for some company a long ways off."

"All Connecticut," Aiken added, "would move up to Vermont anytime they could stay and make a living." His comment leads us to the phenomenal change which came across the Vermont economy, the Vermont land, and the profile of the Vermont population starting in the early 1960s.

The New Economy of the 1960s and 1970s

Between 1850 and 1960, Vermont's total population had advanced at an average of only 2 percent per decade—from 315,089 in 1850 to 389,881 110 years later. If it had not been for the excess of births over deaths, the

* A 1971 poll showed that 46 percent of Vermonters rated the decline of farming as a "very serious" problem, well ahead of such irritations as declining morality, hippies in Vermont, or inadequate care for the elderly.

population in that period would have sunken seriously; in the 1940s and 1950s alone, for instance, Vermont lost 58,000 more people to other states than it gained from them. Then, in the early 1960s, a remarkable transformation occurred. Vermont became a net importer of Americans from other states, and its total population began to expand at a strong clip. The 1970 Census figures would show a 14 percent population gain over the decade, more than the national average. In the first five years of the 1970s, the population would rise another 5.9 percent, to 471,000—again, a growth rate well over the national average and, except for New Hampshire, the biggest gain in New England.

What was happening? The reasons were several but could be boiled down to three chief factors: a rise in factory jobs, especially in sophisticated new industries like electronics; a rapid increase in the ski and summer resort business; and, perhaps most important of all, a heady influx of people from the eastern megalopolis building summer and retirement homes in the Green Mountain State.

Vermont also seemed to be moving away from its ancient moorings when it elected its first Democratic governor since the Civil War, Philip H. Hoff. Hoff represented not only a new political era but an attitude very different from Vermont's old complacency. Elbert G. Moulton, the Republican whom he recruited to head the state's development program, said Hoff fostered "a climate of stimulating courage and enthusiasm and faith, making people more self-confident." New recreational facilities were encouraged, and new industries brought in. Vermont even launched an advertising campaign in Massachusetts and Connecticut papers under the tagline, "Calling All Vermonters Wherever You Are." Replies were received from some 20,000 people, many of them tear-stained letters from *emigrés* who said they would return home if they could find employment in Vermont. Many subsequently did so. The forward movement of Vermont was illustrated a couple of years in the 1960s when the state actually led the nation in growth of per capita income.

It would be an error, of course, to call Hoff the sole force behind Vermont's forward thrust. He symbolized the movement and speeded its velocity, but the forces for change were already there. On the industrial front, for instance, the Vermont development department had already been active in the 1950s, along with a handful of aggressive communities. In the 1957–1958 period, five years before Hoff became governor, announcement was made of a major new IBM plant in the Burlington area. IBM's arrival, one Vermonter told me, was "the most dramatic event in Vermont's economy in a half century." It brought a direct payroll of more than 4,000, engaged in the design and production of computer memories—one of the most capital-intensive, high-technology plants in the United States. All this might well not have come to pass if an affiliate of the Greater Burlington Industrial Corporation, in the late 1950s, had not built a 32,000-square-foot plant on speculation, which IBM decided to occupy. (Also, it is said, IBM chief Thomas Watson liked the location because he loved to ski!)

The work environment of the IBM plant is worlds apart from the clanking, dark atmosphere of a textile mill. In the production plant, consisting of brightly lit work rooms behind glass in long white corridors, one sees people in white coats and masks stamping out circuit modules (a half inch across, mounted on silicone), like a hygenic printing plant. (My notes read: the epitome of the white shirt, short sleeve society. A sign on a wall: "Your Epidermis Sloughs off Keratinized Sratum Corenum during Desquamation. Meanwhile Sebum Secretes from Sebatious Glands and Hair Follicles. Think Clean.")

James Ritchie, the general manager when I visited, said that "for every worker who puts things together to go out the door, we have five in engineering, quality control, systems, programming, finance, industrial engineering, communications, and personnel." About 60 percent of the IBM plant's personnel come from the Burlington area; even without formalized training, those in lower-grade positions have mastered the subtleties of technology with relative ease. Most of the professional types have to be recruited from outside areas, but even in the tight labor market of the 1960s, IBM had little difficulty in drawing them to Vermont. Most of the professionals brought in, Ritchie said, "wanted to get away from the excitements and pressure of big city living. A very few find it too dull and leave. But most adapt to the way of life here, taking to the views, nearby skiing, a lake as beautiful as Champlain, and the cultural assets of the University of Vermont (located at Burlington). Here they feel they can be part of the decision-making—whether a highway, a generating plant, school bonds, or whatever. They feel they can influence things."

Through the late 1950s and all the 1960s, dozens of other light industries constructed plants in Vermont, more than replacing the gap left by the departure for the South of the state's few textile mills. The total employment remained quite small, however. From a base of 33,000 in 1959, total manufacturing jobs went to a peak of 43,000 in 1967 and then dropped off to 36,000 by the early 1970s. The biggest employers were in electrical equipment (chiefly IBM and GE), machine tools (in the Springfield area), and printing and publishing (Brattleboro, Rutland, and Middlebury).

One phenomenon noted by several observers was the high degree of out-of-state ownership in Vermont's industrial, recreation, and natural resource sectors. Professor Lee Webb of Goddard College in Plainfield issued a report in 1971 saying that outside interests owned four of the five Vermont plants employing more than 1,000 people and almost as high a percentage of all those with more than 250 workers. Big business started buying Vermont industries, he said, because poor farmers forced off the land and young housewives trying to supplement their husbands' low incomes were all willing to work for wages well below the national and New England average. The world's largest granite quarries, at Barre and Bethel, were taken over by a land developer and manufacturing conglomerate based in Providence, Rhode Island. Of the state's important mineral resources, only the marble quarries in Proctor remain owned by Vermont-based corporations. All but one of the major machine-tool plants in southern Vermont, Webb noted, were owned by out-of-state corporations. The state's two largest power companies, Central Vermont Public Service Corporation and Green Mountain Power Corporation, have huge blocks of stock controlled by outsiders. The state's biggest landowner is the St. Regis Paper Company, based in New York. Webb called Vermont a "colony," and he put Maine and northern New Hampshire in the same category.

One could question whether out-of-state ownership makes much difference; Professor Webb's point was that it is deleterious. The major profits are siphoned away from Vermont, for reinvestment elsewhere, he said. Even the interstate highways, Webb said, had not helped to develop the state economically, because they permitted the easy transport of raw materials to Vermont's cheap labor market and the quick exportation from the state of the goods and wealth produced there.* A dissenting view was taken by Senator George Aiken, who confirmed the fact that most industry is controlled by outside conglomerates but said "there is no feeling of exploitation in Vermont." The state is also fortunate, he said, in the type of personnel brought in. In Burlington, for instance, I heard that the transient professionals of a firm like IBM had become civically active, and that across the state, bank boards and influential community organizations had been energized by the fresh blood.

Tourism is by no means a recent innovation in Vermont. As early as the 1860s there were a dozen or more hotels and watering places filled during the summer months with wealthy people from Eastern cities, and in the years that followed many less affluent families began to come, too, many of them spending their holidays as boarders at farmhouses. Recognizing the charms of Vermont's mountains, lakes, fields, and country roads for out-of-state visitors, the state in 1911 became the first in the nation to establish an official publicity bureau. It promptly issued an 80-page, profusely illustrated booklet entitled, *Vermont, Designed by the Creator for the Playground of the Continent*. The advent of the automobile, of course, vastly expanded tourism in Vermont during the first decades of the century. The summer camps, now a $10 million-a-year industry, began to sprout up in this period. In 1929, more than a million summer guests visited Vermont, almost three times the state's total population at that time. By the early 1970s, the annual visitor total would approach 7 million, 15 times the state population.

In 1934 a "new thing" arrived on the Vermont scene when Dartmouth ski team captain Bunny Bertram and his friends put up the first ski tow rope in the United States on farmer Gilbert's sheep pasture at Woodstock. That

---

* In 1975 Governor Salmon said Vermont was through building "super-roads"—the expensive, four-lane variety like the interstates. His decision followed a University of Vermont-financed study which found that the ambitious highway net completed in the last two decades generally exceeded the state's real needs and cost more in maintenance than it returned in value to the state's people.

rope-tow, a kind of Rube Goldberg invention powered by a Model T Ford engine, would inaugurate one of the greatest winter recreational complexes on earth. Up to then, the Vermont mountains had been the exclusive domain of hikers, but now the state decided to let private developers put ski trails over many of its slopes. Some Vermonters objected to the commercialism, but George Aiken, then governor, argued there had to be a balance between preservation of natural areas and economic growth. Aiken was present himself when the first commercial ski business was opened at Stowe's Mount Mansfield, now rated one of the great ski areas of the world.

Altogether, the state now has some 40 ski areas, from Stratton and Mount Snow in the south to Jay Peak and Burke Mountain near the Canadian border. An example of the massiveness of these complexes is the one at Killington, which spreads over four mountain peaks with five separate but interconnected ski areas. Opened first in 1958, Killington has 35 miles of trails, with slopes from gentle to near-suicidal, served by 12 lifts, five Pomalifts, and a gondola. Before the ski complex opened at Killington, the tourist accommodations of the area hibernated during the winter, just like the Vermont bears. But by 1970, according to a New York *Times* report, there were 23 restaurants, 10 nightclubs, 20 lounges, and more than 80 lodges, motels, and hotels, with more than 5,000 beds altogether, operating within a 20-mile radius of Killington.

Of Vermont's annual income from tourism, $250 million at latest estimate, the greatest amount comes from skiing; at least 300,000 skiers come to the state each winter, from New York, southern New England, and, in surprisingly high numbers, Canada. Not everyone considers this an unmitigated blessing. Environmentalists have complained of haphazard trails, disregard for wind patterns, and contempt for woodland. One need only glance at the side of a mountain like Mount Snow, which has no less than 80 miles of slopes, to see how seriously the natural landscape is affected. As a general rule, outsiders control the restaurant, motel, and other service facilities that dominate the ski areas. Few Vermont industries and wholesalers have been able to get contracts to supply the ski resorts. But thousands of Vermonters are provided with at least seasonal employment, and in economically depressed areas like the Northeast Kingdom, ski-associated jobs can spell the difference between survival and forced emigration for many people.

The roots of Vermont's big summer- and retirement-home development go back to the early years of this century, when many visitors began to purchase abandoned farms for their summer weekends and vacations. By 1930 out-of-staters had invested close to $20 million in summer property, including $600,000 in the central Vermont town of Fairlee, where they already paid almost half the taxes in town. That same year the state took official cognizance of the summer home boom, publishing an 85-page descriptive catalog, *Vermont Farms and Summer Homes for Sale,* 1930. The summer home influx was slowed down some by the Depression and World War II, but regained its pace afterwards and reached mammouth proportions in the affluent national culture of the 1960s. By 1968 a study showed 22,584 second homes in Vermont, whose owners, on the average, paid half again as much in property taxes as the average Vermont home owner. There were six towns in which more than 50 percent of the property tax came from the second home owners, including one (Maidstone) where the figure was 93 percent.

An ever-growing number of these people came to Vermont to stay. By 1970, the Census found 112,487 permanent Vermont residents—a quarter of the state population that year—who had been born elsewhere. And, amazingly, more than half of these immigrants had made their move to Vermont within the preceding five years. Normal retirees, of course, figured very heavily in this body of new Vermonters. Some people had been drawn to the state for jobs in the tourist industry, or the new-style factories. In addition, there was a strong complement of artists, writers, and people who had decided on an "alternative life style." Hippies had become conspicuous in many towns; communes were springing up in southern Vermont, around the Montpelier-Barre area and Mad River, with scattered colonies in the Northeast Kingdom as well. (By one count, Vermont had 250 communes by 1972.) New-style craftsmen and farmers, representing the back-to-the-soil movement that began in the early 1960s, when the first Harvard Square sandal-makers and potters appeared in Vermont, were present in significant numbers. The Prickly Mountain community in the town of Warren, according to Robert Taylor in the Boston *Globe*, had "developed into a studio community where the residents seek a synthesis of modern design and nature." Young Yale architects started the Prickly Mountain venture, which was said to have but one counterpart, a place called C-Ranch in California.

What makes Vermont so attractive for the counterculturites? The physical beauty of the state was doubtless one factor, but more important is the kind of primal innocence that seems to surround the Vermont character, and the state's tradition—its political conservatism notwithstanding —of tolerating many forms of social dissent.*

Oddly enough, a great deal of the migration into Vermont in the 1960s and early 1970s took place at the same time that many young Vermont natives still felt obliged to leave their home towns, or the state alto-

---

* Back in pre-Civil War days, for instance, there was a famous young Vermont religious fanatic named John Humphrey Noyes, the son of a Vermont Congressman and first cousin of President Rutherford B. Hayes. Noyes had written, in a letter that found its way into the public prints, that "in a holy community there is no reason why sexual intercourse should be restrained by law, than why eating and drinking should be—and there is as little occasion for same in one case as in the other." In 1838 Noyes went to Putney and gathered a band of followers there. Yet, according to the WPA Vermont Guide, "it was nearly a decade before the citizens of Putney realized that he had led his followers from communism of property, through communism of households, to communism of love, or, as he called it, Complex Marriage." Noyes was eventually arrested but managed to flee to New York, where he formed the famous Oneida Community, agreeing to give up Complex Marriage "in deference to public sentiment." In present day Vermont, of course, it would not be difficult to find communes in which Complex Marriage thrives under new guises.

gether, to find suitable employment.* A 1971 poll of a cross-section of people in all regions of Vermont produced this remarkable finding:

To earn a living, young people of this community will:

Find work here	19%
Leave town	31
Leave the state	45

In the same survey, 62 percent of those polled said more jobs in their town were "necessary." And Vermonters appeared, on the whole, to be quite happy about the development that had come to their state. Seventy-six percent of them approved of the recreation industry, 62 percent of the second home industry.

What the Vermonters themselves knew was that a great deal of economic hardship, in need of relief, remained in their state. In 1970 the Census found that some 15,000 families, 14 percent of the total in Vermont, lived under or just above the government-established poverty level. If one looks carefully in back-country Vermont, one can find hovels and shacks strongly reminiscent of impoverished sections of the rural South. In the late 1960s a state-wide Poor People's Congress was formed to protest alleged harassment by welfare caseworkers; the movement was led by David Dorman, a young service station operator from Brattleboro, and was counseled by the late George Wiley, executive director of the National Welfare Rights Organization, who traveled periodically to Vermont for strategy sessions. For the most part, however, Vermont's poor people suffer in silence, jacking a deer, perhaps, to put some food on the family table, but too proud or stoic to turn to the government for help. Less than a fifth of the state's poor people are on welfare, the lowest percentage of any New England state except ultraparsimonious New Hampshire.

In the mid-1970s, Vermont was suffering particularly grievously from the national recession. The hard times had actually come to the state before the rest of the nation, when a winter of "no gas and no snow" undermined the ski industry and the general state economy with it. Delivering his third annual budget message to the legislature in January 1975, Governor Thomas P. Salmon said: "In 1973 the theme was austerity. In 1974 it was severity. In 1975 it is survival. The winter of our economy is with us and it will not end when the snow melts."

The Fate of the Land and Vermont's Epochal Act 250

Robert Frost once described Vermont as "a state in a very natural state." That grand old figure of modern poetry was not precisely correct,

* Even with the influx of new people into the state during the 1960s, the total number of persons 20 to 29 years of age in 1970 was 7 percent less than the total of the same group by years of birth (1941 to 1950) had been 10 years before. This was, of course, a much brighter picture than that of the people born between 1931 and 1940, who reached maturity in the 1950s. During that decade, more than 25 percent of the young adults 20 to 29 left Vermont.

however. A less lyrical but truer summation has been provided by Governor Thomas P. Salmon:

> More than any other state, Vermont reflects the relationship between man and nature. . . .
> Ours is the only state whose landscape is dominated by the small farm, and, indeed, it is the farmer who is chiefly responsible for the delicate interplay between field and forest, mountain and meadow, stream and turnpike, which make Vermont visually unique.
> Because our environment is, in reality, man-made, the social consequences of its disruption are more apparent here than might be the case elsewhere.

In the 1960s, Vermonters learned how immediate and appalling that disruption might be. Bucolic, isolated Vermont suddenly found itself in a vortex of change that threatened to destroy its essential character. Singly, the factors of change might have been absorbable; cumulatively, they seemed to require a rapid jettisoning of Vermonters' laissez-faire attitude toward physical and economic development.

What were the factors of change?

The rapid expansion of the interstate highway system should perhaps head the list. Residents of Springfield and Albany were brought within an hour's drive of Vermont. From Boston or Hartford, the driving time shrank to two hours, from New York City three hours. Jet air travel put the state within an hour of New York, less than an hour of Boston. "Vermont today is a suburb," former Governor Hoff commented to me in 1969.

At the same time, there was a sharp rise in Americans' discretionary income and leisure time. Vermont became accessible and affordable to the masses of megalopolis, not just the affluent. And with the big city riots, the idea of Vermont the pastoral retreat appealed to more and more cityites and suburbanites. Many of them drove through Vermont to Expo 67 in Montreal, and saw that the state was virtually empty.

Finally, the 1960s were the decade when, in the words of conservationist writer Phyllis Myers, "skiing changed from an esoteric sport to a winter mania."

It was in southeastern Vermont's Windham County, with its huge ski complexes at Dover (Mount Snow) and Wilmington (Haystack Mountain), that the first ominous signs appeared of what awaited Vermont at large. Not coincidentally, these areas were first reached by the interstate highways. To accommodate the skiers, dozens of developers swarmed in, buying up large tracts of land into which they crammed as many vacation homes as they could, often on half-acre lots. Frequently, not even the most rudimentary rules of site planning were observed. To spare themselves the cost of sewer systems, the developers installed separate septic systems on each lot; unfortunately, there was impermeable bedrock not far below the surface, and in many locations the tanks overflowed and the sewage seeped downhill into streams or neighbors' wells. By 1970, there were more than 4,000 new vacation homes in Windham County, with thousands more on the drawing boards. Seventy-three developers were in business, one for every 25 residents of Wilmington and Dover. The six miles of Route 100 linking the two towns had become a honky-tonk array of gas stations, restaurants, and nightclubs. The small rural farm communities in the path of such development suffered a kind of cultural shock.*

The effect of the development on land prices and taxes was predictable. Back in 1960, the rock bottom price for an acre of Vermont land had been about $50; by the early 1970s it was $500 and, around ski areas, $2,000 or more. Acre lots around Stratton Mountain were going for as much as $25,000. The Vermont natives in the path of this holocaust of development found their property taxes soaring to pay for increased road maintenance, police, fire protection, and garbage disposal. Even school costs began to rise as the second home owners, initially seen as a net plus for the towns where they lived because of their relatively high property tax payments, began in increasing numbers to commute during the week to jobs in Hartford, Boston, or New York, leaving their families behind in Vermont. Escalating land prices meant that many young native Vermont families could not afford to build homes in their own communities. Many of them were forced to go the mobile home route, and the ugly trailer parks further desecrated the landscape. Moreover, many established Vermont farmers found the new tax rates so high that they could not afford to stay in business. (In overhauling its tax structure, the state had decreed that the local tax "listers" [appraisers] must assess land at its "fair market value." Hence when farmland near a ski development went from $50 to $5,000 an acre, the farmer had to sell to the developer or go broke on his taxes.) So more and more farmers sold out, and the buyers, of course, were the omniverous developers, in need of more land for more subdivisions. And so the vicious cycle went round and round.

"An Ecological Planning Study for Wilmington and Dover, Vermont," prepared by a Philadelphia planning firm, concluded that the towns were "on the edge of disaster," in danger of becoming "Sprawl City, U.S.A." And inexorably, the same pressures were being felt around all of Vermont's ski areas, even those in the far northern part of the state. For the most part,

---

* Example: The board of selectmen of a small town was suddenly confronted with a developer's plan to put up 2,000 chalets on quarter-acre lots selling for $2,000 to $3,500 each. At a minimum, this meant that town of 320 souls would have 8,000 new semi-permanent residents.

This is not to say that *all* large-scale developments are necessarily bad for Vermont's people and environment. One of the best projects, in fact, is that state's largest, Quechee Lakes, near White River Junction. The development being done there, to include no less than 2,000 houses and 500 condominiums by the 1980s, will be spread tastefully across no less than 6,000 acres, or 10 square miles. And the developers, the multimillion-dollar CNA Financial Corporation, have apparently done all they can to keep the lovely vistas open and to tuck the houses themselves into the trees. Waterfront lots, which normally bring premium dollars, are not being sold at all on the theory that "it belongs to everybody." When the project began, the old town of Quechee was worn and tired, practically a ghost town. The developers began to restore the old buildings and to import houses to surround a village green. An old mill was converted into a theater, for instance. One could question whether any development this size should be permitted in a Vermont preserved as a 19th-century museum piece, and many inhabitants of the area are dismayed by the project. But its general tastefulness is proof that large-scale development need not be a crass assault on the Vermont land and culture.

the Vermont towns lacked any kind of zoning or planning controls, and could not afford the expert help they needed to assess new projects. To clear any legal obstacles in their way, the developers typically hired most of the lawyers in a town or county they attacked, and even undermined the traditional town meetings by packing them with people who would front for them. And the locals could not help but be aware that as the second-home developments multiplied and some of their residents moved to Vermont permanently, "outsiders" would represent a potent and possibly even controlling force in the town meetings.

In 1969 concerned officials and citizens of Windham County carried their concerns about the assault on their communities to Governor Deane C. Davis, who personally appealed to the president of International Paper Company to stop an ill-planned development on some of the 23,000 acres it owned near the town of Stratton. IPC embarrassedly backed off, the first environmental victory on land use planning in modern Vermont.

Even before the IPC incident, Governor Davis had set up a state commission on environmental control to study abuses in the recreation home industry. This commission, headed by Arthur Gibb, a state representative from western Vermont, and including businessmen, conservationists, developers, and influential legislators, was to play a vital role in Vermont's modern history. For out of its deliberations, zealously reported to a concerned citizenry during the last half of 1969, emerged the basic mechanisms to control the developers and plan for the future of the state's greatest asset, its land. These were incorporated in an historic piece of legislation, Act 250, passed by the Vermont legislature in April 1970. Even though the legislation impinged on a cherished Vermont tradition—a man's right to do as he chooses with his land—it passed by overwhelming margins in both houses. The heavily Republican legislature which passed Act 250 was a "landowning" body that included 26 farmers with large open land holdings, 10 lawyers with development interests, and nine realtors. The governor who enthusiastically signed the measure into law was a conservative Republican, Deane Davis. And Vermont's Democrats were equally strong in their support.

How could such disparate groups unite so quickly, behind a law so momentous for the Vermont future? The people's fears of what the land and recreation developers could do to their state was the chief factor. This was a year (1970) of intense national concern about environmental issues, and in Vermont the groundswell of sentiment for Act 250 was skillfully orchestrated by the state's conservationist organizations, most of which were "homegrown" (rather than branches of national organizations) and thus had a natural advantage in dealing with the legislature. The developers and realtors were caught off balance; they did raise a fund rumored at $150,000 to fight the bill, but such overt big spending on lobbying is suspect in Vermont. Finally, there was a consensus among Vermonters of various ideologies that the state they knew, with its unique character, must be protected. "We were always aware that we had something special, worth preserving," Thomas Salmon later noted. A clue to the political ideology that permitted this consensus on protecting Vermont's natural heritage was provided by a state legislator who said, "We are so conservative that we are surprisingly liberal."*

Act 250 did three principal things: it set up criteria that proposed real estate or housing developments of more than minimal size would have to meet; it set up a review mechanism through local and statewide citizen review boards that could approve or reject new developments; and it called for the phased adoption, in the early 1970s, of steps leading to a state-wide land use plan. All of this was done in quite a hurry, so that the legislation was stronger on broad principles than precise definitions. "This willingness to move ahead despite uncertainty," Phyllis Myers wrote, "was very special in Vermont in 1970."

Vermonters' natural inclination for localism and citizen, rather than expert or bureaucratic, control was reflected in Act 250's stipulation that local citizen-commissioners would constitute the membership of the district environmental commissions (nine in number, later adjusted to seven). These commissions were given broad power to approve, modify, or reject proposed developments or subdivisions. Only on appeal would aggrieved parties be able to obtain a hearing before a new state regulatory agency, the environmental board, but it too consisted primarily of lay citizens working part time. Jonathan Brownell, a partner in a prestigious Montpelier law firm and leading citizen activist in getting Act 250 passed and implemented, said the real strength of the program lay in the prominent role of laymen in the regulatory and planning process. "We're counting on the common sense of Vermonters to come up with the best solution. It drives the professional planners wild, but if other states look to us as an example, that's where we have created the most important model."

The criteria for proposed developments were quite broad.† Before a permit could be issued, the district commissions would have to be satisfied that the project would: (1) not result in undue water or air pollution, (2) have sufficient water available for its needs; (3) not cause an unreasonable burden on existing water supplies; (4) not cause unreasonable soil erosion or dangerously reduce the capacity of the land to hold water; (5) not cause unreasonable highway congestion; (6) not cause an unreasonable burden on the ability of a town to provide for schools; (7) not place an unreasonable burden on other services of local governments; and (8) "not have an undue adverse effect on the scenic or natural beauty of the area,

---

* In a conversation with Phyllis Myers of the Conservation Foundation.
† The types of projects covered by these regulations were subdivisions of more than 10 lots, housing developments of more than 10 units, and commercial or industrial property of more than one acre. If a town had local zoning and subdivision laws, then it, rather than the district environmental commissions, would decide on projects of up to 10 acres. Highways, public buildings, and other government projects were subjected to the same rules as commercial and industrial projects. And all construction at altitudes of more than 2,500 feet, a particularly delicate ecological zone, were subjected to the approval mechanisms. The biggest loophole appeared to be commercial strip development along highways, which Act 250's definitions generally failed to include.

aesthetics, historic sites or rare and irreplaceable natural areas." Tightening amendments to Act 250, added in 1973, protected sensitive shorelines, floodways, and agricultural and forest lands from subdivision development. A new energy conservation provision made it possible to insist that developers put insulation into vacation homes. Wildlife also had to be protected.

Hundreds of applications for subdivisions, condominiums and apartments, commercial establishments, and improvements to recreation and ski areas began to pour into the regional commissions as soon as Act 250 took effect. If anyone hoped the new process would bring development in Vermont to a screeching halt, they were disappointed. Some 94 percent of applications—for projects totaling in value some $100 million a year—were approved by the citizen panels. But in a large proportion of the cases, detailed conditions were put on permits for new development. According to a study by Robert G. Healy, "applicants have been required to change their method of sewage disposal, to reduce the density of development, to increase their setback from highways, to build culverts and retaining walls for erosion control, and even to change their architecture and the size of their signs."

Given the commissioners' lack of expertise, the law was applied somewhat unevenly from district to district, and funds were short for independent technical studies to offset developers' claims about the benign nature of their proposals. In 1970 the legislature had also created a new superagency, the Environmental Conservation Agency, comprised of the departments dealing with water resources, forests and parks, fish and game, the divisions of environmental protection and recreation, the environmental board, and the like. Martin L. Johnson, secretary of the combined agency, said that its technical experts, including water and sewage engineers, foresters, and fish and game biologists, worked closely on the local level with the Act 250 citizen commissions, filling some of the technical-expertise gap. But overall, he said, Vermont was still not willing to invest in enough staff personnel to let the Act 250 apparatus function as effectively as it should.

Whether Act 250 slowed down the overall pace of development in Vermont was hard to say. But most observers agreed that it had done a great deal to improve the *quality* of growth. Trees were protected from bulldozing, septic systems carefully supervised, and aesthetics generally enhanced. Developers doubtless planned their projects much more carefully than in the pre-1970 period. There were rejections of some of the most massive second home developments, and a halt was put to the "cheesiest" development along Lake Champlain and other Vermont shorelines.

A unique measurement of the feelings of a state's people about environmental control emerged from the 1971 poll (to which we have referred previously) in which 561 Vermonters were asked, in 45-minute personal interviews conducted by the Becker Research Corporation of Boston, to state their attitudes on a whole range of issues covering scenic and water pollution, jobs vs. the environment, and the specific provisions of Act 250.

On some questions, the "environmentalist" cause came out with flying colors. Nearly two out of three Vermonters, for instance, said they would be willing to pay substantially to reduce pollution. Sixty-five percent agreed that "it's worth giving up a significant amount of personal freedom to preserve the environment." The major provisions of Act 250 were endorsed by strong majorities, and 69 percent said they favored strong pollution laws over voluntary efforts. A bare majority even favored taking controls away from the towns, and giving them to the state, if they failed to pass strong pollution and development laws.

The other side of the coin was that when they were asked which was the most important, jobs or the environment, Vermonters came down on the side of jobs, 52 to 42 percent. But 62 percent optimistically believed the state would be able to provide jobs *and* protect the environment.

There were some interesting diversions in attitudes, depending on people's individual backgrounds. In short, the younger, the wealthier, the more educated, and the newer a person was to Vermont, the more he or she considered the environment more important than jobs. Older, poorer, less educated, and longtime residents of the state saw things precisely the other way around:

Which is more important?	Jobs	Environment
Age:		
18–29	41%	56%
65 or over	59	32
Income		
$15,000 or more	42	49
Under $5,000	62	32
Education		
College completed	35	59
Less than high school	68	27
Residence in Vermont		
10 years or less	34	57
20 years or more	58	37

(One sees in the poll findings the emerging political coalitions of our time—the young, the rich, and the well educated on one side, with the old, the poor, and the less educated on the other. National-level surveys by Louis Harris and others have shown precisely the same division on a number of major social and economic issues of the 1970s.)

The least understood part of Act 250 was its requirement that planning be begun that would lead to eventual adoption of rather vaguely defined plans, each one building on the other, to culminate in a full-blown statewide land use plan. The idea of these plans, Governor Salmon has said, has been to "express not merely physical standards for development"—the negative restraints spelled out in the initial permit system—but also *"what, where, for whom, how fast,* and *for what purpose* development will be considered desirable." The first step in that direction was a so-called "interim land capability plan," approved in 1972. This was followed in 1973 by a "land capability and development plan," also approved by the legislature, which clarified and tightened some of the environmental criteria of Act 250 and sought to put a damper on the conversion of agricultural soils, forests, and mineral lands to other uses.

The 1973 plan was complemented by a tough capital gains tax on land deals, designed to discourage the rampant land speculation that was pricing real estate beyond Vermonters' own ability to pay and resulting in rapid subdivision of the state's farms and forests. If someone purchased a piece of land and resold it in less than a year for a profit of 200 percent or more, for instance, he or she would be obligated to pay a heavy 60 percent tax on that profit. A sliding scale was established, so that the longer a person held the land, and the less profit was realized from reselling and/or subdividing it, the less the tax would be. Land held more than six years was exempted from the tax altogether. At the same time, the legislature approved a "circuit breaker" system of tax credits to Vermonters to relieve them of paying property taxes beyond a reasonable percentage of their household income, with the percentage varying according to income levels. While this system was designed primarily to assist low and moderate income people in retaining their homes, it also had the result of offering farmers, whose property taxes are a large part of their cash outgo, a strong incentive to remain on the land.

The really controversial aspect of implementing Act 250 started in 1974, when the legislature began to debate the full-scale land use plan which the state planners had prepared. The explicit assumption of the plan was that Vermont's permanent population would increase by at least 185,000 in 30 years, and that this population expansion should be principally accommodated by new housing in existing communities. This approach, Governor Salmon said, would promote "a nucleated settlement pattern of clustered, village-type growth which has historically characterized the development of our state prior to the automobile period—and is indeed at the heart of Vermont's charm and way of life, even in the age of mobility."

The proposed land use plan divided all of Vermont into distinct types of areas—urban, village, rural, natural resource, conservation, shoreline, or roadside. Suggested population densities ranged down from some 2,000 persons per square mile within existing larger communities to 10 principal buildings in each square mile of the proposed conservation district. The conservation and natural resource (farming, commercial woodland, and mining) areas, covering about three-quarters of the state's land face, would be barred to most new vacation homes. The vacation complexes would be obliged to seek space in other "rural" areas and would generally have to take place in a cluster pattern of settlement.

By its very specificity, the published land use plan aroused much more concern among Vermont's ordinary citizens than any of the previous steps under Act 250. Late in 1972—actually in the debate stage leading up to the 1973 capability and development plan—they had received in the mail, through a Ford Foundation-financed project, a map of the state, with varying areas marked out in red and green and blue and yellow colors; the map was hard to read, but it suggested the state was about to declare whose land could be developed and whose land could not. Suddenly people began to fear possibly deleterious impact on their own property development rights, and many of them were quite unhappy about it. As Congressman Mallary described the situation:

> When you speak in broad generalities of how we're going to "prevent undesirable development," everybody says, "Yes, go ahead." But when someone sees this means the land he owns can't be developed, or where he lives may be next door to an industrial park, then you get the same kind of problems you do with local zoning.
> The basic environmental support is still there. But the issue we haven't reached is how much regulation of land use can be done under the police powers of the state. And to what extent, when you regulate the use of the land, are you going to have to do it by condemnation and compensation? It's one thing to say that a septic system, which might endanger the public health and safety, should be prohibited on certain types of land. But what if one objects to an A-frame chalet on a hill for purely aesthetic reasons? Most Vermonters would feel that if you're going to stop development on a man's land for purely aesthetic reasons, then you're going to have to pay him for it. Doing it that way, however, the cost of your regulation skyrockets. That's the issue everyone's ducking now in Vermont.

Eventually, Mallary said, there would have to be court decisions or specifically crafted legislation saying how far one can go in using the police power to control the use of the land. Jonathan Brownell said it was clear that Vermont would have to develop a sound plan to equalize the economic impact of land use regulation, through such devices as direct subsidies or transferable development rights. To work on those economic problems, the state planning office asked Professors Dennis and Donella Meadows of the Thayer School at Dartmouth College to set up computer models gauging the interaction of population, resources, public services, private enterprise, and the like, throughout Vermont, as they reflect actual and potential land uses and values. (The change of pace was a startling one for the Meadowses, who had previously occupied themselves with the global-scale projections of trends in population, pollution, and the like, incorporated in their 1972 book, *The Limits to Growth*.) Most likely, the whole property tax system of Vermont will have to be overhauled in the application of any comprehensive land use plan. "A land use plan and land use taxation are inextricably intertwined," Martin Johnson commented. "You can't have one without the other."

Disappointingly, such fundamental issues were not well debated in 1974 as the legislature received the state planners' latest version of a land use plan and proceeded to scale it down drastically. Exaggerating perhaps for the sake of effect, Governor Salmon depicted the opponents, in the tumultuous public hearings, as calling the plan "a communist plot, a socialist plot, the work of 'traitorous whoremasters' and the cause of nearly all Vermont's development and economic ills. It was blamed on New Jerseyites, this governor, former Governor Deane Davis, the devil, state bureaucrats, planners and a bevy of architects."

Certainly the organized opposition to land use regulation was much more formidable than it had been when Act 250 was passed in 1970. Three groups, in particular, fought the plan with ample finances and solid organization—one called "Balanced View," another, "The Northeast Kingdom Landowners Steering Committee," and finally the Vermont Home Builders Association. Opposition came, one friend of land use planning said, "from a lot of people who hoped to make a bundle by selling off their land to some developer." That kind of assertion was vigorously disputed by those who said they opposed land use planning on primarily philosophic grounds. In the words of former state representative John McClaughry, a so-called Jeffersonian Republican, "What the real debate is about in Vermont is not the right of a 'fast buck artist' to 'rape' some supine rural town. It is whether the ancient concept of freehold property, so laboriously extracted from the feudal system, shall now give way to a 'modern' concept of 'social property' where all land use is controlled by the state." McClaughry summed up his argument quite simply: "The threat to liberty is greater than the threat to the environment."

A representative answer to McClaughry's type of argument was provided by the Stowe *Reporter* in a 1973 editorial. The tradition that each person had the right to do with his property whatever he saw fit, the paper argued, was

consistent with a rural agricultural society like Vermont in the 1920s or 1930s. Men had absolute freedom to use their property as they wished because the market in land allowed them to use it only for farming, lumbering or growing brush. There was no need for zoning because the neighbors would put social pressure on any man who threatened to do something destructive of the community. . . .
But by confusing the ethic of the farmer and the old Vermont with the ethic of the developer and the new Vermont, [opponents of land use control] would open the floodgates for a process of social change so overwhelming and so overpowering that everything else in the Vermont tradition would be swept away.

Entwined through the arguments was the emotional issue of local control and distaste for dictation from Montpelier. The city and town governments, in Arthur Gibb's words, had "literally howled for help" from the state just before Act 250's approval. But in the interim, especially in the areas more heavily impounded by development, they had become more planning minded. Recognizing the sentiment for local control, the planners who drew up the 1974 land use plan stipulated that the local governments would have two years time to draw up specific plans for the development of the land within their borders. (Areas like the conservation districts, by contrast, would be mapped entirely by the state planners.) But the land use advocates wanted residual power to institute town plans, if the localities failed to do a satisfactory job themselves. Opponents said that would not do; in McClaughry's words: "Holding a club over the head of local government that the state will act if it doesn't is not local control." In reply to that, backers of the land use plan pointed out that some two-thirds of Vermont's 246 towns had not adopted permanent planning and zoning, and doubtless would not do so without a powerful spur from the state.

Thus, the land use plan became hopelessly bogged down in the legislature in 1974–75—a period of "hard times and regression in environmental attitudes," as Governor Salmon put it. Former Governor Deane Davis even said he was concerned that an organized move was afoot to repeal Act 250—which he said would be a disaster for the state. Davis, Salmon, Hoff—all of Vermont's recent governors, of both parties—were for enactment of a land use plan, and so, according to polls as late as the winter of 1974, were a solid majority of the state's people. An anomalous situation had developed in which the most prickly individualists, of opposing fundamental philosophies, favored land use planning. On the one side were young, "ultraliberal" people from out of state, who wanted to "do their thing," whether it be a commune or a hardscrabble farm at the end of some road. On the other were the conservative rock-ribbed Republican farmers, who resent anyone telling them what they should do with their land. The common enemy of both groups were the developers; the sentiment frequently heard was "we're damned if we want some board of directors of a development firm in New York or Chicago deciding for us." The only alternative, Vermonters could see, was control through their own town government or, if need be, the state government. There have been cases of Vermont towns turning down what appeared to be highly desirable, ecologically conscious developments that would in fact reduce local tax rates. Vermonters often seemed to prefer higher taxes to having a lot of strangers move into town. One could call it high-mindedness or stubbornness, but the phenomenon was there, and meant that land use planning was not about to die as a concept in Vermont. The way it would eventually be perfected, it appeared, would also be typical of the Vermont way—through citizen action on the local level, leaving a minimum of discretion to the statewide planners.

From Billboards and Bottles to the Public Power Issue

Act 250 and the efforts to control land use are only one facet of the remarkably broad efforts which Vermonters have been making to protect their cameo state from the many forms of modern pollution.

In 1968, for instance, Vermont joined Hawaii as one of the two states of the Union with legislation aimed at the eventual elimination of all highway billboards. Theodore M. Riehle, Jr., the man who initiated the antibillboard campaign in the legislature, stated its rationale quite simply: "Vermont is a tourist state and tourists can actually be discouraged by signs that detract from our physical beauty. A billboard has no value at all if a road isn't there; the public paid for the road; the public may therefore decide how the road can be exploited."

The billboard ban was not passed, of course, without strong opposition from the billboard lobby and some legislators (one of whom proclaimed on the senate floor that "in the name of aesthetics, we're on the merry road to socialism.") But the hotel, motel, and restaurant associations decided to back the ban, accepting the theory that rampant billboards detracted from the scenery their patrons were coming to see. There was strong support for the ban from the press and groups like the League of Women Voters. And while Democratic Governor Hoff backed the bill, Republican legislators including Riehle made it a partisan issue and got it passed over the opposition of a number of Democrats (especially, Riehle noted, "big city ethnic type Democrats—it wasn't their bag").

The blow to the highway advertisers was softened by provisions allowing existing signs to stay up for five years from their date of licensing, and a system of state-owned directional signs to direct visitors to tourist services. A seven-member travel information council, set up by state law, adopted a system of tasteful designs and symbols prepared by Paul Arthur of Toronto, the graphic artist who coordinated signs and symbols for Expo 1967. The signs, in varying colors for varying types of services, are located every few miles along principal roads; close to larger towns or resorts, there are illuminated, sheltered panels where the names and short written advertisements for local tourist businesses are available to the public. The system was inaugurated in the heavy ski areas of southeastern Vermont and then began to spread to all areas of the state. The state became engaged in a legal tangle with the federal government, which withheld 10 percent of its highway funds to Vermont because the state wasn't paying billboard owners compensation when it had signs removed. (The federal Department of Transportation, pressured by the billboard lobby, didn't want to let Vermont get away with a no-compensation policy and could point to the 1965 highway act as justification for its stand.) In addition, the billboard law did not cover municipalities, so that some gross eyesores were left in cities like Montpelier and Waterbury. Nevertheless, most of Vermont had been swept clear of the offensive outdoor signs by 1974. The contrast to the gaudy roadside advertising of neighboring states like New Hampshire or New York could not be more striking.

In 1972 Vermont again made environmental news by becoming the second state to ban nonreturnable bottles and cans, following Oregon's lead. Under the Vermont law, consumers pay at least a five-cent deposit on all bottles or cans of soft drinks or beer, which they get back when they return the used containers to the stores. The 1972 law did not require that containers be reusable, but after a fierce fight against the law in the legislature and the courts, several of the major beer and soft drink companies decided to switch to refillable bottles. In the meantime, a tax of four mills was placed on bottles and cans, with proceeds going to Vermont communities to establish sanitary landfills. The Vermont bottle bill did cause a sharp rise in the price of beer and soft drinks, but public support for the measure seemed strong and before long it was clear that roadside litter had been reduced sharply. The legislature in 1975 went a step farther by banning throwaway bottles and flip-top cans altogether, confirming Vermont's status as the first state in eastern America to do something about the throwaway society.

Sound pollution even came within the purview of Vermont legislators in 1972 when they wrote a tough control law for the pesky snowmobile, setting maximum decibel levels and requiring that snowmobile owners get written permission from landowners before riding on private lands. Without such a measure, proponents said, it would not be many years before the entire state was posted against trespassing, including hunting and fishing.

Although Vermont had pioneered in sewage treatment legislation and facilities, it decided in 1970 that it would have to do even more about water pollution, one of its oldest and most perplexing problems. Governor Davis defined the problem:

> Fifty years ago, we could swim without fear of pollution in most of our streams such as the Winooski, the Lamoille, and Otter Creek. We could drink the water from many of our lakes, and fish were plentiful in most of our streams. This is not true today. We must look for "safe" places to swim in our rivers. Even sections of Lake Champlain and Lake Memphremagog are closed to swimmers because of pollution. Pure water is fast becoming a thing of the past.

The chief sources of pollution were municipalities and industries which had failed to build adequate waste treatment facilities. One example was the Ottauquechee River, which flows easterly past the delightful town of Woodstock and into the Connecticut River. Many town and village residences were found to be emptying raw sewage directly into the Ottauquechee; a mill in Bridgewater was adding dyes and other solutions to the sewage it pumped into the river; and the village of Woodstock was dumping oil cans, asphalt debris, and other polluting debris directly onto the river's banks, in violation of state law. Similar violations were reported in practically every section of Vermont.

The legislature responded by passing Act 252, a sister law to Act 250 on land use. Act 252 was widely hailed as the nation's first "pay as you pollute" water purity legislation. Patterned after waste management practices in Germany's Ruhr Valley, it required an individual, factory, or municipality to have a permit to discharge wastes into public waters; offenders would be forced to pay stiff fines until they installed adequate water treatment facilities. Subsequently, imposition of the fees was delayed, and their dollar amounts sharply reduced, as a result of intensive lobbying by the Vermont League of Cities and Towns and lobbyists for several industries. The towns, in particular, claimed that the fees might be greater than their entire annual revenues.

Nevertheless, the combined pressures of Act 252 and federal water control legislation went a long way towards cleaning up Vermont's waters by the mid-1970s. Virtually all industries and municipalities were on pollution abatement schedules. Industrial polluters, including plants like that mill in Bridgewater and the granite industry at Barre, which used to sluice its sludge straight into the Winooski, had licked their problem. Several river basins were so improved that the state authorities could not find a single polluting source within them, and it was possible to swim again in many formerly forbidden rivers, including the Winooski and Ottauquechee. The Vermont enforcement effort was so far advanced that the environmental conservation agency had six inspectors going house-to-house through the entire state, checking on sewage systems. One great problem remained, however—the host of smaller towns that had not yet installed water treatment plants. The culprit in this case was the federal government, which failed to produce, on schedule, the promised flow of grants to build the needed plants. The usually mild-mannered environmental secretary, Martin Johnson, called the cutoffs and slowdowns of the federal money, and their unhappy consequence in Vermont, "one goddamned nightmare." The other states, of course, shared the same predicament.

An interesting case of water purity disputes between the states was provided by the way Vermont went hammer and tongs after New York State to stop the gross pollution of Lake Champlain by an International Paper Company plant at Ticonderoga, on the western shore. When New York and IPC failed to heed Vermont's entreaties to stop befouling Champlain's waters, Vermont filed suit in the U.S. Supreme Court, which has original jurisdiction in disputes between the states. In 1974 IPC and New York finally capitulated, agreeing to pay Vermont half a million dollars "for preservation and protection of the Champlain basin," and to install extensive new water and airborne waste emission controls at IPC's plant. New York State also agreed to build a sewage plant at the town of Ticonderoga to stop the dumping of raw sewage directly into the lake. Governor Salmon rightfully hailed the out-of-court settlement as "a great victory for the little state of Vermont." *

Vermont still has a long way to go in assuring the purity of its lakes, however. The U.S. Environmental Protection Agency in 1974 reported that 59 percent of the polluted lake acreage in all of New England was in Vermont, in large part because so many of the state's lakes are around highly populated areas.

Pollution problems of another sort have been raised by the massive Vermont Yankee Nuclear Plant built in the late 1960s and early 1970s on the Connecticut River at the town of Vernon, near the Massachusetts line. The plant was hurried onto line in 1972 in the face of what the power companies said was a serious shortfall of electric power. As a result, adequate testing and quality controls apparently did not take place. The plant has periodically "belched" radioactive gases into the atmosphere in excess of state minimums, has frequently been forced to close down temporarily for safety reasons, and has operated at only 80 percent of its 540,000 kilowatt capacity because of repeated problems with faulty fuel rods. From the standpoint of conservationist groups, which fought the nuclear power plant proposal from the start, the major victory has been in averting thermal pollution of the Connecticut River. This was done through the addition of two huge cooling towers. The combination of inadequate testing and planning, plus the cooling towers, other unscheduled environmental controls, and inflation,

* As early as 1963 a "Lake Champlain Committee," with leadership from both Vermont and New York citizens, had been formed to fight "to eliminate water pollution from all sources in Lake Champlain and its tributaries and to conserve the natural resources and scenic beauty of the Champlain Valley." New York State's multibillion-dollar sewage treatment projects, of course, have helped greatly to clean up the lake.

boosted the originally estimated costs $88 million, to $220 million. And as a result, the price of power from the plant has been four times more expensive than the original estimates used to persuade the state to approve its construction. The political fallout has been correspondingly high, because the plant produces about half of the state's electricity. In 1975 the legislature voted to require that any future nuclear plants receive explicit legislative approval—a measure regarded as the strongest nuclear plant control bill in any of the 50 states. Passage of the bill was regarded as an important victory for the Vermont Public Interest Research Group, which is closely tied to the Ralph Nader organization in Washington, and a major defeat for the state's private power companies and the Westinghouse Corporation, a producer of nuclear components which sent lobbyists from Washington to fight the measure.

Vermont might have spared itself the headache of the Vernon nuclear plant if its legislature in 1967 had not turned down, by a narrow margin, a proposal by Governor Hoff for a state power authority to import a vast amount of power from Canada. Lobbyists for the Central Vermont Power Service Corporation and other private power interests fought feverishly to defeat the Hoff proposal, claiming that the nuclear plant would provide adequate and cheap power—a false promise, as it turned out.

The public-versus-private power issue, in fact, is one of the most enduring of Vermont history over the past four decades. The grandfather of the public power faction was George D. Aiken. When he became governor in the 1930s, half of Vermont's 27,000 farms lacked electricity because the private utilities saw no prospect of profit in stringing lines to distant locations. (The attitude of the private utilities, Aiken told me, was "we'll serve whom we damn please—whom we can make the most money on.") * Aiken proceeded to name a new public utilities board, friendly to farmer and consumer interests, with the result that the national Rural Electrification Administration came into Vermont and delivered service to the farmers. Thus a firm public power tradition was planted in the state, witnessed by the fact that today 21 percent of its power plants are publicly owned (as opposed to 2.7 percent in New England as a whole).

Later Aiken backed the St. Lawrence Seaway because of the inexpensive power it could deliver; as a result Vermont receives 150,000 kilowatts from that power supply and has the lowest power costs in New England. But in 1957, Aiken (then already a U.S. Senator) failed to persuade Vermont to create a state authority to build and operate a power distribution system. While the bill was being debated in the legislature, the conservative, business-oriented governor of the moment, Joseph B. Johnson, outfoxed the public power camp by signing a contract with the privately-owned Vermont Electric Power Company (Velco) to build the system. The state's consequent loss of annual revenue has been estimated at $2 million, not to men-

* Aiken's displeasure with the utilities has never abated. "The son-of-a-guns," he said ". . . they never built the fishways they were ordered to 30 years ago on their dams on the Connecticut River. The result is that the salmon have disappeared from the Connecticut River and all its tributaries in the four New England states."

tion lower costs to consumers that might have been effected. As recently as 1973, however, the head of one of Vermont's electric cooperatives suggested that the state buy up a controlling interest in Velco so that it would be run with consumers' interests foremost. (Velco transmits 91 percent of all the electricity sold in the state. It is directly owned by the state's two largest private utilities, one of whose presidents until recently was also president of Velco *and* of Vermont Yankee, which owns the nuclear power plant at Vernon. A neater interlocking directorate could hardly be imagined.)

A sign of the times was the decision of several town meetings in 1975 to start exploring the possibility of building their own, town-owned power companies. The city of Springfield actually took the plunge, voting more than $50 million in bonds to set up its own electric company, a move certain to drive the Central Vermont Public Service Corporation, the state's largest utility, out of town.

From this discussion I have omitted the Vermont public services board, which began to switch to a consumer orientation when Aiken was governor and moved dramatically in that direction under Charles R. Ross, who was appointed its chairman in 1959 by then Governor Robert T. Stafford. The board also has a strong voice in environmental matters; under a 1969 law, for instance, it has veto power over any electric utility capital construction, including power plants and transmission lines, and may consider aesthetic questions in its decisions. Starting in the early 1970s, however, some critics said the board had become overly friendly to the utilities and slanted its rate-making decisions in their direction.

Predictions are a risky thing, but in the proconsumer atmosphere of our times, it seems likely that the public-versus-private argument will remain a lively one in Vermont. The connection of that dispute with straightforward environmental issues may appear tenuous, but in reality the connection is a compelling one. The question is whether Vermonters will collectively plan for the economic and environmental future of their state, or whether they still feel they can safely leave the resolution of essentially public questions in private hands.

Politics and Government: From the 1860s to the 1960s

The fabled Republicanism of Vermont, which denied the unhappy Democrats a single victory for President, governor, or Congress for more than a century after the founding of the Republican party, is a familiar story. Time and again, Vermont stood out as a lonely island of Republicanism: in 1912, for instance, when Utah alone joined it in voting for William Howard Taft, and in 1936, when Maine was the only other state to withstand the FDR landslide. Why did Vermont remain so obdurately Republican, so long? The Civil War memory was a major reason; as an early governor had noted, "hostility to slavery is an instinct" with Vermonters, and the people did not soon forget their sacrifices in that conflict. In time, political preference merged into social orthodoxy. "It was not easy to be a Democrat in Vermont," William Moran has written. "Any man who told his neighbors he was a Democrat was regarded as contrary and a little queer. Unruly children were frightened by parents who warned that the Democrat down the road had a black tongue and would come after them if they did not behave." Religion played no little role in all of this; the Democrats were generally viewed as the Catholic party in a very Protestant state. (Interestingly, the first two Democrats to make real breakthroughs—William Meyer and Philip Hoff— were Protestants both.)

Republicanism was bolstered by the overwhelmingly rural, small-town complexion of the state, which had only a few cities, and most of them small, where a Democratic working class could take root. Finally, there was the Republican organization, or "machine." Oddly enough, its leaders were industrialists rather than farmers. Generations of "railroad governors"— men who had been presidents of important railroads—dominated from the 1840s on. Then, the marble governors of Proctor took over in the 1870s, to rule directly or through their front men with only brief interruptions for some 80 years. Important candidates were hand-picked by the Proctor bosses and nominated in closed caucuses, without so much as a primary to check them prior to 1912. Vermont's hard-pressed farmers, through all these years, were a kind of powerless majority at the hands of the well-financed, skillful Proctor operatives.

The Proctor dynasty was begun by Redfield Proctor, who founded the Vermont Marble Company at Rutland, carving out a separate town (named, of course, Proctor) in which he owned or controlled 97 percent of the property. In the sparsely populated Vermont of that era, marble was one of the few industries of any importance, and the Proctors established cozy working relationships with the railroads, National Life Insurance Company of Montpelier, and when it rose to prominence, Central Vermont Public Service, the biggest utility. Redfield Proctor was elected governor in 1878, his son Fletcher in 1906, Redfield Jr., in 1923, and finally Fletcher's son, Mortimer, in 1945. The Proctors were to Vermont what the Byrds were for so many years to Virginia. The political wars, all fought out within the Republican party, were a factionalized matter of pro-Proctor and anti-Proctors, and the antis rarely triumphed. The only exceptions to Proctor rule were in the Progressive period (1910–15) and George Aiken's governorship (1936–40). But for the most part, opposition to the Proctors was sporadic and weak. "Most Proctor-faction governors," Duane Lockard wrote, were "conservatives of the 'do-nothing' school. Representatives of the business and financial interests of the state, they [wanted] to keep government costs, government regulation, and service functions at the lowest reasonable levels. . . . In earlier times, they opposed factory inspection, regulation of child labor, workmen's compensation." Of course, they opposed public power when it reared its ugly head in the 1930s.

The result of all this was abysmal government. The quality of public education was poor, state homes for the mentally ill and retarded were approved only grudgingly and provided anemic funds, and the poor had to depend on the dubious charity of "overseers" in each town. One opposition newspaper called Proctor administration of Vermont affairs "a Study in Still Life."

A sign of change to come was provided in the depths of the Depression when Warren Austin fought the Proctors to win election to the U.S. Senate, where he broke with Republican orthodoxy to support some New Deal measures and later made his mark as an early internationalist. Elected three times to the Senate, Austin left it in 1946 to become the country's chief delegate to the United Nations, which he helped father.

About the time Austin went to the Senate, the town of Putney sent to the legislature "a quiet, unassuming, prematurely white-haired nurseryman" named George David Aiken. What happened then is instructive about how accidents can shape politics. "They put me on the conservation committee because they thought I knew wildflowers and the beautification of highways," Aiken said in an interview. "But it so happened that the generation of power and use of the streams came under that committee too. It was then I got the idea that somebody beside politicians should get into politics." Aiken advanced to the house speakership, then to lieutenant governor, and, with powerful backing from the so-long ignored farming interests, to the governorship in 1936. In office, he urged the hard-pressed dairyfarmers and maplesugar producers to band together to market their goods and encouraged farmers to form electric and insurance co-ops. By the end of his two terms, Aiken was revered by the rural Vermont families, detested by the Proctor-style conservatives, and feared by the public utilities. In effect, he founded the progressive wing of the Republican Party, which ever since has been at odds with the conservative wing backed by the utilities, business, and industry.

Ralph A. Flanders, the favorite of the private utilities whom Aiken defeated in a heated primary race for the U.S. Senate in 1940, was able to win the state's other Senate seat, succeeding Austin, six years later. Flanders was to win enduring national fame as the man who offered the resolution to censure Senator Joseph R. McCarthy. A self-educated man, philosopher, and prodigious inventor in the machine-tool field (he had been president of Springfield's Jones and Lamson Company), Flanders became an apostle of universal disarmament and traveled abroad extensively in the early 1950s. "It became clear that in the outside world McCarthy was the United States and the United States was McCarthy," Flanders said later. "The conviction grew that something must be done about this, even if I had to do it myself." Flanders' censure motion led to a special committee's investigation and the eventual Senate condemnation of the conscienceless Wisconsin Senator.

The conservatives regained control of the governorship in 1941, when Aiken went off to the Senate. But the Proctor dynasty, like all dinosaurs, was dead before the body knew it. The man who administered the coup de grace was Ernest W. Gibson, Jr., a liberal, energetic hero of the Pacific campaigns who returned from World War II to challenge the last head of the old cartel, Governor Mortimer Proctor, in the 1946 primary. Gibson, the son of a former U.S. Senator of progressive Republican leanings, was a protegé of George Aiken and, like Aiken, had the support of the Farm Bureau, which was a much more progressive force in Vermont than in most states.

Reflecting the fresh spirit of his times, Gibson in two terms as governor did even more than Aiken to bring Vermont into the 20th century. Before his election, for instance, Vermonters had been extremely reluctant to accept federal aid. They had, in the mid-1930s, been one of the first states to cooperate with the federal government on all phases of the Social Security Act, and the REAs had come in under Aiken. But as recently as 1936, the people in a referendum had rejected a proposed $18 million Green Mountain Parkway and National Park, to run the whole length of the state, which would have been an enormous boon to tourism. The ostensible reason: uneasiness about having a strip of "foreign territory" traversing Vermont. Two years later farmers at West Dummerston had armed themselves with rifles to stop federal engineers from building a flood control dam in their pleasant valley.

Gibson, by contrast, was able to sell the proposition that Vermont would not surrender its sovereignty by accepting federal aid for highways, education, hospitals, and social welfare programs. Pointing to the state's gross negligence in many areas, he was able to increase the state budget rapidly, adding a sharply graduated rate structure to the state's income tax to finance his projects.

Education was one of Gibson's major interests. When he took office, there were many teachers in one-room country schools who had no more than grammar school training themselves. Women 80 years of age were still teaching because younger and better trained people would not accept the $1,000-a-year minimum salary. Gibson attacked the problem with a compulsory retirement program for teachers and a million dollar increase in state aid to boost teachers' salaries. The Weeks school for delinquent children, he discovered, was operated as a penal institution rather than a corrective home; Gibson responded by banning corporal punishment and instituting a "rule of love" in the home. After lagging behind the country for years in social services, Gibson's Vermont became the first state to establish a comprehensive program for the care and protection of homeless and dependent children. His other reforms extended to the areas of expanded health services, welfare reform, and rehabilitation of criminals.*

If Gibson had remained active in Vermont politics, he might well have strengthened the progressive camp in the Republican party so substantially that it would have become the dominant faction. But in 1950, during the last year of his second term as governor, President Truman appointed him to a federal judgeship. Gibson became an innovative jurist, calling the insurance companies, the utilities, and other special interests to heel. Vermont political reporter Vic Maerki commented to me in the late 1960s that Gibson had become "perhaps the biggest plaintiff's federal judge in the United States—

* For several specifics of the Gibson record, I am indebted to Melvin S. Wax of the Rutland *Herald* in a report for *The Nation* of June 11, 1949.

he sees his role as redistributing the wealth."

In Vermont politics, however, Gibson's influence vanished almost over-night. The progressive Republicans left the governor's office, not to return for many years. Gibson was succeeded by a string of conservative and gener-ally uninspired Republican governors.

"High on the list of never-accept-defeat politicians of this country," Lockard wrote in the late 1950s, "are the Vermont Democrats." They were unlike the Republicans of the South, who were so spineless that they rarely bothered to put up candidates for office. But while the Democrats almost always had candidates, they resembled the Dixie GOP in that a small coterie of leaders, primarily interested in patronage crumbs from national Demo-cratic administrations, preempted their leadership posts and kept newcomers out. Then there was the fact that most Democratic leaders were Roman Catholic Irishmen from the larger cities, usually Burlington and Rutland, whom the Yankee farmers distrusted. Moreover, the Irish did not get along too well with their fellow Catholics, the French-Canadians. The Franco-American factory workers joined the Democratic party, but their middle class co-ethnics frequently became Republicans. The rise of a viable Democratic party was further undermined by the habit of many Democrats of voting in Republican primaries whenever a progressive Republican, like Gibson or Aiken, was in a contest with a conservative.

The grounds for an upset of Vermont's old partisan imbalance, however, were all present by the 1950s. The Civil War was almost a century past; mass communications were gnawing away at the orthodoxies of a once iso-lated society; the urban working class share of the state population was up significantly since the turn of the century; and finally the eclipse of the Re-publican progressives after Gibson donned his judicial robes was inducing more and more liberal Republicans to move to the Democratic side. In 1952 an energetic Democratic gubernatorial campaigner made the first serious showing for his party in the century, garnering 47.7 percent of the vote in the face of the Eisenhower landslide. In 1958 another Democrat received 49.7 percent of the vote, forcing the first recount in a Vermont gubernatorial election. And in the same 1958 election, a forester named William H. Meyer, running for the U.S. House on the Democratic ticket, capitalized on a bit-ter split in Republican ranks to become the first Democratic Congressman from Vermont in more than a century. Meyer was a liberal, "peace" type can-didate (several years before the Vietnam war made that a popular issue), and he was defeated after two years in Washington. But he had shown other Democrats that victory *was* possible.

At the start of the 1960s, the Vermont voter pool began to move still further from its dependable Republicanism with the arrival of the indepen-dent-thinking people associated with the new electronics firms, the owners of new recreational facilities—often young couples with young ideas—the growth of political activism in the university communities, and the appear-ance of more and more people in their fifties for early retirement.

Then, in 1962, came Democrat Philip H. Hoff's election to the governorship and the real arrival of two-party politics in Vermont. For the times, Hoff was the perfect candidate—a young, activist state legislator born of Republican parents, an articulate intellectual, a good-looking man with one of those perfect campaign-poster families (attractive wife and four children), and, in a shift of pace for the Democrats, their first Protestant candidate for governor in living memory. (During his political career Hoff even manufactured some fights with the ethnic-based Burlington Democratic organization, to make him look like a nonmachine, independent figure.) In his campaign Hoff pressed the theme that Vermont was lagging because of a century of Republican rule—though he always praised the records of Aiken and Gibson. He was helped by the way the Republican governor of the moment, F. Ray Keyser, Jr., had scrapped with the legislature, as well as feuds within the GOP that had led two disgruntled Republicans to form a Vermont Independent Party, which listed Hoff as its candidate on the ballot. The independent party gave more than 3,000 Republicans, who could not bear the thought of actually voting Democratic, a way to vote for Hoff. The growing independent vote bloc went for Hoff also, and he emerged the winner by a narrow but certain margin of 1,348 votes (50.6 percent). The scene that election night, by Moran's account, deserves recording:

> The deliriously joyful people in Winooski filled the streets of their small city on election night in November 1962 when the tall, blond lawyer from across the river in Burlington arrived for the victory celebration. They lifted him on their shoulders. Philip Henderson Hoff grinned at the sea of French-Canadian faces as he celebrated with them his election as Vermont's first Democratic governor since the founding of the Republican party.
> "One hundred years of bondage—broken!" Hoff shouted. The roar of the crowd echoed off the grimy buildings of the mill city, one of the poorest communities in Vermont and, in all the nation, one of the most faithful to the Democratic party.

For six years Hoff remained as governor, winning reelection in 1964 by a startling plurality of 49,035 votes (64.9 percent) and in 1966 by 21,092 votes (57.7 percent). His first reelection, in 1964, was associated with another Vermont "first"—the victory of a Democratic Presidential candidate in the Green Mountain State. Barry Goldwater proved anathema to many traditional Vermont Republicans, enabling Lyndon Johnson, campaigning in tandem with Hoff, to win Vermont with 66.3 percent—more than his national average. By 1966 the Republicans realized they could not beat Hoff; Richard Snelling, the industrialist who was the GOP candidate that year, told his inner circle: "At least we can be soldierly about it, as the Democrats were for a hundred years."

If it was Hoff's intent to upset the equilibrium of "old" low-service, high-unemployment, communal Vermont, one would have to say that he accomplished his goal. His years in office, of course, were in the heart of the expansionist 1960s, years when millions of outsiders' money began to pour into the state and the "Great Society" programs made all manner of previously impossible innovation in social services possible. Thus it might have been impossible for Hoff to "fail" in any event.

Hoff did not hesitate, however, to use what he later called the "shock treatment" to get Vermonters to think anew. "With a population of less than 400,000 persons," he declared, "Vermont has 800 school directors, 246 road commissioners, and 246 overseers of the poor. It's ludicrous, utterly ridiculous and wasteful. It may be political suicide but I am determined to end this sort of provincialism." Hoff proposed, for example, that there be only 12 school districts in the entire state. Similarly, he said, there should be regional highway districts, regional tax districts, and other devices to let groups of towns share expensive services and thus save money by avoiding duplication. Such proposals quickly ran aground in the conservative and still overwhelmingly Republican legislature, where opponents argued that the town government structure was still a very viable one and much closer to the people than a depersonalized regional approach. There are, however, many Vermont towns with such small populations that they are scarcely viable governmental entities. Friends of Hoff's regionalization proposals maintain that he was simply two or three decades ahead of the times on the issue.

Hoff was able, however, to put state planning in Vermont on a thoroughly professional basis, laying the groundwork for measures like Act 250 and the other environmental projects of the 1970s. With the federal spigot turned wide open, he implemented more than 80 Washington-funded programs in such areas as rural and urban development, manpower training, welfare, and education. After his 1964 election victory, in which he amazingly pulled a full ticket of Democratic state office-seekers to victory on his coattails,* Hoff had the happy task of pushing through a legislative reapportionment bill to conform to the "one-man, one-vote" dictum of the federal courts. Many of the conservatives who had frustrated his programs in his first term were then forced out of office, and the newly reapportioned legislature in 1966 worked with him to pass an historic group of laws. The antiquated "overseer of the poor" positions in each town were abolished; a state educational television network was set up; a fair housing law was passed; the tax system was reformed; and a modernization of the penal system was inaugurated.

Even Hoff's warmest admirers, however, admitted that by his third term (1967–68) he had run out of energy and was a rather poor governor. By this point, he was becoming preoccupied with national issues including the Vietnam war (on which he eventually shifted from "hawk" to "dove," even endorsing Eugene McCarthy for the 1968 Democratic nomination) and the riots in the country's big cities. He startled Vermonters by announcing in 1967 that the basic conditions behind the riots were present in their own placid state, including hidden poverty in the green hills, bad

---

* The Democrats were as stupefied as the Republicans when the GOP treasurer, auditor, and secretary of state, who had been State House fixtures for years, went down to defeat. Peter J. Hincks, an 81-year-old banker who had hardly bothered to campaign, said of the Republican incumbent he ousted: "George Amidon has done a good job as treasurer and he's a fine guy. I was awfully surprised about being elected and I hadn't expected to be taking his job away."

housing, and hunger. One of his most controversial programs was the Vermont-New York Summer Youth Project, which tried to bridge the racial gaps of the time by bringing several hundred black children from Harlem to live with Vermont youngsters during the summer of 1968. That year he did not seek reelection, leaving the state treasury with a deficit of $7 million.

Two years later, when he tried to unseat incumbent U.S. Senator Winston L. Prouty—a rather wintry, shy Republican—Hoff could garner only 40.2 percent of the vote. In that campaign he was embarrassed by a whispering campaign about his personal drinking; like a man, he tried to face up to the issue by admitting he had had a serious problem with alcohol since about 1966 but had licked it with help from a famed cured alcoholic, Iowa's Senator Harold Hughes. In 1973 he decided to help his party in Vermont by taking on a new assignment as Democratic state chairman—the first time, as far as I can recall, any former governor of any state has been willing to return to the political trenches in such an inglorious position. Across New England, Hoff in the mid-1970s was still remembered as one of the most outstanding governors the region had ever had. Among other things, he had revitalized the New England Governors' Conference and helped to set the stage for the intensive forms of intraregional cooperation that began to flower in the 1970s. As citizen, politician, and visionary, it might be a long time before Vermont produced his equal.

Politics and Government: Recent Past and Futures

There is a natural flow and ebb to politics, and after the hyperactivist Hoff years it was probably inevitable that Vermont would look next to more staid, conservative leadership. It found it in Deane C. Davis, whose position as president of the National Life Insurance Company of Montpelier had made him the state's most prominent businessman. Davis was already 68 when he ran for governor in 1968, his first bid for statewide office, but he plunged with vigor into the person-to-person campaigns little Vermont expects (as opposed to mass media appeals). A natty dresser and devotee of Vermont's famous Morgan horses, Davis proved to be a personable campaigner and made points by stressing his business experience and promising to clean up the "fiscal mess" Hoff had left behind. The Democratic candidate, John J. Daley of Rutland, who had been Hoff's lieutenant governor for two terms, proved a lackluster contender unable to appeal to the independents and intellectuals as Hoff had. Davis won by a decisive margin and moved immediately to put the state on a sound fiscal basis through institution of a sales tax. He endeared himself to the conservatives by launching a campaign against welfare "freeloaders," hiring Pinkerton detectives to turn up cases of welfare cheating. (They found five in the entire state.) On the other hand, it was under Davis's administration that the state passed its historic land use and water control bills of 1970. With a legislature heavily weighted to his own party, Davis was also able to make a start at combining Vermont's 156 separate agencies, commissions, and boards under a cabinet system—a reform which Hoff had sought without success.*

Davis was labeled a stick-in-the-mud conservative by some of the state's more liberal voices, the Rutland *Herald* in particular. Liberal Republicans including his 1970 primary opponent (when Davis won a second term), said Davis was neglecting mental health needs in particular and human needs in general. But in fact, Vermont's "conservative" leaders—those who frequently win office—would be called outrageous spenders and socialist meddlers in a state like next door New Hampshire, or in many states of the South and the Mountain West. At least since World War II and the Gibson era, Vermont has been a high-tax state, striving to provide commensurately high levels of services. In relation to personal income, the combined state and local taxes have ranked near the top of all states, and absolute first, in some recent years.† There is no other state in which the citizens pay a greater share of their income to support elementary and secondary education. In dollars spent per capita, Vermont in the early 1970s ranked 10th among the states in higher education,‡ sixth in welfare (up from abysmally low levels in the past), and fifth in highways. Health and hospitals are the only major area in which the financial effort is below par for the United States. Vermont has not shied away from capital improvements, reflected in the fact that only nine other states have a larger per capita debt of state and local governments.

This is not to say that there are not, in Vermont, some ultraconservatives who would gladly junk most of these spending programs. Mallary defined them as those "who don't think we should have taken over welfare at the state level, don't think we should have given up the local overseer of the poor, don't think we should have given up the county lock-ups for prisoners in exchange for state supervision, and don't approve of state subsidies to schools to equalize opportunities." But, he added, "that has not been a dominant tradition in either party."

In the 1960s, for instance, several railroads in Vermont were on the

* The administrative consolidation was only half a loaf, however. New cabinet-level agencies of human services, environmental conservation, administration, and development and community affairs were set up. But the vested interests were able to prevent the creation of four more that had been recommended, covering such areas as education, highways, transportation, industrial relations, and employment security. By 1975, the cabinet system was still incomplete.

† Property taxes take the heaviest bite, about 38 percent of the state-local tax collections, followed by sales taxes (32 percent) and the personal and corporate income taxes (20 percent). Despite the graduated feature of the state's personal income tax, the overall tax system is highly regressive. Property taxes have been estimated to take 4.7 percent of the income of families earning $5,000–$6,000 a year but only 1.8 percent of those earning over $25,000. Sales taxes hit poor families much harder than more wealthy ones. The state income tax, while mildly graduated, is tied to the federal income tax with all its loopholes. Since the overall tax burden is so heavy, one would be surprised if the state's low- and middle-income people did not rise up in protest, demanding a thoroughgoing reform in the next few years to make the structure a more progressive one.

‡ The aid of higher education goes to four state colleges and to the University of Vermont, familiarly known as UVM. Oddly enough, that institution did not become the official state university until 1955, though it was chartered in 1791. It has the state's only medical school and several respected academic departments, but tuitions rank high compared to other state universities.

brink of bankruptcy and the state had the choice of foregoing their services or actually buying the affected lines. Without state intervention, the railroads could have made a lot of money by selling their materials, and especially their lands, and then, "the public be damned," going out of business. But the state stepped in to make the purchases, including the Rutland Railroad, and now there is state or public ownership of about two-thirds of the railroad lines in Vermont. "It's paradoxical," Senator Aiken said, "that some of our people considered ardent conservatives were right in the forefront of buying the railroads and putting them into public ownership. In Vermont you see 'conservatives' going along with what used to be considered very radical ideas." The "conservatives" Aiken referred to in this context, of course, are those within the Republican mainstream, not the bitterenders described by Mallary.

After voting for Lyndon Johnson in 1964, Vermont returned to its Republican habits in presidential elections, giving Richard Nixon 53 percent of its vote in 1968 and 63 percent four years later (though it was only four months after the 1972 election that several town meetings were publicly calling for Nixon's impeachment). Through all these years, the legislature has remained Republican by its customary two-to-one and three-to-one margins. All this does not mean, however, that Vermont has reverted to its old one-party habits, or that the Democratic years under Hoff were simply an aberration. This was proven decisively in 1972 when Vermonters, on the same day they voted to reelect Nixon, were choosing a new Democratic governor by a clearcut 55 percent margin. Thomas P. Salmon, a 40-year-old attorney and former minority leader in the state legislature, was a Hoff protegé, opposing a Republican candidate who was a Davis protegé. Salmon's chief issues were calls to slow down recreation home development (to keep "Vermont for the Vermonters") and blaming the Republicans for high power costs because of their refusal to approve the low-cost Canadian power deal during the Hoff years.

In 1974, facing yet another conservative Republican opponent, Salmon won reelection with 56.5 percent of the vote. Salmon could easily have obtained the Democratic nomination for the Senate seat George Aiken was vacating, and polls showed he might well win the general election. But he announced for governor instead, saying he wanted to complete the programs he had begun. "Vermont finds itself today in the hurly-burly for unprecedented political jockeying in the wake of Senator Aiken's announced retirement," Salmon added. "I for one want no part of this carnival atmosphere at a time when credibility in government at all levels is at its lowest ebb."

On the same day as Salmon's 1974 landslide reelection—and partly because of his coattails—the Democrats elected their first Senator from Vermont in 120 years, 34-year-old Patrick J. Leahy. A veteran of eight years as state's attorney for Chittenden County, the equivalent of a district attorney for the Burlington area, Leahy had built an aggressive record on such issues as fighting the death penalty and investigating major oil companies. With a forceful campaign, he was able to squeeze past the favored Republican, Congressman Richard Mallary, who had been the top vote getter in the state only two years before.* The Salmon sweep also helped the Democrats capture three other statewide offices and gain major blocs of seats in both houses of the legislature. Helped by Republican defections, they actually elected one of their own as house speaker in January 1975.

The development of a two-party system has siphoned off enough liberals from Republican ranks to give the edge to conservatives in most GOP primaries. One could not say, however, that the progressive Republican tradition is dead. Aiken was its living embodiment as long as he was in the Senate. Senator (and former Congressman) Robert T. Stafford, who describes himself as a "moderate-liberal" is another. One of the most progressive younger Republicans, James M. Jeffords, made waves in Vermont (alienating many conservatives) through his support of and vigorous enforcement of the state's environmental laws as attorney general in the 1969–73 period. Jeffords narrowly lost the Republican nomination for governor in 1972, but came back to win nomination (and later election) for the U. S. House in 1974.

Yet all is not well in the GOP liberal wing, because in the same 1974 primary Charles Ross, a former member of the Federal Power Commission and champion of consumer interests, lower utility rates, and tougher regulation of the power companies, could garner only 36 percent of the vote in a contest with the more conservative Mallary for the Senate nomination. From the early 1960s through the mid-1970s, most of the Republican nominations for governor have gone to party conservatives who have difficulty winning support from the large and growing number of independent voters in the state. This helps to explain why, with the exception of Davis's two victories, the Democrats won every gubernatorial election from 1962 through 1974.

The future conservative vs. liberal balance in the GOP has been made harder to discern by the changes in Vermont's primary system enacted in 1970. The law, the first of its kind in New England, provides that each voter will receive an individual packet of ballots for each party; he or she marks one and throws the others away, without having to disclose in which party primary he or she is voting. This has increased participation in the Democratic primary, since citizens can "secretly" mark a Democratic ballot, even in towns where there is still a residual prejudice against Democrats. On the other hand, the law also makes it possible for Democrats and the broad mass of independents to go into Republican primaries

* Mallary, a prosperous dairy farmer and mild-mannered and soft-spoken man in his mid-forties, saw a lifetime ambition thwarted in his defeat. He is the type of down-to-earth, self-effacing Vermonter who—until the 1970s—would have been a totally appropriate representative for his state in the Senate. Ushered into his sparsely furnished Capitol Hill office for an interview one day, I found he had positioned his desk modestly facing the wall. He turned to greet his visitor as if one were entering a small-town Vermont law office. (Most Congressmen, of course, position their desks and furnish their offices for maximum dramatic effect.) After an hour-plus of open conversation, Mallary quietly thanked *me* for coming and turned to face that wall and the desk and the paperwork on it, before I even had a chance to reach the door.

and, if they wish to, be the balance of power in tight conservative-liberal contests. The problem is that the independents, largely a "liberal" group, generally abjure the primaries altogether, leaving an advantage with the conservative contenders in both parties' primaries.

Vermont's old political ways received yet another jolt in 1975 when the legislature voted to remove the provision for straight-party ticket voting on ballots in future elections, opting instead for the Massachusetts-style ballot which requires the citizen to vote individually for each candidate.

"Reforms" of other types have come to Vermont politics in recent years. In the early 1970s, for instance, the legislature approved a "right-to-know" law which prohibits elected bodies, state and local, from holding secret sessions. (There are some exceptions, but if meetings are held behind closed doors, the minutes must be made available to the public later.) Vermont also has a new campaign spending disclosure law, coupled with fairly stiff limitations on the amounts candidates may spend.

On the other hand, the voters in 1974 rejected a constitutional amendment which would have extended the terms of the governor and other constitutional officers from two to four years; the people apparently prefer a frequent check on their officials, even if the results are more nonstop campaigning and less time for officeholders to develop and implement programs. Also, despite repeated attempts at repeal, Vermont's poll tax law, which dates from Civil War days and has been called "an affront to human dignity" in our day and age, remains on the books.

In several programmatic areas, Vermont has established itself as a markedly progressive state since World War II. Environmental and land use legislation are the leading examples, but there are others. Model mental health laws have been passed, deemphasizing the old custodial institutions for the insane in favor of community centers that treat mental problems in their earliest stages and try to keep people well and functioning in their own towns and cities. Major advances have been made in vocational training for the state's young people, as well as rehabilitational services for the physically and mentally handicapped. The state's department of corrections is considered one of the most advanced in the United States, aimed at reintegrating prisoners into their home communities in terms of work; under a 1972 law, sentences can even be suspended for up to five years if the judge and state's attorney agree that a person is not likely to commit further crimes. There is a statewide legal defender system, and in 1971 Vermont Legal Aid was rated by an independent evaluation firm as one of the best legal-service programs for the poor in the entire United States. In the early 1970s, Vermont became the first state to couple the vote for 18-year-olds with full rights for persons of that age to purchase liquor, make binding legal contracts, and marry without parental consent.

The distinguishing traits of Vermont public life would appear to be personalism, tolerance, and a feeling that the state's society and government are still on a scale small enough to be both workable and humane. Vermont leaders I spoke with referred to the problems of sheer scale faced by the larger industrialized states, with their crushing social problems centered in big cities and massive, impersonal suburbs; the suggestion was that Vermont was fortunate indeed to be able to work out its own problems without such burdens.

A corollary to this is the remarkable trust and admiration most Vermonters still seem to have in their elected leaders, and the apparent attitude that government is one's friend and servant, not one's enemy. The startling absence of corruption in government may help to account for the phenomenon. The late William Allen White, according to an account in the *American Mercury* in 1945, at first refused to believe there was no corruption in a state where one political party had so long been in power. But he later concluded that Vermont was so small, and everyone seemed to know so much about his neighbor's business, that graft was practically impossible. Whatever the reasons, the honesty theme appears to hold true today. Mallary said that as secretary of administration in the Davis cabinet, he had the major auditing functions of state government under him, as well as the purchasing department and state buildings department—"both of which in other state governments create the largest problems." But, he said, "we just haven't had the problems. The tradition of clean government and honesty still exists in Vermont."

And from political reporters who ought to know, I heard the opinion that no small group of men or interests control Vermont government from behind the scenes. The vast majority of Vermonters appear to share this confidence—a remarkable expression of faith in the legitimacy of government I think is paralleled in only a handful of other American states, of which Minnesota, Wisconsin, Oregon, and Hawaii are the salient examples. Since Minnesota and Wisconsin are heavily Scandinavian and German in ethnic origin, and Hawaii principally Asiatic, Yankee probity cannot be put down as the sole reason for honest and straightforward government. But in each of these examples, one does find the tradition of English common law operating in an ethnic-historical background where the people have thrown off grave oppressions in times past and gone on to use government as their instrument in creating the kind of society they want. The similarity between Vermont and Hawaii, which I suggest here, may come as a surprise to many readers, but the strong New England influence on the island state should not be forgotten. New Englanders were also important in the settlement of Oregon. And in the last 15 years, Hawaii, Oregon, and Vermont have all developed a finally attuned environmental consciousness based on their fears of what greedy recreation-industry developers can do to their precious and delicate landscapes and ecosystems. They are also among the most advanced states of the Union in land use planning.

This is not to say that special interest lobbies do not have influence in the legislative halls at Montpelier. In the past there were occasions when their role was particularly malodorous, as in the era of railroad dominance

when the rail lobby bought votes and managed to fend off state regulation
for decade after decade. At one point no less than 59 employees of the Central Vermont Public Service Corporation were in the legislature. To this
day, lobbyists are important to the legislative process because of the rapid
turnover of legislative membership and a woefully inadequate staff. For
the 180 members, there are only one fiscal analyst, one research assistant,
and two bill draftsmen. Lobbyists are omnipresent to testify before committees and help with bill drafting. In the Justin Morgan Room, a cocktail
lounge close to the State House, the lobbyists spend many evening hours
with legislators. But, as William Moran has noted, "the lobbyist who depends too much on this convivial way of doing business risks creating a bad
image with the considerable number of legislators who don't drink and
who don't think much of those who do."

In recent times the most visible lobbies have been the private utilities,
the Farm Bureau, the Associated Industries of Vermont, the Wholesale
Beverage Association (informally referred to as the "beer lobby"), the
Federated Fish and Game Clubs of Vermont, Green Mountain Park (the
state's only racetrack), truckers and the "highway lobby" in general, education groups, and, of course, the recreation-land developers. All, however, operate quite openly, and there is still some protection in the large
membership of the house in particular. It was reduced from 246 to 150
in the 1960s apportionment but remained the ninth-largest legislative body
(tied with New York and Texas) in the country. Thus the Vermont legislator continues to represent few enough people so that they can know him
personally. He's elected on the basis of who he is and what he does at
home and what kind of a person his neighbors consider him to be—rather
than how much campaign money he spends or what special interests support him. The net result is to make him (or the handful of hers) relatively
immune to improper special interest group pressures. One should not, of
course, carry too far the argument that a large legislature is more resistant
to manipulation than a small one. "The smaller the legislature, the more
they're sitting ducks for lobbyists and special interests," Senator Aiken told
me. But then he quickly added there were exceptions, including the New
Hampshire legislature in the days that the Boston and Maine Railroad literally "ran the place."

Especially prior to reapportionment, the leadership of the Vermont
house often fell by default to a dozen or so lawyers, wealthy farmers, and
successful businessmen. Since the apportionment, approved by the legislature itself with some tears in 1965, the small town influence has been radically reduced. (Up to then, each of the 246 towns and cities had a single
house member; the U.S. Supreme Court, in fact, cited the Vermont house
as the most malapportioned legislative body in the country.)* Now the
larger towns and especially the cities are much better represented, and the

* The city of Burlington, with 33,155 people, had a single representative—and so did the
town of Stratton with 38.

reflexive conservatism and habit of turning down controversial bills, for fear of making a mistake, has waned appreciably. The reapportioned legislative sessions have been much more willing than their predecessors to take prerogatives away from the towns and enhance the authority of the state government. It is doubtful, for instance, if Act 250 and the whole idea of district and state-wide environmental commissions could ever have been approved before reapportionment. Legislative coalitions of liberal-to-moderate Republicans with the minority Democrats are often sufficient to pass progressive bills. Nor is the Vermont legislature any longer a farmers' assembly. As recently as 1955, 37 percent of the membership were farmers, but by the early 1970s that figure had dropped to 10 or 11 percent. The legislature in the last few years has been overwhelmingly white collar in complexion, with teachers, engineers, real estate brokers, small businessmen, and lawyers all heavily represented. As in times past, however, there is a seemingly inordinate proportion of retirees; the average age of the membership is about 55 years. Many working age people simply cannot afford the long weeks of sessions in Montpelier, especially when the pay remains a scant $30 a day, plus expenses—with none of the boodle available in other states.

Vermonters themselves still criticize the legislature for inaction on important issues. But the overall record, especially in recent years, has been a good one, and the unique personalism of Vermont government is still preserved. As a veteran legislator said, in remarks quoted by the Vermont *Times:* "I read every bill carefully and listen to the pros and cons with an open mind. Before I vote I ask myself one question: 'Will this bill make Vermont a better place for my kids to live in?' If the answer is 'yes' I vote for the bill. If the answer is 'no' I vote against it and I don't give a tinker's dam who's sponsoring it! It's as simple as that."

That is, of course, not far from the philosophy of the town meeting, which remains the bedrock of government in the state. In 200 years little has been done to change this remarkable institution, although some of the larger cities have abandoned it in favor of city elections of representatives to town meetings in which delegates speak for the citizens. In the great majority of Vermont towns, however, town meeting day—the first Tuesday in March—remains the great civic event of the year, and every citizen, if he wishes, can attend and speak his mind. There the tax rate is set, selectmen and other local officials are chosen, and every issue decided from maintenance funds for the town roads to care of the local cemetery.

Many premature obituaries have been spoken over the town meeting, and its obvious defects are easy to spot. Often the crucial decisions are made the night before in a local living room where a small ruling group, the local "establishment," meets to map strategy. Only 10 to 20 percent of the townspeople are usually in attendance. And complex modern issues, like proposals for comprehensive town zoning, are surely beyond the ken of many of those who do show up.

All the same, Vermonters treasure their town meetings. On town meeting day 1971, research teams from St. Michael's College and Johnson State College distributed questionnaires at the meetings in 57 small communities, querying town officers, others who participated in the floor debates, and a random selection of silent attendees. Mailed replies from some 60 percent were received. The tabulations showed that less than 5 percent agreed with the statement: "Town meeting is too old fashioned to be of real value in today's world." Less than 12 percent agreed that "The trouble with town meeting is that a few big shots run the whole show and the regular guy never gets a chance." Less than 4 percent believed that "The towns would be a lot better off if they let the state handle more of their problems." In written comments, the participants did ask for some reforms, including "pre-town meeting" sessions to help clear up issues and better explanations of reports by town officials. But the study seemed to record a desire for political education rather than institutional change.

Asked what issues concerned them the most, the respondents put taxes and education at the top of their lists, far ahead of such issues as pollution, zoning, loss of land to outsiders, or even "help for farmers." And that order of priorities, interestingly, held true for all classes of respondents, including farmers and professionals, Vermonters and "out-of-staters," Democrats and Republicans, people from the larger and from the smaller towns, and people from growing and declining places.

Will there be town meetings when the 21st century dawns, or perhaps a century from now? One guesses so, even if it might seem more "logical" to go to a regional approach as Governor Hoff recommended in the 1960s. To Vermonters, the town meeting is a kind of symbol of their personalized society. They need only look to southern New England to see how great the problem of citizen "voicelessness" is becoming in America's mass culture. And paradoxically, the more complex the governmental forms of the United States become, and the more citizens feel alienated from impersonal institutions of their society, the more thoughtful leaders across the country are looking to the simple exercises in grass-roots democracy embodied in the New England town meeting for clues to preserving and enhancing the social fabric of American communities.

A Postscript on George Aiken

Throughout this chapter, I have had occasion to make frequent reference to the career of George D. Aiken, the horticulturist from Putney who left his plants in the 1930s to become one of the most innovative governors in Vermont history. Then, in the Senate from 1941 to 1975, Aiken became a kind of living embodiment of the simple Vermont virtues of honesty, decency, and independence of mind. Aiken was the despair of more partisan Republicans throughout his years in public life; in the 1930s, for instance, he called on the party's leadership to end the "hate Roosevelt campaign" and told a Lincoln Day dinner: "The greatest praise I can give Lincoln on this anniversary is to say that he would be ashamed of his party today." The year he retired, he told me: "I haven't paid much attention to party politics; you can't do your work if you do." He liked to boast he had never asked for a vote after 1940. "Get into a community and find out what their problems are. That's the best politics," he said. By his last race, in 1968, the Democrats had given up and even endorsed him as their own candidate.*

When Aiken retired, he was the dean of the Senate, the oldest Senator, and the ranking Republican on both the Agriculture and Foreign Relations Committies. In his last decade of service, he became a leading advocate of "lowering the American profile" on the world scene; in 1970, for instance, he told a Vermont group that the United States must find "a halfway house between the innocence of isolationism and the arrogance of trying to dominate the world." Perhaps his most famous piece of Aiken advice was his Vietnam peace plan of 1966: "The United States should declare victory and get out." (What Aiken actually said was that the U.S. should announce "victory" in its limited objective of deterring North Vietnamese aggression and redeploy its troops to strategic centers; then, if the communist attacks ceased, he said, the U.S. could start to withdraw entirely from Vietnam). On legislature matters, Aiken considered U.S. participation in building the St. Lawrence Seaway one of his most important accomplishments. He also took a lasting interest in rural development, advocated antitrust regulation of the utilities conglomerates and a share for rural and municipal electrification associations in the power generated by government-backed nuclear plants, and sponsored in 1945 a bill which was a forerunner of the food stamp program of recent times.

Advice, rather than legislation, was Aiken's chief stock in trade, however. A friendly, keen-witted man, he was described as a man having little power but immense influence. Presidents from Franklin Roosevelt onwards turned to him for private counsel, and he also served with former President Herbert Hoover on the Hoover Commission. Lyndon Johnson, in particular, consulted frequently with Aiken but, of course, failed to heed his counsel on the Vietnam war. (Aiken was fond of saying that if LBJ would only do what Aiken told him, he'd be the best President in history.) Every morning for some 20 years, Aiken had breakfast with Montana's Mike Mansfield, Johnson's successor as majority leader. In a chamber of prima donnas, Harry McPherson has suggested, Aiken's and Mansfield's was one of the few enduring simple friendships. Shortly after Aiken announced his retirement, Mansfield said: "Senator Aiken is a man of outstanding integrity and unquestioned patriotism, a man of independence, a man who represents, to me, what I was led to believe, in my younger days, is the characteristic of all New Englanders."

* Aiken reported spending $17.09 on his reelection campaign that year—mostly for postage to thank people for circulating his nominating papers, "which I didn't ask them to do."

Aiken said he was retiring because, "when I came to Washington, I left much unfinished work at home and I now want to get back to it." What he meant was that he wanted to get back to his orchard and wildflowers in Putney. (He was a pioneer in propagating wildflowers for domestic cultivation, and was proud that the book he dictated in less than a week in the early 1930s—*Pioneering in Wild Flowers*—was back in print and selling at a brisk clip.)

And so 82-year-old George Aiken, Vermont's gift to the nation for 34 years, left the national capital. He would miss old friends, he said, but not Washington. "I've never felt at home in Washington. No, no, Washington's not home. Home's up on the mountain in Vermont where I always lived."

NEW HAMPSHIRE

MAJESTIC DISAPPOINTMENT

NEW HAMPSHIRE! The words evoke the majesty of Mount Washington and the Presidential Range, lovely Chocorua, the Grand Monadnock. They speak of rivers running headstrong and clean over their rock-strewn beds, of deep pine forests, of the radiance of a clear October day when the red maples and yellow birches, framed in evergreen, create a scene of such loveliness that one would like to make time stop and live forever in the perfection of the moment. Since earliest childhood days, those magical words have also meant for me a lake clear and deep, ringed by mountains, and a bright cottage by the water that will always be more home than any other place on earth.

The granite character of New Hampshire—and by inference, the New Hampshireman—is legendary. As Daniel Webster wrote in *The Old Man of the Mountain:*

Men hang out their signs indicative of their respective trades: shoemakers hang out a gigantic shoe; jewelers, a monster watch; and the dentist hangs out a gold tooth; but up in the mountains of New Hampshire, God Almighty has hung out a sign to show that there He makes men.

Perhaps Webster was a little carried away by his own New Hampshire birth when he penned those lines. For the thesis of this chapter will be that

Ralph Waldo Emerson was far more correct when he remarked that "the God who made New Hampshire taunted the lofty mountains with little men." That judgment cannot, of course, be extended to all of the state's leaders, past or present; some have been and are men and women of courage and decency. But compared to most of the other 13 original states, New Hampshire offers a strikingly undistinguished history and tradition. One reads and rereads the state's history in search of great leaders and finds embarrassingly few; one looks for an important tradition in literature, the arts, or public policy and finds practically none; one tries to detect a sense of historic mission and is disappointed again.

There was, of course, and to a degree there remains the classic New Hampshireman—a character of either English or Scotch-Irish stock sparing in words, frugal, stubborn, fearsomely independent. You have to get to know him to discover, as Cornelius Weygandt once wrote, that he is the "merriest of the Puritans." The sense of a good story is there, told with a rhythmic northwoods accent beyond compare. Emerson found his "poets of tavern hearth" around Monadnock; Thornton Wilder's poignant *Our Town* was laid in New Hampshire; Stephen Vincent Benét told a famous New Hampshire story in *The Devil and Daniel Webster*; and it was New Hampshire folk customs and loggers and witches and deserted farms and sugar orchards that created the warp and woof of so much of Robert Frost's poetry. "It is restful just to think about New Hampshire," Frost once wrote. The character of the old New Hampshireman, indeed, *used* to make it that way. Yet when one looks at New Hampshire public life over most of the years since World War II, one finds an appallingly smug and uncreative atmosphere, and in many policies the prototype among the 50 states of the unresponsive and irresponsible society.

Those words, I know, sound harsh and categorical. But consider these New Hampshire phenomena:

In this state of professed granite character, the chief pillars of state government have been sin taxes—the take on booze and butts sold at discount prices to out-of-staters, dog and horse racing, and the nation's first modern-day state-run sweepstakes lottery. Collectively, New Hampshire's tax structure adds up to a tawdry effort to (1) fleece visitors to pay for internal functions, and (2) trick the state's citizens into thinking they have a good deal because New Hampshire stands alone in having no broad-based state tax (sales or income). As a result, local property taxes are at an almost confiscatory level, and a poor New Hampshire citizen pays twice as high a percentage of his total income in taxes as does a rich one. In an early 1970s study of the tax system of the various states, awarding "bonus" points for well-balanced revenue structures and progressivity in taxation, New Hampshire received an incredibly low 3.3 points out of a possible 100, compared to 74 for Vermont and 45 for Maine. No other state received less than 16 points in the study, by John Shannon, assistant director of the Advisory Commission on Intergovernmental Relations.

Mediocre public services are another result of the meager tax base.

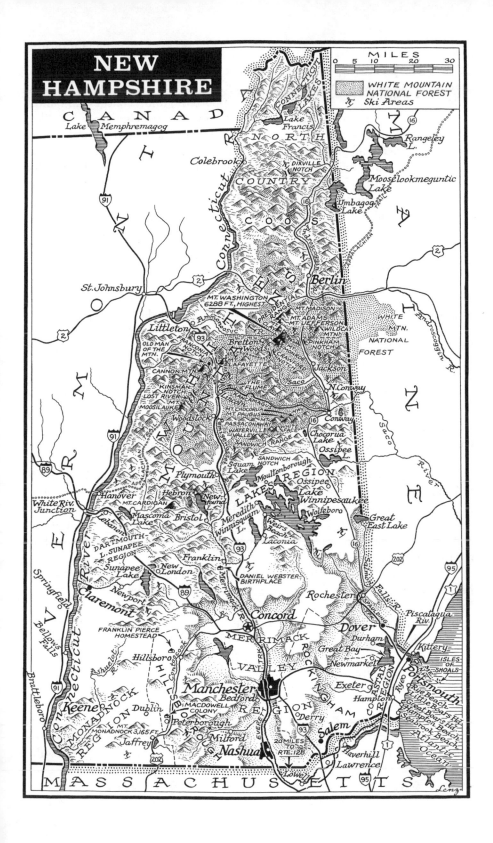

On a per capita basis, counting the expenditures of both state and local governments, New Hampshire spends less than any other New England state on local schools. It has no state-supported junior colleges and must charge inordinately high tuitions for attending the University of New Hampshire. Public kindergartens, vocational education, and special classes for the retarded and handicapped lag far behind the remainder of the region. Less is spent for welfare, less for hospitals and mental health, less for parks and recreation and overall programs for preservation of natural resources than in any other New England state. And largely because its own tax base does not yield enough to match federal dollars, New Hampshire receives less per capita in federal aid than any other state of the region.

In the face of that record, one former governor, Dr. Robert Blood, complained to me that "the state government has become too extravagant." But another onetime chief executive of the state, taking quite a different tack, said that parts of the New Hampshire government were "in a state of atrophy." Asking not to be quoted by name, he added: "Making state government responsive is a task which the people of New Hampshire have not had the political intelligence to face up to." It was the severest indictment that I have ever heard a U.S. governor, past or present, make about his state.

Underlying New Hampshire's dreary public performance—and cited by many as a major reason for it—is the dominant state-wide newspaper, the Manchester *Union Leader*, which rants and raves against any progressive reform. It is owned by an extremist publisher whose diatribes have frightened many decent people from speaking their minds or entering public life at all.

But there are some classic New Hampshire attitudes that have made the state fertile ground for a reactionary press, for obdurate opposition to any broad-based tax, and for New England's dreariest record on land use control. One is: "Why do we need any more taxes? Things seem alright as they are." And another: "Nobody's going to tell me what to do—not by a damned sight."

This is not to say that such attitudes, in proper measure, are not healthy antidotes to overbearing government. But in New Hampshire they have all too often blanked out broader questions of human concern, of government's responsibility to provide a basic minimum of services to people.

And it is into *this* kind of an atmosphere that leaders in search of the presidency of the United States pour every four years in search of some kind of a mandate from the nation's early-bird presidential primary. In unseemly fashion, the candidates cater to a minuscule primary electorate quite unrepresentative of the nation at large—demographically and attitudinally. Sometimes the New Hampshire voters provide an early warning to the nation about the personal or electoral weaknesses of a prospective candidate, or the potential of some new movement in national politics. But making New Hampshire a weathervane of the national pulse, as the media is wont, is a risky business. By national standards, public dialogue about government and services is antediluvian. And while it does not always triumph, the dominant, bile-ridden newspaper stakes out the battlefield for each campaign.

People, History, and Tradition

In his *Study of History*, Arnold Toynbee announced that New Hampshire lay north of the "optimum climatic area." It was, he suggested, a "hard country" fit only for northwoods guides, woodsmen, and hunters. Apparently unaware of this warning, people have been pouring into New Hampshire at an astounnding rate in recent years. By 1975 the state's population was estimated at 818,000, a third more inhabitants than in 1960 and up 64 percent from 1940, when the figure was 491,524. For the last decade and a half, no other New England state has had a growth rate comparable to New Hampshire's. The lion's share of the population increase has come in the extreme southern part of the state, giving Census maps of New Hampshire the appearance of a bottle whose contents have all settled to the bottom like a thick residue. Most of this has been Massachusetts-Route 128 spillover, a thoroughly miscellaneous group of people not easily categorized along traditional racial-ethnic lines.

The newcomers of the post-World War II era have joined a population pool comprising not only the old Yankees but also northern New England's largest concentration of non-Anglo-Saxon—i.e., "ethnic"—folk. At the climax of 70 years of rapid immigration in 1920, for instance, 49 percent of New Hampshire's people were either foreign-born or the sons or daughters of immigrants. (The comparable figures for Maine and Vermont were 35.2 percent each). The descendants of the foreign-born still constitute distinct population groupings which play a vital role in New Hampshire's public life.

The first big "ethnic" group to arrive had been the Irish, starting well before the Civil War. Many came to build with the sweat of their brow the 44 railroads (now mostly abandoned) which once webbed the state. The Irish were an affable, outgoing people who managed by sheer perseverance —as would the Poles, Scandinavians, Italians, Greeks, and most other immigrant groups that followed later—to carve a comfortable niche for themselves in the Puritan environment.

Starting in the mid-19th century, however, New Hampshire began to receive vast numbers of a group not so easily assimilated—the French-Canadian. The French were to become and remain New Hampshire's largest ethnic group, about a quarter of the total population (more, proportionately, than any other state of the Union). They have come from the land in French Canada, where they had experienced a bitter struggle for survival. Desperately poor and little educated, they brought with them an encapsulated parish culture—their own language, customs, and priests. The French-Canadians were not only clannish (albeit far less so in recent years) but instinctively conservative. In Canada they had learned to dislike the English and the English tax, and to resent anyone who sought by taxation to take away from their meager, hard-earned incomes. By transference, any New Hampshire Yankee suggesting new public revenues was just another taxing Englishman. In Manchester and Nashua, in the north country's Berlin and several smaller industrial towns, the French either approached or surpassed the 50 percent mark in the population. One cannot even begin to understand New Hampshire politics without taking into account this massive culture-within-a-culture.

The mediocre character of public life in modern New Hampshire, however, is rooted in more than the state's peculiar ethnic composition. One has to look to two other roots—the geophysical and the historical.

This granite-strewn land was endowed with a thin soil—no match for Vermont's fertile valleys or the plentiful harvests to be taken from the sea along Maine's long coast. The early settlers, in an age still agricultural, "pried the sun with a crowbar" trying to wrest a livelihood from the resistant land. It was largely a losing battle, so New Hampshire became an early recruit to the Industrial Revolution as one after the other mills sprang up beside the rivers racing down their tight little valleys. At first displaced Yankees from the farms provided the manpower for the mills, but soon that labor source became too scarce—or, as the mill owners saw it, too high priced—and thousands upon thousands of foreign workers, principally French-Canadians, were brought in to run the looms of the textile plants, ensconced in grim multistory red brick buildings. The great Amoskeag mill at Manchester was to become the world's largest textile manufacturing plant; Nashua and several smaller cities became major textile centers as well. Long before Maine or Vermont, New Hampshire became a principally urban state. The factory culture of New Hampshire's cities was marked by child labor, meager wages, and ferocious opposition to unions by the mill owners. Too early, too brutally, an industrial urban culture robbed New Hampshire of its agrarian innocence.

One needs to look back even further in history to detect the roots of other factors which colored the state's development by generating among New Hampshire people a deep suspicion of their own government. And in the colonial period, one finds questionable land claims, a succession of native-born royal governors who lorded it over their compatriots in a style reminiscent of the most pretentious European nobility, and dishonesty in high places.

The original grantee to the territory was a London merchant, Captain John Mason, who in 1629 named the colony New Hampshire in honor of the English county of Hampshire where he had lived. Mason was interested in the rich fur trade of the interior, and also sought to establish a semifeudal domain in the New World. The welter of land grants he issued, with confusing and overlapping boundaries, were to cause litigation clear down to 1787. Thus New Hampshire's early settlers had to cope not only with forbidding winters and Indian maraudings, but with fear that they might not hold true and permanent title to the land they settled.

Mason's land grants were one reason that New Hampshire, outside of the four settlements begun along or near the coast in the 1630s—Portsmouth, Dover, Exeter, and Hampton—filled very slowly with people, preventing development of a strong New Hampshire society before the mid-1700s. In 1641, only 1,000 people lived in the colony, such an exposed group of settlements that they asked to be taken under Massachusetts' protective wing. Ninety years later, in 1732, the total population of the colony was still only 12,500.

Made a separate royal province in 1679, New Hampshire for years shared a governor with Massachusetts though it had its own legislature and council. In 1741 the colony received its first governor in its own right, Benning Wentworth, a third-generation New Hampshireman who determined to use the office to enrich himself, his relatives, and his friends. Holding office for 25 years, Wentworth created, according to the WPA Guide, "more townships than all his predecessors put together. . . . Distributing about two hundred tracts of land of generous proportions to various groups of persons, it was his practice in each case to reserve for himself a personally selected lot of five hundred acres. In less than twenty years he thus acquired, without expense to himself, one hundred thousand acres scattered over New Hampshire in such a manner that whatever direction the growth of population and trade might turn, he could not fail to become rich." Another who became rich was Wentworth's serving maid, Martha Hilton, whom the governor suddenly summoned forth from the ranks of a party at his regal Portsmouth house, ordering the thunderstruck local cleric to marry him to "the maiden" on the spot. When the old man died, Martha inherited not only his money but Wentworth Hall itself—"the mansion by the sea whose tables and rambling rooms still breathe of the eighteenth century, of lace and satin and white wine." (To understand something of the difference between Vermont and New Hampshire, one need only remember that Vermont's great pre-Revolutionary leader was Ethan Allen, a legitimate folk hero who in fact made his fame fighting the land claims Benning Wentworth had sought to extend across Vermont as well.)

As the American Revolution approached, New Hampshire was growing rapidly in population as shipbuilding, fishing, lumbering, shoemaking, and the manufacture of linen prospered. The last of the royal governors, John Wentworth II (Benning's newphew), tried to retrieve some of the land grants his uncle had made to Martha Hilton, and revoked and reissued grants to unsettled tracts (sometimes to himself). But he was a great developer of roads to the interior, helped to gather money for the founding of Dartmouth College (on 500 acres of Benning Wentworth's land), and might have been a great New Hampshire leader if the Revolution had not intervened—a development which forced him, as the King's representative, to flee his native land.

Seven months before the Declaration of Independence, in fact, New Hampshire broke its ties with Great Britain. New Hampshiremen served long and with distinction in the war—a "fighting" tradition (the state motto is "Live Free or Die!") that has recurred in every war the nation has since faced. In the war of 1812, for instance, New Hampshire supplied 35,000 fighting men out of a total population, women and children included, of only 215,000. In the Civil War, 39,000 New Hampshiremen went off to defend the Union; of these more than one out of 10 died on the battlefield or from wounds or disease suffered while in service.

What New Hampshire has lacked has been outstanding native leaders. Look down the list of New Hampshire Senators and Representatives over the years and you find scarcely any names to match Maine's Hannibal Hamlin, James G. Blaine, or Edmund Muskie, or the stature of Vermont's Justin Morrill, Warren Austin, or George Aiken.

To be fair, one must add that the record does show some "middling-great" New Hampshiremen of the early years of the Republic. One of these was John Langdon, a delegate to the Constitutional Convention of 1787, where he performed fairly creditably, speaking up frequently for the cause of moderate nationalism. (By contrast, the state's other delegate, Nicholas Gilman, has gone down in the history books as one of "the ciphers" of the convention, never opening his mouth to say a word.)

Langdon returned home to help persuade New Hampshire (albeit by a narrow margin) to ratify the Constitution. He then became one of the state's first Senators and helped organize Jefferson's Democratic-Republican party in New Hampshire, though he himself was a wealthy man of originally Federalist sympathies. (Parallel acts of political courage, one might add, are hard to find in modern New Hampshire.)

Another noteworthy figure of the era was Levi Woodbury, U.S. Senator, Secretary of the Treasury under Presidents Jackson and Van Buren, and subsequently a Supreme Court Justice. Woodbury left his mark by helping to lead the fight for an independent federal Treasury and championing the cause of free public education. But on the Supreme Court he upheld the states' rights doctrine on the issue of slavery. In this respect Woodbury was representative of New Hampshire, where the Democratic party was in control before the Civil War, its leaders among the most faithful Northern apologists for the Southern slaveholders. In Vermont, by contrast, the Whigs and abolitionists were in the overwhelming majority —another taproot of the profound difference of politics and public temper between the states, as striking in our own time as ever.

The most illustrious native son of New Hampshire was Daniel Webster, the great orator and legislative craftsman who contributed immeasurably, over a long career, to solidifying American nationalism and loyalty to the Union. New Hampshire remembers him for his famous exposition in the Dartmouth College case before the Supreme Court in 1818, successfully defending the charter of his alma mater: "It is, sir, as I have said, a small college—and yet there are those who love it!" Yet the fact is that after two terms in Congress, early in his life, New Hampshire refused to reelect Webster. He moved to Boston, and it was Massachusetts which would be his personal and political home during the last 36 and most productive years of his life, the years in which he would establish his record as one of the greatest United States Senators of all time.

New Hampshire would also claim credit for such distinguished jurists as Salmon P. Chase and Harlan F. Stone, Chief Justices of the United States Supreme Court in their day. But both men, at an early age, had left their native state—Chase for Ohio, Stone for New York. The famous New Hampshire-born editors—Horace Greeley of the New York *Tribune* and Charles A. Dana of the New York *Sun*—also made their mark many years after leaving the state.

Robert Frost wrote in his poem, "New Hampshire":

> She had one President (pronounce him Purse,
> And make the most of it for better or worse.)

Most people have made the worse of Franklin Pierce. He was first of all a rather accidental President, having won nomination on the 49th ballot at the Democratic National Convention of 1852. Dark horse though he was, he carried all but four states in the election because he combined the best of two worlds in the politics of the time—a Northerner with strong Southern sympathies who had denounced the abolitionist cause as destructive to the Union.

Emerson wrote of Pierce that he "was either the worst, or one of the weakest of all our Presidents." Modern-day assessments are not much kinder. In the words of historian Philip S. Klein: "Inexperienced and burdened by personal tragedy, Pierce was unable to cope with the glaring domestic issues of his administration, notably the conflict over slavery in the territories. Naturally amiable, he had little inclination to philosophize but preferred the conviviality of good fellowship and tended to make decisions based on expediency. . . . Stereotyped as weak and shallow, he probably was neither, but he was not equal to the task before him." Another historian noted that Pierce "suffered from an overfondness for alcohol and a violent allergy to it."

Tragedies and mishaps plagued the Pierce presidency, a record thoughtfully assembled by a Washington attorney, David Epstein, founder of Friends of Franklin Pierce. (The society's motto: "To rescue him from the obscurity he so richly deserves.") The tragedy began shortly before inauguration day, when the Pierce family was involved in a train wreck that killed the only surviving child and unhinged Mrs. Pierce for the rest of her life. (In the White House, she would never receive visitors.) On the cold and blustery day of his inauguration, Pierce delivered an extemporaneous address of more than 3,000 words; by the time he finished, 65,000 of the 85,000 people in the crowd had left. One who stayed was Abigail Fillmore, wife of the outgoing President. She caught a cold that led to her death a few weeks later. Arriving at the white House, Pierce found the servants had left with the Fillmores; he could find but a single candle to light and spent his first night as Chief Executive sleeping on the floor on the only mattress he could locate. Pierce is distinguished in being the only President ever to have his entire Cabinet remain for as long as he was President. One of these was Secretary of War Jefferson Davis, soon to be President of the Confederacy.

Even a George Washington, of course, could not have contained the fires of sectional antagonism building over the slavery issue in the 1850s. The issue caused furious debate in Congress, and in those years the issue killed the Whig party, split the Democrats, and precipitated the birth of the Republican party.

In 1856 Pierce sought renomination but was denied the honor by his own party's convention—the only incumbent President ever so treated, before or since. Leaving Washington, he set out on a European tour. Then he returned to Concord, from which vantage point he attacked the Lincoln government for provoking the Civil War and expressed sympathy for those in the North who wanted to stop the conflict and let secession succeed. For this, charges of treason were hurled against him.

And that is the record of New Hampshire's only President. A century later, Pierce's modest home in Concord was in danger of demolition because it stood in the path of urban renewal. The New Hampshire government solved the problem in a fitting (and typical) way: it sold $75,000 worth of bourbon in $15 commemorative bottles, thus raising the money to move the Pierce homestead without dipping into the public treasury.

One looks to the era since the Civil War for great New Hampshire leaders, and is even more disappointed than with the record through Pierce's years. The Republican party came to rule supreme, and one can divide its leaders into three general groups—those of the Gilded Age, so corrupt that they virtually sold New Hampshire to the railroad interests; a group of reformers, from the 1910s onwards, who cleaned up the worst of the corruption, enacted some progressive laws, but failed to grace the national scene with figures of exceptional stature; and finally the school of snarling conservatives, running from Styles Bridges to Meldrim Thomson, obsessed with Communist witch-hunting (an idea laughed out of court in Vermont) and fighting progressive taxation as though it were a plague.

The Republican machine of the half century following the Civil War, according to Duane Lockhard's account, was an arrogant combine in which "railroad interests along with timber barons and a few others had control over the party organizations, and local party barons held their fiefs at the grace of the leadership." The system operated "in the best feudal tradition —votes from the bottom up and pay-offs and patronage from the top down." The distinguished Missouri-born American author, Winston Churchill, moved to a river estate at Cornish, where he wrote a delightfully revealing, muckraking novel, *Coniston:*

> Never, since the days of Pompadour and Du Barry, until American politics were invented, has a state been ruled from such a place as Number 7 in the Pelican House—familiarly known as the Throne Room. In this historic cabinet there were five chairs, a marble-topped table, a pitcher of iced water, a bureau, a box of cigars and a Bible, a chandelier with all the gas jets burning, and a bed, whereon sat such dignitaries as obtained an audience—railroad presidents,

governors and ex-governors and prospective governors, the Speaker, the President of the Senate, Bijah Bixby, Peleg Hardington, mighty chiefs from the North Country, and lieutenants from other parts of the state. . . .

"All Gaul," said Mr. Merrill—he was speaking to a literary man—"all Gaul is divided into five railroads."

As an absolute power, the old Republican machine went into rapid decline when the old convention form of nominating candidates fell with passage of a party primary law in 1909. New Hampshire was to remain a solidly Republican state for another half century, but now insurgencies were possible and sometimes successful. Reformers like Churchill and former U.S. Senator William E. Chandler,* some of them Bull Moose Republicans, stirred such public resentment against the organization that a high-grade independent Republican, Robert P. Bass, was able to win the governorship in 1910. Charged that he was a wealthy man trying to buy the governorship, Ralph N. Hill records in *Yankee Kingdom*, Bass replied that he was at least spending his own money to get elected, not that of the Boston and Maine Railroad. Taking the torch from the Bull Moose insurgents, Bass and his spiritual successors—men like John G. Winant, governor for three terms in the '20s and '30s and later U.S. Ambassador to Great Britain, and Charles W. Tobey, who was governor, U.S. Representative, and then Senator in the years between 1929 and 1953—were able to establish a significant beachhead of liberal Republicanism in New Hampshire. Winant, for instance, pressed for social reforms and welcomed New Deal welfare programs, a record that prevented the Democrats from gaining the governorship in the 1930s as they did in so many normally Republican states, including Maine. Tobey was a colorful, Bible-quoting "Truman Republican" who voted a consistently liberal line in the U.S. Senate.

Just to the right of this group, and occasionally allied with it, were the middle-of-the-road New Hampshire Republicans of whom the chief exemplar was probably Governor Sherman Adams (1949–53), the man who organized New Hampshire for Dwight Eisenhower in the 1952 primary and subsequently became his all-powerful White House chief of staff until the Bernard Goldfine scandal brought him down.

But the conservative Republicans, heirs of the old machine, remained the most powerful faction in the party. Their leader for many years was George H. Moses, a Senator from 1918 to 1933 and a chief ally of Henry Cabot Lodge in blocking U.S. entry into the League of Nations. Moses sneeringly referred to the progressive Republicans as "sons of the wild

---

* Chandler was a fascinating character whose career spanned the years from the Civil War to the Progressive era. As a journalist writing for the Concord *Monitor* and *Statesman* in his early years, he was nicknamed the "stormy petrel" of state politics. He supported the Union cause in the war, was elected speaker of the New Hampshire house in 1863, held several appointments under Presidents Lincoln and Johnson, became a Republican National Committeeman and directed several presidential campaigns, helped swing disputed electoral votes to Rutherford B. Hayes in the bartered election of 1876, and received appointment as Secretary of the Navy under President Chester Arthur. In the latter post he began a modern shipbuilding program but was obliged to resign amid accusations regarding contract favoritism. From 1887 to 1901 he was a U.S. Senator. Even before he left the Senate, however, Chandler was on the warpath against the New Hampshire Republican regime, attacking the railroads and their use of money in political life.

jackass"; as for himself, he epitomized the party's Old Guard. He finally met defeat in the Democratic landslide of 1932.

Not long after, the conservatives' most skillful organizer of the century arose in the person of Styles Bridges, governor from 1935 to 1937 and then U.S. Senator until his death in 1961. Bridges was no member of the old New Hampshire aristocracy. He had been the eldest child of a poor Maine tenant farmer and moved to New Hampshire as a young man, gaining his entry into politics, ironically, through the progressive Republicans. Former Governor Bass made Bridges his personal secretary in the 1920s, and Tobey, as governor, appointed him to the public service commission in 1930. The appointment was initially blocked by the governor's council out of a fear—which turned out to be groundless—that Bridges would be hostile to the private utilities. Bridges was still considered a progressive when he won election to the Senate in 1936, defeating none other than an aged George Moses trying for a comeback.

In the style of the old Southern Populists who so often sold out to the "Big Mules" after winning office, Bridges turned coat early in his Senate career, voting a rigidly conservative line and toadying up, sometimes for cash, sometimes for other favors, to a motley crew of five-percenters, out-of-state liquor dealers and distillers, and to John L. Lewis of the United Mine Workers. (He received $45,000 for serving as a trustee of the UMW's pension fund, for which sum he attended a total of nine meetings). One of Bridges' closest chums, according to a remarkable piece of investigative reporting by Douglass Cater in *The Reporter* in 1954, was the master Washington fixer, Henry Grunewald, who eventually landed in jail—but only after Bridges had sought to influence several government agencies in behalf of Grunewald clients.

All of this caused little consternation in New Hampshire, where Bridges became fabled as the man who could and often did do anything for a constituent, or for New Hampshire interests in general, including landing a multimillion-dollar Air Force base through the power he exerted in 1953–54 as chairman of the Senate Appropriations Committee. Nor was any opponent ever able to make anything of Bridges' conservative voting record, well to the right of any New England Senator except perhaps Maine's Owen Brewster. This onetime progressive, for instance, became a bitter opponent of TVA. At one point an aging Senator George Norris, outraged at Bridges, called him during Senate debate "the one Member outstanding in the Senate of the United States who does exactly what the Power Trust of America wants done."

Bridges also became the China Lobby Senator *par excellence*, working assiduously for Chiang Kai-shek's Nationalist Government in its struggle with the Chinese Communists. Eventually the Chinese Nationalists purchased a sumptuous summer residence on the shores of Lake Winnipesaukee, establishing what Cater called the "strange New Hampshire division of the China lobby." Bridges set up a vacation home on adjoining land partially carved from the estate, and so did a Bridges protegé, Louis C. Wyman, then the Red-hunting attorney general of New Hampshire and later a U.S. Representative.

Bridges may have believed sincerely in the Chinese Nationalist cause, which he had at one point identified as a goal of American foreign policy above almost any other. Certainly anti-Communism was a theme that came naturally to Bridges. With a little more imagination he might have performed the public role later assumed by Wisconsin's Senator Joseph R. McCarthy. Before McCarthy surfaced with his crusade against Communists in government, Bridges had perfected the theme of treason at home as an explanation for disaster in Asia. In 1950 he delivered a Senate speech in which he demanded to know the name of "the master spy, the servant of Russia who moves the puppets . . . using them and using our State Department at will."

Yet it seems more than coincidental that in 1946 William Loeb, the president of the American China Policy Association, the strong right arm of the China Lobby, had suddenly become the most powerful molder of public opinion in New Hampshire through his purchase of the Manchester *Union Leader*. Loeb quickly transformed the paper, New Hampshire's leading and only morning daily, into a propaganda organ for the China Lobby and his assorted other pet peeves and causes. He and Bridges became fast friends and political allies. Loeb's purchase of the *Union Leader* was the paramount event in setting the tone and direction of New Hampshire public life since World War II, and we must turn our attention to it next. Even in doing so, however, one should remember New Hampshire's thin political tradition, its lack of great leaders, its proclivity for official corruption. To this one can add the facts of life in modern-day New Hampshire which mute the liberal bases of opposition that would normally be offered to a publisher like Loeb. In the words of Bill Kovach, writing in the New York *Times Magazine*:

> Largely because of the parsimony of its fragmented legislature, government is weak and has few of the civil-service jobs which tend to develop—through job security and detailed information about conditions—a liberalizing resource. New Hampshire banks have traditionally sent their money out of state for investment, and, while they are concerned about corporate laws and the tax structure, they lack the deep interest in other economic matters that widespread local investment would produce. Finally, the university system is fragmented. Dartmouth, dependent on outside resources, has never developed as an institutional leader. The University of New Hampshire is so poorly funded that high tuitions have driven away many potential undergraduates. Here, as in the rural South, military service is a prime vehicle for social mobility for the young, and both enlistment rates and high-school drop out rates are high—offering yet another reservoir of support for Loeb's pro-military, anti-Communist views.

One might say that if Loeb was ready to make the Granite State his object of personal manipulation, it is also true that New Hampshire lacked the inner resources to resist very well.

One Publisher's Power

We might start by pointing out that Loeb's purchase of the *Union Leader* was an event that need not have happened at all. The paper had belonged to Frank Knox, Franklin Roosevelt's wartime Secretary of the Navy, who died in 1944. When Knox's family decided to sell the *Union Leader* after the war, a group of New Hampshire leaders headed by John McLane, a moderate Republican who was head of the most influential law firm in the state and the son of a former governor, expressed interest. But when McLane's group turned to New Hampshire's business leaders for the necessary financial backing, they were refused. And so, in what must be called one of the most fateful failures of indigenous leadership in any state's history, the paper went instead to the outsider William Loeb. The purchase price was $1.5 million—for a paper most recently valued by Loeb himself at $25 million.

Who was William Loeb? His father had been President Theodore Roosevelt's secretary, confidant, and chief of White House staff, and when Roosevelt left the presidency, the Loebs had moved to Sagamore with the President's family. Young William picked up a lot from his godfather, TR, including a love for the rough outdoor life, an aversion for big business, and faith in armaments and a militant foreign policy. He went to Williams College, tried Harvard Law School for a couple of years because he wanted to own a newspaper one day instead of being a lawyer, held a number of jobs in business and journalism, finally obtained control of a paper in Vermont, and in 1946 was ready to make his big purchase in New Hampshire. Oddly enough, however, Loeb has never become a resident of New Hampshire. His legal domicile is in Nevada; he owns a baronial house of "30 or so" rooms at Pride's Crossing, Massachusetts, some 60 miles south of Manchester; and he visits the *Union Leader* offices only about once a month.

Those who have visited the Loeb estate at Pride's Crossing describe it as an armed camp—the half-mile private driveway, electronic security devices planted all around the 100-acre property, a doberman pinscher and German shepherd at the door. Loeb himself is cordial and friendly, a stocky and balding man and the picture of the country squire. But he says there have been threats on his life; in 1974 he startled Bill Moyers during the filming of a public television program at the estate by saying: "I always carry a gun. I have a Walston 38 on me right now." Outside the house there is a shooting range, where Loeb enjoys shooting dummy figures "right in the middle of the head."

There is a "progressive" side to Loeb which should be recognized. He prides himself on supporting labor unions,* in opposing inherited wealth, or sometimes opposing the rate increases of the telephone company

---

* The labor union which Loeb supports the most enthusiastically is the Teamsters, a fact not unrelated to the fact that he is deeply in hock to it. In 1957 Loeb began a paper in Haverhill, Massachusetts, and tried to squeeze out the older Haverhill *Gazette* through an agreement with local merchants to pay them a fixed sum of money if they would advertise exclusively in

and New Hampshire Public Service. Loeb entertains antitrust views and fought to destroy the state milk control board, which pegged milk prices at artificially high levels in the 1950s. "When I took over the paper," he said in 1973, "it was essentially the voice of the special interests in New Hampshire. We side with the people against the special interests." Loeb established a profit sharing plan at the *Union Leader*, and made provision for the ownership to pass to the employees when he dies. (At this writing, he is in his late sixties.)

Despite this, Loeb has to be marked down as probably the most opinionated and certainly the most intemperate publisher in the United States. His opinions—relayed to readers in prominent page-one editorials, and in every column of government or political news coverage—drip with acid invective. He thinks American newspapers are dull and bore their readers; his own surely does nothing of the sort. A modest collection of his editorial phrases to depict prominent state and national figures includes the following:

John F. Kennedy—"the Number One threat to America"
Eleanor Roosevelt—"Ellie and her belly-crawling liberal friends"
Margaret Chase Smith—"Moscow Maggie"
Leverett Saltonstall—"that fatuous ass"
Henry Kissinger—"Kissinger the Kike?"; "Tool of the Communist Conspiracy"
Nelson Rockefeller—"Rocky the Wife-Swapper"
Sherman Adams—"Sherm the Worm"
Dwight Eisenhower—"Dopey Dwight"; "that stinking hypocrite"
Harry Truman—"the little dictator"
Gerald Ford—"Jerry is a jerk"
Robert Kennedy—"the most vicious, vindictive, egotistical man on the face of the earth"
Edward Kennedy—"just plain stupid"
Eugene McCarthy—the "skunk's skunk's skunk"
George Romney—"George Romney Can't and Shouldn't Win"; "It would be hard to think of a more irresponsible leader for this great nation than the Mexican-born George Romney."
Richard Nixon—"Foul Ball Nixon"; "The Great Devaluator"; "Tricky Dicky"
Martin Luther King, Jr.—"really asked for what happened to him" (Loeb uses every opportunity to play up crimes by "negroes," whom he considers as a group to be "years back in evolution and development" compared to whites. Black criminals are "without moral re-

his paper, causing the demise of the *Gazette*. There was then a court case in which Loeb was charged with violating antitrust laws. Loeb's opponents among the other New England publishers saw a chance to bring him down and closed off his credit sources. He was saved only when James Hoffa came to his rescue with a $2 million loan from the Teamsters pension fund. Loeb called repeatedly for Hoffa's release from prison after Hoffa's conviction on jury-tampering charges, and sang hosannas when President Nixon finally sprang him prior to the 1972 election.

straint" and like "jungle savages." "We are hopeful the black population of New Hampshire will never increase from its present
minimal figure.")

Robert Welch (John Birch Society head)—"bloody nut" (Loeb says he dis-
approves of the way the Birch Society labels people as Communists, although the paper picks up stories from Birch publications
and regularly prints columns by Birchers without mentioning their
connection with the Society.)

Edmund Muskie—"Senator Flip-Flop Muskie"; "the Vietnam War-dove-
chicken"; "hypocrite"

Jane Fonda—"Shoot Jane Fonda"

Small wonder, it would seem, that many New Hampshire people like
a distinguished former governor whom I interviewed, find the *Union
Leader* "gives you a well-developed sense of nausea." But many New Hampshireites feel obliged to read the paper because it does provide fairly thorough if unimaginative reporting of statewide news in nonpolitical areas,
and because the public life of the state so often revolves around William
Loeb's latest vendetta(s). The more sophisticated folk learn to read the
paper with a discount, to build up their immunities. For those with less
education—and thus fewer defenses—it is another matter. "*The* people in
New Hampshire have never supported or liked me," according to Loeb. "I
find my support among the common people, the factory workers, not among
the politicians or publishers." Loeb purposedly dictates his editorials to
give them "more punch" and get his point across to the unsophisticates.
The self-appointed guardian of their morals, he mixes his diatribes against
disfavored politicans with a constant stream of editorials on highly emotional issues—prayer, the Bible, abortion, pornography, homosexuality, gun
control, the death penalty. Gordon Hall, an authority on extremist movements has suggested that the *Union Leader* is largely responsible for a
streak of "primitive right-wing extremism" that runs throughout the state.

While he refuses to live in the state himself, Loeb has taken unto himself the task of forcing the public dialogue and range of public policies
into his own ideological straightjacket. "It has always been my hope we
could make New Hampshire an example to other states," he said in 1972,
"and in many ways we are. The state has no sales tax, no income tax." This
is done by harping on the antitax theme to the exclusion of all other debate
and excoriating anyone who dares to take an opposing stand. Noting that
New Hampshire is littered with the carcasses of reputations fallen victim
to the wrath of Loeb's hyperboles, Bill Moyers quoted this letter from a
state representative:

William Loeb is a permeating, deadly, sickening, horrible, frightening load on
the entire state of New Hampshire. Because of Mr. Loeb, New Hampshire is
the only state in the Union with no sales or income tax. But he never mentions
that we also rank 50th in state aid to education, 50th in support of mental

health, and 54th in aid to vocational rehabilitation—behind Guam, Puerto Rico, and the Virgin Islands.

Senator Thomas J. McIntyre told me that "if the New Hampshire tax system is regressive, it's because anyone who came out for a sales or income tax has been pilloried by this paper." The abuse opponents must suffer can take on sinister form. One hears time and again of citizens who fear to raise their voices in public meetings, or decide not to run for office, for fear of what Loeb's paper might do to them—or their families. When Governor Walter Peterson bucked Loeb by supporting a state income tax, Loeb picked up an innocent remark made by Peterson's daughter Meg at a White House conference on drugs in 1968—namely that she knew that some of her high school classmates smoked marijuana but thought it was their own business. Loeb seized on the incident to depict the Petersons as misguided parents and Meg as a symbol of a generation destroyed by drugs. He ran her picture, her father's picture, the school's picture. Governor Peterson bought space on the front page of the paper to say: "I am fair game, Mr. Loeb, but I must ask you to stop picking on my 15-year-old daughter, who, after all, is only a young girl with many years of life ahead." The plea fell on deaf ears; three years later Loeb was still mentioning the incident*

Another example: when Dr. Thomas Bonner was appointed president of the University of New Hampshire in 1971, Loeb decided Bonner was not to his liking and assigned an investigative reporter to look into his background. The result was a 25,000-word series of six articles which *Newsweek* described as "one of the most brutal newspaper assaults ever directed at a U.S. university official." Without attribution of proof, the paper charged that Bonner, while provost of the University of Cincinnati, had fostered "all-night drinking parties, marijuana parties, the sharing of showers by male and female students, and around-the-clock sex." New Hampshire was told that Bonner would "destroy your most precious possession—your children." Replying to such charges, Bonner discovered, was a risky business: "I discovered that there is just no vehicle for another view. Everything is so fragmented that it is always a fight on his [Loeb's] terms and in his field. Every day I opposed him gave him more fodder to continue the attack and in the end it was the university that suffered."

Nor are such attacks reserved for the "big fish." Senator Thomas McIntyre posed the not-so-hypothetical case of a legislator voting for a bill Loeb opposed. "You'd likely see your name appear in red" in the *Union Leader,* he said—with little if any way to reply. If there is any American state in which the public dialogue is more distorted or polluted, this writer

* For a detailed account of and assault on Loeb's use of his power, the reader is referred to *Who the Hell Is William Loeb?*, a self-published 1975 biography by former *Union Leader* reporter Kevin Cash. The book dredged up a number of embarrassing incidents in Loeb's past life. Of Loeb, Cash told a reporter: "Sometime between the time he turns out the light at night and hits the pillow, he knows I'm telling the truth." Loeb refused initially to comment and threatened to sue Cash.

—having interviewed extensively in all 50 states in the past few years—is unaware of it.

A not surprising corollary is that the last strong governor New Hampshire had, Sherman Adams, was first elected in 1948, when Loeb's process of propagandization and intimidation was just in its infancy. Adams proudly recalled, in a talk I had with him, the vote held in the state in the spring of 1945 on the question of whether the United States should join in the United Nations. The vote was affirmative, by a 20–1 margin. In the Loeb-influenced climate of more recent years, a strongly positive referendum vote by New Hampshire's people on the progressive side of *any* important issue would be inconceivable.

Back in the 1930s, William Loeb was associated with an organization he claimed became infiltrated by Communists, whom he exposed. The experience is often cited as the cause of the fierce anti-Communism of his later career. But Loeb has employed one tactic typical of Communist newspapers—the use of news columns, not just editorials, to sell a chosen ideological line. His chief editors and writers are just as much True Right believers as he, and in any event would never think of presenting a deviationist line. His long-time chief editor, B. J. McQuaid, says he has always "felt it would be confusing to the reader to hold a different editorial opinion" from Loeb's. One glances at any day's front page and detects the approved line in headlines and story placement. Bill Kovach cited a particularly choice front page, that of October 15, 1969:

The *Union Leader* published above its masthead . . . a welter of red and black type delivering this notice of Moratorium Day marchers: "ATTENTION ALL PEACE MARCHERS: Hippies, Yippies, Beatniks, Peaceniks, yellow-bellies, traitors, Communists and their agents and dupes—HELP KEEP OUR CITY CLEAN! . . . Just by staying out of it!—The Editors." Below that was an eight-column picture of *Union Leader* employees atop the newspaper's building "proudly" displaying a sign that said: "AMERICA love it or leave it! VICTORY IN VIETNAM." Under the picture appeared an eight-column headline, "MORATORIUM DENOUNCED," and a two-column editorial by Loeb entitled, "Hanoi's Little Helpers."

If the politicans who buck Loeb or his policies are, as the Boston *Globe* once noted, "consigned to the crowded kennels of his disfavor," it is equally true that the *Union Leader* has become skilled in picking figures from near or total obscurity and puffing them up into serious candidates for public office. One such "instant candidate" was retired Air Force Brigadier General Harrison Thyng, who was persuaded by a *Union Leader* editor to move back to New Hampshire after 25 years of absence and run for the U.S. Senate in 1966. Loeb, through his contacts, raised thousands of dollars for Thyng from right-wing sources across the country, including $3,500 from H. L. Hunt. The other candidates—including two former governors and Styles Bridges' widow, who by then had fallen into Loeb's disfavor—were mercilessly attacked, while Thyng was given maximum favorable publicity, day in and day out. "The only people opposing Harry Thyng in New Hamp-

shire," the *Union Leader* declared, "are the left-wing, anti-God, anti-pa-
triotism newspaper publishers and the usual Ivy League eggheads, who are
against God and country and are in favor of world government and appeasement." Thyng won the primary but proved to be a rough martial type
on the hustings and lost to Senator McIntyre by 18,647 votes in the general
election.

Loeb's next big project—the election of a governor—took three years
of build-up but was finally crowned with success when Meldrim Thomson,
Jr., little-known law book publisher raised in Georgia, finally toppled moderate Republican Governor Peterson in the 1972 primary. Thomson then
won the general election—defeating, ironically, a conservative Democrat
who had been Loeb's favorite in *that* primary. Before Loeb plucked Thomson from obscurity, his total public record consisted of serving a term on
his local school board and losing a race for the legislature.

In the midst of Thomson's first primary race, the *Union Leader* carried a story typical of its treatment of its favored boys. A four-column picture, at the top of page one, showed Thomson atop the Presidential Range,
right hand thrust out toward the heavens, his left hand around his wife's
waist. Both were smiling, with uplifted faces. And below the picture was a
Loeb editorial headed "Mel Thomson's Credo," beginning with a slightly
altered Biblical quotation, "I will lift mine eyes unto the hills, from whence
cometh my strength."

Thomson's election and reelection in 1974 represented a big breakthrough for Loeb, who had previously backed a string of losers. Even when
his favorites failed to win, however, Loeb was often able to cut up promising
and rising figures in both parties so badly that their careers were prematurely truncated.

Just how many votes, one asks, can Loeb normally influence to his way
of thinking? Professional surveys conducted for the state Republican party
in the late 1960s showed that 40 to 45 percent of Republicans likely to vote
in primaries read the *Union Leader*; the Thyng and Thomson nominations
indicate this is sometimes sufficient to create a plurality, if not a majority,
among Republican voters. Some believe the *Union Leader* is just as strong,
if not stronger, in influencing Democratic voters because some 60 percent
of the Democratic vote is concentrated in the Manchester area, where the
paper is most widely read and where Loeb's influence over the heavy
French-Canadian population has reinforced that group's natural proclivity
to conservative politics. It would seem no accident that in the 1970, 1972,
and 1974 Democratic gubernatorial primaries, conservative contenders par-
roting the Loeb view on taxes emerged as the winners. Generally, it was the
Manchester vote which won them their nominations. Loeb's influence has
generally been the strongest in gubernatorial primaries and general elections, because he sets the terms of the debate—taxes, not services. As an
aide to former Governor Peterson put it, "a campaigner spends all his
time putting out brush fires started by Loeb and never has time to speak

to the issues." Except, one might add, as William Loeb has defined them.*

The New Hampshire presidential primary provides Loeb with a unique opportunity to influence the course of national politics in the state's early-bird, highly overrated primary. It is then, as Dom Bonafede of the *National Journal* has noted, that Loeb "emerges from the wintry cocoon of New Hampshire as the abominable snowman of the national political scene." Whether Loeb has the influence attributed to him, Bonafede added, "is almost beside the point: the fact is that the candidates and a good portion of the state's voters think he has is virtually the same thing."

Yet if one is to assess the final Loeb impact on the presidential sweep-stakes, one would have to say he is far more the spoiler than the kingmaker. In 1964, for instance, while he backed Goldwater, he attacked Rockefeller viciously, opening the way for Henry Cabot Lodge's write-in victory on the Republican side. Before the 1968 primary, George Romney received a 117-page analysis of the state situation from William R. Johnson, the liberal former Republican state chairman who had been skewered himself by Loeb in the 1966 Senate primary. As a result of his study, based largely on the circulation pattern of the *Union Leader*, Johnson urged Romney to shun New Hampshire. Romney disregarded the advice, found himself pummeled daily by Loeb, and as a result of dismal poll showings withdrew from the New Hampshire contest and the entire Republican presidential picture before primary day.

The 1972 Democratic primary proved to be a classic case of Loeb inter-vention. It had long been assumed that Edmund Muskie, a Senator from neighboring Maine and a helpmate in the rebirth of the New Hampshire Democratic party, would win the state by a handsome margin. But Loeb was determined to upset Muskie, whose turn against the Vietnam war had upset him. A full year before the primary, Loeb began a series of meetings with Los Angeles Mayor Sam Yorty, a veteran anti-Communist and Vietnam hawk. No responsible journalist or national leader regarded Yorty as a serious candidate, but Loeb began to build him up as if he were one, and Yorty entered the primary. At the same time Loeb began his series of slashing attacks on Muskie—granting the two other candidates, George McGovern and Indiana's Vance Hartke, rather benign treatment. Jules Witcover, for the *Columbia Journalism Review*, did a count of column inches devoted to each candidate in the final five weeks of the primary cam-paign. Yorty received 53 stories totaling 870 inches, Muskie 52 stories with 420 inches, McGovern 40 stories with 262 inches, and Hartke 34 stories with 241 inches. Without exception the Yorty copy was favorable; the overwhelm-

* A thorough analysis of Loeb's impact was presented in Eric Veblen's excellent book, *The Manchester Union Leader in New Hampshire Elections* (Hanover: University Press of New England, 1975). Political strategists take the paper most seriously, Veblen noted, because of its circulation dominance and the potential impact (positive or negative) of its strong editorial attacks. In some cases, he reported, candidates deliberately provoked *Union Leader* attacks to gain public notice and to garner support of the state's other dailies, many of which auto-matically take the other side of any debate from Loeb's. By careful voting analysis, Veblen also demonstrated Loeb's greater success in influencing votes in the Manchester area than in other parts of the state.

ing bulk of the Muskie coverage was unfavorable, some of it slanderous.

Then, two weeks before primary day, *Union Leader* readers were suddenly exposed to a page one editorial entitled "SENATOR MUSKIE INSULTS FRANCO-AMERICANS." This was the charge, allegedly from a Florida letter writer, that Muskie had maligned New Hampshire's biggest minority group by calling them "Cannucks." (Later it turned out that the letter originated in the dirty tricks department of the Nixon White House, but no one knew that at the time.) A day after the famous "Cannuck" letter, the *Union Leader* reprinted a short item from *Newsweek* quoting Jane Muskie, the candidate's wife, as saying during a day of campaigning with woman reporters, "let's tell dirty jokes" and "pass me my purse—I haven't had my morning cigaret yet." The two articles and accompanying Loeb commentary so outraged Muskie that he made his famous appearance in the snow before the *Union Leader* building to call Loeb a "liar" and a "gutless coward." Discussing the article about his wife, Muskie in his anger broke down and some observers believe he cried. And at that very moment, because the national media would subsequently make so much of it, Muskie may well have lost his chance to be the Democratic nominee for President.

All Loeb's efforts did little for Yorty in the primary—he got only 6 percent of the vote. Muskie ended up with 47 percent, less than the magic 50 percent figure national pundits and even some of his own staff had said he would need to claim victory. The vote returns suggested Loeb's role was decisive in denying Muskie a clear majority of the votes cast. Most of the state's cities and working class wards went heavily for Muskie—but not Manchester's. Muskie barely edged out McGovern in the city, and lost two heavily French-American Manchester wards to him. But far to the north, in Berlin, where Loeb's "Cannuck" editorial had not been seen, Muskie carried strongly Franco-American wards by about 60 percent of the vote. The conclusion was unmistakable: Loeb had played his spoiler role with grand success.

But what, the reader may ask, of New Hampshire's other newspapers? Are they not, collectively, a match for the *Union Leader*? The answer is no, for several reasons.

There are nine other dailies, with a combined circulation of about 100,000, compared to the *Union Leader*'s 63,000 (and 57,000 for Loeb's Sunday *New Hampshire News*). But in circulation none holds a candle to the *Union Leader* (the closest is the rather mediocre Nashua *Telegraph*, with 22,500). All the other dailies—nicknamed "the pipsqueak press" by Loeb—are afternoon papers, an increasingly difficult position for papers across the country. Five of them finance a State House News Service, begun in 1962, which provides some stories with in-depth quality. But most of them are dependent on the wire services for the bulk of their state coverage; the wire services, in turn, are loath to offend the *Union Leader*, their biggest client, and the shocking fact is that both the Associated Press and United Press International each morning put members of their rather meager staffs to work rewriting stories from the morning *Union Leader* for transmission to the afternoon dailies. Some of the most controversial material from the Loeb paper is excluded, but the fact is that *Union Leader*-generated news infuses the afternoon papers and is also received and repeated by radio and television.

Some of the afternoon dailies are mediocre in quality and even fail to send a reporter to cover the legislature first hand when it is in session. The best of the lot are the Portsmouth *Herald, Valley News*, Keene *Sentinel*, and Concord *Monitor*. The *Monitor*, in particular, offers original, quality coverage. Its State House reporter, Rod Paul, is the state's best. Its editorial page, under the direction of editor Thomas Gerber, former Washington correspondent for the Boston *Herald*, is well written, lively, and fiercely anti-Loeb. The *Monitor* would in fact be the most logical paper to compete with the *Union Leader* on a statewide basis. But Concord is no match for Manchester in the broad advertising base needed for expensive statewide distribution, and the *Monitor*'s circulation in 1975 was still a rather disappointing 17,600.

The Boston *Globe* does circulate fairly widely in the southern part of the state, but New Hampshire affairs remain a matter of secondary interest for it. On quite the other end of the spectrum is the *New Hampshire Times*, a weekly begun in 1973 which provides the state with a kind of respectable alternative press. Similar in format and orientation to the *Maine Times*, the *New Hampshire Times* had quite a different genesis. It actually began as a throwaway advertising sheet known as the *Flea Market* in 1971, its editors just-out-of-college-or-the-army young New Hampshire natives with little if any journalistic experience. Given away free at some 800 outlets statewide, the *Flea Market* hit a circulation peak of 45,000; eventually the costs of distribution proved oppressive, leading to the decision to print a regular weekly newspaper "that cared about New Hampshire, her history, her land and her people." Studiously ignored by the regular state press, the *New Hampshire Times* began to break a number of important stories, especially in the environmental field, and to put in historic and political perspective some of the strange goings-on in the state's public life. Editor Dick Wright, a cofounder with publisher Susan Salls, said that by the end of 1974 the paper had more than 4,000 paid yearly subscriptions and 6,000 to 10,000 weekly newsstand buyers, depending on the season. Despite its thin editorial staff, the *Times* was offering an invaluable service for aware New Hampshireites; on the other hand, it was unlikely, by its very nature, to become a real news alternative for the masses of the state's people.

The electronic media—especially through network news programs—offer something of a non-Loebian view of the world. But the overall impact is as fragmented as that of the daily press. There is "one nice little television station," as Senator McIntyre put it, located in Manchester; its news coverage quality has improved in recent years, but its VHF signal fails to pierce the White Mountain barrier to the north and it has to cope with fierce competition from the Boston stations. Vermont and Maine stations are heard in several areas of the state, but of course with scarcely any New Hampshire news. The state does have a high-grade VHF public television station, located in Durham, and other UHF public stations in Berlin, Hanover, Keene, and Littleton. And there are 40 radio stations; though most have limited listening areas, New Hampshire is considered a "radio state," particularly during morning and evening "drive times." Many younger radio newsmen are liberal and see themselves as a counter to Loeb, but the wire copy they receive, as with the daily press, is often rewritten from the *Union Leader.*

So for New Hampshire-oriented news and public affairs coverage reaching broad numbers of people, the *Union Leader* retains its dominance. If New Hampshire's leaders really wanted a reliable, fair, and constructive state-wide newspaper, they could have one—by starting a competing daily in Manchester or finding a way to expand the *Monitor* or some other paper. But it would cost the leadership group many times over what McLane and his associates needed but couldn't raise to buy the *Union Leader* in 1946. And one suspects they really don't care enough.

Tempestuous Politics

Writing about New England in the late 1950s, Duane Lockard singled out New Hampshire as a state with particularly "tempestuous" politics.

He had no idea of what was coming. It is as if the state set out on a conscious course to prove the description correct, perhaps a little restrained. Consider this partial list of strange goings-on:
- Senator Styles Bridges, the master power broker, passed on to his eternal reward in 1961,* and the once mighty New Hampshire Republican party broke up into innumerable factions, fighting viciously for power. In the 1962 primary for his Senate seat, no less than four prominent Republicans entered the fray. Ranged ideologically, from right to left, they were Doloris Bridges, the Senator's widow, who seemed to believe she had a claim on the seat by reason of inheritance (and William Loeb's backing); Maurice Murphy, a colorless lawyer and crony of the incumbent governor who had been appointed to the seat on an interim basis; Perkins Bass, a Congressman, son of the former governor, and a party moderate; and Chester Merrow, another Congressman, who was such an outspoken liberal that he would later desert the Republican party entirely (but never again win office).

When the smoke had cleared, Bass had defeated Mrs. Bridges by a narrow margin, with the other candidates not far behind. The enraged Mrs. Bridges refused to support him in the general election, and the seat went to an attractive Democratic contender—Thomas J. McIntyre, a

---

* What Bridges could not take with him was the considerable wealth he had accumulated over the years, most of it spent in public office. When he died, in fact, several bundles of cash were found among his effects—a phenomenon, like many others concerning the powerful senior Senator, never adequately explained to his trusting constituents.

former mayor of Laconia, and New Hampshire's first Democratic Senator in 30 yeaars.

▪   In that same 1962 primary, Governor Wesley Powell, a controversial and unpredictable man who had cut his political teeth on Bridges' Senate staff back in the 1940s, was defeated for renomination. But Powell then turned on the man who had beaten him, John Pillsbury, the Republican leader in the state house. Powell said the ballot count had been dishonest, and that the voters should elect the Democratic candidate, John W. King, minority leader in the legislature. King proceeded to win the election by some 40,000 votes and proved to be a popular governor, winning by wide margins again in 1964 and 1966. But he was so conservative that the Republicans, at least on a programmatic basis, had little reason to quarrel with him.

(Powell, in the following years, would run twice again for governor and twice for the U.S. Senate, losing each time. He is a sometimes Loeb ally, a staunch conservative, a former close political friend of Richard Nixon, and a maverick. It is considered a truism that if he runs for any job, Powell can pick up 20,000 votes from people who remember and like him—but not enough to win. His divisive career in Republican politics started in 1950, when he tried unsuccessfully to unseat Senator Charles Tobey in the primary.)

▪   A touch of normalcy returned to New Hampshire with the 1968 election as governor of a moderate, decent, but not very forceful Republican, Walter R. Peterson. But Peterson, who had been speaker of the State House, had a rough time in Republican primaries, which would eventually provide his nemesis. In 1968 he had to cope with opposition from both Powell and the *Union Leader*'s new-found creation, Meldrim Thomson. But Peterson won with only 34 percent of the primary vote in 1968 and, with Thomson again his adversary in 1970, by just 51 percent. Intellectually, Peterson understood New Hampshire's desperate tax and services problem, and he knew the need for a broad-based tax, probably on personal income (the recommendation of a blue-ribbon citizens advisory committee, including Sherman Adams, which he appointed). But Peterson's style was so low-key, so muted, that he failed to provide the leadership New Hampshire needed. (Rod Paul wrote in the Concord *Monitor:* "Showing little emotion, other than what fatigue has wrought, Peterson has displayed no zest for politics—his profession. . . . The governor tiptoes in and out of controversy, disavowing rough and tumble political debate." Paul deplored Peterson's unwillingness to provide "blunt talk tuned into the frustration of unmet need" in the state.)

▪   As Peterson waned, Meldrim Thomson rose in power until in 1972 he was strong enough to topple Peterson in the primary and then, in an unusual three-way general election, to become the chief executive of New Hampshire. "Ax the tax" was his slogan, combined with a smokescreen of fear he managed to generate about youth, reform, and any form of social dissent. It would be mistaken to call Thomson a throwback to anything as basic as old-style Yankee frugality and conservatism. He was, to put it crudely, a know-nothing "cracker" from Georgia, the state where he was reared—elected governor of New Hampshire at just the time in history that Georgia was shucking off its segregationist officeholders in favor of moderate, semi-"populist" leaders, men of tolerance and decency like Jimmy Carter. (Some have labeled Thomson a "Lester Maddox of the North." The appellation is unfair, however, to Maddox, who at least had a touch of humor, of regard for the "little man," and willingness to reform some areas of state government.)

Our story will return shortly to the administration of New Hampshire's Stone Age governor, but note should first be made of his Republicanism. In 1970, the second time he lost to Peterson in the GOP primary, Thomson actually bolted the party and ran in the general election as the candidate of the American Independent party—the George Wallace party. As an AIP'er, Thomson got 8 percent of the vote. His apostasy led some old-line Republican leaders, like Senator Norris Cotton, to express their deep shock. But the *Union Leader* saw no harm in Thomson's excursion into third-party politics and began to puff him up as a regular Republican, putting him on his course to eventual victory in 1972. By then, the regular Republican leaders had forgotten their shock and were on record for Thomson's election.

Liberal candidates for governor, largely because of the *Union Leader*'s influence in both parties' primaries, were becoming a virtually extinct species by the early 1970s. Both in 1970 and 1972, the Democratic nominee was Roger Crowley, a rigid conservative and antitax man who beat liberal primary competitors with the avid support of the *Union Leader*. In 1972, when Thomson had finally downed Peterson, Loeb exulted in one of his page one editorials: "For once the voters of New Hampshire have an opportunity to choose between two fine men, equally qualified in competence, integrity, character and in their private lives to be governor." (Later Crowley, though defeated in the general election, turned up as executive director of the commission on crime and delinquency in the Thomson administration.) The choice between two ultraconservatives in 1972 was so unpalatable to liberal Republicans that one of their number, Concord Mayor Malcolm McLane of the illustrious New Hampshire McLane family, ran as an independent. Though he had only seven weeks to campaign, McLane garnered 20 percent of the vote—compared to 41 percent for Thomson and 39 percent for Crowley.

Thomson, running for renomination in 1974, easily defeated a more moderate Republican, state senate president David (no relation to Richard) Nixon. Nixon won cities like Concord, Keene, and Portsmouth, but was swamped by a Thomson landslide in Loeb's Manchester and the traditionally conservative North Country around Berlin. Again in 1974, the liberal Democratic contenders were killed off in the primary and the only candidate pledged to veto any broad-based tax, Richard W. Leonard, won the right to oppose Thomson. Thomson was to win the general election—albeit by a rather narrow margin.

If the reader finds this succession of primaries and general elections, of intrigues and counterintrigues and party-boltings confusing, he might have pity on the poor New Hampshire voter also. Actually, it is a wonder that the state's voting participation level remains one of the highest in the country.

In its 1974 election for the seat of retiring U. S. Senator Cotton, New Hampshire illustrated in a startling way how important every last vote can be. The contest presented the voters with one of their clearest choices in many a year. On the right was another onetime Senate aide to Styles Bridges, Louis C. Wyman. As a fire-eating state attorney general in the 1950s, Wyman had established his reputation as Northern New England's top Red hunter. In 1962 he went to Congress, broke with New England tradition by voting against the 1964 Civil Rights Act ("it makes a mockery of the Constitution"), voted consistently against liberal spending programs and for the Vietnam war, and in 1972 proved his conservatism by getting a voting record score of zero from the Americans for Democratic Action. On the left was John Durkin, who in five years as state insurance commissioner had established a reputation as a persistent fighter for the interests of the consumer, pressing for no-fault auto insurance and for lower medical insurance rates. Durkin had been replaced by Governor Thomson in 1973, despite petitions circulated by a group of legislators and citizens to "keep Durkin working."

In a "normal" year (if there are such in New Hampshire), Wyman would probably have won by a comfortable margin. But it was revealed that Wyman had played a role in 1971 in soliciting an ambassadorship for a fat-cat Republican campaign giver, Ruth Farkas of New York, who it later turned out gave $300,000 to the Nixon reelection effort before being named ambassador to Luxembourg. Testimony by former Nixon lawyer Herbert Kalmbach seemed to involve Wyman in the affair up to his ears, but a letter from Watergate Special Prosecutor Leon Jaworski, released in September 1974, indicated the on-going investigation into the Farkas ambassadorship had "not uncovered evidence which would support the bringing of any criminal charges against Congressman Wyman." Nevertheless, the Farkas affair doubtless hurt Wyman, and he was probably not helped any when Wesley Powell—who had first put Wyman on the Bridges staff back in the '40s—announced there were "absolutely no circumstances under which I could or would support Louis Wyman for the U.S. Senate." Powell warned that more irregularities "involving Louis and his political money" would come to light.

When the initial vote tally was completed, Wyman was shown to be the winner by a margin of 542 votes. Durkin then demanded a recount, and he emerged with an incredibly slim lead of 10 votes—out of 221,838 cast. On the basis of that, Durkin got a certificate of election, but then the

Republican-controlled ballot law commission probed further into disputed ballots and decided Wyman had won after all, by a margin of two votes. The U.S. Senate refused to seat either man and plunged into months of committee hearings, laboriously reviewing hundreds of disputed paper ballots. Then came a long Senate debate in which Republicans charged the Democrats were trying to "steal" the election, rather than returning it to New Hampshire for another vote. A Republican filibuster prevented any resolution of the issue, and after eight months the Senate gave up and a new election was called.

The special election of September 1975 was a remarkable affair that may have been a crucial turning point in New Hampshire politics. Both Durkin and Wyman hired professional campaign managers and waged intensive campaigns. But what was expected to be another close vote turned out to be a landslide for Durkin in which he won by a plurality of no less than 27,771 votes—a landslide by New Hampshire standards. President Ford campaigned personally for Wyman, putting his own prestige on the line. But many moderate and liberal Republicans shunned Wyman, recalling his ultraconservatism and witch-hunting tactics of the past and recoiling at his political embrace of Governor Thomson and Loeb. Wyman foolishly made no bid for independent voter support, and continued to be plagued by reports that he might still be indicted in the Farkas affair.

Durkin, by contrast, emphasized the sad state of the economy, criticized the Ford administration's oil policies, and played the role of a spunky consumer advocate. He became the first candidate in a statewide election to purchase television time on Boston stations, blaming the Republicans for New Hampshire's high unemployment (8.6 percent at the time). The Durkin campaign would probably have been unable to afford that luxury without major cash assistance from organized labor, which chipped in manpower and more than half the $150,000 he was allowed to spend under federal election law. The vital role of labor money is becoming familiar in the state's Democratic Senate campaigns. After McIntyre's successful 1972 campaign, it was revealed that at least $41,000, largely secret labor money, had been "laundered" for him (i.e., passed along to conceal its source) by the Democratic Senatorial Campaign Committee.

Aside from Durkin's big plurality, the two most remarkable things about the 1975 special election outcome were the high turnout—about 60 percent of the eligible electorate, a rare phenomenon in a special election —and the heavy shift to the Democrats, even in normally Republican small towns. The euphoric Democrats said the Durkin election symbolized the successful "coming of age" of their party as a broad-based, progressive force in New Hampshire. But whether the outcome presaged an early liberal Democratic capture of the governorship was another question: for one thing, the state's stringent campaign spending limitations would preclude the Boston television advertising Durkin used; in addition, it would be hard to get organized labor to focus its national shock troops and money on a general election contest for the governorship.

That the political ground was shifting to a significant degree had already been signaled, however, by the November 1974 election to Congress (replacing Wyman) of Democrat Norman D'Amours, a 37-year-old former state assistant attorney general. D'Amours ran a populist-style campaign shrewdly geared to the theme (so appropriate for tax-conscious New Hampshire): "I'm for the people who pay taxes, not for the people who don't, like the big oil companies." He became New Hampshire's first Democratic Congressman in a full decade.* He was able to beat a Loeb-sponsored candidate, both because of his French-Canadian name and because he was able to do so well in his home city of Manchester.

Indeed, the more one studies New Hampshire voting patterns, the more one is impressed by the pivotal nature of the Manchester vote. In Democratic primaries, where it makes up a full quarter of the vote, it is more often than not decisive; in general elections, when it casts 12 percent of the state-wide vote, it quite often swings the result one way or the other. Durkin, for instance, would probably not have been able to do as well as he did, either in 1974 or 1975, if he had not been a Manchester resident. It would seem that when a "local boy" runs, especially if he is a Democrat (and preferably French-Canadian), Manchester voters are much more likely to disregard the advice of the *Union Leader*.

A different formula for success is the one Democratic Senator McIntyre has used—to slip into office the first time when the *Union Leader* is preoccupied, as it was in 1962 because of its distaste for Congressman Bass, and then to campaign assiduously against the paper and Loebism in general, building up support among voters across the state who can't stand Loeb. McIntyre pointed out to me that in his first race, in 1962, his entire state-wide plurality of 10,413 votes was accounted for by his margin in normally Democratic Manchester. Two years later, running for a full term, he carried the state by 18,647 votes but dropped to a margin of about 8,000 votes in Manchester. In 1972, he won state-wide by a handsome margin of 44,643 votes against Loeb's candidate, Wesley Powell. But in Manchester his margin was down to some 6,700 votes.

In time, Hillsborough County, which includes Manchester and often like-voting Nashua, may yield some in importance to fast-growing Rockingham County, which lies between Hillsborough and the sea and has been receiving a high proportion of the Massachusetts Route-128 working force population influx. In 1960, Rockingham's total vote was not much more than a third of Hillsborough's; by the early 1970s, it was over 60 percent of its biggest neighbor's.† The original assumption was that the Massachusetts

---

* On an apparent fluke in 1964, the Democrats had unseated Wyman—but only for two years. Otherwise, the Republican hold on New Hampshire's two House seats had been unbroken since the 1930s. The holder of the other seat, from 1963 to this writing, has been James C. Cleveland, who was once viewed as a moderate-to-liberal Republican (he excoriated Loeb when I first met him in 1960) but later turned rather cautious and conservative. Cleveland did, however, distinguish himself as one of the leading exponents of House reform, including adequate minority staffing on committees.

† As a share of the state-wide vote, Hillsborough has been stationary at just over 30 percent since 1960 while Rockingham has moved up from 15 percent to almost 20 percent. By

expatriates had, in many cases picked New Hampshire residence to avoid the Bay State's high taxes and would therefore vote a conservative and usually Republican line. In recent elections, however, there has been a noticeable trend to the left in Rockingham's vote. One could reason that the new residents are a touch more sophisticated than folk influenced over years by the *Union Leader*; another explanation is that the Portsmouth *Herald,* the Boston *Globe,* the Lowell *Sun* and other Massachusetts papers read widely in the county are chipping away at Loebian thinking.

Describing his fellow Democrats, Dartmouth's Herbert Wells Hill, a former gubernatorial and Senate nominee, noted "there's no resemblance whatever between a small-town Democrat and a fellow from Ward 12 in Manchester and the Democratic chairman in the college town of Hanover —they're three totally different creatures." The small-town Democrats are of an ancestral type, either perpetual "agginers" in the overwhelmingly Republican environment of their areas or throwbacks (though they would have no memory of it) to the time when Andrew Jackson used to come and hold court in Concord.

The city Democrats are overwhelmingly ethnic types—generally Irish or French-Canadian (although some of the more affluent Franco-Americans, in particular, are Republican). For decades, the ethnics have been the backbone of Democratic strength in the state; in 1951, for instance, they made up 63 percent of the Democratic membership in the legislature, and by one account the state Democratic leadership contained 41 persons of whom "14 were of French or French-Canadian descent, 13 were Irish, nine were English, Scottish or native American of many generations, two were Jewish, one was mixed French and Irish, and one Polish and one Greek." Bitter internecine warfare between the ethnic factions, Lockard observed, long retarded Democratic growth in the state. But the sociological base which underlay the old antagonisms and French-Canadian clannishness, Senator McIntyre observed, is now dissipating "as the Catholic schools begin to fall by the wayside and a generation rises that has almost lost track of its special ethnic heritage." It would be hard to conceive now, he said, of the situation in Laconia when he was a boy, when the rector of Sacred Heart, the local French Catholic church, who had come down from Canada to take the job, wouldn't even take part in civic affairs like saying the benediction at a chamber of commerce dinner. (By contrast, McIntyre said, at the Irish church, St. Joseph's, "we had a monsignor who was right out of Pope John's book—when we buried him three of his pallbearers were his golf buddies, all Protestants.")

Finally, there are the liberal-intellectual Democrats, many of them young people, often resident in the few university towns (notably Hanover and Durham), who were wakened to new political consciousness by Eugene McCarthy's campaign in 1968 and George McGovern's in 1972. Even

---

contrast, Merrimack County, which includes liberal-voting Concord, accounts for 11 percent of the state vote. The remaining seven counties, scattered from the Massachusetts to the Canadian borders and including many of the smaller Republican towns, represent only 40 percent of the state total.

a number of bright young French-Canadians are now joining the liberal group. In 1975 the state Democratic chairman was a Dartmouth government professor, Lawrence Radway, who told me that moderate liberal Democrats had taken full control of the party apparatus with women and younger people playing a large role. The right wing of the Democratic party, he said, had no natural leader left. And it was expected that with two Democratic U.S. Senators, both with politically expert staffs, there would be strong and ongoing Democratic leadership for the first time in living memory.

Interestingly, many Democrats credit their initial post World War II rejuvenation to the 1952 presidential primary campaign of Tennessee's Estes Kefauver, whose common touch and person-to-person campaigning gave the ethnic Democrats a sense of their own importance and encouraged the blue-collar workers in the mill towns to challenge the Yankee Republican hegemony.

The Democrats have also been blessed by the support—organizationally and financially—of New Hampshire's remarkable Dunfey family, the six sons of Mrs. Catherine Dunfey who have built or acquired so many hotels and motor inns across the U.S. in recent years that they are the country's seventh largest lodging operator. This corporate empire is run out of a renovated 100-year-old inn in Hampton, New Hampshire, with major financial backing from Hartford's Aetna Corporation—a far cry from the brothers' start running a family luncheonette and variety store in Lowell, Massachusetts, right after World War II. William Dunfey, in particular, is credited by McIntyre as being "the father of whatever Democratic party we have." Jean Hennessey, another prominent Democrat in the state, called Dunfey "the shrewdest political mind in New Hampshire." He has refused suggestions by McIntyre and other Democrats that he run for office, but in several years as Democratic state chairman he put vitality into the party and also provided a link to young Democrats in the universities.

At least through the early 1970s, it was safe to call New Hampshire a "normally Republican" state. Even in 1974, a banner year for Democrats in most states, the Republicans held on to about 58 percent of the seats in the state's lower house (though the senate, interestingly, ended up in a dead tie between the parties). But the Republican edge in party registration has been declining steadily to a 1975 level of 165,000, compared to 115,000 Democrats and 145,000 independents. In the first half of the '70s Republican registration advanced a minuscule 1.5 percent, while the Democrats increased by 15 percent and the independents 13 percent. Moreover, there seems no early resolution of the bitter struggle for control within the Republican party. One scenario would be for the party moderates simply to give up the ghost and leave control in the hands of the Loeb-Thomson-Wyman wing. Already most of the avowed Republican liberals have either deserted to the Democrats or become paralyzed by successive defeats.

What then of the moderate-to-liberal Republicans—politicians in the Adams-Bass-McLane tradition? State senator C. Robertson Trowbridge, who with a few others represents the present-day incarnation of that school, claims that it has "by and large provided what little leadership" the Republicans have offered in state public policy. But Loeb, he notes, has dulled the effectiveness of the activist Republicans. Yet "it turns out that the types he [Loeb] sends up to the legislature can't do anything." The result is all-around stalemate.

When the liberal and moderate Republicans venture into formal party politics, they are quickly bloodied in their constant fights with Loeb and Thomson. The "regular" Republican conservatives, like U.S. Representative James Cleveland and former U.S. Senator Norris Cotton, generally oppose Loeb and Thomson but have been unwilling to mount or join a concerted attack on the party's increasingly dominant right wing.

This has, of course, spin-off effects on the Democrats. Richard Wright noted in the *New Hampshire Times* in 1975 that "the Democratic party has an inner strength now, but is still young, brash, and idealistic. It needs the temperance of Republicanism, but will have, instead, the intemperance of the radical right."

The Presidential Primary: Exercise in Perversity

The first question to ask about New Hampshire's presidential primary, which generates such an inordinate amount of attention each four years, is why it's held so early in the year. For the past quarter century, since presidential hopefuls and the mass media obediently following them into the snowy Granite State scene began to make so much of the contest, the answer has been obvious enough. New Hampshire loves the attention. And it loves the money brought into the state by the presidential hopefuls, their staffs and volunteer entourages, and the small army of print and electronic media correspondents and support personnel who fill up hostelries in the slow season. No one has ever made an accurate count of how much the primary brings into New Hampshire, but the sum pumped into the local economy for lodgings, food, gasoline, rented autos, campaign literature, billboards, handcards, bumper strips, telephones, newspaper and radio and television advertising, for "purchasing" the support of local politicos, and all the rest, must be formidable indeed. New Hampshire would not think of relinquishing its first-in-the-nation primary date. Before the 1972 contest, when Florida opted for the second Tuesday in March, the Granite State's traditional date, the legislature rushed to pass a law making the New Hampshire primary the *first* Tuesday of March. In 1975, when sentiment mounted in other New England states for a common regional primary day on the first Tuesday in March, the New Hampshire legislature passed a law automatically setting its primary date for a week before *any* other state's. (With Massachusetts choosing the first Tuesday in March, that meant the New Hampshire primary was actually in February.)

Historically, the reason for New Hampshire's early date was much simpler: mud. The primary was set on the day of the annual town meeting. "You have to beat the spring thaw," an oldtimer explained to a credulous visiting reporter in the 1950s. "In the old days, the roads were impassable on account of mud when the thaw set in. Some of 'em still are today. So town meetin', and later the primary, had to be held at a time when people could come in from the farms to vote."

The state's first presidential primary law was actually passed in 1913, at the height of the Progressive era. For years it was one of only middling importance, because primaries were not considered as important as they are today (the bosses still made the final decisions at conventions) and in any event there was no spot on the New Hampshire ballot where a citizen could vote directly for a presidential candidate. Instead, there was only a choice (and usually a very limited one) between slates of convention delegates who might or might not be pledged to support any particular candidate.

Nevertheless, the early New Hampshire primaries did have some impact. A Woodrow Wilson slate won on the Democratic side in 1916, showing his popularity for renomination. Calvin Coolidge, who had succeeded to the presidency on Warren G. Harding's death, saw his slate win in 1924. In 1928 the slates of the two eventual winners—Alfred E. Smith and Herbert Hoover—were victorious. In 1932 Franklin D. Roosevelt beat a Smith slate and started the bandwagon rolling toward his eventual nomination. (FDR would win three times again, including 1940 when he had to break the third-term barrier.) A Truman slate won in 1948. That year, on the Republican side, though an unpledged slate got the most votes, the then very serious candidacy of Harold E. Stassen got a forward boost when he piled up a significant vote. The next spring, the legislature changed the law to include a straight presidential preference vote (including write-ins), and New Hampshire was headed for the big time. (The fact that nationwide television arrived on the scene about the same time, making New Hampshire's early-bird contest a media event of formidable proportions, was not coincidental.)

Between 1952 and 1972, the New Hampshire primary on eight occasions had what could be called a significant impact on the course of presidential nominating politics:

1952—Democratic. Estes Kefauver, the man in the coonskin cap, defeated the incumbent President of the United States, 55 to 44 percent. Before the New Hampshire vote, Harry Truman had said that primaries were "eyewash"; three weeks after the vote, he announced his withdrawal from the presidential race.

1952—Republican. In a classic contest between the party's conservative and liberal wings, General Dwight D. Eisenhower—then an officially unannounced candidate, still in uniform as NATO supreme commander in Europe—received 50 percent of the vote compared to 39 percent for Ohio's Senator Robert A. Taft. The primary was dramatic evidence of Ike's vote-pulling power; a month later he would move ahead of Taft in the Gallup Poll ratings for the first time and, with other primary victories, defeat the

"Mr. Republican" of that day to win the nomination and then the presidency.

1956—Republican. Vice President Richard M. Nixon received 22,141 write-in votes for Vice President—82.5 percent of the total Republican vote cast. The returns helped to stop growing speculation (perhaps Eisenhower's own plan) to drop Nixon from the ticket. It was to be the beginning of a long love affair between Nixon and the state's GOP voters, who would give him 89 percent of their presidential preference vote in 1960, 16 percent (even as a write-in "noncandidate") in 1964, 78 percent in 1968, and 69 percent in 1972.

1960—Democratic. Senator John F. Kennedy, without serious opposition, received 85 percent of the preference vote. Kennedy's status as a fellow New Englander may have helped; also it must be remembered that this was the year of the great religious test in presidential politics, and that Kennedy's Catholicism was sure to appeal to the overwhelmingly Roman Catholic Democratic voter pool of New Hampshire. (In the overall Granite State population, Roman Catholics account for 36 percent—more than all but four other states.)

1964—Republican. This was a contest between the outstanding representatives of two ideological wings of the Republican party—Senator Barry Goldwater of Arizona and Governor Nelson Rockefeller of New York. Both campaigned assiduously in the state; both had prestigious New Hampshire campaign chairmen (Senator Norris Cotton for Goldwater, former Governor Hugh Gregg for Rockefeller); both spent immense amounts of money on the effort. But in the end, both were to lose to a phantom—Ambassador Henry Cabot Lodge, then halfway around the world in Vietnam, a man who had previously promised Rockefeller his support. A write-in effort for Lodge was engineered by four young Bostonians in what Theodore White later described as a "madcap adventure." The opening for Lodge was created by the handicaps of the official candidates. Goldwater ran an incredibly inept, foot-in-mouth campaign, making bellicose foreign policy proposals, suggesting that Social Security be made voluntary (thus losing support from New Hampshire's big retiree community, which began to fear for the stability of the system), and generally creating a picture of himself as a callous and reckless man. Rockefeller ran a competent enough campaign, capitalizing on Goldwater's goofs. But Rockefeller was bedeviled by resentment against his recent marriage and divorce (an offense to Yankee morality constantly recalled by the Manchester newspaper). Lodge, the unannounced candidate who entered the state not once during the primary season, had no one to answer to and provided a handy alternative for New Hampshire Republicans thrown off by the "front runners." The final count: 34 percent for Lodge, 21 percent for Goldwater, 20 percent for Rockefeller, 16 percent for Nixon (like Lodge, a write-in), 3 percent for Margaret Chase Smith of Maine.

In the long term, New Hampshire could not and did not do anything for Lodge, who was not a serious possibility for the Republican nomination in any case. But what happened there may well have sealed Goldwater's doom in November, because Lyndon Johnson had only to recall Goldwater's statements—and Rockefeller's critique of them—in the national campaign. (The Goldwater people, according to one report, "saw this as an example of New Hampshire's *capacity for delayed mischief.*") As for Rockefeller, his only chance to win the Republican nomination probably went a-fleeting in New Hampshire. Theodore White later ventured the guess that if there had been no write-in effort for Lodge, "Nelson Rockefeller would have won by a flat majority, gone on to a larger majority in Oregon and then probably carried California to defeat Goldwater conclusively."

1968—Republican. Richard Nixon won in one of his customary New Hampshire landslides, thus "proving" his electoral viability after his defeats of the early '60s. The New Hampshire Republicans helped Nixon immeasurably in his road to the White House; only later history would show what an incredible mistake they had made. This was the same campaign, as I noted earlier in this chapter, in which Michigan's George Romney, pilloried by the *Union Leader*, lagged so egregiously in the polls that he withdrew before primary day.

1968—Democratic. President Lyndon Johnson never said he would run for reelection, but the Democratic hierarchies—in Washington and New Hampshire—assumed that he would and decided that a massive write-in for the President in New Hampshire would be a healthy psychological send-off. In normal times, this might have worked well, but it failed to take account of several phenomena: Johnson's personal unpopularity in New Hampshire, the heavy-handed ineptness of his campaign managers, the mounting fury of the Vietnam war (the Tet offensive would commence January 31), and Eugene McCarthy—or more particularly the amazing army of student activists who would go to work on McCarthy's behalf by primary day, rather than the often diffident and aloof candidate himself. Moral abhorrence with the war (combined in some cases with fear of the draft) was quite enough to send literally thousands of student activists, some from hundreds of miles, pouring into New Hampshire to campaign for McCarthy. Curtis Gans, McCarthy's staff director, would hold briefing sessions for the young people offering this general counsel: "You came here because you're against the war; we're here because we believe the war can best be ended by removing LBJ. Understand this is a conservative, 'hawkish' state. When you go around, talk about the endless nature of the war, the disruption it's causing in the country, and the image of truthfulness of our candidate as opposed to Johnson's deviousness. But steer clear of making arguments on the war *qua* war."

The tactic proved immensely successful. As Mary McGrory reported in the Washington *Star:*

What is happening is that violet-eyed damsels from Smith are pinning McCarthy buttons on tattooed mill-workers, and Ph.D.s from Cornell, shaven and shorn for peace, are deferentially bowing to middle-age Manchester housewives and importuning them to consider a change of Commander-in-Chief. Some of the best young minds of the country are sitting in the cellars of Manchester, Nashua, and points north, poring over precinct lists . . .

McCarthy's New Hampshire success was particularly surprising because it was not until January 3—on the basis of an encouraging situation report drawn up by his young in-state activists, and on the urging of Blair Clark, the former New Hampshire *Sunday News* editor and CBS executive —that he formally announced he would run in the state. The McCarthy campaign was aided immensely by the blunder of the Johnson managers in sending out postal pledge cards for LBJ with serial numbering that smacked of intimidation and control. Another factor was the Johnsonian style, abhorrent to New Hampshireites more accustomed to taciturn ways—and officeholders. McCarthy's standing, according to canvass reports by his workers, rose rapidly to about 43 percent of the vote. Then the Democratic establishment, alarmed by the turn of events, turned nasty. Governor King called McCarthy "a champion of appeasement and surrender"; Senator McIntyre referred to him as the friend of "draft dodgers and deserters."

The counterattack apparently stopped McCarthy's upward movement. President Johnson did win the primary, receiving, as a write-in candidate, 49 percent of the Democratic total. But McCarthy was amazingly close at 42 percent, losing in Manchester, Nashua, and a couple of other cities, but winning practically everywhere else. He ran particularly well in Rockingham County and the Massachusetts-orbit suburbs, and swept the university towns. Moreover, McCarthy received an interesting 5 percent in write-ins on the Republican side, so that when one totaled the votes for the two men in both primaries, Johnson led McCarthy by the slimmest of margins— 29,021 to 28,791. Johnson later denied that New Hampshire had anything to do with his decision, but the fact is that within a month, following very gloomy reports about the upcoming Wisconsin primary, he had announced, like Harry Truman in 1952 that he would not be a candidate for reelection.

1972—Democratic. This is the primary Edmund Muskie "lost" by winning only 47 percent of the preference vote, compared to 38 percent for his nearest rival, George McGovern. This was considered a great moral victory for the relatively unknown South Dakotan running in northern New England; later I even saw a number of press stories flatly stating McGovern had "won" in New Hampshire. That McGovern had taken a daring gamble in New Hampshire, and enhanced his national campaign through his showing there, is certain. A lot of the credit for that was given to Joseph Grandmaison, a 23-year-old Nashua alderman and master of grassroots political organizing who turned out the youthful precinct brigades just as impressively as the McCarthy forces had in 1968.* The results in working-class areas, which would normally seem to have little affinity for McGovern, were particularly impressive (though those same areas were to turn dramatically against McGovern in the general election). After the

* Three years later Grandmaison also masterminded Durkin's successful special election campaign for the U.S. Senate.

primary, McGovern's 21-year-old professional pollster, Patrick Cadell, complained that in the more affluent suburbs and southeastern New Hampshire in general, McGovern had been unable to match McCarthy's showing. In those areas, he said, McGovern's drive was blunted by "liberal pragmatism," the belief that "Muskie is as liberal as a guy can be and still win." That, of course, was precisely the point: by giving their neighbor from Maine such a lukewarm endorsement, and advancing the McGovern candidacy, New Hampshire voters were undermining the chances of perhaps the only Democrat with a serious chance of defeating Richard Nixon in the general election, and building up a contender who would become the most overwhelmingly defeated Democratic presidential candidate in the 20th century.

Reading again the reports on Muskie's campaign in the national press and transcripts of the network news broadcasts, one is shocked to see how cavalierly the media took unto itself the responsibility of saying that unless Muskie got 50 percent or more of the New Hampshire vote, he would have failed in the state. It is true that Muskie's own aides, at one time or another, said as much, but as far as I can determine Muskie himself never said that he would have to get more than half the votes in the six-candidate field. Indeed, Muskie saw what was coming when he complained on March 2 that he was locked in combat with a "figment of the press imagination." "I'm not campaigning against just physical opponents, I'm campaigning against a phantom that has been created by the press," he said. Predictably, when Muskie fell three percentage points short of the magical 50-percent figure in the final count, the results (starting in the lead sentence of one network news report) were reported to the nation as a defeat for the man from Maine.

There were plentiful other reasons for Muskie's eventual demise as a presidential candidate, ranging from Nixonian dirty tricks and the campaign of vilification Loeb waged against him (reviewed on pages 304–305 above) to problems of his own temperament (pages 382–385, in the Maine chapter of this book). Nevertheless, one can seriously doubt if the Democratic party—or the nation—benefited from the perceived rebuff to the most outstanding public servant northern New England has produced in several generations.

The standard argument of justification for New Hampshire as a legitimate test tube of presidential candidates is that the Granite State—far from being the rural redoubt of monosyllabic Yankees perceived from afar—is actually a place of heterogeneous population, highly industrialized, with a goodly complement of professional, technical, and skilled workers and a fair representation of Suburbia U.S.A. Defenders also point out that New Hampshire has two counties (Coos and Strafford) which have voted for the winner in every presidential election since 1892, with the exception of 1968.* Correct as all this may be, it misses two salient facts about New

* There are only three other counties in the nation with similar "bellwether" credentials—Palo Alto (Iowa), Crook (Oregon), and Laramie (Wyoming). It may be that New Hampshire's

Hampshire—the polluted nature of its public dialogue, as noted earlier in this chapter, and the sheer madness of the way presidential primaries are run there.

It takes, for instance, only 50 petition signatures from each of the two congressional districts to qualify a candidate for the preference ballot. As a result, any Tom, Dick, or Harry can easily cloud the waters of serious deliberation about a future President. Consider the also-rans of the 1972 Democratic contest. There was Sam Yorty of Los Angeles, blown up to allegedly presidential proportions, as we noted previously, by the Manchester *Union Leader*. Yorty was to get 6 percent of the vote. Then there was Indiana's Vance Hartke, whose candidacy for the presidency of the United States seemed to have been taken seriously only by himself, his family, and some paid New Hampshire ward heelers in his corner. He clocked in at 3 percent. Wilbur Mills, then chairman of the House Ways and Means Committee and considered one of the most powerful men in Washington, waged an extremely expensive media campaign financed by special interests dependent on decisions of his committee. Few people of sound mind ever believed Mills's personality, or his skill as a wheeler-dealer in the House, qualified him for the presidency (even before his affinity for stripteasers became a matter of public record). But no matter, Wilbur Mills could make a "serious" effort in New Hampshire and end up with 4 percent of the vote. Add together the votes of Yorty, Hartke, and Mills, and you have 13 percent of the Democratic vote—most of which would probably have gone to Muskie if this triumvirate had not entered the contest.

In the interests of "equal time," we should perhaps mention another candidate of the 1972 campaign—Ned Coll, a 32-year-old social activist from Hartford, Connecticut. Coll was to end up with the grand total of 280 votes (.3 percent of the total), but not before he had made his mark. According to a March 5 report by Don Oberdorfer in the Washington *Post*:

> Durham, N.H.—Four minutes into the first televised debate of the 1972 Presidential campaign, a little-known candidate named Ned Coll reached into his suit coat pocket and produced a rubber rat. As spectators in the control room gasped, Coll held the rodent up to the camera and declared, "Until we do something about the rat in America, I think the politics of 1972 is meaningless." . . .
>
> By the luck of the draw, Coll sat on the left and spoke first, and Los Angeles Mayor Sam Yorty sat on the right and spoke last. The two of them provided something of a Greek chorus, framing the views of the three United States Senators seated between them. . . .
>
> To an observer watching from the corner of the studio, there was no clear winner unless it is the cause of rat control in America.

1976—Republican. In April 1975, anticipating a 1976 primary challenge in the state from either Ronald Reagan or Governor Thomson, President Gerald R. Ford saw fit to leave his official duties in Washington to make a

---

Coos and Strafford, as some political scientists claim, are microcosms of the entire nation in important demographic features. But between them, they cast only 13 percent of the state's vote. Another factor overlooked by champions of New Hampshire as a national barometer is the almost total absence of black people (.3 percent of the state population in 1970). This is a particularly distorting factor in Democratic primaries.

"nonpolitical" trip to New Hampshire. In a speech before the legislature, he somehow made virtues of the state's grossest failings:

> Amid the climbing costs of federal and state budgets—particularly in the past decade—New Hampshire has truly balanced its budget. You grapple with your problems without a general income or sales tax. I admire your spirit of self-discipline and self-reliance. You have gone about your business quietly—with restraint—without the exaggerated rhetoric which divides people and without excessive promises that create so much false hope.

It would be naive to think that Mr. Ford's advisers had not briefed him on the realities of New Hampshire—the state of sin taxes, inadequate services, and the public dialogue of Loebian vituperation. Again, New Hampshire was showing what mischief it can work with national leadership.

Ford's praise for New Hampshire's ways was not enough to get the endorsement of Loeb and Thomson, who supported Reagan in the primary. Yet Ford beat Reagan 51 to 49 percent. It was a narrow victory but a setback to Reagan's strategy of winning primaries and shattering the incumbent's natural command of party allegiance. Of the 13 largest cities in the state, Ford carried nine and Reagan four. Reagan carried Manchester, but not by the margin predicted by Thomson, indicating that voters may not have rallied as loyally to Loeb as in times past.

1976—Democratic. The same anti-Washington sentiment that led to the close Ford-Reagan vote also propelled former Georgia Gov. Jimmy Carter to a clear win over his four more liberal rivals, Morris Udall, Fred Harris, Birch Bayh, and Sargent Shriver. Carter got 30 percent of the vote. To the surprise of his opponents, he piled up 32 percent of voting moderates and 20 percent of voting liberals in addition to 44 percent of voting conservatives, an NBC News survey showed. Carter's New Hampshire victory gave his campaign early momentum and placed him on the covers of both *Newsweek* and *Time*.

A serious question can be raised about the ability of New Hampshire voters, under the onslaught of national media attention and immense expenditures by presidential primary candidates in their state (totaling close to eight dollars per Democratic voter in 1972, for instance), to keep their perspective. Senator Norris Cotton, who had been burned by his chairmanship of the Goldwater campaign, commented later: "Is the New Hampshire primary a fair test of the voters' real choice? No! You get no considered judgment of the people. The average voter in New Hampshire feels ten feet high. He is thinking of how his vote will have this terrific meaning for the whole country. He gets too thoughtful and self-conscious."

One could argue that it is a fine civics lesson for high school students in remote New Hampshire towns to have the cream of a national party's presidential talent parade before them and answer questions. As Charles McDowell wrote in the *Atlantic* in 1967:

> On the record of past performance, at least four generalizations can be made about the importance of the New Hampshire primary. One: it gives a candidate a little help or a lot of trouble. Two: It does not necessarily offer a clue to who

will win the nomination, but it has the power to kill off candidates who might. Three: It can reveal a man to be a hopeless candidate for President without doing much to stop him. [McDowell must have had Goldwater in mind when he made that comment.] Four: It has a close kinship to a lottery, and the odds are quite good that everyone who gets in will be a loser.

What is easily forgotten is that if the candidates are sometimes all losers, so is the country. Leadership and its corollary—respect for leaders —is a fragile quality, easily shattered in a destructive atmosphere like the primaries of this bizarre little state. And when the electoral system cannot produce legitimate leaders, then the nation suffers, as the record of the last several years has so dramatically illustrated.

State Government: Anatomy of a Disaster

New Hampshire has a fine highway system. Even before the federal interstate system was inaugurated, the state had built an impressive north-south turnpike in the heavily populated southern area. Then with the generous federal funds—nine dollars for each one dollar raised locally—the interstate system connected most regions of the state. Where the interstate system fails to reach, regular state highways are of generally high quality. In per capita expenditures for roads, New Hampshire ranks a very respectable 12th in the country, even though its land area is only 44th.

But in practically any other area one examines, the performance of New Hampshire state government is abysmal. Indeed, the splendid highway system in a state starved for other services provides a dramatic illustration of New Hampshire's warped priorities.

One can start with the organizational structure of the state government itself. A quarter century ago, under Governor Sherman Adams, the first executive department reorganization of New Hampshire history was effected. Adams put together a blue-ribbon commission of citizens, jurists, legislators, and business leaders, and they produced a plan reducing the number of boards and agencies from 83 to just over 40. "It was only a partial job," a leading figure of that era noted, "but it was absolutely necessary."

Since that 1950 organization, as most other states have streamlined and modernized their operations, New Hampshire has made scarcely any change at all. Most departments remain governed by boards or commissions, minimally responsive to the governor; indeed, most have terms which are not coterminous with his, so that a new governor is encumbered with a whole administrative machinery that can as easily resist his policies as support them. Moreover, when any top executives of the state government die or resign, the governor can only offer New England's lowest salaries to any replacement person he selects. The state government operates without any executive recruitment, training, or promotion plan. Also, the governor must clear many of his official actions with an executive council that remains as a useless appendage of colonial days.

One looks in vain to the state legislature for any relief from this dismal picture. Its chief problem is its lower house, which has no fewer than 400 members—the largest body of any state legislature in America and in fact (after Congress and the British Parliament) the third largest legislative body in the English-speaking world. The standard mythology used to justify this huge membership—an argument John Gunther thoughtlessly repeated in *Inside U.S.A.*—is that there are so many members that it is difficult for the selfish interests to "buy" their way in it. The fact is that special interests like the liquor companies, racetracks, insurance brokers, groups of firemen and policemen, state employee associations, and the telephone and power companies exercise marked influence, sometimes through their own employees who get elected to the house and then vote freely on matters affecting their own interests. (The state lacks a strict conflict-of-interest law to hold this practice in check.)

Then there is the problem of doing much rational at all in a milling herd of 400 citizen legislators, a body so large and fragmented that there is a practically infinite possibility for competing leadership clusters. One legislator cited to me the trials and tribulations of getting over to 400 people the nuances of a piece of legislation that is at all comprehensive without having a large number of them say, "You have nothing in there for field mice and therefore I'm going to vote against the bill." Getting a consensus in such a fragmented body, he said, is exceedingly difficult unless the legislation "is so complicated that no one understands it at all." Party discipline is practically nonexistent; both the formal leaders and the committee chairmen lack the power to knock heads and get much of substance accomplished. And that leaves the onnipresent lobbyists and lobbyist-legislators as the glue of the legislative process.

The pay of a New Hampshire legislator is $200 for his two-year term; even with travel money the compensation is only some $1,500. With one legislator elected for every 1,300 adults, candidates often have to be "drafted" because no one is really too interested in serving. The result: a legislature packed with grizzled oldsters plus a sprinkling of ambitious younger attorneys. The average age in recent years has been 66 or 67 years! A moment of silence is observed for each recently deceased member when the legislature assembles every two years; so long is the roll that the ceremony lasts for an almost macabre length of time. Inevitably, such an "old" legislature is unresponsive to the needs of a younger generation interested in quality schools, progressive mental health programs, and environmental laws; elderly people, many scraping by on fixed incomes, naturally fear anything new and untried, especially if new taxes might result. In recent years, a large number of young people, much less wed to the orthodoxies of New Hampshire's recent past, have been running for the legislature. More are being elected each election, so that some change may be in the offing— though any move to make New Hampshire progressive will run head-on into the formidable Loeb-dominated conservative bloc from Manchester.

Any surgery less radical than halving the size of the house would probably do little to make it more responsive to the "new" New Hampshire. A cut to 300 has sometimes been suggested, but as it is, only 300 usually show up now anyway—the "no-shows" generally representing legislators from the cities and the several multiple-member districts, who only appear to vote on racetrack bills or when their employers tell them to. With a 200-member house or, even more sensibly, 100 or less, it would at least be easier to have one-on-one election battles in individual districts, eliminating the wild draws and fuzzed issues of multi-member elections. In addition to being smaller, however, the legislature would also have to pay adequate compensation. The joint result of huge size and minimal pay is that highly educated individuals account for but a small part of the membership (and must do the lion's share of the work). The others, Lawrence Radway notes, "view the house as part social club and part theater." The inevitable result is mediocre legislating.

One could add that the New Hampshire legislature (officially known as the General Court) operates inefficiently because it meets only once every two years and has an exceedingly thin professional staff. Indeed, the list of disabilities of this legislature—ranging from the nation's lowest pay to the unmanageable house size to the lack of annual sessions, the high geriatric quotient, and inadequate staff—is staggering. On several occasions in recent years, New Hampshire voters have been given a chance to reform their legislature on a number of these issues. They have consistently voted "no" on change, partly because a two-thirds vote is required for constitutional change. If they are discouraged by the low level of performance they are getting, they have no one to blame but themselves.

Following through on a 1968 campaign pledge, Governor Peterson in 1969 persuaded the legislature to authorize a thorough management review of New Hampshire state government. Royden C. Sanders, Jr., president of Sanders Associates in Nashua, the state's leading electronics firm, was appointed chairman of the citizens task force to oversee the study. Among the other 15 executive committee members were Sherman Adams, Robertson Trowbridge, and Joseph A. Millimet, an outstanding attorney and Democrat from Manchester. The task force recommendations represented a bare minimum of reforms which were needed to give New Hampshire an adequate state government. But pitifully few of them were enacted—a measure of Governor Peterson's own weak leadership and the paralysis of government in the state in modern times. By the time of a special 1970 legislative session called to act on the proposals, Peterson had already watered down the package to make it politically "feasible." And by the time the legislature was finished, only two reforms of any great note had survived—setting up a state planning agency, and establishing a consumer protection division in the attorney general's office. What did *not* get approved was the real story. A partial list includes these points:

- A four-year term for the governor. The existing two-year term, the citizens task force said, makes "it difficult, if not impossible to initiate a program having any breadth of purpose and follow it through to completion. . . . A four-year term for the governor is the foundation of the edifice of reorganization." But the legislature refused to submit a constitutional amendment to lengthen the governor's term, and so did a constitutional convention that met in 1974.

■   Executive reorganization. The evidence was "overwhelming," the task force said, that the governor lacked adequate staff or clear authority. It was recommended that a secretary to the governor, to serve as his "administrative right arm," as well as an assistant for planning and a counsel to the governor, be authorized. It was also suggested that posts for four deputies to the governor, responsible respectively for fiscal affairs, administration, human concerns, and natural resources be set up. All existing executive departments, agencies, and commission would be regrouped within those administrative divisions.

Net result by 1975: virtually no executive branch reorganizations.

■   Executive council. The task force said the executive council should be reduced to an advisory role only, to be followed by a reexamination of whether the council was necessary at all. But by 1975, the council remained intact, its power essentially unchanged since the 19th century.

■   Legislative reform. The legislature should have annual (instead of biennial) sessions, the house should be reduced in size, and the pay of legislators should be increased, the task force said. Net result by 1975: zero. The 1974 constitutional convention did, however, recommend that legislators be paid the same daily rate as the lowest grade of classified state employee rather than the existing $200 per biennium. That change was to be submitted to the people in 1976. In addition, while refusing to change the 400-member figure for the lower house, the convention did recommend that the senate be increased from 24 to 36 members. That change—generally recognized as desirable by experts on the state government—was submitted to the people in November 1974 and rejected.

■   Revitalizing county government. The task force said the counties should be given broader powers, because so many city or town problems had become regional in character. Redrawing of county lines along more rational and convenient lines was also suggested. Net result by 1975: no change.

■   Create a state housing authority. The task force said there was an urgent need for more and better housing in the state, and that the lack of it worked to the detriment of the general welfare of New Hampshire's people and as an extreme deterrent to the state's economic growth. By 1975, however, the state housing authority was still not a reality.

■   School reform. The glaring inadequacies of elementary and secondary education in the state were noted: inefficient and uneconomical small school districts, a state department of education without adequate staff to execute existing laws to organize and lead education, lack of free public kindergartens in 158 of the 183 school districts, nonexistent special education programs for 82 percent of the state's handicapped children, and the lowest level of state aid to local school districts of any state in the Union. "The property tax thus bears the giant share of education costs, and this has chilling implications for the future, with the per pupil rate for the cost of education outrunning enrollment increases by 2 to 1," the task force noted. Figures were cited showing that the 25 poorest districts in the state were taxing themselves at twice the rate per pupil as the 25 richest, yet were able to raise only two-thirds as much money for each pupil. Moreover, the state foundation aid program, designed to reduce financial inequalities between districts, was being funded at only 18 percent of its authorized level (a figure that was to drop to 7 percent in 1973–74 because of the skinflint attitude of the state legislators).

A broad array of school reforms was recommended: drawing up a master plan to effect a substantial reduction in the number of school districts, additional appropriations for a revitalized state department of education, mandatory state-wide kindergarten programs with state assistance, making special education available for all handicapped children, and full foundation aid funding.

Instead of moving in these fruitful directions, it might be noted, New Hampshire instead decided in the mid-'70s to experiment with the so-called school voucher plan, under which parents can cash in educational vouchers at any private, nonsectarian school. However promising the voucher plan, proposed originally by conservative economist Milton Friedman, might appear as a way to provide freedom of choice to parents and stimulate the sometimes lethargic public education community, New Hampshire with its tradition of poorly funded public schools seemed like a very poor place to inaugurate it on a wide scale.

■ Higher education. New Hampshire, the task force noted, ranks third among the states in the number of students who leave for higher education elsewhere. Erratic funding of the University of New Hampshire and the state colleges, growing out of "a marathon battle of wits" between the university, the governor, and the legislature each biennium, was cited as a key problem; the solution was said to lie in finding a consistent budgetary formula. Major improvements were also urged in the junior college and vocational technical school area; in vocational education in particular, it was noted, the state was losing millions of dollars of available 4–1 formula federal matching funds because of its own anemic effort. Again, no major change was effected in the four years following the recommendations, except for some notable advances in vocational education.

■ Mental health. The task force touched lightly on this perennial disaster area of New Hampshire government, urging that the New Hampshire State Hospital at Concord—the state institution for the mentally ill—be given increased appropriations lest it lose its accreditation, and that more adequate state funds be made available for the series of 17 community health centers begun in the mid-1960s. There has been widespread agreement in the state that the community mental health centers, offering treatment in a patient's home area, offer much better chances for rehabilitation than the distant, understaffed and underfinanced state hospital.

Some increase in funds did result from the citizens task force report. But not nearly enough. In August 1972 the state hospital, a grim collection of 30 buildings, some more than a century old, lost its national accreditation. As writer Daniel Yergin noted: "It deserved to lose it. The treatment is substandard. Records are poorly kept. Overcrowding in some wards has run as high as 50 percent. There is only one kitchen, and food is invariably cold when it reaches patients. Heating and ventilation are inadequate, and the stench of urine creeps through the buildings. The only time some wards get cleaned is when the patients in them are well enough to do the work. Only a children's center, the most recently constructed building, meets the national Life Safety Code. The present hospital has even lacked a superintendent for much of the last six years."

In 1974 Dr. Margaret M. Riggs, chief psychologist of the state division of mental health, pointed with pride to the steadily decreasing number of patients at the state hospital as a result of screening that diverts many potential admittees to the community health centers. But as for the patients still at the Concord facility, many of them long-term cases, she noted: "There is still not enough active treatment to go around. New Hampshire Hospital will not be reaccredited until there is."

■   Welfare. The task force recommended that benefits in the four family service programs—aid to the aged, blind, disabled, and families—"be raised in accordance with evident needs."

Indeed, between 1968 and 1974, the budget for the state division of welfare did more than triple, from $14 million to $53 million. Even with the increased appropriations, New Hampshire could not be called particularly generous in the welfare area. There had been a time (in the 1950s) when New Hampshire's welfare levels were well above national averages in all categories, but in recent years that has been far from the case. The amounts of its grants for the old, blind, and disabled stand well below the rest of the nation; only in aid for families and dependent children is the average New Hampshire figure above the national average, but even there it lags behind every New England state except Maine. The state's eligibility critera are so tough that overall, it spends just $4.88 per inhabitant for welfare each year, a figure that looks rather miserly compared to a national average of $8.70. The figure for Vermont is $8.14, for Maine $8.59, for Massachusetts $14.07.

Conservative New Hampshire politicians, particularly Governor Thomson, have virtually made a career of attacks on welfare chiseling—but failed to prove that it exists in very large measure. Based on a 1974 interview with Thomas Hooker, the state welfare director, the *New Hampshire Times* reported:

You don't hear of chiselers and gold bricks, of women paid to have babies, or of men paid not to work.
What you hear about are New Hampshireites who are alone, without the

money, youth, health or skills which would enable them to care for themselves or their children.

You hear about 254 blind people who are unable to earn a decent living either because they lack employment opportunities or employable skills.

You are told about 1,900 foster children whose fate and future are in the hands of the welfare agency.

He talks of the 4,127 persons over 65 who have worked and saved, but not enough to keep up with the rising costs of food and medical care, of rent and fuel.

And of battered and neglected children whose physical wellbeing depends upon the swift intervention of his agency's social workers. . . .

"Welfare departments," asserts Hooker, "are the receptacles of the failures of other systems. They should assume a more aggressive role in pointing up the inadequacies in those systems and the need to eliminate the deficiencies as the means of slowing the rate of welfare growth."

▪ Human rights. Interestingly, the citizens task force recommended a rather full resolution "recognizing the primacy of individual human rights as the foundation of law and justice in our state." In most states, the listed rights would be accepted and guaranteed with little question. But when one reads some of the recommended articles in the light of subsequent developments in New Hampshire, one wonders: Examples:

"Each New Hampshire citizen has the right to decent shelter, clothing, and food as basic necessities of existence. This right cannot be abrogated because of a citizen's inability to produce." Yet in recent years the state has dragged its feet on making food stamps generally available, done little to foster better housing, and watched its governor and leading newspaper launch vendettas against welfare recipients.

"Each New Hampshire citizen has a right to privacy of his personal life and economic affairs. Such rights may not be usurped for economic expediency or bureaucratic convenience." The framers might have added— "or for political gain or reprisal," for that indeed seemed to be Governor Thomson's motivation in searching the government-held records of his political opponents (of which more later).

"Each New Hampshire citizen has the right to join peacefully with others to communicate on any issue public or private, either in person or through the media without harassment." Our previous subchapter on the Manchester *Union-Leader*, particularly the point that so many actual or potential participants in New Hampshire public life have to fear below-the-belt attacks on themselves or their families, suggests that this right is in dire jeopardy in the modern-day Granite State.

In the human rights area, one might also take note of the hostile legislative reaction to the more important of the recommendations made by the commission on laws affecting children, appointed by Governor Peterson in 1972 and chaired by a former majority leader of the New Hampshire house. In its final report in 1973, the commission blamed "publicity seeking politicians, pretentious publishers, indifferent officials, insensitive probation officers, regressive magistrates and apathetic disciples of the revulsionary press" for the defeat of so many of its legislative proposals—every one of which, the commission claimed, was a "constructive, impartial humanizing piece of legislation."

■   Environment. "Unspoiled surroundings," the citizen's task force said, "are essential not only to our peace of mind and our health, but also to our economy. Unless our incomparable environment—our fields, forests, lakes, streams, mountains, and the air—is protected against further damage by uncontrolled encroachment of man-made ugliness and pollution, our recreation and tourist industry will deteriorate with the environment."

Since the task force's 1970 report, New Hampshire has made some progress in these fields—a record we will review in a following section. But the state's overall record on environmental and land use control is clearly inferior to those of Vermont and Maine, and in fact worse than any other New England state.

■   Taxes. The state's revenue structure, the task force observed, failed to meet any one of the three commonly accepted criteria of a good tax system—fairness, ease of collection, and growth potential.

What the state would eventually need, the citizens said, to raise additional revenues for needed expanded state programs, would be a personal income tax, together with a business profits tax, or a sales tax, or a combination of both. "Both the personal income tax and the general sales tax and use tax," it was observed, "possess the qualities of fairness, ease of collection and responsiveness to increases in economic activity. In addition, they are flexible and allow a wide choice of possible exemptions to shield low-income and fixed-income citizens from hardship."

In response to the task force suggestions, the legislature in 1970 did enact two reforms. It abolished a number of outmoded business taxes on factory machinery, inventory, and the like, instituting in their place a 6 percent tax (later raised to 7 percent) on business profits. It also enacted a 4 percent tax on the income of people who commute to work in New Hampshire but have residences outside (a law declared unconstitutional by the U.S. Supreme Court in 1975). But a sales tax or income tax on its own residents? Heaven forbid!

Instead, while local property taxes have soared from $66 million a year in 1960 to well over $200 million annually in the early 1970s, New Hampshire has sought to nickel and dime its way through with its familiar array of taxes on all "sins" except sex. These include beer, liquor, cigarette, and racetrack taxes, plus the revenues realized from the state-owned liquor stores and sweepstakes. Together, they make up close to two-thirds of the state government's revenues (excluding federal aid). The rationale for them was spelled out by John W. King, the three-term Democratic governor of the 1960s: "The plain truth is that we could not run New Hampshire without these so-called 'sin taxes.' They pay the state's bills. They also introduce an element of choice into taxation. No ordinary person can escape a sales tax or an income tax. But he can choose not to smoke, drink, or play the horses, and thereby avoid the taxes on these activities." Then Governor Peterson made the same argument in an interview I had with him, calling all these sources of revenue "voluntary" taxes. (By the same reasoning, one supposes, New Hampshire could set up a string of gambling casinos and state-run brothels and reap the profits which they could also bring from "sinning" Massachusetts citizens crossing the border. Indeed, there might be all-purpose "houses" crowding the Massachusetts border. Downstairs, one could buy liquor and cigarettes, gamble and buy lottery tickets. Upstairs, the ladies of pleasure could wait. The morals of the Granite State's own citizens might be protected by requiring out-of-state identification for anyone wanting to sample the upstairs delights. If all this sounds preposterous, consider this: in 1975 Governor Thomson did come out squarely for casino gambling in New Hampshire, and as requested in his capital budget, two state-run stores have just been constructed on the turnpike, a few miles from the Massachusetts border, to sell liquor and lottery tickets. They are open seven days a week, including evenings.

New Hampshire's biggest source of "sin tax" revenue—more than a quarter of its budget—is from liquor sales. And the state is not modest about advertising its cheap booze or encouraging people to burn up gasoline in a petroleum-scarce era in order to get to New Hampshire and buy it. I quote from the state liquor commission's introduction to its 1974 retail price list:

> New Hampshire's liquor pricing structure has remained unchanged since May 6, 1968. This policy decision has made our retail prices attractive enough to bring consumers throughout the Northeast to our stores.
> Even throughout the energy crisis customers have found that the dollars saved buying in New Hampshire more than offset the increase in gas prices. . . .
> Since New Hampshire's gasoline allocation was a generous one, we expect supplies to remain plentiful. . . . Come on up, over or down to New Hampshire, it's your best investment in your gasoline dollar.

Leaving aside the questionable patriotism of this pitch, it also reflects the parasitic nature of New Hampshire financing. Each bottle of liquor bought by outsiders means that much less tax revenue for their own home states—revenue their own states need to finance necessary government services. The same applies when outsiders drive into New Hampshire to buy "big tag" retail items (television sets and the like) and thus avoid their own state sales taxes.

New Hampshire's sweepstakes program—pegged to the horse races at Rockingham Park—was voted by the legislature in 1963 on the theory that it would be a big help for local schools, for whom the revenues were earmarked, and help obviate the need for a broad-based tax. Governor King, who signed the legislation setting up the first legal sweepstakes lottery in 20th-century America, dismissed opposition as an outmoded vestige of the Puritan ethic. The idea has certainly taken hold; from 1964, when New Hampshire was the lonely leader and grossed $5.7 million, the lottery idea spread until in 1974 12 states were running lotteries with a gross of $681 million.* But if New Hampshire hoped for a financial panacea for its school funding problems, it was sorely mistaken. The net proceeds per pupil for education were $24.15 in 1964, the first year; they declined to a measly $5.79 in 1970 but then climbed again to the $15–$17 range in 1972–73 when the sweepstakes commission reduced the price of tickets from $3 to 50 cents and instituted drawings every week (instead of a few times a year). The "take" hardly dented actual school expenditures, which ranged from $775 a year for each elementary school pupil to $1,004 for a senior high school student. And New Hampshire still ranked 50th among the 50 states in its level of state aid to education.

No scandals marred the sweepstakes program in its first decade of operation, but there had long been—and remained—serious doubts about the racetracks themselves. Until quite recently, between 10 and 15 percent of the members of the legislature were visibly in the employ of the racing interest, either through jobs at the track or in other capacities.† The New Hampshire Jockey Club fought long and hard to keep out dog racing, but that battle was lost in 1969, and two dog tracks were operating by the early 1970s. The state gets a part of the take from the tracks, but the dog lobby is so powerful that it has persuaded the legislature to give a higher percentage of the take to the track operators. Governor Thomson has had secret meetings with the dog track operators. In 1973 Thomas Thessier, a law partner of senate president David Nixon and a member of the state greyhound racing commission, incurred the wrath of the operators when he voted against allowing a certain dog racing company to set up a track in New Hampshire. He received a telephone call threatening to murder him and his family if he refused to change his mind; when he didn't, he was beaten gangland style outside his home in Manchester.

Scandal has also touched the immensely powerful state liquor commission, which controls prices, advertising displays, and in effect the relative success of various liquor brands in the state stores. The commission can—and does—arrange for gifts of free liquor, for having campaign contributions made or not made, and the like. In 1972 Rod Paul of the Con-

* The others were Connecticut, Massachusetts, New York, New Jersey, Pennsylvania, Maryland, and Michigan, with Rhode Island, Maine, Illinois, and Ohio joining the pack in 1974. The reader will note that every New England state save Vermont was on the lottery list. What most New Englanders failed to realize was that the lotteries, in terms of making any significant dent on the bill for state and local government, were a dismal failure. They accounted for only five-tenths of one percent of government costs in New Hampshire, the same percentage in Massachusetts, six-tenths of one percent in Rhode Island, four-tenths of one percent in Connecticut, and two-tenths of one percent in Maine.

Washington State would have joined the group if Governor Daniel Evans had not vetoed a bill to make his state the first west of the Mississippi to sponsor a lottery. Lotteries, Evans said, had been shown to be "an unreliable source of steady income." And he added: "For the first time, our state government would be engaging itself in a gambling activity as a principal participant. . . . I am extremely reluctant to approve a measure which would result in the state, by its actions, fostering a climate of gambling that may . . . lead to professional gambling and the various forms of criminal activity associated therewith." It was the kind of sentiment one might have expected, in years past, to hear from a New England governor.

† Under a bill of recent vintage, members of the legislature are forbidden to work at the racetracks.

cord *Monitor* revealed that the liquor commission chairman had accepted a $7,000 "finder's fee" from a Massachusetts advertising firm to which he had directed one big liquor company, Schenley's. The implication was that Schenley's whiskey would be taken off the state liquor list or relegated to back shelves if it was not willing to use the designated Massachusetts firm. Informed of the affair, the governor and executive council gave the liquor commission chairman a light slap on the wrist.

If one subscribes to the theory that "where there's smoke, there's fire," then the likelihood is that aggressive investigation would reveal substantial corruption in the various "sin"-related activities of New Hampshire state government. One could mark it down as yet another price of the polluted public process in the state.

Unless New Hampshire chooses to abrogate totally its responsibilities for education and social services, the day of an income tax or sales tax—or both—is probably not far distant. Robertson Trowbridge noted that liquor revenues and "sin-tax" type revenues were peaking out, and that a big short-fall was in sight on the general state budget in the latter part of the '70s.* New Hampshireites may not like taxes, he noted, but they also expect services—a decent university education for their children, treatment for relatives in mental institutions, and the like. A general sales tax would relieve the pinch on the general state budget; an income tax could be used to rebate some $150 million a year to the local school districts on a per capita basis, thus canceling out some 70 percent of the local property tax currently used to support the schools.

The *Union Leader*, everyone agrees, will continue its ferocious opposition to any kind of broad-based tax—probably even if William Loeb himself passes from the scene. Moreover, the tax phobia among the less affluent, ethnic-heritage part of New Hampshire's population remains formidable. Trowbridge recited an experience he had trying to sell his legislation to institute an income tax to pay the lion's share of local school costs. He went to the town of Greenville, heavily populated by French-Canadian and Finnish textile workers—a town with a per capita property tax close to the highest in the United States. "I could prove with geometric logic," Trowbridge said, "that 90 percent of the population of Greenville would gain moneywise from my bill. But the reaction was: 'You change it and who knows where it's going to go? How can you guarantee that the next legislature won't take it [the tax rebate] away, or up the tax, or something else?'" Workers of this heritage, Trowbridge said, have barely made it economically. Their horizons are often limited to keeping the mortgage under control and holding on to their jobs. Concepts like improving the quality of life are often beyond their ken; in fact, Trowbridge suggested, they have "a low level of life expectation" fused with a fear they may lose what they

* Indeed, a budget deficit of as much as $25 million loomed in the winter of 1975 when the Supreme Court declared invalid New Hampshire's income tax on out-of-state workers. But Massachusetts inadvertently bailed out New Hampshire again, by enacting such stiff increases in its liquor and cigarette taxes that New Hampshire could expect that much more across-the-border business.

have. Their attitude on schools reflects their attitude toward a great deal of the society around them: "leave the schools alone, leave me alone."

But there is a new ingredient in New Hampshire—the recent arrivals in the southern part of the state. And they may be the progenitors of change in the near future. They may have come into New Hampshire to avoid taxes, Trowbridge noted, but they then demand precisely the level of services they had in Massachusetts. According to this line of reasoning, New Hampshire, the state which apparently abhors taxes more than any other constituency in the English-speaking world, will finally be obliged to bite the bullet and face fiscal reality before too many more winters pass. One can only imagine the bloody donnybrook the tax battle will occasion.

Governor Thomson: Calendar of the Bizarre

I hesitate to devote an entire subchapter to a single small-state governor, but the temptation in the case of Meldrim Thomson, Jr., is irresistible. Within the past generation, to the best of my knowledge, there has not been another governor of an American state who has acted in such a bizarre (and often illegal) fashion. Citizens of other states occasionally upset with their governors should consider just these highlights * of Thomson's first term in office:

Jan. 4, 1973—Thomson got his term off to a secure start by having all the locks changed in the State House executive offices. The same day, he spoke of the "leniency" within the state judiciary and called it the "weakest" branch of state government.

Jan. 22—By executive order, the governor ordered the summary resignations of all members of the governor's commission on crime and delinquency without advance notice to them. One of the members was William Grimes, a state supreme court justice and nationally noted authority on crime.

Jan. 23—Thomson secretly dispatched his administrative assistant to search through the business profits tax returns of his political enemies, including associates of Walter Peterson. Also sought out were tax records on businesses in which Dartmouth College—a favorite enemy of the state's archconservatives—might have owned an interest. On the same day, Thomson secretly slipped out of the state to drive to Wellesley, Massachusetts, to the offices of the federally supported New England Organized Crime Intelligence System. There he demanded to inspect the files of political foes, including Senator Thomas McIntyre. When the state supreme court subsequently ruled the search of business profits tax files illegal, the governor said he was entitled to interpret the state constitution as he saw it "and not as it is understood by others."

At a later state legislative hearing on Thomson's probe into the crime

* For major portions of the chronology cited, I am indebted to an anonymous Thomson watcher who relied solely on the public record.

files in Massachusetts, Senator McIntyre charged that the governor's actions represented "misuse of official authority for either vengeful politics or, to put it gently, bizarre and inexplicable purposes." "Good Lord, enough's enough!" McIntyre said. "This is America. . . . This is *New England!*"

Feb. 12—Thomson summarily canceled an agreement with Maine on the extension of the states' border into the Atlantic, without either consulting Maine officials or trying to work out a compromise. His action, along with the arrest of a lobsterman in disputed waters, was to balloon into an all-out border "war" with Maine.

March 1—The comptroller's office revealed that the governor's office was overspending its monthly budget by 30 percent, in seven different areas. In his campaign, Thomson had pledged to cut spending in the governor's office by 25 percent.

April 6—Thomson at a news conference displayed his disdain for environmental groups ("governors have been frightened by the environmentalists") and began what would become a personal crusade to locate an oil refinery in New Hampshire: "I would be willing to do anything I can to encourage the establishment of a refinery. . . . Let's get a refinery here and get the crude oil here." Later, speaking to the New Hampshire petroleum council, he said that to bring oil to the state, it would be necessary to "drill in the mountains and drill in the valleys."

April 10—Thomson threatened to revoke the charter of Franconia College after a conference was held there on prison problems. Charter granting and revocation is exclusively the power of the legislature.

July 12—After some damage occurred during a conference at Plymouth State College, allegedly caused by black students, Thomson found it appropriate to wire President Nixon calling for a federal investigation.

Aug. 4—Thomson became terribly upset and fell into an argument with auxiliary police at the North Haverhill Fair because they would not salute him.

Aug. 10—The governor declared he would not allow newsmen into the state prison to cover legislative hearings because such an act would be "a first step toward allowing citizen observers inside. . . . Citizen observers will never be permitted inside that prison as long as I am governor. I am not going to turn this state over to the hoodlums."

Aug. 26—Thomson lashed out at environmental groups trying to halt further construction of interstate highways, declaring: "Our civilization as we know it is going to be brought to an unfortunate halt" by such actions.

Sept. 24—Thomson exchanged letters and telegrams with U.S. Senators Sam C. Ervin, Jr., and Lowell P. Weicker, Jr., accusing Watergate investigators in New Hampshire of "Gestapo tactics." Ervin dismissed the charges for lack of substantiation, and Weicker returned Thomson's letter with a postscript reading: "Some nut is using your official letterhead and signing your name to it."

Oct. 16—It was disclosed that Thomson had written to the Department of the Navy, inviting location of the communication grid network called Operation Sanguine in New Hampshire. He apparently failed to realize that the project would require an area at least half the size of the entire state.

Nov. 9—Just after announcing drastic measures deemed necessary to deal with the fuel crisis (including a 50-mile-an-hour speed limit), Thomson raced to Newport High School at 85 miles an hour, using his blue light to pass "slow" cars on the way. This was but one of several occasions on which he used his blue light and siren to pull over slower cars, even attempting to give people tickets for failing to get out of his way.

Nov. 29—Thomson denounced the New Hampshire Legal Assistance program and declared that he intended to veto "with great relish" a federal grant of $350,000 to support its activities.

Dec. 15—Thomson delivered an ultimatum to the University of New Hampshire board of trustees: "Either you take firm, fair and positive action to rid your campus of socially abhorrent activities (i.e., a gay students organization) or I, as Governor, will stand solidly against the expenditure of one more cent of taxpayers' money for your institution." (Court orders stopped university officials from banning the homosexuals' organization.)

Jan. 4, 1974—Thomson said he directed the state purchasing officer to order a new 1974 Lincoln Continental despite its poor gas mileage. "I would not advise the average citizen to do this, but the state benefits from the tremendous amount of work I can do in the car."

Jan. 31—The impeachment charges against President Nixon, Thomson said, were "without any substantiation" and would "fall flat on their face."

April 23—Thomson criticized Vice President Ford, saying he "has apparently joined the noisy pack that would drive President Nixon out of office without presenting any evidence of wrongdoing."

June 13—Complaining that New Hampshire wasn't getting any money from the arrangement, Thomson threatened to withdraw the state from the New England Regional Commission.

June 21—"Thoughtless" judges were making "downright stupid decisions" out of a misguided sense of social concern; they represented, Thomson said, "the greatest internal danger to our American civilization."

Sept. 1—Thomson suggested moving the state capital out of Concord to some suburban location a few miles distant.

Sept. 14—President Ford, Thomson said, was on "sound ground" when he pardoned former President Nixon "as an act of mercy." Three days later, Thomson said Ford's proposal for amnesty for draft-dodgers and deserters was "the most disgraceful act ever perpetrated against American veterans by an American President." Thomson then declared an "Anti-Amnesty Week" in New Hampshire.

Oct. 8–12—Rod Paul of the Concord *Monitor* reported that between January 1973 and June 1974, no fewer than 138 telephone calls were made from Thomson's office to the homes of William Loeb in Massachusetts and Nevada. The pattern of calls showed clearly that Thomson had been in touch with Loeb most frequently just prior to a number of his most controversial statements, vetoes, and executive orders.

The *Monitor* story, in fact, led inexorably to the conclusion that Meldrim Thomson, the man of William Loeb's creation as a viable New Hampshire politician, remained at the publisher's beck and call.

Three weeks later, Thomson was elected for another term. As many interviews with voters showed, he remained a popular man because he stood as a bulwark against higher taxes—a fighter, they said, for the little man.

Economy: The Bright Side

However grave New Hampshire's public policy failings may be, there is no gainsaying the spectacular economic growth of the state in the past quarter century. The population rate growth, which lagged behind the national level for almost a century after the Civil War, began to pick up in the 1950s, reached a remarkable level of 21.6 percent between 1960 and 1970, and was 9.5 percent in the first four years of the 1970s alone. The most impressive increase has been in the 15-to-29-year-old age group, where the young and potential workers—the promise of a society's future —are located. And while it still has a large retiree population, New Hampshire was one of only eight states in the United States in which the percentage of people 65 or older actually declined during the 1960s. (Two of the others were Vermont and Connecticut.) New Hampshire now has so much fresh blood as a result of in-migration that barely half its population was born there. Reflecting the heavy spillover from Massachusetts, 15 percent of New Hampshire residents were Massachusetts-born in 1970.

Even discounting for inflation, one has to be impressed by the growth of the gross state product—up from $1.6 billion in 1960 to $3.1 billion in 1970. Anyone who still has a vision of New Hampshire as a bucolic state will be quickly disabused of the idea when he looks at the breakdown of the gross state product. Some farming remains, concentrated in dairy farming, apple orchards, maple sugar production, and the like, but only Alaska and Rhode Island have lower farm income and fewer farm acres. Farming accounts for a scant one percent of the gross state product. Manufacturing, by contrast, represents 34 percent. Only Indiana, Michigan, Ohio, and South Carolina have a greater percentage of their work force employed in factories. New Hampshire's unemployment rate, which used to be above that of the country at large, dropped below the national average in 1955 and has stayed there ever since. In 1966 and 1968 it dipped to 1.8 percent, the lowest figure recorded for any state of the Union since World War II. In 1973, when the national figure was 4.8 percent, New Hampshire's jobless percentage was just 3.9 percent; until the national recession began to worsen rapidly in late 1974, New Hampshire's unemployment percentage was still only 4.7 percent, compared to 7.0 percent for New England as a whole and 5.3 percent for the nation.

The essential reason for New Hampshire's robust economic health is that the state's "Golden Triangle" from Manchester to Nashua to Portsmouth is fast replacing Massachusetts' Route 128 "Golden Horseshoe" as the industrial growth center of New England. New Hampshire has attracted (some would say pirated) dozens of large and small Route 128 companies in the past several years. Between 1960 and 1970, some 300 new manufacturing plants opened in the state; of these, only a third were firms already doing business in New Hampshire. Some of the growth, particularly in southern New Hampshire, was probably an inevitable spillover from the Route 128 complex. But New Hampshire leaders claim that their low tax, low spending, probusiness climate had a lot to do with it. The tax argument is a strong one—particularly when figures (for 1972–73) show a per capita tax of only $454 in New Hampshire, compared to $714 in Massachusetts or $618 in Vermont. But the New Hampshire business profits tax —important to employers considering a move into the state—is not significantly lower than the Massachusetts corporate income tax, and actually higher than the comparable levy in Vermont. Moreover, New Hampshire businesses must help to pay the fearsome local property taxes necessitated by the absence of a broad-based state tax.

So to the low-tax explanation for New Hampshire's industrial growth, one should add other significant factors: low wages; exceedingly weak unions, which have succeeded in organizing only 17 percent of the work force (the lowest level in New England); and comparatively lax environmental standards. All these factors, plus gimmicks like state-guaranteed loans for new businesses and tax-exempt revenue bond financing for new plants and equipment, have succeeded handsomely in drawing industry. But there is a real question as to how long it can all last. In the words of an official of the New England Regional Commission, "New Hampshire may look good on paper, but in fact it is on the verge of bankruptcy because of its imbalanced tax structure. Northern New Hampshire is in classic decline and decay, and schools and housing are inadequate. Sooner or later it has got to come up with better revenue sources to provide government services."

The low-wage profile of New Hampshire merits special attention because it raises serious questions about the quality of life for the state's people. Ever since the Civil War, wages for New Hampshire workers have lagged 10 to 20 percent behind the national and the New England-wide level, and even with all the job growth of recent years, there are few signs that the income gap for New Hampshire workers is closing appreciably. Traditional New Hampshire industries like textiles and shoes are notorious low payers, and except for a certain percentage of highly skilled personnel, the new growth industry of electrical components is also a low wage paying industry. Whether old or new, New Hampshire industries tend to be of the labor-intensive type not heavily dependent on employees of higher skills, training, and education, who can demand higher wage rates. The same low-skill, low-wage profile dominates the big recreation industry, which brings some $400 million a year into New Hampshire. Per capita income figures for the state mirror the problem: while they have risen sharply since

World War II, as in all states, in 1974 they were still 9 percent behind the national average and 13 percent behind the figure for New England as a whole. Since 1960, in fact, New Hampshire's income picture relative to the nation and New England has actually deteriorated somewhat. The picture would be even worse if a high proportion of male family heads in New Hampshire did not "moonlight" on second jobs or if the state did not have one of the highest percentages of working mothers in the entire nation. "It's a bad thing," Senator McIntyre noted, "when Johnny comes home from school."

New Hampshire people can, of course, take much comfort in the fact that while they may be employed at somewhat substandard wages, at least they do have jobs. And just a few decades ago, it was not at all sure that their future would be so secure. There are still thousands of New Hampshire people who recall vividly the day in 1936 that the Amoskeag Manufacturing Company at Manchester, the colossus of the textile world, collapsed. Fifteen thousand people lost their means of livelihood and New Hampshire's greatest city was thrown into a state of semiparalysis. For Amoskeag had been more than a single textile company; it had been the world's largest, the very embodiment of capitalistic success in New England. The first mill had been begun at Manchester in 1805; five years later the name Amoskeag appeared for the first time; overcoming initial difficulties, Amoskeag prospered and expanded for a century thereafter in its 45 acres of red-brick mills in double and triple tiers beside the Merrimack River, filled with 700,000 spindles and 23,000 looms, turning out 147,000 miles of cloth every year. It was an exploitive industry in the truest sense. In the early days, many children were employed, no woman worker would be paid more than one dollar a day; later the company assiduously recruited French-Canadian and other foreign workers because for $1.50 a day they would work from 6:40 in the morning to 6:00 at night, uncomplaining and unlikely to join labor unions.

The factors that brought Amoskeag down were multiple: pay reductions which enraged the workers; a series of costly strikes in the 1920s and early 1930s; Southern competition; the Depression; Amoskeag's inability to shift from its ancient specialty of simple cotton gingham ("grey goods," as the saying went) to the newly popular rayon fabrics; absentee ownership that let the equipment become obsolete; and finally unseemly financial machinations of the trustees who were charged with putting their own winnings aside and callously letting the mill die. The psychic blow for Manchester—and the entire New Hampshire textile industry—could scarcely be underestimated. Francis Brown wrote in the New York *Times* in November 1936:

> The grilled gates are locked and the fallen leaves swirl beyond them in the mill yard which the weeds have occupied. In places grass has overgrown the railway sidings, while around newer buildings on the river's right bank the shrubbery is already tangled and unkempt. Paint peels from exposed woodwork. Electric lights are broken. On the clock tower the hands stand obstinately at 8.

Textiles and the other nondurable goods manufacturing that had always dominated the New Hampshire industrial scene did not, of course, fade away with that single factory closing. Despite the influx of new types of factories during World War II, in 1947 some 74 percent of the workers in the state still were in the nondurable line—23,000 in textiles, 21,000 in footwear and other leather goods, 7,500 in paper products. But in 1948 there was another spectacular closing—that of Nashua Manufacturing Company, a firm founded in 1823 with Daniel Webster as one of the incorporators, which had been turning out textile goods under the famed Indian Head label for the following 125 years. Textile firms continued to flee, contract, or go out of business, until in the early 1970s they had only 6,600 employees in the entire state. Footwear and leather were down to 14,000 workers—still the largest single job provider. But by the '70s it was clear that New Hampshire had effected a basic transformation of its manufacturing base. The electric equipment industry, which had only 700 workers back in 1947, had 13,000 employees (albeit down from a peak of 18,000 in 1968); nonelectrical equipment manufacturers employed another 10,000 workers; the rubber and plastics industry was up to 7,000 from an insignificant number at the end of World War II. And if one measured value added by the various industry groupings, these "new" industries accounted for substantially more of New Hampshire's output than the traditional ones. The close association of New Hampshire industry with that of Massachusetts was now clear, because in both states the combination of electrical and nonelectrical equipment accounted for the largest employment pool and the greatest amount of value added.

Significantly, New Hampshire's largest corporation and employer—Sanders Associates of Nashua—was a Massachusetts transplant. Royden Sanders, Jr., began his enterprise with several other Raytheon executives in a blacksmith shop in Waltham, Massachusetts, in 1951. Sanders had been in charge of the missile laboratory at Raytheon, where he had been responsible for the United States' first land-to-air missile. Looking around for a large laboratory and manufacturing facility, Sanders discovered that a Nashua development group was searching for a company to occupy the vast empty textile mill where the Nashua Manufacturing Company had once prospered. So the new firm moved to Nashua, and within a few years had established itself as one of the country's leading developers and makers of military electronic countermeasure systems. For many years, as much as 90 percent of the firm's business was with the Defense Department, but gradually it sold more and more of its sophisticated computer display terminals in the commercial markets. By the early 1970s the firm had moved to a gleaming seven-story corporate headquarters in a suburban location near Nashua, Manchester, and Concord. Sanders Associates' importance to New Hampshire could be measured by the fact that the second largest employer in the state, the Brown Paper Company at Berlin, had 1,920 workers, less than a third of the Sanders total.

New Hampshire, Sanders executives told me, was an easy place to relocate top scientific and technical people because they could work in a sub-urban-type setting—away from the urban "rat race"—but still be within an hour of metropolitan Boston with its arts, culture, and educational facilities. Technical personnel, they pointed out, had to stay up with their fields through special courses, and institutions like Harvard, MIT, Tufts, Northeastern, and a branch of the University of New Hampshire at Manchester provided those opportunities—at the same time workers were 45 minutes from the seacoast, an hour from the mountains, and 20 minutes from Route 128.

Geographic New Hampshire: From Connecticut Lakes to Monadnock . . .

Precious little public planning takes place in New Hampshire; indeed a Dartmouth scientist remarked to me that "New Hampshire has a planning perspective that extends no further than the next payday." Nevertheless, the state government has divided the state into six planning and development regions, and they serve quite nicely as a division of the Granite State.

The first district encompasses the upper third of the state, the lumberman's North Country and the White Mountains with their multitudinous attractions for the visitor. I like Eugene McCarthy's description of the North Country—

It is Maine or better—a land of lakes, of forests of pine and balsam and cedar and birch, of pulpwood and paper mills, with the smell of sulphur hanging over the towns. The inhabitants are either what are called native whites or French Canadians. Wood and woods are their livelihood. In Berlin and Groveton and other places the people are silent, purposeful and committed; their plaid shirts under padded blue jackets, is almost a uniform. No singing voyageurs, but men knowing the hard life, near poverty, they pay little attention to visitors and have little regard for the recreation or resort trade.

There is a modicum of tourism in the North Country, centered around the Connecticut Lakes, four small bodies of water where the Connecticut River is born. The lakes are surrounded by hunting and fishing camps, and the locals make a decent living as guides. But overwhelmingly, the North Country is woods, woods, and more woods—and isolation. Vast stretches of land are uninhabited wilderness, the refuge of the bear, the beaver, the moose, and deer in grand number. Once the area was hotly contested between Canada and New Hampshire, and the people formed their own independent Republic of Indian Stream, which existed briefly in the 1830s before New Hampshire dispatched troops to establish its ultimate control.

Berlin (1970 population 15,256) is so heavily French-Canadian that one of its two radio stations broadcasts frequently in French. The giant mill of the Brown Paper Company (now a subsidiary of Gulf & Western) has contributed grievously over the years to the pollution of the Androscoggin River, which dips briefly here into New Hampshire and then returns (with effluents added) to Maine.

Close to Berlin is the northernmost tip of the White Mountain National Forest, 1,127 square miles encompassing the everlasting hills which are the crown of New England. There are 86 well-defined mountain peaks here, of which eight rise more than a mile above sea level. The Indians—Pennacook, Coosuc, Sokoki and other Algonquin tribes—never dared ascend to the heights of these great granite hills, whence, as Ernest Poole wrote in *The Great White Hills of New Hampshire*, "great spirits launched thunder and lightning, snow and hail, avalanches and river floods down upon the mortals below." Even now these mountains can strike one with more awe than ranges of higher elevation elsewhere on the continent, simply because of the dramatic changes of elevation. At Franconia Notch ("notch" being the Yankee word for a sharp valley pass, or gap in the mountains) the visitor standing on the valley floor looks up a sheer 1,500 feet to see the stern visage of the Old Man of the Mountains, almost straight above him. At Pinkham Notch, itself more than 2,000 feet in elevation, there is the breathtaking rise of Mount Washington, another 4,000 feet in the sky.

At 6,288 feet, Washington is the highest peak in Northeastern America; so fierce is its climate that there is no timber growth above 4,800 feet, compared to more than 10,000 feet in the Rockies. The strongest wind ever recorded by man, 231 miles an hour, was noted on the summit on April 12, 1934; about every third day, year in and year out, the wind reaches hurricane velocity (74 miles an hour). During the winter of 1968–69, 569 inches of snow were recorded on the summit—though as the late Joe Dodge, who was Appalachian Club hut master and manager at Pinkham Notch for 37 years, once noted, "We'll probably never get a true measurement of snow on Mount Washington because it snows horizontally up there. It comes at you, it doesn't fall on you." Dodge also pointed out that though the lowest temperature ever recorded at the summit was 46 degrees below zero, the chill factor at minus 15 degrees with a 150-mile wind could be well below 200 degrees below zero. A weather station has been located at the summit for several decades, along with a 1952-vintage television tower; one wonders what ever could compel the weather and broadcasting crews to endure the climatic conditions of this peak where clouds blot out the view of the world some 60 percent of the time. Perhaps it is the spectacular sunrises, the northern lights, and, on a clear night, a view so unimpeded that one can see the lights of Montreal to the northwest, those of Boston to the southeast.

Viewing Mount Washington, P. T. Barnum once commented: "This is the second greatest show on earth." One assumes he was referring to the entrepreneurs' indefatigable effort to exploit the mountain for private gain. The first Summit House, anchored by foundation bolts drilled into bedrock and cables over the roof to withstand the gale winds, was built in 1852; despite demolition and a fire that destroyed all other buildings on the mountaintop in 1908, there has been a "little city" of structures there ever since. In 1861 the eight-mile, 99-curve spiral of the carriage road was completed to the summit. Eight years later came the cog railway, "the first rack-and-pinion type mountain railroad in the world." Its rickety little steam engines and passenger cars have been chugging up Washington in fair weather ever since. Anyone who has ever ascended the mountain on foot, coming perhaps over the Appalachian Trail as it traverses the Presidential peaks, or up from Pinkham Notch by the famed Tuckerman Ravine or treacherous Huntington Ravine Trails, has to be a little offended when he reaches the top. There, instead of an unspoiled summit, he finds all the tawdry buildings and the less adventurous souls stepping out of their automobiles or railway cars. I remember first climbing Washington as a boy and being shocked by the intrusion of so much "civilization" on a noble mountaintop; now that the word has become popular, I guess I had a classic "environmentalist's" reaction.

The White Mountains are served by the greatest network of foot trails in America, most of them the handiwork of the Appalachian Mountain Club, which also operates a string of nine huts with simple eating and sleeping facilities at the high elevations. One could spend the better part of a lifetime getting to know all the trails, the peaks and ravines and splendid vistas of this magnificent region; one only wishes he had the time.

Considerations of space will not permit me to review all of the attractions in or just beside the White Mountain National Forest, ranging from the famed notches (Franconia, Crawford, Pinkham) to fascinating natural sights (like Lost River), the great ski areas (including noteworthy newcomers like Waterville Valley and Sherman Adams' Loon Mountain development at Lincoln) to the exciting Kancamagus Wilderness Highway. The towns, one might add, are blessedly few and far between; the largest is Conway (4,865), a pleasant and sophisticated resort town with two of New Hampshire's famed covered bridges, many fine houses of the early Republic, and not too much of the gross commercialism that has creeped in at other places on the forest's periphery.

Of all the White Mountains, my own favorites are the peaks of the Sandwich Range in the southern part of the national forest. They bear the names of Indian chiefs—Passaconaway, Wonalancet, Kancamagus, Paugus, and Chocorua. All are lovely mountains, but the noblest of all is Chocorua, a beautifully shaped mountain topped by a pyramidal white granite cone. Seen across two small lakes at its base, it is, as one of its thousands of admirers once wrote, "everything that a New Hampshire mountain should be." Rich legend and fact surrounds the chiefs for whom the Sandwich peaks are named. Passaconaway (Child of the Bear), for instance, was a great warrior in his youth, granted land to the English settlers in 1629, was converted to Christianity, and, according to Indian belief, lived to the age of 120. "When the end of his long stay on earth drew near," according to Arthur Vose's account based on Indian legend, "he was carried in a sleigh drawn by wolves to the top of Agiochook (Mount Washington) and rose toward heaven in a chariot of fire." A less happy fate awaited Chocorua, who made friends with an English settler in Conway, Cornelius Campbell, even leaving his small son with Campbell when he went on a trip. But when Chocorua returned, he was told the boy had died of maple-syrup fox poison in Campbell's cabin; not believing the story, he brooded and then, when Campbell was at work in the fields, massacred the settler's family. At sunrise, Campbell tracked Chocorua to the top of the mountain and fired his musket at the chief. Chocorua, before giving up the spirit, then uttered his famous last words: "A curse upon you white men. May the Great Spirit curse you when he speaks in the clouds and his words are fire. Lightning blast your crops. Wind and fire destroy your homes. The Evil One breathe death on your Cattle. Panthers howl and wolves fatten on your bones."

The greatest curse that ever came to the White Mountains, though, was the work of the white man himself—the rape of their slopes for timber in the latter 19th and early 20th centuries. In 1867 the state government sold the bulk of the land in the mountain region to lumber companies for the pittance of $26,000. As Ernest Poole later wrote:

So began the era of wholesale forest slaughter by men who from small beginnings rose to employ thousands in immense areas of timberland, built little railroads, bought control of others and with them went into politics in order to be left free to wring the last dollar from the trees, first from our virgin spruce and pine and later from pulp to our second growth. . . . Fearless, ruthless, colorful men; there were a score of them at least. . . .

By 1907, seven big lumber and pulp companies owned or controlled most of our White Mountain timberlands. Two of them had adopted conservative cutting, but the others slashed down both large and small spruce, pine, balsam, birch, maple and beech. All along the mountain slopes great areas were stripped so bare as to bring our valley farms alternative floods and droughts through rapid runoffs of rain and snow from mountains where the forest-crown cover and floor were gone.

Yet this was not the worst of the damage, for as big tracts were left heaped with "slash" dry as tinder, in place of the old damp forest "swamp," the stage was set for the roar and smoke of forest fires.

Agitation to stop this despoliation began to mount around the turn of the century, symbolized by formation of the Society for the Preservation of New Hampshire Forests (SPNHF) in 1901. This group soon became and has since remained the leading conservationist organization of the state. The SPNHF and its allies fought for a full decade to have a national forest created in the White Mountains; time and again they were repulsed by timber interest lobbying, but finally in 1911 Congress passed a bill authorizing many of the early acquisitions of the U.S. Forest Service, including a million acres of timberland for a White Mountain National Forest. The purchase price was $6 million—230 times the amount for which the state had sold essentially the same land 44 years before. The sponsor of the bill was Senator John B. Weeks of Massachusetts. (Fittingly enough, Weeks was directly descended from one of a group of early New Hampshire mountaineers who had ascended Mount Washington in 1820 and, in a well-juiced party on the summit, proceeded to name the neighboring peaks Madison, Adams, Jefferson, Monroe, *et al.*) The year 1911 also marked the beginning of the state of New Hampshire's own purchase of important tracts in the heart of the mountain district. Nor, over the years, has the Society for the Preservation of New Hampshire Forests ever tired of purchasing lands when it could, or encouraging others to do so. One can easily perceive how much more difficult the preservation of natural treasures has been in the East than it was in the West, simply because of the time differential in settlement. (Another great New England example, cited in the Maine chapter, was the purchase of what is now Baxter State Park, including Mt. Katahdin.)

Environmental threats to the White Mountains have, of course, continued over time. The ever increasing number of visitors to the national forest, and especially its public campgrounds, have sometimes become intolerable. In 1970 the U.S. Forest Service was obliged to announce tight restrictions on use of parts of the forest because "the soils and vegetation cannot stand the amount of use they are getting, and the forest must be protected from further degradation."

Then there has been the threat to build a stretch of Interstate 93, massive four-lane right-of-way and all, straight through Franconia Notch. Groups like the SPNHF and Appalachian Mountain Club have fought assiduously to prevent any major widening of the existing two-lane road, arguing that an interstate would defile the narrow valley and that the rumble of heavy interstate traffic and blasting to widen the pass to accommodate four lanes would increase the chances of crumbling the Old Man of the Mountain (whose face is already tied together with metal braces to prevent further disintegration). After 15 years of dispute, Congress finally passed an amendment by New Hampshire's Senator Norris Cotton permitting (but not mandating) making the stretch of the interstate through the notch a more modest "parkway" instead. What Cotton had in mind, he said later, was a two- or three-foot widening of the two-lane road, possibly with a dividing barrier down the middle to prevent head-on accidents. But his amendment hadn't said so specifically, and conservationists still feared the highway interests would push through a four-lane interstate-type road, open to heavy commercial traffic.

Finally, environmentalists have been concerned about the efforts of developers to build large ski- and summer-vacation home projects in some of the choice parcels of land abutting the White Mountain National Forest. A substantial project was indeed built at Waterville Valley, by Tommy Corcoran (a nephew of Washington's famous "Tommy the Corc," who first rose to fame in New Deal days). But the grim economics of second-home developments in the early '70s spelled the demise of the two most massive proposed projects—one by Boise Cascade, for close to 4,000 units, and another by a Philadelphia developer for a 7,000-unit project on 10,000 acres of privately held land at Bretton Woods, directly beside Mount

Washington. The latter effort, which would have been the largest single development ever attempted in the state, ended in bankruptcy in early 1975. It had envisaged using the historic Mount Washington Hotel, one of those great snow-white summer hotels so popular with the affluent of yesteryear, as the focal point of the developer's new "sports paradise." Despite the high quality the developer wanted to bring to the Bretton Woods project, opponents contended a development of its intended scope would be an intolerable incursion in the shadow of the Presidential Range and beside one of the few remaining wild areas of the state. Nearby roads, they argued, "could be transformed into neon strips of commercial development to capitalize on increased traffic flows."

Proceeding southward, our attention turns now to the Lakes District. New Hampshire has a total of some 1,300 lakes, scattered from one border to the other, but it is here that one finds the greatest number, the largest, and the most beautiful—cool, clear bodies of water created by the glaciers, set exquisitely in the foothills of the White Mountains. The grandfather of them all is Winnipesaukee, a deeply indented body of water some 22 miles long with 274 wooded islands. This is summer camp and summer resort area *par excellence*; indeed (and somewhat alarmingly) an exploration of the sheltered coves, the islands, the headlands and wooded peninsulas reveals precious few stretches of lakeside not filled with summer places. The worst excretion of all is Wiers Beach, on the western shore, an egregiously overdeveloped, carnival-like spot that a sensible state government would have long since swept away as a public nuisance. Few other spots on the lake smell of such gross commercialism, but Winnipesaukee—once likened to "a liquid sheet of burnished silver"—has had serious problems with water pollution in recent years. They result from thousands of private septic systems lining its 175 miles of shoreline and 75 inhabited islands, the treated wastes from three municipalities, the thousands of registered power boats, and high concentrations of public bathing. The dangers of large outbreaks of algae growth have prompted an ambitious regional water control program, aimed particularly at adequate sewage treatment for the effluent of the cities and towns in the area. The public began to recognize the dimensions of the threat to the Winnipesaukee region when a new citizens group, the Lakes Region Clear Water Association, revealed in 1969 that Lake Winnisquam, beside Laconia on Winnipesaukee's western flank, was suffering serious eutrophication. The culprit turned out to be the city of Laconia and its overburdened sewage treatment plant.

All of the other lakes of the region—Squam, Ossipee, Newfound, and farther to the west, Lake Sunapee—have come under close scrutiny for incipient algae problems. The cleanest of them all, state officials told me, is Newfound (once named Pasaquaney), a piece of news I received with no little joy since it is there that my Boston grandfather had the wonderful foresight to acquire a delightful gingerbread-style summer house, directly by the water's edge, soon after the turn of this century. From the balcony of that cottage, which my wife and I now own, we can look down and see our school of "pet" fish swimming in for scraps of bread. Indeed, it is easy to be spoiled by a lake where you can see every detail on the sand and rock bottom, to several tens of feet depth, and drink the water without a qualm. A lifetime of summers at Newfound have made me, of course, hopelessly prejudiced in the lake's favor, but in research for this book I was gratified to find many writers alluding to it as the most beautiful in New Hampshire. The glacier fortuitously scooped very deeply to form Newfound, leaving steep and lovely hills close-in on its sides and a body of water of "human" scale, just seven miles in length. Add to that the continued presence of several large parcels of little-developed land, and the absence of any polluting town on the shorelines, and you have the prescription applied to Chocorua among the mountains—"everything a New Hampshire lake should be." I have friends, of course, who would say the same of Sunapee or other lakes, and even Newfound suffers from a few stretches of ticky-tack development testifying to developer avarice and townfather shortsightedness.

For the most part, the Lakes Region remains deeply rural, though the cities of Laconia (14,888) and Franklin (7,292), and even some very lightly populated towns, offer a variety of manufacturing jobs to balance the tourist income. Many people commute to jobs in the Concord and Manchester area; the growing commuter population, combined with the ski and summer resort business and activities like the regional Vocational College in Laconia, have led to state projections that the regional population will rise from 57,200 in 1970 to 160,000 by the year 2020. In this instance, one can only hope the planners are grossly overestimating the growth to come. Because the charm and uniqueness of this part of New Hampshire, aside from its lakes and mountains, lies in the pristine beauty of its little towns and villages—places like Plymouth, filled with historic 17th- and 18th-century homes and the home of a state college, Ossipee and Moultonboro and picturesque Center Harbor at the head of Lake Winnipesaukee, hilltop New London with its Colby Junior College and summer theater, and precious little town green villages like Goshen and Hebron.

Over to the west, one comes on Lebanon (9,725), Hanover (8,494) with its Dartmouth, and other settlements along the Connecticut River. This region is marked by its fertile intervales, rising in geologic terrace along the eastern rim of the Connecticut Valley. Dartmouth contributes heavily to the character and economy of the region, not only because of the undergraduate college, but through its major schools of business administration and engineering, the medical school and hospital, and the outstanding Hopkins Center for the Performing Arts opened in recent years. Despite Dartmouth's apparent close ties to New Hampshire, ranging from its founding by Governor Wentworth to the striking numbers of Granite State governors who went to college there, it has not been very relevant to the problems and life of New Hampshire in the last several decades. Its ties to Vermont, in fact, seem even closer—if for no other reason, because Vermont provides a more hospitable climate for the contribution of intellectuals.

Just to the south, also in the middle Connecticut River area, are Newport (9,195) and Claremont (14,221) both old mill towns fairly static in population in recent years. Several covered bridges and pleasant river scenes grace this part of the state.

The southwestern, or Manadnock region, centers around Keene (20,-467) and the lesser population centers of Peterborough-Jaffrey (9,082) and Hillsborough (4,559), the home of President Pierce. Keene is a city of diversified light industry and one of the state colleges; it has been growing in recent years and captured an All-American Cities award in the 1960s. Peterborough is famed chiefly as the home of the Macdowell Colony, a resident colony of artists, musicians, sculptors, and writers established in memory of the composer Edward Macdowell, on land where he had had his home and did his work. The artists work at cabins scattered throughout the grounds; among those who have done their work at the colony have been Thornton Wilder (writing there *The Bridge at San Luis Rey* and perhaps gathering background for *Our Town*), Stephen Vincent Benét, Edwin Arlington Robinson, Willa Cather, and James Baldwin. Such noteworthies (attendance is by invitation only) eat dinner together at a central building, but lunch is left for them in a basket on their cabin doorsteps. A Peterborough resident who knows the colony well, Mrs. Walter Peterson, wife of the former governor, pointed out to me that "the discipline means productivity."

Close to Peterborough is Dublin, where the fabulously successful *Yankee Magazine* and *The New Englander* are published and Mark Twain and Amy Lowell used to summer; also nearby is the sleepy town of Nelson with a monument to "her heroic Sons who fell in the War of Great Rebellion for the Preservation of Liberty and the Unity of the Republic, 1861–1865." Such references to the Civil War are frequent in New England—vivid reminders of the way the people of the region felt about that conflict, and why Republicanism could hold on so long afterwards.*

Between Dublin and the lovely old town of Jaffrey rises, in imperial and lonely majesty, Mount Monadnock, beloved of Thoreau and Emerson and countless other 19th-century writers and artists. The solitude of this 3,165-foot peak gives it its uniqueness; by 1900 it was so famous that it became a noun in Webster's dictionary, meaning a mountain that towers alone above the surrounding countryside. With the unimpeded 360-degree view from the summit, it is the only spot from which all six New England states are visible at once.

For almost a century now, conservationists have sought to protect Monadnock. When commercialism threatened the mountain in the early 1880s—some feared an unsightly structure on the summit—the selectmen of Jaffrey claimed the mountaintop as public land. "Wild land reservations for public recreation were almost unheard of in those days, especially in rural communities," Allen Chamberlain later wrote in his *Annals of the*

---

* For a contrast to Confederate monuments, see the Mississippi chapter of a prior volume in this series, *The Deep South States of America* (page 173).

Grand Monadnock. Early in this century, however, most of the upper portions of the mountain were still held by 70 scattered descendants of the original towns who bought up the claim of Captain John Mason in 1746. The Society for the Protection of New Hampshire Forests, through its first and illustrious forester, Philip Ayres, launched a "Save Monadnock" project and after diligent search of the genealogical lists and conveyances persuaded the "Masonian Proprietors," as they were called, to vest the rights and title in the land to the SPNHF. The deed was a classic of conservationist-historical sentiment—

That the Society for the Protection of New Hampshire Forests shall forever hold this part of Monadnock Mountain in trust, to maintain forever its wild and primeval condition, where the forest and rock shall remain undisturbed in wild state, and where birds and game shall find natural refuge. That the forest shall be unmolested and free to grow and decay as untold ages past. . . . That the entire tract shall be forever kept open to the public for use in accordance with the expressed objects for which the reservation is made. . . . That this reservation shall be known as the Masonian Monadnock Reservation in commemoration of the romantic history of the Masonian Grant and the Masonian Proprietors in New England.

The SPNHF was left the guardian of 4,000 acres, including the summit. But in 1974 the SPNHF warned that developing pressures on the mountain and its environs, occasioned by rapidly increasing numbers of visitors and new land use patterns in the area, were endangering the wilderness environment and causing some physical deterioration of the mountain. A program encompassing additional land acquisitions, land easements, and stiffer controls on camping was developed. "You look at a map of New Hampshire," SPNHF forester Paul Bofinger said, "and you can see that that area is the backbone of the state—the highest, hilliest, rockiest land in the southern and central portion of the state. There is land there still in the wild. If there is ever going to be any such thing as a greenway, or any strip left for public recreation, it has to be done now."

. . . And the Merrimack Valley and Coastal Provinces

Now we come to the Merrimack Valley and coastal regions of New Hampshire, where two-thirds of the state's people live. The state planners would have one believe that from 481,100 people in 1970, the population of these areas will rise to a staggering 1,858,000 by 2020. If the projection is anywhere near correct, and the state continues its haphazard tax and land use policies, one can expect a continuation of the repulsive kind of development which has engulfed communities on the Massachusetts border in recent years. Consider this description of Salem, by Jay McManus in the *New Hampshire Times*:

A little more than 20 years ago, Salem still lay in bucolic splendor on the banks of the Spicket River near the New Hampshire-Massachusetts border—a quiet mill town of 4,000 people. . . .

Suddenly, the completion in 1958 of Interstate Route 93 placed Salem squarely in the path of the horde of disillusioned refugees fleeing north from the cities. Even the most farsighted planner couldn't have calculated the impact: an incredible growth rate of 118 percent in the past decade, a population of 29,000 and a desperate demand for roads, schools and housing. The explosion is multiplying and no one is certain when—or if—it will end.

Entering Salem from Interstate 93, your eyes are immediately assaulted by a three-mile strip of commercial blight along Route 28—an ugly montage of traffic lights, discount department stores, trailer parks and fast food franchises.

The story goes on to describe soaring local land values, property taxes, and pressures on the schools. State support covers less than a 20th of the $10 million town budget. Salem appears to have lost its identity in the avalanche of growth, the old and conservative Republican power structure having given way to overwhelmingly young newcomers of every political stripe and little cohesion. The local attitude, in the words of area planner John Gilmore, is: "If I don't like it, I'll move away in 10 years. I only sleep here." In that situation, he added, "public policy planners aren't making the decisions. The marketplace makes them by default."

A cooled-off national economy, fewer Route-128 jobs and fewer new industrial parks could well stop such growth in its tracks in the next years. And in that event, southern and southeastern New Hampshire might be able to save more of its rural innocence and livability.

There remain lovely towns in southern New Hampshire, some struggling hard to contain the growth pressures on them. One thinks of Exeter (1970 population 8,892), not far from the coast. It was the Revolutionary capital of New Hampshire and home of famous old (1781) Phillips Exeter Academy, the best known of the state's private schools. Despite heady population growth (23 percent in the '60s), Exeter is still linked to its past by elm-shaded streets, lined with old homes, churches, and public buildings. In 1970, Exeter citizens rose up in protest when a local bank sought to tear down Dudley House, a distinguished 19th-century frame structure of Federalist design. A hundred people showed up for a demonstration on a snowy December day, hearing historian Henry Bragdon issue the warning: "You cannot destroy symbols without doing violence to the values they represent—craftsmanship, hard work, trust in one's neighbors, a sense of proportion, putting public good ahead of private gain."

The famed New Hampshire cities of the Merrimack Valley are Concord (30,022), Manchester (87,754), and Nashua (55,820). Concord, which at its center is one of the nation's less attractive capital cities, still has some of the earmarks of a faded industrial town. But it has sprouted several shopping centers including one, oddly enough, only a block off the main street. Economically, the city is something of an island to itself, heavily geared to government employment, including close to 1,000 workers at the state mental hospital alone. Many visitors head for the New Hampshire Historical Society, where the displays include one of the old Concord Coaches that were made by the thousands in the city in the 19th century and played such a role in the settlement of the American West. On a pleasant tree-shaded street in the northern part of Concord one can also find the display of the New Hampshire League of Craftsmen, an exemplary state-level organization which has been encouraging potters and weavers and woodcarvers since the early 1930s and selling their handicraft to the public. The state government, under Governor Winant, helped to launch the organization through a special commission on the arts and crafts—making New Hampshire the first state to take an official interest in native crafts.

If all of New Hampshire had the liberal Republican and independent cast of Concord voters, the state's public life would have a very different complexion. A major reason for the overwhelming conservatism, as we noted earlier in this chapter, is the heavily ethnic and *Union Leader* influenced city of Manchester, a few miles downstream. Here, in 72 separate social clubs where the working folk drop by for a drink on the way home or a Saturday evening get-together, you can identify the ethnic heritages by the clubs' names—the Lafayette Club, the Sweeney Post of the American Legion, the Russian-American Club, the Pulaski Club, and so on. Greeks are also represented in goodly number (even in the 1930s the WPA Guide reported that "the Greeks own more than a million dollars worth of real estate in Manchester"), and by the early '70s there were some 1,000 Spanish-speaking people from at least 16 Latin American countries living in Manchester, imported to work at minimum-wage levels in the mills just as the old Amoskeag owners, seeking cheap labor in the last century, used to lure French-Canadians to the sweatshops beside the Merrimack.

The first settlement on the Amoskeag Falls occurred in 1722, but it was in 1810 that the town, then named Derryfield, received its present name. This stemmed from the inspiration of Judge Samuel Blodget, who had visited England's Manchester and returned to proclaim as he stood by the river's banks: "For as the country increases in population, we must have manufactories, and here at my canal will be a manufacturing town . . . the Queen City of New Hampshire . . . *the Manchester of America.*"

The city the Amoskeag Company built was considered in its time "the handsomest manufacturing city in the world," an embodiment of the early 19th-century utopian idea of creating a completely organized world for the men and women who worked in the mills. The company laid out the whole city on paper first, and then proceeded to build it: the long procession of red brick mill buildings, adorned by an occasional Victorian tower and gateway, power from two gently curving, mile-long canals, rows of neat brick houses for the workers, and bridges over the canals providing the workers easy access to their place of work.

After the fateful Christmas Eve of 1935, when the lights flickered out for the last time in the great company's mills, a group of Manchester businessmen bought all the physical property, including the two and a half miles of buildings, and proceeded to lease and sell them to smaller industrial firms. Smaller textile firms came, along with shoe, printing, lumber, metal products, and electronics companies (the latter the largest single employer in recent years). Unemployment remained high for years, and wages have never come close to New England-wide levels. But at least in recent years it has been a labor shortage, not a surplus, which has been Manchester's problem.

One could wish now that no one had ever meddled with the old Amoskeag buildings, leaving them as a great outdoor museum commemorating the best and worst of New England's 19th-century industrial culture. But in recent years, to relieve Manchester's crushing parking and traffic problems and make way for other modern "improvements," many of the buildings have been demolished and the canals filled in. This was made possible by the nation's first urban "renewal" project for a strictly industrial area, financed with federal money. Fortunately, a number of the narrow-windowed old four-to-seven story buildings, some announcing in chiseled stone their hoary ages of 1844, 1855, and the like, have been spared.

Like so many older American cities, Manchester let the first waves of post-World War II growth go to its suburbs; foolishly it thwarted the plan of Boston's big department store, Jordan Marsh, to build within the city, so that the state's premier retail facility went instead to neighboring Bedford, on the interstate. Belatedly, however, some growth has come to the center city including the Hampshire Plaza Project, a commercial project including a 20-story office building ("the tallest thing north of Boston") and a covered mall retail shopping center. And while most of the population growth has gone to the suburbs, Manchester retains its colorful ethnic communities, plentiful parkland, and even a couple of "silk stocking" wards.

Manchester has a rather primitive city government structure, based on a weak mayor-council charter, commissioners who appoint agency heads, and no civil service—a device which permits the powerful aldermen to keep the pool of some 1,000 city jobs a patronage preserve for themselves.

Nashua, still farther downstream on the Massachusetts border, grew much more rapidly than any other New Hampshire city in the 1960s—by 42.8 percent. It remains heavily Franco-American, at least in the core city, but has a very mobile new population, much of it in its suburbs, which have expanded even more rapidly than the city proper. Nashua has long since shucked off the effects of the massive mill closings of yesteryear, not only by virtue of Sanders Associates, but also through firms like the Nashua Corporation (a labeling and photocopying concern with world-wide holdings), Sprague Electric, and other diversified industries. The city has been rated (by David Franke, coauthor of *Safe Places*), as one of the 10 most crime-free cities of over 50,000 people in the United States.

Not all of the new industry that has come to southern New Hampshire has been "clean" and problem-free. The classic example is the big Anheuser-Busch brewery that the people of the river town of Merrimack (population 8,594) agreed to in the 1960s on the theory that 350 local jobs would be provided and that taxes paid by the company would cover costs of a big new local sewage treatment plant. The factory and the sewage plant were indeed built, but the waste flow from the brewery was so massive that Merrimack soon found itself blighted with a three-acre pool of slimy, brownish sludge. Then came the demand that the residents pay hundreds of thousands of dollars toward building an incinerator to burn the mess away.

Our attention now turns to the southeast and New Hampshire's 18-mile window to the sea, an area rich with the history of early settlement, the high-living royal governors, the days of the West Indian trade and clipper ships. The seacoast, if one will overlook the more commercial elements, is an exquisite mixture of broad sand beach and boiling surf against the rocks, of perfect little colonial towns and sumptuous mansions. Whittier wrote of Great Boars Head as the place where the "Grisly head of the boar . . . tosses the foam from tusks of stone"; Longfellow described the Benning Wentworth mansion, where the governor held court in the aristocratic tradition of beeswing port and high play at cards, as "a noble pile, baronial and colonial in its styles," with "gables and dormer windows everywhere, and stacks of chimneys raising high in air." The flavor of the sea, of the days when brigantines and clipper ships set forth for distant oceans, and of lobstering to this day, characterizes the coastal settlements. They run from Seabrook on the south through Hampton Beach, Rye, and lovely North Castle north to Portsmouth, across the Piscataqua River from Kittery, Maine. Lying in the haze a few miles offshore are the famed Isles of Shoals, "barren and bleak, swept by every wind that blows and beaten by the sea." Captain John Smith discovered these white-ledged isles in 1614, and would have named them for himself; instead they gained their present name from early fishermen who took note of the shoaling or schooling of fish off their shores. Tourism is naturally the big business of the coast these days, with diversions ranging from ocean swimming to summer theater; for the tradition-minded there is that grand old white elephant, the massive Wentworth-by-the-Sea hotel which has catered to the elite ever since the first carriages rolled up to its portals in 1874. (The Wentworth reached its pinnacle of fame when it hosted the diplomats who signed the Russian-Japanese peace treaty in 1905; my own remembrance is capped by a 90th birthday party of my Philadelphia grandmother, who summered there in an opulent style her descendants rarely know.)

Portsmouth is the queen of the coastal cities; though its population (25,717 in 1970) remains modest, it can rightfully claim to be the first commercial settlement of any size after Jamestown. In its early years, the town was New Hampshire's capital and prospered as a commercial fishery, a builder of masts and ships for the Royal Navy, and as a seaport rivaling New York and Boston. The peak of its glory came in 1800, when it was the 10th largest city in America. Major fires and the Embargo Act soon reduced Portsmouth to an also-ran in the race for eminence among the young country's cities; there was some revival as it became one of the chief producers of clipper ships, and again as it became, for a while, a major beer brewing center. But decline set in from the mid-1800s onwards, as the wharves and elegant old homes began to crumble. Only the Navy Yard saved it—a partial fulfillment of the prediction of a French traveler, Francois Jean de Beauvoir, who had written in his diary in 1782 that Portsmouth would become to New England what the other Portsmouth was to Old England—"the depot of the Continental Navy." To this day, the city depends in great measure on the uncertain fortunes of the Navy Yard, as well as nearby Pease Air Force Base.*

The stagnation of old Portsmouth had its positive side, for while the 18th- and 19th-century homes and wharves slowly crumbled, no economic forces arose to cause their destruction. The old streets, as narrow and winding as Boston's, never got straightened out; the business district remained quiescent; not knowing it, Portsmouth awaited the era of restoration that would come to so many old American cities in the years after World War II. The occasion for the most exciting renewal came when the old South End neighborhood, an area beside the Piscataqua River known in the early days as "Puddle Dock," was slated for demolition in an urban renewal project. The area seemed to deserve destruction: it was overrun by junkyards, the old homes had boarded up windows, and all the remaining structures appeared in the most advanced stages of decay. But local leaders, inspired by the city librarian, Dorothy Vaughan, were led to turn this section of old Portsmouth into an historic and tourist district instead. The neighborhood was given the early name of Portsmouth–Strawbery Banke, a description applied by the first settlers in 1630, who had noted the river embankments covered with strawberries. In the "new" Strawbery Banke, all but 27 historic houses were torn down, and then the painstaking process of house-by-house restoration begun. Unlike such "outdoor museums" as Sturbridge Village, or much of Williamsburg, Strawbery Banke consists entirely of original structures. The restoration idea has proved contagious; in another part of the city, for instance, 14 historic houses of Georgian or Federal design, built between 1715 and 1826, have been incorporated into a new shopping center and office complex, rather than feeling the wrecker's ball.

A sister city to Portsmouth, and with it one of the four oldest New Hampshire settlements, is Dover (20,850), a place where textiles once reigned supreme but diversified industry, ranging from rubber and plastics to electrical equipment, has grown in recent years.

Also an integral part of the coastal region setting is the pleasant colonial-era town of Durham, which has been the site of the University of New Hampshire ever since that institution broke away from Dartmouth's protective wing in 1893. Some 5,500 people, including university personnel, make Durham their home; when the university is in session, some 10,000

* *The Wall Street Journal* was undoubtedly correct in 1971 when it noted of the Portsmouth Navy Yard, "clearly [it] has survived mainly for political reasons." Senator McIntyre said it had been "a continual thorn—a political football." In the early 1960s, Robert McNamara, as Secretary of Defense, ordered the yard closed. "So the New Hampshire delegation," McIntyre recalled, "went down on its knees to McNamara, who gave us a 10-year phase-out on the argument that a sudden closing would be an economic disaster. Then, when Richard Nixon came campaigning in New Hampshire in 1968, he was quickly advised by Cotton and Wyman to say he would reconsider the phase-out. He did reconsider—a major reason the yard survives to this day." One of the yard's severest critics is Hyman Rickover, who once said that the "Portsmouth Naval Shipyard is the most inefficient nuclear submarine yard, private or public, I have ever seen."

students augment the total. If Aristotle Onassis, Meldrim Thompson, William Loeb, and the Federal Energy Administration had had their way in 1974, Durham would have become the home of a $600 million oil refinery, handling 400,000 barrels a day—enough to supply a quarter of New England's total petroleum demand. An offshore terminal, near the Isles of Shoals, would have received the crude oil from Saudi Arabia, carried by Onassis' fleet of tankers; from there a 15-mile pipeline, going underwater and underground, would have brought the oil to the refinery on Durham Point, an unspoiled piece of land which juts out into Great Bay. The refinery, Onassis promised, would be "clean as a clinic" and camouflaged by a 1,000-foot-wide belt of trees; moreover it would add 1,000 permanent jobs and add enough to the Durham tax base to reduce the town's tax rate by 80 to 90 percent.

But all those inducements, plus a heavy-handed public relations campaign by Onassis and his agents, *Union Leader* editorials calling refinery opponents a "small, noisy and vocal group of leftists," and heavy pressure by the governor, were not enough to convince the people of Durham that they wanted their college town transformed into an oil town. Nor were the pressures enough to persuade the state legislature to override Durham's wishes and make a refinery possible against its wishes. It was not that New Hampshire people were not interested in a dependable, less expensive oil source; 65 percent, in a Boston *Globe* poll, endorsed the idea of a refinery in the state. But Durham voted against a local refinery 1,254 to 144 in its town meeting. And the sacred principle of home rule could be raised to stop state intervention; the key vote in the legislature, in fact, went 233 to 109 against giving the state government sole authority in refinery siting.

The two key figures in Durham's successful resistance to a refinery were both young women—Nancy Sandberg, leader of a local group known as "Save Our Shores," and a state legislator with the wonderfully New England name of Dudley Dudley. How they used the hoary home rule principle to defeat all the established powers, including the tanker tycoon rumored to be the richest man in the world, is a story of citizen activism fit for the textbooks.

Despite the defeat at Durham, the possibility of a refinery along the New Hampshire coast seemed far from dead in early 1975. Onassis' firm, Olympic Refineries, had gone to the Federal Energy Administration to sound out the possibilities of a superport located at the Isles of Shoals. Albeit by narrow margins, the neighboring cities of Rochester and Newmarket had both voted in favor of having a refinery in their towns and opened the door for future consideration of a refinery in the state. "Although we won the battle," Dudley Dudley said, "we have far from won the war."

Sometimes, indeed, it seems as if the debates about energy needs in New Hampshire and the other northern New England states will never end. Since 1969, for instance, a spirited debate has been underway about the proposal of the Public Service Company of New Hampshire to build a nuclear power facility beside the marshes at Seabrook, close by Hampton Beach. From an original proposal for a single 860 megawatt unit, the proposal has been expanded to *two* 1,150 megawatt-producing nuclear reactors —compared to the single 540-megawatt Vermont Yankee plant across the Connecticut River on the state's other border. As this book went to press, it appeared that the final hurdles to the $1.2 billion project would soon be overcome. Why, one asks, was New Hampshire's narrow coastal region selected for a plant that would ship a substantial portion of its power out of state? A clue was given in a site survey done for the utility in the late '6os, which noted: "The site shall preferably be in New Hampshire due to public relations and tax considerations."

Saving Natural New Hampshire

In 1974 the *Valley News*, published at West Lebanon, provided a unique native's-eye view of what has happened to the Granite State in our time. The native was one Fred Talbert, a 94-year-old lumberjack-farmer from East Plainfield, and this in part is what he had to say.*

I used to be able to cut one, two tons of hay per acre where it's all grown into woods now." It makes you sick to see it.

The highways. They went through the best farmland we had in this valley. And a few years ago the land where that shopping plaza down by the river is, that was all farmland.

Everything you eat has to come from the ground. Now we pave it over. Kill it all.

The damn fools couldn't see it in the beginning. There's so many more people to feed now, and the local farms are all gone. The promise is short hours and big pay. Now we have trouble feeding people. But why shouldn't we? Look at the way we've treated this area. The nit-wits. We just throwed away what we had.

Farmers were once the backbone of a community. It was that way right here in New England. But the idea that the west was going to feed everybody was ridiculous. You eat up half the food getting it here. We need self-supporting agriculture right in this area. . . .

Look: right out there is where the Shakers used to live. I've seen those hills covered with cattle and sheep. Today, you couldn't pasture a jackrabbit out there.

Down by Goose Pond there was lots of good meadow land. And lots of lumber to cut.

I remember seeing fields in this valley filled with flowers. I'll never forget that.

And I used to see fields and gardens with 15, 20 men and boys—all ages— working side by side.

On Grantham Mountain—hunted and fished all over up there—you could see stands of virgin spruce that ran straight and tall and right into the sky.

And now . . . God . . . now all of that is gone.

There are few who would disagree, in fact, that the central public policy problem in present-day New Hampshire, deeper than its political-governmental malaise, is the problem of growth.

---

* In an interview with writer John Griesemer.

The years since World War II have seen the face of the state inexorably altered. Interstate highways have bisected the pretty little valleys, suburban subdivisions have preempted field and forest land, condominiums have crept up into the glories of the White Mountains, cheap roadside development has obscured the view of the grand natural landscape, mobile home parks have sprouted in alarming proportions, shopping centers have grown like mushrooms. "Beautiful, rural New Hampshire," the state's leading charitable trust warned in 1965, "faces a calamity. The quality of life is threatened by the fastest growing population in the nation—by spreading urbanization."

There are those in New Hampshire who have labored hard over the years to protect the state's priceless natural environment. The Society for the Protection of New Hampshire Forests has been the catalytic force, but it has had many allies—the Associations of Conservation Commissions and Lake and Stream Associations and their local affiliates; the New Hampshire Audubon Society, which owns a substantial amount of land and operates a number of nature centers; the New Hampshire Fish and Game Clubs; the state chapters of the Nature Conservancy and the Sierra Club; the New Hampshire Environmental Education Council; the New Hampshire Clean Air Alliance; the Land Use Foundation; the Seacoast Antipollution League, and many others. Jean Hennessey, executive director of the New Hampshire Charitable Fund and Affiliated Trusts and a leading environmental leader on her own, told me she could think of no other state "as well organized for the environment from a citizen base."

All of this has made a substantial difference over the years. In terms of conservation commissions and local governments acquiring scenic lands, in shoreline protection, and in state government aid to localities in building water pollution facilities, New Hampshire was long a leader in northern New England and to a substantial degree it still is. Years were required after the passage of the first major water pollution control legislation in 1959 until any one of the major river basins in the state was cleaned up, but under combined state and federal pressure results were finally noticeable by the late 1960s and early '70s. There were still grave pollution problems to be resolved on the Merrimack and Androscoggin Rivers, but the state could point to at least one shining success—the clean-up of the smaller Pemigewasset. For more than 60 years, the Pemigewasset had been befouled by sulfite liquors, acidity, scum, and noxious vapor from paper pulp mills, particularly a large plant at Lincoln. Fish died in the murky waters; at Bristol, a few miles downstream from Lincoln, vapor from the river turned houses yellow. Under pressure to install pollution-abatement equipment, the Lincoln mill finally went bankrupt. Hundreds of jobs were lost in the process, but now the Pemigewasset, as it had for centuries, flows blue and clear over its rocky bed, all the way from the point where it rises in Profile Notch under the Old Man of the Mountain to its junction with the Merrimack at Franklin, some 70 miles to the south.

Major credit for the local land acquisition programs should go to the now extinct Spaulding-Potter Charitable Trusts, headed from 1959 to 1972 by one of New Hampshire's most dedicated leaders of recent times, Eugene C. Struckhoff (at this writing vice president of the Council on Foundations in New York). Based on the bequests of wealthy New Hampshire and Boston families, the Trusts expended $16.8 million in their 15-year history, about 60 percent in New Hampshire. Among many projects, Struckhoff made available money from the trusts to New Hampshire towns, on a matching basis, for permanent land acquisition funds. As secretary of the trusts, which were due under the bequests to expire in 1972, Struckhoff also took a leading hand in creating the New Hampshire Charitable Fund in 1961—creating a permanent way for various family bequests to be applied to educational, cultural, health and environmental projects in the state.*

One of the most interesting activities of the Spaulding-Potter Trusts was the organization, in 1969, of a project known as "New Hampshire—Tomorrow," a multifaceted program to alert New Hampshire people to the threats to their environment, and encourage them to confront those threats. Under the project umbrella, more than 50 projects were undertaken, including studies of environmental threats to the coastline, mobile homes, access to public waters, the Appalachian Trails, roadside blight, solid-waste disposal, the siting of power plants, and eutrophication of the lakes. At a final conference in October 1970 more than 2,000 people discussed the demonstration projects and, probably for the first time in New Hampshire history, got a sense of the need for unified action to save the state's natural heritage.

The lesson was an important one, because until the 1970s the activities of the various conservation groups in the state had been quite fragmented. This was especially harmful in getting good environmental legislation passed, because the organizations interested in wetlands and forestry, clean waters, and the removal of billboards rarely got together. This situation was finally corrected in 1972 with creation of an Environmental Council, also known as SPACE (Statewide Program of Action to Conserve our Environment) in 1972. This group, with participation by all the leading conservation groups of the state, draws up a list of legislative priorities and then fights for its bills in a coordinated manner.

The unhappy fact, however, is that in terms of new legislation and effective state enforcement, the environmental cause in New Hampshire has lagged badly since the mid-1960s—precisely at the moment when growth pressures have made bold action an imperative to save New Hampshire's landscape, and when neighboring Vermont and Maine have forged to the national lead in land use and other conservationist measures. The rise of Loebism, the parsimony of the state government, and stiff opposition by influential private interests seeing a threat to their profits and activities, have all played a part in the picture. In a broader sense, one could almost say

* For a discussion of coordination of family trusts to maintain flexibility in meeting the needs of a state or city, the reader is referred to the review of the Kansas City Association of Trusts and Foundations in a previous volume in this series, *The Great Plains States of America*, pp. 76–78.

that as soon as environmental protection became a really important political issue, the conservationist organizations discovered how thin their base
of support had always been. Particularly among the factory-oriented ethnic
groups, one notes a certain irreverence for the land in New Hampshire—
in sharp contrast, for instance, to the Vermont dairy farmer who treasures
his land as his present security and hope for his children. The early decline
of agriculture in New Hampshire accounts for much of this, but it seems
to go even further in a low level of life expectation—the attitude that "with
a camper in the backyard and a motorbike and a skimobile, that's all I
need."

One could trace the environmental backwardness of New Hampshire
through a dozen major issues, ranging from unfettered billboards and
loose snowmobile laws to the lack of state-wide controls on mobile home
parks and the legislature's refusal to approve creation of a single, unified
environmental protection agency. The issue which underlies all others, however, and which has caused the bitterest legislative fights, is the fundamental
one of land use control. By the midpoint of the 1970s, New Hampshire
still had no state-wide land use regulatory control. No regulations existed
for big-scale developments other than power plants. Many municipalities
had enacted zoning laws of varying quality, but the state had no land use
controls for unincorporated areas. There was no regulatory mechanism to control development in the coastal zone. The state had no mining controls, no
flood plain control legislation, no regulations of wilderness areas, and only a
rudimentary set of statutes for solid waste management. There were no state
controls for new towns and no controls for critical areas other than wetlands. The state had no land use inventory, no procedure for monitoring
land use impacts across the state, no growth and development plans (though
there was a possibility they might be forthcoming), and no state standards
or inducements for granting open space easements. As Maine and Vermont
moved forthrightly in most of these areas, Malcolm Taylor of the SPNHF
commented: "There's a definite disadvantage in having states with tough
environmental laws on both sides. New Hampshire is becoming the happy
hunting ground of shoddy, ticky-tacky developers."

About the only significant restrictions on haphazard growth were zoning restrictions in some of the state's towns and cities, a current land use
tax assessment law (which allowed owners of farm, forest, and recreation
land to get lower assessments in return for an agreement to leave their
land in "open space"), and finally a fairly tough 1967 law requiring state
permits for septic or sewage systems within 1,000 feet of lakes or streams.
At least in the short term, the latter statute had delayed some ill-planned
large real estate developments.

In each legislative session of the early 1970s, the environmentalists
pressed for comprehensive land use legislation, only to meet defeat at the
hands of suspicious legislators, hostile developers, agricultural blocs fearful
of loss of control over land they wanted to subdivide and sell, and general
"home rule" sentiment. Shocked by its reversals on Vermont-style envi-

ronmental and land use bills, the groups in the Environmental Coalition in 1973 decided to ask for just a third of a loaf—a "critical lands" bill that would have controlled new construction on flood plains, high elevations, prime agricultural lands, and unique natural areas. At the most, the measure would have affected 6 percent of the state's land area. But despite its limited scope and orderly review and hearing procedures, the bill was voted down by a margin of almost two to one in the legislature. Typical of the pressures against it was this passage from a letter to legislators from a well-known realtor-developer: "The attitude of the makers of this bill has been one of 'no growth,' more concentralized state control over private property, and a shameful disregard for the viability of our state economy and its people. The bill is voluminous and fraught with concepts that, if passed, would close the doors to the Granite State."

As the legislature headed into yet another land use debate in 1975,* however, it was becoming clear that some of the groups most opposed to controls in the past were having reason to rethink their position. Many developers had become painfully aware that the most desirable towns were zoning themselves in such a way as to exclude practically any new development. Unzoned or politically supine towns were still open to massive second-home developments or trailer parks, but there were an increasing number in which local zoning and planning boards were turning down anything but one-to-four-acre single-home proposals they were sure wouldn't add to their local property tax burden or destroy their intrinsic town character. As the law stood, there was no way for the developers to force their way into the towns that were on an "antidevelopment" bent.

A second factor was that many local officials, fearful of pressure for large-scale development in their domains, found they lacked the technical expertise needed to make rational decisions. One survey found 90 percent of local officials in favor of state resource planning and development guidelines to assist them, including data on the nature of soils, environmentally sensitive areas, and the economic impact of large-scale residential or industrial developments.

The legislature was presented with a land use proposal drawn up by a so-called "Study Group, Inc.," whose ranks, according to one report, "read like a Who's Who of the land business in New Hampshire." Only two or three recognized environmentalists were among the incorporators. The Study Group recommendation was that the state draw up largely optional guidelines on critical areas and then leave it up to the local governments to decide on whether they wanted to approve new developments. But appeal could be made to a state-wide review board. Critics said the plan was a scheme to get around recalcitrant local zoning boards. They also questioned the power left in the hands of local political figures to make essentially scientific decisions about critical environmental areas, the relationship of new development to the ecosystem, and the like. But the alternative

---

* In a well-functioning democracy, this issue would have been well aired in the 1974 gubernatorial election. But in fact the candidates scarcely mentioned it at all.

generally favored by the environmentalists—strong regional and state land use control commissions—flew in the face of fervid home rule sentiment ("don't let those Concord bureaucrats tell us what to do"). It was also just the kind of comprehensive, integrated control the developers wanted to avoid. And without developer support, savvy State House hands said, there was no chance for any kind of land use legislation at all. (Despite strong attempts, the land use bills again failed in the 1975 session.)

The fate of natural New Hampshire thus remained in the hands of that same political system of which I wrote earlier in this chapter—a system of uncompromising conflict, of special interest influence, and of a people's endemic distrust of the government that is really their creation. The odds against further degradation of a magnificent natural landscape were not very good. One could only read with bittersweet apprehension the quotation from Thoreau, so often used by the state's conservationists—

I long for wilderness . . . woods where the woodthrush forever sings, where the hours are early morning ones, and there is dew on the grass, and the day is forever unproven . . . a New Hampshire everlasting and unfallen.

MAINE

THE TIDES QUICKEN

THE STATE OF MAINE, set beside the "Down East" tides on America's northeastern extremity, is a place of marvelously unique qualities—natural and human.

Consider, for instance, how the last glacier created the picturesque coast of Maine we know today, with its seeming infinity of bays, inlets, harbors, and islands. Before the glacial age, the coastline had been fairly straight and unspectacular, with mountain ranges rising some distance inland. Then, from the polar cap, came the great ice sheet, so massive that even its "thin" tip, near Nantucket, rose a sheer thousand feet. The weight was too much for the earth's crust to bear, so that a great fault appeared near Long Island. The land to the north tipped down and below the ocean's cold, green waters for many centuries.

When the glacier finally receded, some 12,000 years ago, the resilient earth rose again—but not to its former height. So one sees just the tips of the preglacial mountains that were closest to the sea, in their new incarnation as the galaxy of 2,000-odd islands off the Maine coast, surrounded by dangerous reefs and shoals. The high flanks of the more inland mountains have taken form as the capes and promontories of the coast proper. And the former hollows and ravines of the old mountains are under water entirely, apparent now as the coves and harbors of the drowned coast of the state of Maine. This is perhaps the most irregular, rugged coastline of the world. As the crow flies, the distance from Kittery, on the New Hampshire border, to Eastport, beside New Brunswick, is only 228 miles. But if one were to follow each bay and cove and inlet, one would see a shoreline of more than 3,500 miles. Maine has, indeed, half the tidal line of the entire east coast of the United States.

The glacier did more. As it shrank to the north, it left in its wake great deposits of sand, gravel, and clay which distorted, almost beyond recognition, the watersheds of former ages. The torrents of melting water from the ice sheet formed new rivers, which when backed up against the dams created by the glacial litter, created countless lakes and ponds, of which some 2,500 survive to this day. The inland water area of Maine today, in fact, is about twice the *total* area of Rhode Island. Moosehead Lake, some 40 miles long with no less than 300 miles of shoreline, is the largest lake encased within the borders of any American state.

By New England standards, Maine is a fantastically large state. Put together, the other five states of the region are only a shade larger, in total area, than Maine's 33,215 square miles. By road, the distance from New York City to Kittery is 268 miles, a considerable stretch. But from Kittery north, especially to parts of the state where there are no superhighways, the distance becomes immense. To reach Eastport, one must drive close to 300 miles— substantially more than the New York-to-Kittery stretch. From Kittery to Madawaska, high in Aroostook County, the distance is a full 400 miles, at least eight hours of nonstop driving. (One can forget doing any of this by train; Amtrak's passenger service fails to service Maine at all, though there has been some talk of reviving rail transportation.)

A kind of continental cul-de-sac, Maine is the only one of the 48 coterminous states which borders on only one other (New Hampshire). The only section of the state feeling direct population pressures from outside is York County, on the state's southernmost flank, where the natural sea and farm and woodland setting is being invaded by ticky-tacky subdivisions and condominiums populated by people who work in the nearby coastal cities or in Massachusetts' Route 128 orbit. This is the northernmost extension of the East Coast megalopolis, a county that rapid rail commuter service could put within 45 minutes of Boston.

Few shorelines of the world have been more written or painted than the Maine coast with its quaint, historic fishing and vacation towns hugging the granite-ledged shoreline. Just the briefest listing is evocative of the variety and delight of the coast—York Village of colonial fame; once elegant Old Orchard Beach with its broad, smooth beaches; Cape Elizabeth and the view toward Portland Head Light (built in 1791 under instructions from George Washington); Casco Bay and the lovely Calendar Islands beside Portland City; Brunswick and shipbuilding Bath and the scores of little rock and hill-bound harbors on their seaflank; famed Boothbay Harbor with its intricate network of islands and coves and pine-clad peninsulas and sleek sailboats on the waters; Thomaston with its stately captains' homes; spacious Penobscot Bay ringed by towns like Rockland, where Andrew Wyeth's paintings are on display; flower-bedecked Camden, sometimes called "Maine's prettiest town," and Camden's twin, the famed resort town of Rockport; and finally the natural wonders of Mount Desert Island, the site of part of Acadia National Park. Here Cadillac Mountain rises a sheer 1,532 feet directly by the sea; here are deep forests and ragged cliffs and coves carved by the glacier and the ocean. The most famous towns are Bar Harbor and Little Seal Harbor, where Nelson and David Rockefeller and numerous other luminaries have had or have their summer homes. Rockefeller calls the area "one of the loveliest spots on God's earth," and there are many who agree.

One must also pause to mention the islands that lie miles off the coast— still primitive Matinicus, the farthest out inhabited place on the coast, where, as Edna St. Vincent Millay wrote, "island woods were pushed by winds that flung them hissing to leeward like a ton of spray," and ruggedly beautiful Monhegan, first touched by John Cabot in 1497, the historic home of Atlantic seafarers, lobstermen, rumrunners in Prohibition times, and a distinguished art colony, where seals inhabit the ledges and whales slip darkly through the waters.

There is more to coastal Maine than the popular southern and central coast. Even at the height of the tourist season, one need only leave Mt. Desert Island and turn up U.S. Route 1 at the nearby town of Ellsworth to find a very different world. The motel-every-mile culture ceases; the country and the traffic quiet down, and soon one is in vast Washington County, 2,420 square miles of forest, lake, and blueberry barren, where only 30,000 people live, most of them in a narrow file along the coast. By every economic index, Washington County is a disaster area: regularly high rates of unemployment, which soar to estimates as high as 60 percent in the winter; a per capita income $1,200 below the New England average; housing that includes many tarpaper shacks with dirt floors; low health standards; constant outmigration of young people who can't find decent jobs. Such figures have been cited time and again to justify proposed deepwater oilports and refineries at places like Eastport and Machias. Many have made the point, however, that Washington County people are not quite as badly off as it might seem. Many are lobstermen, a breed known to keep the sketchiest records about their income. People hunt a great deal, grow their own food, chop their own wood, own their own homes, and exchange goods and services. Theirs is a barter and subsistence economy that most Americans would reject—but which these remaining far-Down Easters seem content to live with.

Washington County does symbolize a physical fact about Maine that always comes as a shock to people familiar with the neat, tailored look of most of New England. The fact is that the county, together with hundreds of settlements throughout Maine's "outback," evidences an extreme frugality and scruffiness more reminiscent of Appalachia than pristine, picture book New England.

The diversity of Maine is exemplified by vast Aroostook County, at the state's northern tip along the St. John River. The county covers 22 percent of Maine's land area and is larger than Connecticut and Rhode Island combined. Aroostook was Maine's—and New England's—last frontier; in fact it

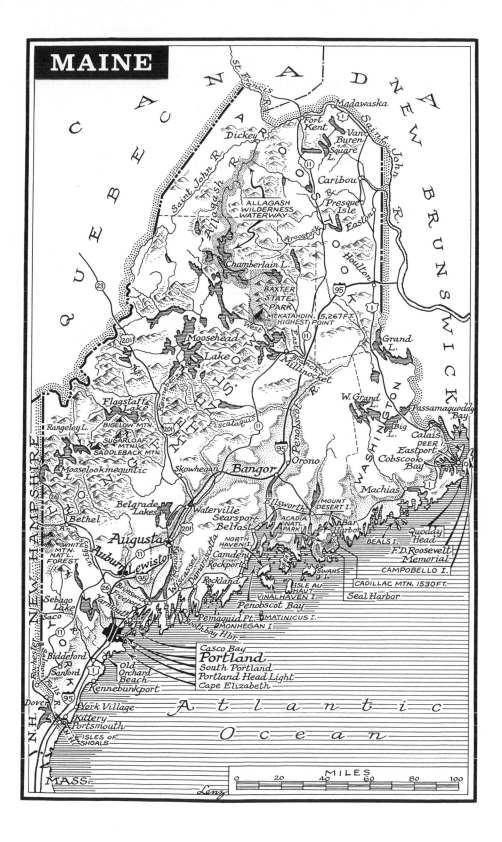

MAINE

QUEBEC

CANADA

NEW BRUNSWICK

St. Francis
Saint John R.

Madawaska
Fort Kent
Dickey
Van Buren
Square
Caribou
Presque Isle
Easton
Houlton

Allagash R.
ALLAGASH WILDERNESS WATERWAY
Aroostook

Chamberlain L.
BAXTER STATE PARK
MT. KATAHDIN, 5,267 FT. HIGHEST POINT

West
East Branch

Grand L.

Moosehead Lake
Millinocket

W. Grand L.
Big L.
Passamaquoddy Bay

Flagstaff Lake
BIGELOW MTN.
Rangeley L.
SUGARLOAF MTN.
SADDLEBACK MTN.

Piscataquis

Calais
DEER I.
Eastport
Cobscook Bay

Mooselookmeguntic

Skowhegan
Bangor
Orono
Machias

Belgrade Lakes
Waterville
Searsport
Belfast
Ellsworth
MOUNT DESERT I.
ACADIA NATL. PARK
Bar Harbor
BEALS I.
Quoddy Head
F.D. Roosevelt Memorial
CAMPOBELLO I.

Bethel
WHITE MTN. NATL. FOREST
Augusta
Auburn Lewiston
NORTH HAVEN
Camden
Rockport
SWANS

Sebago Lake
Saco
Brunswick
Freeport
Yarmouth
Wiscasset
Damariscotta
Rockland
ISLE AU HAUT
VINALHAVEN I.
Seal Harbor
CADILLAC MTN. 1530 FT.

Biddeford
Sanford
Boothbay Hbr.
Pemaquid Pt.
MATINICUS I.
MONHEGAN I.
Penobscot Bay

Old Orchard Beach
Kennebunkport

Casco Bay
Portland
South Portland
Portland Head Light
Cape Elizabeth

Dover
York Village
Kittery
Portsmouth
ISLES OF SHOALS

N.H.

MASS.

NEW HAMPSHIRE

Atlantic Ocean

Lenz

MILES
0 20 40 60 80 100

was still pioneer country in 1870, when southern Maine was a well-developed region of farms and factories. Ask anyone from southern Maine about Aroostook, and he will tell you it is like a totally different state, as representative of the rest of Maine or New England as an Alaskan wilderness would be if appended to Ohio or Indiana. Aroostook's lifeblood is the potato, which prospers in the red glacial soil, growing free of parasites and diseases because of the cold, deep winters and short summers. But the growing conditions vary wildly from year to year, and the potato farmers are gamblers down to their last Cadillac. Some years, when crop yields are poor or national markets adverse, they lose practically all they have; by contrast there have been vintage years like 1925 when Aroostook prospered so mightily that 3,500 farmers paid off their mortgages. Western competition and endemic overproduction, without federal price supports, drove so many Aroostook farmers out of business in the '50s and '60s that the number of farms dropped from 4,600 to 1,300. One out of four of the county's residents departed between 1960 and 1970. But good growing years brought back good times in the mid-1970s, and the prospect of continuing global food shortages boded well for the county and its farmers. Presque Isle and Caribou, the two biggest towns of the county, began to recover from a long slump and even to indulge themselves in some tasteless strip development.

Despite its potato reputation, only a seventh of Aroostook is farmed. The rest is forest and wilderness (including part of the great Allagash Wilderness Waterway, a 92-mile corridor of forest and water approved in the 1960s).

This brings us to forests, the dominant feature of the state. Ninety percent of Maine's land surface is covered by woods, and even a century ago, when about three-quarters of the land in the other New England states was cleared for farms, less than a third of Maine's landscape was in open fields. To this day, some 50 to 60 percent of Maine consists of so-called "wild lands," largely wilderness areas outside the jurisdiction of any municipal government. These "Unorganized Territories"—great tracts of forest simply labeled as "Township 6, Range 8," or the like—are mostly owned by huge paper companies, semi-sovereignties within the greater sovereignty of Maine. The Great Northern Paper Company alone, for instance, owns two million acres, or almost a tenth of the entire state.

Maine also has some magnificent mountains—97 more than 3,000 feet above sea level, and nine over 4,000 feet. The most famous of these is Mount Katahdin (5,267 feet), the highest point in Maine, set in the midst of a seemingly limitless wilderness. To have climbed to the top of this mighty granite monarch, as this writer and countless thousands of others who have made the ascent can testify, is an unforgettable experience. No other ranges rise to obscure the view on any side, and on a clear day one can see more land and water than from any other point of land in America. The feeling of Katahdin itself is arctic, and around one spreads a domain of lesser peaks and lakes and streams and forest rolling on and on through northern and central Maine.

Katahdin lies within Baxter State Park, which itself is a kind of miracle— the perseverance and wise foresight of Republican Governor Percival Baxter

(1921–25). Baxter asked the state legislature to set aside a preserve of mountainous wild land, but after the legislature six times failed to act, Baxter in disgust set out to accomplish the deed on his own. An independently wealthy man, he began in 1931 by purchasing 5,960 acres of game preserve land including Katahdin; to this he later added 12 more great tracts for a total parkland of 201,018 acres which "forever shall be held in its natural wild state" for the people of Maine. Baxter died in 1969 at the age of 92, leaving more than $6 million to be added to the $1.5 million park trust fund he had established during his life. Without Baxter's grand bequest, Katahdin and its mighty wilderness could easily have fallen prey to unconscionable logging and commercialized development.

Katahdin is the northern anchor of the 2,000-mile-long Appalachian Trail, the continuous mountain footpath which ends in the south at Springer Mountain, Georgia. Each day, Maine greets the rays of the morning sun before any other place in the United States; depending on the time of year, the first place to be bathed in light will be Katahdin's peak, Cadillac Mountain, or West Quoddy Head. (So vast is the nation's territorial reach now that it will be another six hours before the sun filters through to the slopes of fiery Mauna Loa and Mauna Kea on the "Big Island" of Hawaii, a quarter of the way around the globe.)

Although modern modes of transportation make the distances within Maine a little less intimidating than they once were (providing one can afford an automobile), it is easy to imagine how profoundly they worked to shape the state's character in times past. For centuries, in fact, Maine seemed to exist in splendid isolation. Just as in part of Appalachia and the Ozarks, clear representations of Elizabethan English could be heard in places like Washington County's Beals Island. (And like Appalachia's, the original Maine stock was heavily Scotch-Irish.)

Until the last few decades, the great majority of Maine people lived in small towns, with scant contact with the outside world. For hundreds of thousands, small-town life is still the norm in Maine. Richard Saltonstall, in *Maine Pilgrimage*, quotes a native as saying: "The small town life has its appeal. But there are three big drawbacks that you've got to keep in mind. Medical facilities generally are not available. The schools are awfully provincial. The teachers are good people but they live in a small world with no exposure to outside thought, so education falls into a rut. The third problem is lack of outside recreation and culture, activities that get people out and doing things." Captain Littlepage made the same point in *The Country of the Pointed Firs*, when he commented that "a community narrows down and grows dreadful ignorant when it is shut up to its own affairs, and gets no knowledge of the outside world except from a cheap, unprincipled newspaper."

Along the coast, which one normally thinks of as a gateway to the wider world, communication even between towns is complicated by the deep indentations of inlets and estuaries which may require an auto trip of 50 or 75 miles to get to another place a mere 20 or 25 miles away, but separated by a river or arm of the sea. To this day—and in some respects even more seriously than in the past—Maine people suffer from peculiar types of isolation. Rural postal service has deteriorated; phone rates are high, with toll charges even for calls from town to town within a single county; and there is an appalling dearth of public transportation.

And then one must mention the weather, which alone seems to have done so much to seal folks off over the course of Maine's history. As Louise Dickinson Rich wrote in *State O' Maine*:

Great storms sweep in from the seas—three day nor'easters, drenching line storms, real old lamb-killers and goose-drownders—to be followed by spectacular clearings. The ocean turns in an instant from dull gray to deep blue. . . .

Sometimes epic fogs move in from the Bay of Fundy in a mile-high wall to shroud the land for days on end. The world is reduced to a dim circle of low-bowed, moisture-beaded grass tops, dripping blueberry bushes and spectral, perimetrical trees. . . . Visitors find these fogs depressing, but to Down-easters they are restful, beautiful and right.

Out of all this developed the fabled Down-easter character, so devoid of the hail-fellow-well-met exuberance of many Americans. Little affection is shown unless there's a disaster; then if one's house burns down or his traps are stolen or broken in a storm, Maine neighbors are there to help—and one would never have reason to expect it otherwise. Mrs. Rich wrote that the old-style Maine Yankees

somehow give the impression that behind the watchful eyes detached judgments are being made and uncompromising conclusions drawn. This is frequently a false impression, rising from Down-easters' disinclination to expose their feelings. Ever since they first came to the Maine coast, they have necessarily been on guard against unexpected attacks from a variety of quarters, including Indians, the weather, the wrath of God, and smooth-talking, out-of-state salesmen. These centuries of defensiveness have trained the Yankee face not to lend itself to merely polite smiles. . . . Such might lead to commitment, and Down-easters have learned not to commit themselves readily. . . .

The aversion to squandering anything, including time, energy and words, is ingrained. . . . The Down East Yankee is busy, thrifty and practical, and he uses a language as direct, graphic and economical as he himself is.

That very wariness and disinclination to commit oneself was complemented by the character attributes of Maine's principal "ethnic" group, the French-Canadians. Drawn to Maine as lumberjacks, and then to man the low-wage textile mills in the last half of the 19th century, the French felt themselves linguistically and religiously separate from the rest of Maine. It has taken generations for the most educated French to work their way into positions of leadership in government and politics, and still there is a great deal of separation. The French still tend to live together, to listen to French language radio broadcasts in their communities, and to visit a great deal back and forth with New Brunswick and Quebec. A Canadian-American Solidarity Day is held each year at Lewiston, and for decades the "Canadian-American Atlantic City" has been Old Orchard Beach, a honky-tonk resort, where 75 percent of the visitors are from Quebec and in the summertime French is spoken more than English.

Television and intermarriage are breaking down some of the Franco-American isolation now, but roughly 15 percent of Maine's people are still only one or two generations away from Canadian birth, not to mention the Franco-Americans whose families have been in Maine for up to a century or more. In the process there has been a noticeable merging of the flat Yankee twang with the French-Canadian patois.*

Maine has always had, of course, a minority of well-traveled and literate professionals—businessmen, bankers, lawyers, politicians, college professors—for whom Maine has only been one window on a wider world. Since the last century, wealthy out-of-staters have vacationed at places like Mount Desert Island, though their initial impact on the state's culture was slight. In the last decades, however, Maine has begun to take more note of its distinguished sometime residents—Buckminister Fuller, IBM's Thomas Watson, the Fords of auto fame, the Rockefellers, the late Rachel Carson, Walter Lippmann, E. B. White, and others. Even more important on the permanent Maine scene have been the many artists, writers, physicians, business executives, intellectuals, and other sensitive people who began to question the urban civilization of modern America in the years following World War II and turned Down East to find a safe harbor, a touchstone with a more basic civilization they felt missing in the heart of megalopolis. One of the latter-day arrivals, Richard Goodwin, who had been a speechwriter for Presidents Kennedy and Johnson and bought a farm near Sugarloaf Mountain, described to students at Bowdoin College the conditions in America's national life that had driven him to Maine (though it's worth noting that he continued to spend a good portion of his time out of the state). "It is almost impossible for the individual to escape the vast and frenzied throng of the stranger, stripping him at once of isolation and a place in the community," he said. "The dissolution of family and neighborhood and community deprive him of those worlds within a world where he once could find a liberating sense of importance and shared enterprise as well as the security of friends."

Out of such motives, looking for a place where they can be more in tune with nature and community, many hundreds if not thousands of Americans have turned to Maine as their new residence in the last several years. Some have become homesteaders working long-abandond farmland; some have provided important new sources of leadership within the state. An example is J. Russell Wiggins who retired from the editorship of the Washington *Post* to publish the influential weekly Ellsworth *American*, aided by his son-in-law, Thomas N. Schroth (former editor of *Congressional Quarterly*) and daughter Patricia Schroth (a former United Press correspondent). The Wiggins-Schroth clan are typical of people who used to vacation in Maine but found themselves drawn more and more into its public life. Another is my friend Frederick H. Sontag, a public affairs and research consultant, who

---

* Maine's other principal ethnic groups are the Irish, long-time competitors with the French-Canadians in Democratic party politics, plus scatterings of Scandinavians, Poles, Jews, blacks (only 2,800 in 1970), and the original Mainers, the Indians (2,195 in 1970).

spends his winters in New Jersey and Washington, D.C., but long summers and autumns at Seal Harbor, from which point he does commentary on national affairs for Maine Public Broadcasting and guest lecturing in political science at Colby.

Even more important for Maine, the breakdown of the old political orthodoxy pioneered by Edmund S. Muskie has enlivened public debate and the public process in a state once known for its rock-ribbed, change-me-not attitudes. The change in Maine's mood and outlook on life in the past quarter century has probably been greater than in the entire previous century. One might fear for a destruction of the best qualities of the old Down East character—self-reliance, thrift, and realism—in these changes. As we shall note, there have been and are some very serious concerns about the preservation of the natural environment, and the motivations of the fast-buck developer and oilman. But in character, Maine's evolution toward the last years of this century arouses less concern than the change of practically any other American state. I make that observation because the Maine oldtimer and newcomer alike seem united in the determination that the state will retain the core of integrity, of sticking to basics and essentials, that makes Maine the distinctive civilization it is.

Discovery, Statehood, and Past Glories

The early history of what is now Maine is one of constant discovery and rediscovery, starting most probably with the Viking expeditions in the early years of the 11th century, skipping almost 400 years to the exploration of the coastline by England's John Cabot and his sons in 1496. As the 1500s passed more European ships, many of them French, came to visit briefly. In 1607–08 a colony was tried briefly, but abandoned by its British sponsors; had it succeeded, history would record that in the same year of 1607 America received its first two permanent settlements—Jamestown, Virginia, and Popham, Maine. Seven years later Captain John Smith visited the coast from Penobscot to Cape Cod and made a map of the territory which he named "New England." Smith was perhaps the first man to perceive the true potential of the Maine coast; as his famous account reads:

I have seen at least forty habitations upon the seacoast and sounded about twenty-five excellent good harbors. . . . From Penobscot to Sagadahoc [the Kennebec River] this coast is all mountainous, and isles of huge rocks, but overgrown with all sorts of excellent good woods for building houses, boats, barks, and ships, with an incredible abundance of most sorts of fish, much fowl and sundry sorts of good fruit for man's use. . . . I made a garden upon the top of a rocky isle [Monhegan] in 43½ degrees, four leagues from the mainland in May, that grew so well that it served us for salads in June and July. . . . All sorts of cattle may here be bred and fed in the islands or peninsulas securely for nothing. . . . You will scarce find any bay, shallow shore, or cove of sand where you may not take many clams or lobsters, or both at your pleasure, and in many places load your boat if you please; nor isles where you find not fruits, birds, crabs, and mussels, or all of them for taking at low water . . . Worthy is that person to starve that here cannot live, if he have sense, strength, and health, for there is no such penury of these blessings in any place but that a hundred men may in an hour or two make their provisions for a day.

Permanent English settlements did indeed come to spots along the Maine coast in the 1620s; some 20 years later the settlers affiliated with Massachusetts. But the question of ownership and control of the province was constantly in dispute, and Maine was so poor and weak because of its seemingly constant wars with the French and Indians that at one point, in 1690, only four settlements continued to be inhabited. With its broad sea exposure, Maine would suffer during the Revolutionary War more than any other part of New England.

In the years following the Revolution, and particularly the War of 1812, when the province was left virtually undefended by Massachusetts and the British seized and occupied much of the Maine coast, Maine's people became increasingly unhappy about their status as a virtual colony of the commonwealth to the south. It was clear that the interests of Maine and Massachusetts were quite divergent, that the seat of the government was distant, the tax system unbalanced, and that it was quite illogical for Maine to remain part of a state it did not even adjoin physically. Massachusetts' leaders also came to the conclusion that they had little to gain from governing such a large, distant, and not very rich area, and agreed to separation. So it was that Maine separated from the Bay State, winning admission to the Union in 1820. In that year, Maine had 298,335 people—three times as many as in the first U.S. Census, 30 years before. The state would continue to expand rapidly in population to 1850; since then, it has lagged behind the national growth rate, usually by wide margins, in every decade.

The reasons for heady growth, followed by relative stagnation in population, are easy enough to perceive. It was only natural that the Maine coast would fill with fishermen, that a goodly complement of fur traders and guides would head off to its wilderness, and that the lumberjacks would follow soon thereafter, together with farmers in the time that New England's small-bore agriculture was still feasible. Boat building rose up as a natural early industry, both because Maine had its long seacoast and because its forests could supply the masts and timber. In the 1840s Maine was building more tonnage than any other state and Maine captains and their crews circled the globe; often the captains took their wives with them, and Maine children were born in such far-flung places as Rangoon or Shanghai. But when shipbuilding shifted from wood to metals, Maine lacked the basic natural resources. The state was an illogical place for any kind of heavy industry. When farming began its long decline, soon after the Civil War, textile mills did come to Maine, utilizing the power from the fast-running rivers. But the textile mills and shoe factories could absorb only part of the surplus of able-bodied young men and women coming off the farms; in any event, it was cheaper to import French-Canadian labor for the mills. In time, textile and shoe employment in Maine began to drop precipitously, as in the other New England states. Someday they might disappear from the scene entirely, just as another product for which Maine was one famed—ice—is no longer a viable commodity. (In the

19th century, ice was a great cash crop. Cut from Maine's lakes and rivers for shipment to the rest of the United States, and even to Europe, ice-cutting hit a peak in 1890 when some 25,000 men were employed in cutting three million tons of ice in the state. This was prototypal seasonal employment in an industry destined for extinction in the age of electrical refrigeration.)

The essential fact was that once the United States became an industrialized and rail-borne (and later highway-borne) nation, Maine would be at the end of the line—and fail to grow apace. Its prime export has always been its young people, looking for brighter opportunity far afield. Tens of thousands of them have left every decade; one looks at the Census figures and the story is unmistakable: every 10 years there is a dramatic dropoff in the population group moving into its productive years. There are now some signs that the population outflow may be tapering off, or that immigrants to Maine may more than make up for it statistically. We will look at that story later in this chapter; for now it is sufficient to note that the population and economic tides of the years have left that state with a per capita income ranking only 43rd in the entire United States, and the lowest of all the New England states.

Early Maine was a relatively classless place, a frontier where the differentials of rank or wealth were not great. As the authors of the WPA Guide on Maine noted, "there was little law or respect for law" in the early days; "rum was the common beverage, and spirits were consumed on all occasions." (Again, one notes a striking parallel to the sociology of old-time—and not so old-time—Appalachia.) The disregard for law was gradually brought under control by the spread of Congregationalism and the Puritan movement from Massachusetts, although in Maine the sternest Puritan types of laws—prosecution of religious "heresy," limited suffrage, and hidebound conventional morality, including the banning of games and dances and strict controls on public houses—were not very zealously enforced. And Maine was fortunate to gain from Massachusetts an early public school system and basic respect for learning, a benefit Appalachia never had.

As in Massachusetts, a strong abolitionist movement sprang up in the early 19th century; although it was resisted in the coastal towns, with their strong trade ties to the South, antislavery sentiment prospered inland and eventually across the whole of Maine, leading to the state's enthusiastic (and costly) involvement in the Civil War. Simultaneously, a strong effort to ban alcohol spread through Maine, leading to prohibition laws from 1846 clear through the national Prohibition era and not finally erased from the statute books until 1934. As in so many states, the issue of prohibition diverted people's attention from more important issues of government awaiting resolution. Another diversion was the virulent anti-Roman Catholicism that surfaced in Maine in the 1850s, allied with the national "Know-Nothing" Party and its strong prejudice against foreign immigrants, the Irish in particular. Catholic churches in Maine were desecrated and burned by angry mobs, and while the Catholic Church eventually survived the attacks upon it (rising to 80,000 members by 1874), one hears to this day of deep anti-Catholic prejudice, especially along the coast.

During the last half of the 19th century, Maine enjoyed a kind of national heyday during which it contributed three men of immense stature—Hannibal Hamlin, James G. Blaine, and Thomas B. Reed—to the country at large.

During the 1850s, the antislavery movement had gone into politics, resulting in the organization of the Republican party. Maine quickly embraced the new party, and in 1856, two years after its birth, made Hannibal Hamlin the first of a long string of Republican governors. Hamlin had served previously in Congress as a Democrat, albeit in that party's antislavery wing, fighting battle after battle from the 1840s onward to stop the spread of slavery into the new states and territories. In 1856, when the national Democratic party nominated James Buchanan for President on a proslavery platform, Hamlin rose in the Senate to make the decisive political speech of his life, denouncing his party for giving in to the South and announcing, "I am leaving the Democratic party forever!" Maine voted that fall for Republican Charles Fremont for President. Four years later, after Abraham Lincoln had been nominated by the Republicans—with Maine's support—Hamlin was chosen as the candidate for Vice President. After the two men took office, he constantly pressured President Lincoln to move rapidly toward the abolition of slavery. In 1864, however, he was dropped from the ticket in favor of Tennessee's Andrew Johnson, a Democrat who had supported the war. Had Hamlin been retained, he, rather than Johnson, would have succeeded to the presidency to preside over the Reconstruction era, and the freed slaves would have had a much better friend in the White House.

Hamlin returned to the Senate in 1868 and served another two terms, becoming the senior figure in terms of service, called "The Father of the Senate." Only he remained of the strong leaders who had fought slavery before the war. Hamlin died peacefully at his Bangor home on the Fourth of July, 1891.

James Blaine, like Hamlin, might well have become President with a luckier draw of the cards; in fact he was almost nominated in two years (1876 and 1880) when his Republican party won nationally, and barely lost the 1880 election to Democrat Grover Cleveland. Blaine was a master orator of his age, an opponent of slavery and backer of Negro suffrage, and a high-tariff man. For 20 years he was the commanding "general" of Maine Republican politics, and he served as the speaker of two houses of representatives—Maine's and the nation's. Personal ethics, including a connection with the scandals of the Grant administration and the fairly mysterious accumulation of a personal fortune, proved his political undoing. His most enduring contribution was in the field of foreign relations; under Presidents Garfield and Harrison he was Secretary of State, and he fathered the Pan-American Union, seeking hemispheric solidarity based on "friendship, not force." In the words of one historian, Blaine was a pioneer in coordinating the strategic, diplomatic, and economic elements of foreign policy, "thus setting the stage for America's rise to world power. Blaine's diplomatic fame outlived political defeats and surly epithets."

Thomas B. Reed, who went from the Maine legislature and attorney generalship to serve continuously in Congress from 1876 to 1899, was a master of parliamentary law who raised the office of Speaker, which he occupied for three terms, to a position second only to that of the President of the United States. A corpulent man, over six feet in height, Reed was the master of any debate and as Speaker in 1889 overrode the rebellious minority Democrats to effect some vital reforms in House rules. In 1896 Reed was a prominent candidate for the Republican presidential nomination; when asked if he thought the convention would nominate him, Reed replied: "They could do worse, and probably will." The nomination went to William McKinley.

No Maine Republican, from Reed's departure from Washington to this day, has had an impact on the national scene comparable to the giants of the last century. Some of the reasons for this may emerge from our subsequent account: the Maine Republican party's fall into the hands of special interests, the ossification of the one-party system that prevailed until the 1950s. Political editor Donald C. Hansen of the Portland *Press-Herald* suggested to me that the emigration of the most imaginative young people from Maine depleted it of its leadership reserve. Perhaps the explanation is simply that the leaders of a retrenched, status quo society, as Maine was until a few years ago, are unlikely to make much of an impression on the nation at large.

Political Metamorphosis

"Thirty-two state central committeemen, a few score town councillors, an occasional mayor, a sprinkling of rustic selectmen and assessors, and several thousand hereditary voters, without a program and almost without a hope—such is the party of Jefferson in the Pine Tree State." In those words political scientist Lane Lancaster summed up the sorry condition of Maine's Democratic party in an article for the *National Municipal Review* in 1929, going on to explain that in ballot support, the Democrats' mainstay was a half dozen cities where "the foreign element of the population"—French Canadians and some Irish—was strong.* Whatever Democratic support there was in rural areas, Lancaster suggested, came from patriarchal adherents of Jeffersonian Democracy who stayed true to their founder by fighting against state control of local affairs.

It is true that the Democrats won occasional elections for governor during the long winter of their discontent; in 1910 they even won control of the legislature for a year. But the Republicans always rose up to overwhelm them, the voters selecting the Grand Old Party partly out of Civil War memory or tradition, partly because the Republicans for generations kept themselves on the politically popular "dry" side of the prohibition issue, while the Democrats were avowedly "wet." For years there was a remarkable complacency among the Democrats, particularly their leaders who liked the patronage they

* The French-Canadian and Irish adherence to the Democratic party had its roots in the 19th century, when the Democrats were at low ebb and welcomed all and any recruits, in contrast to the dominant, overwhelmingly Wasp Republicans. As recently as the 1920s, there was a powerful, virulently anti-Catholic Ku Klux Klan movement in the state. U.S. Senator Owen Brewster, finally defeated in a 1952 primary, had been a Klan leader in the '20s.

got from national Democratic administrations ("post office" Democrats like the fabled "post office" Republicans of the South) and defaulted in many election contests by not even nominating candidates.

The result of all this was a rather issueless type of politics. As the Lisbon *Enterprise* complained editorially in 1948: "Nobody is allowed to say anything that has the least to do with government or the office being sought. Those running for governor comment how noble it is to dig clams, grow blueberries, teach school, and wait on table. Our senatorial aspirants touch on ancient Roman roads, winter sports. . . ."

Yet another factor was the close alliance between the Republicans and the big corporate interests—the timber companies and paper mills, the power companies which moved into politics to secure or protect hydroelectric sites and defend their flank against the rate cutters or competition, and the textile and shoe manufacturers. As recently as 1959, in his book *New England State Politics*, Duane Lockard could write that "in few American states are the reins of government more openly or completely in the hands of a few leaders of economic interest groups than in Maine. . . . They have done more than merely 'influence' Maine politics; 'control' is probably a more appropriate term."

Together with the banks and railroads, the Big Three of pine, power, and manufacturing are still factors to be reckoned with. In 1974 the Maine *Times* alleged that five men "run" Maine:

William Henry Dunham, chief executive officer of Central Maine Power, whose influence spreads to practically every New England power company; an officer or director of the Maine Development Credit Corporation, the Oxford Paper Company, the First National Granite Bank, WCBB-TV, etc.

Robert Nelson Haskell, president of Bangor Hydro Electric Company, the state's second largest utility, who "ruled the Legislature with an iron hand for four years"; briefly governor in 1959; director or trustee of Merchants National, Diamond International Corporation, University of Maine.*

Horace A. Hildreth, governor for two terms in the 1940s, former president of Bucknell University, former U.S. Ambassador to Pakistan; head of a mini-conglomerate in Maine radio and television; "still a major force in Maine Republican politics."

Edward Spence Miller, president of the Maine Central Railroad since 1952; director of Keyes Fibre, Great Northern Paper, Maine National Bank, and First National Bank of Boston; supporter of oil development in Maine "who emerges as the tough guy of the group."

Curtis Marshall Hutchins, founder of Dead River Company (oil distribution, timberlands, and lumber); director of Guilford Industries, Merrill Trust Company, State Street Bank and Trust, Scott Paper Co., New England Council, American Association of Railroads.

Even the Maine *Times*, however, had to acknowledge that this group (all aging Protestant Republicans), did not provide quite the united front of their historic predecessors, who used to fight tooth and nail against environmental control legislation. Hutchins, for instance, has served on environ-

* Haskell was described as "perhaps the finest, most knowledgeable student of Maine government to serve in the state Legislature in this century" by Theo Lippman, Jr., and Donald C. Hansen in their 1971 book, *Muskie* (New York: W. W. Norton & Co.)

mental boards and study groups for the state's educational future, while Hildreth threw his television and radio stations into the battle against oil development on the Maine coast.

Nor is Maine any longer a normally or predominantly Republican state, so that one can relegate to the history books the state's one-time reputation as being only less Republican than Vermont (which it joined in the lonely two-state coalition that voted for Alf Landon for President in 1936).

The Republican "machine," dominated by the major economic interests, began to lose its touch in the late 1940s as intraparty squabbles increased and younger party members became increasingly dissatisfied with the secondary position to which the party patriarchs relegated them. A sign of the disquietude was the success of Margaret Chase Smith, then a relatively little-known Congresswoman, in winning the Republican nomination for the Senate in 1948, defeating two former governors, Horace Hildreth and Sumner Sewall. Then, in 1953–54, Republican Governor Burton W. Cross ran into the kind of difficulties that can be expected when a dominant political party loses touch with the public. Though he could be faulted for parsimonious budget-cutting, Cross was actually a very able governor; he reformed the patronage-ridden highway commission, for instance, and reorganized the state liquor commission that had become mired in scandal. Politically, however, Cross's manner was disastrous; he seemed to lack any kind of tact, and gratuitously suggested to the people of poverty-ridden Washington County that they "lift up their own bootstraps." The remark, writers Theo Lippman, Jr., and Donald C. Hansen have suggested, "was the kind of unfeeling aristocratic comment that could only have been uttered by a politician leading a firmly one-party state."

The Democrats surely seemed in poor condition to score a statewide victory. They had only 99,386 registered voters, compared to 262,344 Republicans (and 118,928 independents); in some counties the Republicans had an 8–1 advantage. There was no permanent state Democratic headquarters; Democratic committees existed in only 132 of Maine's more than 400 towns; Democrats held only 14 percent of the seats in the state legislature and had no representation at all on the congressional delegation. To wage their 1954 campaign for governor, the U.S. Senate, and three U.S. House seats, they could raise only $18,000.

Early in 1954, however, control of the Democratic party shifted into the hands of a group of young reformers including Frank M. Coffin, a brilliant Harvard Law School graduate and representative of a family that had worked for Maine's Democratic party over three generations. According to the Lippman-Hansen account,

Even before his election [as] state chairman, Coffin had put his imprint on the 1954 campaign as chairman of the platform committee. The platform, a masterpiece of political showmanship, was developed as a "grass-roots" statement of Maine beliefs and aspirations. It was drafted not by party workers behind closed doors, but by schoolteachers, mill workers, and farmers. Questionnaires were circulated throughout the state, exploring citizen sentiment on a broad range of issues. The public reaction was enthusiastic: Mainers, long accustomed to being either scolded or ignored by the Republican party, took the formation of the platform seriously. By February 1954, Coffin had held an open "issues conference" that attracted about 250, including many who had never before participated in politics.

The platform exercise, of course, was a harbinger of the new, "open" style of party activity which in recent years has become so widespread in the nation but was so little known in the early 1950s. But it did not settle on the question of a candidate for governor. For that slot, the Democrats agreed on the initially quite reluctant candidate—Edmund S. Muskie, a state legislator since 1947, lawyer, and son of a Polish-born tailor named Stephen Marcis-zewski who had come to America in 1903, changed his name to Muskie when he became naturalized, and moved to Rumford, Maine, in 1911. Edmund Muskie was the second of six children of Stephen and Josephine Muskie (nee Czarnecka); they were one of only three Polish families in Rumford, and experienced bitter prejudice in the years following World War I. At school, Edmund found himself called a "dumb Polack" and heard his Roman Catholicism held up to ridicule. Silently, he bore the abuse, and from his father, as Lippman and Hansen wrote, he "inherited a quizzical combative instinct, a thirst for knowledge, and a temper." With great financial difficulties, he made his way through Bates College, graduating Phi Beta Kappa and president of his class in 1936; then came Cornell Law School, a fledging law practice in Waterville, service in the Navy during World War II, and a request to run for the legislature in 1946, after his return home. Muskie won the election and by 1949 had risen to be the house minority leader; as a state legislator his reputation was chiefly for caution and careful attention to issues.

In 1954, Muskie had originally thought he might run for Congress if any higher office at all. But as he helped to survey candidates for governor, he was increasingly asked why he didn't run himself, and finally decided to take the chance. "The campaign," according to Lippman and Hansen, "was laughable even by rustic Maine standards." Apparently Muskie never spent a night in a hotel or motel during the campaign, bedding down in the houses of Democratic supporters instead. He was constantly scratching for cash throughout the race. But gradually the thoughtfulness and openness of the rawboned young candidate came across, together with his message of the need for a viable two-party system and industrial development for Maine. The state's campaigns had traditionally consisted of nighttime rallies and shaking hands at factory gates; Muskie shook thousands of hands but had an advantage in the advent of television. Television in those days was inexpensive— $200 for 15 minutes, for instance—and the Democrats made wise use of it, bringing the image of their gubernatorial candidate into thousands of homes, even those of rock-ribbed Republicans who might well never have listened to a Democratic leader before in their lives. Muskie also benefited from some key endorsements by dissident Republicans, from Governor Cross's unpopularity, and from Coffin's masterful management of the campaign.

Few people in Maine seriously believed Muskie would win in 1954, but when the returns started to pour in it was never even close. The victory was based on two pillars: huge margins in the Democratic mill towns—Lewiston went to Muskie by a 5–1 margin, for instance—and Muskie's ability to cut deeply into the massive Republican margins usually registered in rural Maine. The final count was 135,673 for Muskie, 113,298 for Cross.

Campaigning for Vice President 14 years later, Muskie recalled for a Texas crowd the election night of that first great victory: "I never had an experience like that. If I win elections from now until the year 2000—this election, if we win it, won't be nearly the exhilarating experience of that one. We won against hopeless odds. We won with almost no resources. We had to literally walk that state from one end to the other. We had to talk to Republicans who had never seen a live Democrat in their lives. We had to learn the political skills that none of us had ever developed. We had to do it against an establishment, against a machine, against a political organization which had had a century to entrench itself, and we did it."

Muskie's election was the vital breakthrough Maine Democrats needed, and his personality had a great deal to do with the party's general rise. As Michael Barone commented in *The Almanac of American Politics*, Muskie's "serene and plain manner, coupled with his clearly honest idealism, persuaded many Yankee Republicans that not all Democrats were big-city hacks, and that some like Muskie were decent men who could be trusted with government." Whatever weaknesses Muskie was to show as a national politician in later years, there was no gainsaying the skill with which he constantly put the overwhelming Republican legislature on the defensive, keeping the public on his side yet agreeing to compromises at just the right moments to get legislative approval for the great bulk of his program.

Moreover, Muskie was a party builder—just as Hubert Humphrey was in Minnesota, George McGovern in South Dakota, G. Mennen Williams in Michigan, and William Proxmire and Gaylord Nelson in Wisconsin. He made such a good impression in his first term in Augusta that in 1956 he was able to win reelection with a plurality of 56,000 votes, his total vote larger than any Maine governor had ever before received. That same year, Frank Coffin won the first of two terms he would serve in the U.S. House. In 1958, Muskie won election to the Senate with an astounding margin of 61,000 votes and the Democrats elected their second Maine Congressman. Another Democrat was elected governor in 1958: he died during his first year in office, and in the 1960 and 1962 elections the Democrats could elect neither governor nor a Congressman.* In 1964, however, they rebounded, and for the next 10 years they held at least half of Maine's two Senate and two House seats. One of their number, Kenneth M. Curtis, was governor for the eight years from 1967 to 1975; at the time he first took office, Curtis was only 36, the nation's youngest governor, but he proved to be an exceptionally able and innovative one.

* Frank Coffin was the unsuccessful Democratic gubernatorial candidate in 1960, a year when strong anti-Catholicism was credited with a strong defeat for John F. Kennedy of nearby Massachusetts, a Democratic reversal which hurt the party's candidates for almost all lower offices.

The Democrats are no longer a hopeless minority in the legislature, either; at this writing, for instance (1975), they control the house by an ample margin and trail by only a few seats in the senate.

In presidential voting, Lyndon Johnson carried Maine by an astounding 69 percent of the vote in 1964. Four years later Maine gave 55 percent of its vote to the Democratic ticket of Hubert H. Humphrey for President and Edmund S. Muskie for Vice President. In 1972 George McGovern could win only 38.5 percent of the Maine vote—though it might have been much different, of course, if Muskie had been the Democratic nominee. But in the same 1972 election Maine voters ousted an aging and out-of-touch Margaret Chase Smith as U.S. Senator, installing in her place an attractive younger Democrat who then represented the state's northern congressional district, William D. Hathaway.

The Republican registration edge—162,958 when Muskie first won—has dwindled steadily; in 1974 it was only 16,653. It would be an overstatement to say that Maine is or is about to become a normally Democratic state; the Republican strength remains formidable, even if eclipsed in most major offices. But the destruction of the monolithic Republican façade of Maine politics which Muskie and Coffin began in 1954 has been total, one of the great success stories of American politics.

Today Maine is one of the nation's most intensely competitive states in partisan politics. Indeed, so much time has now passed since the Democratic renaissance that the Republicans may be ripe for one of their own. One of their most promising leaders of the early and mid-'70s was the young former mayor of Bangor, William S. Cohen, who undertook a 550-mile trek across the Second congressional district (the largest east of the Mississippi) to get close to the people and learn their concerns and thus win election to Congress in 1972. In 1973 and 1974 Cohen was back on the road again in his working outfit of blue workshirt and patch-pocket khakis; in the meantime, as a member of the House Judiciary Committee, he cast early votes leading toward Richard Nixon's impeachment, impressing national television viewers and particularly his own constituents, who became convinced of his sound judgment and honesty.* His voting record in the House was moderate-to-liberal, and he won reelection by a landslide margin in 1974, looking forward to a race for the U.S. Senate in some future year. Also in 1974, Republican Dave Emery, a 26-year-old electrical engineer and state representative, upset the lackluster Democratic incumbent in the state's other U.S. House district.

The problem of Maine Republicans—overcome by only a few candidates, like Cohen and Emery—is that the party's taproot of support remains the cautious small towns, where only orthodox candidates, allied with the state's economic establishments, tend to win. A quintessential candidate of that old, traditional Republicanism was the state's attorney general, James Erwin, who won the party's gubernatorial nomination in both 1970 and 1974, but lost both times. In the latter year, Erwin—once unkindly described as a "young fogey"

---

* Before Nixon's lawbreaking became manifest to all, however, Cohen received some irate mail. One constituent wrote: "May a thousand camels relieve themselves in your drinking water."

in a newspaper column—barely defeated former state legislator Harrison Richardson, a leading environmentalist and skilled lawmaker of maverick bent, for the Republican nomination.

If the Republicans have a conservative-liberal split, the same must be said of the Democrats. A description John Cole wrote for the Maine *Sunday Telegram* describing the 1968 Democratic state convention still holds largely true:

> Fifteen years ago there were still only 90,000 Maine Democrats—recruited from the sweat shops of the mill towns along Maine rivers; from the half-dozen grimy Maine cities where organization was able to make patronage possible; and from the Maine French and Irish Catholics, long a minority in a state run for centuries by Protestants. . . . [But] in the last few years these Maine Democrats have put Democratic machinery in the State House, and now they are about to enjoy the ultimate luxury of fighting among themselves. . . .
>
> The French-Catholics are here: hard-working, thrifty—generally regulated types carefully dressed in new clothes and boisterously excited by the event they look forward to so long. They are like children at a camporee—talking loudly, drinking in the forenoon, back-slapping, smiling and knowing all along that they still control most of their party.
>
> They are courteous but cautious with the new Maine Democrats—the tweed-jacketed campus oriented and more casual and outwardly reserved liberals, intellectuals and middle-class Protestants who know they control only a small part of the party, but who hope they can use their sophistication to maneuver to advantage.
>
> And both groups are excited by the McCarthy people—the virginal teen-age girls, so polite, so smiling, so hopeful; and the college boys in their blazers trying with such touching intensity to be efficient.

(The latter group, in its continuing metamorphosis, is not to be taken lightly; by the 1974 Democratic state convention, it was able to get through platform planks calling for the elimination of jail terms for marijuana for personal use, "to forbid discrimination on the basis of homosexuality," and to declare amnesty for Vietnam war resistors.)

For governor in 1974 the Democrats nominated George Mitchell, a former chief aide to Muskie and able political organizer who had been state Democratic chairman, national committeeman, and a candidate for national chairman. Mitchell ran a campaign based on substantive issues, but he was no more colorful a figure than Erwin, and failed to stir the voters' imagination. Moreover, 1974 was the year of Watergate and as Senator Muskie put it in an interview I had with him later, profound "unhappiness of the American people with the political system, the two political parties, the cost of government, and the irrelevance of government programs."

So the stage was set in Maine for one of the most astounding upsets of modern political history—the election of an independent candidate for governor (the first in any state since William Langer in North Dakota in 1936). The man who did it was James B. Longley, a wealthy insurance man and registered Democrat up to 1974. Longley had first won statewide notice as chairman of the Maine management and cost survey, a position to which he was appointed by Governor Curtis. Without pay, he had spent two years on the survey, which produced 807 recommendations for efficiency in state government. As a result of the commission's work, 92 bills were introduced in a special session of the Maine legislature; of these some 30 passed. According to the Bangor *Daily News*, the only major paper to back Longley's candidacy, the survey saved "Maine people $10 million and without any attendant injury to state government operation or a lessening of the quality of Maine life."

Longley was piqued, however, that neither his friend Curtis nor the Republican-dominated legislature approved more of his recommendations, and so he plunged into the race as an independent—because, he said, he had promised Curtis and the legislature he would keep the cost survey nonpartisan.

After his election, Longley said: "This election is shining like that beacon off the coast of Maine. I can see other candidates all over the country doing what I did."

How, though, had he done it? Prospective emulators had a long list of reasons to pick from. One reason, as Longley himself said, was that he had shaken 400,000 hands around Maine in only five months. Another was that the cost survey chairmanship had given him visibility and credibility, on an issue of concern to people. The state budget, he said, had burgeoned from $165 million to $569 million in 10 years, a growth rate unjustifiable in a slow-growth state. "I'm a businessman," he said repeatedly during the campaign, "and I think through the introduction of business procedures and practices in government we can save a lot of taxpayers' money."

Longley also won, it appeared, because his opponents both ignored him throughout the campaign. "While Mitchell and Erwin battled each other," journalist Robert Merry reported from Portland, "Longley was free to convince voters he was a serious contender with serious ideas." Had Mitchell and Erwin taken Longley seriously, of course, they could have questioned his credibility by suggesting the impossibility of achieving—as Longley seemed to promise—a flawlessly efficient state government, lower taxes, and adequate if not improved state services, all at the same time.

Voter disillusionment seemed to help Longley in two ways: first, because he was a competent executive, who obviously knew a lot about state government, so that a citizen could safely cast a vote for "none of the above" as far as the regular politicians on the ballot were concerned; and second, because Longley's appearance as "an almost painfully sincere man beholden to no special interests" was appropriate for 1974 as in few election years. Longley, in effect, turned the voter disillusionment to his favor. In a year when voter turnout was down 8 percentage points from four years before in the nation as a whole, it was *up* 7 percent in Maine and in fact was the highest total vote of any nonpresidential election year in the state's history.

In many ways Longley's campaign seemed highly amateur. He surrounded himself with only a few "professionals," leaving it instead to his daughters and his wife to assemble a remarkable group of volunteers, many of them young people. A man less convinced of his own abilities might never have succeeded, but Longley had in earlier years sold millions of dollars of life insurance—sure evidence of a super-salesman—and he had risen to be president of the Million Dollar Roundtable of insurance men, the pinnacle of that business. Yet there was no discernible sign that Longley manipulated his own image for political selling purposes. As Jay Neal Martin, president of the state chamber of commerce, commented after the election: "There's no question that Jim Longley is the personification of commitment to God, country, and family. He's a gutsy, hard working, sincere, devoted kind of guy."

(Reading the first draft of this manuscript, one of my Maine readers penciled in beside Martin's quote: "Longley also had a beautifully oversimplified view of reality. There was a lot of 'sincere' bullshit in his campaign.")

Some practical political considerations have to be added. Longley had grown up in and lived in heavily Catholic and Democrat Lewiston, where his father was a streetcar conductor. In his youth he had worked in a textile mill to help support his widowed mother of six. His background helped him to cut heavily into the conservative side of the Democratic vote. But he also stole the march on Erwin by nipping off a large segment of the regular conservative Republican town vote, because he had in effect "expropriated" the favorite Republican theme of fiscal responsibility in government.

Not a single Maine newspaper, or any of the public opinion polls, it is worth noting, gave the public any clue before election day of the impending Longley coup. A Mitchell win was generally anticipated, because it was thought to be a good Democratic year, and because Mitchell had taken the time to ask for and win endorsements from key groups like COPE, the Maine Teachers Association, and the Women's Caucus in the state. (Longley didn't even try to get such endorsements.) Yet when the vote tally was finished, Longley had 39.5 percent of the total. Mitchell trailed fairly narrowly at 37 percent. But so far had Maine's political metamorphosis come that the campaign had left Erwin, the Republican of once-rock-ribbed Republican Maine, trailing in the dust with a scant 23.5 percent.

The Senators

If, in the autumn of 1968, the American people had been free to choose separately between the Democratic and Republican nominees for Vice President, Edmund S. Muskie would in all probability have been their choice. Polls taken during the campaign showed that the voters did indeed prefer Muskie over Spiro Agnew, though their preference between Nixon and Humphrey fell narrowly for the former, and of course there is no way under U.S. law to split one's ballot between presidential and vice presidential nominees. Certainly the image of fairmindedness and candor Muskie projected in that campaign spoke more of the nation's best spirit that did Agnew's thinly veiled racism and contempt for adversaries.

Let the scene shift forward two years in time, to the eve of the 1970 midterm elections, when Nixon and Agnew had been riding the "social issue" of public distaste for youthful dissenters and other malcontents, climaxed by the spurious "rock-throwing" incident involving Nixon at San Jose, California. In a raucous, arm-waving appearance before a partisan crowd at Phoenix, Nixon sought to capitalize on San Jose with a call on Americans to vote Republican and thus repudiate the rock throwers and obscenity shouters. The speech had been taped in black and white, with a barely audible sound track, but the White House insisted on airing it nationally. And the Democrats had decided that Edmund Muskie would be the person to deliver their party's reply, on national television immediately following the Phoenix tape showing.

So onto viewers' screens came (in color) the figure of a dignified Lincoln-esque Muskie, speaking from the quiet fireside of a borrowed Maine ocean-front home. "Honorable men have been slandered," Muskie began (using a text written for him by Richard Goodwin). "They imply that Democratic candidates for high office in Texas and California, in Illinois and Tennessee, in Utah and Maryland, and among my New England neighbors in Vermont and Connecticut—men who have courageously pursued their convictions . . . that these men actually favor violence and champion the wrongdoer. That is a lie. And the American people know it is a lie. How dare they?"

The righteous indignation of Muskie's speech was exquisitely appropriate to the moment, and the Nixonian excess had given him an opportunity to make an address that appealed to every segment of the Democratic coalition. From that evening onward, if he had not been before, Muskie was the leading contender for the Democrats' 1972 presidential nomination.

That it was all to come to naught is now a story well known; in subsequent years Muskie himself has acknowledged many of the mistakes of the 1972 campaign: to become identified (as George Romney had four years before) as the frontrunner too early, thus being called on to be expert on every conceivable subject and to agonize publicly over each; to be lured into running in virtually all the major presidential primaries, thus spreading too thin his financial, organizational, and personal strengths; to be the second choice of too many Democrats but not the first choice of enough; to campaign on a slogan of "trust and confidence" in a year when the voters were more in a mood to send the politicians an angry message. Primary voters, Muskie has commented, "know they're not electing a President," and in 1972 in particular turned to candidates who would "spit in the eye of the establishment." George McGovern fulfilled that need for left-leaning Democrats, George Wallace for those on the right, and in the emotion-filled primaries there was little room left for centrists—and Muskie had to share whatever centrist vote there was with Hubert Humphrey. In earlier years, whatever his problems as an early frontrunner, Muskie might well have emerged with the nomination and waged a creditable general election campaign. But then the "rules" were different, because there were not so many primaries in which a candidate could be cut up, nor was there such a hyperactive and critical national media, ready to pounce on a leading candidate's mistakes (like Muskie's "crying" scene before the Manchester *Union Leader* building, when he thought his wife had been maligned, or Romney's famous "brainwashing" comment.*)

Muskie does, of course, have character traits problematic for a presidential candidate. One is his frequent aloofness, another his towering temper, and still another his insistence on learning all sides of an issue, mulling it over carefully in his own mind, before taking a stand. Finally, he lacks the burning ambition, the steely determination that has sustained men like Humphrey, Nixon, and McGovern in campaigns for the presidency, even when the odds seemed hopelessly against them.

In the light of those factors, Muskie might have failed in 1972 even if he had not been the victim of systematic sabotage by the Nixon operatives (including the spurious letter to the *Union Leader*, in which he was accused of calling French-Canadians "Canucks"), and even if he had not, under the strain of a ludicrously overscheduled campaign covering multi-primaries, returned to Manchester on Saturday morning to utter his outburst against publisher William Loeb and shed that overpublicized tear.

All of this is not to say that Edmund Muskie has not been a superb United States Senator. From his position on the Public Works Committee, an assignment that looked so undesirable when he first went to Washington, he began to work on the environmental issue long before it was fashionable and eventually became the author of the nation's most important air- and water-pollution control legislation. Assigned to another seemingly humdrum committee, Government Operations, he became one of the nation's foremost experts on revenue sharing and the complex interrelationships of the various layers of government, within the U.S. federal system.† Such concerns, Muskie once observed, had led him into areas that "don't sound very glamorous, things that require tough, tedious, nuts-and-bolts work. But that is the only way to make the system work for people, and that, after all, is the real meaning of American politics."

In the late '6os Muskie went on the Foreign Relations Committee and

---

* One wonders about the purported judgment or omniscience of the national political reporters who made so much of these incidents regarding such honorable men as Rommey and Muskie, yet failed somehow to communicate to the voters the character failings of the likes of Nixon and Agnew, the first President and Vice President of the United States ever forced to resign in disgrace.

† One of Muskie's most innovative proposals for revenue sharing—to give states and localities a greater amount of funds if they would institute their own income taxes—was unfortunately watered down to the point of insignificance in the revenue sharing measure finally passed in 1972. The income tax, Muskie had pointed out, was "the most lucrative source of tax revenue," yet one used quite ineffectively by most states. He cited figures showing that each time the national economy expanded by one percent, federal income tax revenues increased by 1.5 percent. But because the states and cities collected only 9 percent of all income taxes in the country, leaving the rest to the federal government, the states had lagged seriously in revenue-raising capacity. (Another point, of course, was that income taxes are far less "regressive"—and thus less discriminatory against poor people—than property and sales taxes, the mainstays of state-local tax raising in the country.) Muskie's proposal was to add an extra $1 billion to the basic revenue sharing fund, to be paid to each state on a ratio of 10 percent of its own income tax collections. This "carrot" would presumably have made it much easier for state officials to persuade their citizenries of the desirability of instituting an income tax, because they would be losing money to other states if they failed to do so.

The point seems especially significant to this writer because of his conviction, based on a study of all 50 state governments, that the states will remain fiscal cripples, and/or discriminate egregiously against their poor citizens, until they institute sharply graduated income taxes accounting for a major part of their total state revenue.

shifted his position from support to eloquent opposition to the Vietnam war. In 1973 he was one of the leaders of the successful effort to open up the highway trust fund to spending for mass transit. He worked to curb, through legislation, the Nixon administration's free-wheeling impoundment of Congressionally appropriated funds. And in 1974 he became chairman of the new Senate Budget Committee, staffing it with outstanding persons in the most significant congressional effort of the past two generations to reestablish the power and responsibility of Congress over federal spending. By 1975 he was frequently taking the Senate floor to oppose new spending programs of Democratic liberals which he said would "break" the budget limit set by Congress under its new budget procedures. Muskie is one of the few Senators who has not become so wedded to past beliefs that he cannot adapt to the times. He may never become President (though the hope has not died entirely within him), but as a legislator he remains an important national resource.

While Margaret Chase Smith was still holding one of Maine's Senate seats, Donald Hansen remarked to me that while she and Muskie differed in many policy areas, they were "alike in personality—reasonable, sensible people, neither great partisans, people who have a sense of moderation and a deep sense of fair play." Thus, Hansen said, both "reflected Maine character."

Even more than Muskie, Mrs. Smith seemed to be the very embodiment of Maine virtues, as independent and straightforward as the Maine coast itself, a person to whom no one could dictate. (In fact, Mrs. Smith fiercely resisted any pressure or blandishment, and on controversial issues might tell no one how she would vote until the roll was called.) For years, Maine tourists to Washington would head straight to the Senate gallery to look for their lady Senator with the white hair and the red rose. Often they found her, because Mrs. Smith took her Senate voting seriously and cast an all-time record of 2,941 continuous roll-call votes, until a hip operation kept her away from the chamber briefly in 1968.

Toward the end of her career, people began to question whether Mrs. Smith had been as effective a Senator for Maine as her supporters advertised; though she was the ranking Republican on Armed Services, for instance, Maine in the early '70s ranked only 43rd in its percentage of defense contracts, and though she was the second-ranking Republican on Appropriations, Maine ranked only 47th in its share of federal expenditures. But still, people liked her independence. While she remained an unreconstructed backer of the Vietnam war and opponent of most welfare legislation, she did vote against the supersonic transport, the ABM (antiballistic missile) system, and the Haynesworth and Carswell nominations for the Supreme Court.

By the time of her eventual defeat in 1972, Mrs. Smith had begun to lose her touch with Maine and national problems. In meetings with young people, for instance, she showed a real lack of knowledge or of concern for their concerns. In retrospect, it is sad that she sought reelection at the age of 74. History will remember her, however, as the Senator who stood up in the Senate in June 1950, during the height of the McCarthy anti-Communist hysteria, and delivered her "declaration of conscience" in which she assailed "certain elements of the Republican party" for "selfish, political exploitation of fear, bigotry, ignorance and intolerance." She said the Senate was being debased into "a forum of hate and character assassination," remarks easily interpreted as a rebuke to Senator Joseph McCarthy, though she did not mention him by name. The remarks came at a time when many illustrious Democratic Senate liberals were fearfully maintaining silence on McCarthy.

Mrs. Smith might have been the heroine of an Horatio Alger story. In her lifetime she was a salesgirl in a five-and-dime store, a telephone operator, a schoolteacher, a weekly newspaper circulation manager, the author of a nationally syndicated column, the first woman ever to seek a major party's presidential nomination (in 1964), and for years the only woman in the U.S. Senate. She was fourth ranking among all Senate Republicans when she retired after 24 years of service there.

A final note on the gentle lady from Maine. On the morning of November 23, 1963, while the Senate press gallery was being deluged with grandiloquent statements of regret on the assassination of the President in Dallas the day before, Margaret Smith entered the chamber before the Senate convened. She walked quietly to John Kennedy's old desk and laid on it one red rose.

William D. Hathaway, the four-term Democratic Congressman who risked a quick return to his law practice in Lewiston when he took the long shot of challenging Mrs. Smith in 1972, has yet to establish himself as a figure comparable to Muskie or Smith. But then again, it often takes a while in the Senate to climb to a position of prominence. Hathaway did successfully engineer passage in 1973, when he had been a Senator only two months, of an amendment to a national economic controls bills requiring large companies to issue price, cost, and profit data when their price increases went 1.5 percent over guideline figures. Later that year, he proposed an ingenious bill to deal with the problem of a double vacancy—in both the presidency and vice presidency. Instead of having the presidency go to the Speaker of the House for the remainder of the presidential term, Hathaway proposed that a special national election for President be held under those circumstances. In the meantime, the highest ranking officer of the House of the same party as the outgoing chief executive would serve as Acting President. The intent was to let the voters issue a new mandate when *both* the President and Vice President they had elected were forced to leave office for some reason.

State Government Turns Responsive;
The Legislative and the Power Lobby

Maine state government has been laboriously working its way into the 20th century, and there have been some bright indications in recent years that the process may actually be completed by the time the century ends.

The state continues to function under the constitution of 1820, which has yet to be subjected to major revision. Its most archaic provision was doubtless the seven-man executive council, that remarkable New England institution harking back to the days of the colonials' desire to put a crimp on royal governors. By the time Maine wrote its constitution, the original *raison d'être* of the councils was gone, but Maine emulated the provision of the Massachusetts constitution anyway—disregarding the advice of one member of the convention, who said: "I believe we can get a governor as capable of doing the business of the executive alone as other states. If we give him a council we not only incur a useless expense but divide the responsibility and open the door for intrigue." The council had right of "advise and consent" over each gubernatorial appointment, was required to approve pardons, and had powers over the state budget when the legislature was not in session. Running for governor in 1960, now-Federal Judge Frank Coffin called the council Maine's "hidden executive." The shelves of Maine libraries groan with official studies recommending its abolition. Over the years the council was variously called "secretive," "wholly undemocratic," "arrogant," "fusty," "narrow-minded," "a clearing house for patronage," "capricious," and "an un-American way of doing things." Governor Kenneth M. Curtis told me that with the council "hung around his neck," it was "virtually impossible for a governor to assume any real executive responsibility and leadership. The only way it can be done is by trying to be a good humor man and a con man all wrapped up into one."

In modern times, only two other states have still had executive councils—Massachusetts and New Hampshire. Both those bodies are anachronistic enough, but at least they have been popularly elected since the last century. Maine's council, by contrast, was still elected by the legislature. That meant it was almost exclusively the domain of Republicans in this century, a terrible hindrance for Muskie when he was governor, and later for Curtis. Since 1954, the Democrats had called for the council's abolition. With a legislative majority following the 1975 elections, they finally made good on their promise, submitting a constitutional amendment for the council's abolition, which Maine's people approved in a referendum that autumn.

Muskie, as governor, had an independent study made of Maine government and even formed a citizens' committee to push for reorganization. But the bureaucracy and most local civil servants fought fiercely against any changes, and the Republicans were not about to give a Democratic governor enhanced power and prestige. Some minor reforms were effected: an extension of gubernatorial terms from two to four years, and a bill to set Maine's elections in November, instead of the odd September date, unique to Maine among the states, that had so long been in effect.

John H. Reed, the timorous Republican governor of the 1959–66 period, was not about to seek major changes, and Kenneth Curtis, despite his vigorous approach to problems, found himself stymied on reform during his first term in the late '60s. Thus, when the 1970s dawned, Maine still had a surfeit of some 226 boards, agencies, commissions, departments, and authorities—a prescription for unresponsive government and faceless bureaucracy. At Curtis's instigation, and with approval of the GOP-controlled legislative research committee, the administrative nightmare was finally brought under some control in 1971–73 by legislation combining the 226 parts into 12 new departments with cabinet-level secretaries.* The laudable intent of the reorganization was to make the parts of state government more accountable by having the cabinet secretaries, with authority to "knock heads" within their departments, directly responsible to one elected official—the governor. A second objective was to break up some of the cozy relationships between lobbyists, legislators, and the almost-invisible heads of the multitudinous and formerly independent agencies.

In education, Maine was long one of America's most regressive states. In 1937 there were more than 200 rural schools operating on annual budgets of less than $360. As recently as the 1940s, John Gunther reported, there was a titanic struggle to get the minimum wage for teachers raised to $720 a year. In 1973–74, teacher salaries still ranked only 32nd in the nation.

There have, however, been some quite spectacular changes in recent years. A starting point was the school consolidation law passed during Muskie's administration. The "little red schoolhouse," whatever its romantic and communal values may have been, had often offered substandard education to grouped-up classes of as many as 40 or 50 students with a single teacher in sometimes dilapidated buildings. With consolidation, Curtis noted, students had "more facilities, guidance, athletic teams that can compete, bands, orchestras—all that goes into rounding out a kid." The better schools, he noted, were the biggest factor in increasing Maine's university and college enrollments, "because the kids were getting motivation and were no longer satisfied with the old standard of living" in backwater rural communities.

Maine still ranks far below the national average in the dollars it expends, either for schools or universities, but its actual expenditure in these areas has risen very sharply. In 1973 the legislature passed legislation designed to eliminate the gross inequities in financing of local schools between poorer and more affluent communities. One feature of the law increased the state share of local education costs, financed from the state's general fund, from 33 to 50 percent. It was the financing of the other 50 percent, through a new uniform property tax for education which drained off money from well-to-do communities and transferred it to poorer ones, that touched off a full-scale taxpayers' revolt in the affluent towns when the bill went into effect for the 1974–75 school year. Residents of wealthy coastal towns, where property values had soared in the previous decade, formed groups like the "Freedom Fighters" to protest the Robin Hood-style skimming off of their taxes to assure quality education in other comumnities which had never before enjoyed quality education. A centralized state bureaucracy, they argued, was stealing

---

* In addition to general government-type departments, the reorganization created separate departments in such areas as environmental protection, consumer protection, and transportation. A recommended department of natural resources was blocked by fish and game interests, however, so that the state instead now has separate cabinet-level departments of inland fisheries and game, of marine fisheries, and of conservation.

their money; proponents of the program answered that the affluent towns had simply not been paying their fair share of state expenses.

Curtis counted as one of his most important achievements the consolidation of the University of Maine at Orono and the other state colleges; the intent was to tame their provincialism in fighting for legislative funds and finally to offer overall better quality in higher education.* The state has also seen a dramatic increase in enrollments at its technical-vocational schools and the start of expansion in community colleges, an area in which Maine lagged for many years.

In welfare, some 19th-century ideas are still heard in Maine. The 1971 legislature, for instance, forced a reduction of 7 to 10 percent in welfare payments for 46,000 children in the state. Republican Harold Bragdon, chairman of the house appropriations committee, in defending the cuts, said: "I don't believe we can continue to live as a welfare nation, and the sooner we stop this trend in its tracks—even to the point that those on welfare have to live upon reduced amounts—then maybe it won't be as attractive to be on welfare as it would be to get out and look a little harder for a job." Presumably, hungry children were to take note of his counsel. Still, the state's per capita expenditures for welfare—most recently about 90 percent of the national average—are a far cry from the early 1950s, when Maine's levels of aid for the blind, disabled, aged, and dependent children were scarcely two-thirds of the prevailing level in the country.

A national guaranteed income plan would be necessary to eliminate the poverty that still plagues the state of Maine. "It's worst in the northeast coastal counties and the St. John Valley, but you can find it about two miles outside of every town," Curtis commented. "The worst situation is found in the tar-papered shack where the father is either unemployed or works for very little. You'll find large numbers of kids crammed in two or three rooms. This is the real problem in Maine. And it's not so much a shiftlessness—a very small percentage of these people don't want to work. The jobs simply haven't been available."

Curtis was prouder of Maine's record in building highways, saying that the state had "done a remarkable job with the money available" to provide roads for its vast distances. But he said the state's mental health and corrections programs had long been in "terrible shape and still are." Some forward strides have been made in mental health, however. And despite periodic complaints by prison inmates that they have been subjected to atrocities and abuses, the state has pioneered in granting furloughs for male prisoners and in 1963 opened the nation's first halfway house for women inmates. Ward E. Murphy, appointed in 1970 as the first woman chief executive officer of a state's prisons, pressed for more reforms "to get people out of institutions as soon as it is safe, logical, and feasible." Garrel Murphy, a 28-year-old ex-

* Better known than Maine's public colleges and universities are a number of highly regarded private institutions, including Bowdoin College at Brunswick, Colby College at Waterville, and Bates College at Lewiston, Muskie's alma mater. Their enrollment, however, is minor compared to the 25,000 enrolled in regular courses or "continuing education" programs of the University of Maine.

Marine appointed warden of the grim Maine State Prison at Thomaston, said, "Our philosophy here is to try to create an atmosphere as much like the community as possible."

In 1975 Maine passed a new criminal code that made it the first state in the nation to abolish those popular but often-abused features of U.S. criminal justice—indeterminate sentences and parole. Maximum terms were set for various types of offenses, with judges given the discretion to choose the terms and conditions of sentences. But except for the authorization of ten days off a sentence for each month of good conduct, a prisoner could not hope for early parole.

A reflection of the growing activism and social concern of Maine state government was the fact that appropriations from the general fund jumped from $118 million to $395 million during the 1960s, even while the population remained relatively static. By the early 1970s, Maine residents were paying 13 percent of their personal income in state and local taxes, the seventh highest rate in the country and more than any of the other New England states except Vermont and Massachusetts.

Maine had always depended primarily on local property taxes, but in 1951, under Governor (and later U.S. Senator) Frederick G. Payne, a sales tax was instituted; from an initial rate of 2 percent, it gradually rose to 5 percent by 1970. The need for additional revenue, particularly for public education and penal institutions, prompted Governor Curtis in 1969 to propose a personal and corporate income tax, even though he had made a no-new taxes pledge in his 1966 campaign. Harrison Richardson, then Republican leader in the Maine house, persuaded his party's caucus to support the income tax despite the hard-core resistance of legislators from several coastal counties, with high numbers of retired people, who regarded income taxes as rampant socialism at best. The tax—graduated from 1 to 6 percent on individuals, and set at a 5 percent for corporations—passed by margins of a single vote in both the senate and house. Voter reaction was predictably negative, almost causing Curtis's defeat in the 1970 election. But when a group of citizens tried to undo the income tax in a 1971 repeal referendum, a bipartisan committee argued that repeal would plunge the state into financial chaos and cause other taxes to rise. The voters easily sustained the income levy. (Actually, it is not a very onerous tax, accounting for only 5.8 percent of combined state and local taxes in Maine, compared to 18 or 19 percent in states like Vermont and Massachusetts.)

In 1973 a reform-minded legislative session set up fulltime property tax assessment districts throughout the state, thus correcting the gross disparities in assessments that had existed since time immemorial. Two taxes that had long been a depressant on business expansion—the local inventory tax and the sales tax on new industrial machinery—were abolished, the revenue gap made up for by increasing the corporate income tax to 7 percent on businesses with profits of more than $25,000. This was the same legislature that enacted the so-called "equal education" tax reform bill to wipe out the difference between poor and affluent school districts.

All these steps have not ended Maine's fiscal problems: more recently, for instance, the legislators have felt compelled to set up a state lottery ("Play Me") of dubious legality and certain impropriety for a state of Maine's professed values. The full steps of complete state financing of schools, to take that burden off the shoulders of local property tax payers, has yet to be accomplished. But in comparison to where the state stood just a few years ago, one would have to say that in services, tax adequacy, and tax fairness, remarkable progress has been made.

Much of that progress would have been impossible without the prompting, cajoling, and leadership of the progressive Democratic governors, especially Curtis. And if the first year of independent Governor James Longley's administration was any test, there was little chance that Maine would return to its ultraparsimonious policies of yesteryear. Longley did insist on a no-new-taxes biennial budget of $703 million, and prevented any break in that policy—even though it threw him into frequent conflict with the Democratic-controlled house of representatives and meant a cut of approximately 5 percent in the 13,000-person state work force. Longley's personal relations with legislators and many leading groups in the state were extremely strained, as he self-righteously accused opponents of rank partisanship. On one occasion, he even called legislators who refused to cooperate with him "pimps." He vetoed a record of 26 bills, but 14 vetoes were overridden (another record.) His administration was marked by erratic appointments and personnel policies; at one point he even asked the entire board of trustees of the University of Maine to resign (a request which was refused). But the spending issue, after a decade of sharp state budget increases and in a year of severe recession, was tailor-made for Longley's appeal: "We're proving you can bring business practices to government." Even critics acknowledged his base of popular support remained very strong.

Despite their informal alliance with Longley on many issues, Maine's Republicans have been changing over the past decade, moderating their rock-ribbed conservatism and taking an active lead in program innovation and needed reforms of the legislature itself.* Harrison Richardson, house majority leader in the late '60s and later a state senator, was one of the GOP's most progressive leaders. Another was Joseph Sewall, a progressive Republican state senator who moved forward to the senate presidency in 1975. Kenneth Mac-Leod, the blunt-spoken senate president of the 1969–74 period, became (partly through Sewall's influence) a leading exponent of legislative reform—which the Maine legislature direly needed. On tests including accountability, independence, and representativeness, the national Citizens Conference on State Legislatures ranked the Maine legislature only 30th in the nation at the start of the '70s. Highly inadequate staffing, some of the most "closed" pat-

---

* There remains, of course, a core of archconservative Republicans, mostly from rural areas, who never think twice before voting "nay" on any liberal or progressive legislation. But their numbers in the house were down to less than 30 by 1973. "A sympathetic observer," the Maine *Times* commented, "could find something almost touching in the profiles of these generally aging lawmakers, products of a rural Maine past which engendered a stubborn independence and a tight fist with money."

terns of committee executive sessions in the nation, and a house of rather unwieldy size (151 members, eighth largest in the country), were among the defects most prominently noted. Since then the staffing situation has been improved somewhat, the number of standing committees has been reduced to a more manageable size, and stiffer lobbyists' expense statements have been required. A reform bill has been passed defining legislative conflicts of interest and requiring legislators to file annual reports listing their sources of income. And a 10-member legislative council, including the leaders of both houses, has been established to guide the activities of joint legislative committees meeting between sessions. In 1975 the legislature also voted to join the growing list of states with annual rather than biennial sessions.

Lobbyists still swarm around the State House in Augusta when the legislature meets; in a recent session, for instance, there were 317 lobbying interests registered, seeking to influence 183 legislators. The most powerful lobbies include the big paper companies (of which more anon) and the truckers, which run a nonstop free bar for legislators. The once powerful railroads, Richardson said, have an "enlightened" lobby but have been reduced to "pathetic power." "The truckers have beat the hell out of them, getting weight increases and absolutely monstrous weight overages," he said. Even Democratic governors have not known how to resist the truckers; Curtis, for instance, signed a bill to increase truck weights on Maine roads as much as 50 percent.

Over the years, the private power companies of Maine have registered a success—in and out of the legislative halls—that would be the envy of their counterparts in other states. New England has the country's highest power rates; and in New England, Maine's rates have generally been the highest with the exception of parts of Massachustts. (The only states with average higher overall rates are Alaska and New York.) Earlier in this century, almost any important legislative decision was cleared in a room of the Augusta House in the presence of the leading lights of the power lobby. A long and complicated history surrounded the Fernald Law, passed in 1909, which forbade the exploration of any hydroelectric power outside of Maine. The law helped the power companies dominate the Maine market to the virtual exclusion of public power; for several years it also permitted them to escape the jurisdiction of the Federal Power Commission, since they were by law intrastate concerns. It was finally repealed in 1955, while Muskie was governor, but by then private power was so entrenched in Maine that to this day there are only three REA cooperatives and five town nonprofit power distribution districts in the entire state. (They buy their power at wholesale rates from the private utilities, and thus can give consumers lower electricity rates.)

In 1973, at the instigation of an energetic young Democratic state senator named Peter S. Kelley, the state's voters were given an opportunity to vote for creation of a Maine power authority that would have given municipalities a strong inducement to buy their power from the public authority instead of the private utilities, thus reducing power bills. The private utilities would not have been put out of business, but they would have been obliged to share a portion of their market. "Dangerous and radical," William Dunham, chairman of the board of Central Maine Power, called the proposal—"the most radical plan ever advanced in these United States . . . it smacks more of Russia than it does Maine." Kelley argued that the public power authority, because it would be eligible for tax-free bonds, would have no common stock holders, and would pay no federal income taxes, would be able to generate and supply power at less than the private companies. Early polls showed a large majority of the people for the public authority, but that was before Central Maine Power invested in a massive public relations campaign, more costly than a typical gubernatorial campaign, to kill the plan. A Boston polling firm was brought in to do motivational research on the best arguments against the proposal, a front organization was set up to look like a broad-based citizens group in opposition, and a scare campaign was mounted on television and radio. In the end, Kelley and his allies spent $66,000 to back the public authority, but Central Maine Power and the other private utilities laid out an estimated $308,440 to kill it. The public vote was 62 percent in opposition. "What is certain," Peter Cox wrote in the Maine *Times*, "is that money won the election. If Peter Kelley had had the money instead of Central Maine Power, he would have won." (Others, however, said Kelley had managed the public authority campaign quite ineptly, so that he might have lost, even with equal money.)

Two great hydroelectric projects, yet to become reality in the 1970s, have colored Maine's public-vs.-private power debate for years. The first was one of the most ambitious hydroelectric projects ever proposed on any continent—to harness the power of the moon, evidenced in the towering tides that pour through rockbound inlets from the Bay of Fundy on the Atlantic into Passamaquoddy Bay on the border of Maine's Washington County and Canada's New Brunswick province. The 26-foot high tides (with velocities as high as 10 feet a second) would be captured in Passamaquoddy Bay, to be released through turbines into adjacent Cobscook Bay, and then back to the sea, providing vast quantities of electric power. A hydroelectric engineer from Boston, Dexter P. Cooper, developed the basic plan for a tidal power plant on "Quoddy" as early as 1919. Then, another American who had witnessed the awesome tides during summers on Canada's Campobello Island, Franklin D. Roosevelt, set the planning mechanism in motion for the tidal project in the 1930s. But critics, including spokesmen for the private utilities, castigated the project as "WPA moondoggling" and the Senate shut off funds in 1936 after engineering surveys had been made and a model village built for the expected construction workers. President Kennedy tried to revive the Quoddy project in 1963 but died before he could move it forward. With advanced technology, Quoddy's backers have claimed in recent years that it could almost double the originally contemplated million kilowatts a day. They argue that tidal power is superior to river power because droughts, floods, ice jams, and silting do not affect it. But the cost—probably more than $1.5 billion—and the fact that Quoddy could provide only peaking power for New England, have discouraged backers. (Ironically, if the project

had been constructed in FDR's time, it would have cost only $150 million—
a tenth as much.)

The other proposal goes by the odd name of Dickey-Lincoln School
hydroelectric project—Dickey for a tiny little hamlet (a Shell pump and
some houses) high on the St. John River, in northernmost Maine, where the
world's 11th largest dam would be built, and Lincoln School for an abandoned
gray brick schoolhouse in a weedy yard, 11 miles downstream from Dickey,
where a smaller dam would be constructed to control the flow of water and
obtain some extra electric power. Some 1.1 billion kilowatt hours of electricity
would be produced by this vast complex each year, chiefly for peaking power
needs. Another benefit would be to stem the raging springtime floods on the
St. John, which sometimes inundate the downriver town of Fort Kent (4,700
population) with chunks of ice floating down its main street.

Even more than Passamaquoddy—with which it has sometimes been
linked in feasibility studies and proposals—Dickey-Lincoln for years was the
vortex of the public-private power fight in New England. The private utilities spent a reported $567,058 to fight against its authorization by Congress
in 1965 and then, losing that fight, successfully to prevent the appropriation
of funds to make it a reality. The 16 largest New England private power companies formed a common lobby with the express purpose of defeating Dickey-
Lincoln, "developing a regional climate of public opinion which would
prevent any expansion of government-owned or tax subsidized electricity
within New England," and instead "permit the gradual elimination of government power operations presently existing in the area." Despite proponents'
arguments that Dickey-Lincoln would provide a "yardstick" to shame the
private utilities into reducing their high rates in the region, only four New
England Congressmen, on one key vote, cast their lot with Dickey-Lincoln.
(One wonders where some of the region's highly valued liberal Democrats
were on such votes.) One of the supporters, Maine's Republican Stanley
Tupper, said after the vote: "There was Boston Edison up in the galleries,
ready to put on the pressure. There were more lobbyists on the Hill against
Dickey than there were Congressmen."

Another power company tactic was to undercut arguments for the need
for Dickey-Lincoln by rushing forward plans for a nuclear power plant in
Maine. Between 1966 and 1972 a gigantic nuclear plant was built at Wiscasset, on Montsweag Bay. The plant does produce 3.5 billion kilowatts of power
a year, three times the contemplated Dickey-Lincoln figure. But the power
companies were not content with announcement of a single power plant,
however great, to combat Dickey, and in 1965 also hastily announced a $1.5
billion, "Big 11" power loop for New England which they claimed would
"lower the cost of power in New England by 40 percent by 1980." The power
loop has also gone forward, but electricity rates in New England have never
shown any signs of making the predicted long-term dip.

The Dickey-Lincoln stalemate—authorization but no funds—continued
until the energy crisis bit heavily into the Maine and New England economy
in 1974. At that point many hydroelectric projects challenged on grounds of

cost effectiveness in the era of cheap oil suddenly gained new attractiveness, and Dickey was one of them. And the power companies, deciding it would be unseemly to be fighting any energy source, quickly shifted to a position of neutrality. The case against Dickey was taken up by the environmentalists, who complained that the project would flood 140 square miles of the St. John-Allagash wilderness territory and destroy the habitats of many species of wildlife and ruin trout fishing. But the environmentalist lobby was a weakling compared to the power companies, and under the altered circumstances of 1974, planning funds were approved by Congress with a heavy majority of the New England delegation in favor. The required environmental impact study and economic analyses by the Corps of Engineers could still sink Dickey-Lincoln. Yet the region's and nation's power shortage, likely to endure for years to come, had dramatically improved the outlook for Dickey-Lincoln and, perhaps one day, for Passamaquoddy as well. Should either project ever be built, public power would finally arrive in a big way in the state and region where it had so long and so effectively been fought by companies accountable to their stockholders, not to the men and women of Maine and New England.

The Low-Wage, Hard-Work State; Big Oil; and Land Use Planning

Maine has a fairly earned reputation as a state of low-wage, high-pollution industries. A glance at the list of the state's five biggest industrial employers—leather (shoes), paper, lumber and wood, shipbuilding, food processing, and textiles—explains the reasons. With the exception of shipbuilding, all tend to be industries of subnormal wages and high pollutant risks. On the average, Maine's factory workers earn 20 percent less than their counterparts in other states. The state's unemployment rate has been above the national average for all but one of the last 20 years. The 1960 Census showed that 39 percent of the housing units in Maine were substandard; the picture has improved some since, but in 1974 there were still some 130,000 people (about 40,000 households) in need of substantially improved housing. Sprawling dirty shacks reminiscent of Appalachia can be spotted all over Maine. In recent years more than half the housing starts have been mobile homes; hearings conducted by the activist Republican attorney general, Jon Lund, brought forth testimony all across the state of practically uninhabitable mobile homes, plagued by leakage, water condensation in light fixtures, shorting out of lights and wires, inadequate insulation, and stains on ceilings and walls. Some 26,000 Maine families—more than 10 percent of the state total, the highest level in the Northeast—live below the federally defined poverty line, and fully 22 percent of them earned less than $5,000 a year at the time of the 1970 Census. The state has a grievous shortage of doctors and dentists and ranks 48th among the 50 states in its per capita public expenditures on health and hospitals.

Moreover, since the bulk of Maine industries require only unskilled or semiskilled workers, there has for years been a dearth of opportunities for skilled workers*—a prime reason that the state has lost so many of its productive youth over the past several generations. Compared to most other states, Maine has lacked the infusions of capital that would create an adequate base to finance development that would break the dreary cycle.

Tourism, often hailed as a "clean" alternative to industrial development, is actually another culprit in the low-wage problem. In 1972, for instance, 3.1 million people visited Maine. But the ski industry, one of the major attractions, was reported to employ only 102 people fulltime and another 738 seasonally. Average ski industry annual wages were only $4,000. Even during the summer, most tourist-related jobs tend to be low-wage—waiting on tables, changing beds, housecleaning, and the like. And a big proportion of those jobs go to students and other out-of-staters.†

The climate makes Maine a rigorous place to live, and an exceptionally large number of Maine people labor in factories or lumber camps or on farms, or make their living from the sea, eking out New England's lowest per capita income at hard, demanding labor under conditions that would make most American wage-earners blanch.

Consider the clam diggers, up each morning in the subzero darkness to wade through the muck exposed by the receding tide and rake for their catch. Or the lobstermen, who work the rugged bays and inlets, out in their boats before dawn to put in 10 or 12 hours on the water, coping with the eternal factors of the sea, the weather, and the vagaries of the catch. Time and again in the past decade, Maine lobstermen have heard grand promises of a dawning age of "aquaculture" and advanced "marine arts and sciences" in which such innovations as selective breeding techniques, improved hauling procedures, "seeding" of specified areas with new food sources to draw a catch, or even enclosed lobster farms, would increase their yields and income to undreamed of heights. But even as live lobsters began to draw $3.50 or more per pound in the early '70s, there was a hard-to-explain shortage of lobsters that resulted in just a handful of usable catches in dozens of traps. Interminable bickering and competition among the marine research institutions and arms of the state government stymied the program of advanced oceanographic research promised by the governor and others. Journalist William Langley reported in the Maine *Times* that "Maine fishermen feel they are being ignored or patronized by the researchers, planners, and bureaucrats." Some felt

---

* Value added per worker in Maine, because of the state's low-technology and labor-intensive type industries, is the lowest of any New England state. Moreover, the *rate* of growth of value added per worker has been slower in Maine since 1955 than in any of the other states of the region.
† According to a full-scale study of the tourist industry completed in 1974, tourism generated $260 million in direct sales and another $460 million in related sales. Thus in cash flow the industry is important to Maine, but the profits of tourist establishments are not high, and the state government—after public expenditures for roads, environmental protection, etc., are deducted from tourist-generated tax revenues—had a net "profit" from tourism of only $15 million a year. The least desirable tourists, from a financial and environmental point of view, were found to be the campers, who spend only a third as much a day as visitors staying in motels.

"aquaculture is going to be for the corporations, not the individual fishermen." And even when the experts sought to meet with the fishermen, few of
the latter—a breed for whom sturdy self-dependence is a way of life—
showed up.*

Consider next the lumbermen, working out of isolated camps, doing most
of their tree-felling in the frigid, short winter days—because in summer the
mosquitoes and those miniature hypodermic attackers, the black flies, make
the wilderness even more perilous than in the months of ice and snow. Lumbering has always been, and remains, the toughest and most dangerous kind of
physical labor; one should forget the Paul Bunyan myths and remember that
by his early fifties, even the strongest man may be pretty well "worked out."

Maine novelist Helen Yglesias invites us to think, too, of the men who
labor in the pulp and paper mills. "How much 'control over his destiny,' " she
asks, "may a paper-mill worker experience, beginning with the noxious odor of
the sulfite process pervading the air he breathes, not only at work but at his
leisure in his own yard and on the main street of his town where heat and
noise and smell and physical danger combine in a hell our literature has produced no Zola to describe?" Sweatshop labor it is, in tanneries and shoe factories, in textile mills, in the paper mills. Writer David Nevin described a visit
with Senator Muskie to a marginal shoe factory at Dexter:

Hundreds of men and women, each responsible for some part of a variety of shoes,
were at machines that clattered and roared beneath low ceilings. The light was dim
and the air heavy with the acrid smell of dyes and new tanned leather. Machines
stamped out the parts and other machines sewed them together. Machines glued
and shaped the finished product, buffed it, packed it. Pay was by the piece and the
people worked at great speed, their bodies moving in strange, jerky rhythms: one
hand guiding a piece through as the other snatched up the next; the great blades,
shears, stamps, presses and needles rising and falling amid the flashing fingers. The
work is sought after; if you are slow, someone awaits your job.

Thus, it was not surprising that Muskie, first seeking the governorship in
the early 1950s, could make such political capital out of the call for increased
industrial development. In Donald Hansen's words, "the attraction of industry—almost any type of industry—became a state goal." A new department of
development of commerce and industry was created, together with an industrial building authority "to stimulate the flow of private investment funds into
mortgage loans for the purpose of furthering economic expansion in the state."
The chosen device was state guarantee of bank loans, arranged through local

* The lobstermen vary in character, of course, as much as any group of human beings.
The Internal Revenue Service has been after some in recent years for conveniently forgetting to
note or report their full income. Yet I am compelled to quote from a 1971 report by a rural
correspondent on Charles D. Murphy, "Maine's No. 1 lobsterman" then retiring at the age of 94.
For more than 75 years, Marion Watson of Five Islands reported, Mr. Murphy had been engaged
in active lobster fishing in the Friendship area waters off the coast. When Maine first licensed
fishermen in 1916, Mr. Murphy received license Number 1—which on retirement he transferred
to his great-grandson, Sherman Stanley, Jr., of Monhegan Island. "Charles Murphy is a proud
man," the report went on. "He never smoked and never drank. He is proud of his family, his
state and his country. . . . When asked the secret of his success as a lobsterman, and as a
citizen, he said, 'That's easy. Proverbs three, verses five and six: Trust in the Lord with all thine
heart; and lean not unto thine own understanding. In all thy ways acknowledge Him and He
will direct thy paths.' "

nonprofit development corporations, to expanding or new industries. Many less affluent states have used similar techniques, starting with Mississippi in the 1930s; the goal, in effect, is to lure, through special advantages, industries which might otherwise not find an area particularly desirable. But as in the South, Maine learned that low-wage and/or high-pollution industries were those most frequently attracted. Chicken and potato processors, shoe factories and textile mills, processed meat and electronic assembly firms, and woodworking firms obtained the state guarantees for their mortgages. But by far the greatest loan guarantee of the building authority's history—in the amount of $8 million—went to Maine Sugar Industries, Inc., to build a massive plant for refining beet and cane sugar at Easton in Aroostook County, close to the Canadian border. Eventually that loan went sour, at an average cost to each Maine taxpayer of $40.90.

Maine Sugar Industries was the creation of a flamboyant entrepreneur of colossal ego, Fred Vahlsing, Jr., who had previously set up a potato processing plant at Easton, enlarged several times with loans from the federal Area Redevelopment Administration. The potato plant's waste was causing horrendous pollution to the Prestile Stream, a once pure trout waterway, which flows a few miles downstream across the border into Canada. In 1964, when the federal government granted Maine a sugar beet quota, the state saw a golden opportunity to diversify its agricultural base and add new jobs through a refinery. "Freddie" Vahlsing offered to build the refinery if he could get $6 million in federal loans and $8 million from the state's industrial building authority. But the state's water improvement commission had served a cease and desist order against Vahlsing's potato plant, which was killing fish (even hardy eels) and causing the Prestile to stink. To get the federal loan, even though no one knew if the new refinery would emit water wastes, Vahlsing felt obliged to get the Prestile officially downgraded to the state's lowest level, so that it could be polluted legally. And indeed, a temporary downgrading of the stream to a level equivalent with a sewer was achieved by vote of the then Democratically controlled state legislature, urged on by Senator Muskie and Republican Governor John Reed—both of whom then apparently thought that Freddie Vahlsing, and particularly the sugar beet refinery, were good news for Maine. Three years later, when a group of Canadian residents became so irate over the befouling of the Prestile from potato wastes that they threw up a temporary dam on the international border, the issue became a profound embarrassment for Muskie and his "Mr. Clean" image. The embarrassment was compounded in 1970 when Vahlsing's sugar plant—partly because of bad management, partly because the Aroostook farmers failed to plant enough sugar beet acreage—defaulted on its loan payments, forcing the state government to start making payments to Vahlsing's creditors.

As the Portland *Evening Express* later commented, New Jerseyite Vahlsing had "taken advantage of Maine's hospitality, our generosity, our friendship, our money, our laws and our good name."

The Freddie Vahlsing episode was the first chapter in Maine's painful learning process about the monumental side costs of "development." Soon it was to be eclipsed by controversy over oil company proposals to build refineries alongside Maine's deepwater ports, ports so deep (100 feet or more) that only they, on the entire U.S. Atlantic coast, would be capable of receiving the great new supertankers being constructed around the world in the late '60s and early '70s.

Not many years ago, the prospect of industrial development worth hundreds of millions of dollars would doubtless have been received with uncritical enthusiasm anywhere in the United States. Indeed, for Maine development officials, oil at first looked like the answer to their fondest prayers. "To break out of our income slump," commissioner James Keefe of the state's economic development department said, "we need some brand new entities on the Maine scene. Oil would provide high-wage paying major investment." Unfortunately for the oilmen, however, their proposals for Maine coincided quite neatly with the rise of the environmental movement in the late 1960s. Before long, as one journalist noted, the oil promoters came to be "perceived by many as villains come to ravage and despoil the state's beautiful coast."

Fortune magazine in 1971 listed the chief players on each side of the Maine oil game; updated to the mid-1970s with appropriate additions and deletions, the list reads like this:

First, those with something to gain from big oil development:
▪ Several major oil companies, as well as promoter-developers who would like to build docking and refinery facilities to sell or lease to the oil companies.
▪ Local businessmen and bankers, whose present-day opportunities are severely limited by Maine's stagnant economy.
▪ Industries that would gain business from an oil complex: utilities, construction companies, and the railroads.
▪ All the Maine firms that would benefit from a nearby source of low-sulfur fuel. (While the proposed refineries would produce some gasoline, the emphasis would be on industrial and heating oils.)
▪ Unemployed and underemployed Mainers, in hope of high-paying jobs (although various independent studies have shown that a refinery complex would produce only a few hundred jobs, and that many of the technical personnel for construction and maintenance of the facilities would have to be recruited from out of state).
▪ Maine towns and state government, looking for an enrichment of the meager tax base.

Second, there are those who have nothing to gain from oil development and perhaps much to lose:
▪ Lobstermen, clam diggers, sea-worm diggers, and other sea and shore fishermen who are convinced that the state's famous thick fogs and treacherous coastal waters would result in occasional oil spills of horrendous magnitude, destroying their livelihood.
▪ The coastal tourist industry, fearful that the mere sight of refineries and monster tankers, not to mention oil washed onto the coast, would drive away their customers.

■   Coastal property owners, ranging from natives and exurbanites to some of America's most elite families, who see the quality and value of their property endangered by oil.

■   The environmentalists, who see in big oil the potential for sullying if not destroying the celebrated natural beauty of the Maine coast. Among the conservationist groups most actively involved have been the Natural Resources Council of Maine (a rallying point for local groups fighting oil), the Maine Audubon Society, the Sierra Club, the Maine Coast Heritage Trust, the State Biologists Association, and the Coastal Resources Action Committee (CRAC). The latter organization, spawned by Maine Audubon and the Natural Resources Council, was set up to hire lobbyists and fight the oil interest in the courts. Its chairman, Portland attorney Horace Hildreth, son of a former governor, is a former Republican state senator and onetime pulp and paper lobbyist who knows the ways of legal and legislative infighting and is proud to have become Maine's first conservationist lobbyist in 1969. "The industrial lobby," he told me, "is made up of attorneys from the good law firms, expert in their trade." Before CRAC was set up, he said, "the conservationists and the public interest were simply not represented." CRAC's board is establishmentarianism personified, including such figures as former U.S. Treasury Secretary C. Douglas Dillon, R. Buckminister Fuller, writer E. B. White, editor James Russell Wiggins, and Jean Gannett Arnzen, publisher-owner of Maine's largest newspaper chain. Maine's present-day conservationists, Hildreth said, are a far cry from the "garden clubbers in their feathered hats."

■   The Maine *Times,* a feisty, fiercely pro-environmental weekly begun in 1968 to provide "expression unfettered by the compromises of commercial journalism." Publisher of the *Times* is Peter W. Cox, son of a prominent Washington attorney; the editor, John N. Cole, is a transplanted New Yorker who has become a kind of hero in liberal journalistic circles in New England and even further afield. "Maine is a small society, with total accessibility. For an editor, you can really do something—even maybe save the coast of Maine," Cole said. The *Times* has gamely taken on a long list of Maine's vested interests, including the banks, utilities, railroads, paper companies, land developers, feudal county governments, state industrial developers, and insensitive legislators and bureaucrats. But the *cause célèbre* of its career has been the fight against oil development.* On that issue, through investigative reporting

---

* By delving into so many areas previously untouched by the Maine press, the *Times* prompted some of the state's nine dailies (none of which previously had an environmental reporter) to become more activist and aggressive. Only those whose special interests were attacked could doubt that the paper has been good for Maine. Nonetheless, some of the praise heaped on the *Times* by outside observers may be excessive. On occasion the writing is long-winded, sometimes sloppy, and the staff is so small and overworked that major issues are often overlooked or given short shrift.

In a commentary for Maine Public Broadcasting in 1974, Lance Tapley said that the *Times,* by accepting spacious real-estate ads to help sell Maine to New Yorkers, while simultaneously advocating a no-growth philosophy for Maine, was "following the accepted American business tradition of always separating the pocketbook from the pulpit." Pointing out that a third of the subscription copies go out of state, Tapley asserted that "in some ways the Maine *Times* is the organ of the liberal summer people."

John C. Donovan, chairman of the department of government at Bowdoin and a veteran of the Muskie-led Democratic revival of the 1950s, complains that John Cole and the Maine *Times* are "irrelevant" to Maine's biggest problem—hard-core, endemic poverty. "It is quite un-

and sound research, the *Times* has played an almost indispensable role in publicizing and stopping poorly planned development.

Since 1967, a succession of locations along the Maine coast have been proposed for massive refineries and deepwater port facilities. The first was near Machias (pronounced Match-eye-us), a poverty-plagued town of 2,300 in Washington County, some 25 miles from the Canadian border. The oil terminal would be built on Stone Island, in Machias Bay, close by the little village of Machiasport. Jack Evans, an independent oil promoter whose interest was soon bought out by Occidental Petroleum, suggested constructing a $150 million refinery beside the bay's 100-foot-deep waters. The Maine Port Authority, in turn, applied to the federal government for a foreign trade zone at Miachiasport so that Occidental could import some 300,000 barrels a day of Libyan oil, process it, and only pay duty when it was ready to sell its product of some 100,000 bbl. a day, mostly residential heating oil, in New England markets. A special import quota in that amount was requested—a proposal which ran into a hornets' nest of opposition from major U.S. oil companies, who wanted to prevent any circumventing of the oil import quota program that had given them a protected, high-price market in New England.*

Senator Muskie, Governor Curtis, and the whole New England establishment fell over themselves in enthusiastic backing for the Machiasport proposal. The area, Muskie said, was "suffering from severe economic dislocation and poverty" and desperately needed new development. Curtis and others said the refinery would create 350 new jobs and, with a petrochemical complex likely to follow, 3,000 or more within a few years. It was claimed that the refinery products would cut the cost of home heating oil in New England by $50 million to $60 million a year. And pollution dangers, it was said, would be minimal because the state itself would control the free trade zone and have complete control over decisions affecting the environment. Even John Cole, in an editorial for the Maine *Times'* inaugural edition in October 1968, predicted glowingly that "one of the nation's first, only and largest free ports may soon be opened at Machias. Not only can it be a boon to that corner down east, but it could benefit the entire New England economy."

The Machiasport proposal never came to reality, ostensibly because neither the Johnson nor Nixon administrations was willing to buck the Texas-Louisiana-major oil producers' combine which fought the foreign trade zone proposal. By 1969–70, however, the conservationists were already in full cry against the idea. "Machias Bay," the Sierra Club warned, "practically invites catastrophic accidents." It was pointed out that the bay, lying near the mouth of the Bay of Fundy, which has the highest tides in the world, is one of the most hazardous navigational areas anywhere with 16-foot tides, countless islands, reefs, and ledges, and stormy weather. A permanent fog bank, opponents noted, lies 25 to 100 miles to sea "except for the frequent occasions when

---

clear to me," according to Donovan, "when Cole was appointed keeper of the 'real' Maine values."

    * The other 200,000 barrels of crude could either have been made into residual fuel, which was exempt from the import quotas, or refined into some other kind of petroleum product and shipped abroad.

prevailing winds blow it in upon the coast." And the massive 300,000-ton tankers, opponents said, needed a two-mile run to come to a stop from full speed. Dr. Max Blumer of Woods Hole testified at a 1970 hearing about the total ruination to sea life that oil spills can cause. (It kills shellfish, releases poisons known to cause cancer, kills bottom plants, penetrates marshes, and is a grave public health hazard, Blumer said.) An oil spill at Machias, it was alleged, would spread the entire length of the Maine coast.

In September 1970, Cole editorialized in the Maine *Times*:

Oil is worse than any of us ever thought it was. . . . Downeast Maine is one of the last great unpolluted, undamaged coastlines in the entire world. It is a magnificent resource of immeasurable value that belongs not only to the people of Washington County and Maine, but to the entire population of the northeast coast, the United States and the world. . . .

The proposed oily work at Machias does not have to be done. The alternative to oil is no oil.

Oil proposal Number 2* surfaced in 1970, the brainchild of promoter David Scoll, head of Maine Clean Fuels, a subsidiary of Fuel Desulphurization, Inc., of New York. The parent company had already been rebuffed twice, on environmental grounds, when it proposed its sulfur-free fuel oil refinery for Long Island, New York and South Portland, Maine. Now it wanted to build at Sears Island in Penobscot Bay, and the selectmen of Searsport, a weather-beaten town of 1,800 souls in an area with 13.5 percent unemployment, endorsed the idea. "I'm not for pollution," a local businessman said. "But if we don't get some kind of added industry, Searsport may just kind of peter out."

The environmentalists had only to dust off the arguments they were using against Machiasport to discredit the Searsport project. The issue was gaining national attention, too. The New York *Times*, some of whose editors summer in Maine, rhapsodized: "The region around Maine's Penobscot Bay, one of the last strongholds of the independent Yankee farmer-fisherman, is largely unspoiled land where wooded hills plunge to the ragged, granite shores of an island-studded sea. The bay, Robert P. T. Coffin once wrote, has 'a loveliness as fresh as the morning of Creation.' " Again, there was talk of the treacherous, fogbound waters and the disaster for fishermen and resort owners that an oil spill would cost in "this magnificent maritime wilderness." The state government turned down the proposal, deciding that Maine Clean Fuels lacked the money or technical ability to meet the state's antipollution standards.

Proposal Number 3: A 250,000-bbl.-a-day refinery and supertanker terminal at Eastport, costing $500 million, to be built and run by Pittston Co., the New York-based energy conglomerate (coal, oil). "This one is the real thing," the Maine *Times* warned after the subdued announcement of Pittston's plans (no fanfare or state government officials on hand to give their blessings) in the spring of 1973. By this point, the energy crisis was looming and Washington seemed in a mood to cooperate, not hinder a Maine refinery.

---

* I have omitted from this account some lesser proposals that also came to naught, including ones by King Resources (owned by Colorado's flamboyant John King) to build a refinery at South Portland, by Atlantic Richfield at Machias, and a proposal by Robert A. G. Monks—a young entrepreneur strangely befriended by the Maine *Times*.

Moreover, Pittston had technical expertise and capital resources unmatched by the earlier bidders.

Eastport, once the sardine canning capital of the world, has little to distinguish itself except that it is the easternmost city of the United States—and very poor (area unemployment was 20 percent in 1974, with a quarter of the population receiving surplus government foods). Around the turn of the century, some 5,000 people lived in Eastport. Now the fishing fleet has been decimated by the rough competition of the foreign factory ships; two sardine canneries and a single fish rendering plant remain, but they provide only seasonal, fitful employment. Aside from that, Eastport has three factories that make pearl essence from fish scales, a Christmas wreath plant, and a woolen mill. Many of the stores in the decaying old brick downtown are closed. Eastport is an enclosed society, plagued by constant departure of its young people. The population has sunk to 1,989. The locals have been strong for the refinery —for anything to alleviate the depressing economic situation. Opposition to the refinery has been largely confined to people "from away"—the nonnative retirees and alternative life-style arrivals who are a class set apart, because they were not born in Eastport.

Pittston proposed importing crude oil in supertankers of more than 250,-000 tons, which would approach the port through the Canadian water of Head Harbour Passage, which is subject to tidal currents of over five knots. The ships would pass many tiny islands and Campobello Island, where an international park commemorating Franklin D. Roosevelt is located. Anchored off a rocky cove, the ships would pump oil into holding tanks; after being refined, the oil would be carried out in smaller tankers and motorized barges for distribution.

The environmentalists' arguments against a refinery at Eastport had a familiar ring. According to CRAC: "Because of the strong tidal currents, bad weather and fog that have made Eastport an historically difficult port, the risk of accident is inordinately high and the difficulties of containing or removing spilled oil are insurmountable." Then CRAC recalled that it was Pittston that gained notoriety when an earthen dam used in its strip mining operations collapsed, drowning 118 people at West Virginia's Buffalo Creek in 1972.* A company with that kind of record of callous disregard for people's safety, it was suggested, should not be trusted to build a refinery on the priceless Maine coast.

In June 1975 the Maine board of environmental protection gave its approval to the Pittston proposal. The outcome, however, was still uncertain. The final stumbling block might be the refusal of the Canadian government to allow the tankers, as every ship entering Eastport must, to pass through the marine waters under its exclusive control. In addition, navigational aids would have to be installed on Canadian soil and Canadian pilots would have to guide the tankers through the turbulent waters of much of Head Harbour Passage. In an official 1973 protest, the Canadian government said the Pitts-

---

* For details of the Buffalo Creek tragedy, see an earlier book in this series, *The Border South States,* pages 182–84.

ton proposal "presents an unacceptable risk in the transport of a large volume of pollutants through these difficult waters."

Sometimes overlooked in the controversies over the exposed coastal refinery sites is the fact that Portland, although it cannot handle the new supertankers, is already the third largest oil port on the East Coast, after Philadelphia and New York. It is capable of handling 100,000-ton tankers, and pipes large quantities of crude oil to Canada. A consortium of several oil and gas companies in 1974 proposed a refinery 35 miles inland, at Sanford, connected to Portland by pipeline. The voters of Sanford approved the proposal, and there seemed at least a fair chance that the $650 million refinery-pipeline-terminal plan would eventually be approved.

The furor over oil contributed significantly to two tough antipollution and industrial control laws, passed in 1970. The first, which came to be known as "the oil handling law," made the spiller of oil absolutely liable, without any common law rules of negligence or misconduct, for any clean-up costs, damage to fishermen or shorefront property owners. A coastal protection fund was set up, financed by a tax of one-half cent a barrel on oil transferred between ship and shore in Maine waters; the funds were to pay immediately for clean-up costs, plus damages to lobstermen or whoever, with the fund then empowered to undertake the lengthy process of suing the company responsible for the spill. Harrison Richardson, the sponsor of the bill, said it was "the toughest oil pollution control law in the United States." The oil companies challenged its constitutionality in a decision the U.S. Supreme Court refused to review.

Concurrently, Maine passed its landmark site approval law, which gave the state government veto power over any proposed industrial or residential project of more than 20 acres, anywhere in the state. Elaborate hearings would be required, but in the final analysis the state gained power to reject any project it thought would have an adverse effect on Maine's air or water. Again, the oil companies fought the bill; again the courts rejected their challenge. The law had the effect of forcing much more careful consideration of new projects, whether in oil or other fields. Governor Curtis, however, acknowledged in 1974 that it had two chief drawbacks. The first was that it was not based on any comprehensive plan of where industrial development *ought* to be located. Secondly, he said, there was too much uncertainty in the process:

Conservationists are never sure from which port their Paul Reveres will ride in next. Coastal towns continue to hope for bonanzas few will receive. Some companies continue to assume that they can replace planning with promises and pollution control with politics. When these dreams and nightmares converge, the state must go through an expensive six-month hearing process that diverts resources from our continuing efforts to clean up the pollution we already have.

In 1971, the legislature went two steps further toward land use plans for Maine. One measure expanded the scope of authority of the two-year-old land use regulation commission from 2 to 51 percent of the state's land area—namely, 10:5 million acres of the Unorganized Territories that fill the northern part of the state. The commission was given power to classify these vast land tracts into various types of districts—some to be protected totally against recreational or industrial use, some to be made available for those purposes, some to be managed by the timber companies for commercial forest production, etc. The essential purpose was to safeguard most of the northern lands against irresponsible recreation development, strip-mining or other activities that would harm water and land resources.

The second bill required municipalities to adopt subdivision and zoning controls for all areas within 250 feet of the coast or any "navigable" pond, lake, or river. If they failed to do the job, the state department of environmental protection or the land use regulation commission would step in and do it for them.

Theoretically, the various land use and natural resources measures should all be coordinated by the state planning office, which is attached directly to the governor's office and is charged by statute with developing a "Maine comprehensive plan." But as the state planning director, Philip M. Savage, wrote in 1973, "We do not have a comprehensive state land use plan." He proposed that in view of the state's town meeting tradition and distaste for bureaucracy, most land use regulation decisions should be left in local hands. But he also recommended that the regional planning commissions, operating in the planning and development districts into which Governor Curtis had divided Maine by executive order in 1972, should guide planning and project review in the major drainage basins with which their borders coincide. He looked to having the "p&d" commissions prepare regional segments of the state land use plan.

In all this, there seemed to be many a slip 'twixt cup and lip. In setting land use control for the half of Maine under its jurisdiction, for instance, the land use commission was hampered by a skeleton staff and an infinity of objections from timber companies and other landowners. Many municipalities were also dragging their feet in zoning, and there was still no proof that even when the zoning came, it would stop the garish strip development that has begun to blight U.S. 1 along the coast and many of the coastal towns. Maine has experienced pressure for big second-home and ski developments, but not on an intensity scale comparable with Vermont, a state much closer to the megalapolitan population centers.*

Some other environmental measures passed in recent years are noteworthy. A "great ponds protection" measure inhibits ecologically hazardous development on Maine's inland waters; where there is no sewer system, newly sold lots must be of substantial size. Wetlands are protected against filling, dredging, or draining, but court orders make it necessary to compensate owners for not undertaking these activities except in the case of clear-cut pollution or public health hazards. "Current use" tax laws, to put a damper on land speculation and prevent Maine residents from being taxed out of their homes

---

* By the 1970s there were two big-scale ski resorts, at Sugarloaf and Saddleback in the northwestern part of the state, plus many smaller ski slopes and accommodations. But developers' proposals for a huge four-season resort on untouched Bigelow Mountain appeared to have been stymied.

and property because of development pressure, apply to farms, forest lands, and open spaces. The board of environmental protection must approve new mines, which cannot be dug without reclamation schedules for the affected land. A billboard law, passed in 1969, outlawed several thousand existing boards and prevented construction of more—but was not as thoroughgoing as the comparable Vermont statute. And the state has a fairly effective air pollution law.

Water Pollution, Pulp and Paper, and the Debate on Maine's Future

Water pollution has been one of Maine's most intractable problems. Pristine and fast-moving rivers and tree-shrouded lakes that were pools of clear cold water—these were the legacy of nature to early Maine settlers, and for generations, in a primitive, agricultural economy, they were not threatened. But then, in the early 1800s, sawmills began to dump their dust into the rivers, coating the riverbeds and altering their ecology. The paper and pulp plants began to open in the latter part of the century, taking in vast quantities of water and then returning it to the waterways, contaminated with chemicals and laden with organic substances. "Paper and pulp effluent," Richard Saltonstall has written, "created oxygenless barriers on the rivers, through which fish could not pass alive." The highly noxious effluents of leather tanneries, dyes from textile plants, and potato starch wastes added to the problem until there were several rivers wholly given over to carrying away industrial wastes. The offal from chicken processing plants—fat, blood, guts, bones, and feathers—choked some of the state's waters, including the port of Belfast near the head of Penobscot Bay. And to this list one must add the most serious single cause of pollution for the past century: the runoff of sewage from towns and cities, with the problems raised by bacteria and potentially dangerous coliform counts. Long stretches of river became unswimmable and undrinkable unless heavily treated; the Androscoggin was labeled the nation's ninth filthiest river; with uncontrolled vacation home development, a number of lakes became polluted as well.

The state's first pass at pollution control came in 1945, when four different classes of water were established by law, running from "class A" in which no pollution would be permitted to "class D"—waters "primarily devoted to transportation of sewerage and industrial wastes." But the law, as Duane Lockard wrote in the 1950s, was "more amusing than effective" because it contained a section exempting from its provisions 12 major rivers of the state —including practically all with any kind of pulp and paper mill along their banks. The hopeless inadequacy of the state's laws, Lockard noted, was due to the political muscle of the controlling vested interests—paper and potato starch industries, those most intent on preserving freedom to pollute; municipalities anxious not to bear the cost of sewage treatment plants; and the power companies intent on protecting the interests of the industries to which they sold power. When controls were proposed, the bugaboo of fleeing industries was always raised to scare off the legislature.

Eventually somewhat better bills were passed, but "grandfather" clauses guaranteeing existing polluters the right to keep on polluting for years were included, along with other hard-to-enforce control provisions inserted by legislators who were at the beck and call of the industrialists and labor unions. The federal clean water bills of the 1960s, passed under Muskie's sponsorship, did have a beneficial effect through their requirements for factories to control their pollution and authorization of generous federal matching funds to help towns and cities build sewage treatment facilities. Maine became the nation's second biggest spender, on a per capita basis, in passing state bonds for sewage plants. Maine bankers cooperated through a policy of not making loans to potential polluters.

But then the Nixon administration began to impound and otherwise thwart the flow of federal grants for treatment facilities. Instead of the mid-1970s, Maine's people probably had to look to the 1980s—if then—for a final solution to the problem of their polluted, abused waterways.

Significant progress in cleaning up the rivers has been made by the pulp and paper mills, which have invested huge sums in pollution control equipment over the past several years. But that behemoth of Maine industries, with close to 17,000 employees and by far the highest level of gross wages and value of any Maine industry, in recent years has been on the receiving end of some of the stiffest criticism ever leveled against any industry in any American state. Ralph Nader, whose Center for Study of Responsive Law in 1973 released the results of a two-and-a-half year study of the Maine pulp and paper industry,* declared:

> Maine is a paper plantation—a land of seven giant paper and pulp companies imposing a one-crop economy with a one-crop politics, which exploits the water, air, soil, and people of a beautiful state.
>
> The goal of the paper industry is the maximum profitable extraction of pulpwood. And it dominates the state as it pursues this goal, with a tunnel vision unique even for large absentee corporations.

The seven great corporations which control 6.5 million acres of Maine timberland, about a third of the total land area of the state, are Great Northern Paper, International Paper, Scott Paper, Diamond International, St. Regis Paper, Georgia-Pacific, and Oxford Paper (a division of Ethyl Corporation). Collectively, they produce 90 percent of the pulp and paper. All have headquarters outside of Maine and are controlled by non-Maine interests. The Nader report alleged that "each represents an economic force and power as great as, if not greater than, the state of Maine itself." In 1970, every one of the big seven had gross revenues exceeding Maine's total tax revenues; International Paper, in fact, took in six times as much as did the Maine government. "Instead of using its enormous resources for the long-term benefit of

---

* The study was begun in 1970 by a task force of law students, primarily from the University of Maine in Portland. In 1972 leadership of the project was assumed by William C. Osborn, who wrote the final report, *The Paper Plantation,* published in 1974 (New York: Grossman Publishers).

all Maine people," the Nader report asserted, "the paper industry has concerned itself with a narrower goal—that of maximizing short-term profits and increasing the value of its shareholders' investment."

The long-standing water pollution practices of the industry received the bitterest condemnation in the report: "The pollution has destroyed valuable fisheries, forced industries and municipalities to seek new water supplies, depreciated property values and discouraged recreational use of the rivers. The result is nothing less than a major theft of public and private resources." The leading polluters were said to be Oxford Paper and Diamond International, each of which was pouring more than 50 tons of suspended solids into the Androscoggin and Penobscot Rivers daily. The report accused the industry, as many in-state environmentalists have, of dragging its feet on pollution abatement until forced by a 1967 law to comply, and then pressuring the legislature "with false threats of environmental shutdown" to grant an extension for abatement facilities to 1976, even though the technology existed to do the job in a much shorter period of time. (Harrison Richardson told me, for instance, that the threats of paper mill shutdowns were a ruse. "Any time the Great Northern Paper Company wants to pack its goddamn paper plants on flatcars and ship them south," he said, "I will meet them at Kittery with a brass band!" Edward Penley, an editorial writer for the Portland *Evening Express*, put it a little more delicately: "The paper companies can't pick up their woods and go.")

The 1970s have seen the last of the great log drives which used to occur on the Kennebec, the Machias, Dead River, Moxie Stream, and a hundred unnamed water courses from ice-out to summer each year. The accumulation of wood would be gathered upstream during the winter cutting season. Then, as the ice broke and the melting snow turned the riverbeds into fast-moving torrents, millions of lengths of fir and spruce would be released for their rapid, exciting trip to the mills downstream. Unless the loggers guiding the flow of logs, keeping them free from snags and jams, were agile indeed, their working days could be limited. "No employment that I am aware of threatens the life and health more than river driving," John Springer wrote in 1851. "Many a poor fellow finds his last resting-place on the bank of some wild stream, in whose stifling depths his last struggle for life was spent."

The log drives were an affront and hazard to the rivers. Dumped into lakes or river coves during the winter, the logs grew heavy with water and a portion of them (some 6 percent) sank to the bottom. Wyman Lake on the Kennebec today has 80 feet of sunken logs on its botom. Then the grinding ice ripped off the bark, covering the spawning grounds of trout and salmon and reducing the oxygen count of the water. Finally, the log drives, some extended to the fall, deprived Maine residents of the recreational use of their rivers. A landmark lawsuit against the Kennebec Log Driving Company and the big paper companies which were its major owners, instituted by a University of Maine graduate student and taken up by the state government, stopped logging on the Kennebec in 1971. But already, most paper companies had found it more economical to use trucks to get deep into the woods. So the log drives ended—and with them, a romantic era, dangerous employment, and an egregious case of industry's preemption of public property for private profit.

The average pulp and paper mill worker in Maine earns 22 percent less than factory workers elsewhere in the United States, but the real hardship falls on the independent loggers who purchase and cut wood from non-paper company lands and then sell it to the mills. Some 57 percent of the cordage used in the mills is obtained in this manner. The independents, according to writer William Osborn in the Nader report, constitute a "pulpwood peonage." Since they are not mill employees, they must purchase and maintain all the equipment required for modern logging—chain saws, skidders,* bulldozers, and trucks. Usually they work in three- or four-man crews, as partners or on contract, an arrangement which frees the logger in charge from paying workmen's compensation, social security, or unemployment. "There is general agreement," Osborn wrote, "that pulpwood simply could not be cut and furnished to the mill for the prices paid if the contractors had to pay all the employee benefits required by law." The report backed up the contention of a group of independent cutters who staged a strike in 1970: that the big paper companies, whether through collusion or *de facto* monopoly, fix the prices paid for pulpwood. The rise in those prices over the past decades has been only a fraction of average price increases in the country. The independents find themselves working long hours under one-sided contracts written by the mills. Pressed financially, they overload their trucks, thus exposing Maine drivers to added dangers on the state roads. Working under conditions where time is of the essence, they tend to neglect safety.

Finally, there has been the charge that the big paper companies own so much woodland that they lack the incentive or need to adopt intensive forest management practices. The Nader report alleged that they could grow twice as much wood on their acreage as they do, but refuse to make the necessary investments in stocking their lands with desirable trees, removing rough or rotten trees between harvests, or in cultivating hardwoods (birch, maple, and beech) that can be used by independently owned Maine-based wood products firms. (According to the U.S. Forest Service, total hardwood removals are in danger of exceeding growth within the next few years. Hardwoods can be used in producing pulpwood, which accounts for two-thirds of the timber harvested in the state, but the preferred types for pulp are softwoods—white pine, red pine, white spruce, balsam, fir, and white cedar.) An example of "something wrong" with the management of Maine's forest industry is the fact that although the state ranks third in the nation in the lumber it produces ($715 million in 1972), 90 percent of its housing is constructed with timber shipped in from Washington and Oregon, 3,500 miles distant. Critics say there are countless ways that the forests could be developed for the benefit

---

* The skidder is an odd-looking double-jointed machine that has replaced horses in dragging trees from the woods. The cost per skidder is some $25,000.

of Maine-owned and run industries, but that the big paper companies have little or no interest in a diversified, prosperous local economy.

Rapidly rising prices for timber, coinciding with the international energy crisis that began to mount in 1973–74, after completion of the Nader report, did change the outlook for Maine's forests to rapid and more intensive development. By the end of 1974, some half billion dollars of new investments had been made for plant expansion and improvements to expand production. "We are only using half the forest products in Maine right now," John Cole said. "The rest of the trees are just falling over and dying. But that is going to stop." There were predictions that a deepwater port would indeed materialize in eastern Maine—not for oil, but to put the state's forest products on the global market. Robert A. G. Monks, after unsuccessful thrusts as an oil developer and U.S. Senate candidate in 1972, became director of the state's new office of energy resources and began to look to wood as an alternative energy source for Maine. (By 1975 Monks had moved on to head a new corporation planning to produce large quantities of methanol, a competitive and desirable fuel, from wood presently being wasted.) The big new fight in the Maine legislature, Cole predicted, would be over the forest practices act, which controls whether wood can be harvested and taken to market with minimal destruction to the landscape. The paper companies, he said, would abandon any more ideas of setting aside portions of their land for large-scale recreational developments. "They won't want the public on their lands because they are going to be in such a hurry to harvest that wood that they don't want people driving around in snowmobiles or camping out when they have their big machines rummaging about," he observed.

In 1974, it appeared that the emotions generated in Maine over the oil issue in the late '60s and early '70s might be transferred in significant measure to the question of the public's interest in the millions of acres of forest, Maine's most formidable resource. An indication of battles to come was the unsuccessful effort of Harrison Richardson and others to organize millions of "unorganized" acres of Maine woodlands into eight "grand plantations"—in other words, to bring municipal government, with representation for the scattered residents, resource management, and equitable taxation to the half of Maine that had been under total control of the paper companies since the late 19th century. An immediate effect of the bill would have been to terminate the paper companies' timber cutting rights on some 320,000 acres of those vast territories classified as "public lots." The legislature had never actually sold those lots, but rather sold cutting rights on them, for as little as five to 10 cents an acre "until the said township or tract shall be incorporated into a town, or organized into a plantation." The tenuous nature of the paper companies' cutting rights to the public lots had been a deep secret in Maine until 1972, when reporter Bob Cummings of the Portland *Press-Herald* looked into the agreements, sparking a full study by the populist-oriented Republican attorney general, Jon Lund. In a 1974 hearing before Richardson's public lands committee in the legislature, Lund attacked the pulp and paper interests for launching "a gargantuan lobbying effort" to block the grand plantation bill:

> No issue of these dimensions has been before the legislature [Lund said] since the 1920s when Governor Percival Baxter fought many of these same private interests over ownership of the water resources of the state. At that time, private interests brought a powerful lobby to bear against the state in an effort to acquire for nothing the lakes and rivers of the state. Governor Baxter saw the issue then: Shall the resources of the people of the state that belong to all the people be deeded to corporate interests forever, or shall the people be entitled to share in the benefits accruing from these resources? The issue here is the same. . . .
>
> Well over one-half of the cutting rights are claimed by only five corporations, which own, in the aggregate, more than 35 million acres of fee title and cutting rights throughout the United States and Canada. . . .
>
> In contrast, for a state that is so heavily forested and thinly populated, Maine has a remarkably small acreage of public recreational lands. If the enactment of this proposal results in termination of cutting rights on the 320,000 acres of woodlands, it will be more than double the amount of state-owned public land which would be available for recreational purposes. . . .

The grand plantations bill—entangled in Richardson's gubernatorial ambitions, opposition of some residents of the unorganized territories, and the intensive opposition lobbying efforts—went down to defeat in the 1974 session. (The object of the bill, state senate president Kenneth MacLeod said, was little more than "to steal back from the paper companies and large landowners what they stole from us in the 1850s.") But the big landowners apparently decided that public opinion was turning against them on the issue, and in 1975 started negotiations to return tens of thousands of acres of the public lots to state control, also trading land to avoid the sudden emergency of 1,000-acre state-owned "islands" in the midst of their domains.

The "issue" facing Maine is, in fact, a great deal broader than public lots, oil refineries, low wages, pollution, land use controls, or any of the other issues which I have deliberately brought together in the last two subchapters because of their intimate interconnection. On the one side one finds the major corporate and business interests, labor unions, and the traditional-style development officials who say that the only solution for Maine's low income problem is the heavy importation of capital for the generation of new jobs. With varying degrees of sincerity, this group has shown an interest in environmental questions in the last several years. But its primary concern is economics, not ecology.

The opposition point of view—expressed by young people, back-to-the-earthers, new Maine immigrants, academics, and the Maine *Times*—is that the last thing Maine needs is more heavy industry. Cole takes perhaps the most extreme view when he speaks of a "critical transitional phase," all across the United States but particularly in Maine, "from a high energy, centralized system, to a low energy decentralized system." Multitudes of cottage industries, self-sufficient agriculture, wind, wood, and solar substitutes for nonrenewable energy sources like oil, a ban on nuclear plants, fewer roads, fewer big recreational developments, waterless toilets,* the return of passenger rail service, and community control of people's lives—these are the salient features of the future Cole predicts for Maine. Richard Saltonstall, Jr., another nonnative, took a similar view in his 1974 book, *Maine Pilgrimage: The Search for an American Way of Life.*

Critics accuse people like Cole and Saltonstall of being hopeless romanticists, trying to turn the clock back to a condition never likely to recur in a highly interdependent, high-consumption, high-demand society. At a colloquium in Washington in 1974, at the Woodrow Wilson International Center for Scholars, Elliot Richardson replied to John Cole by belittling the prospect of Maine people returning to pot-bellied stoves and giving up the material advantages of a mass production economy. "I think most of the mill-owners and the descendants of the French-Canadians and others who came there for a better living and even the descendants of the New England farmers who have left the land would very much welcome the opportunity to make a better living than they do now," Richardson said. In an interview I had with Senator Muskie, he made almost exactly the same point, saying that Maine people living on the edge of poverty in a city like Lewiston "aren't content with and can't be persuaded that they shouldn't be able" to rise above their present standard of living. Muskie said he would be intrigued to see how Cole or like thinkers could sell their low-key development approach to such people.

Cole and his friends, however, can produce some interesting statistics to suggest that Maine should diversify its production units, "think small," and keep ownership close to home. During the years that Maine's per capita income has been dropping further and further behind the national average, the percentage of outside ownership in the 47 firms employing more than 500 workers in the state has dropped from about 50 percent to 13 percent. Between 1958 and 1969 the employment rolls of firms with headquarters outside Maine rose eight percent, while the employment of larger Maine-owned companies went up 82 percent. Moreover, there are signs that the century-long population flight from Maine may be ending, even without the infusion of big out-of-state capital. Between 1970 and 1975, the state population rose 65,000—from 994,000 to 1,059,000, a growth rate of 6.6 percent, more than the national average. Interestingly, the growth was minor in the southern Maine counties on the outer edge of megalopolis; rather it was moving into remote, rural, nonindustrial counties, especially those farthest "down east."

No one has a very clear picture of the kind of people most heavily represented in the new influx to Maine. Retirees represent part of the pool. Some are exurbanite homesteaders. Others are young middle-class entrepreneurs starting up antique shops, craft centers, inns, and other service enterprises. Others are footloose professionals—lawyers, architects, nurses, even a few physicians. All seem willing, as one state official put it, "to exchange the

---

* The modern American flush toilet, according to Cole, is symbolic of the high energy society and its foolishness. "If you engineer a system that requires eight gallons of water for an eight-ounce cargo, and take clean water out, and then you turn around and spend millions upon millions of dollars to clean it up again, then you expend a great deal of energy."

psychic income of the Maine life style for the economic benefits of the city."

Even allowing for the arrival of such people, however, it is possible that if job opportunities had not been shrinking so rapidly in the country's metropolitan centers in the early '70s, Maine youth would still be emigrating as rapidly as they did in the preceding decades—offsetting, in total population, any infusion of new stock into Maine. The same reversal of population loss noted in Maine since 1970 has also been apparent in other quite rural, isolated states, including those of Appalachia and the Mountain West. One cannot yet answer the question of whether recent population growth in these states is anything more than a temporary phenomenon in a time of shrinking national job markets.

So the debate about economic planning and the ideal future pattern is likely to go on in Maine for some years to come. Actually, it seems unlikely that Maine will opt either for unfettered economic development based on big projects financed by outside corporations, *or* totally for the Cole-Saltonstall version of a low-energy, low-demand Maine society. Politically, the most attractive course could well lie with neo-populists like Harrison Richardson and Jon Lund, or people like them in either political party. This course would include rigorous defense of the people's rights in any development, and in righting past wrongs—but not in opposing development *per se*. The solution, in short, might be in Maine people putting some stiff controls on the corporations which have so often exploited them but still welcoming the infusions of capital those corporations can bring to a still-poor state. A growth in Maine's still rather limited, unimaginative labor movement could increase incomes, as it is just beginning to in Appalachia and the South.

One could question the internal consistency of asking for a fairly pristine environment, political control close to home, stronger labor unions, and the benefits of capitalist development all at the same time. But American voters, whether they live in Maine or elsewhere, have rarely been characterized by the consistency of their attitudes and expectations.

City and Townscape

The city of Portland, Maine's closest pass at a metropolis, is not very large by national standards. In 1970 it had only 65,116 inhabitants—fewer than it could boast in 1920—and a modest-sized metropolitan area of 141,625. Such diverse places as Lima, Ohio, or Lubbock, Texas, have more.

Portland is, however, a town with a colorful history ranging back over more than 300 years. Few dispute its claim to be New England's most important financial, trade, and cultural center north of Boston. And it is one of those medium-sized—i.e., manageable—American cities with unique assets (Portland's is its harbor) and a quality of livability and potential for citizen action that draws able and talented people. Philadelphia's famed architect-planner, Edmund N. Bacon, put it well in a 1972 visit: "Portland is a remarkable city. It's therefore very important that you don't mess it up."

Bacon compared Portland to an ancient Mediterranean city built on a T-design, the arms of the T corresponding to the handsome Eastern and Western Promenades, which are boulevards on the heights of either side of the peninsula which extends into lovely Casco Bay with its 365 Calendar Islands (one for every day of the year). Bacon was urging Portlanders to avoid development that would destroy any of the basic parts of the T, or free movement between them, or to neglect the city's waterfront, which he said "could become world famous."

Bacon also had praise for the renewal activity in the Old Port Exchange district on the waterfront, long a seedy, rundown area where century-old Victorian buildings are being converted into nostalgic specialty shops, craftsmen's workbenches, and gourmet restaurants. New life has been returning to the area, which sank to the status of a red light district during World War II. Improvements of this type come none too soon for Portland, whose inner city has the grimy visage of an old industrial town, its curving and irregular streets (marked by some of the worst street signs in America) clogged with traffic even though a lot of the retailing vitality has gone suburban. In 1970 the first major downtown building since 1925 was completed. Having missed the postwar business building boom may in the long run turn out to be a blessing in disguise, however, because the core area can now be revived with an eye to restoration of architecturally significant old structures, rather than stamping out the old in favor of massive demolition to make way for undistinguished skyscrapers. A group known as Greater Portland Landmarks, Inc., has had a fair degree of success (though some failures) in protecting Portland's fine old buildings.

Over its history, Portland has been visited by a remarkable series of successes, usually keyed to its maritime role, interspersed by disasters physical and economic. Between 1750 and the Revolution, the city (then known as Falmouth) prospered through the export of great quantities of pine masts for the British Navy. Then, in 1775, as a prelude to the Revolution, a British fleet shelled the town and landed, putting the torch to most of its buildings and leaving 2,000 persons homeless. Maritime prosperity returned quickly after the war, and Maine's first banking house was organized. These were the years when Portland's Commodore Edward Preble won world-wide fame for subduing the Barbary pirates; it was the era Henry Wadsworth Longfellow, Portland's most famous literary figure, would later recall in his poem *My Lost Youth:*

> I remember the black wharves and the slips
> And the sea tides tossing free;
> And Spanish sailors with bearded lips
> And the beauty of mystery of ships
> And the magic of the sea.

The Jefferson Embargo of 1807, however, plunged Portland into a deep depression, the worst of its history. The ships on the waterfront literally rotted at their moorings and citizens lined up in Market Square to be fed from public soup kettles.

Recovery came with the War of 1812, and through the next half century ocean commerce boomed, the city became a winter ice-free port for the Canadian Martime provinces, and shipbuilding added to the general prosperity. Then, late on the afternoon of the Fourth of July, 1866, a clear and happy Independence Day gloriously celebrated in Maine's biggest and most prosperous city, a small boy tossed a firecracker into the wood shavings of a boat yard. A high wind came up, fanning the flames and showering sparks for miles about. John Neal later wrote in *The Great Conflagration in Portland*: "On swept the whirlwind of fire, spreading out like a fan as it went, directly through the wealthiest and busiest part of our city; and with such inconceivable swiftness, that people knew not whither to fly for safety." Fire companies came from near and far, laboring in the midst of "falling chimneys and tumbling walls, and showers of broken slate, and clouds of smoke, and blazing cinders all about them, and a suffocating, scorching atmosphere." Only 15 hours later did the wind shift and the fire die out; in its wake it left 1,500 buildings destroyed, a burnt over area of 200 acres, and 10,000 people homeless. Longfellow wrote to a friend a few weeks later: "I have been in Portland since the fire. Desolation, desolation, desolation! It reminds me of Pompeii."

As has ever been its custom, Portland rebuilt quickly and became a prosperous shipping center in the wake of the fire. Streets were widened, rail connections extended, and an enviable city park system inaugurated. But as Richard Saltonstall has observed, "Something was lost in that 1866 fire, if only the chance to keep up with the competitive pace." Each world war brought bursts of economic activity, but a precipitate slump in maritime activities began in 1924 when Montreal shifted the bulk of its winter shipments to St. John and Halifax. Between 1919 and 1939, Portland lost more than half its manufacturing establishments, and its income levels fell well below national averages. By the late 1940s the waterfront was spectacularly dilapidated, and shipbuilding, so intense in war years, practically disappeared. The 1950s saw completion of a pipeline to Montreal, making Portland the major oil port it remains today. But rotting, fire-blackened piers along the waterfront symbolized a general decay, and by 1972 Portland was "putting far more raw sewage into its harbor (20 million gallons a day) than tons of cargo into ships."

Portland in the 1960s did try to revive its core with liberal panaceas like urban renewal, public housing, and model cities. Talented city managers have done a lot to revive the city, including the Old Port Exchange project. The young city manager, John Menario, was the key negotiator in reviving the era of passenger ships making Portland their port of call. Regular ferry service, on well-appointed ships, was inaugurated between Portland and Yarmouth, Nova Scotia. The service has been very popular, and talk has even been heard of future ferry lines to New York or Philadelphia. The city has a fine new medical center; the University of Maine has its law school and an undergraduate branch there; the lively arts have prospered with theatrical groups, a symphony orchestra, and the like. The Portland *Press Herald* and Maine *Sunday Telegram*, lackluster, rock-ribbed Republican papers in the days of founder Guy Gannett, who died in 1954, have become politically independent, boast some excellent writers, and have even dipped a toe into exemplary investigative reporting on environmental issues. The papers serve a broad region—practically all of Maine south of Bangor.

New hope for the port has also been rekindled in recent years. There was hope in 1974, for instance, that the commercial waterfront might get the largest dry cargo port facility north of Boston, capable of handling the big containerized ships which have become the key to successful port operations. The containerized port, it appeared, might be financed by the Gibbs Oil Company as part of the deal to construct facilities for oil tankers to unload large quantities of crude oil at Portland for transfer inland to the projected refinery at Sanford. Were this to come to pass, Portland's real prosperity, as through all its history, would come from the sea—fitting enough, one might say, for a town that has emblazoned on its city seal the motto *Resurgam*— "I will arise."

A review of Maine's other cities in the 20,000-plus population range leaves one with the vague feeling that Maine might be just as attractive and well-off a state if they were not there at all, or alternatively could be built again from the ground up.

The state capital at Augusta (1970 population 21,945) is a case in point. Set on both sides of the Kennebec River, 45 miles from the open sea, the city has ample parks, many streets lined with century-old elms, and of course the State House—designed by the illustrious Charles Bulfinch in the 1820s but unfortunately redesigned and expanded in Greek Renaissance style some 80 years later, so that only the "Bulfinch front" remains. Looking around Augusta, some attractive structures can be found. The excellent Romanesque granite post office building of the 1890s, for instance, was saved from destruction when the Postal Service moved to larger quarters in the 1960s and reopened as an attractive downtown shopping arcade and office building. But it is hard to argue with John Cole's charge about the low-grade development of Augusta in the years since World War II. "Someday," Cole wrote, "someone should document just how the retching sprawl of shopping centers, two-bit restaurants, used car lots, beer joints, cheap apartments, rundown hotels and tottering homes swallowed Augusta in a relatively few years. [There are] beer signs and filling stations within a horseshoe pitch of the State House. . . . For every Maine citizen, Augusta is an insult as a capital, because it is in no way an accurate or inspired representation of Maine."

Then there are Maine's textile and shoe towns, crowded with French-Canadians who by choice or necessity occupy acre after acre of bleak wooden tenement buildings, some of the ugliest housing I have seen anywhere in the United States. Add to the scene the massive and dreary brick mill buildings (many vacant with "for rent" signs), the stench from polluted rivers, and the congested streets, and one somehow wonders if Maine couldn't have done better.

The largest of these are the twin cities of Lewiston (41,779) and Auburn (24,151), on the Androscoggin, and two other twins, Biddeford (19,983) and

Saco (11,678), on the Saco River. Despite the physical blight of these towns, one must recognize that they offer real *communities*, which so much of America cannot. Lewiston, for instance, has dozens of social clubs, run by veterans and other organizations, where people can gather together for an evening of dancing and card games and social drinking—a welcome relief from the austerity of their daily lives.

The mill towns, however, also offer very high unemployment—not just because of the long decline of textiles and shoes, but because many young people won't accept the dirty, unglamorous, monotonous employment those industries offer.

The northernmost spot in Maine one could seriously call a city is Bangor (33,168); in fact it has no competitors within its own realm, so that the circulation area of the Bangor *Daily News* can and does cover one-third of New England or 68 percent of Maine's land surface. (Delivery routes of the *News*, which has become a quite high quality paper in recent years, even reach Madawaska on the Canadian border, 235 miles distant.) Bangor is a feeder city for this vast domain of some 390,000 people, and its chief supplier of goods and services.

The big success story of modern-day Bangor is how it recovered in rather tidy fashion from the closing of the Dow Air Force Base, where some 5,000 civilians had been employed up to the mid-1960s. Some thought the Air Force pullout could spell Bangor's obituary, but the city fathers responded imaginatively—not by putting on one of those fruitless lobby campaigns to retain the facility, but rather by deciding to live with its consequences. "We knew it had to come down one day," publisher Richard Warren of the *Daily News* said some years later. "A lot of us felt it might be a good thing in the long run to get the town back where it was not so dependent on the base." For the grand sum of $1, the city bought the airfield and potential commercial buildings from the government—a facility valued at $100 million. Another $1 bought base facilities to start up a satellite campus for the University of Maine. And some 1,000 housing units were purchased by low-income Bangor residents.

The city used some of the buildings and land it acquired to open an industrial park, which drew firms that took up some of the employment slack. The most imaginative step, though, was to turn the airfield—which had a 11,400-foot runway, big enough to accommodate any known aircraft—into the Bangor International Airport. Bangor lies fortuitously on the Great Circle Route to Europe, and thus could offer major inducements to scheduled and nonscheduled transatlantic carriers—a place for diverted aircraft to land because of congestion or poor weather at New York JFK Airport, much lower landing charges, fast turnaround times, aircraft maintenance, quick customs clearance, and a stopover and base for charter flight crews. From virtual ground zero in 1968, Bangor International became a port of call for more than 300,000 international passengers by 1972, thus becoming the sixth largest point of entry in the continental United States.

The city of Bangor itself, however, leaves a lot to be desired. Its streets are lined by dirty, old red brick buildings, the skyline is monotonous in the extreme, and the Penobscot River, which in centuries past ran clear and sparkling to the sea, is plagued by industrial pollution. Nor is there any of the exuberance of 19th-century Bangor, when the lumber barons of the Gilded Age put up their great mansions and made the town the cultural center of Maine. In and out of the harbor came literally hundreds of ships, taking out the pine boards, bringing in molasses and sugar and rum from the West Indies. Bangor then was a national and world port, peopled by lusty sailors and lumberjacks, against whom today's international air passenger is a pallid passer in the night. According to the WPA Guide, the section of old Bangor known as the Devil's Half Acre was comparable to San Francisco's Barbary Coast:

> It was here in spring that hundreds of lumberjacks, fresh from the log drives, with a winter's thirsts—and a winter's wages—and ready for pleasure, thronged to the fleshpots of Bangor. No trace remains of the taverns and grogshops, lodging houses and brothels that catered to the teeming life of the busy seaport; gone are the salt water shellbacks and tall timber men who swapped tales, drinks, and blows. . . .

One can feel less sorry about the kind of lumbering that made all that possible. Rapaciously, the lumber companies stripped the forests of their tall timber. Henry David Thoreau had written prophetically in 1846 of the mission of Bangor's lumbermen: "like so many busy demons, to drive the forest all out of the country as soon as possible." Today, all that remains in place of the sawmills are the pulp and paper operations—an essential enterprise, of course but, like modern Bangor, no match in color for what went before.

A quick p. s. on Bangor: the principal University of Maine campus is located at Orono, eight miles distant, largely because Bangor's own Hannibal Hamlin wanted it there. Among other things, the Orono campus is now headquarters of the Maine Public Broadcasting network, which carries exemplary television and radio programs to Maine's people. (This helps to fill, one might add, the gap left by the poor quality of news and public affairs programming on most of Maine's television and radio stations.) And to ·show one can't predict where classes of people will show up in this country, a report comes of a rather large, sophisticated Jewish community in Bangor, engaged in quite enterprising new textile-related manufacturing industries.

In contrast to the cities, the towns and rural areas have positively benefited from Maine's lethargic economy of the past century. Writing in *Historic Preservation*, Marius B. Peladeau of the Maine League of Historical Societies and Museums has classified his state as a prime example of "negative preservation"—the leaving alone of past architecture and town scenes because of a dormant economy. His observations also have a lot to say about the interaction between physical setting and a people's state of mind:

> Maine's rural communities appear practically as they did 25, 50, or 75 years ago. The typical Maine town is still composed of a Grange Hall for the local chapter of the Grange fraternal organization, a feed and grain store, a hardware store, a

general store, and a church or two, all clustered about an intersection, with some houses filtering out onto side streets once bordered by farmland. . . .

If a church has served well for 50 or 100 years, why build a new one? The same applies to the Grange, the town hall and everything else in town. The buildings have served well, they are well built, remain sound and are of attractive design. Thus they need not be replaced. This is the Maine instinct.

The reminders of the Maine past, rarely altered, are scattered across the landscape—thousands of the sturdy Maine Cape style houses, unaltered and in excellent condition though some are 200 years or more old; the quaint "porthole" cottages built by shipwrights-turned-housewrights; Victorian castles built by lumber magnates of the Gilded Age in Portland and Bangor; the opulent shingle-style summer homes of wealthy families like the Vanderbilts and Rockefellers; mansions along the coast put up by sea captains or men who had made their fortunes in shipbuilding or whaling; and some of the textile mills, shoe shops, barrel plants, and other remnants of the innumerable self-contained manufacturing firms of 19th-century Maine.

This is not to say that garish strip development does not blight several areas around and between Maine's towns and cities—along the tourist traps of coastal Route One, from Kittery to Saco, from Portland to Boothbay, around Augusta and Waterville and Bangor. But on the whole, Maine remains the most primitive of the states east of the Mississippi River. Feeling that what was good enough for their fathers was good enough for them, the Maine Yankees have preserved the modest houses, the solid schoolhouses and simple town halls of yesteryear; even where many of the old structures fell into disrepair, they are being restored today by natives and new Maine people alike, sometimes for their old purposes, sometimes for new.*

The social equation is not quite as bright. For all its appearances of stability, Maine is not immune to the problems of social disaffection, of rural crime, of broken up families, even of drugs, alcoholism, unwanted pregnancies, and suicide, which afflict the nation at large. Any social class can suffer from those ills, but it does seem that the Maine families who have the heaviest burden to bear are those who also live in comparative or real poverty, like the inhabitants of Lewiston's shabby wood tenements.

During a talk in his office one afternoon, Senator Muskie recalled that his own family had lived in a wood tenement for a few years. "It was comfortable for that day and time," he said, "and we had plenty to eat. But if most Americans had to live now by heating the cold bath water on top of the stove, or carrying the wood in for the range, for sleeping in cold rooms, as we did—we'd consider it poverty." Back then, he said, "our lower level of material comfort was more than offset by the sense of family and doing things together. We had fun at Christmastime, for instance, not because the toys were stacked high under the tree—in fact my sisters got the same dolls as last Christmas, with new clothes. Rather, it was because we did everything

---

* The wrecker's ball has most frequently struck the old railroad stations, seemingly useless relics in the highway age. But not always: in Minot, for instance, Peladeau reported that the turn-of-the-century station has been converted into a dwelling. The owners have kept the original exterior appearance, even to the point of leaving the old signboards on the end walls.

together. Father, mother, the children, and often neighbors would be together at the table, eating, playing games, listening to the first phonograph in town that my father had. Often all eight of us in my family would sit around together—and that sort of thing wasn't as destructive of communication as television is today. The destruction of the sense of family and of doing things together adds a bleakness to life which, taken with a lower material standard of living, as many Maine people experience to this day, makes life pretty hard. People need each other as much as they ever did, but they don't know how to reach out to each other."

Still, Muskie observed, Maine remains a unique place in America— where one can find community, or solitude if one wants it, and a place where a person can set his own pace. "Maine," he added, "still seems like a place of relative repose to me, and many others. The other side of the coin, of course, is its lack of economic viability."

Perhaps, Muskie seemed to be saying, Maine can't be both prosperous and itself. For the most part, it has chosen to remain itself.

PERSONS INTERVIEWED

THE FOLLOWING PERSONS kindly agreed to interviews with the author in the preparation of this book. Affiliations shown are as of the time of the interview.

ADAMS, Sherman, Former Governor of New Hampshire, Lincoln, N.H.

AIKEN, George D., U.S. Senator from Vermont

ALSOP, John, Republican National Committeeman, Hartford, Conn.

BABCOCK, Robert S., Former Provost, Vermont State Colleges, South Burlington, Vt.

BABBIDGE, Homer, Master, Timothy Dwight College, Yale University, and Former President of the University of Connecticut, New Haven, Conn.

BAILEY, John M., Chairman, Democratic State Committee, and Former Chairman, Democratic National Committee, Hartford, Conn. (deceased)

BENOIT, Arthur, Member, Board of Regents, University of Maine, Portland, Maine

BENSON, Lucy Wilson, Secretary of Human Affairs, Commonwealth of Massachusetts, Boston, Mass.

BLOOD, Robert O., M.D., Former Governor of New Hampshire, Concord, N.H.

BOWLBY, Rita, Director of Government Relations, Connecticut Resources Recovery Authority, Hartford, Conn.

BRADFORD, Peter A., Commissioner, Maine Public Utilities Commission, Augusta, Maine

BROWN, Edwin, Secretary-Treasurer, Rhode Island State AFL-CIO, Providence, R.I.

BROWN, George, Staff of Gov. Francis Sargent of Massachusetts

BROWNELL, Jonathan, Attorney, Montpelier, Vermont

BUCKLEY, John, Vice President, Northeast Petroleum Corporation, Boston, Mass.

BULGER, William M., State Representative, South Boston, Mass.

BURKE, John, Suburban Editor, Boston Globe, Boston, Mass.

BURNS, James MacGregor, Professor of History, Williams College, Williamstown, Mass.

CAIN, Francis J., Mayor of Burlington, Vermont

CALDWELL, William, Editorial Writer, Maine Sunday Telegram, Portland, Maine

CASEN, Bernard, Director, New Hampshire Fish and Game Department, Concord, N.H.

CHAFEE, John, Former Governor of Rhode Island, Providence, R.I.

CLARK, Blair, Former Publisher, The Sunday News of Manchester, Princeton, N.J.

CLEMOW, Bice, Editor, West Hartford News, West Hartford, Conn.

CLEVELAND, James, U.S. Representative from New Hampshire

COLE, John, Editor, Maine Times, Topsham, Maine

COLLINS, John F., Former Mayor of Boston; Professor, Department of Urban Studies, Massachusetts Institute of Technology, Cambridge, Mass.

CONTE, Silvio O., U.S. Representative from Massachusetts

COSTLE, Douglas, Commissioner, Connecticut Department of Environmental Protection, Hartford, Conn.

CURTIS, Kenneth M., Governor of Maine

CURVIN, Harry F., Chairman, Rhode Island Board of Elections and Former Speaker of the Rhode Island House, Providence, R.I.

DARMAN, Richard, Fellow, Woodrow Wilson International Center for Scholars, Washington, D.C.

DONOVAN, John, Professor of Political Science, Bowdoin College, Brunswick, Maine

DROUGHT, James, Administrator for Staff Services, Boston Redevelopment Authority, Boston, Mass.

DUKAKIS, Michael S., Governor of Massachusetts

EWING, James D., Publisher, The Keene Sentinel, Keene, N.H.

FEINBERG, Mark, Director of Development, Connecticut Department of Commerce, Hartford, Conn.

FINE, Ralph, Chairman, Boston Finance Commission, Boston, Mass.

FRANK, Barney, State Representative, Boston, Mass.

FRANKLIN, Robert, Executive Director, Connecticut Public Expenditure Council, Hartford, Conn.

GANS, Curtis, Director, 1968 McCarthy campaign in New Hampshire, Washington, D.C.

GERBER, Thomas, Publisher, the Concord Monitor, Concord, N.H.

GORDON, Lincoln, Fellow, Woodrow Wilson International Center for Scholars, Washington, D.C.

GRANDMAISON, Joseph, Director, Massachusetts Office, Washington, D.C.

GRASSO, Ella T., Governor of Connecticut

GREGG, Frank, Director, New England River Basins Commission, Boston, Mass.

GRENDAY, Charles A., Sr., Corporate Manager for Administrative Services, Sanders Associates, Nashua, N.H.

HACKETT, John P., Political Editor, Providence *Journal* and *Bulletin*, Providence, R.I.

HAGENSTEIN, Perry, Director, New England Natural Resources Center, Boston, Mass.

HALL, Ray, Manager of Public Affairs, Sanders Associates, Nashua, N.H.

HANSEN, Donald C., Portland *Press-Herald*, Portland, Maine

HARDY, Rudolph W., Regional Research Coordinator, New England Council of Water Center Directors, Boston, Mass.

HARRISON, David E., Chairman, State Democratic Committee, Boston, Mass.

HARSCH, William, Aide to Governor Philip Noel of Rhode Island and State Co-Chairman's Special Representative, New England Regional Commission, Providence, R.I.

HEALY, Robert, Executive Editor, Boston *Globe*, Boston, Mass.

HENNESSEY, Jean, Executive Director, New Hampshire Charitable Fund and Affiliated Trusts, Concord, N.H.

HILDRETH, Horace, Jr., Attorney and Former State Senator, Portland, Maine

HILL, Herbert W., Professor of History, Dartmouth College, Hanover, N.H.

HOFF, Philip H., Former Governor of Vermont, Burlington, Vermont

HOSTETLER, James, The New England Council, Boston, Mass.

HOWELL, James M., Vice President and Chief Economist, First National Bank, Boston, Mass.

HUFFMAN, Benjamin L., Planning and Program Coordinator, Vermont Central Planning Office, Montpelier, Vt.

JOHNSON, Martin L., Secretary, Agency of Environmental Conservatism, State of Vermont, Montpelier, Vermont

KEEFE, James K., Commissioner, Maine Department of Economic Development, Augusta, Maine

KUMEKAWA, Glenn, Executive Assistant for Policy and Program Review, Office of the Governor, Providence, R.I.

LANE, Carleton G., Chairman, Maine Industrial Building Authority, Portland, Maine

LEE, Richard, Former Mayor of New Haven, Conn.

LIBASSI, Peter, President, The Great Hartford Process, Hartford, Conn.

LICHT, Frank, Governor of Rhode Island

LINSKY, Martin A., State Representative, Brookline, Mass.

LODGE, Henry Cabot, Former U.S. Senator from Massachusetts

LONDON, Paul A., Director, New England Research Office, Washington, D.C.

LONGLEY, James, Governor of Maine

MAERKI, Vic, Legislative Assistant, Office of Senator Robert Stafford of Vermont

MAHAN, James F., Attorney, Boston, Mass. (deceased)

MALLARY, Richard W., U.S. Representative from Vermont

MANN, David L., Executive Director, New Hampshire Municipal Association, Concord, N.H.

MARTIN, David B. H., Assistant to the Secretary, Department of Health, Education and Welfare, Washington, D.C.

McALISTER, Scott, President, Hartford School Board, Hartford, Conn.

McGARRY, Lawrence P., Democratic City Chairman and Former State Democratic Chairman, Providence, R.I.

McGLENNON, John A. S., Regional Administrator, U.S. Environmental Protection Agency, Boston, Mass.

McINTYRE, Thomas J., U.S. Senator from New Hampshire

MEADOWS, Dennis, Professor, Thayer School, Dartmouth College, Hanover, N.H.

MERRIMAN, Russell, Federal Co-Chairman, New England Regional Commission, Boston, Mass.

MITCHELL, George J., Democratic National Committeeman, Portland, Maine

MOCCIA, Thomas J., Director, Public Affairs, Greater Boston Chamber of Commerce, Boston, Mass.

MORAN, William, Former Vermont Newspaperman; Writer, CBS News, New York City

MOULTON, Elbert G., Republican State Chairman, Montpelier, Vermont

MUSKIE, Edmund S., U.S. Senator from Maine

NEWALL, Arthur, Biologist, New Hampshire Fish and Game Department, Concord, N.H.

NOEL, Philip W., Governor of Rhode Island

NOLAN, Martin, Washington Correspondent, Boston *Globe*, Washington, D.C.

O'HARE, Robert J. M., Director, Bureau of Public Affairs, Boston College, Chestnut Hill, Mass.

PANAGGIO, Leonard J., Chief, Tourist Promotion Division, Rhode Island Department of Economic Development, Providence, R.I.

PARADISE, Scott, Director, Massachusetts Tomorrow, Cambridge, Mass.

PARSELITIE, Frank, Restaurant Owner, Hartford, Conn.

PAUL, Rod, Correspondent, Concord *Monitor*, Concord, N.H.

PENLEY, Edward, Editorial Writer, Portland *Evening Express*, Portland, Maine

PETERSON, Walter, Governor of New Hampshire

PETERSON, Mrs. Walter, Concord, N.H.

PROFUGHI, Victor, Professor of Political Science, Rhode Island College, Providence, R.I.

RADWAY, Laurence I., Professor of Government, Dartmouth College, and Democratic State Chairman, Hanover, N.H.

REILLY, Charles T., Democratic State Chairman, Providence, R.I.

RICHARDSON, Elliot, Fellow, Woodrow Wilson International Center for Scholars, Washington, D.C.

RICHARDSON, Harrison, Attorney, Former State Representative and Senator, Portland, Maine

RIEHLE, Theodore M., Jr., Director, Vermont Central Planning Office, Montpelier, Vt.

RITCHIE, James, General Manager, IBM-Burlington, Burlington, Vt.

ROBERSON, James, Director, Rhode Island Department of Economic Development, Providence, R.I.

ROBERTS, Dennis, Former Governor of Rhode Island, Providence, R.I.

SALMON, Thomas P., Governor of Vermont

SALOMA, John S., III, Associate Professor of Political Science, Massachusetts Institute of Technology, Cambridge, Mass.

SCHUCK, Victoria, Professor of Political Science, Mt. Holyoke College, South Hadley, Mass.

SCHUKER, Jill A., Executive Director, New England Congressional Caucus, Washington, D.C.

SMITH, Howard N., Secretary of Economic Affairs, Commonwealth of Massachusetts, Boston, Mass.

SNELLING, Richard W., Shelburne Industries, Shelburne, Vt.

SNOW, Wilbert, Poet, Former Governor and Lieutenant Governor of Connecticut, Middletown, Conn.

SONTAG, Frederick, Public Affairs Consultant, Seal Harbor, Maine

SPILMAN, Charles, Editor, Providence *Journal-Bulletin*, Providence, R.I.

SPEERS, Jerrold B., Majority Leader, Maine Senate, Winthrop, Maine

STEVENS, Jerald L., Commissioner, Massachusetts Department of Public Welfare, Boston, Mass.

STOCKFORD, Chapman (Chip), Executive Director, New England Governors' Conference, Boston, Mass.

STRUCKHOFF, Eugene C., Founder, New Hampshire Tomorrow, Concord, N.H.

TROWBRIDGE, Robertson C., State Senator, and Publisher, *Yankee Magazine,* Dublin, N.H.

TURNER, Robert L., Correspondent, Boston *Globe,* Boston, Mass.

WARNER, John, Director, Boston Redevelopment Authority, Boston, Mass.

WECHSLER, James, State News Service, Concord, N.H.

WHITE, Kevin P., Mayor of Boston, Massachusetts.

WILLARD, Edward, Manager of Community Relations, IBM-Burlington, Burlington, Vt.

WILSON, Leonard, Robert Burly Associates, Fayston, Vermont

WINSHIP, Thomas, Editor, Boston *Globe,* Boston, Mass.

WRIGHT, Dick, Editor, New Hampshire *Times,* Concord, N.H.

WOOD, Dr. Robert, President, University of Massachusetts

ZAIMAN, Jack, Political Editor, Hartford *Courant,* Hartford, Conn.

BIBLIOGRAPHY

IN ADDITION TO THE EXTENSIVE INTERVIEWS for these books, reference was made to books and articles on the individual states and cities, their history and present-day condition. To the authors whose works I have drawn upon, my sincerest thanks.

NATIONAL BOOKS

Barone, Michael, Ujifusa, Grant, and Matthews, Douglas, *The Almanac of American Politics—1972*, and *1974*. Boston: Gambit Publishing Co., published biennially.

Birmingham, Stephen. *The Right People—A Portrait of the American Social Establishment*. Boston: Little, Brown, 1968.

Book of the States. The Council of State Governments. Published biennially, Lexington, Ky.

Brownson, Charles B. *Congressional Staff Directory*. Published annually, Washington, D.C.

1969 Census of Agriculture, Bureau of the Census, Washington, D.C.

1970 Census of Population, Bureau of the Census, Washington, D.C.

CBS News Campaign '72 handbooks—Democratic National Convention, Republican National Convention, various primary states, and general election. New York: CBS News, 1972.

Churches and Church Membership in the United States—An Enumeration by Region, State and County, by Douglas W. Johnson, Paul R. Picard, and Bernard Quinn. Washington, D.C.: Glenmary Research Center, 1974.

Citizens Conference on State Legislatures. Various studies including *The Sometime Governments: A Critical Study of the 50 American Legislatures*, by John Burns. New York: Bantam Books, 1971.

Congress and the Nation, 1945–64, Vol. II, *1965–68*, and Vol. III, *1969–72*. Congressional Quarterly Service, Washington, D.C., 1967, 1969, and 1973.

David, Paul T., *Party Strength in the United States, 1872–1970*. Charlottesville: University Press of Virginia, 1972.

Editor and Publisher International Year Book. New York: Editor and Publisher. Published annually.

Employment and Earnings—States and Areas, 1939–71. U.S. Department of Labor, Bureau of Labor Statistics, Washington, D.C., 1972.

Encyclopedia Americana. Annual editions. New York: Americana Corporation. (Includes excellent state and city review articles.)

Facts and Figures on Government Finance. Published annually by the Tax Foundation, Inc., New York.

Farb, Peter. *Face of North America—The Natural History of a Continent*. New York: Harper & Row, 1963.

Federal-State-Local Finances—Significant Features of Fiscal Federalism. Published periodically by the Advisory Commission on Intergovernmental Relations, Washington, D.C.

Fodor-Shell Travel Guides, U.S.A. Fodor's Modern Guides, Inc., Litchfield, Conn.

From Sea to Shining Sea—A Report on the American Environment—Our National Heritage. President's Council on Recreation and Natural Beauty, Washington, D.C., 1968.

Gunther, John. *Inside U.S.A.* New York: Harper & Row, 1947 and 1951.

Jacob, Herbert, and Vines, Kenneth N. *Politics in the American States: A Comparative Analysis*. Boston: Little, Brown, 1971.

Life Pictorial Atlas of the World. Editors of *Life* and Rand McNally. New York: Time, Inc., 1961.

McPherson, Harry. *A Political Education*. Boston: Little, Brown, 1972.

The National Atlas of the United States of America. Geological Survey, U.S. Department of the Interior, Washington, D.C., 1970.

Phillips, Kevin H. *The Emerging Republican Majority*. New Rochelle, N.Y.: Arlington House, 1969.

The Quality of Life in the United States: 1970, Index, Rating and Statistics, by Ben-Chien Liu with Robert Gustafson and Bruce Marcy. Kansas City, Mo.: Midwest Research Institute, 1973.

Rankings of the States. Published annually by the Research Division, National Education Assn., Washington, D.C.

Ridgeway, James. *The Closed Corporation—American Universities in Crisis*. New York: Random House, 1968.

Saloma, John S. III, and Sontag, Frederick H. *Parties: The Real Opportunity for Effective Citizen Politics*. New York: Knopf, 1972.

Sanford, Terry. *Storm Over the States*. New York: McGraw-Hill, 1967.

Scammon, Richard M., ed. *America Votes—A Handbook of Contemporary American Election Statistics*. Published biennially by the

Government Affairs Institute, through Congressional Quarterly, Washington, D.C.

Sharkansky, Ira. *The Maligned States: Policy Accomplishments, Problems, and Opportunities.* New York: McGraw Hill, 1972.

State Government Finances. Published annually by The U.S. Department of Commerce, Bureau of the Census, Washington, D.C.

Statistical Abstract of the United States. Published annually by the U.S. Department of Commerce, Bureau of the Census, Washington, D.C.

Survey of Current Business. U.S. Department of Commerce, Bureau of Economic Analysis, Washington, D.C., monthly. April and August editions contain full reports on geographic trends in personal income and per capita income.

These United States—Our Nation's Geography, History and People. Reader's Digest Assn., Pleasantville, N.Y., 1968.

Tour Books. Published annually by the American Automobile Assn., Washington, D.C.

Uniform Crime Reports for the United States. Published annually by the U.S. Department of Justice, Federal Bureau of Investigation, Washington, D.C.

Who's Who in American Politics (New York: R. R. Bowker Co., published biennially).

Williams, Joe B. *U.S. Statistical Atlas.* Published biennially at Elmwood, Neb.

The World Almanac and Book of Facts. Published annually by Newspaper Enterprise Assn., Inc., New York and Cleveland.

REGIONAL BOOKS AND SOURCES

Among the more helpful books treating New England as a whole were: *New England State Politics*, by Duane Lockard (Princeton Univ. Press, 1959); *New England*, by Joe McCarthy (New York: Time-Life Library of America, 1967); *The Changing Face of New England*, by Betty Flanders Thomson (New York: Macmillan, 1958); *A Southerner Discovers New England*, by Jonathan Daniels (New York: Macmillan, 1940); *Collected Poems of Robert Frost* (New York: Henry Holt, 1930). A brief review of political trends was included in *Party Politics in the New England States*, by George Goodwin, Jr., and Victoria Schuck (Durham, N.H.: New England Center for Continuing Education, 1968); *The Case for Regional Planning with Special Reference to New England*, by the Directive Committee on Regional Planning (New Haven: Yale University Press, 1947).

ECONOMY *The Dynamics of Growth in New England's Economy, 1870–1964*, by Robert W. Eisenmenger (Middletown, Conn.: Wesleyan University Press, 1967); *New England Economic Almanac* (Boston: Federal Reserve Bank of Boston, 1971 and 1973 supplement); *Prospects for the New England Economy*, monograph by the First National Bank of Boston, 1972; *The Manufacturing Structure of New England: The Alternative Before Us*, monograph by the First National Bank of Boston, July 1972; "What's the Matter with New England" by John F. Kennedy, *New York Times Magazine*, Nov. 8, 1953; "The New Wrinkles in New England Textiles," by Grant B. Southward, *The New Englander*, August 1973; "New England Criticizing Shoe and Textile Imports," New York *Times*, July 13, 1969; "Footwear Gains a Toehold on the Future," by Jack Shea, *The New Englander*, March 1974; "Absentee Owners of America—Colonial New England," by Geoffrey Faux, *New Republic*, Nov. 25, 1972; *A Short-Range Action Plan for New England*, New England Regional Commission, June, 1974.

Is There Still Hope for Farming in New England?" by Malcolm Cowley, *Country Journal*, August 1974; "Resort Farming Blooms in Northeast," by Robin Wright, *Christian Science Monitor*, Jan. 20, 1972.

"Destroying Myths About Energy and New England," by K. Dun Gifford, *Maine Times*, Oct. 25, 1974; "It's Time to Stop Pumping Special Favors to Big Oil," by Thomas J. McIntyre, *The New Englander*, August 1973; "The Oil Issue," *New England River Basins Commission Regional Report*, December 1973; "Fisheries Anchor All Hope on 200-Mile Limit," by Frederick J. Pratson,

The New Englander, November 1973.

New England Regional Railroad Study Summary, New England Regional Commission, Nov. 8, 1973; *The New England Economy and the Boston and Maine Railroad System*, a preliminary report of the Boston and Maine Study Group, Oct. 26, 1973; "The B&M May be Bankrupt, But It Wants to Try Again," by Lucy L. Martin, *Maine Times*, April 5, 1974; "Commuter Lines: NE's Only Hope for Air Service," by Robert H. Wood, *The New Englander*, February 1974; "New England Economic Outlook—Industry, Finance, Energy, Tourism, Farming, Education," supplement to *Christian Science Monitor*, Feb. 24, 1975.

NATURAL RESOURCES, LAND USE *New England River Basins Commission Regional Report*, April 1974; *Strategies for Natural Resource Decision-Making* (Boston: New England River Basin Commission, 1972); "New England's Natural Resources and Its Economic Future," by Robert W. Eisenmenger, *New England Economic Indicators*, March 1974; *A Report to New England* (Boston: New England Natural Resources Center, 1973); "Let's Launch the United States of New England," by Phillip H. Hoff, *The New Englander*, May 1973; *Protecting New England's Natural Heritage* (Boston: New England Natural Resources Center, 1973); *Prospects for Massachusetts Tomorrow*, position paper by Scott Paradise, dated Feb. 14, 1974; *Policies for the Use of New England's Forested Lands*, prepared by the American Forest Institute and New England Natural Resources Center.

REGIONALISM "The Obstinate Concept of New England: A Study in Denudation," by George Wilson Pierson, *The New England Quarterly*, March 1955; "The Withering of New England," by Oscar Handlin and Howard Mumford Jones, *Atlantic Monthly*, April 1950; *Regionalism in America*, ed. Merrill Jenson (Madison, Wisconsin: University of Wisconsin Press, 1951); *Between State and Nation: Regional Organizations in the United States*, by Martha Derthick (Washington: Brookings Institution, 1974); "Toward A United New England," remarks by James C. Cleveland, midyear meeting 1973 of the New England Council; "Business Forms Economic Study Unit to Support Bipartisan New England Caucus," by John L. Moore, *National Journal*, Feb. 17, 1973; *Prospects for New England*, A Conference of the Woodrow Wilson International Center for Scholars (Washington: 1975); "The Case for Regionalism," by Chapman Stockford, *Country Journal*, January-February 1975.

MASSACHUSETTS

Two books offer excellent insights into Massachusetts politics: *The Political Cultures of Massachusetts*, by Edgar Litt (Cambridge: MIT Press, 1965), and *The Compleat Politician: Political Strategy in Massachusetts*, by Murry B. Levin with George Blackwood (New York: Bobbs Merrill, 1962). The state's culture and geography are well covered in *New England*, by Joe McCarthy (New York: Time-Life Library of America, 1967), and *Massachusetts: A Guide to the Pilgrim State*, ed. Ray Bearse, a second edition of the American Guide Series volume (Boston: Houghton Mifflin, 1971). For information on the Boston suburbs, I am indebted to John C. Burke, suburban editor of the Boston *Globe*, who prepared a special review used as background in the chapter.

The chapter draws on regular coverage of Massachusetts newspapers, especially the Boston *Globe* and *Christian Science Monitor*, and the following articles in particular:

GENERAL "Massachusetts Builds for Tomorrow," by Robert De Roos, *National Geographic*, December 1966; *Some Facts About Massachusetts* (Boston: Massachusetts Department of Commerce and Development, 1969); and other publications of state government.

POLITICS "Bay State GOP Missed a Comeback Chance," by George B. Merry, *Christian Science Monitor*, Aug. 7, 1970; "Mass. Legislature . . . Imbalance by Default," by Kenneth D. Campbell, Boston *Globe*, Oct. 20, 1970; "Figures Prove Democrats' Advantage in State," by Cornelius Dalton, Boston *Herald Traveler*, Nov. 17, 1968.

"Bay Staters Shun Ceremony—Even the Political Variety," by David S. Broder, Washington *Post*, June 16, 1970; "Chaos Wins as Massachusetts Democrats Stage a Donnybrook," by R. W. Apple, Jr., New York *Times*, June 14, 1970; "How to Run & Win," by James Higgins, *The Nation*, Dec. 21, 1970.

"Why The Bay State Countered Trend," by Robert Reinhold, New York *Times*, Nov. 9, 1972; "O'Neill: Impeachment Stage Manager," by Martin Nolan, Boston *Globe*, Jan. 6, 1974; "Dukakis Stirs Governor's Race With Grass-Roots Campaigning," and "Bob Quinn Charges up Beacon Hill," by Stewart Dill McBride, *Christian Science Monitor*, March 18 and July 22, 1974; "With '76 Ruled Out, Kennedy Could Run in '80, '84, '88 or '92," by Stephen Isaacs, Washington *Post*, Sept. 24, 1974; Politics and the Kennedy Factor," by Richard J. Whalen, Washington *Post*, Sept. 29, 1974. "Spotlight on John Davoren and His Milford Machine: Clique Translates Public Power into Private Profit," by Gerald M. O'Neill, Stephen A. Kurkjian, Arthur L. Jones, and Ellen S. Zack, Boston *Globe*, June 20, 1973.

STATE GOVERNMENT "Governor's Council: Going—or More Pay?" by George B. Merry, *Christian Science Monitor*, Dec. 22, 1970; "Massachusetts Passes Cabinet Bill," by Victoria Schuck, *National Civic Review*, July 1969.

"Bay State's Moral Crisis," by Edgar M. Mills, *Christian Science Monitor*, April 9, 1962; "Era May Be at End in Massachusetts," by John H. Fenton, New York *Times*, Nov. 16, 1969; "Massachusetts Is Aroused by Corruption Scandals," by Anthony Lewis, New York *Times*, June 19, 1961; "Poisoned Politics," by Elliot L. Richardson, *Atlantic*, October 1961.

"Sargent Sees 'No-Fault' Success," by Monty Hoyt, *Christian Science Monitor*, April 24, 1971; "Will Reform Slash Bay State Property Tax?" by George B. Merry, *Christian Science Monitor*, Nov. 11, 1970; "$2 Billion Budget?" by George B. Merry, *Christian Science Monitor*, Jan. 15, 1971; "Bay State Foes Rap Racial-Imbalance Law," by George B. Merry, *Christian Science Monitor*, Feb. 23, 1971; "Apartheid in Urban Schools," by Peter

Milius, Washington *Post*, April 4, 1971; "The Public vs. Its Servants in Mass.," and "Mass. Ex-Official Says Civil Service Strangles Quality," by Robert G. Kaiser, Washington *Post*, Sept. 2, 1975.

"Amendments, Initiative Bring Changes to Mass.," by Victoria Schuck, *National Civil Review*, February 1975; "Private vs. State Power Battle On," by Benjamin Taylor, Boston *Globe*, Feb. 20, 1975; "Secretary Benson Quits Dukakis Cabinet," by Jonathan Fuerbringer, Boston *Globe*, Dec. 19, 1975.

LEGISLATURE "Legislators Apply Polish to Their Image," by George B. Merry, *Christian Science Monitor*, Dec. 12, 1970; "David Michael Bartley: The Speaker," by David Ellis, Boston *Globe*, June 27, 1971; "Higoodtaseeyahowsitgoin? or What I Do All Day," by Rep. Martin F. Linsky, *Ripon Forum*, August 1969; "Lobbyists Bend Sargent Tax Bill," by Joanne Leedom, *Christian Science Monitor*, March 12, 1971; "Youth Wins More Votes," by George B. Merry, *Christian Science Monitor*, Nov. 16, 1970; "I Wish to Change My Vote—Story of House Cut Defeat," by David Nyhan, Boston *Globe*, March 22, 1970; "Membership in the Club: Denizens of the Massachusetts House of Representatives," by Barry M. Portnoy, *Harvard Journal on Legislation*, January 1969.

"Massachusetts: Vox Pop," *Newsweek*, Jan. 10, 1972; "Two-Session Roundup for General Court," by Victoria Schuck, *National Civic Review*, October 1972; "How Bay State Lawmakers Move Out and Up," by George B. Merry, *Christian Science Monitor*, Jan. 22, 1973; "Massachusetts Legislative Scorecard—'74," by George B. Merry, *Christian Science Monitor*, Aug. 5, 1974.

EDUCATION "Conditions Favoring Major Advances in Social Science," by Karl W. Deutsch, John Platt, and Dieter Senghaas, *Science*, Feb. 5, 1971.

"Harvard Clings to Shaky Peace," by Jim Mann, Washington *Post*, May 3, 1970; "My Several Lives," book review by Harold Taylor, New York *Times Book Review*, March 22, 1970; "Harvard Picks a Young Face for the '70s," *Life*, Jan. 22, 1971.

"MIT's Main Problem: Determining Its Role," by Eric Wentworth, Washington *Post*, Nov. 10, 1969.

"Gathering Storms Over Once Quiet Campuses," by Michael Dorfsman, *Boston Magazine*, May 1970; "The First Hurrah," *Newsweek*, Jan. 4, 1971; "Quest for a Silver Unicorn," by Edward Kern, *Life*, June 4, 1971; "Bitterness at Brandeis," *Newsweek*, Nov. 9, 1970; "A Jewel in the Rough," *Newsweek*, Sept. 28, 1970; "Broader Scope for Higher Ed Urged," by Muriel L. Cohen, Boston *Herald Traveler*, June 27, 1971.

"What's Happened to Harvard?," by Stephen Isaacs, Washington *Post*, Nov. 25, 1973; "Scorpions in a Bottle," *Time*, Feb. 18, 1974; "Harvard Bracing For Hard Times," by Robert Reinhold, New York *Times*, Dec. 22, 1974; "MIT Hopes to Make Itself the Mother of Salable Inventions," by Patricia Sagon, *Wall Street Journal*, Jan. 22, 1975; "After 339 Years, Does Harvard's Butter Still Stinketh?" by Nina McCain, Boston *Globe*, June 29, 1975.

ECONOMY *Massachusetts Trends in Employment and Unemployment*, Division of Employment Security, Herman V. Lamark, Director, May 1971; "Slowdown on Route 128," by Gene Smith, New York *Times*, Oct. 11, 1970; "Raytheon Co. Prospers Despite Big Slowdown in the Defense Industry," by David Gumpert, *Wall Street Journal*, March 5, 1971; "Down and Out Along Route 128," by Berkeley Rice, New York *Times Magazine*, Nov. 1, 1970; "Polaroid: Make It Unique—and

Wanted," *Forbes*, June 1970; "Ex-NASA Lab Gets Down to Earth," by John Lannan, *Washington Star*, Oct. 26, 1970.

"Route 128 Learns to Live in Commercial Markets," *Business Week*, April 21, 1973; "What, Why and How of the Economy in Massachusetts," by Albert J. Kelley, Boston *Globe*, Dec. 15, 1974; "Layoffs Tarnish 'Golden Horseshoe,' " by Ward Morehouse III, *Christian Science Monitor*, Dec. 26, 1974; "New England Economic Outlook," *Christian Science Monitor*, Feb. 24, 1975.

FARM AND FISH   "Record Cranberry Harvest?" by Dorothea Kahn Jaffee, *Christian Science Monitor*, Sept. 23, 1970; "Depression, Despair Mark Fishing Industry," by Frank Donovan, Boston *Globe*, June 27, 1970; "Business Is Good, but Fishing Isn't," by Frank Donovan, Boston *Globe*, June 28, 1970.

RELIGION   "The Many Mansions of Cardinal Cushing," by John Fenton, *Boston Magazine*, August 1970; "Big Man in a Long Red Robe," *Time*, Nov. 16, 1970; "Cardinal Cushing Dies in Boston at 75," *New York Times*, Nov. 3, 1970; "Medeiros Installed Before 2,500 as Boston Archbishop, Succeeding Cushing," by Robert Reinhold, *New York Times*, Oct. 8, 1970; "Clergymen Reply in Boston Dispute," *New York Times*, Jan. 3, 1971; "Negro Is Installed as Bishop of Mass. Episcopal Diocese," UPI Dispatch, *Washington Post*, Jan. 18, 1970; "Court Overturns Birth Control Law: Baird Is Freed," by Diane White, Boston *Globe*, July 7, 1970.

CRIME AND JUSTICE   "Computer War: Massachusetts Bucks the Trend," by Robert A. Jones, *Los Angeles Times*, Aug. 17, 1973; "Shoot-Out," by Alan L. Otten, *Wall Street Journal*, June 6, 1974; "State High Court, Under Tauro, Breaking New Ground," by William F. Doherty, Boston *Globe*, July 7, 1974; "Massachusetts Prison Reform: Delayed but Not Forgotten," by Clayton Jones, *Christian Science Monitor*, Oct. 8, 1974; "Tough New Gun Law Takes Effect April 1," by Gary Thatcher, *Christian Science Monitor*, March 10, 1975.

BOSTON—GENERAL   "The Two Most Exciting Cities in the Nation?" by Ian Menzies, Boston *Globe*, Sept. 27, 1970; "Boston," by George Sessions Perry, *Saturday Evening Post*, Sept. 1945; "Boston's Marvelous Marathon," *Reader's Digest*, April 1971; "Boston: The Livable City," supplement to Boston *Globe*, June 24, 1973.

BOSTON—GOVERNMENT   "Regional Government Proposed for Mass.," *National Civic Review*, February 1971; *The Economics of Air Pollution*, a symposium by Harold Wolozin (New York: Norton, 1966); "When 'Go It Alone' Breaks Down," by George B. Merry, *Christian Science Monitor*, April 29, 1970; "Boston Tests Public Transit," by William Raspberry, *Washington Post*, Feb. 25, 1971; "Bay State Transit Agency Hit by Revolt," *New York Times*, March 14, 1971; "Drive in Boston May Bring a New Urban Transit Mix," by Bill Kovach, *New York Times*, July 25, 1971; "What's Wrong with the MBTA?—Everything," by Alan Lupo, *The Real Paper*, Sept. 17, 1975.

"White Plans for City Hall," by Brad Knickerbocker, *Christian Science Monitor*, June 2, 1973; "How Mayor Kevin White Is Running for President," by Robert A. Jordan and Martin F. Nolan, Boston *Globe*, April 14, 1974; "Boston Holds Tax Line, but Debt Climbs," *Christian Science Monitor*, Aug. 26, 1974; "City Hall's Wily Politico," by Brad Knickerbocker, *Christian Science Monitor*, Dec. 13, 1974; "MBTA: Future Bright for Aid, Passenger Level Still Low," by David Rogers, Boston *Globe*, Dec. 22, 1974; "Boston's Bulging Bureaucracy Eyed," by Brad Knickerbocker, *Christian Science Monitor*, Jan. 14, 1975; "The Anatomy of a Close Election," by David Farrell, Boston *Globe*, Nov. 6, 1975; "In the End Performance Counted," by Mike Barnicle, Boston *Globe*, Nov. 6, 1975.

BOSTON—URBAN RENEWAL   "A Boston Interview with I. M. Pei," *Boston Magazine*, June 1970; "Construction at Full Speed," by Richard W. McManus, *Christian Science Monitor*, Aug. 22, 1970; "Tall Stories About Boston," by Arthur Monks, *Boston Magazine*, November 1970; "Boston's New City Hall: A Public Building of Quality," by Ada Louise Huxtable, *New York Times*, Feb. 8, 1969; "A New City Hall: Boston's Boost for Urban Renewal," by John Conti, *Wall Street Journal*, Feb. 12, 1969; "A Noble Sequence," by Brigitte Weeks, *Boston Magazine*, February 1969; "Housing and Renewal," by John D. Warner, *Boston Magazine*, January 1970; "Massachusetts Tries Mixing Income Groups in Subsidized Housing," by Liz Roman Gallexe, *Wall Street Journal*, June 25, 1974.

BOSTON—CULTURE, COMMUNICATIONS   "Fiscal Performance," by Bernard Taper, *Boston Magazine*, March 1970; "Accounting for the Arts," by Bernard Taper, *Boston Magazine*, November 1969; "Spiraling Look into the Sea," *Time*, March 1970; "Herald Traveler TV Split Would Hurt," by Richard W. McManus, *Christian Science Monitor*, Dec. 2, 1970; "Who Really Runs the Globe," by George V. Higgins, *Boston Magazine*, May 1971.

BOSTON—ETHNIC, GEOGRAPHIC   "Only 22 Percent of Hub Is Irish," by Bruce McCabe, Boston *Globe*, July 8, 1970; "The Little People of East Boston Fight Back," by Arnold R. Isaacs, *Baltimore Sun*, Nov. 3, 1969; "East Boston: A Fighting Comeback," by Ian Menzies, Boston *Globe*, Jan. 10, 1974.

"The Back Bay as a Work of Art," by Lewis Mumford, Boston *Globe*, Nov. 2, 1969; "Back Bay —Historic Monument, a State of Mind," by Diggory Venn, *New York Times*, Nov. 9, 1969; "The Boston Ritz: Only Birch Logs in the Fireplace," by Gordon Cotlier, *Holiday*, April 1969; "Whatever Happened to Newbury Street," by Patricia Linden, *Boston Magazine*, July 1971; "A National Park for Charlestown," by Oren McCleary, *Boston Magazine*, November 1970.

BOSTON—SCHOOL BUSING   "South Boston: Symbol of Urban Resistance," by Alan Lupo, Boston *Globe*, June 2, 1974; "Parades Livelier in Curley's Day, Says Old Bostonian," by Bill Kovach, *New York Times*, March 18, 1971; "South Boston Feels Betrayed," by William Claiborne, *Washington Post*, Oct. 14, 1974; "Boston Busing: 10 Bitter Years of School Woes," by Robert A. Jones, *Los Angeles Times*, Oct. 14, 1974; "Southie Is My Home Town," by Robert Sam Anson, *New Times*, Nov. 15, 1974; "School Committee Has Failed the City," by Robert Healy, Boston *Globe*, Dec. 15, 1974; "Report Says Boston Suburbs Help Segregation," by Douglas Rogers, Boston *Globe*, Jan. 14, 1975; "White Pupils' Rolls Drop a Third in Boston Busing," by John Kifner, *New York Times*, Dec. 14, 1975; "Boston Ghetto School Uses Academic Merit as Integration Lure," by Liz Roman Gallese, the *Wall Street Journal*, May 17, 1975; "Boston Busing Dispute Disrupts the Education and Lives of Students," by David Gumpet, the *Wall Street Journal*, April 7, 1975; "Court Takes Over South Boston High," by Ed Schumacher, the *Washington Post*, Dec. 10, 1975; "Violence Erupts After New Busing," by Ed Schumacher, the *Washington Post*, Dec. 11, 1975.

CAMBRIDGE, SUBURBS   "The Disparate Worlds of Cambridge," by Caryl Rivers, *New York Times*, Sept. 13, 1970; "Blowing My Mind at Harvard," by Larry L. King, *Harper's*, October 1970; "Harvard Square: A Place to Enjoy?" by Patricia Reid, *Christian Science Monitor*, Jan. 15, 1971; "Roads to Ruins," by Roy Mann, *Boston Magazine*, January 1970; "In a Time of Change, Plymouth, Mass. Looks Back 350 Years," *New York Times*, Sept. 14, 1970; "Plymouth Mass. Gets With It," by John H. Fenton, *New York Times*, May 3, 1970; "Nuclear Power Plant Proving Mixed Blessing for Plymouth," by Leslie Burdick,

Christian Science Monitor, May 31, 1974.

OTHER CITIES AND REGIONS "Thoreau and the Endless Beach," by Eugene Kinkhead, *Saturday Review*, March 13, 1971; book review of *Cape Cod and the Offshore Islands*, by Edward B. Garside, New York *Times Book Review*, June 14, 1970; "Cape Cod Moving Toward Year-Round Economic Stability," by William J. Lewis, Boston *Globe*, Aug. 9, 1970; "Island Periled By Prosperity," by Marquis Childs, Washington *Post*, July 9, 1971; "Nantucket Fears Urbanism Blight," New York *Times*, Oct. 4, 1970; "Can the Cape Survive Suburbanization?" by Deckle McLean, Boston *Globe*, Aug. 12, 1973; "When Cape Cod Becomes a Playground, Increases in Rent Force Winter Tenants Out," by John Kifner, New York *Times*, June 9, 1974; "Residents' Efforts to Save Martha's Vineyard Aided," by Susan Watters, *Christian Science Monitor*, May 1, 1972; "Guardians of Martha's Vineyard," by David Langworthy, *Christian Science Monitor*, Jan. 16, 1975.

"Worcester Rescues Poverty Programs With Revenue-Sharing Funds," by Susan Watters, *Christian Science Monitor*, April 12, 1973; "A New Building of the West (Worcester)," by Jane Holtz Kay, Boston *Globe*, Sept. 5, 1971; "An Urban Park for America's Industrial Revolution," by Geoffrey C. Upward, *Preservation News*, May 1974; "National Park Lifts Lowell Outlook," by Grant B. Southward, *The New Englander*, February 1974; "Aging Fall River Battles Unemployment Lines," by Richard W. McManus, *Christian Science Monitor*, Feb. 11, 1971; "New Bedford Racial Tension at a Simmer Since Last Summer," by Noel Stern and Andrew Grannell, *Christian Science Monitor*, June 4, 1971; "New Bedford's Trouble Laid to Unemployment, Lack of Aid for Slums," by Monroe W. Karmin, *Wall Street Journal*, Aug. 11, 1970; "New Bedford Ready to Go on Urban Renewal," by Paul J. Deveney, Boston *Globe*, Feb. 17, 1974.

"Development: A Healthy Kick in the Pants" (regarding Springfield), *Time*, May 10, 1968; "Springfield Expects Smooth Busing," by Muriel L. Cohen, Boston *Globe*, May 19, 1974; "A Very Special Place," *Newsweek*, July 27, 1970; "Tanglewood," by Michael Zwerin, *Holiday*, June 1969; "Housatonic Shows How a River Can Stay Clean," by John William Riley, Boston *Globe*, July 12, 1970; "Shaker Village: God Is in the Details," by Hilton Kramer, New York *Times*, July 25, 1971; "All-America Cities Democracy at Work: North Adams, Massachusetts," *National Civic Review*, April 1974; "A Town Seeks a New Identity: That of an All-America City," by Diane K. Shah, *National Observer*, Dec. 1, 1973.

RHODE ISLAND

No outstanding general book is available concerning Rhode Island in recent years. The most helpful general reference sources included: *Rhode Island: A Guide to the Smallest State*, compiled by writers of the Writers' Program of the WPA (Cambridge: Houghton Mifflin, 1937); "Rhode Island: One-Party Façade and Two-Party Reality" and "Politics on the Seamy Side," chapters of *New England State Politics*, by Duane Lockard (Princeton: Princeton University Press, 1959); *Theodore Francis Green: The Rhode Island Years, 1906–1936*, by Erwin L. Levine (Providence: Brown University Press, 1963); *The Democrats and Labor in Rhode Island: 1952–1962*, by Jay S. Goodman (Providence: Brown University Press, 1967); "New England's Experiment, Rhode Island," by Robert De Roos, *National Geographic*, September 1968; *This Is Rhode Island*, Rhode Island Development Council, Providence, 1972.

ECONOMY "Rhode Island Takes Hard Line Toward Economic Renewal," by Richard N. Livingston, *The New Englander*, September 1973; "Response to Economic Crisis," by Phillip W. Noel, *Innovations In State Government—Messages from the Governors Conference* (Washington: National Governors Conference, 1974); *Rhode Island Basic Economic Statistics* (Providence: Rhode Island Development Council, 1972); "State's Economy Sails Off with Navy," by Stephen Isaacs, Washington *Post*, April 30, 1973; "Panic in the Face of an Exodus," *Business Week*, May 26, 1973:

STATE GOVERNMENT "Rhode Island Convention Is Over and Out," *National Civic Review*, April 1969; "Rhode Islanders Vote on Seven Amendments," *National Civic Review*, December 1973; "Rhode Island Debate on Open Caucuses," *Christian Science Monitor*, Jan. 15, 1974; "Rhode Island Legislators Try Again for Pay Raise," *Christian Science Monitor*, May 14, 1973; "Rhode Island Ponders Pay Hike for Legislators," *Christian Science Monitor*, Oct. 23, 1973.

POLITICS "Rhode Island: A State for Sale," by Lincoln Steffens, *McClure's Magazine*, February 1905; "A Block Breaks Up," *The Economist*, Nov. 24, 1956; "Rhode Island Swindle," *The Nation*, July 30, 1973; "Ethnics Vote Ethnic Study Finds," by M. Charles Bakst, Providence *Journal*, March 20, 1974; "Providence and Chafee: A Study in Fairness," by Gerald S. Nagel, *Columbia Journalism Review*, Jan.-Feb. 1973.

"The White House's Resident Jesuit," by Lawrence Stern, Washington *Post*, June 2, 1974; "Jesuit Superior Disavows Nixon Aide's Views!" by Jerry Taylor, Washington *Post*, May 23, 1974.

CONGRESSIONAL DELEGATION *Ralph Nader Congress Project* reports on John Pastore and Claiborne Pell, by F. N. Khedouri (Washington: Grossman, 1972); "The Quiet Success of Claiborne Pell," by Clayton Fritchey, Washington *Post*, Aug. 10, 1973; "Sen. Pastore Rules Roost Despite Size," New York *Herald Tribune*, Sept. 15, 1973; "3 Democrats Waging a Brisk Fight for Senate Whip," by E. W. Kenworthy, New York *Times*, Jan. 1, 1965.

UNIVERSITIES "Experiment with Radical Reform," by James Cass, *Saturday Review World*, June 1, 1974; "At Brown, Trend Is Back to Grades and Tradition," by Robert Rheinhold, New York *Times*, Feb. 24, 1974.

PLACES Various publications of the Rhode Island Department Of Economic Development, by Leonard Panaggio, Chief, Tourist Promotion Division; "Resort In The Sea," by Paul Stewart, *Ford Times*, June 1968; "America's Oldest Summer Cottage," by Leonard P. Panaggio, The *Atlanta Journal and Constitution Magazine*, Aug. 5, 1973.

"Who Knows What Providence Really Needs?" by Phillip M. Perry, *The New Englander*, May 1974; "Patronage Clicks in City Hall," by Richard C. Halverston, *Christian Science Monitor*, October 26, 1970; "A New and Vital Downtown Providence for 1995," by William E. Collins, Providence *Journal*, Oct. 5, 1975.

"What's Doing in Newport," by Jay Walz, New York *Times*, Aug. 4, 1974; "Newport's Mayor Wears a Blue Collar," by Ginny Pitt, Boston *Globe*, July 7, 1974; "Newport: One City for the Rich, Another for the Poor," by Bill Kovach, New York *Times*, September 21, 1970; "After Navy Departs, a Belt Tightening," *Christian Science Monitor*, April 18, 1974; "A Picture is Worth . . . (regarding Doris Duke)," by William M. Kutik [MORE], June 1975.

CONNECTICUT

There is no single outstanding book on modern Connecticut history, government, and culture. Among the more helpful volumes in preparing the state chapter were: *Connecticut in Focus*, by League of Women Voters of Connecticut Education Fund (Hamden, Conn., 1974); *The Power Broker* (regarding John Bailey), by Joseph I. Lieberman (Boston: Houghton Mifflin, 1966); *Let's Go into Politics*, by Raymond E. Baldwin (New York: Macmillan, 1952); *The Collected Poems of Wilbert Snow*, (Middletown, Conn.: Wesleyan University Press, 1923); *A Campaign Album*, by Howard Goldbaum and Eric Rennie (Philadelphia, Pennsylvania: United Church Press, 1973); *Above the Law*, (regarding Thomas Dodd), by James Boyd (New York: The New American Library, 1968); *Many Sovereign States*, by Dan Lufkin (New York: McKay, 1975); *Connecticut: A Guide to Its Roads, Lore, and People*, compiled by the writers of the writers' program of the WPA (Cambridge: Houghton Mifflin, American Guide Series, 1938).

STATE GOVERNMENT *Lawmaking in Connecticut: The General Assembly*, by Wayne R. Swanson (Washington: American Political Science Association, 1972); "Income Tax Urged for Connecticut," "Attempts to Modify Income Tax Reported Gaining in Connecticut," and "Both Connecticut Houses Approve 6.5% Sales Tax," by Joseph B. Treaster, New York *Times*, Jan. 27, July 18, and Aug. 13, 1971; "Connecticut Sales Tax to Top Nation," *Christian Science Monitor*, Aug. 25, 1971; "Connecticut Labor Asks Equity in State Taxes," *AFL-CIO News*, Oct. 9, 1971; "Tax Revolt in Connecticut," by Vivien Kellems, *Human Events*, March 4, 1972; "Connecticut: No New Tax," *Christian Science Monitor*, Aug. 28, 1973; "Gov. Grasso Offers $1.4-Billion Budget" by Lawrence Fellows, New York *Times*, Feb. 14, 1975.

"Supreme Court Refines Apportionment Standards," *National Civic Review*, September 1973; "Realigning Accord in Connecticut?," by George B. Merry, *Christian Science Monitor*, June 6, 1972; "Connecticut Remap Invalidated by Court," by Rosaline Levenson, *National Civic Review*, May 1972; "Connecticut: Disagreement over Reapportionment," *Ripon Forum*, November 1971; "Connecticut Reapportionment Struggle," *Christian Science Monitor*, July 14, 1971.

"Connecticut Abortion Ruling Stayed," *Christian Science Monitor*, Oct. 17, 1972; "Tough Abortion Law in Connecticut Is Attributed to Meskill and Catholics," by Jonathan Kandell, New York *Times*, May 25, 1972.

"Connecticut Seeks Regional Units," by Rosaline Levenson, *National Civic Review*, October 1969; "Connecticut Government Undergoing Review," by Rosaline Levenson, *National Civic Review*, September 1971; "A Catalogue of Corruption," *New Times*, Sept. 6, 1974; "Connecticut Gets an Energy Agency," by Lawrence Fellows, New York *Times*, June 1, 1974; "Budget Cutter Stirs Up Connecticut," by Brian Kelly, Washington *Star*, Sept. 5, 1971; "Connecticut Deals with Its Deficits," by Frederick J. Pratson, *The New Englander*, March 1974.

POLITICS "The Cities: State Democrats Face Real Trouble," by Jack Zaiman, Hartford *Courant*, Oct. 20, 1968; "Bailey Loses a Rein," by R. W. Apple Jr., New York *Times*, June 29, 1970; "A Onetime Kingmaker Suffers Unkind Cut: Everyone Ignores Him," by Albert R. Hunt, *Wall Street Journal*, July 12, 1972; "Bailey, John M[oran]," *Current Biography*, 1962; "Politics, Bailey-Style," by David S. Broder, Washington *Post*, April 16, 1975; "Democrats in Disarray," by R. W. Apple, Jr., New York *Times*, June 19, 1970; "Connecticut Democratic Party Is Called 'Shattered,' " by Joseph B. Treaster, New York *Times*, Feb. 22, 1970; "New Democratic Era Foreseen in State," by Jack Zaiman, Hartford *Courant*, Nov. 6, 1974; "Connecticut Labor Gains in the First 5 Months Under Democrats," New York *Times*, June 9, 1975; "Reformers Facing Realities of Ethnic Game in Politics," by David S. Broder, Boston *Globe*, July 1, 1970.

"Two Establishments," by Jack Zaiman, Hartford *Courant*, May 20, 1968; "1970 Outlook: Can State GOP Spring the Trap," by Jack Zaiman, Hartford *Courant*, Nov. 17, 1968; "Group Taking GOP Reins; Steele's Status Uncertain," by Jack Zaiman, Hartford *Courant*, Nov. 9, 1974; "As Meskill Works to Build a Republican Empire in Connecticut . . . ," by Joseph B. Treaster, New York *Times*, Dec. 6, 1970; "Reaganism in Connecticut," by James Quinn, *The New Republic*, May 29, 1971.

"Lowell the Lion-Hearted: A Profile of Senator Weicker of Watergate Fame," by Lloyd Shearer, *Parade*, July 14, 1974; "Sen. Weicker Assails 'Gutter Goals' in Politics," by Douglas Watson, Washington *Post*, July 28, 1973; "Lowell Weicker Gets Mad," *Time*, July 9, 1973; "No Way, Mr. President," by Lowell Weicker, *Ripon Forum*, April 1972; "That [Expletive Deleted] Senator from Connecticut," by Bice Clemow, *Esquire*, August 1974; "Weicker Will Stay a Republican," *Christian Science Monitor*, Jan. 14, 1975.

"Ribicoff Attacks Schools in North; Supports Stennis," by Warren Weaver, Jr., New York *Times*, Feb. 10, 1970; "Ribicoff: No Clichés," by William Greider, Washington *Post*, Feb. 20, 1970; "Ribicoff Rides the Tide," by Robert G. Sherrill, *The Nation*, March 16, 1970; "Ribicoff Bill Sets Timetable for City, Suburban Schools," by Gayle Tunnell, Washington *Post*, Nov. 29, 1970; "Ribicoff Abandons Drive for Nixon Welfare Plan," by Marjorie Hunter, New York *Times*, Jan. 29, 1972; "The Crusader," *Newsweek*, May 3, 1971; "Ribicoff's Charmed Life: From Poverty to Power," by Martin Tolchin, New York *Times*, July 30, 1974.

"Dodd in 1970: Big Decision Faces Democrats," by Jack Zaiman, Hartford *Courant*, Nov. 24, 1968; "Ex-Senator Dodd Dies at 64," Washington *Post*, May 25, 1971; "W. B. Benton, Ex-Senator, Businessman, Dies," by Martin Weil, Washington *Post*, March 19, 1973.

"A Sheepish Bailey Pushes for Duffey," by Mary McGrory, Washington *Star*, Oct. 1, 1970; "1968 Backers of McCarthy, Dormant Elsewhere, Run Strong Drive in Senatorial Race in Connecticut," by R. W. Apple Jr., New York *Times*, April 5, 1970; "G.O.P. Candidates Sweep to Victory in Connecticut," by Joseph B. Treaster, New York *Times*, Nov. 4, 1970; *Connecticut's Challenge Primary: A Study in Legislative Politics*, by Duane Lockard (Rutgers, N.J.: Eagleton Institute: Case Studies in Practical Politics, 1959); "A Connecticut First," *Christian Science Monitor*, August 14, 1970.

"Mrs. Grasso Tops Democrats for Connecticut Nomination," *Christian Science Monitor*, Feb. 20, 1974; "Posts in Hartford Sought By Women," by Lawrence Fellows, New York *Times*, March 17, 1974; "Mrs. Grasso Advances for Governor," by Jack Zaiman, Washington *Post*, May 24, 1974; "Female Politicians Say This May Be the Year Tide Turns Their Way," by Albert R. Hunt, *Wall Street Journal*, June 19, 1974; "Woman to Head Grasso Campaign," by Jack Zaiman, Hartford

Courant, Sept. 4, 1974; "A Low-Key Candidate," by Linda Greenhouse, New York *Times,* July 22, 1974; "She May Not Look Like It, But She May Be Governor," by Benjamin Taylor, Boston *Globe,* Oct. 27, 1974; "On the Run with Ella," *Newsweek,* Nov. 4, 1974; "Grasso Won by 200,000; 2nd Biggest Edge Ever," Hartford *Courant,* Nov. 7, 1974; "Connecticut's Grasso," by Maria Karagianis, Boston *Globe,* Nov. 10, 1974; "A Year of 'Storm' for Governor Grasso," by Lawrence Fellows, New York *Times,* Jan. 26, 1976.

"GOP Nominates Steele for Connecticut Governor," by Malcolm Johnson, Boston *Globe,* July 28, 1974; "Killian Runs Uphill in Connecticut Race," by Lawrence Fellows, New York *Times,* May 20, 1974; "Babbidge Withdraws from Race for Nomination in Connecticut," New York *Times,* March 31, 1974; "State Income Tax Becomes Major Connecticut Issue," *Christian Science Monitor,* Aug. 8, 1974; "Grasso Says Abolish PUC," and "PUC Is Key Gubernatorial Race Issue," by Michael Dorfsman, Hartford *Courant,* Oct. 4 and 20, 1974.

ECONOMY   "Life Companies Widening Role in Realty Investing," by Daniel F. O'Leary, Philadelphia *Bulletin,* October 1968; "Diversification Haunts the Insurance Industry," *Business Week,* Aug. 24, 1974; "Insurance's Belated Awakening," *Time,* Aug. 29, 1969; *The American People: The Findings of the 1970 Census,* by E. J. Kahn, Jr. (New York: Weybright and Talley, 1973); "Connecticut to Stake Promising Products," by David T. Cook, *Christian Science Monitor,* March 3, 1973; "Connecticut Gives Seed Money to New Ideas," *Business Week,* Feb. 24, 1973; "Connecticut Plans a Recruiting Raid on Companies Here," by Lawrence Fellows, New York *Times,* March 20, 1973.

"Fairfield County: Time to Scrap the Welcome Wagon," by Resa W. King, *The New Englander,* February 1974; "Greenwich Rebuffs Xerox on Plan for Office Campus," by Michael Knight, New York *Times,* Nov. 24, 1973; "The Great Corporate Get-A-Way to Connecticut," *Fortune,* April 1971; "Tobacco Field Jobs More Attractive Now," by Michael Knight, New York *Times,* July 24, 1975.

EDUCATION   "A Tale of Two Universities," by Ernest Holsendolph, *Fortune,* February 1971; "Salute to Brewster, the Hardy Whiffenpoof," by John Mathews, Washington *Star-News,* March 7, 1974; "Yale's Brewster: '70s College Head," by Marquis Childs, Washington *Post,* March 12, 1971; "Yale Rallies Behind Brewster," by Karl E. Meyer, Washington *Post,* April 30, 1970; "Student Zeal at Yale Switches From Politics to Learning," by Joseph B. Treaster, New York *Times,* Nov. 8, 1971; "Yale Facing Crisis on Panthers," by Karl E. Meyer, Washington *Post,* April 27, 1970; "Agnew Asks Ouster of Yale's President," by Bruce Galphin, Washington *Post,* April 29, 1970; "Brewster Explains Campus Unrest," by Peter Kihss, New York *Times,* April 22, 1970; "Yale Fund Drive Asks $370-Million," by Michael Knight, New York *Times,* April 9, 1974; "Unhappy Yale Alumni Charge Bias, Cut Gifts," by Eric Wentworth, Washington *Post,* Aug. 4, 1975.

"School Boundaries Blamed for Blight," by Theodore A. Driscoll, *National Observer,* June 10, 1972; "Connecticut Parochiaid Tested," *Christian Science Monitor,* June 29, 1972; "Connecticut Plan Seeks Equitable Schools Taxes," by Gene I. Maeroff, New York *Times,* Jan 11, 1973; "The Education Gap That's Under Growing Attack," *U.S. News & World Report,* Nov. 8, 1971; "Private Colleges in Connecticut Seek State Help," by M. A. Farber, New York *Times,* Sept. 20, 1970.

ENVIRONMENT   "Lufkin Urges Land Use Plan," Hartford *Courant,* May 17, 1974; "A Super Recycling Project," *Business Week,* Oct. 6, 1973; "Connecticut to Recycle Most Solid Waste," Los Angeles *Times,* Sept. 3, 1973; "L.I. Sound Pollution Challenged," by John Darnton, New York *Times,* June 20, 1970; "Private Talent Joins Fight on Connecticut Pollution," by Lawrence Fellows, New York *Times,* March 29, 1972; "New Grass on the River Bank," *Saturday Review/World,* Nov. 16, 1974; "Can Dan Lufkin Clean up Connecticut?" by Sylvia Dowling, *Fairfield County Magazine,* September 1972; "Dan Lufkin Goes Public," by Charles G. Burck, *Fortune,* January 1972.

NEW HAVEN   *The Mayor's Game,* by Allan R. Talbot (New York: Harper & Row, 1967); *Political Entrepreneurs and Urban Poverty,* by Russell D. Murphy (Lexington, Mass.: D. C. Heath, 1971); "A Coalition Dissolves," *Ripon Forum,* March 1968; "The Flight from City Hall: Lee of New Haven," by Fred Powledge, *Harper's,* November 1969; "Richard Lee: Urban Pioneer," New York *Times,* Jan. 11, 1970.

"The Example of New Haven," *The Nation,* Sept. 14, 1970; "Justice in New Haven," *Time,* Sept. 14, 1970; "A Conservative Calm Pervades 'Radical' New Haven," by Martin Arnold, New York *Times,* May 26, 1971; "Connecticut Cities Progress with Civic Center Plans," *National Civic Review,* October 1970; "Model Poverty Program Falters," by Michael Knight, New York *Times,* Nov. 18, 1974; "New Haven's CPI Wonders Where It Can Go from Here," by Andrew L. Houlding, *City,* Fall 1971; "Model City New Haven Is Taking a Breather," by Peter Braestrup, Washington *Post,* Aug. 2, 1970; "New Haven: Triumph and Trouble in Model City," by Fred Powledge, *Washington Monthly,* February 1970; "New Haven's Mayor Is Upset in Primary," by Michael Knight, New York *Times,* Sept. 13, 1975.

HARTFORD   "Hartford, Hurt by Looting, Wonders Why It Happened," by John Darnton, New York *Times,* June 13, 1969; "Hartford Area Broadens Scope," by Clyde D. McKee, Jr., *National Civic Review,* February 1970; "Hartford Undertakes Projects to Improve Municipal Services," by Rosaline Levenson, *National Civic Review,* July 1972; "Transition Seen for Hartford Area," by Clyde D. McKee, Jr., *National Civic Review,* September 1971; "Hartford's Development Catalyst," by Stephen Silha, *Christian Science Monitor,* April 21, 1973; "Hartford Takes Another Giant Step," by Marion Steinberg, *The New Englander,* April 1974; "Hartford: Prototype for Self-Renewal," by Frederick J. Pratson, *The New Englander,* June 1973; "Processing Hartford: An Idea-Laden Interim Report," by Allan R. Talbot, *City,* Summer 1972; "Hartford Process Proposes Changes," by Rosaline Levenson, *National Civic Review,* June 1972; "Officials Debate Hartford Plan," by Clyde D. McKee, Jr., *National Civic Review,* September 1973; "Tale of Two Cities," *National Geographic,* September 1972.

OTHER CITIES   "Charge of Racism Tarnishes Waterbury's Yankee Image," by John Darnton, New York *Times,* March 24, 1969; "Aldermanic Battle Brings Racial Politics to Waterbury," by Michael Knight, New York *Times,* Sept. 6, 1973; "New London's New Mall Fights Decay in Downtown," by Michael Knight, New York *Times,* Oct. 20, 1973; "Tension Is Rising in Middletown," by Wlliam E. Farrel, New York *Times,* July 2, 1969.

"The Bridgeport Story," by Joseph Alsop, Washington *Post,* Oct. 6, 1972; "Bridgeport Shines by Standards Here," by Murray Schumach, New York *Times,* Aug. 27, 1970; "The Rebirth of Bridgeport," by Paul and Helen Deegan, *Connecticut,* February 1974; "Bridgeport Lack of Beauty More than Skin Deep," by Joseph B. Treaster, New York *Times,* Oct. 19, 1970.

FAIRFIELD COUNTY   "New York's Best Address," by Stephen Birmingham, *Holiday,* April 1969; "Plan for Candlewood Lake 'City' Stirs Fears of Urbanized Suburb," by Michael Knight, New York *Times,* Aug. 21, 1973; "Corporations Aid Stamford Housing," *National Civic Review,*

September 1974; "Downtown Renewal Gives Stamford Lift," by James F. Clarity, New York *Times,* Sept. 7, 1971; "Once-Sleepy Stamford Awakening to New Eminence," by Michael Knight, New York *Times,* June 22, 1974.

"Greenwich Changes and Many Lament It," by John Darnton, New York *Times,* Jan. 7, 1970; "Office Buildings Fail to Please All in Greenwich," by Joseph B. Treaster, New York *Times,* Nov. 29, 1971; "Xerox Stirs Zoning Fight in Greenwich," by Michael Knight, New York *Times,* June 9, 1973; "A Company Adjusts to the Suburbs," by Linda Greenhouse, New York *Times,* Nov. 22, 1970; "Exclusionary Zoning in the Suburbs: The Case of New Canaan, Conn.," by Ellen Szita, *Civil Rights Digest,* Spring 1973.

VERMONT

In preparing the chapter, I benefited particularly from access to an excellent unpublished manuscript about the state by William Moran, a former Vermont newsman. General reference books of most usefulness included: *Vermont: A Guide to the Green Mountain State* (Cambridge: Houghton Mifflin, American Guide Series, 1937); *Yankee Kingdom: Vermont and New Hampshire,* by Ralph Nading Hill (New York: Harper, 1960); "Vermont: Political Paradox," chapter of *New England State Politics,* by Duane Lockard (Princeton: Princeton University Press, 1959); *The Hill Country of Northern New England: Its Social and Economic History 1790–1930,* by Harold Fisher Wilson (New York: Columbia University Press, 1936); *The Vermont Story: A History of the People of the Green Mountain State, 1749–1949,* by Earle W. Newton (Montpelier: Vermont Historical Society, 1949); and *Vermont Tradition: The Biography of an Outlook on Life,* by Dorothy Canfield Fisher, (Boston: Little, Brown, 1953); *Abby Hemenway's Vermont: Unique Portrait of a State,* by Abby Maria Hemenway, selected and edited by Brenda C. Morrissey (Brattleboro: Stephen Greene Press, 1972).

OTHER SOURCES Regular coverage of the Burlington *Free Press,* other Vermont dailies, the *Vermont Times,* the Boston *Globe,* and *Christian Science Monitor,* and specifically the following articles:

GENERAL CHARACTER "Vermont—The Last American Eden?" by Robert Taylor, Boston *Globe,* August 16, 1970; "How to Live Among the Vermonters," by Bernard DeVoto, *Harper's Magazine,* August 1936; "Vermont: Where Are All Those Yankees?" by Miriam Chapin, *Harper's Magazine,* December 1957; "What Is Vermont Tradition?" by Dorothy Canfield Fisher, *Vermont Times,* June 1973; *Vermonters on Vermont,* public opinion survey released by Vermont Natural Resources Council, January, 1972.

AIKEN *Ralph Nader Congress Project* report on George D. Aiken, by Claudia Townsend (Washington: Grossman, 1972); "Senator Aiken Is Retiring," by William Greider, Washington *Post,* Feb. 15, 1974; "Maverick Republican," New York *Times,* Dec. 16, 1958; "Aiken Opts for Time Off," by Jeff McCulloch, *Christian Science Monitor,* March 7, 1974; "Senator George Aiken— An Institution Returns To Vermont," by Tom Slayton, Boston *Globe,* Feb. 17, 1974.

ECONOMY, GEOGRAPHY "Outsiders Own Vermont Resources, Professor's Study Shows," *Christian Science Monitor,* July 24, 1971; "Vermont's Maple Business," by Bradford W. Ketchum, Jr., *The New Englander,* November 1973; "Vermont Would Like Bananas—but No Fog," by Richard M. Klein, Washington *Post,* Jan. 25, 1970.

"How the Ski Complex Grew Up and Became So Complex," by I. Herbert Gordon, New York *Times,* Feb. 1, 1970; "America's First Ski Resort Is Over the Hills," by John and Frankie O'Rear, *Holiday,* November 1971.

"Woodstock and Rockefeller," by Linda Dunn, *Vermont Times,* June 1973; "In Friendly Upstate Vermont Sans Skis" by Virginia Creed, New York *Times,* Feb. 8, 1970; "The Champlain Monster," *Vermont Times,* Sept. 14, 1970; "Bread-loaf Writers' Conference," by Richard Wien, *Vermont Times,* September 1974; "Practical Foreign Relations In Springfield, Vt." by Marquis Childs, Washington *Post,* July 31, 1973; "Burlington: Stability Goes Boom," by Phillip M. Perry, *The New Englander,* October 1973.

ENVIRONMENT "Vermont Draws Bead On Polluters," *Christian Science Monitor,* Dec. 7, 1970; "Vermont 'Pay To Pollute' Law Attacked," by Mavis Doyle, *Christian Science Monitor,* Feb. 16, 1972; "Vermont, Paper Firm Settle Lake Champlain Sludge Case," by Howard Coffin, *Christian Science Monitor,* April 26, 1974; "Vermont Set For Removal Of Billboards," *Christian Science Monitor,* July 19, 1971; "One-Year Test In Vermont Shows Bottled-Drink Deposit Law Is Working," by Clayton Jones, *Christian Science Monitor,* July 30, 1974;

"Vermont Yankee: Walking the Tightrope of Nuclear Safety," by Edward G. Picket, *Vermont Times,* September 1973; "Vermont Yankee: The Tightrope Grows Taut," *Vermont Times,* June 1974; "A-Power Means Prosperity to Vernon," *Christian Science Monitor,* April 17, 1974; "Vermont Clamps Down on Nuclear Plants," by Howard Coffin, *Christian Science Monitor,* March 31, 1975.

LAND USE *So Goes Vermont,* by Phyllis Myers, The Conservation Foundation, Washington, D.C., February 1974; "The Land Use Plan," *Vermont Times,* November 1973; "Vermont Weighs Ecology Vs. Property Rights," by Brad Knickerbocker, *Christian Science Monitor,* Dec. 16, 1972; "Land Use Regulations and Property Tax Relief," by Thomas P. Salmon, *Innovations In State Government—Messages from the Governors* (Washington: National Governors' Conference, 1974); "There's More Than a River Separating Those Two States," by Bill D'Alessandro, *New Hampshire Times,* July 31, 1974; "Controlling the Boom in Vermont," by Thomas P. Salmon, New York *Times,* Jan. 5, 1974; "Vermont Land Rush—Controls Only Slowed Pace," by R. S. Kindleberger, Boston *Globe,* Oct. 28, 1973; "Non-Yankee, Stay Home," *Newsweek,* July 10, 1972; "Vermont Struggles to Balance Land Use Pressure," by Brad Knickerbocker, *Christian Science Monitor,* Dec. 14, 1972.

"Vermont Gets Tough on Land Sale," by William G. Connelly, New York *Times,* May 27, 1973; "Naughty," by John McClaughry, *Ripon Forum,* September 1973; "State Control of Land Use Favored," by Paul Langner, Boston *Globe,* March 3, 1974; "Land Use and Development," presentation to the National Governors Conference by Thomas P. Salmon, March 1, 1973; "Saving Rural Scenes for 1992," by Louis Chapin, *Christian Science Monitor,* Dec. 3, 1971; "Vermont: Public Support for Land Use Controls," by Thomas P. Salmon, *State Government,* Summer 1973; "Salmon Says He Expects to Attend Presidential Conference on Economy," by Neil A. Davis, Burlington *Free Press,* Sept. 5, 1974; "GOP Emphasizes Local Control," by Frederick W. Stetson, Burlington *Free Press,* Sept. 17, 1974; "Why Does Vermont Look Different?" by Jerry Kelly, *Vermont Times,* July 1974.

NEW HAMPSHIRE

Among the books and articles providing the best general background on the state were *New Hampshire: A Guide to the Granite State*, compiled by the Federal Writers' Project of the WPA, American Guide Series (Boston: Houghton Mifflin, 1938); "New Hampshire Politics: Triumph of Conservatism," chapter of *New England State Politics*, by Duane Lockard (Princeton: Princeton University Press, 1959); *Yankee Kingdom: Vermont and New Hampshire*, by Ralph Nading Hill (New York: Harper & Row, 1960); *The Story of New Hampshire*, by James Duane Squires (Princeton, N.J.: Nostrand, 1964); *Let Me Show You New Hampshire*, by Ella Shannon Bowles (New York: Knopf, 1938); "New Hampshire—The Granite State," by Cornelius Weygandt, *Think*, August 1947; "Profile of the 'Spotlight' State," by Penn Kimball, New York *Times Magazine*, March 9, 1952; "New Hampshire Key: A State in Transition," by Bill Kovach, New York *Times*, Feb. 2, 1972; "It's a Nice Place to Visit," by James Stack, Boston *Globe*, Aug. 23, 1970.

GOVERNMENT   *Report of the Citizens Task Force*, Royden C. Sanders, Jr., Chairman (Concord: 1970); *A Better New Hampshire*, by Citizens' Council for a Better New Hampshire (Concord: 1968); "Budget Showdown on N.H. Horizon," by Stewart Dill, *Christian Science Monitor*, March 8, 1973; "Commission's Swan Song," *New Hampshire Times*, Oct. 17, 1973; "Welfare: The Fastest Growing Social Service," by A. Downey, *New Hampshire Times*, May 1, 1974; "Instead of the State Hospital," by Robert Gillmore, *New Hampshire Times*, July 18, 1973; "Link-Plan-Screen Is Working: A New Evaluations Policy Has Dramatically Reduced Admissions at New Hampshire Hospital," by Margaret M. Riggs, *Human Services*, March 1974; "New Hampshire Con Con Rejects Controversy," *State Government News*, September 1974; "Will N.H. Vouch For Free-Choice Education?" by David R. Bickford, *The New Englander*, March 1974.

"State-Local Tax Systems: Proposals and Objectives," by John Shannon, *National Civic Review*, April 1972; "How New Hampshire Bucks the Trend," *U.S. News & World Report*, Jan. 1, 1973; "Governor: Forthright or Cautious," by Rod Paul, *Concord Monitor*, July 7, 1970.

"New Hampshire Legalizes Nation's Only Sweepstakes," by Thomas P. Ronan, New York *Times*, May 1, 1963; "I'm Not Ashamed of Our Lottery," by John W. King, *This Week Magazine*, July 14, 1963; "A Look at the Lottery 10 Years After," by Hank Nichols, *New Hampshire Times*, July 3, 1974; "Legal Gambling—No Jackpot For States," *U.S. News & World Report*, April 1, 1974.

"Meldrim Thomson—Furor, Fun and the Fear of God," by John B. Wood, Boston *Globe*, Nov. 11, 1973; "The Blockhead Who Runs the Granite State," by Daniel Yergin, *Boston Magazine*, May 1974; "Granite State Another Watergate?" by Jeff McLaughlin, *The New Englander*, June 1973; "Watergate North," *Newsweek*, May 21, 1973; "N.H. GOP Platform Mirrors Thomson's Political Views," by Adolphe V. Bernotas, Concord *Monitor*, Sept. 30, 1974; "Thomson Prompted Firing, Says Calley," by Adolphe V. Bernotas, Concord *Monitor*, Sept. 25, 1974; "Thomson-Loeb Phone Calls Total 138 in 18 Months," by Rod Paul, Concord *Monitor*, Oct. 12, 1974.

POLITICS   "Remembering Franklin Pierce (Which Few People Do)," by David Epstein, Washington *Post*, Nov. 27, 1971; "Senator Styles Bridges and His Far-Flung Constituents," by Douglass Cater, *The Reporter*, July 20, 1954;

"Adams Won Fame for State Budget," New York *Times*, Nov. 25, 1952; *Dynamics of the Party System*, by James L. Sundquist (Washington, D.C.: Brookings, 1973); "Restless New Hampshire," by W. David Gardner, *The Nation*, March 6, 1972; "Let Me Tell You About New Hampshire," by Eugene J. McCarthy, New York *Times*, Nov. 7, 1971; "2 Conservatives Vie in New Hampshire," by Robert Reinhold, New York *Times*, Oct. 13, 1972; "Durkin, Powell May Talk about Senate Campaign," AP Dispatch, Concord *Monitor*, Sept. 13, 1974; "Wyman Testified Before Grand Jury," Concord *Monitor*, Sept. 6, 1974; "Wyman Resignation Demanded by Durkin," AP Dispatch, Concord *Monitor*, Sept. 18, 1974; "The Democrats' Best Hope," by Tom Ferriter, Concord *Monitor*, Oct. 24, 1974; "Wesley Powell: Watching and Waiting in Hampton Falls," by Hank Nichols, *New Hampshire Times*, Sept. 25, 1974; "Democratic Stronghold," *New Hampshire Times*, Nov. 13, 1974; "The N.H. Barometer Is Broken," Baltimore *Sun*, Oct. 6, 1970.

"Report: New Hampshire," by Charles McDowell, Jr., *Atlantic*, December 1967; "Press Invented 'Phantom' Foe for Him, Muskie Complains," by Don Oberdorfer, Washington *Post*, March 3, 1972; "The New Hampshire Debate: Benefit Is Minimal," by Don Oberdorfer, Washington *Post*, March 6, 1972; "McGovern Drive: Shrewd, Intensive," by David S. Broder, Washington *Post*, March 9, 1972; "On the Morning After, Surprise Over Durkin Victory Still Fazes N.H. Pundits," by Benjamin Taylor, Boston *Globe*, Sept. 18, 1975.

PRESS   "William Loeb: A Gunfighter Who Relishes Quadrennial Role as Abominable Snowman of American Politics," by Don Bonafede, *National Journal*, March 18, 1972; *The Man Who Made Muskie Cry*, televised interview by Bill Moyers, WNET-TV, New York, March 19, 1974; "Publisher Loeb's Word War," by Mary Russell, Washington *Post*, March 1, 1972; "Citizen Loeb," by Gerry Nadel, *Boston Magazine*, May 1973; "Publisher's Choices Run Strong in N.H.," by Haynes Johnson, Washington *Post*, Sept. 7, 1970; "William Loeb and the New Hampshire Primary: A Question of Ethics," by Jules Witcover, *Columbia Journalism Review*, May/June, 1972; "Nixon's Too Left-Wing for William Loeb," by Bill Kovach, New York *Times Magazine*, Dec. 12, 1971; "New Hampshire's Union Leader," by David Gardner, *The Nation*, March 31, 1969; "How News Gets From the State House to You," by Charlie Calley, *New Hampshire Times*, April 4, 1974; "The Story Behind the Times," *New Hampshire Times*, May 8, 1974; "The Political Power of the Loeb Press: Real or Imaginary?," by Hank Nichols, *New Hampshire Times*, April 23, 1975; "Boss Loeb and the Closing of the Ring," by Richard Wright, *New Hampshire Times*, Sept. 3, 1975.

GEOGRAPHY AND ENVIRONMENT   "New Hampshire, a Booming Vacationland, Fights to Preserve Its Natural Beauty," by Bill Kovach, New York *Times*, Feb. 1, 1971; *A New Hampshire Everlasting and Unfallen*, by Paul E. Bruns (Bennington, N.H.: Society for the Protection of New Hampshire Forests, 1969); *The Orange Tree and the Inch Worm*, final report of the Spaulding-Potter Charitable Trusts, by Eugene C. Struckhoff (Concord, 1972); "Good Earth Gone," by John Griesemer, *Valley News* (Lebanon), Nov. 30, 1974; "An Environmental Look at the Past Year," by Bill D'Alessandro, *New Hampshire Times*, May 8, 1974; "New Englanders Buck Trend Toward Bulldozer," by Bill Kovach, New York

Times, Jan. 17, 1971; "A Story of Teamwork That Rescued a River: Pemi Showcase," by John Dodge, *Forest Notes,* Winter 1971–72.

The Great White Hills of New Hampshire, by Ernest Poole (Garden City, N.Y.: Doubleday, 1946); *The White Mountains: Heroes and Hamlets,* by Arthur W. Vose (Barre, Mass., 1968); "In Fair Weather Or Foul, Loners Man Mountaintop Outpost," by Laird Hart, *The Wall Street Journal,* Sept. 17, 1974; "The Second Greatest Show On Earth," by Christina Tree, Boston *Globe,* June 24, 1973; "Mountain Man," by Peter Taber, Boston *Globe,* Nov. 11, 1973; "Ring Around the Mountain," by Susan Redlich, *Forest Notes,* Winter 1973–74; "Franconia Notch Road Strongly Criticized," AP Dispatch, *Christian Science Monitor,* Aug. 10, 1973; "Cotton Explains His Amendment," *New Hampshire Times,* Oct. 23, 1974.

Annals of the Grand Monadnock, by Allen Chamberlain (Concord: Society for the Preservation of N.H. Forests, 1968); "A Land Use Study: Monadnock and Gap," by Stephen H. Foster, *Forest Notes,* Summer 1974; "Trying to Protect and Guide Monadnock's Future," by Bill D'Alessandro, *New Hampshire Times,* July 3, 1974.

"A Bit of Boston in the Granite State," by Jay McManus, *New Hampshire Times,* Aug. 28, 1974; "When You Say Sludge You've Said It All," by Ronald A. Frank, *The New Englander,* September 1973; "The 10 Safest Cities," *Esquire,* December 1973; "New Hampshire Waters," by Monty Hoyt, *Christian Science Monitor,* Sept. 18, 1970; "New Hampshire Waters: A Murky Future?" by Bill D'Alessandro, *New Hampshire Times,* July 3, 1973; "Nuclear Power at Seabrook: Let's Take a Closer Look," by Robert Backus, *New Hampshire Times,* June 12, 1974.

"Will Quiet N.H. College Town and Oil Mix?" by Nina McCain, Boston *Globe,* Dec. 2, 1973; "The Refinery that Ran Aground," by Daniel Ford, *The Nation,* May 4, 1974; "The Heavy Burden of Dudley Dudley," by Charles Calley, *New Hampshire Times,* Jan. 2, 1974; "A Sleepy Town Battles Onassis' Oil-Refinery Plan," by Diane K. Shan, *The National Observer,* Feb. 9, 1974.

"The Land Use Issue: Where Is the Voice of the People," by Bill D'Alessandro, *New Hampshire Times,* Nov. 27, 1974; "The Land Use Issue: Existing Laws and Problems," by Bill D'Alessandro, *New Hampshire Times,* Dec. 4, 1974; "The Land Use Issue: Heading for the Legislature with No Compromise in Sight," by Bill D'Alessandro, *New Hampshire Times,* Dec. 18, 1974; "New Hampshire/Vermont: There's More than a River Separating These Two States," by Bill D'Alessandro, *New Hampshire Times,* July 31, 1974.

CITIES   "Epitaph for an American Landmark," by David G. McCullough, *American Heritage,* April 1970; "Taxing the Fun Out of Manchester," by Charlie Calley, *New Hampshire Times,* June 19, 1974; "Manchester Buries Mill Town Image," by Phillip M. Perry, *The New Englander,* March 1974; "Tax Sharing and Tax Relief," by Bernard D. Nossiter, Washington *Post,* May 9, 1971; "The Latino Trail to Manchester," by Charlie Calley, *New Hampshire Times,* June 27, 1973.

"Portsmouth on Its 350th Birthday Reflects Prosperity, Depression Eras," by Christina Tree, Boston *Globe,* July 29, 1973; "Where Urban Renewal Means Recovering History," by Sando Bologna, Washington *Post,* May 17, 1970; "Preservationists, Developer to Build Shopping Center," *Preservation News,* July 1973.

MAINE

The most helpful books on the general Maine scene were: *Maine: A Guide "Downeast,"* second edition, ed. Dorris A. Isaacson (Rockland, Maine: Courier-Gazette, 1970); *Maine Pilgrimage,* by Richard Saltonstall, Jr. (Boston: Little, Brown 1974); *Where the Place Called Morning Lies,* by Frank Graham, Jr. (New York: Viking, 1973); *Maine and Her People,* by Harold B. Clifford (Freeport, Maine: Wheelwright, 1963); *State O'Maine,* by Louise Dickinson Rich (New York: Harper & Row, 1964); *A Portrait of Maine,* by Berenice Abbot and Chenoweth Hall (New York: Macmillan, 1968); "Maine: Pine, Power, and Politics," chapter of *New England State Politics,* by Duane Lockard (Princeton: Princeton University Press, 1959); *Muskie,* by Theo Lippman, Jr., and Donald C. Hansen (New York: W. W. Norton, 1971); *Muskie of Maine,* by David Nevin (New York: Random House, 1972).

STATE GOVERNMENT   "The Council: Maine's Bureaucratic Dinosaur," by William Langley, *Maine Times,* Oct. 22, 1971; "The Dinosaur Has Teeth," by William Langley, *Maine Times,* Oct. 29, 1971; "Maine Restructuring Slowly," by George B. Merry, *Christian Science Monitor,* March 6, 1972; "Maine Provides Tax Relief," *State Government News,* September 1973; "Taxes and Finance," by Peter W. Cox, *Maine Times,* March 22, 1974; "Maine to Cut Aid to 46,000 Children," *Christian Science Monitor,* June 23, 1971; "Maine Prison Relaxes Rules, Tensions, and Violence," by Robert M. Press, *Christian Science Monitor,* Aug. 6, 1973; "Maine Administrator Pushes Prison Reform," by Robert M. Press, *Christian Science Monitor,* Aug. 2, 1973; "Maine Defines Legislative Ethics," *State Government, News,* July 1974; "Ken MacLeod: Legislative Architect or the Terrible Tempered Mr. Bang," by John N. Cole, *Maine Times,* April 6, 1973; "Maine

Legislature Votes End of Executive Council," by Kent Ward, *Christian Science Monitor,* July 1, 1975; "Uniform School Tax Surviving Trials in Maine," by Jerry Harkavy, *Christian Science Monitor,* Aug. 1, 1975.

POLITICS   "The Democratic Party in Maine," by Lane W. Lancaster, *National Municipal Review,* December 1929; "Congressional Campaign: Maine Elects a Democrat," by John C. Donovan, *Eagleton Foundation Studies in Practical Politics,* 1958; "The Maine Democrats," by John Cole, *Maine Sunday Telegram,* May 26, 1968; "Q: How Much Does It Cost to Buy a Maine Election? A: About A Dollar a Voter," by Peter W. Cox, *Maine Times,* April 12, 1974; "Pols Scratch Heads over Upset in Maine," by Robert W. Merry *National Observer,* Nov. 16, 1974; "Pollsters Find Longley Striking Responsive Chord," Portland *Press Herald,* Nov. 2, 1974; "Flurry of Promises, Voter Apathy Mark Maine Campaign," by Kenneth Bredemeier, Washington *Post,* Oct. 21, 1974; "Maine's Longley," by Peter Anderson, Boston *Globe,* Nov. 10, 1974.

"There Are Five Men Who Form the Core of Maine's Power Elite," by Phyllis Austin, *Maine Times,* Feb. 15, 1974; "Meet the Men Who Say No," by John N. Cole, *Maine Times,* Feb. 16, 1973.

CONGRESSIONAL DELEGATION "Muskie: A Sketch from The Inside," by Joseph H. Nicholson, Jr., *Washington Monthly,* July 1971; "The Remaking of Muskie," by J. F. Richard, *The Nation,* Feb. 22, 1971; "To Understand Muskie You Must Understand Maine," by Peter W. Cox, *Maine Times,* May 7, 1971; "Muskie: Presidency Still Appealing," by Jack Germond, Washington *Star-News,* April 1974.

"Maggie Smith: Roses, Thorns," *Newsweek,* Nov. 20, 1972; "Sen. Smith: Maine Changed, She

Didn't," by Maxwell Wiesenthal, Washington *Post*, Nov. 9, 1972; 'Is the Great Lady from Maine Out of Touch?" by Berkeley Rice, New York *Times Magazine*, June 11, 1972; "Leaping Lady from Maine," by Richard Spong, *Editorial Research Reports*, Feb. 21, 1964.

"Long-Shot Senator from Maine," by Shirley Elder, Washington *Star-News*, March 26, 1973; "Naming an Interim President," by William Raspberry, Washington *Post*, Nov. 14, 1973.

"Cohen of Maine," Boston *Globe*, July 21, 1974; "Maine Congressman Walks to His People," by Stewart Dill McBridge, *Christian Science Monitor*, Aug. 29, 1973; "Rep. Cohen Has Sent Back Rockefeller Money," Portland *Press Herald*, Oct. 6, 1974.

ECONOMY "Mitchell: Industrial Development," Portland *Press Herald*, Sept. 10, 1974; "Play the Maine Development Game," by John N. Cole, *Maine Times*, March 22, 1974; "Freddie Vahlsing Has Something to Tell Us About Industrial Development," by Peter W. Cox, *Maine Times*, March 24, 1972; "Erwin: Industrial Development," Portland *Press Herald*, Sept. 9, 1974; "Perpetuating the Maine Myth," by John N. Cole, *Maine Times*, Aug. 20, 1971; "Wrong Doctors, Wrong Patient, Wrong Cure," by John N. Cole, *Maine Times*, Sept. 18, 1970; "Mobile Home Horror Stories," by Lynne Langley, *Maine Times*, May 6, 1973; "Hard Test for Maine," *Time*, April 12, 1971; "From Rags to Riches," by William H. Williamson, *Maine Telegram*, Sept. 29, 1968.

"Aquaculture: A Drastic Change in the Lobster Industry," by Paul Lazarus, *Maine Times*, June 5, 1970; "Maine Fishermen Fire Both Barrels at the Experts," by William Langley, *Maine Times*, May 12, 1972; "The 'Red Tide' Leaves Clam Diggers Destitute," by Homer Bigart, New York *Times*, Oct. 2, 1972; "Tax Audits Complicate the Problems of Maine's Lobstermen," by John Kifner, New York *Times*, July 14, 1974; "Number One Retires," by Marion Watson, *Maine Times*, Jan. 29, 1971.

"Recreation," by Peter W. Cox, *Maine Times*, March 22, 1974; "Tourists: Good or Bad," by Peter W. Cox, *Maine Times*, June 28, 1974.

ENVIRONMENT "Computing Pollution," *Maine Times*, March 22, 1974; "Is the River Clean-Up Program a Smokescreen?" *Maine Times*, May 18, 1973; "Congressman Hathaway on Maine Myths," *Maine Times*, Sept. 17, 1971; "The Philosophy Behind Making Them Open Sewers," by Lynne Langley, *Maine Times*, April 5, 1974; "A Grand Horrendous Mess," by Lucy L. Martin, *Maine Times*, April 27, 1973.

"Designing a State Land Use Program," by Phillip M. Savage, *State Government*, Summer, 1973; "Land Laws," by Richard L. Robbins, *Maine Times*, Jan. 5, 1973; "'People Push' Spurs Tougher Maine Laws," by R. S. Kindleberger, Boston *Globe*, Nov. 11, 1973; "Maine's Treasure," by John N. Cole, *Maine Times*, July 12, 1974.

OIL "Senators Feel Oil Fight Lost," by Donald R. Larrabee, Boston *Globe*, Jan. 1, 1969; "Balancing Oil with Environment," by Kenneth M. Curtis, *Innovations in State Government: Messages from the Governors* (Washington: National Governors' Conference, 1974); "Oil and the Environment: The View from Maine," by John McDonald, *Fortune*, April 1971; "Maine Governor Vows to Bar Pollution if Refinery Is Built," New York *Times*, April 21, 1969; "Machiasport Project Catches Muskie in Middle," by Crosby S. Noyes, Washington *Evening Star*, Feb. 14, 1970; "Eastport Divided over Risk and Benefit of Refinery Planned for Its Harbor," by John Kifner, New York *Times*, June 21, 1973; "Canadian Opposition to Pittson Grows Stronger," by John N. Cole, *Maine Times*, Nov. 23, 1973; "The Pittson Refinery: This One Is the Real Thing," by Lynne

Langley, *Maine Times*, April 27, 1973; "Refinery Faces Ballot Test," by Kenneth McCormick, *Christian Science Monitor*, May 16, 1974; "Oil Discovers Maine," by La Rue Spiker, *The Nation*, June 1, 1970; "Gibbs Will Give the State a Dry Cargo Pier if the State Will Let Gibbs Have Its Oil Pier," by John N. Cole, *Maine Times*, March 15, 1974.

PUBLIC POWER ISSUE "Searching for the Central Issue in the Power Debate," *Maine Times*, Nov. 2, 1973; "An Aswan Dam for Maine?" by Arlen J. J. Large, *The Wall Street Journal*, July 25, 1974; "A Good Idea Is Hard to Kill," by Karl Keyerleber, *The Nation*, Feb. 26, 1973; "Dickey-Lincoln Dam Lobbied to Death, Looks Great In 1974," by Stan Wallerstein, Boston *Globe*, Feb. 10, 1974; "Maine and Neeco—for Now," by John N. Cole, *Maine Times*, Sept. 27, 1974; "Quoddy Revisited: Here's How It Works," by Lucy L. Martin, *Maine Times*, June 15, 1973.

FOREST INDUSTRIES *The Paper Plantation*, by William C. Osborn, (New York: Grossman, 1974); "Timber Rights Maine Campaign Issue," by Emmet Meara, Boston *Globe*, Feb. 17, 1974; "The Timber Companies May Deny Harry Richardson Governorship if He Doesn't Knuckle Under on Public Lands," by John N. Cole, *Maine Times*, Feb. 15, 1974; "Victory for the Timber Interests," by John N. Cole, *Maine Times*, March 29, 1974; "The Forests," *Maine Times*, March 22, 1974; "The Pulpcutters," *Maine Times*, March 14, 1969; "Are Maine Woods Cut Too Fast?" by Stewart Dill McBride and Stephen Silha, *Christian Science Monitor*, Jan. 9, 1974; "Maine's Forests Are an Absurd Mismanaged Resource," *Maine Times*, May 25, 1973; "How the Maine Woodsman Is Kept in Peonage," by Peter W. Cole, *Maine Times*, May 18, 1973; "Maine Trying to Settle Future of 322,000 Acres," by John B. Wood, Boston *Globe*, March 31, 1974; "Lawsuits May Terminate Annual Log Drive Down the Kennebec," New York *Times*, April 17, 1971; "Maine to Recover More Forest Land," New York *Times*, Sept. 2, 1975.

GEOGRAPHY "The Coast of Maine," New York *Times*, March 23, 1971; "Megalopolis and Maine's Fastest Growing County," by Lynne Langley, *Maine Times*, June 22, 1973; "Small Town in Maine Calls Rockefeller's 'Neighbors,'" by James T. Wooten, New York *Times*, Aug. 23, 1974; "Matinicus," by David B. Wilson, Boston *Globe*, July 12, 1970; "'Sunrise County' Provides a Respite from the Madding Crowd," by Emmett Mears, Boston *Globe*, Aug. 19, 1973; "Good Days Are Coming for the County but They May Bring Bad Spinoffs," by John N. Cole, *Maine Times*, July 12, 1974; "Preservation Yankee Style," by Marinus B. Peladeau, *Historic Preservation*, October 1973.

"Mt. Katahdin, Maine," by Joe Michael Leigh, *Holiday*, May 1970; "Katahdin: Huge . . . Powerful . . . Permanent," by Robert Coxe, *Maine Times*, July 11, 1969.

CITIES "Portland: Victorian Mini-Hub," by Frank Perrotta, Boston *Globe*, July 7, 1974; "Renewal by Fire," by Don Stofle, *Maine Times*, June 25, 1971; "Portland: Don't Mess It Up," by (LLM), *Maine Times*, Nov. 10, 1972; "The Waterfront: Where the City Starts," by Peggy Fisher, *Maine Times*, July 23, 1971; Chapter in *Cities of America*, by George Sessions Perry, from his *Saturday Evening Post* articles (Freeport, N.Y.: Books for Libraries Press, 1970).

"John's Column (About Augusta)," by John N. Cole, *Maine Times*, Oct. 22, 1971; "Behind Bangor's Rebound," by David R. Bickford, *The New Englander*, June 1973; "Little Canada: Maine's French-Canadian Heritage, in Trouble on an Urban Island," by Wayne E. Reilly, *Maine Times*, Sept. 10, 1971.

INDEX

Page references in **boldface** type indicate inclusive or major entries.

Scale of Miles

100 200 300 400 500

CAN

WASH.
Seattle
Olympia
Spokane
Portland
Salem
ORE.
Eugene
IDAHO
Boise

MONT.
Helena
Butte
Billings
YELLOWSTONE
NATIONAL
PARK
WYO.

N.D.
Bismarck
S.D.
Aberdeen
Pierre
NEB.

CALIF.
Oakland
San Francisco
Reno
Carson City
Sacramento
YOSEMITE
NAT'L. PARK
Mt. Whitney
Las Vegas
Santa Barbara
Los Angeles
San Diego

NEV.

Pocatello
Great
Salt Lake
Ogden
Salt Lake City
UTAH

Casper

Cheyenne
COLO.
Denver
Colorado
Springs

KAN

Wichi

GRAND
CANYON
NAT'L. PARK

ARIZ.

Phoenix
Tucson

Farmington
Santa Fe
Albuquerque
N.M.
Lubbock
El Paso

Oklo
Cit
Amarillo
Wichita
Falls
Fort Wort

TEXA

Pacific
Ocean

Austi

San
Antonio

U.S.S.R.

U.S.S.R.
U.S.

Kotzebue
ALASKA
Nome
Fairbanks

Anchorage

Bering
Sea

CANADA

Juneau

MEXICO

MILES
200 400 600

Lonz